SOMERSET RECORD SOCIETY
Volume 82

SIR STEPHEN GLYNNE'S CHURCH NOTES FOR SOMERSET

edited by

Michael McGarvie

SOMERSET RECORD SOCIETY

c/o Local History Library, Taunton Castle, Taunton, Somerset

1994

ISBN 0-901732-30-3

Produced for the Somerset Record Society by Alan Sutton Publishing Limited, Stroud, Gloucestershire

CONTENTS

INTRODUCTION

1. *The Life of Sir Stephen Glynne*

In its obituary of Sir Stephen Glynne *The Daily Telegraph* paid tribute not merely to his memory but also to his powers of remembrance, powers considered by W.E. Gladstone the most remarkable of his generation and country, superior even to those of Macaulay. The *Telegraph* declared that

'. . . his memory in his own orbit was so tenacious that, at the mention of some little parish church and even in the most out-of-the-way corner of Westmoreland, Cornwall, or some other little visited shire, he would at once describe the architecture of the fabric, rehearse the name of the incumbent and add any special details of interest as regards any peculiar features of the structure, or exceptional monuments that building, or its churchyard contained'.

Sir Stephen's contemporaries echoed this view, including D.R. Thomas who edited Glynne's Welsh church notes. 'Those who had the pleasure of his acquaintance,' he recalled, 'will remember how complete and accurate were the details that he could so readily call to mind, and that an extraordinary memory underlay his quiet and unassuming manner'.[1]

This forerunner of Pevsner was born on 22nd September 1807, the son of Sir Stephen Glynne, eighth baronet, of Hawarden Castle in Flintshire (now Clwyd) and of his wife Mary, daughter of Lord Braybrooke. The Glynnes were an ancient family of Glynillion in Cardiganshire who claimed descent from the fourth of the Royal Tribes of Wales. A younger son, Sir John Glynne (1602–1666), a successful lawyer and later Lord Chief Justice of the Upper Bench, established the family in Flintshire, buying the Hawarden estate in 1653. A new mansion built near the ancient castle between 1752 and 1757 was gothicized in 1809 and the name changed from the prosaic Broadlane House to Hawarden Castle. By this time the Glynne estate ran to nearly 7,000 acres with a rent roll of £9,000.

Young Stephen's father died of tuberculosis in France in 1815, so at the age of eight he succeeded as ninth baronet and squire of Hawarden, although he did not come into the estate until 1828. He developed early intellectual tastes and interests quite at variance with the traditional rural occupations of his class. Mr A.G. Veysey[2] has suggested that he may have inherited these from his mother's family, the Braybrookes, who were literary and historically minded.

1. *Archaeologia Cambrensis*, 5th. series, I (1884), 82.
2. Sir Stephen Glynne, 1807–74, in *Journal of the Flintshire Historical Society*, vol. 30 (1981–82), 152, note 6.

Glynne spent much of his childhood at their famous Essex seat, Audley End. He was a precocious child, reserved and aloof but determined; his mother wrote of him with what seems like resignation that 'he cared little or nothing for other people's opinions, having taken a line of his own at two years old'.[3]

Glynne's journals reveal that the child was truly father of the man, the absorbing interest of his manhood being clearly evident in the jottings of the boy, as are latent powers of observation and discernment. Passing through France at the age of seven he records seeing 'the cathedral of Abbeville which was Beautifull. I saw some saints which were plentiful'. Near Tarascon he noted 'a fine old castle. It contained an old tower and the Keep, 2 other towers, one was ornamented with a window like a church. There was another castle at Tarascon but it was not near so handsome'.[4] During a European tour in 1815 Glynne visited Louvain and saw 'a most beautiful church' and 'a very handsome cathedral with an extra-ordinary pulpit carved in wood & a beauty[ful] stone carving'.

The eight year old Glynne considered the Hotel de Ville at Genoa 'the most stately palace you ever saw' and after an excursion, 'went out again to see 2 churches. The first was the most beautiful'. He saw the Pope go into the cathedral, 'that great black and white church' and noted a house 'with a floor of solid speckled marble, red, green, black and white & a very curious clock'. These aesthetic pleasures had to be paid for: Glynne found in his bed '17 vermin, 14 fleas & 3 bugs' and had to partake of 'a most horrid dinner of gruel-soup, brains, mostly bones formed into a sort of pudding in sauce & I do not know what the other was & cutlets fit for a pig & a nasty raw burnt bird & then plumbs and a tart which were tolerable'.[5]

As a boy, Glynne was already renowned among his fellows for his phenomenal memory and knew the words and tunes of most of the psalms. He attended the funeral of George III at Windsor and was able to note the fine music despite a headache brought on by the scent of the burning candles. A love of church services and music remained with him through life. At Eton (where he was considered one of the cleverest pupils) he could list the names of all the boys and was 'as good as a pocket peerage' in his wide knowledge of members of the House of Lords and their families. Although said at school to be 'wholly engrossed with Botony, Conchology, Optics, in short the Taste of the day',[6] at the tender age of thirteen Glynne was already riding 20 miles a day in search of old churches near Hawarden. At seventeen he was described as 'quiet and slow, retaining a singular indisposition to mix or associate even with his school fellows'.[7] This unusual young man had no interest in hunting, shooting, or even dancing, let alone 'common occurrences'.

3. Glynne–Gladstone MS. 1068: notes of Mary, Lady Glynne, 1815–22.The Glynne–Gladstone MSS. have been very completely catalogued and are available in the *Handlist of the Glynne–Gladstone MSS. in St. Deiniol's Library, Hawarden*, compiled by C.J. Williams (List and Index Society, volume 24, 1990).
4. Glynne–Gladstone MS. 1075.
5. Glynne–Gladstone MS. 1076.
6. Glynne–Gladstone MS. 1068.
7. Racheal Leighton (ed.), *Correspondence of Charlotte Grenville, Lady Williams-Wynn* (1920), 306.

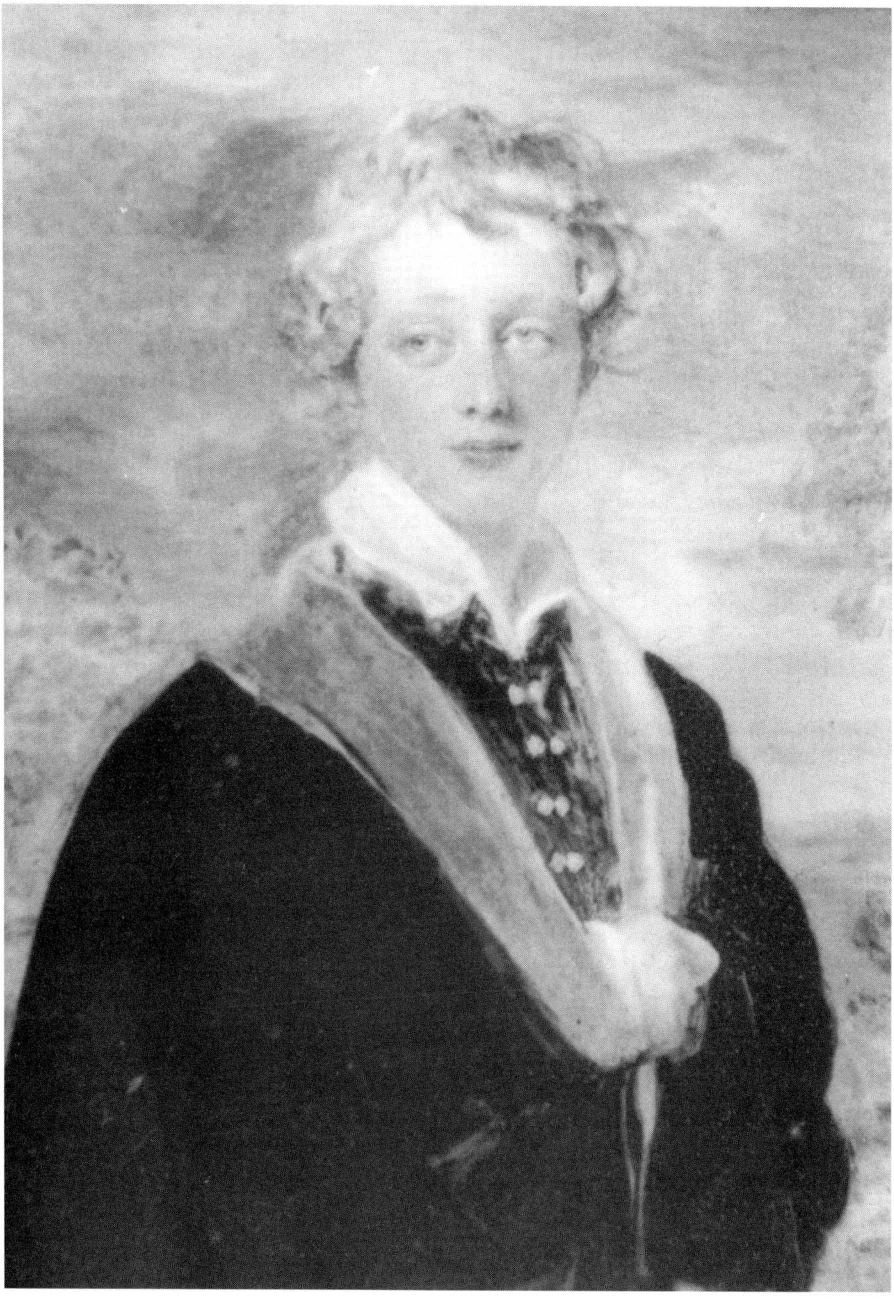

'Pretty, small, shy, timid, gentle looking': Sir Stephen Glynne as a boy from a miniature at Hawarden Castle. By the age of 13 he was riding 20 miles a day in search of ancient churches. Reproduced by kind permission of Sir William Gladstone, Bt.

The intellectual promise shown by Glynne at Eton did not blossom at Christ Church, Oxford. The rather spoilt young man, heir to a fortune, had little incentive to work and achieved only a third class degree in classics. He spent much of his time at Oxford playing the piano and, as we might expect, visiting old churches.[8] He returned to Hawarden where Mrs Edward Stanley met him at the age of twenty four. She calls him 'the topographical baronet' in contrast to 'the geological baronet' Sir Philip Egerton, and found Rickman's *Architecture* on his table 'interleaved with observations & notes of his own'. She considered Glynne 'pretty, small, shy, gentle-looking' and remarked on his grave and deliberate mode of speech. Mrs Stanley found the young baronet amiable and discovered that he was much loved and respected by his own people; 'such a good young gentleman', was the constant refrain. 'His study and pursuit is Antiquity & Cathedrals – there are only two in England that he has not seen, & that so thoroughly as to know all the details by heart.'[9]

At Hawarden, Glynne was much respected. He was not the sort of man who would ever be popular, although what *The Chester Chronicle* called his 'unaffected manners and invariable urbanity' made a good impression. Close friends found him a pleasant and cultured companion. He was genuinely kind-hearted and modest, doing good by stealth throughout life. The gift of a pound to an impecunious old tenant was found in his wallet after his death. Glynne was an old-fashioned churchman of a type which disappeared with the coming of the Oxford movement. He loved old church music, Bach, Corelli, and Handel and compiled a hymn book for Hawarden church. When at home he always read a psalm, prayers and a chapter of the Bible to his assembled family before breakfast.

There was no escaping the public duties expected of the landed gentry. Glynne accepted them dutifully but reluctantly. It was remarked that few made 'less personal effort to bring himself to the front' than did Glynne. He discharged his public responsibilities as quietly as possible. Nevertheless, he was an active magistrate and even chairman of the Board of Guardians in his locality. From 1832 to 1837 he was M.P. for Flint Boroughs, continuing for 10 years thereafter as M.P. for Flintshire, but his heart was never in it. Sir Stephen was frequently abroad and was annoyed when such matters as the dissolution of Parliament interrupted his 'flying about'. He never spoke in the House of Commons. Not even the marriage of his sister, Catherine, to W.E. Gladstone, then a rising politician and still 'the last hope of the stern unbending Tories' in July 1839 whetted his appetite for political life. Glynne began as a supporter of Reform but soon came to feel 'the restless spirit of innovation . . . which *unchecked* might cause the overthrow of the monarchy itself' and became a Conservative. The hurly-burly of the hustings were never to his taste and it hurt him deeply that after the election campaign of 1841 he had to bring a libel action against *The Chester Chronicle* which had accused him of homosexuality. Gladstone thought this particularly hard on a man 'with a tone of character such as . . . is most of all remarkable for its peculiar purity'.[10]

8. Glynne–Gladstone MS. 12: Henry Glynne to Mary, Lady Glynne, 21 June 1829.
9. Glynne–Gladstone MS. 999: Mrs. Edward Stanley to Mrs. Augustus Hare, January 1831.
10. Glynne–Gladstone MS. 22: W.E. Gladstone to Sir S.R. Glynne, 3 June 1841.

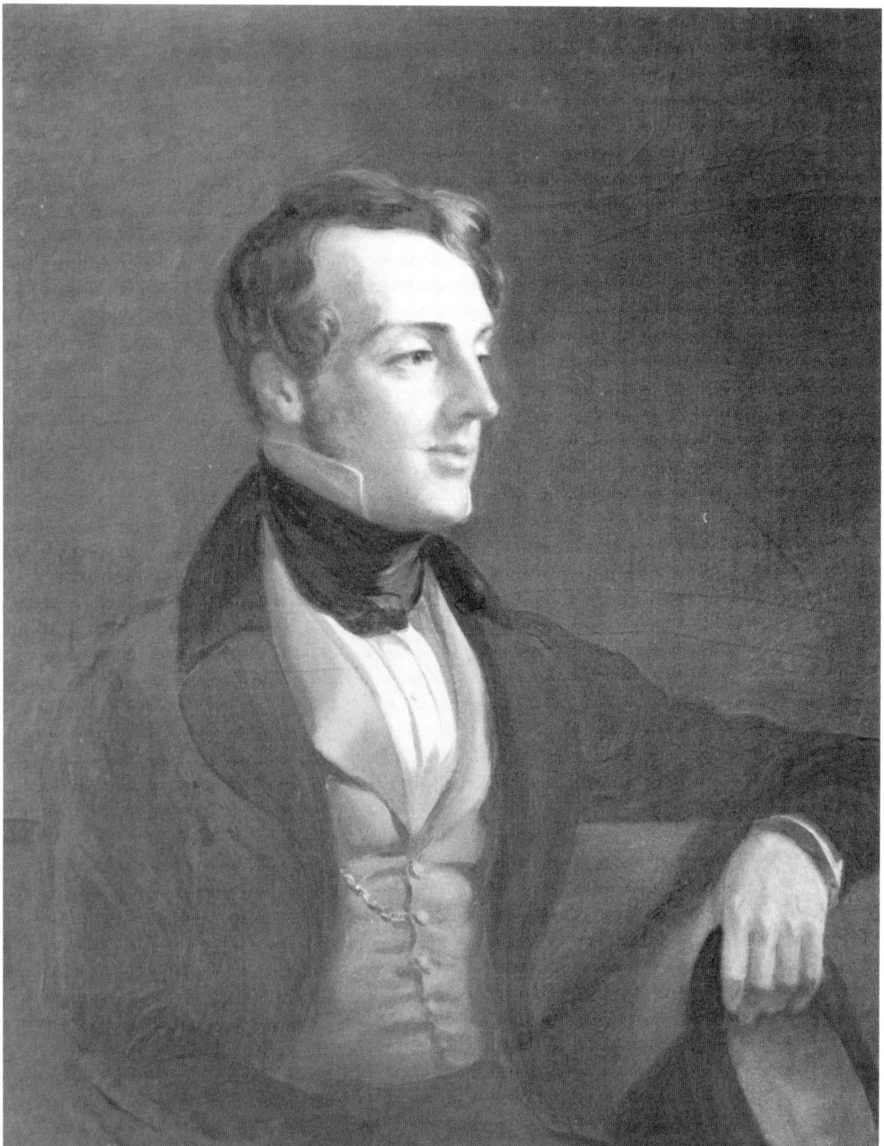

Already in 'pursuit of Antiquity and Cathedrals': Sir Stephen Richard Glynne, ninth baronet, aged about 25 from a portrait by Sir George Hayter at Hawarden Castle, probably painted in 1832. Reproduced by kind permission of Sir William Gladstone, Bt.

Those who knew him said he was as innocent as a lamb. Sir Stephen moved out of the fray in 1845 as Lord Lieutenant of Flintshire, being persuaded by his brother-in-law, Lord Lyttleton, who told him that he would find it 'hardly any trouble in quiet times' and that he would get 'a great deal of butter & deference at public meetings'.[11]

A practical man of business Glynne was not. He was less extravagant than careless, even reckless. He travelled widely and built schools and churches, taking little interest in the running of his estates which he left to his staff, not always reliable. In particular an attempt to exploit the coal on his Oak Farm estate in Staffordshire was mismanaged. By 1847 he was on the edge of bankruptcy, his mortgages and debts totalling £250,000. His uncle Lord Braybrooke blamed his 'apathy and want of firmness'[12] but in fact he had not lived within his income since he came of age in 1828. When his financial affairs were at crisis point, Sir Stephen went off on a three month tour to Constantinople. It is difficult to decide whether to condemn his irresponsibility or to admire his *sang-froid*. At one point he had £17 only in his account. The situation was resolved by Gladstone taking over the whole management of his brother-in-law's financial affairs which he did with great success, gradually reducing the debts by judicious sales and sound policy. For a time, Glynne's income was reduced to £700 a year. Hawarden Castle was closed, to be re-opened in 1853 when the Gladstone family moved in to share it with him. He called the Gladstones 'the great people' and was glad not to have to entertain 'unsupported'. Although the 'excitement & want of quiescence' at weddings was a trial to him, Glynne enjoyed the society of his sister's children. He never married.

Much more congenial than business matters was Glynne's membership of the Ecclesiology Society of which he was a Vice-President. This had been founded in 1839 as the Cambridge Camden Society 'to promote the study of ecclesiastical architecture and antiquities and the restoration of mutilated architectural remains'. The insistence of the Society that church buildings should reflect the Christian faith had a considerable influence on Glynne, whose church notes ceased to be only antiquarian but became larded with liturgical observations. He contributed to its journal and helped to write *The Hand-Book of English Ecclesiology*, published in 1847. Even the learned ecclesiologists conceded that Glynne was 'the most accurate of observers'. He was also first President of the Cambrian Archaeological Society in 1847 expressing the wish that it would be 'eminently useful in bringing to light the antiquities of the country'.

The years of Glynne's 'retired and unobtrusive' (but by no means unproductive) life passed serenely by, filled with ecclesiology to the last. He came to London on his way to see his sister at Wellington College after visiting churches in Essex. He collapsed and died in Shoreditch on 17th June, 1874. The private nature of the man is underlined by his reluctance to give any personal details about himself to those who attended him as he lay dying. Glynne was buried at Hawarden on the 24th June in a ceremony which,

11. Glynne–Gladstone MS. 25: Lord Lyttleton to Sir S.R. Glynne, 19 April 1845.
12. Glynne–Gladstone MS. 19: Lord Braybrooke to Sir S.R. Glynne, n.d.

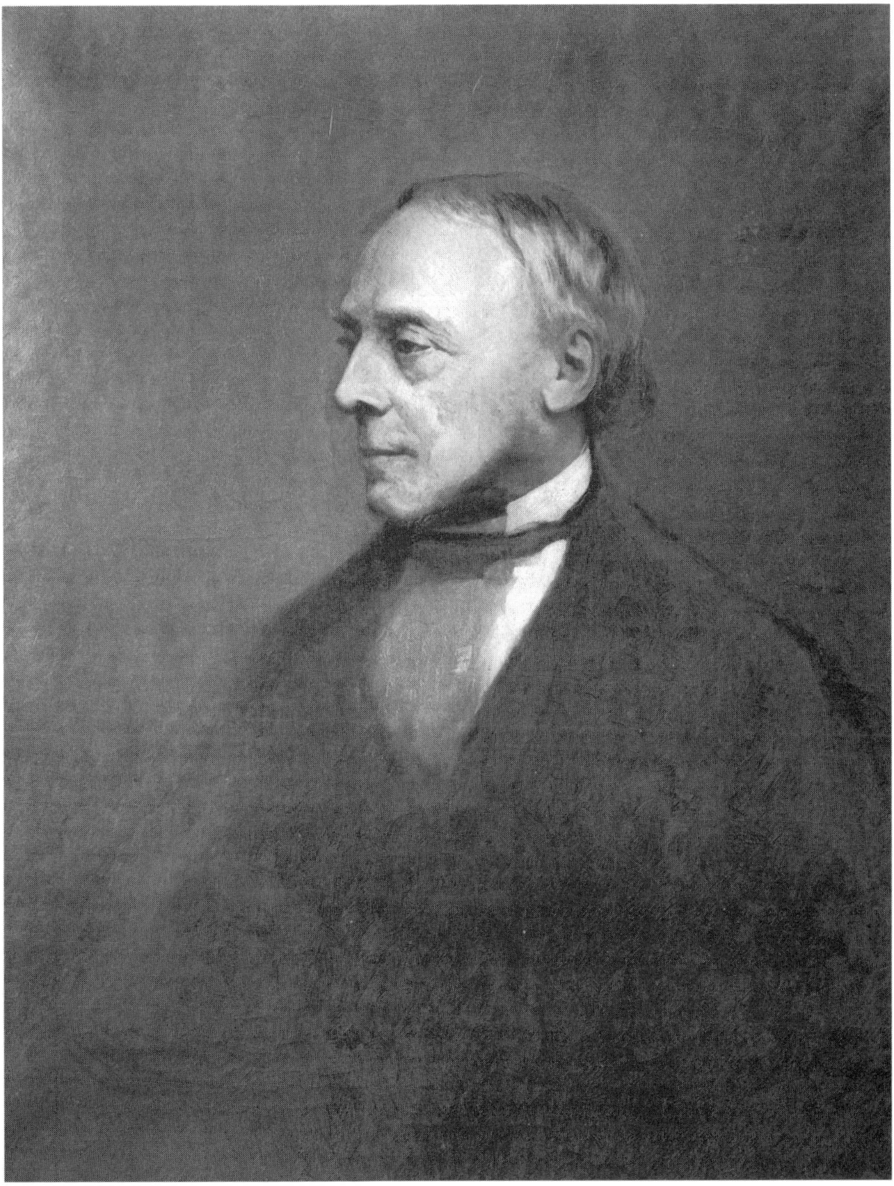

Sir Stephen Glynne as he was towards the end of his life from a posthumous portrait by W.T. Roden at Hawarden Castle, commissioned by his family as a memorial to him. Reproduced by kind permission of Sir William Gladstone, Bt.

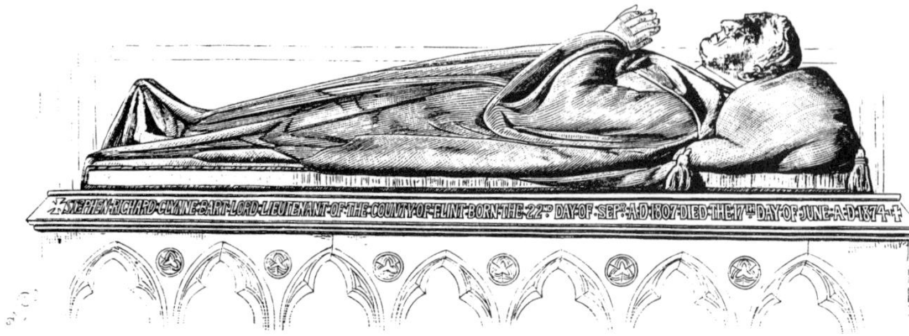

Memorial effigy of Sir Stephen Glynne by Matthew Noble in the Whitley chancel, Hawarden Church, Clwyd.

Gladstone recorded, 'was a most soothing, most Christian funeral, such as *he* deserved, such as *he* would have loved'.[13] His sister, Mrs Gladstone, told Queen Victoria that her brother 'was no ordinary person with very considerable gifts and with kindness and affection unbounded'.[14] Gladstone thought his brother-in-law's life 'pure, beautiful and peaceful'. Sir Stephen Glynne may not have been well-known in his day but as Mr A.G. Veysey has remarked 'after reading his many travel journals, diaries and the massive collection of church notes he left behind, one cannot but admire and be grateful for the energy and determination of a Victorian antiquarian whose researches and life work are of lasting value'.[15]

2. *Glynne's Somerset Church Notes*

As we have seen, Sir Stephen Glynne began looking at churches as a small child, but his life's work did not start in earnest until 1824 when he visited Beddgelert in North Wales. He was then sixteen or seventeen and would continue the task for the next fifty years. It is difficult to be sure of the exact number of churches that he saw in that time. The Revd Benjamin Webb, of the Ecclesiastical Society, estimated 5,530. A contemporary list gives 5,521 and the index at the Clwyd Record Office 5,150. Sometimes visits to minor churches are hidden away in accounts of greater ones and this accounts for some discrepancy. Rumour had it that Glynne visited every parish in the kingdom, surely an exaggeration, but certainly he reached more than half of all pre-Reformation churches. These were mostly in England and Wales, but included a few in Scotland and Ireland, the Channel Islands and the Isle of Man as well as those seen on continental tours.

Viewing churches became Glynne's favourite occupation and he spent some months each year on this pleasant task. As an ecclesiologist he was largely self-taught, but in time his knowledge of church architecture became 'so extensive

13. *The Gladstone Diaries*, VIII: 1871–74 (1982), 501–505.
14. Glynne–Gladstone MS. 1016: Mrs. Gladstone to Queen Victoria, 22 June 1874.
15. A.G. Veysey, *Sir Stephen Glynne*, 167.

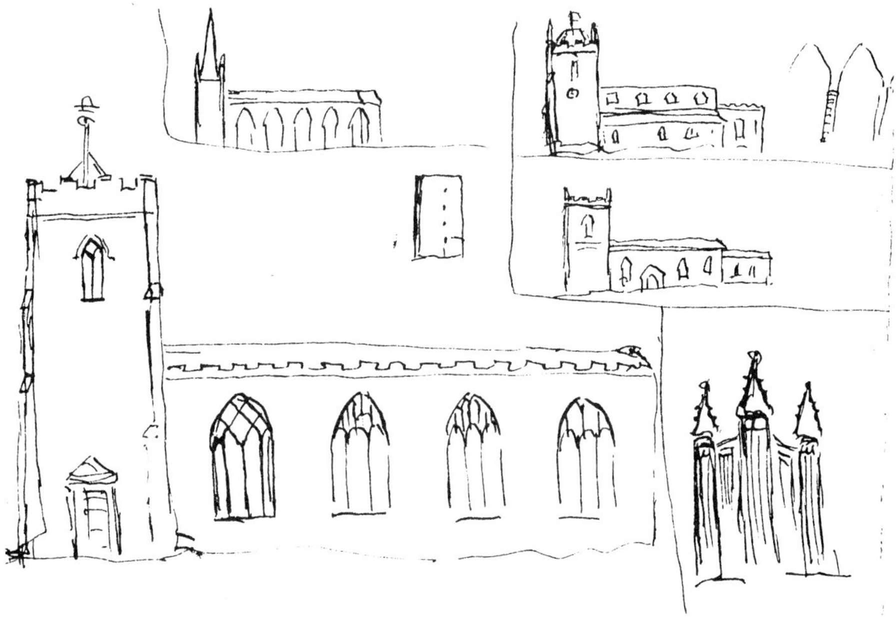

Rough sketch of an unidentified church made by Sir Stephen Glynne.

and exact that he could take in at a glance the features of a building and his descriptions are remarkable for their accuracy'.[16] His nephew W.H. Gladstone summed up Glynne's skill even more succinctly: on seeing a church he 'would at once, as if by instinct, read its architectural history'.[17] We may agree with R.D. Thomas that 'probably no one in the Kingdom ever visited so many of the old churches of the land; certainly no one ever examined so large a number so thoroughly and intelligently or recorded so minutely their details and salient features'.[18]

As far as Somerset is concerned, Glynne's own list shows that he inspected 244 churches in our county out of a total of some 500, but when the notes came to be transribed descriptions of 256 Somerset churches were found. Glynne's methods were determined and energetic. He did much of his church visiting on horseback and usually alone, although occasionally he would take a friend or join a clergyman on his Visitation. The aid of the incumbent was 'rarely invoked or required'.[19] Few are mentioned and those being the days of open churches (although even Glynne was faced with locked doors sometimes) the local clergy could easily be by-passed.

Glynne delighted in 'roaming', as he called it, 'and the very act of exploring the country to its furthest recesses, and acquiring all sorts of local information

16. Revd. J.A. Atkinson, *Notes on the Churches of Lancashire by the late Sir Stephen R. Glynne, Bart*, Chetham Society, vol. 27, new series, (1893), iii.
17. W.H. Gladstone, *Notes on the Churches of Kent*, London, John Murray, (1877), v.
18. *Archaeologia Cambrensis*, 6th. series, 2, (1902), 113–114.
19. Gladstone, *Churches of Kent*, iv–vi.

by the way, was a process thoroughly congenial'[20] to him. In South Wales in 1824 he travelled 930 miles in 48 days visiting not only 84 churches but also 43 castles with five cathedrals and six ruined abbeys thrown in for good measure.[21] The next year he drove 120 miles round Lincolnshire in a gig taking in '40 churches at the rate of 10 a day – all splendid'.[22] Glynne had no objection to using his legs and once walked 17 miles to see a new church. Otherwise he rode, took some kind of carriage, or even sailed. He thought nothing of missing his way – an occupational hazard – or of ending up ankle-deep in mud.

Advice from fellow antiquaries was always welcome and the congenial intercourse between them is revealed in a letter to Glynne from a Mr Parker. It is undated but written before the death of Sir Richard Colt Hoare of Stourhead in 1838. After advising Glynne on a trip to Devon – 'in some parts you will find much to interest you' – Parker tells Glynne:

> 'I must now speak for myself a little & wish anything might bring you towards the north of that county, or into Somerset so as to be at Sturton about Easter. From Taunton or Shaftesbury you are a very short distance. There is the nicest inn in the kingdom at Sturton close to my friend Sr. Rd. Hoare's garden, & I am sure he will be most happy to be introduced to a Brother Antiquarian so versed as yourself, & shew you his British museum as well as beautiful place, from there so much is to be seen, Longleat 6 miles only, Wardour 8, Stonehenge, Wilton, Wardour [*sic*], etc. & so on to the coast at Brighton'.[23]

The first tour of Somerset by Glynne was made in 1825 with his observations written up in the form of an antiquarian journal. He came into the county from Devon, sweeping through it from Ilchester to Chard, Ilminster, Langport (on a 'dreadfully wet day which prevented us from enjoying the country'), Somerton, Glastonbury, Wells, Castle Cary, Bruton, Yeovil, Crewkerne and Shepton Mallet as well as many small churches in between. Ecclesiastical buildings and their architecture are, of course, the centre of interest, but the vision is slightly broader than it later became, giving glimpses of the countryside, old houses, and some general comments. This is also true of his French tour of 1826 when he writes of Falaise from a typically insular point of view: 'certainly a delightful town and more resembles an English town than almost any French town I know, there being a general appearance of cleanliness'.[24] Later such frivolous comments disappear from his notes.

Before 1840 Glynne's notes are undated, which is unfortunate, but from that time forward he kept his own index with the precise date of every visit. He saw 65 Somerset churches before 1840 and a further 107 before 1860. That was generally before the Victorian programme of church restoration got into its stride. The last Somerset church he saw was Clutton on 16th May, 1874, a month before his death. Considering that Glynne was visiting churches in many other counties, he did well to reach so many in Somerset, more than in

20. Gladstone, *ibid.*, iv.
21. National Library of Wales: Glynne of Hawarden MS. 57, f. 50.
22. Glynne–Gladstone MS. 14: Sir S.R. Glynne to Mary, Lady Glynne, 8 May 1825.
23. Glynne–Gladstone MS. 27.
24. Glynne–Gladstone MS. 1077.

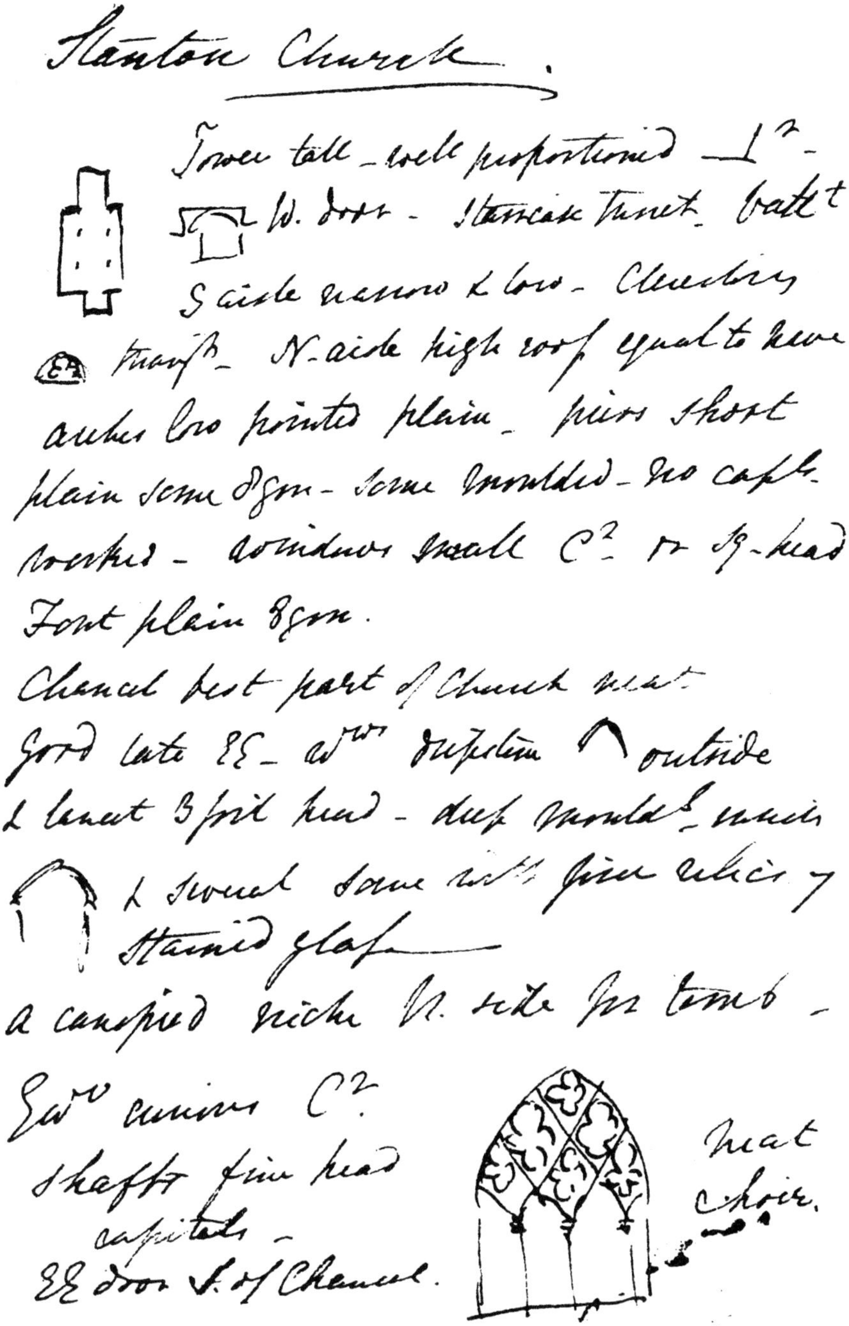

Stanton Church.

Tower tall – well proportioned ⊥r –
W. door – Staircase turret – battt
S aisle narrow & low – Clerestory
transt – N-aisle high roof equal to nave
arches low pointed plain – piers short
plain some 8gon – some moulded – no capls.
worked – windows small Cr or Sq-head
Font plain 8gon.
Chancel best part of Church neat
good late EE – wdws deeply outside
& lancet 3 foil head – deep mouldgs – much
& several some with fine relics of
stained glass
a canopied niche N. side for tomb –
Eastw curious Cr.
shafts fine head
capitals –
EE door S. of Chancel.
neat
choir.

Aide-memoire for an antiquary: brief details of Stanton Church jotted down by Glynne on the spot. Such jottings formed the basis of the future church notes.

any other county except Kent and Lincolnshire. Nevertheless, his coverage of the county was patchy. The north was pretty thoroughly recorded, but the eastern march from Cucklington towards Bath was much neglected. He saw Rode and Freshford but missed such gems as Farleigh Hungerford and Witham Friary.

Likewise many churches around Radstock and Midsomer Norton were omitted including Norman Lullington and the island church of Orchardleigh. The western Mendips and the levels below them saw Glynne hardly at all. He failed also to penetrate the south and west borderlands of Somerset from Pendomer to Oare or that triangle of country between the Parrett estuary, Bridgwater and the Quantock Hills, so leaving important churches such as Cannington and Stogursey unvisited. Glynne did travel along the northern seaboard as far as Culbone but recorded few of the churches in the interior of Exmoor.

As Glynne grew older the character of his notes changed. As a young man they are antiquarian, but under the influence of the Ecclesiological Society he takes an increasing interest in liturgical arrangements such as whether or not there were crosses on the gables or candlesticks on the altar and the dignity and correctness of a church from an Ecclesiological point of view. The youth had been able to judge 'unscholarly' Georgian Gothic on its merits; the man was less certain of his judgment. Glynne saw Holy Trinity, Dorchester, in 1827 and described it as having been rebuilt 'in a very neat style', but re-visiting in 1852 he states baldly that it 'now must be condemned as excessively bad'. Besides this new slant, his passion for distinguishing between the various architectural styles present in the churches came to dominate his view of a church. That in itself posed a problem for at the beginning of the 19th century

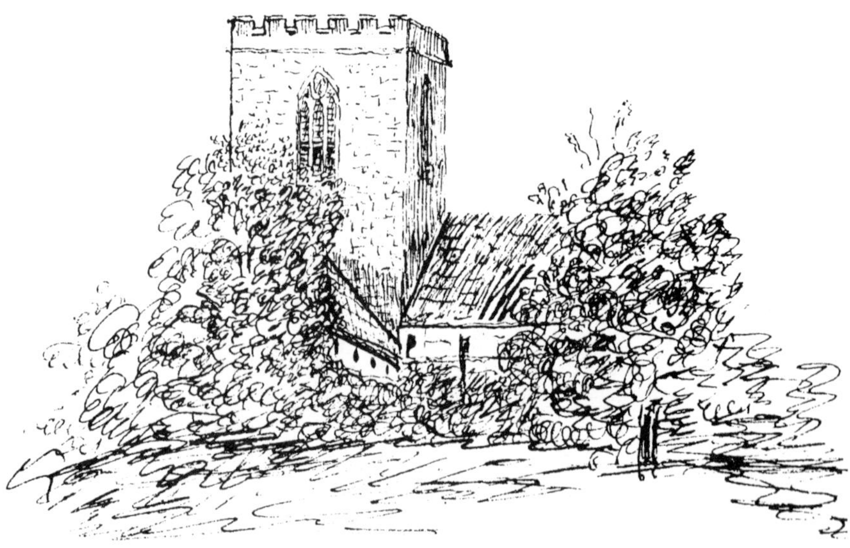

Glynne was a competent artist. This pen and ink sketch of St. Asaph Cathedral was done when he was 19.

there was no universal agreement as to the names to be given to these styles. In 1819 Thomas Rickman published his *Attempt to Discriminate the Styles of English Architecture* in which he gave the name Early English to the style of the 13th century, Decorated to that of the 14th, and Perpendicular to that of the late 14th and 15th centuries. These terms are now standard, but in Glynne's day they were considered awkward and disliked by many scholars. Glynne accepted Rickman's nomenclature at first, but later adopted other terms, although not exclusively the others. So throughout these notes a mixture of terms will be found. After starting out as a Rickmanite, broadly between about 1830 and 1842, Glynne was inclined to use 'Curvilinear' for Decorated and 'Rectilinear' for Perpendicular. Sometimes he combines the two, as in his note on Selworthy church. In the later 1840s and early 1850s, he opted for 'First', 'Second' and 'Third Pointed' before finally returning to Rickman's Early English, Decorated and Perpendicular.

To be found in the notes also are some obscure architectural terms, fashionable in Glynne's day, but which have long since been discarded. Such are '*benetura*', a stoup or basin for holy water, 'lychnoscope', 'sanctus window', 'hagioscope' for a squint, and '*fenestella*', a niche containing a piscina, a basin with a drain used for washing the holy vessels after communion. He also uses the word 'feathering' for what we now call cusping. Once he had sorted out the architecture of the church, Glynne spared a cursory glance for other features of the building such as tombs, brasses, monuments, organs, stained glass and bells. Although these objects sometimes forced themselves on his attention, they were of much less interest and are generally treated in a perfunctory manner and sometimes omitted. Ironwork and heraldry, especially 'obituary' glass, are mentioned occasionally and sometimes the notes are enlivened by the recounting of a legend like that of Sir John Hauteville at Chew Magna.

Nevertheless, Glynne's notes are far from being a mere catalogue of architectural details. He knew his own mind and did not hesitate to express his views. Those inject a vibrant element into the notes. He had a particular detestation of pews, preferring open benches, disliked galleries and modern monuments (anything after 1500 'a date subsequent to which rarely anything good can be found') and hated whitewash. The 'frightful' white pews of Keynsham filled him with disgust and he found Pawlett church 'so glaring white as to be almost spectral'. He was appalled by the 'neglect, dirt and ruin' of Dunster and holds up the Wyndham tombs at St Decuman's as an example of 'the decline of monuments to downright paganism'. The paintings at East Chinnock were 'barbarous' and the gallery at Norton Fitzwarren 'hideous'. At Charlton Horethorne the details did not bear inspection.

All the same, Glynne was a fair-minded man and he rarely let prejudice overcome reasoned judgment. He generously commends the 'handsome pews' at Crewkerne and the galleries, also handsome, at Ilminster while the tower gallery at Dinder was 'a far better arrangement than when it intrudes on the nave'. There is high praise, too; the tower at North Petherton is one of the finest and Martock church 'one of the largest and most beautiful' in the county. As for the roof at Somerton it was simply 'one of the finest that can be seen'. Like all Ecclesiologists, Glynne believed that Decorated was the true Christian style but tolerated decent Early English and Perpendicular. He could even acknowledge that neo-Norman could be well done (as at Corfe). Much could be forgiven as long as ecclesiastical propriety was observed. Glynne could accept most fittings if tasteful and generally welcomed restoration and improvement, whatever the style, but had little enthusiasm for new churches, however correct ecclesiastically.

As a young man Glynne had quoted in his commonplace book some lines from St Ronan's Well by Sir Walter Scott:

> 'Knowledge that is unimparted is necessarily a barren talent & lost to society like the miser's concealed hoard by the death of the proprietor'.

Despite this wise self-admonition he failed to impart his own knowledge except in conversation. That he knew much about churches was well-known to the Victorian *cognoscenti* and he was several times asked to write a book but could never be persuaded to do so. When Glynne's death was announced, discerning contemporaries were immediately concerned about the possible loss of so much knowledge. 'There will be general anxiety,' commented *The Daily Telegraph* in its appreciation of Glynne, 'to learn whether he leaves behind him any ms. notes, or document susceptible of publication.'[25]

The challenge was taken up by Glynne's nephew, W.H. Gladstone, who proposed to publish the 307 notes on the churches of Kent, the largest single county collection. He showed them to the Revd Benjamin Webb, of the Ecclesiastical Society, who commented that it was 'indeed a happy thing (and truly characteristic of his ordered and exemplary life) that the rough notes of the observations of so many years are so fully and so intelligently written up . . . no attention seems needed, and no curtailment possible'. He concluded that the notes were 'of lasting value and interest which would become a standard work of reference as to the state of our churches in the middle of the 19th century'.[26] Word got round stimulating Archdeacon Benjamin Harrison to write to Gladstone in May 1876 that he was 'heartily glad to hear there is a prospect of Sir Stephen's wonderful notes being published. I felt and expressed at the time of his lamented death, great regret that his vast stores of knowledge in regard to our old churches should be lost'.[27] The following year *The Churches of Kent* appeared, being printed directly from the original manuscript which was subsequently lost. Glynne's notes on the churches of Wales and Monmouth were published next in the pages of *Archaeologia Cambrensis* from 1884. But it was the West Country which was most active in getting the notes into print, those of Cornwall, Devon, Wiltshire and Gloucestershire being published over the years. Somerset is the 13th county to be published plus Wales and Monmouth and the notes on Ipswich in Suffolk (see appendix 1). Those of Rutland, transcribed by the present editor, will be published shortly.

It is surprising that more of Glynne's church notes have not appeared in print as they have long been known as a source of ecclesiastical history and open to researchers. There is much interest in individual parish churches, but

25. Glynne–Gladstone MS. 1016.
26. Sir Stephen Glynne's church notes, vol. 107.
27. *Ibid.*

less in transcribing the notes by county. This is all the more astonishing given the value of the notes which have been described by a modern scholar as 'one of the most valuable available sources for the appearance and condition of British churches in the second and third quarters of the nineteenth century.'[28] Students may have been put off by Glynne's concern with architectural features and periods of construction to the exclusion of more colourful details. Nevertheless, the notes contain descriptions of many churches which are unique, including the condition of the fabric in Glynne's time, the features of the building, information about early restorations and additions, and records of fittings and artefacts later swept away.

Glynne's church notes are deposited in St Deiniol's Library at Hawarden in Clwyd which was founded by his brother-in-law, W.E. Gladstone. They are available through the Clwyd Record Office (which is next door), the County Archivist acting as honorary archivist to the Library. The notes are contained in 107 volumes, 7ins. by 9ins., with leather spines and marbled covers. Generally, each volume runs to 85 folios. The recto page is used for the description of the church, the verso for additions and occasional sketches, sometimes of a whole church or tower, but more often showing details of window tracery or the mouldings of a pillar. The Revd J.A. Atkinson, editor of Glynne's notes on the churches of Lancashire, who knew him, tells us that Glynne wrote these notes 'for his own satisfaction' although in fact remembering the details.[29] W.H. Gladstone, another of Glynne's editors, who should have been *au fait* with is uncle's methods, says that he 'jotted down brief memoranda respecting the fabric and its appurtenances to be afterwards drawn up into the full but compendious form'.[30] It is true that a few of these memoranda survive, such as those of Stanton church, yet the notebooks themselves give no impression of finished form, often showing evidence of hasty writing, interlinings and crossings out. It is difficult to believe that the rough sketches were not done at the time. Glynne writes as a rule in a fine but crabbed hand which can pose problems for the transcriber when he was writing quickly; it deteriorates as the years go by.

I intended to transcribe Glynne's church notes in 1985, but quailed before the huge pile of photocopies and did not start in earnest until February, 1991. I decided to arrange the notes alphabetically for easy reference and this accounts for why a few notes taken from the early journals begin rather abruptly. I have corrected some minor spelling (such as storey for story) and punctuation. Glynne often refers to pews as pues and rere-arches as rear-arches. I have let these stand as sensible and characteristic. He uses also 'ye' and 'hath' on occasion. Editorial interpolations (such as dedications of churches left out by Glynne) are in square brackets. Material in round brackets represents Glynne's own additions or after thoughts.

28. Nigel Yates, 'Sir Stephen Glynne and Kentish Ecclesiology', in Alec Detsicas and Nigel Yates, *Studies in Modern Kentish History*, Kent Archaeological Society, Maidstone, (1983), 192.
29. Atkinson, *Notes on Lancashire Churches*, iii.
30. Gladstone, *Churches of Kent*, v.

NOTE ON THE ILLUSTRATIONS

by David Bromwich

Most of the illustrations which appear in this volume have been chosen from two large collections, both put together during the period when Sir Stephen Glynne was writing, but independently of him and of each other.

The Pigott Collection was commissioned by John Hugh Smyth-Pigott, F.S.A. (ca 1792–1853) of Brockley Hall and of Grove House, Weston-super-Mare.[1] It consists of six large volumes containing 1,154 wash drawings entitled 'Illustrations of the Ecclesiastical and Domestic Architecture of Somersetshire. . .' The artists were John Buckler, F.S.A. (1770–1851) and his son John Chessell Buckler (1793–1894). Their work also survives in copies retained by them, which are now in the British Library, as well as in the ones which they supplied to other patrons.[2] Smyth-Pigott's drawings were bequeathed to the county of Somerset, placed at Quarter Sessions under trustees, and deposited by them with the Somerset Archaeological and Natural History Society, which has published a catalogue of them,[3] and has retained them ever since.

The Braikenridge Collection, or rather collections, as there are parallel ones covering Bristol in the Bristol Central Library and in the City Art Gallery there, were formed by George Weare Braikenridge, F.S.A., F.G.S. (1775–1856) of Broomwell House, Brislington.[4] His Somerset collection originally took the form of an extra-illustrated copy of J. Collinson's *History and Antiquities of Somerset* (1791) enlarged from three to fourteen large volumes with the addition of prints and watercolours. The majority of the latter were commissioned from William Walter Wheatley (1811–1885), who provided similar work for W. Adlam and for Prebendary J.S.W. Horner, which is now in the possession of the Society of Antiquaries of London and of the Earl of Oxford and Asquith respectively.[5] Another artist represented in the present selection is Samuel Griffiths Tovey (1808–1873). On the death of G.W. Braikenridge the Somerset collection passed to his son William Jerdone Braikenridge, and on the latter's death in 1907 it was bequeathed to the Somerset Archaeological and Natural History Society. By 1975 the condition

1. See *Portraits of the Smyth-Pigott family: a catalogue of the oil paintings and busts in Woodspring Museum, Weston-super-Mare.*
2. M.W. Barley, *A guide to British topographical collections*, (1974), p. 62.
3. S.A.N.H.S. *Proceedings*, 8, (for 1858), pp. 149–190.
4. See S. Stoddard, *Mr Braikenridge's Brislington*, 1981.
5. M. McGarvie, 'A letter from W.W. Wheatley,' *Somerset & Dorset Notes & Queries*, 32, part 325, (March 1987), pp. 583–4.

of the heavy volumes had deteriorated, and they were broken up and the prints and drawings re-housed in a filing cabinet.

Some of the illustrations from both these collections have been published before,[6] but the present selection is the largest single one to have been made so far.

The two drawings of Glastonbury Abbey ruins come from a small collection by Samuel Hieronymus Grimm (1733–1794), also in the hands of the Somerset Archaeological Society. The interior view of Shepton Mallet Church is not taken from the Pigott Collection, although it too is by John Buckler, but from a separate drawing in the private possession of Mr T.W. Mayberry, who has given permission for it to be reproduced here. The Skinner view of Street Church is from the British Library, and is reproduced here by permission.

Copies of illustrations in the collection of the Somerset Archaeological Society may be obtained from the society's secretary, Taunton Castle, Taunton, Somerset, TA1 4AD.

6. See especially A.K. Wickham, *Churches of Somerset*, (1952).

GLOSSARY

Abacus	The uppermost division of a capital (French *abaque*, a tile).
Apse	Semi-circular or polygonal east end of a church.
Ashlar	Finely cut masonry blocks.
Aumbrye/aumbry	Cupboard in the north wall of the sanctuary where the sacraments or sacred vessels were kept.
Ballflower	Petalled, globe-like ornament used as decoration in the early 14th century.
Benetura	Stoup; a basin for holy water usually near the church entrance.
Billet	An ornament used in Norman architecture; an imitation of billets, round sections of sticks, alternating with spaces.
Boss	A carved stone placed at the intersection of the ribs of a vault.
Cable	A Norman moulding cut in imitation of twisted rope.
Capital	The crown of a column.
Cavetto	A hollow moulding.
Chamfer	The paring off of the angle of a corner or sharp edge.
Chancel	The eastern part of a church containing the main altar usually divided from the nave by a screen (*cancellus*).
Chantry	A family sepulchral chapel in which masses for the dead were performed.
Chevron	Norman zig-zag or inverted 'V' ornament.
Cinquefoil	Five-leafed decoration in tracery.
Clerestory	Range of windows in the top storey of a nave or chancel.
Corbel	Projecting stone in a wall to support an arch, vault, or roof timber.
Collegiate church	One served by a college of canons or prebendaries.
Cornice	Moulding which projects from the top of a wall, column or entablature.
Cove	A concave moulding linking a wall and flat ceiling.
Crocket	A small carved ornament on the side of a pinnacle or colonette.
Curvilinear	Early 14th-century Decorated style using tracery of a flowing pattern.
Crypt	Vaulted chamber, usually for burial, under a church.

Cusp Connecting point between arcs in Gothic tracery and ornament, often richly carved. Glynne calls cusping 'feathering'.

Decorated Gothic style of the first half of the 14th century.

Dripstone A projecting moulding over doors and windows to keep off the rain.

Early English The first Gothic style, of the 13th century, characterized by simple forms and tracery.

Feathering See cusp.

Fenestella Niche containing a piscina and sometimes a credence shelf usually on the south side of the altar.

Finial Ornament (usually of carved foliage) crowning pinnacles, canopies, gables, etc.

First Pointed Alternative name for Early English sometimes used by Glynne.

Flying Buttress Buttress in the form of an arch used to support the thrust of a high vault.

Hagioscope Squint allowing a view of the altar from side chapels.

Hatchment A board painted with the coat-of-arms of a deceased person hung outside their house after death and later in the church. The word is a corruption of achievement.

Grisaille Grey-white monochrome glass with enamelled patterns on the quarries.

Hood Projecting moulding above a door or window originally applied to those inside a building.

Impost Horizontal mouldings at the springing of an arch or pilaster.

Jamb Sides of a window or door (or chimney).

Label Projecting moulding above a door or window to keep off the rain.

Lancet Tall, narrow pointed window characteristic of the Early English style.

Lychnoscope A sanctus or low side window on the south side of the chancel through which people outside could hear the sound of the sanctus bell rung at the Elevation of the Host.

Mullion An upright bar of stone or wood dividing a window into lights.

Nailhead A Norman and Early English ornament in the shape of a small pyramidal stud.

Niche A recess in a wall or pillar, often semi-circular.

Ogee An arch moulding incorporating double curves, convex and concave.

Panelled Usually a wooden lining on interior walls divided into compartments, but used by Glynne mostly of battlements and roofs implying square, recessed panels surrounded by a moulding.

Parapet A wall, solid or embattled, round the top of a building. It is often pierced with quatrefoils or waved lines.

Parclose screen One which enclosed part of an aisle or chapel.

Parvise	A small room above a church porch sometimes used as a school, library or for storing records.
Pilaster	Pier or pillar attached to a wall.
Piscina	Recess with basin and drain usually in the south wall of the sanctuary used for washing the sacred vessels.
Quatrefoil	A four-leaf decoration in tracery.
Quoin	A dressed corner stone.
Quarry	A small, lozenge-shaped piece of glass leaded in a window.
Rectilinear	Alternative name for Perpendicular.
Reredos	Carved or decorated screen behind the altar.
Rib	Projecting band of stone supporting a vault.
Rood	Cross with a figure of Christ.
Roodloft	The gallery on which the rood was placed, usually between the chancel and the nave.
Sacrarium	Sacristy, part of a church used for storing sacred vessels.
Second Pointed	Alternative name for the Decorated style.
Sedile, sedilia	Stone seat, or seats, usually three but sometimes less, attached to the chancel wall and used by the clergy.
Soffit	The underside of an arch, lintel, cornice, etc.
Spandrel	A triangular space between two arches often found in the corners of arches and chimneys.
Splay	Diagonal surface caused by cutting away a wall especially the jamb of a window to allow more light to enter.
Stilted	Used of an arch which does not rise directly from imposts but from uprights rising from them, so said to rest on stilts.
Stoup	Stone basin used for holy water.
Stringcourse	Projecting horizontal band of masonry dividing the stages of a tower, etc.
Tabernacle	Receptacle in which the Sacraments were kept.
Tabernacle work	Traceried decoration on walls and fittings.
Third Pointed	Alternative name for the Perpendicular style.
Tracery	Intersecting decoration in a window. **Subarcuated tracery:** having subordinate arches within the tracery of a window.
Transom	Horizontal bar dividing a window.
Trefoil	Three-leaf decoration in tracery.
Tudor flower	Cresting used in the Tudor period as decoration consisting of a lozenge-shaped flower with three spiky lobes.
Tympanum	Semi-circular space over a Norman doorway often containing carved scenes.
Vault	Arched covering of a space in stone.
Vestry	Room attached to a church where vestments were kept and where clergy robed.
Voussoirs	Wedge-shaped stones usually supporting the keystone of an arch.

ACKNOWLEDGEMENTS

I am grateful to the Somerset Record Society for undertaking the publication of this substantial work and in particular to the Society's honorary editor, Dr R.W. Dunning, F.S.A. and to its chairman, Mr Gerard Leighton. The book has been greatly enhanced by the paintings of Somerset churches with which it is illustrated. These come from the Pigott and Braikenridge collections of the Somerset Archaeological and Natural History Society and I thank the Society and its honorary secretary, Mr Bruce Watkin, for allowing them to be reproduced. I owe much gratitude to Sir William Gladstone, Bt., owner of the Glynne manuscripts, for permission to publish and for kindly showing me portraits of Sir Stephen Glynne at Hawarden Castle. He also allowed them to be photographed and reproduced.

Without the support and co-operation of the Clwyd Record Office this book would never have come to print and I record my appreciation to the County Archivist, Mr A.G. Veysey M.A., and to Mr C.J. Williams. Mr Veysey also allowed me to draw on his scholarly and entertaining article on Glynne published in *The Journal of the Flintshire Historical Society* and I have made full use of this in my introduction. Dr J.H. Harvey, F.S.A. with his customary generosity helped me transcribe some of the more illegible parts of Glynne's notes. I thank Mr David Bromwich and Mr Barry Hamilton for work on the photographic side and Mr L.V. Bowring and the Frome Society for Local Study for a grant towards the considerable costs involved in the project.

Michael McGarvie
Marston House, October 1993.

APPENDIX 1

Published Editions of the Church Notes

The following editions of the church notes have appeared in print. The list includes only those publications which cover whole counties.

CHESHIRE:	*Chetham Society Remains*, N.S. XXXII (1894).
CORNWALL:	*Notes and Queries*, CLXVII–CLXIX (1934–5).
DEVON:	*Notes and Queries*, CXLIII–CLXVI (1932–4).
DORSET:	*Proc. Dorset Nat. Hist. and Ant. Field Club*, XLIV–XLV (1923–4).
GLOUCESTERSHIRE:	*Gloucestershire Church Notes* (London, 1902).
KENT:	W.H. Gladstone (ed.), *Notes on the Churches of Kent* (London, 1877).
LANCASHIRE:	*Chetham Society Remains*, N.S. XXVII (1893).
NORTHUMBERLAND AND DURHAM:	*Proc. Soc. Ant. Newcastle-upon-Tyne*, 3rd series, III (1907).
SURREY:	*Surrey Arch. Coll.*, LV (1958).
WILTSHIRE:	*Wilts. Arch. and Nat. Hist. Mag.*, XLII (1986).
YORKSHIRE:	*Yorks. Arch. Jnl.*, XII–XV (1893–1900), XVII–XVIII (1903–5), XX (1909), XXIII–XXIV (1915–17), XXVI (1922).
WALES:	D.R. Thomas (ed.), *Notes on the older Churches of the four Welsh Dioceses* (London, 1903). (Previously published in *Archaeologia Cambrensis*, 1884–8, 1897, and 1902).

APPENDIX 2

Sir Stephen Glynne's Church notes: list of volumes

This list was compiled by the Clwyd Record Office which has also indexed the notes and arranged them under counties. The churches are entered in alphabetical order with date of inspection, volume and folio number.

1–2. Bedfordshire and Huntingdon: Diocese of Lincoln.
3. Berkshire, Buckinghamshire and Oxfordshire: Diocese of Oxford.
4. Berkshire and Buckinghamshire: Diocese of Oxford.
5. Berkshire.
6. Berkshire and Buckinghamshire: Diocese of Oxford.
7. Cambridgeshire: Diocese of Ely.
8–9. Cheshire and Lancashire.
10. Cumberland and Westmorland: Dioceses of Carlisle and Chester.
11. Derbyshire.
12. Derbyshire and Nottinghamshire.
13–14. Devon and Cornwall: Diocese of Exeter.
15. Devon.
16–18. Devon and Cornwall: Diocese of Exeter.
19. Dorset, Devon and Somerset.
20. Dorset, city of Bristol and that part of Gloucestershire in the Diocese of Bristol.
21. Durham and Northumberland: Diocese of Durham.
22–24. Essex and Hertfordshire: Diocese of Rochester.
25. Essex and Hertfordshire: parts of original Diocese of London.
26. Hampshire and Isle of Wight: Diocese of Winchester.
27. Hampshire and Surrey: Diocese of Winchester.
28. Hampshire, Surrey and Channel Islands: Diocese of Winchester.
29. Hampshire and Surrey: Diocese of Winchester.
30. Hertfordshire and Buckinghamshire: Diocese of Lincoln.
31–33. Leicestershire and Rutland: Diocese of Peterborough.
34. Lincolnshire and Nottinghamshire: Diocese of Lincoln.
35. Middlesex.
36–39. Suffolk and Norfolk: Diocese of Norwich.
40–41. Northamptonshire.
42. Northamptonshire and Rutland: Diocese of Peterborough.
43. Northamptonshire: Diocese of Peterborough.
44–45. Oxfordshire.
46–47. Salop: Diocese of Lichfield.

48. Staffordshire and Derbyshire: Diocese of Lichfield.
49–52. Somerset.
53. Staffordshire: Diocese of Lichfield.
54. Suffolk: Diocese of Norwich and Ely.
55. Sussex: Diocese of Chichester.
56. Warwickshire: Diocese of Lichfield and Coventry.
57. Wiltshire and Dorset: Diocese of Salisbury.
58. Wiltshire.
59. Wiltshire, Hampshire, Isle of Wight and Dorset.
60. Miscellaneous Counties.
61. Cathedrals.
62. Scotland, Ireland and Isle of Man.
63. Gazetteer incomplete of dioceses, listing churches, county in which located, style of architecture etc.
64. [Lists of] churches classified according to architecture.
65. [Lists of] churches classified according to architecture.
66. South Wales.
67. North and South Wales.
68–69. North Wales.
70. South Wales and Monmouthshire.
71. North Wales.
72. Lincolnshire.
73. Lincolnshire and Nottinghamshire: Diocese of Lincoln.
74–75. Lincolnshire.
76. Lincolnshire and Nottinghamshire.
77–78. Gloucestershire: Diocese of Gloucester.
79. Diocese of Gloucester and Bristol with South Wales and Herefordshire. [Gloucestershire: 4 churches only].
80–81. Gloucestershire and Bristol: Diocese of Gloucester.
82. Gloucestershire and Wiltshire: Diocese of Gloucester.
83. Dorset, Wiltshire, and that part of Wiltshire which lies in the Diocese of Gloucester.
84. Yorkshire: Dioceses of York and Durham.
85. Miscellaneous.
86–88. Yorkshire.
89. Hereford, Monmouthshire and Salop: Diocese of Hereford.
90. Herefordshire and Monmouthshire.
91. Warwickshire and Worcestershire.
92–94. Worcestershire and Warwickshire: Diocese of Worcester.
95. Dioceses of Worcester and Gloucester.
96–97. Hereford and Salop: Diocese of Hereford.
98. Dioceses of Hereford and Llandaff.
99. Dioceses of York and Ripon.
100–3. Sussex.
104–6. Yorkshire.
107. Sir Stephen Glynne's Index (incl. correspondence and related papers).
108. MS. copy [by Revd. Gilbert C. Joyce, Warden of St. Deiniol's Library] of entries in vol. 11 (Derbyshire), *c.* 1900.

Ash Priors

50/86–87 Holy Trinity 7 May 1855

The plan: chancel and nave with north and south parallel aisles, west tower and south porch. The whole rather ordinary south-western Perpendicular. The exterior walls covered with yellow plaster, except the tower. The tower is embattled with square turret at the south-east with gargoyles but of a poor character. The tower arch from the nave springs straight from the walls. There is a great ascent eastward from the nature of the ground so that the chancel is unusually elevated and approached by several steps but this only serves to show off the hideous pues in the chancel to still greater disadvantage. The nave arcade on each side has 2 ordinary Perpendicular arches with a clustered pier of 4 shafts . . . the capitals being moulded.

The chancel arch springs from capitals only. The aisles of the chancel appear to be of the nature of chapels, each opening to the chancel by a double arch of small size, looking as if it had formerly contained a tomb there being

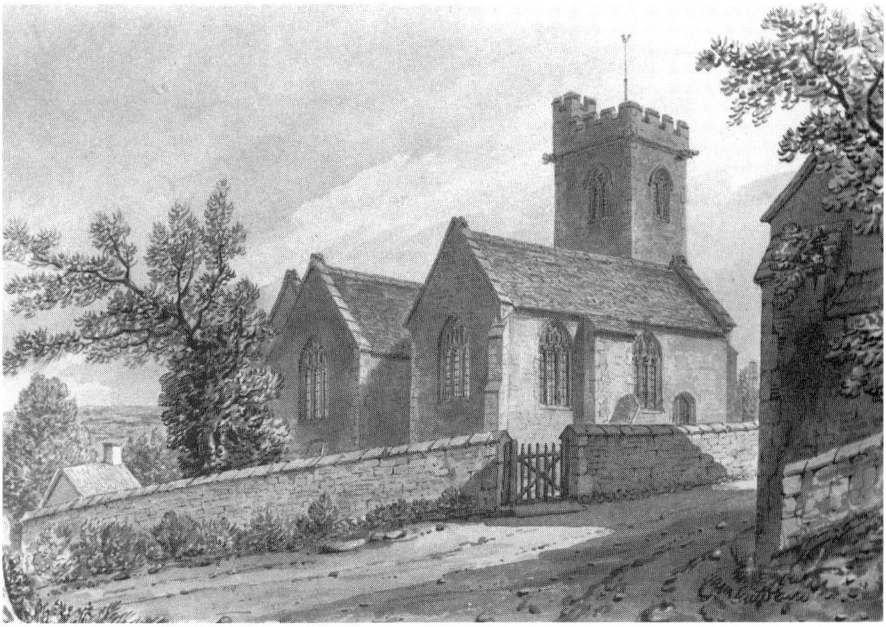

North east view of Ash Priors Church, 1835, by J. Buckler

shafts with moulded capitals to each face and the soffit forming, as it were, the covering of a tomb.

There are no arches between the aisles of the nave and those of the chancel. The windows are all of 3 lights. The chancel is ceiled. The nave and aisles have coved roofs with ribs and bosses. The chancel extends a little beyond the aisles. The font has an octagonal bowl, panelled with square quatrefoils, the same in the slope beneath the bowl and the pedestal all panelled. There is a projection on the north side or further rood steps. A few open benches exist, but not old. A west gallery contains a barrel organ. In some of the windows appear amber coloured floriated quarries.

Ashcott

19/67–68 [All Saints] Before 1840

The church is a neat structure consisting of a nave, chancel, and tower at the west end. The tower is embattled and has an octagonal staircase turret on the south side. At the angles under the battlement are grotesque water spouts and the belfry windows are of two lights and simple. On the western side of the tower is a piece of antique carving of square form in which are represented a mitre and crosier with other devices. The tower contains 5 bells and is divided from the church by a pointed arch. The church is mostly of Rectilinear period and has some very good work. The nave has a very beautiful open work parapet formed of *pierced quatrefoils*, set within lozenges, a form common in

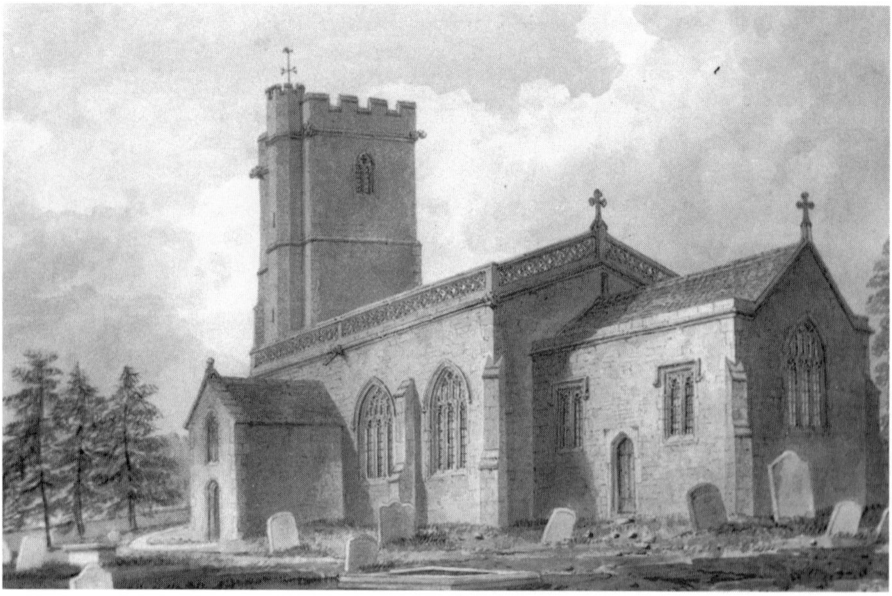

South east view of Ashcott Church, 1834, by J. Buckler

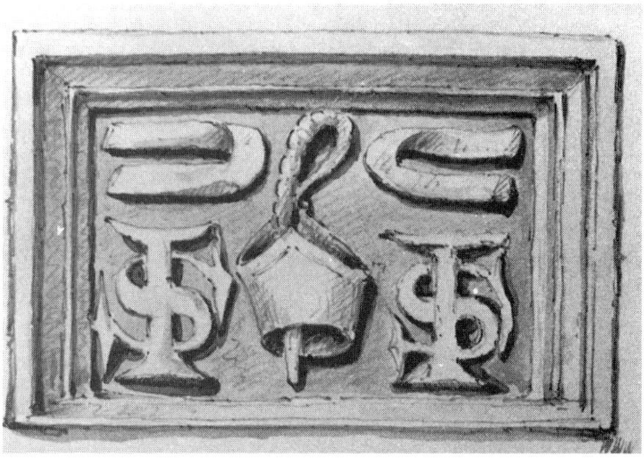

Ashcott Church, west side of the tower, 1843, by W.W. Wheatley

this county and occurring in St. Mary Magdalen's Church, Taunton. The chancel is tiled and without parapet.

The windows of the nave are of very good Rectilinear tracery with dripstones and some good fragments of painted glass. The pulpit is of stone with good panelling and band of quatrefoils and around the top a small cornice of square flowers. The font is circular upon a cylindrical pedestal, without ornament. The arch between the nave and the chancel is wide and pointed and springs from shafts, one of which has a foliated capital of early Gothic work. The roof of the nave has been handsomely painted and gilt but the colours are now quite faded. Between the beams and the roof is some handsome pierced panelling. The nave windows are mostly 3 lights. The chancel is of late Rectilinear work and has some square-headed windows. The eastern window, however, is pointed. On the south side of the altar is a piscina and there are remnants of 2 stone stalls now destroyed. The nave has a modern porch on the south side with a pew over it. On the right of the south doorway outside the church, is a stoup. There is a little carved woodwork within.

Ashill

51/15–16 [St. Mary] 12 February 1857

A small church having chancel and nave only, west tower and north and south porches, with portions of every style and much that is curious. The chancel arch is plain Norman, at least its eastern face is entirely so. On the west, it has chevron mouldings and springs for imposts which terminate in a kind of receding brackets causing a shouldered appearance. On each side of the arch on the west face is a shallow round arch in the wall, not pierced, nor reaching to the bottom. The door within the north porch (now made into a gloomy pue) is also Norman with segmental arch and shafts with cushion capitals. (On the gable of the north porch is a pretty cross).

The south doorway has also a flat segmental arch on shafts with varied

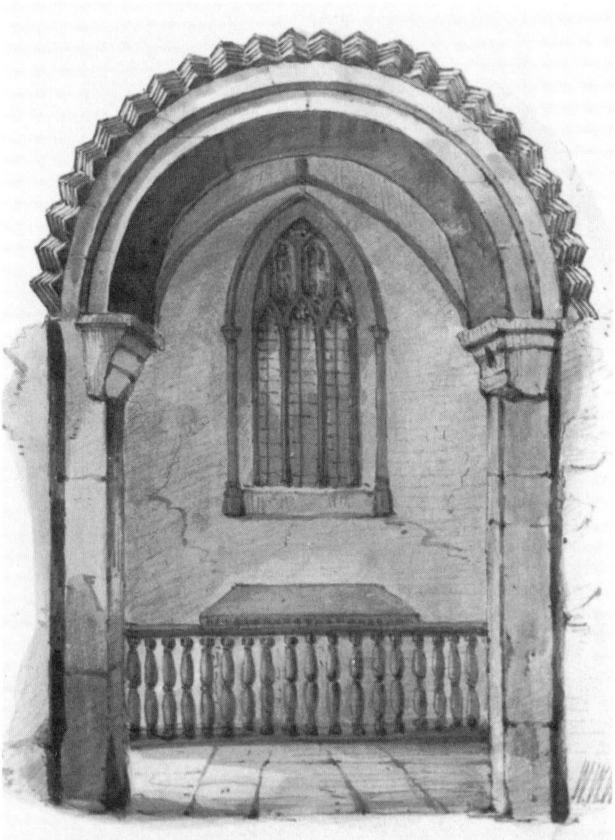

Chancel arch, Ashill Church, 1849, by W.W. Wheatley

capitals and abaci moulded. One shaft is fluted and the capitals have a very curious Egyptian look. The porches are Perpendicular having labeled outer doorways with panelled spandrels. The nave has the original lead roof. One window on the north of the nave presents a rear arch with cinquefoil foliation on Early English shafts, a feature not uncommon in this county. Some windows of the nave are Perpendicular, others modern.

The chancel has, on the south, 2 Decorated windows of 2 lights: on the north a Perpendicular one square-headed: at the east a Perpendicular one of 3 lights which has stilted shafts to the rear arch and contains fragments of painted glass. On the north are indications of another Decorated window, but the arch has been altered. Some of the Decorated windows are close at the top.

The chancel is disfigured with pues. Its roof is tiled. In the north wall of the nave is a fine Decorated sepulchral arch having bold foliations and mouldings, slightly of ogee form, having at the point a canopied niche. Beneath the canopy is the effigy of a Lady with hands joined, her head under a pedimented canopy with double cusping and angels supporting the head.

Eastward of this is another sepulchral arch under a window with double feathering. The effigy, apparently that of a lady, is hidden by a pue. There are

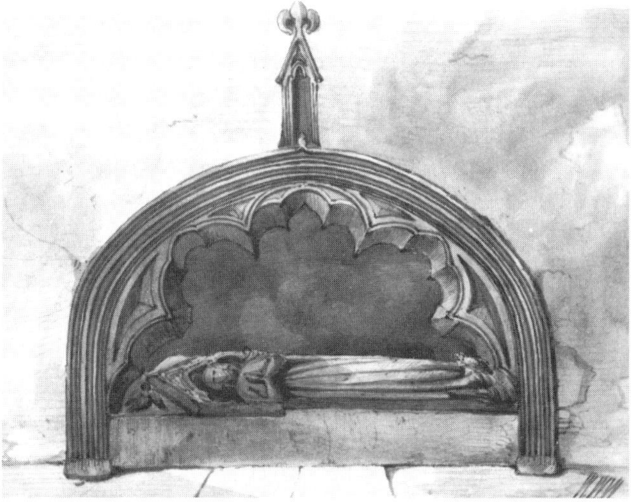

In Ashill Church, south side, 1849, by W.W. Wheatley

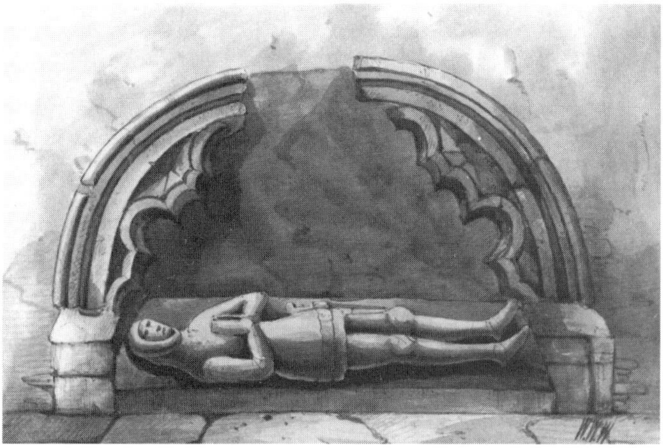

In south side of Ashill Church, 1849, by W.W. Wheatley

some plain, open seats in the western part of the nave, but the remainder is pued. The tower arch is pointed upon octagonal shafts. The font is Perpendicular, the bowl octagonal and panelled with sexfoils and shields: the stem also panelled. The pulpit is most absurdly cocked up at a great height and there is a western gallery.

The exterior is entirely covered with plaster. The tower is Perpendicular, embattled, with an octagonal turret at the north-east, also embattled, rising above the parapet. The belfry windows of 2 lights, the buttresses at the angles. On the west side a 3 light window and a labeled door having panelling with quatrefoils in the spandrels.

The churchyard very nicely kept and has a large yew tree.

Ashton, Long

49/1–3 All Saints Before 1840

This church is a large good building of Rectilinear character with rather a plain exterior and consisting of a nave and chancel, each with side aisles of equal height without a clerestory, and a well proportioned embattled tower at the west end, 3 stages in height and crowned with a pinnacle at each angle. On the west side is a window of 4 lights immediately over the door. The windows of the upper stages are of 2 lights. The side aisles and porch are embattled and there is an octagonal turret on the south side of the nave. The east gable of the nave is surmounted by a bell niche.

The north porch is very large and placed unusually, much farther to the eastward than is commonly found and being thus near the centre of the building has the appearance of a transept. The character is very plain, but there is a niche over the doorway. The interior is handsome and neatly fitted up. The nave is divided from each aisle by 4 pointed arches, the piers of which are of lozenge form with shafts at the angles and mouldings carried down the intermediate spaces. The windows in the aisles are of 3 lights. The roofs have plain panelling with bosses. Between the nave and chancel is a rich and beautiful wood screen extending across the whole breadth of the church. It is in a very perfect state, painted and gilt, and has fine open tracery and 4 beautiful cornices alternatively of Tudor flower and vine leaves with grapes.

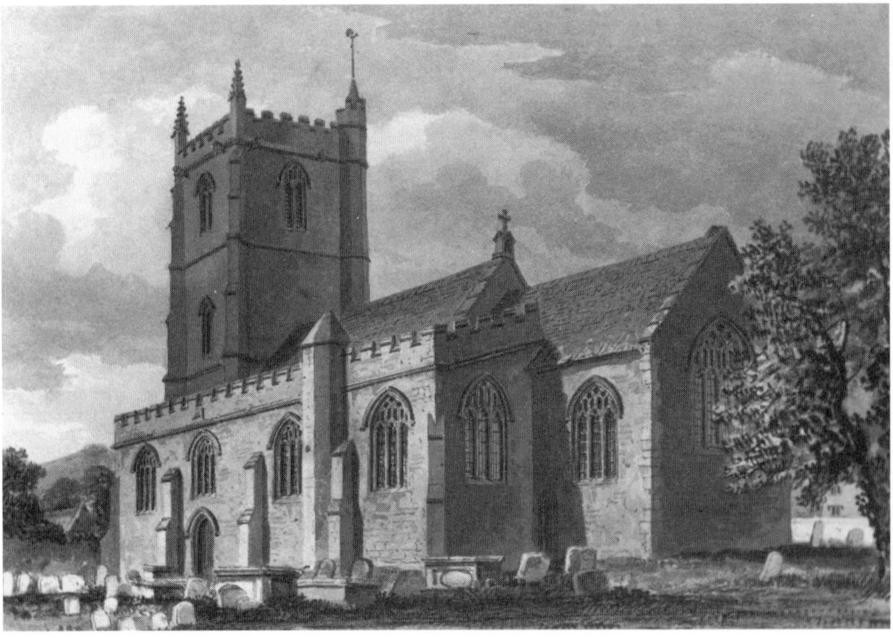

South east view of Long Ashton Church, 1827, by J. Buckler

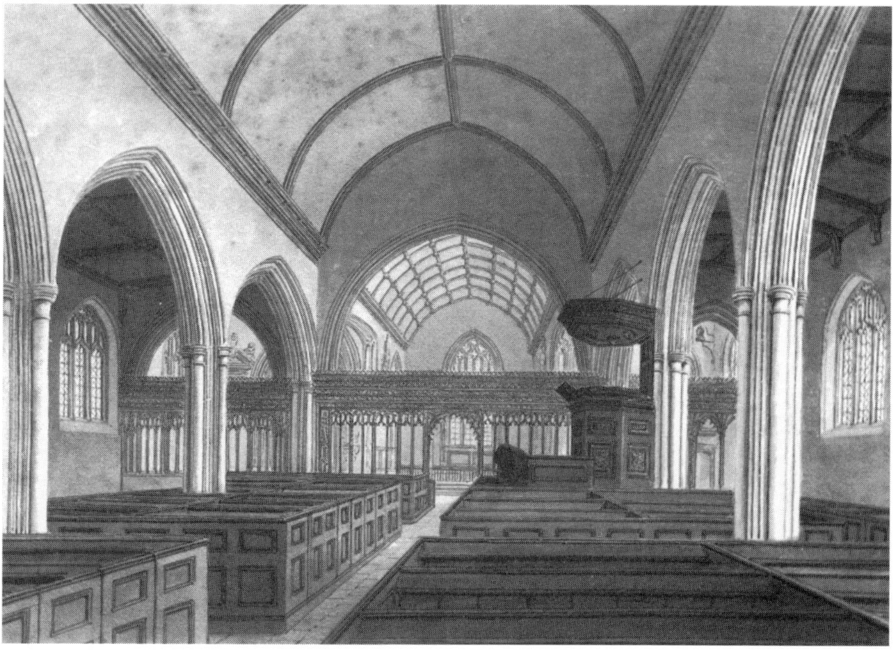

Interior view of Long Ashton Church, 1829, by J.C. Buckler

The chancel opens to each of its aisles by one pointed arch, one of which has panelling in the soffit. The chancel extends somewhat eastward of the aisles and the east window is of 4 lights. Several of the windows of the chancel contain rich portions of painted glass. In the north aisle of the chancel is a very rich altar tomb of Rectilinear character, the tomb having its sides panelled with quatrefoils and large shields. Above it rises a splendid canopy of tabernacle work with a cornice of vine leaves and grapes and groining on the under side. On the tomb are the effigies of a man and woman with angels at their heads commemorating Sir Richard Charlton [sic] and his Lady, 1486. The doorway leading into the roodloft remains on the north side.

The west gallery is furnished with a good organ. In the churchyard is a flat stone, sculptured with a cross.

In the churchyard two ancient cottages with square headed windows having labels.

Axbridge

50/12–13 St. John Baptist Before 1840

This church is . . . Perpendicular and a spacious structure but inferior in elegance to Cheddar. The form comprehends a nave and chancel each with side aisles, a tower in the centre and small transepts not projecting beyond the aisles and a small south porch. The latter is low but has a stone roof with rather good panelling and the door within has foliated spandrels and is flanked by crocketed pinnacles. The south aisle of the nave has an elegant open parapet of pierced panelling with quatrefoils and pinnacles as at Cheddar, but not the north aisle which has no parapet.

The nave is of equal height with the aisles and has no clerestory. The roofs are leaded except that of the chancel which is of slate. There is an octagonal turret in the south transept which has a panelled parapet. The tower is massive and its parapet of open panelling as the south aisle; at each angle a small crocketed pinnacle and at the north-east is an octagonal panelled turret rising above the parapet. The belfry windows are 3 on each side, each of 2 lights and good tracery. The stage below has single windows and on the east side a niche containing a statue. The windows are mostly of 3 or 4 lights, but the tracery not extremely good. In the south transept is one of 6 lights.

The nave is divided from each aisle by 4 good pointed arches with light piers formed of columns clustered in lozenge form. The shafts at the south have foliated capitals, the others plain. The tower rises upon 4 fine Perpendicular arches in the centre having a handsome stone groined roof. The roof of the nave and the chancel is coved and plastered, adorned with pendants in a mixed and mongrel style, executed 1636. The side aisles of the nave had wood panelled ceilings differing in character: that on the north is in small compartments, that on the south has them larger. There are bosses and the ribs spring from stone shafts. The transepts have coved,

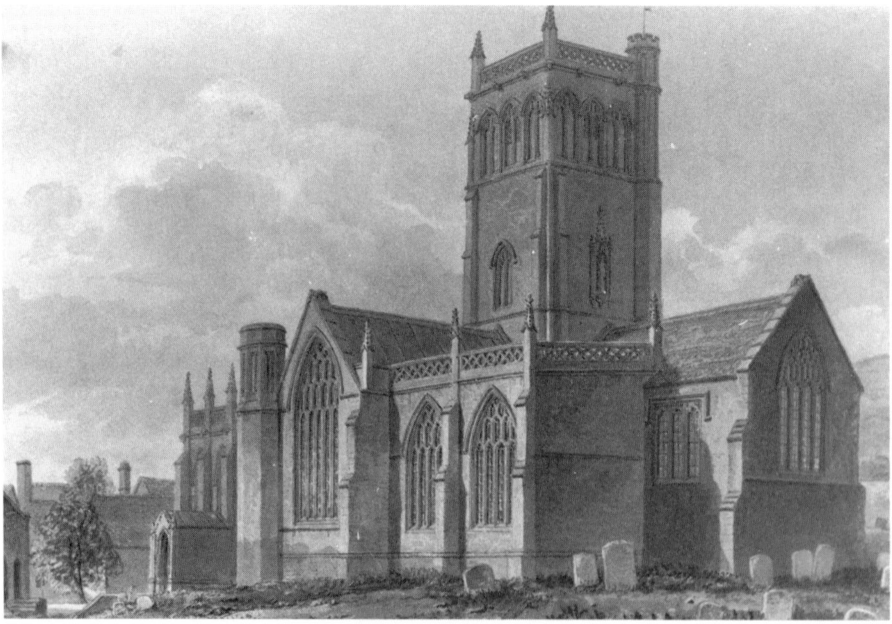

South east view of Axbridge Church, 1829, by J. Buckler

boarded roofs with fine foliated bosses, especially on the south where the roof is flatter than on the north. The stair turret of the tower is entered from the north transept.

The chancel is divided from each aisle by 2 elegant Perpendicular arches with light piers of shafts and moulded intervals. The capitals on the north have angels bearing shields, those on the south are plain. The aisles of the chancel have panelled wood ceilings in small compartments. On the south side is a boss sculptured with some sacred subject. The chancel extends a little beyond the aisles, the eastern part having square-headed windows, but the eastern window is blocked up by tasteless Italian reredoes. The space enclosed by the altar rails is large. The font is a fine Perpendicular one, the bowl octagonal with quatrefoiled circles below which are angel figures, bearing shields and the shaft is octangular and panelled. There is a large old organ. In the north transept a brass to Roger Naper [sic] and Johanna his wife 1483.

Babcary

19/84 [Holy Cross] Before 1840

Babcary is a village situated about 4 miles east of Somerton, 5 from Ilchester and about 7 from Castle Cary. The church consists of a nave and chancel with a plain embattled tower (having a square turret on its north side) situated at the west end. On the south side of the nave is a large plain porch. The church is built of the stone obtained in the neighbourhood and is wholly of Rectilinear character. There are some good windows in the nave of 3 lights with square

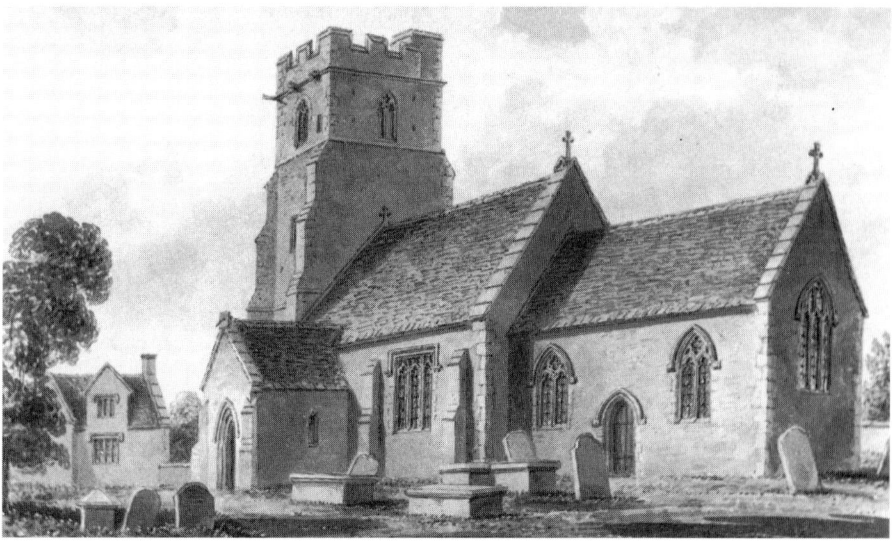

South east view of Babcary Church, 1840, by J. Buckler

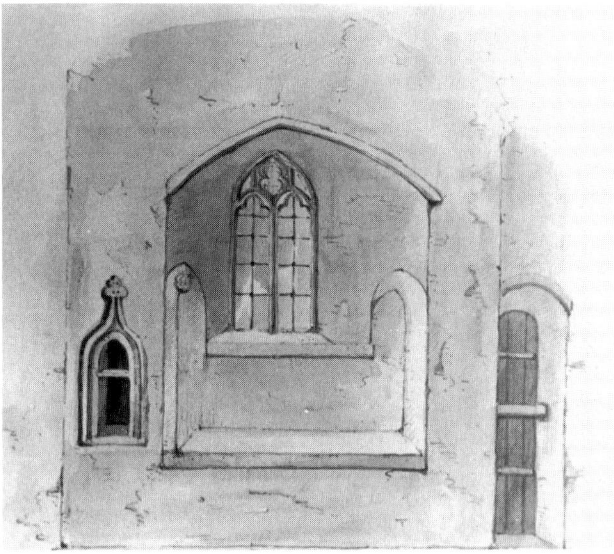

Babcary Church chancel, south side, by W.W. Wheatley

heads and labels. The chancel has, on each side, small, neat windows of 2 lights, one of them square-headed. The eastern window is of 3 lights. The arch from the nave to the chancel has but slight curvature, is wide and springs from shafts of true Rectilinear character.

On the south side of the altar is a water drain with a plain ogee niche terminated by an elegant finial and without crockets. The font is very elegant of octagonal form, panelled with quatrefoils and gradually decreasing in size towards the base and supported on a slender panelled pedestal of octagonal form. The gable ends of the nave and chancel are surmounted by crosses two of which are plain and one (the western) elegantly worked. There are 5 bells.

Backwell

50/29–31 St. Andrew 7 July 1845

A large church comprising a nave and chancel with aisles carried along the whole of the former and part of the latter, a lofty western tower and south porch. The work is nearly all third-Pointed, but there are earlier indications in the chancel. The parapet of the south aisle is moulded, but the north aisle is plainer and without one, has a very plain door. Over the east gable of the nave is a fine, large sancte bell niche surmounted by a kind of tabernacle work. The nave has a chantry with leaden roof of better pitch than late roofs usually are. On the south side, corresponding with the roodloft's place, is a square embattled stair turret. The south porch is embattled; its outer door has plain mouldings and within is a benatura. The nave has on each side, an arcade of 5 bays, pointed arches with octagonal piers.

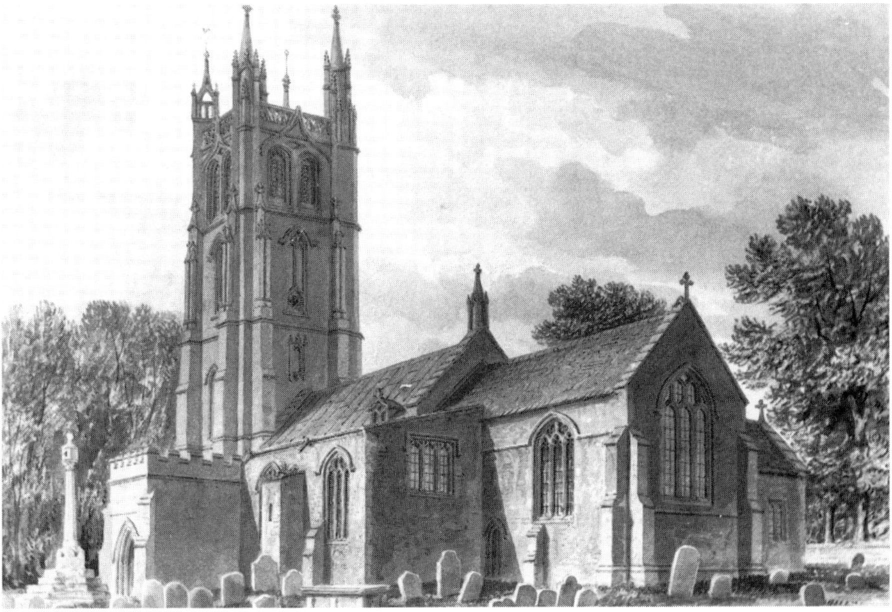

South east view of Backwell Church, 1827, by J. Buckler

The chancel arch lofty, also from octagonal shafts. There is only one clerestory window which is over the lectern arch on the south side and is surmounted externally by a gable with cross. The tower arch is lofty with continuous mouldings. The roof of the nave is coved with plain ribs and bosses, but over the roodloft, the ceiling is panelled. The aisles have flatter roofs with spandrels on head corbels. The windows are of 3 and 4 lights, one on the north of 2 only, some have fair third-point tracery, some inferior and without feathering. There is a little stained glass. The rood screen extends across both nave and aisles with pierced tracery, projecting foliage in the spandrels and above are 2 cornices of vine leaves and grapes. The chancel is large and has on the south, a small first-Pointed priest's door, also 3 equal sedilia of the same style under a 3d Pointed window on the south. These have plain mouldings and circular shafts with capitals and bases moulded. In one of the capitals appear the nailhead.

There is the trace of a piscina, east of there now walled up. The sacrarium is laid with marble. The east window, a poor third-Pointed one, is much encroached on by an Italian reredos. The south east window is of 3 lights of rather odd tracery. On the north side of the chancel is a third-Pointed altar tomb with canopied niches on the sides and crooked pinnacles, within the niches angels bearing shields. Upon it the effigy of a knight with dog at his feet. At the back of this tomb is a gorgeous stone screen with pierced tracery in 3 compartments, one being a door opening to the chapel behind. Above the horizontal parapet is an ogee arch of large size with finial containing some panelling and shields. This is flanked by pinnacles and the whole surmounted by a fine pedimental canopy with crockets and finial.

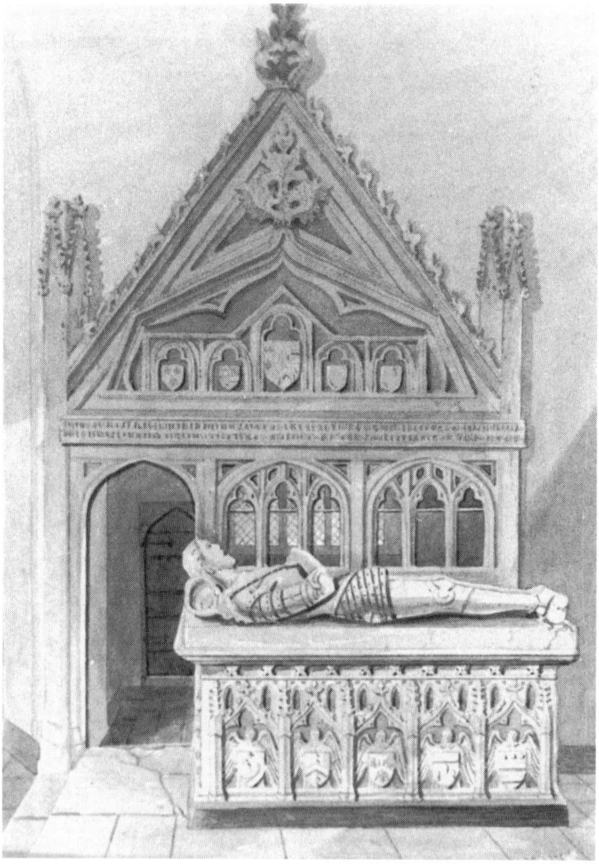

Backwell, 1831, by J. M(anning?)

On the horizontal bend is an inscription: 'Withen this chapell lyeth Elizabeth the first founderys of this chapele and of the flocke of shepe to the Quarter times late wife of Sir John Chaworth, Knight and before that wife to Sr. Walter Rodney, Knight and sister to Sir William Compton, Knyght which Elizabeth departyd the 111 day of June in the yere of grace MCCCCCXXXVI'. This is a curious specimen of late work and the foundress does not seem to have been a Romanist. The chapel behind it is oddly vaulted in stone and has feathered arched ribs. The back of the tomb is panelled and its arch has bold feathering. There is a niche and bracket in the east wall of this chapel and a 3 light window; east of it is a small sacristy opening internally only. There is a battlement to the north chapel of the chancel. The font is a bad made one and there is a barrel organ.

The tower is lofty and imposing having a rich general effect but the details are late and not very good, probably of the same date as the chantry north of the chancel. It is 4 stages in height with pierced parapet and corner turrets with smaller pinnacles attached. At the north-east angle is a large octagonal turret rising higher than the parapet. The belfry windows are odd, of 2 lights with large interval between, surmounted by a flat ogee arch rising high and each light filled with an odd kind of quatrefoil pierced stonework. In the 2d stage there is a pinnacle set upon the set off of the buttress. The window of this stage is of 2 lights not glazed, the mullion rising from a pierced quatrefoiled circle ogeed in the upper part. The 3d stage has 2 light windows of great length. There is a west window of 5 lights and below it a door with good continuous mouldings deeply cut. On the west side of the 3d stage is a legend in which occurs the monogram I H C. The stone and masonry of the tower are very fine, but the details almost debased. The situation very lovely on a woody hillside with rich views.

Badgworth

82/29–31 St. Congar 26 April, 1863

An interesting church, though not very spacious, comprising nave with north aisle or chapel, chancel, west tower and south porch. The chancel is disproportionate in length to the nave, being very nearly equal to it. The features are mainly Decorated, but the north aisle greatly surpasses all the rest in richness and beauty and was probably once a chantry chapel dedicated to St. Margaret. It has a separate high roof with stone tiles, the pitch of the two gables being very good and both surmounted with crosses. The stone masonry is

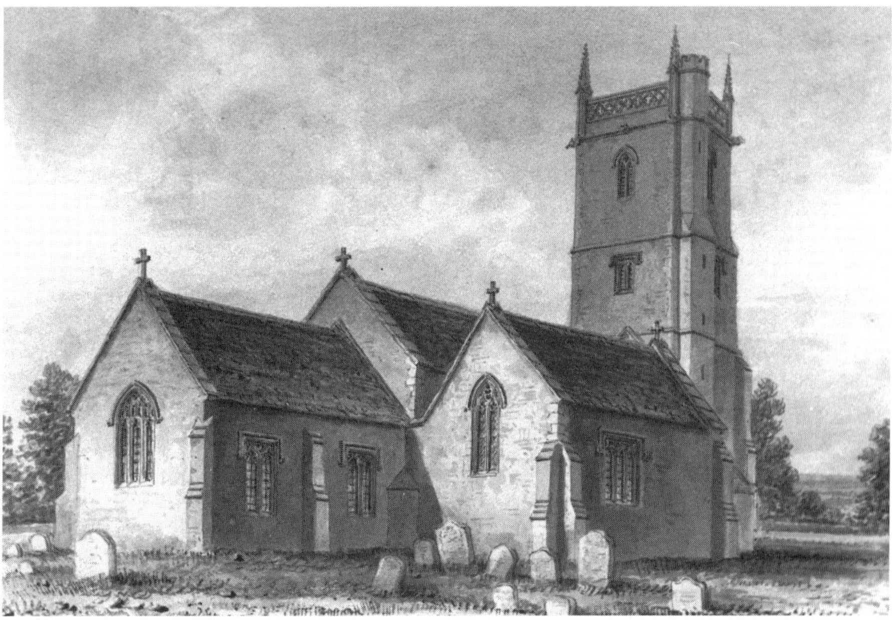

North east view of Badgworth Church, 1831, by J. Buckler

excellent and a ball flower cornice runs externally under the eaves of the roof. The windows are similar on the west and on the north, of 2 lights and all richly studded in the jambs and mullions with ball flower, both externally and internally, mostly having a rear arch internally. (The jambs internally have octagonal bases.)

The east window is a Perpendicular insertion of 3 lights. The north doorway is curious, contemporary with the rest and similar in ornamentation, but singular in having a semi-circular arch with deeply recessed mouldings which are flowered. The inner arch, however, surmounting the doorcase is slightly ogeed. The hood is on head corbels and over it is a single head. Beneath the windows externally runs a moulded band. This chapel is divided from the nave by 3 pointed arches on octagonal columns with capitals, the arches somewhat stilted and no east or west responds. The nave and aisle have open roofs with tie-beams. Over the eastern portion of the nave is a more intricate piece of panelled roof with a good deal of colour, chiefly red.

In the aisle, the monogram I H C and other figures appear in white upon red on the roof. The aisle has, on the south side of the east end, an odd piscina with double feathering and a wood door on the north. The nave has on the south, a Decorated 2 light window containing stained glass and near it a piscina with trefoiled ogee head. The tower arch is open to the nave and very lofty, the outer moulding continuous, the inner is on concave octagonal shafts with caps and base. The west window containing some good stained glass is seen through this arch. The chancel arch is pointed, springing straight from the wall. The chancel is lower than the nave and has on the north a trefoiled lancet and one 2 light Decorated window. On the south are 2 square-headed windows of 3 lights which are trefoiled.

The east window is an odd one of 3 lights with radiating tracery not unlike one in Gloucester Cathedral and of late Decorated but it is concealed by some tapestry forming a reredos. The south side of the chancel seems to be Perpendicular. There is a board against the north wall of the chancel with a long and not very legible inscription of 1591. North and south of the altar are longitudinal seats.

There is room for improvements in internal arrangement as the ugly pues still continue. The font is new, has an octagonal bowl on a stand. The south porch is plain and used as a vestry. There is a niche over one of its doors. The tower is substantially Decorated, of 3 stages in height and corner buttresses. The west window is a very good reticulated one of 3 lights, slits in the 2d stage, belfry windows Decorated of 2 lights, the parapet embattled and panelled, evidently a Perpendicular addition and probably pinnacles were intended at the angles, but not completed. The western doorway also a Perpendicular addition with Tudor arch and good mouldings set in square compartment with panelled spandrels. There are 6 bells. The churchyard is very large and planted with beautiful elm trees.

There is an odd little carved box in an angle dated 1626.

A harmonium is in the north chapel.

In the east wall of the nave, south of the chancel arch, is a shallow niche with trefoiled ogee head.

Baltonsborough

19/78 [St. Dunstan] Before 1840

The church of Baltonsborough, about 2 miles from Butleigh, consists of a broad nave, a chancel and tower at the west end. (The whole is Perpendicular and plain.) The tower is plain, low and embattled, of Rectilinear work with a west window of 3 lights and 2 rather singular apertures on each side of the belfry windows. There is also a south porch. The windows of the church are small but good Rectilinear ones of 2 lights. The gable ends of the nave and chancel are crowned by crosses. The tower and chancel are divided from the nave by plain pointed arches with plain mouldings. The windows have no drip stones. The font is [a] handsome, octagonal one of Rectilinear work with panelling and quatrefoils. The pulpit is of stone with simple but good panelling. In front of it is an iron stand formerly used for supporting the hour glass. The chancel is, as usual in this county, of less breadth and height than the nave. At the south side of the altar is a cinquefoiled piscina with ogee canopy crowned with a finial and the south-east window forms a sedile in its cill with skulls and armorial bearings. On the north an aumbrye. There are some plain carved pew ends.

1849

Baltonsborough Church has been carefully restored and fitted with neat open benches and low reading desk and stalls in the chancel.

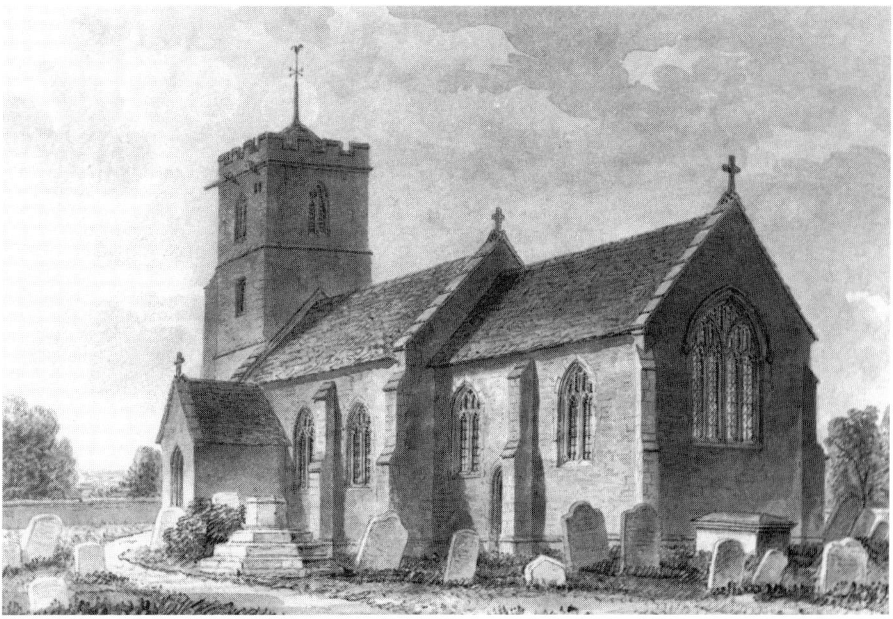

South east view of Baltonsborough Church, 1833, by J. Buckler

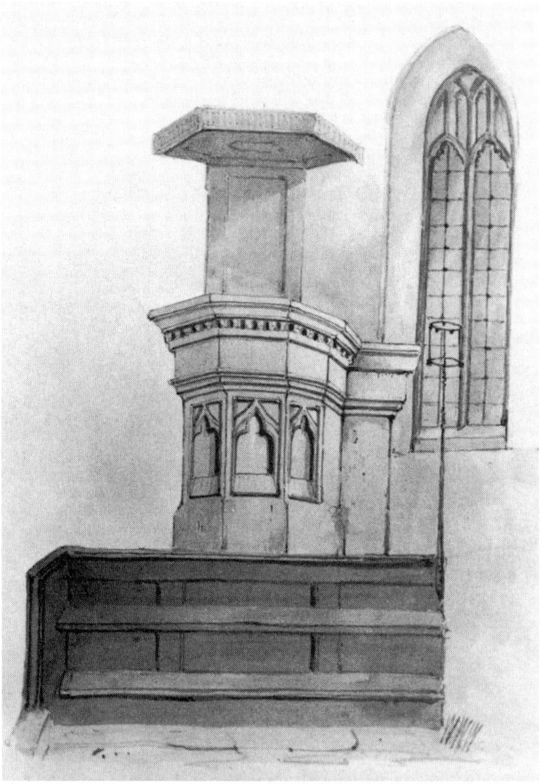

Stone pulpit, Baltonsborough Church, 1846, by W.W. Wheatley

The tower arch is continuous, also that to the chancel which is rather inelegant. The east window is of 4 lights. On the north of the chancel arch is a rood turret. At the south-east end of the nave is a plain piscina.

The roof of the nave in coved and ribbed, that of the chancel is painted blue with gilt stars.

It is intended to fit the chancel windows with stained glass.

The south door has good wood tracery.

Banwell

51/41–44 St. Andrew 25 January 1862

A very fine church, wholly Perpendicular and one of the first examples of the genuine Somersetshire church.

The plan is nave with north and south aisles, chancel, west tower and south porch. The nave has a chantry and the roofs are leaded and there is a good pierced panelled parapet to the chantry and aisles with pinnacles at intervals. There are numerous well sculptured gargoyles and there is great predominance

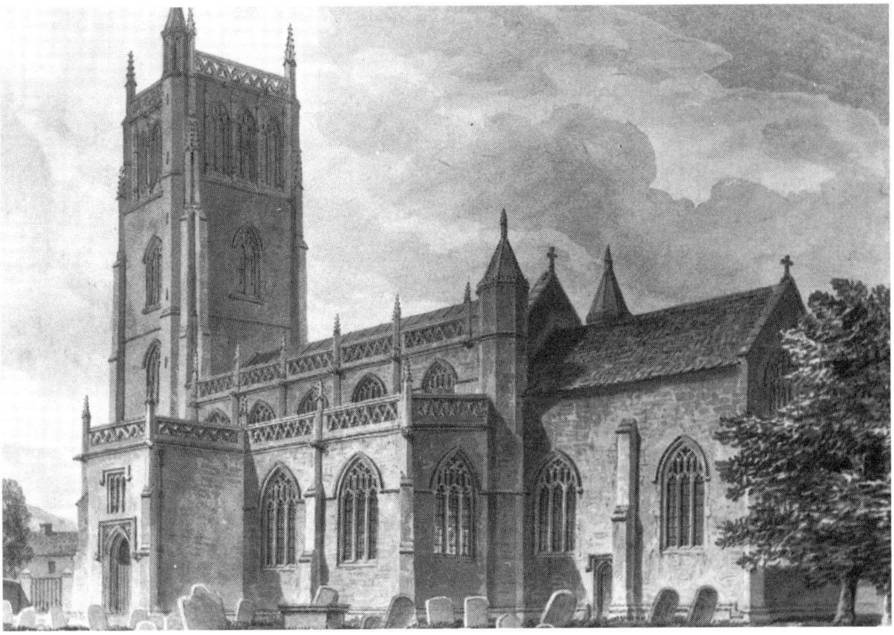

South east view of Banwell Church, 1827, by J. Buckler

of angel figures, both within and without. The masonry of every part is very good, but some part of the exterior is, according to a local custom, stuccoed.

(The roof of the chantry is of high pitch . . . and there is a stair turret crowned with a pyramid at the south-east of the nave containing the rood stair.

The chancel is plain and has tiled roof.)

The tower is lofty and grand of 3 stages divided by string courses, has double buttresses at the angles, not of great projection and charged with pinnacles in the upper stage. There is a parapet of pierced panelling and 4 crocketed pinnacles at each angle. On the south-east [is an] octagonal turret ending in a large pinnacle. (The turret is lighted by slits and contains a staircase.) The west doorway has fine arch mouldings and the hood on large head corbels. Above is a 4 light window not of very good character. The next stage above has a 2 light window between canopied niches the opening being partly filled up with stone work upon which appears sculpture representing the lily pot of the Annunciation. The next stage has on each side a 2 light window. The highest or belfry stage has on the west, 3 closely set windows of 2 lights divided by pinnacles.

The porch has a pierced parapet ranging with and resembling that of the aisle. It has a stair turret at the angle that led to a parvise. The outer doorway is large, labeled, with panelling in the spandrels. The inner has richer arch mouldings, flowered, and panelled spandrels.

The tower has fine stone groining within and a large continuous arch open to the nave. The interior is fine and lofty, moreover in good case. The nave has, on each side, an arcade of 5 good Perpendicular arches with light piers of the usual western form, the shafts having separate capitals of foliage. The chantry windows are of 3 lights and those of the aisles are very much of the same character. The roof is fine, coved, with moulded and flared ribs and bosses. Over the chantry windows is a good cornice of pierced panelling and displayed angel figures and the chantry windows have internally hood mouldings on corbels of angel figures.

The aisles have flat panelled roofs with bosses. The nave has all the seats open and most of the bench ends are original with fair carving. The pulpit is of stone, panelled with tracery and Tudor flower upon a panelled stem. The rood screen and loft remain and have lately been restored. The screen is remarkably fine, has at the top a range of Tudor flowers and beautiful vine leaf cornices and groining. It has 7 compartments filled with tracery of 4 lights, the central being the door to the chancel and the whole is richly gilted and coloured.

There is at the east end of the north aisle, an ogee headed doorway leading to the rood stairs. The chancel arch is pointed upon corbels, Somersetshire fashion and reaching up nearly to the full height of the chancel. The chancel is spacious and has lately been much repaired and ornamented. It has an east window of 5 lights, lateral ones of 2 and a coved roof panelled and illuminated. There is a small piscina south of the altar with a division having a small battlement and Tudor flower along the top. There is a modern reredos and the chancel is fitted with stalls of recent work. The whole has received much colour, the windows are fitted with stained glass of modern work and the window jambs illuminated.

There are several windows with stained glass by Warrington and some pieces of ancient stained glass may be seen in some. The font is early, the bowl circular, sculptured with rude foliage and round the top, a sort of quatrefoil band. It may be Early English.

The gallery has been moved so as to be wholly within the tower and contains a barrel organ.

Barrington

49/37–39 [St. Mary] Before 1840

This is a curious church in the form of a cross, without aisles, and having in the centre, an octagonal tower, a feature not very uncommon in this part of Somersetshire. There is a good deal of Early English work, especially about the transepts. The nave has a leaded roof and a plain parapet. The west doorway has a flat arch and the window above has lost its tracery. The character of the nave is generally Rectilinear and there is a large north porch with an ogee arch to its outer doorway and panelling about it which has been left unfinished. Near this door is a small niche. In the south porch is a stoup, in shape like a Norman capital. The roof of the nave has the tie-beams ornamented with a small battlement.

The tower is octagonal, much resembling that of Somerton. The lower part above the roof is early English with lancet openings. The belfry windows may be Decorated and the embattled parapet later. It stands upon 4 plain pointed arches opening to the low portions of the cross and has, on the north-west side, a projecting half octagonal staircase turret which does not reach to the belfry

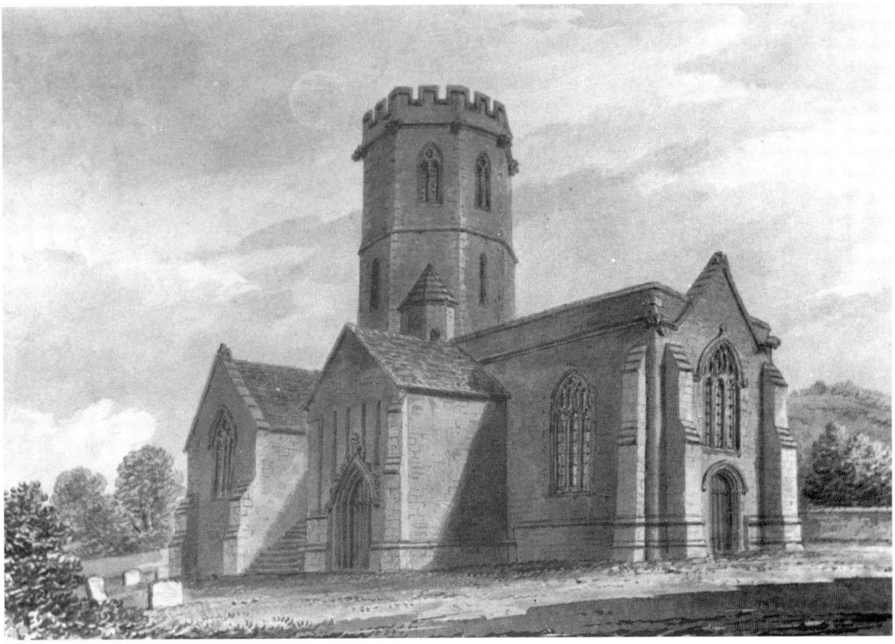

North west view of Barrington Church, 1835, by J. Buckler

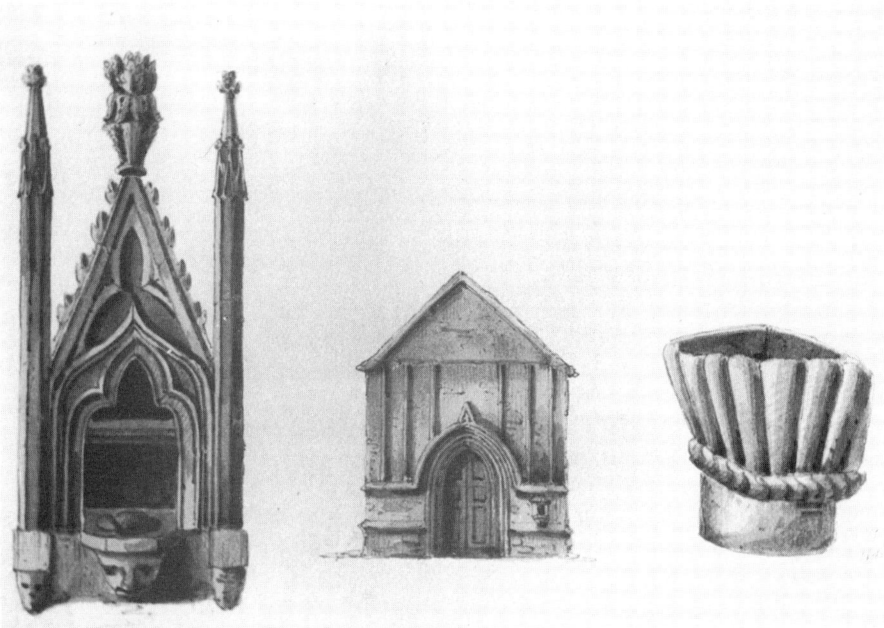

In Barrington Church, 1850, by W.W. Wheatley

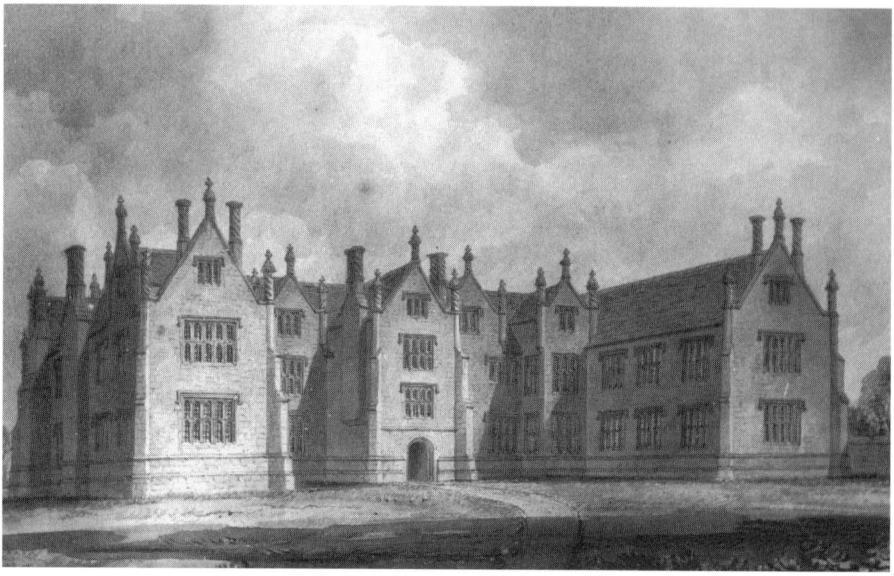

South view of Barrington Court, 1835, by J. Buckler

stage. The transepts are of advanced Early English varying to Decorated; indeed, the end windows of each may be considered entirely Decorated and of 3 lights (the dripstone resting upon good corbel heads) and presenting to the interior shafts of Early English character with good capitals and bases.

On the east side of each transept, is a double lancet; in the north transept these lancets to the *interior*, are included under a kind of plain scolloped arch. In the east wall of the north transept is a fine trefoiled niche with a shelf and piscina crowned by a handsome triangular canopy with a finial. There is in the south transept, one of still richer description with crockets and a very grand finial set between pinnacles. The orifice of the piscina is in a head set within a quatrefoil and there is also a shelf set quite in the back. There are oblique openings [hagioscopes, interlined] into the chancel both north and south of the arch which opens into it.

The chancel is nearly equal to the nave in length but is almost wholly of poor Rectilinear character. On its south side, is a plain, trefoiled piscina with a shelf. Near the east end of the nave, is a small door on the north and a window so high up on the south as if to light the roodloft. There are some open seats in the nave. The transepts and chancel have high pitched tiled roofs and the former have good corbel tables, decided Early English with billet corbels.

At the further extremity of the village from the church is Barrington Court, a very beautiful ancient mansion of the time of James I. The exterior is in very fair preservation and the style and taste superior to what is usual at that period. The form is a half H and an excellent and highly picturesque effect is derived from the great number of projecting gables and the quantity of pinnacles (rather unusual at that period) which surmount them. Some doors are decidedly Gothic in their forms.

Barrow, North

51/78–79 St. Nicholas 1 February, 1864

This church seems to have been recently rebuilt except the tower, but is evidently of the same plan and scale and probably may retain some part of the original walls. It has nave and chancel, properly developed without aisles and western tower. The latter is plain and embattled with a kind of saddle roof within the parapet. There are 2 dividing string courses, corner buttresses and west doorway with hood, over which is a 2-light Perpendicular window. The belfry windows of 2 lights and one single light in the middle storey.

The tower arch to the nave is pointed and small on shafts with octagonal capitals. The chancel arch is pointed, on shafts and may possibly be the original one. The church is generally of rather tame modern Perpendicular work, but roofs of fair pitch and tiled and crosses on the gables. The chancel is too much blocked with seats and the interior, though neat, is very ordinary.

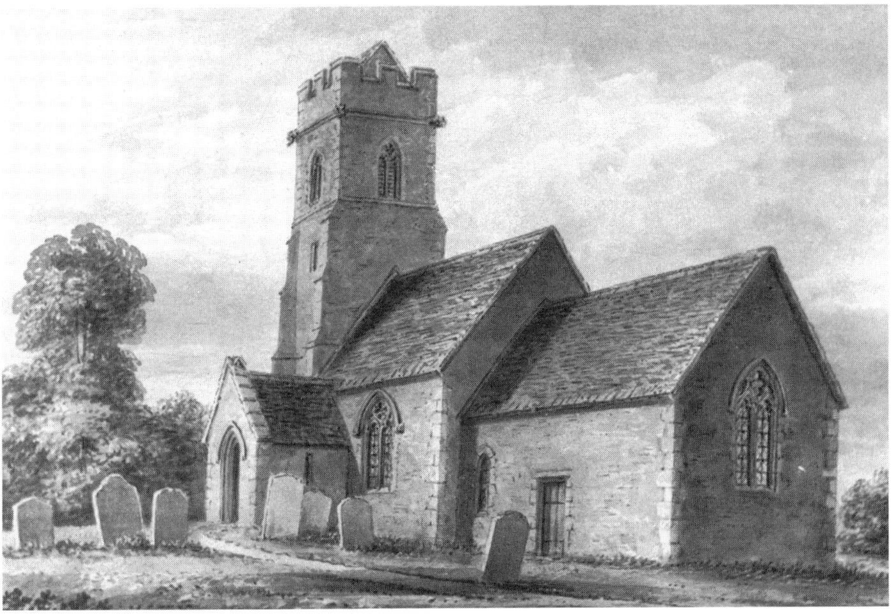

South east view of North Barrow Church, 1840, by J. Buckler

Barton St. David

19/61–62 [St. David] Before 1840

Barton St. David about 2 miles west of Lydford over the river has a small church consisting of a nave and chancel, a small north transept or chapel and

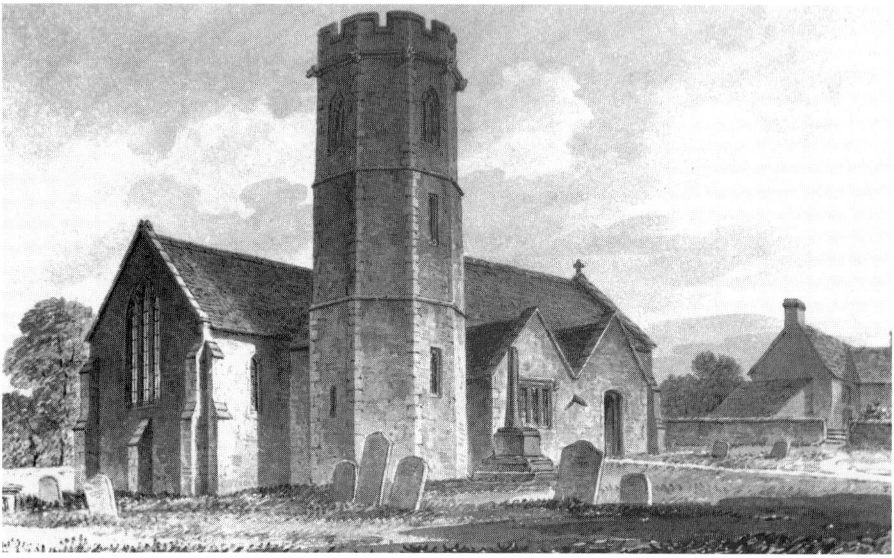

North east view of Barton St. David Church, 1834, by J. Buckler

an octagonal tower very singularly placed on the north side of the chancel and contiguous to the east side of the transept. There is also a large porch on the north side of the nave, the inner doorway of which, is a good Norman one, having two bands of moulding, the outer one having small chevrons, the inner and larger one worked with 3 ranges of lozenge work, resembling network. The shafts are plain. The tower is of Rectilinear work, plain, octagonal and embattled.

On the south side of the nave, is an arch in the wall, which seems to have opened to a transept or chapel now destroyed. The windows of [the] nave are

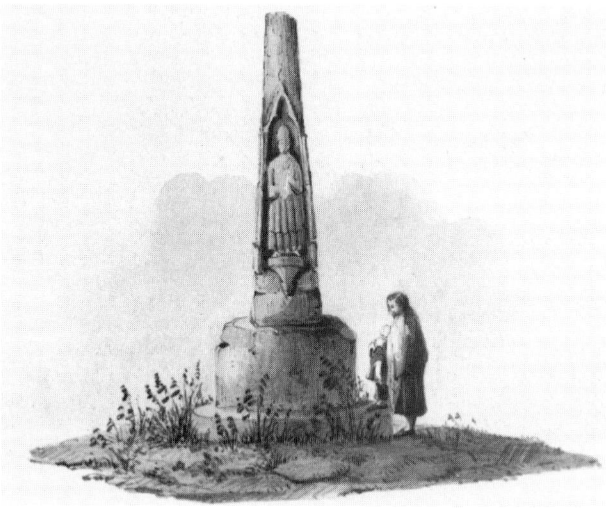

In Barton St. David churchyard, 1847, by W.W. Wheatley

mostly square and Rectilinear. The east window of the chancel seems to be of Early English of late period, of 3 lights under one arch. The other windows of the chancel are small, with feathering and have hanging feathering to their arch opening within. South of the altar is a feathered niche with plain triangular canopy and finial. The arch open to the north transept is pointed and springs from round shafts. The chancel arch springs from brackets of Early English character. There is an aperture in the wall between the nave and chancel. The font is a plain octagon. In the churchyard is the stone shaft of a cross of elegant workmanship and enriched with the figure of a saint beneath a rich, crocketed canopy.

Batcombe

51/27–29 St. Mary 27 July 1873

A good church wholly Perpendicular having clerestoried nave and aisles, chancel, western tower and south porch. The clerestory is lofty and, as well as the aisles, well finished externally, the parapets having pierced battlement. The tower is very lofty and fine, has an octagonal turret at the north-west, a pierced parapet and 8 crocketed pinnacles. It is divided into two very long stages, has on the north, 2 long blank windows with tracery and lattice work. On the west side, 3 of these and a 4 light window over the doorway which has label and panelled spandrels. The turret rises higher than the tower parapet.

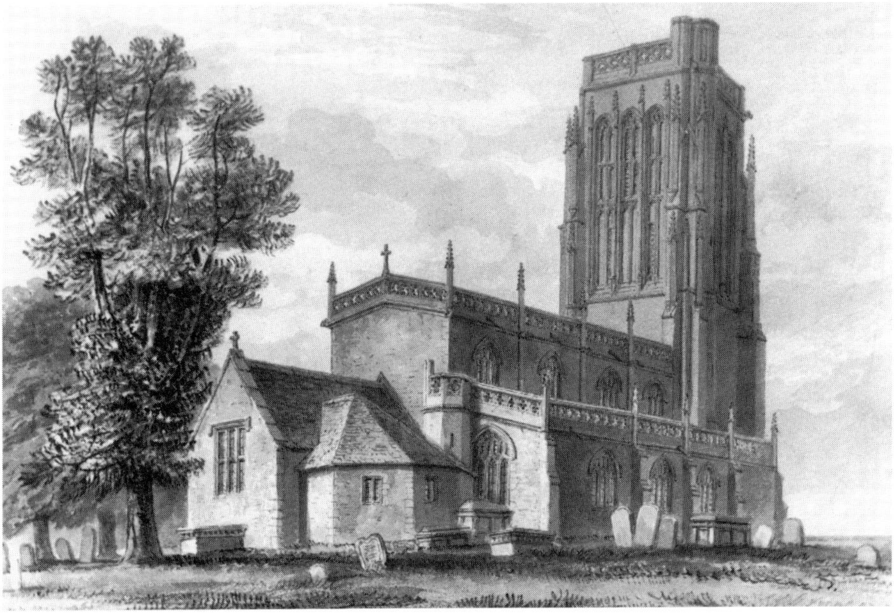

North east view of Batcombe Church, 1829, by J. Buckler

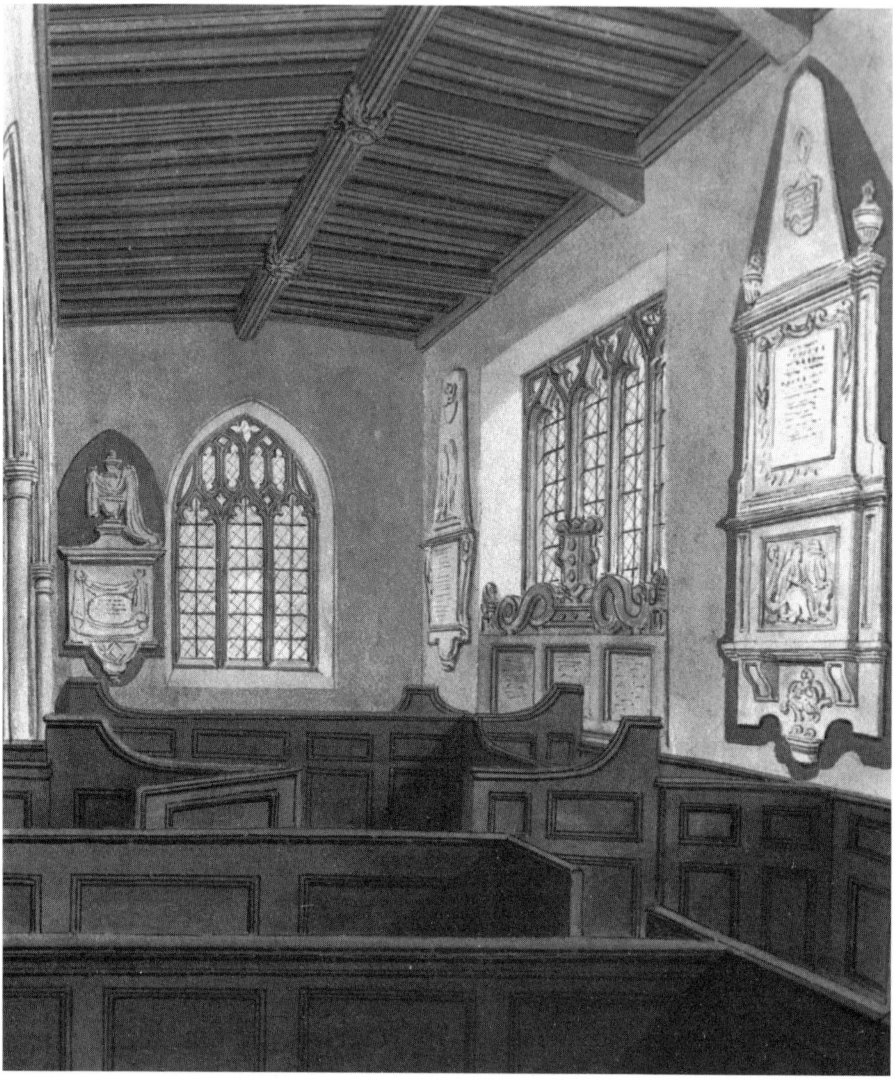

South aisle of Batcombe Church, 1829, by J.C. Buckler

On the west side is a fine canopied niche over the west door containing a statue and 3 angel figures on each side. On the south are 3 canopied niches. The belfry windows are of 3 lights flanked by pinnacles. The tower arch to the nave is lofty and grand and somewhat stilted and richly panelled with slender shafts in the jambs. The lower storey of the tower has beautiful stone groining seen well from within.

The arcades of the nave are lofty and good; each of 4 bays with good pointed arches on light piers of lozenge form with 4 light shafts. The clerestory windows have 3 lights.

The south aisle has square-headed windows of 4 lights, not equal in style to some of the other features. In the north aisle, they are ordinary pointed windows of 3 lights and there are none at the west end of the aisles. The roofs are of flat pitch. In the north aisle is a sepulchral arch with feathering and at the east of the same aisle, a door with panelled spandrels to the vestry. The nave is fitted with new open seats.

The chancel is much inferior to the nave, short and low and looking as if funds had failed for carrying on the work in equally good style. The chancel arch is Perpendicular but low, on stilted shafts with circular caps and octagonal bases. The east window is particularly ugly. On the south, is a square-headed window of 2 lights. On the south is [a] piscina with trefoil head which may be part of an earlier building. The altar is remarkably mean. On the north, is a vestry of debased work and without form or beauty.

The font is good Perpendicular; the bowl octagonal with panelling containing shields and foliage, well and deeply cut; the stem has shafts attached to the angles and there is a good band of foliage. The south porch is plain and ordinary. The door within it has good foliaged spandrels.

(There are buttresses set square, have fine panelling on the different stages. The tower arch is superior in workmanship and richness of moulding to those of the arcades.

In the south aisle, is a monument to James Bisse 1606.)

Bath Abbey Church

49/63–65 SS. Peter and Paul Before 1840

This very spacious and imposing edifice is principally remarkable as perhaps of the latest specimen existing of a church of the same scale, its dimensions being those of a cathedral. The date 1518, a period subsequent to which rarely anything good can be found, and even within this church and all its magnificence, symptoms of decadence appear and the proportions are in general far from good or pleasing.

The plan is simple and regular, a nave and chancel each with parallel aisles, a north and south transept, narrow but lofty, and a central tower of much beauty but chiefly remarkable for not being square. In the transepts, being narrower than the nave and chancel, the tower is larger from north to south than from east to west. The west front is fine with a good doorway, a pierced parapet with niches and above the window are images on each side ascending as if on a ladder. The west windows of the aisles are of 4 lights with less good tracery.

The aisles are rather low, the clerestory very large and, as in most late churches, out of proportion. There are flying buttresses from the clerestory. All the whole church has parapets of open panelling and the ends of the nave, chancel, and transept are flanked by large, crocketed pinnacles. The large windows of the transepts are of 3 lights, long and narrow. The east front is fine and bold, the window very large of 7 lights divided by 3 transoms and set in a kind of square frame, having circles and panelling in the spandrels.

The tower has a pierced battlement and corner turrets upon which have

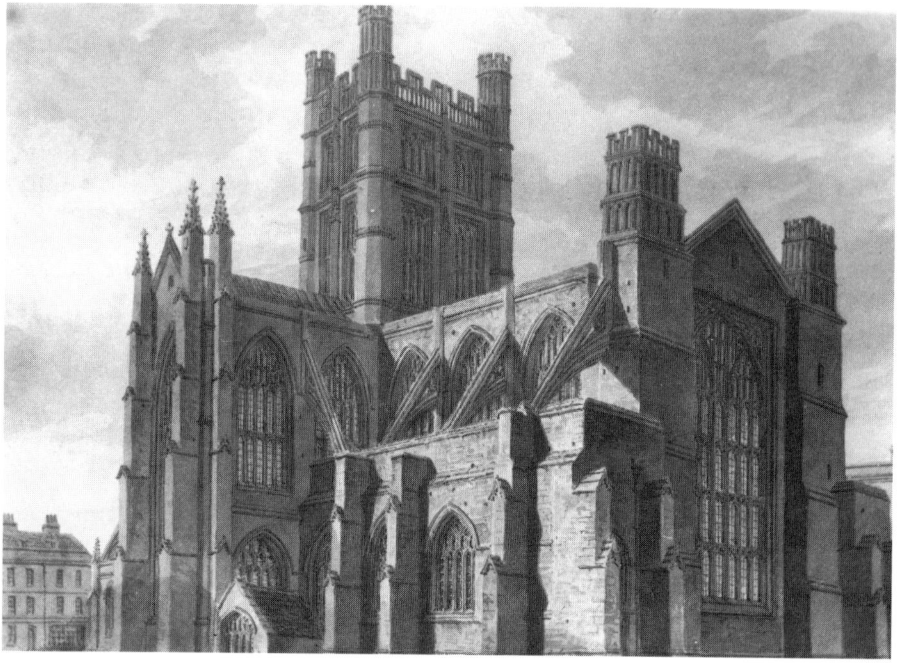

South east view of Bath Abbey Church, 1815, by J.C. Buckler

been raised large crocketed pinnacles, which rather impair its appearance and are too heavy. The belfry windows are large and double set in square compartments. The chief singularity of the tower is that it is not square . . . a circumstance that does not add to its beauty.

The interior, fine as it is, wants both the interest and the grand proportions of earlier buildings. The nave has on each side, 5 arches of Tudor form with piers which are not very light or elegant. The arch mouldings are continued, only stopped at intervals by large shafts. The chantry windows are much too large, those of the aisles too small, and their tracery very ordinary. The organ screen has lately been brought to the west arch of the tower, in order to give more room for the congregation in the choir, the nave being wholly vacant and serving as a vestibule to the choir.

The transepts, in consequence of the tower not being square, are extremely narrow, though lofty and not available at present for the congregation. In the southern is the font. The choir is only 3 arches in length and the aisles are carried quite to the east end, where are small doorways contrary to custom. The only point of difference between the choir and nave is the roof, which in the former, presents very magnificent fan groining in stone. In the latter, is a plastered ceiling worked in rich pattern.

On the south of the choir, within one arch, is the elegant chantry of Prior Bird, a fine specimen of late Perpendicular agreeing with the rest of the structure. The choir is too full of pews and galleries tho' elegantly carved in Gothic design. The pulpit far too large. The organ case is rich Gothic carving but too ponderous. The altar reredos of stone and rather good.

1843

It is a pity that in the restoration of Bath Abbey Church, a more Catholic arrangement was not adopted. If the organ had been placed in one of the transepts, a large portion of the nave might have been used by the congregation by which means, the choir might have been relieved from some portion at least, of the truly Protestant pues and galleries which now encumber and disfigure it, for although they are executed in a rich and expensive way, they are wholly out of place, especially in a choir. The backs of the pews are so high that the people in the free benches placed behind them at the extreme west of the choir, can scarcely see or hear.

[Another note Volume 61] Before 1840

This is one of the latest examples of the pure Gothic having been completed in Henry 7th's time. The west front is elegantly adorned. The ceiling is richly decorated, the chantry of Prior Bird beautiful and the whole edifice light and neat, but the nave is much disfigured by paltry modern monuments.

Bathampton

49/67–68 St. Nicholas 1843

This small church scarce 2 miles from Bath is delightfully situated near the Avon, opposite Batheaston. It is chiefly Perpendicular with earlier indications in the chancel and consists of a west tower, nave, south chapel and porch and chancel. The tower is neat but late Perpendicular, 2 stages in height with a

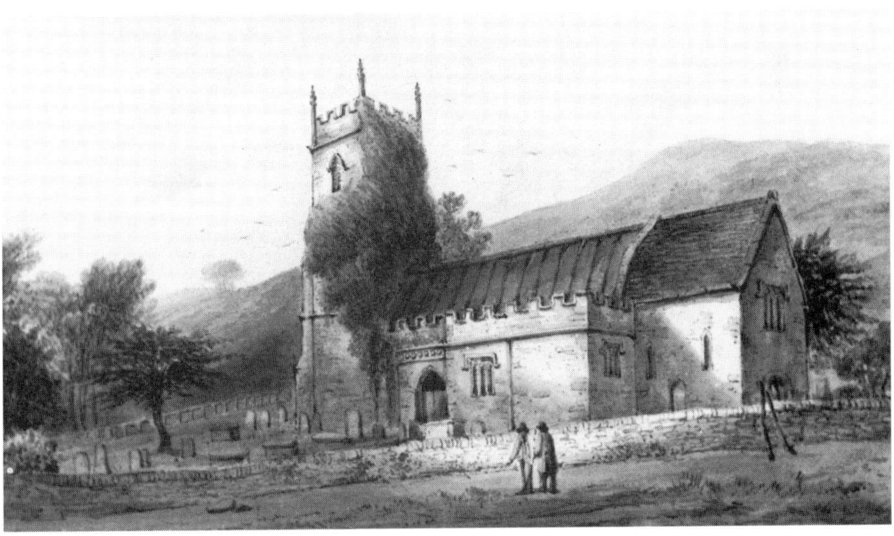

Bathampton, 1844, by W.W. Wheatley

battlement and 4 crocketed pinnacles and buttresses at the angles and a turret at the north-east angle. The west doorway has foliage in the spandrels and a label and over it a window of 3 lights. The belfry windows are of 2 lights and, in the fashion of the county, have stone lattice work.

The nave and south chapel are embattled. The porch has a panelled quatrefoiled parapet. The nave has a high tiled roof as has the chancel, but without parapet. The windows on the north side, are square-headed, of 3 lights, and in the chancel there is one of 5 lights. The south chapel has Perpendicular windows. The chancel is earlier than the nave and built of rough stone and its roof is higher. On its south side, are 2 plain Early English lancets, one of which is walled up. The east window has a square-headed Perpendicular one but is completely blocked up by an ugly altar screen.

The arch from the tower to the nave, is of Tudor form with shafts; that to the south chapel has mouldings and shafts and that to the chancel, plain and springing abruptly from the wall as in the north of Devon. The nave and chancel have coved roofs with ribs framing panels, the chancel an embattled cornice. There are, in the porch, effigies of armed knights much defaced. The interior of the chancel has many monuments of the 15th and 16th centuries. Under the east window externally within the arch, is a small effigy, rudely executed, in a singular head dress much defaced and one hand holding a book. There is a good deal of ivy on the walls of this church.

Batheaston

49/67 St. John 1836

The church consists of a very elegant west tower, a nave with north aisle, south porch and chancel. The whole Perpendicular, the north aisle a modern addition but in good style and uniform with the rest. The tower is very lofty as well as rich, 5 stages in height in the Somersetshire style, with a parapet of pierced panelling and crocketed pinnacles. There is at the south-east corner, a stair turret of octagonal form, terminating in a pyramidical finishing. On the west side, is a 3 light window. The other stages have 2 light windows and those of the belfry have enriched stone lattice work and on the east side of the middle stage, is a fine canopied niche containing the statue of an apostle.

The whole of the church is embattled and there, in the east gable of the nave, is the arch for the saints' bell. The south doorway arch is well moulded with flowers and crocketed canopy. Above is a niche and on the porch is a band of panelling. There is one pointed and one square-headed window at the south. The chancel has the east window with contracted arch, the others square-headed. The northern windows are modern, but good and there are 5 elegant pointed arches upon the usual light Perpendicular piers dividing the aisle from the nave. There is an organ and the interior is altogether neat.

The situation is beautiful.

1865

The chancel has been rebuilt with Decorated windows.

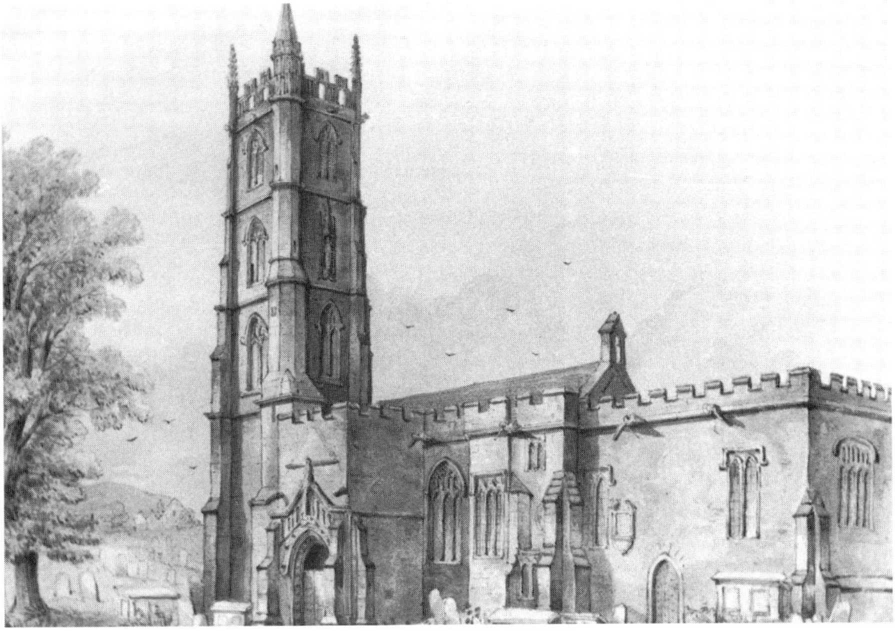

Batheaston, 1843, by W.W. Wheatley

Bathford

49/67 St. Swithin 1843

This church has a west tower, a nave with modern, south aisle and a chancel, the whole much altered and modernized. The tower was built only a few years' ago in imitation of the Perpendicular style and though not altogether bad, is

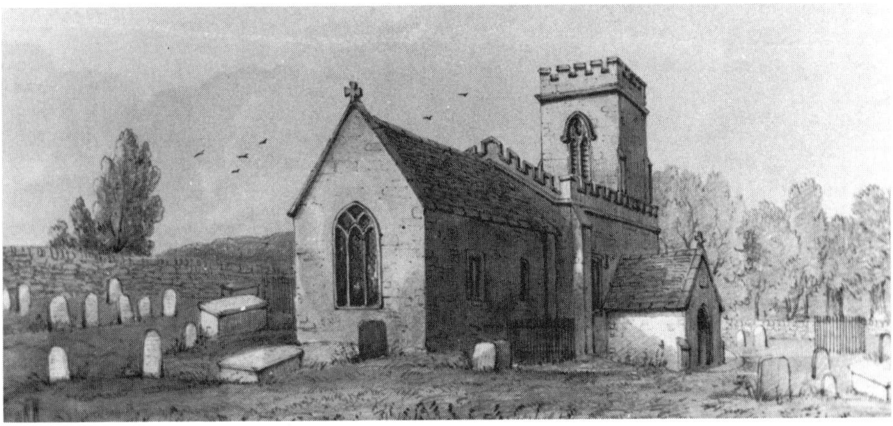

Bathford, 1846, by W.W. Wheatley

bald and wanting in effect. The extreme whiteness of the stone, causes an almost ludicrous contrast with the dinginess of the nave and the plain embattled parapet without pinnacles has a meagre effect. The north doorway within the porch is Norman with fine mouldings containing the chevron and knob ornament springing from shafts. The head of the arch is filled with stone work. The porch is large and of plain, Perpendicular work.

There are a few ordinary square-headed, Perpendicular windows on the north of the nave and south of the chancel, but the whole has been so badly altered that few of the original features remain. The south aisle is an addition of the worst modern Gothic but the original moulded parapet of the nave, is still perceptible on the south and also the east gable of the nave. Within, there is nothing worthy of remark. The chancel arch is altered and the interior is filled with large pues and ugly monuments. The font appears to be Norman, of circular form, but mutilated. There is a south gallery and west. The situation is beautiful on an eminence commanding a fine view over the woody vale of Avon.

Beckington

50/41–43 St. George 3 October 1848

An interesting church with more of early work than is often found in the district. It comprises a nave with aisles, chancel with south aisle, western tower and north and south porches. The nave has a clerestory at the east end of which, is a sancte bellcote. The parapet of the clerestory is moulded, the aisles have high roofs. The tower is a curious Norman one, though much cased and altered. It opens to the nave by a Third-Pointed, panelled arch. On its west side, is a flat buttress. The east and west belfry windows still retain their original character, of 2 lights with shafts contained within a large semi-circular arch and flanked on each side, by a plain Norman arcade with shafts. On the south, the original work is best preserved and the mouldings enriched with chevron and other ornaments. Some of the western stone lattice work, of late date, is inserted in these Norman windows. Those on the south and west, have been altered. There are Norman shafts in the angles of the upper part of the tower. The parapet is plain and there are 4 ugly modern pinnacles. On the south side, is an octagonal stair turret, projecting, and evidently a late addition. Within, the tower has stone groining.

The porches are Third-Pointed. On the northern one, is a niche over the door. The nave is wide. On each side, it has a Third-Pointed arcade of 4 arches with light lozenge piers which have 4 shafts with separate octagonal capitals and Tudor flower over the capitals. Between the arches are head corbels on which the timbers of the original roof rested. The nave and aisles are now unfortunately ceiled. The clerestory has square-headed windows deprived of tracery. Most of the windows of the aisles have also been mutilated but one on the south has a richly panelled arch internally. That at the east end of the north aisle is square-headed, of 2 lights, perhaps Mid-Pointed.

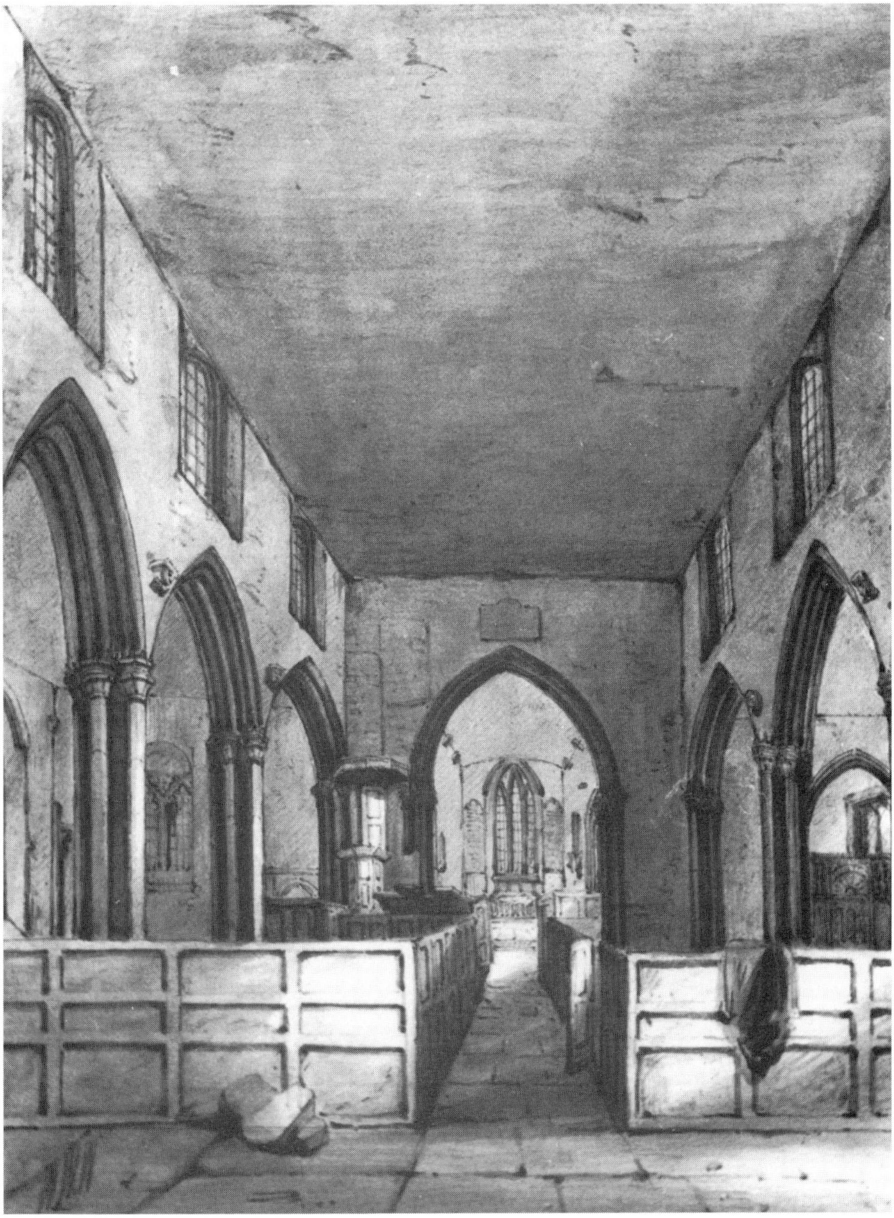

Beckington Church 'before the alteration', by W.W. Wheatley

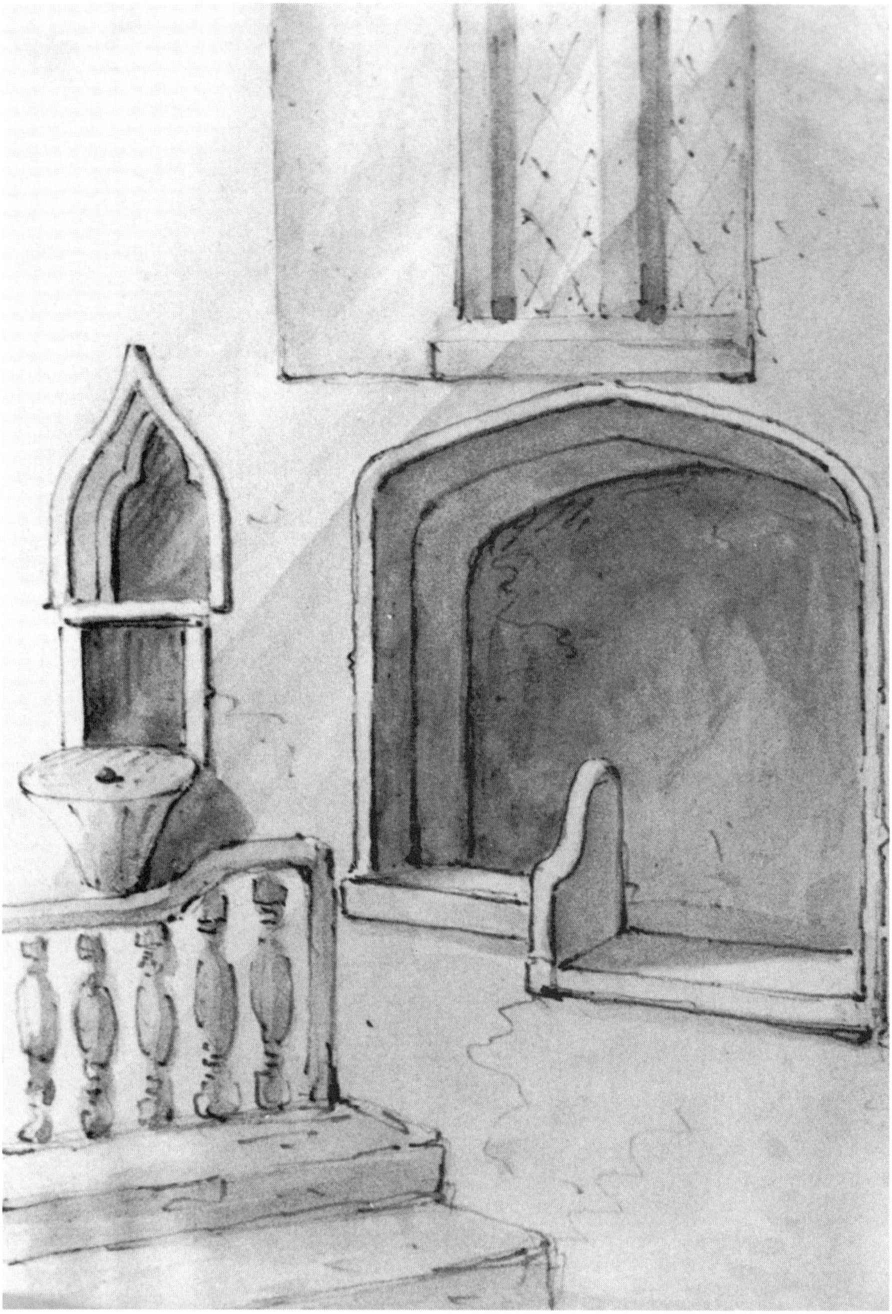

Lately discovered in Beckington Church, 1844, by W.W. Wheatley

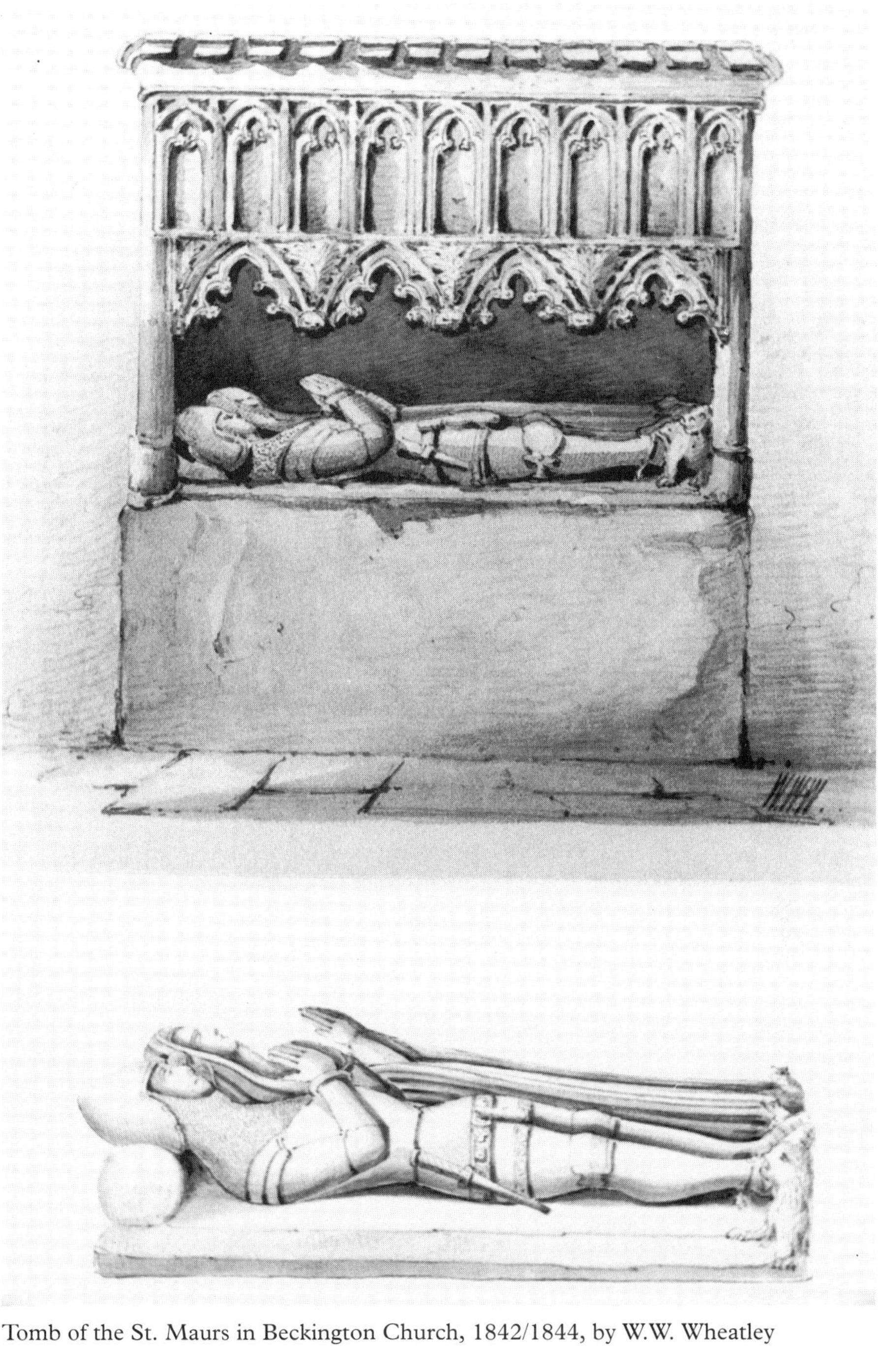

Tomb of the St. Maurs in Beckington Church, 1842/1844, by W.W. Wheatley

The chancel arch resembles those on the north and south. The chancel has indications of earlier work than the nave. Its east window is a plain triplet in a containing arch. That on the south-east is Mid-Pointed of 2 lights. On the north is a square-headed Third-Pointed one of 4 lights. In the same wall is a plain arch which projects outward within which is the effigy of a lady with joined hands and square reticulated head dress in very good preservation. On the south side of the altar, are 2 sedilia, ascending eastwards, under one arch, with only a stone elbow between them; also a piscina of ogee form, trefoiled, with stone shelf and round basin.

The east end of the north aisle has some Third-Pointed stone panelling looking like the remnant of a reredos; also a large ogee niche with embattled cornice and piscina with trefoiled arch in a square, containing a stone shelf and a trefoil orifice. Near it is a late doorway opening to the rood turret, which is seen projecting on the outside. The arch between the chancel and south aisle, is very plain. The floor of the latter is raised on several steps. Its east window is Third-Pointed of 4 lights, another is square-headed of 6 lights cinquefoiled.

In the chancel on the north side, near the east end, is a fine Third-Pointed tomb, of considerable depth into the wall, having a rich horizontal canopy with panelling and small battlements below which are 4 small arched compartments with foliations and heads at the points. On the tomb, are effigies of a knight and lady. The former has a pointed helmet, chain breast piece and lion at his feet. The lady has a mantle over her head which is supported by angels – and seems elderly – and 2 little dogs at her feet. On the wall is a brass plate thus inscribed: 'Hic jacet Johes Sayntmour armig et Elizabetha vxor eivs q. quidm Johes obiit V die octobr A° dni MillCCCCLXXXV cuius aie ppiciet de' Amen.'

On a slab in the middle of the chancel is a brass of a knight and lady, the latter in butterfly head dress, the former with a dog at his feet.

The font is early, the bowl octagonal upon a cylindrical stem and 8 legs upon octagonal base and all of marble. There is a west gallery with a finger organ.

(At the east end of the north aisle, is a brass with English inscription: 'Thomas Webb Clotheman who dyed in the feare of God and departed this transitory lyffe the X daye of August in the yeare of our Lorde God one Thousande fyve hundred and eyghty fyve being of the adge of 74 yeares.')

Bedminster

20/62–63 St. John 25 February 1849

A plain church, comprising a nave with north aisle, chancel, west tower and north porch. The tower is massive and low, of First-Pointed character with plain lancet belfry window with later parapet of pierced panelling, such as is common in the neighbourhood, and 4 crocketed pinnacles. The arch to the nave has very good First-Pointed mouldings.

The north doorway within the porch is First-Pointed having also good mouldings and shafts with capitals of foliage. The east window of the aisle is

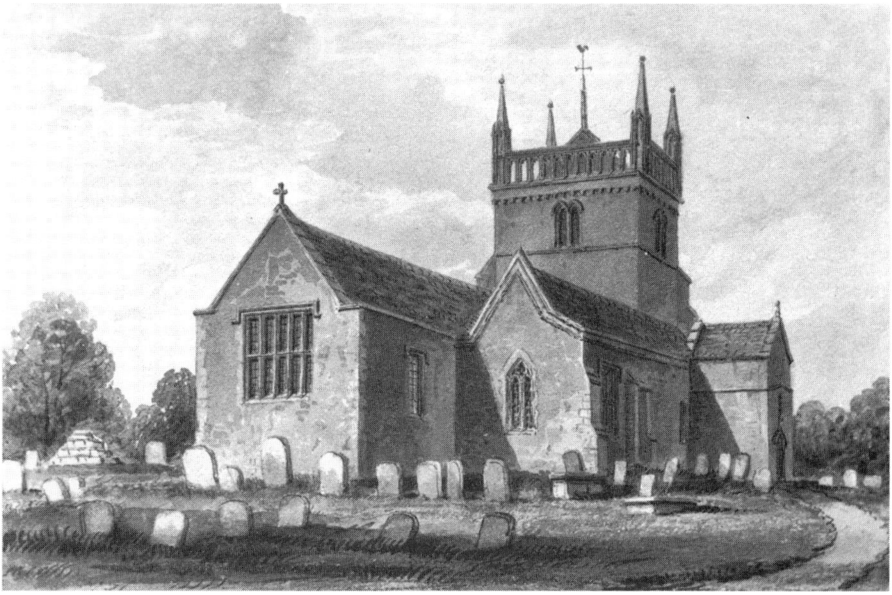

North east view of Bedminster Church, 1827, by J.C. Buckler

Middle-Pointed of 2 lights. All other windows are square-headed of debased character. The arches have been removed and the colonnade now existing, appears of very questionable kind, the columns heavy of a diagonal form. There is no chancel arch. The outer walls are covered with black rough cast. The interior is plain and ordinary in its fittings, has a west gallery, an organ and a poor modern font.

Beercrocombe

50/95–96 St. James 13 February 1857

A small church in plan, resembling [Stoke St. Mary] in a bleak, lonely situation. Entirely Perpendicular except part of the north wall which contains a single lancet window, which is the only opening on that side of the nave. The other windows, south of the nave, are of 3 lights. In the chancel the east window is of 3 lights, the others of 2. The chancel arch is pointed on octagonal pillars. The nave is wide. There is a plain, Perpendicular rood screen. The roofs coved with ribs and bosses. In the chancel, the roof is coloured with blue. The tower arch is open and has for corbels, grotesque animal figures. The interior is remarkably neat and has undergone recent restoration. The nave is fitted with open seats, the chancel stalled. The font has a plain, octagonal bowl with panelling.

The tower is a pretty good Perpendicular [one], embattled and divided by 2 horizontal string courses, has buttresses at the angles and an embattled turret at the south-east angle, lighted by slits. In the centre storey on the west side, is

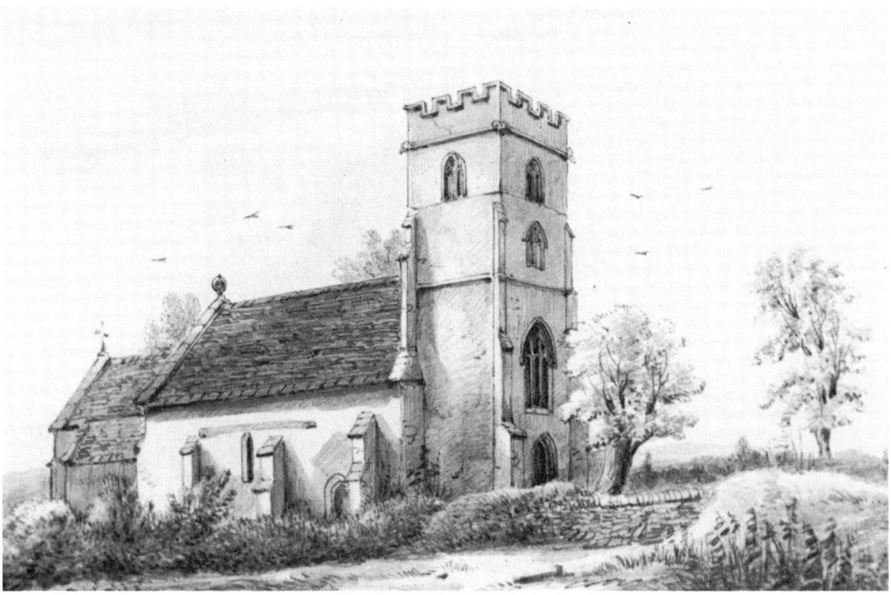

Beercrocombe, 1850, by W.W. Wheatley

a 2 light window, which looks Decorated. Between it is a 3 light Perpendicular window on the west and [a] doorway of which the door has new ironwork. The belfry windows are of 2 lights. Over the east gable a good cross.

Bishop's Lydeard

49/71–72 St. Mary 1843

A Perpendicular church with a magnificent tower but the body is rather inferior to that of Wellington. The tower is at the west end and the general arrangement is as at Wellington but the south side only being continuous along part of the chancel. There is a south porch but no clerestory. The tower has 4 stages. The west window [is] of 5 lights with a transom and beneath it a doorway with a label and foliated spandrels. The three upper stages of the tower have each windows with pierced stone lattice work. Those of the belfry are double and each of 3 lights. In the 3d storey, from the ground, are niches on three sides. The battlement of the tower has open panelling and there are 8 crocketed pinnacles. The buttresses are enriched with pinnacles on the belfry storey and there are smaller ones in the other storeys. There is the usual stair turret all up the north side of the tower. (There are 8 bells.)

The tower and nave are of a fine red stone. The chancel appears to be modern and is stuccoed. The south side of the body has a handsome battlement. The south porch has a moulded parapet without battlement. The north side is very plain and windowless.

The side aisles open to the nave each by 4 pointed arches, those on the south,

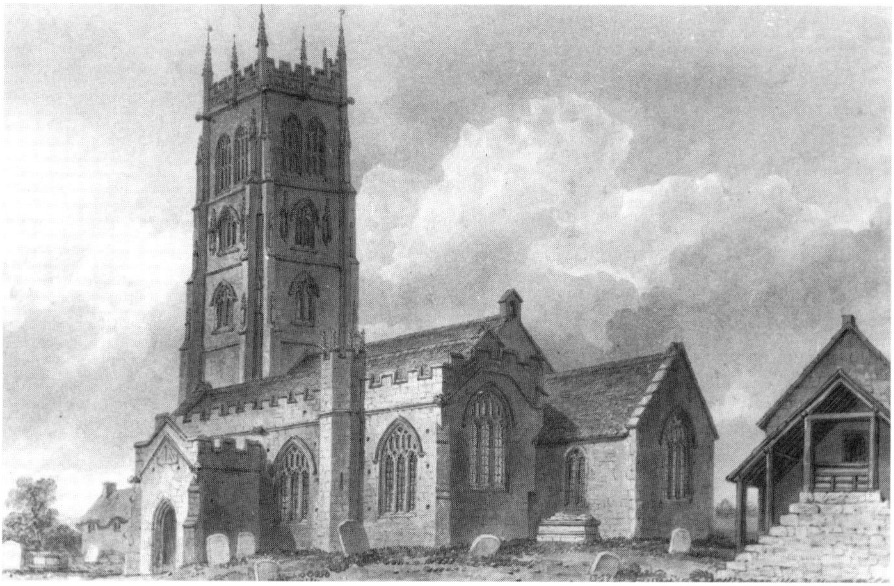

South east view of Bishop's Lydeard Church, 1835, by J. Buckler

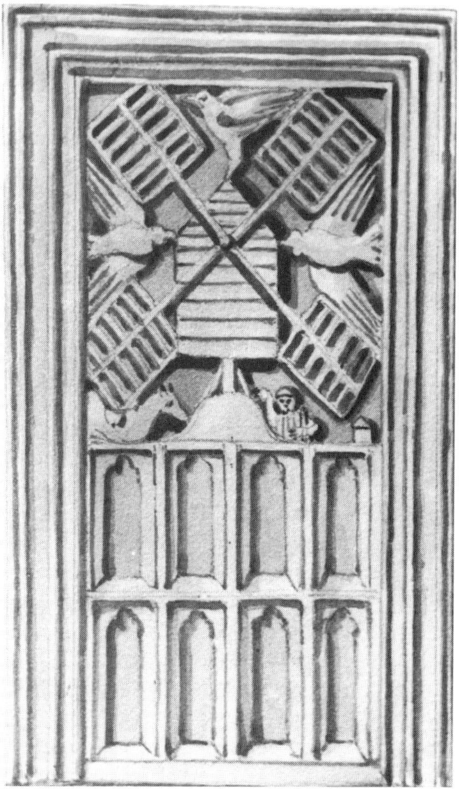

Pew door, Bishop's Lydeard, 1848, by W.W. Wheatley

lofty and elegant, rising from piers exactly resembling those of Wellington. The northern arches are much lower and plainer but with nearly similar piers.

The north aisle is much narrower than the southern, the tower arch lofty with continuous mouldings. Within the tower is placed a large and handsome organ. The front of the west gallery has good wood carving and tracery which may perhaps be composed from portions of ancient benches of which, however, a great many remain in the nave and exhibit very rich wood sculpture at the ends. There are no closed pues except in the side aisles. The roof is coved in the usual style with ribs, but over the roodloft exhibits more intricate and elaborate panelling.

The windows of the south aisle are large and of 3 lights, those in the north aisle of 2 lights. There is an octagonal turret on the south side, with stairs to the roodloft. The roodloft screen extends across the chancel and the south aisle, the screen of great beauty, with fine tracery in a very perfect state. There are 5 compartments in the centre portion, 3 at the south side. The loft itself is complete and exhibits elegant courses of foliage and one cornice on which is inscribed the creed in Latin.

The chancel arch is wide and above it are two ugly modern windows. There is also some ugly, modern painting just above the roodloft. The chancel opens to its south chapel by a Tudor arch on shafts. The chancel is entirely modernized in a very poor style and the east window blocked up by a hideous screen.

The south chancel aisle opens to that of the nave by a pointed arch. There is an ugly, modern addition on the north side, forming the pue of the Lethbridge family. The font is a good, octagonal one on a pedestal of like shape. The sides of the bason are panelled in a rather curious style.

Blackford

52/25–26 St. Michael 28 July, 1873

A small church having only chancel and nave with a south porch and western tower. The south doorway is Norman, with 2 orders much enriched. One is a course of bold chevrons, one is of lozenges, the outer on shafts with sculptured capitals. That on the east has a special ornament, on the west, chevroned. The door has a very flat arch and there is a tympanum between that and the outer arch. The rest of the church is later and mainly Perpendicular. The chancel has a 3 light, Perpendicular window, with coloured glass, the other windows mostly square-headed of 2 lights, one on the north, very narrow and labeled.

There is a projection at the north-east of the nave for the rood stairs and the rood door is seen high up on the north-east internally. The chancel arch is on clustered shafts of the Somersetshire type, of pointed form and stilted. In the nave, in the south wall, is a square recess, with orifice, having a rose for piscina. The roof of both nave and chancel, is coved, with ribs and bosses. The font has a circular bowl with mouldings round it upon a base. The nave is pewed. The tower arch is pointed and very narrow on octagonal corbels. The tower arch is small and wholly Perpendicular, has battlement and corner buttresses, west door and small 2 light window over it and the same in the belfry storey.

(There is a stoup on the east side of the porch. The porch has an outer door pointed and chamfered. The tower is covered with ivy.)

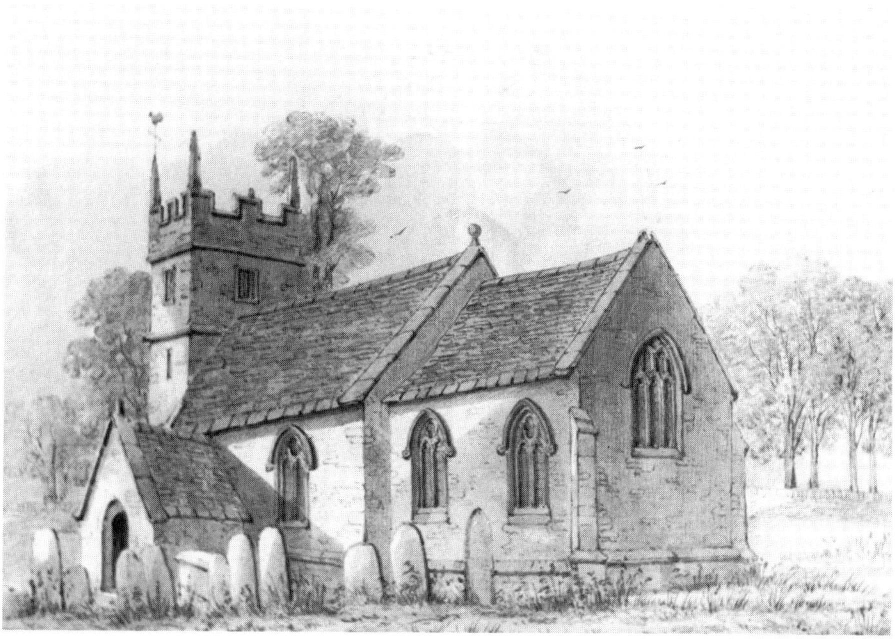

Blackford, 1846, by W.W. Wheatley

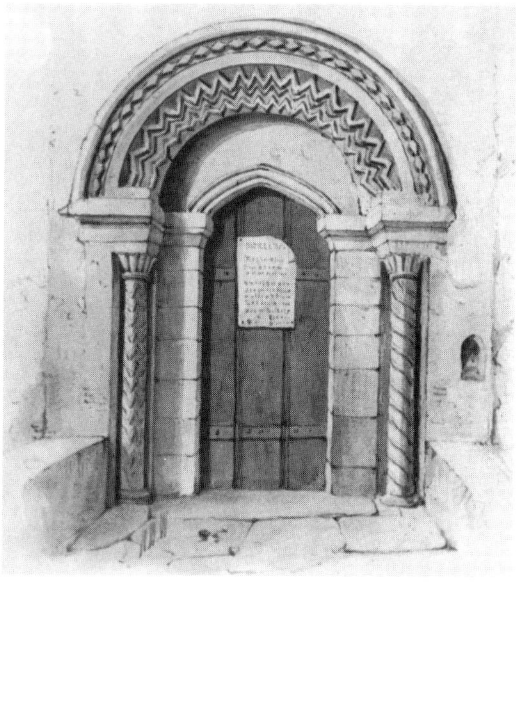

Blackford Church, south door, 1846, by W.W. Wheatley

Bleadon

50/82–83 St. Peter 21 May, 1855

A poor church, with only chancel and nave, south porch and western tower. The tower is much the most remarkable feature of the church and is really a very fine Perpendicular one of 3 stages with panelled parapet and pinnacles at the angles, an octagonal pyramidical turret and pinnacle at the north-east rising to some height. The belfry windows of a range of 3 and each of 2 lights, the central one only open. On the west side is a 4 light window and a labeled doorway with head corbels.

The chancel is very long in proportion to the nave. The whole of the body of the church, both within and without, much neglected and out of repair and the outer walls partially stuccoed. On the north, the windows are few, of 2 and 3 lights, and there is a square projection on the same side for the rood stairs. The chancel is Decorated: said to have been built in 1317. The chancel arch is continuous. The east window has been closed.

On the north, is a Decorated, 2 light window and a 3 light Perpendicular one closed. On the south, is one Perpendicular window of 3 lights and 2 Decorated ones of 2 lights, one of which, near a buttress, is continued low down with a kind of transom, like a lychnoscope but not glazed below. On the same side, is the trace of an early string course and door with good and rich double feathering. On the south of the nave, are Perpendicular windows of 3 lights. The porch, plain. There is a trace of hagioscope north of the chancel arch.

Just outside the churchyard, on the west side, is the lofty shaft of a cross on several steps.

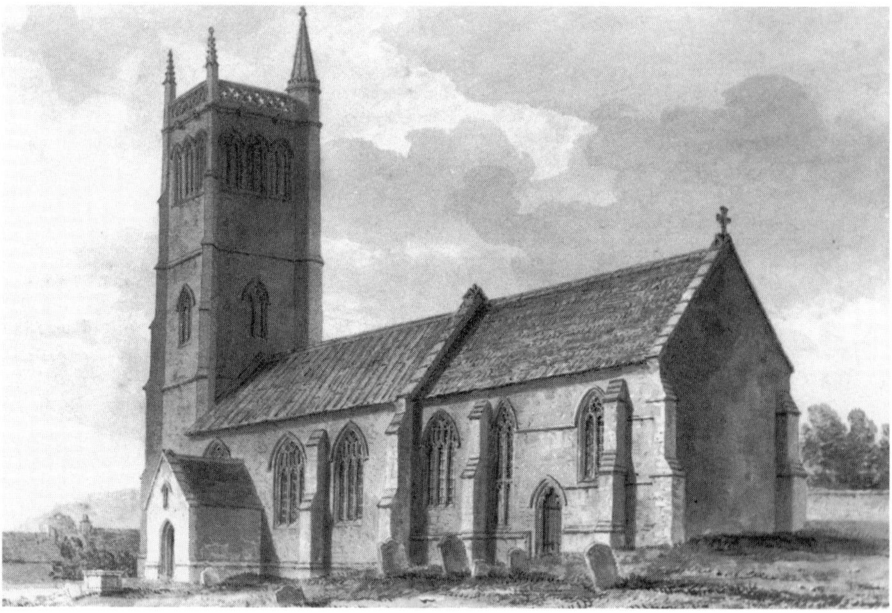

South east view of Bleadon Church, 1828, by J. Buckler

Bradford-on-Tone

50/66–67 St. Giles 24 January, 1854

A fair sized church, the exterior of genuine Somersetshire character and all Perpendicular. The plan is a common one, nave with aisles, chancel with side chapels, west tower and south porch. The nave and chancel have tiled roofs. The aisles of the nave and the porch are embattled. The chapels of the chancel have tiled, separate roofs. The walls of good stone masonry but partially rough cast. The tower is of 3 stages and embattled with 4 diagonal, crocketed pinnacles at the angles, an octagonal stair turret on the south side occupying the centre and carried up above the parapet and embattled. The buttresses are at the angles. The belfry windows of 3 lights with the mullions hidden by buffer boards. On the west side, a good, continuous doorway and a 3 light window. The windows are all Perpendicular of 3 lights, except a wide lancet in the south chapel of the chancel.

Internally, the arcades of the nave are Early English. On each side are 3 pointed arches, upon circular columns with capitals. The chancel arch following a Somersetshire fashion, springs from brackets only and forms a very simple division between chancel and nave, which are of equal height. The chapels, or aisles, north and south of the chancel, extend wider than those of the nave and the chancel is continued eastward of them. There are also arches between the chapels of the chancel and the aisles of the nave, which are continuous. There is a priests' door on the north. The interior contains some good, ancient bench ends, but several pues and a gallery with an organ.

The porch has a bold, continuous outer door.

(There is a new grave stone coped with a fine cross flory to Bridget Tulip obt. 1850.)

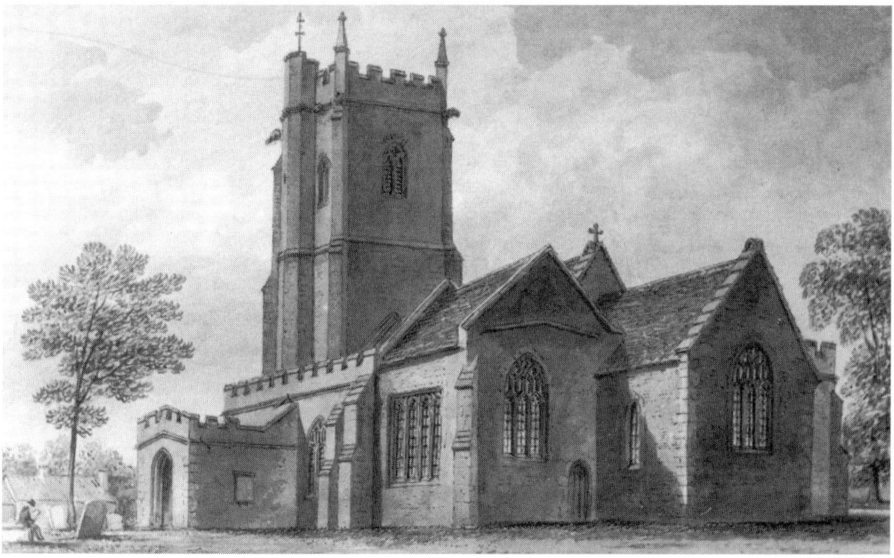

South east view of Bradford-on-Tone Church, 1837, by J. Buckler

Bradley, West

49/24–25 [Unknown] 1835

This is a small church with a nave, chancel and small west tower, all of plain, but good Rectilinear architecture. The parapet of the nave is well finished but there is no battlement. The windows are without labels, those in the chancel, square-headed. A low side one on the south, resembles in its tracery, those of the old quadrangle Christ Church, Oxford; the others are plainer. There is a south porch with a fine, plain arch with mouldings and the inner door is enriched with elegant tracery in woodwork. The tower is small and of 2 storeys. The upper [storey] has a good battlement and the roof is raised in the centre into a pyramidical form crowned by a cross of stone. The belfry windows are square-headed; the western one resembles that of the nave.

On the north side of the nave, opposite the chancel arch, is a staircase turret to the roodloft, with small window, now stopped. The tower is open to the nave by a pointed arch upon shafts and a similar one open to the chancel. A little stained glass appears in the windows. In the chancel is a plain niche on the south and pedestals for statues in the east wall.

The situation is pleasing and sequestered.

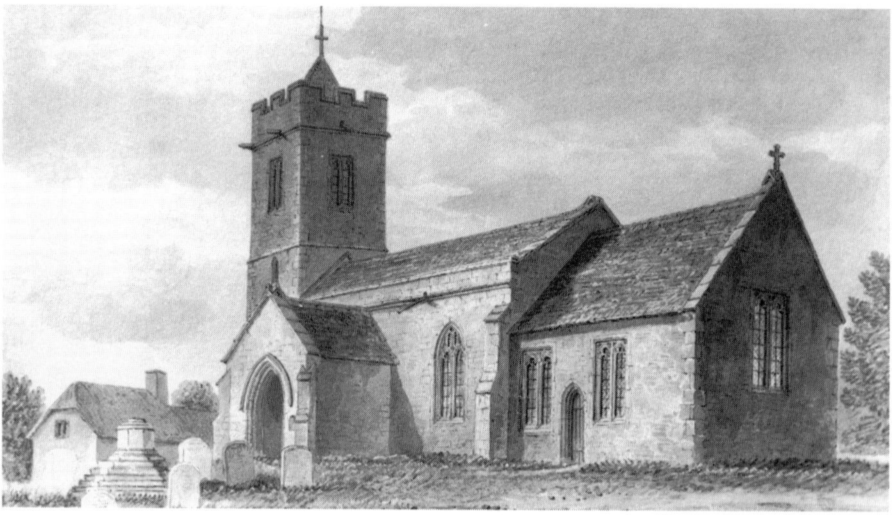

South east view of West Bradley Church, 1833, by J. Buckler

Brent, East

50/79–80 St. Mary 21 May, 1855

A handsome church, all Perpendicular with many points resembling that of South Brent. The plan is a chancel and nave with north and south aisles

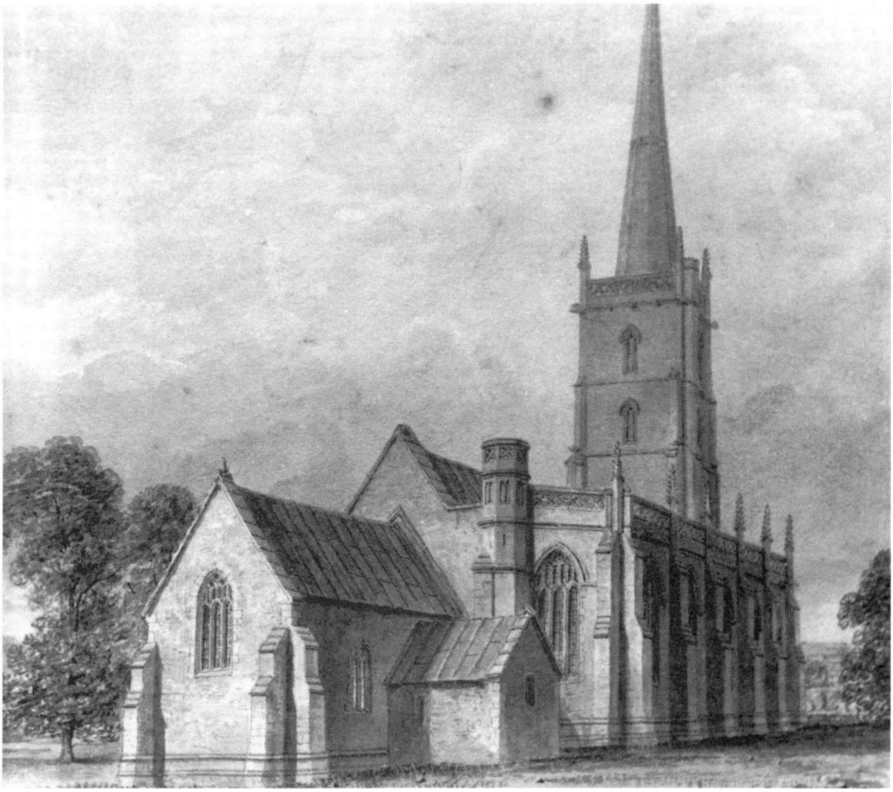

North east view of East Brent Church, 1831, by J. Buckler

and south porch, the south aisle being short and only carried from the porch eastward; a western tower and spire. The walls are all covered with rough cast.

The north aisle, as at South Brent, has a fine open parapet, panelled in form of lozenges, and pinnacles and on the buttresses. The windows are all Perpendicular throughout and of 3 lights. There is an octagonal rood turret on the north side with a parapet of pierced panelling.

The north arcade is of 5 pointed arches on light, Perpendicular piers of shafts of the usual Western form, with separate capitals and stilted. On the south side, beyond the porch, are only 2 arches, lower than those opposite (and not quite resembling them) with clustered piers. Chancel arch resembles those of the north arcade. The roof is coved with ribs and bosses with a kind of debased ornament. Several windows contained good pieces of ancient stained glass and there is some of rather inferior modern character. There is a west gallery and a good organ and several ancient open benches with poppy-headed standards. There are some monumental effigies in the windows, apparently ecclesiastics. The font has an octagonal bowl panelled.

The outer doorway of the porch, is apparently Early English and has some beaded [?] shafts, some octagonal ones with stilted bases and foliated capitals.

The inner door has continuous mouldings of later character and the door itself has fine wood tracery.

The porch itself is very large.

The tower is 80 feet in height, the spire 60 more: all Perpendicular, the tower divided by horizontal strings into 5 stages, has buttresses and an open panelled parapet. The belfry windows are of 2 lights and on the north side, are other 2 light windows and at the north-west, a square stair turret, terminating in an octagon. There are pinnacles at the angles. The spire is light, octagonal and ornamented with a band of foliage. On the west side of the tower, are 3 canopied niches in 3 different storeys. The highest contains the statue of a king, with another figure in the act of embracing him. The middle contains what seems to be a representation of the Trinity. The lowest, another king crowned and bearing the emblems of majesty. In the churchyard is the shaft of a cross.

Brent, South

50/77–79 St. Michael 21 May, 1855

A handsome church in a pretty situation on the side of Brent Knoll. The plan: chancel, nave with north aisle, south transept, south porch and west tower. The whole Perpendicular except some small portions on the south side.

Within the south porch is a good semi-Norman doorway with pointed arch, the other member chevroned on imposts and the chevron moulding continued

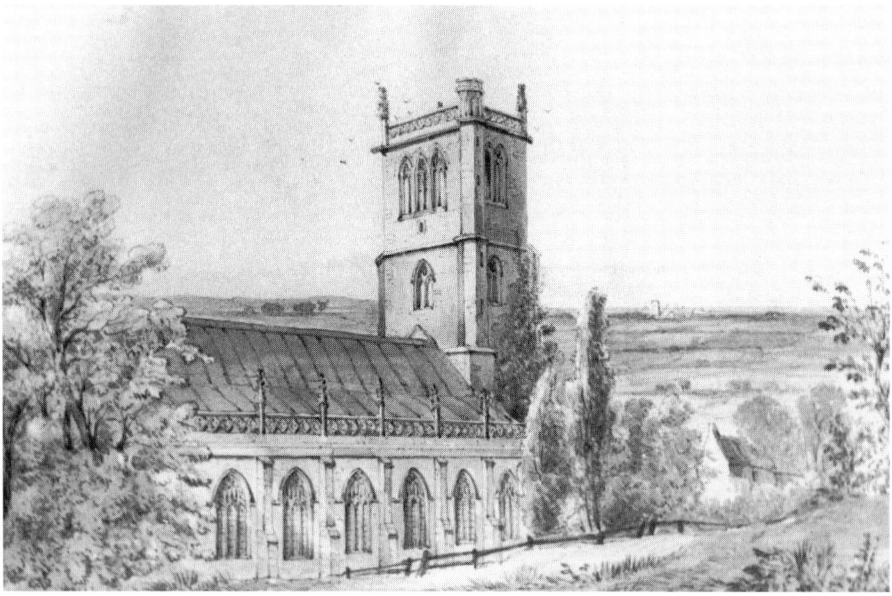

South Brent, 1843, by W.W. Wheatley

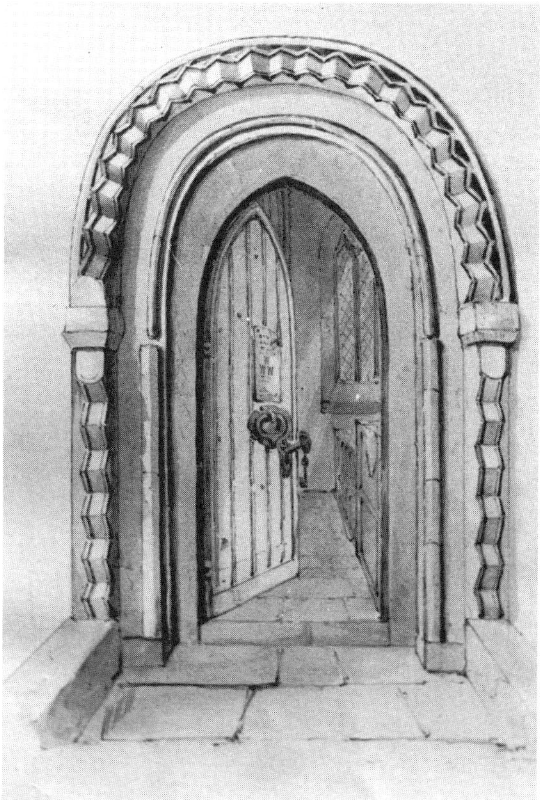

South Brent, 1843,
by W.W. Wheatley

longitudinally down the jambs. Over the door is a niche. The outer door of the porch is on shafts; the porch itself is large. The whole of the north aisle, though not on the show side, has a fine pierced parapet in lozenge work and roof turret on the same side, which rises to some height, has the same ornamental parapet. On the same side, the buttresses are pinnacled. The south side is plainer and without parapet. The nave has a lead roof. The transept is tiled.

The chancel is modern, (of rather meagre imitation of Perpendicular), but is fitted with stalls.

The interior is very light and handsome. The windows of the north aisle are set very closely and many in number; those on the south, fewer and further between. All of good Perpendicular character and of 3 lights.

The arcade is good and of considerable length, of 6 arches having the usual light, clustered piers of 4 shafts, which are stilted and have octagonal, separate capitals. The chancel arch is similar. The south transept is earlier and appears to be early Decorated. It opens to the nave by a low, continuous pointed arch and is in a great measure, cut off from the church and appropriated as a vestry and approach to the pulpit. On its west side, it has a single cinquefoiled window, which has its rear arch feathered, according to a Somersetshire practice.

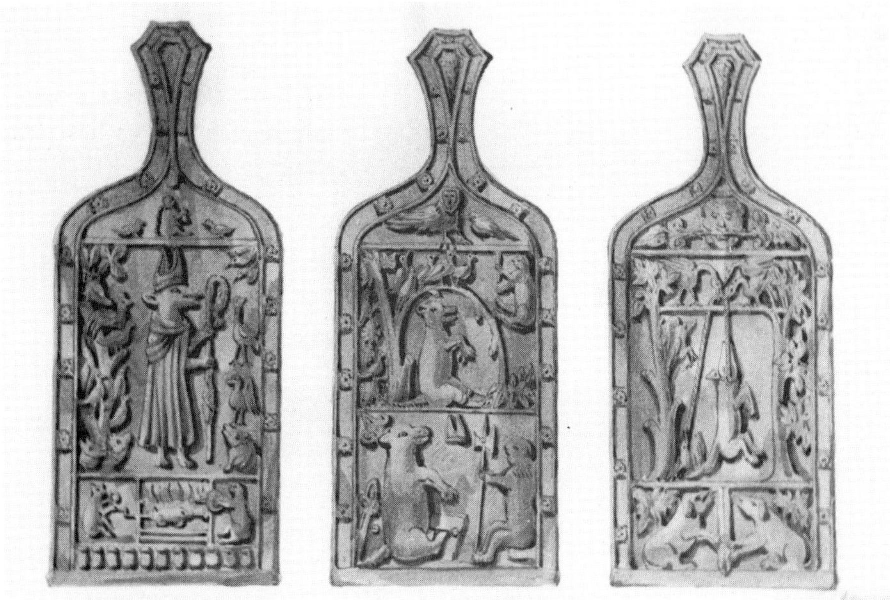

Pew ends, Brent (Knoll) Church, 1843, by W.W. Wheatley

The south window, which is of 3 lights, early Decorated, has also the interior feathering. The east window is Perpendicular and square-headed. In the south wall, is a large ogee piscina, trefoiled, with quatrefoil orifice and a niche.

There is an ascent to the chancel by 2 steps.

The roof of the nave is coved with the usual ribs and bosses. That of the aisle is flat and panelled elegantly with enriched bosses and brackets and figures of angels and saints. The tower arch is fine and open, unencumbered by gallery and springing from tall shafts. In the tower stands the organ, but the large west window is seen through the arch. At the east end of the north aisle and in the very angle is a figure on a bracket; also an odd spiral shaft with octagonal capital and base having rather an Early English look and probably meant to support a statue. Near to it, is the rood door.

In the nave, the original bench ends remain very perfect on the north side, having poppy heads and excellent wood sculpture, both figures and tracery, in some instances grotesque figures as a fox drawn up by a rope; monkeys roasting a pig; a bishop with a mitre and the face of an ass or a fox, etc. On the south side, new benches have been erected also with well carved ends and poppy heads so as to be tolerably uniform with those opposite but these have low doors added.

The font is curious and early. The bowl is a sort of quatrefoil form with the rim and base moulded, the stem octagonal with moulded sides to which are attached 4 marble shafts without capital or bases and set lozenge wise.

The tower is a fine one with a parapet of pierced panelling and 4 crocketed pinnacles divided by 3 horizontal strings; the belfry windows, three in number of equal size, each of 2 lights. The west window [is] of 5 lights and below it a labeled door with enriched spandrels, flanked by canopied niches and there is an octagonal turret on the side.

Bridgwater

49/13–16 St. Mary 1830

This is a large and handsome church, is principally Rectilinear but has some portions of Curvilinear character. The plan comprises a low west tower, crowned by a lofty octagonal spire, a nave with side aisles, north and south transepts with aisles and chapels adjoining and a chancel with side chapels. There are also large porches both north and south. The whole, except parts of the transepts, is embattled. The west door of the tower has a label and the spandrels highly enriched. Above it, is a Curvilinear window of 2 lights.

The north porch adjoins the transept and is a very beautiful specimen of Curvilinear work, especially the outer doorway, in which the head of the arch above the door is filled with singularly elegant, open tracery in which there is a fine wheel. The arch of the door itself is of contracted form but has a fine, foliated band in its moulding and springs from shafts with rich capitals of foliage. The inner doorway has an ogee head, but is plain. The south porch ranges with and adjoins the transept and its outer doorway has shafts and appears Curvilinear.

In the south transept is a curious oriel window with a square head, surmounted by an embattled cornice. The north transept has a large, Curvilinear window of 5 lights and there is, likewise, one in the adjoining chapel with a wide arch. The south aisle of the nave has also Curvilinear

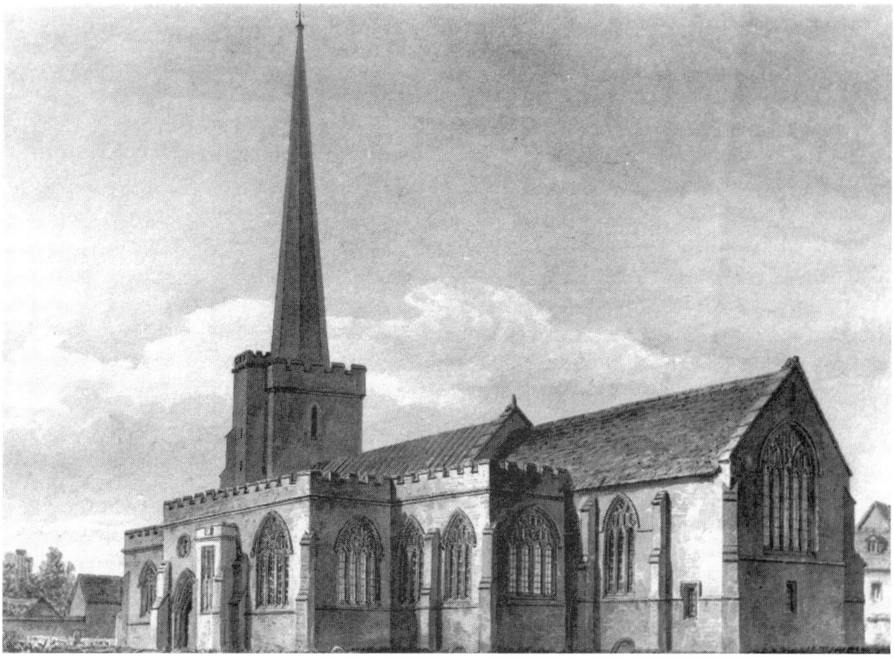

South east view of Bridgwater Church, 1832, by J. Buckler

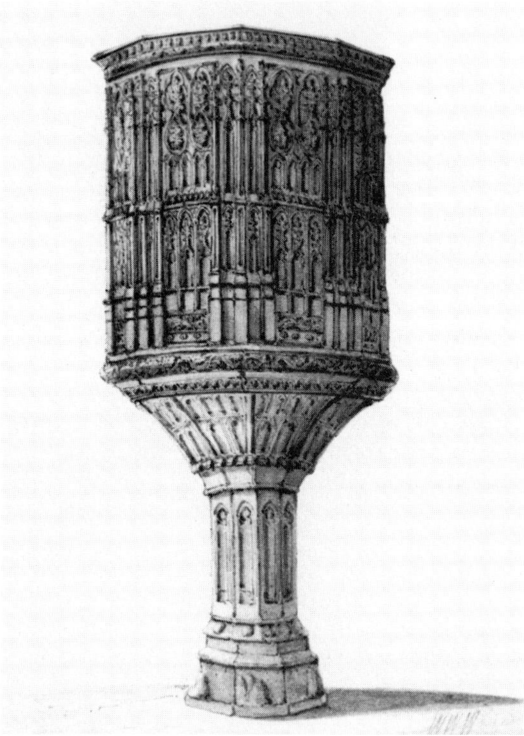

In Bridgwater Church, 1851, by W.W. Wheatley

windows, mostly of 4 lights. Those of the north aisle, are Rectilinear of 4 lights.

The interior is spacious and rich. The nave is divided from each aisle by 6 lofty arches of Rectilinear character with light piers of lozenge form with a small shaft set at each angle. Above is a clerestory which has a square window of 3 lights over each pier. The nave has a modern ceiling, but those of the side aisles are good, plain ones of wood. The transepts are both divided into aisles. The south transept is the largest and opens to its aisles by arches similar to those in the nave. It has also a handsome panelled ceiling of wood.

The north transept has a modern roof and is walled out from one of its aisles. Beneath one of its windows, are 2 arches in the wall, with feathering and containing some mutilated effigies.

The pulpit is a very fine one, beautifully carved in wood and enriched with Rectilinear panelling and niches. There is also the base of [an] ancient desk of octagonal form, enriched with open tracery and panelling but the upper part is modern. There is some very rich screen work surrounding the Corporation Pew in the style of the 17th century with arabesque ornament.

The roodloft screen, between the nave and chancel, is of Rectilinear character and is continued across both aisles. It is very rich with open panelling, niches and crocketed pinnacles, but parts of it are modern and less good. The chancel opens to each of its chapels by a wide, pointed arch but extends beyond them. Its roof is coved and panelled and all its windows are of

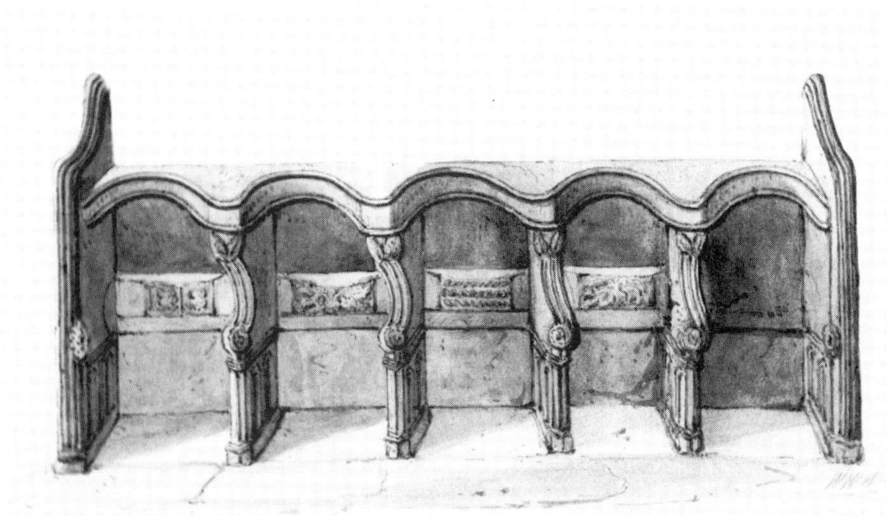

In Bridgwater Church, 1851, by W.W. Wheatley

Rectilinear character. There are some remnants of the ancient stalls. The altar piece has a modern, Gothic screen, in which is inserted a very fine painting of the 3 Maries presented to the church by the Honourable Ann Paulett. The artist is unknown.

The font is octagonal, panelled with quatrefoils. In the west gallery of the nave, is a very fine organ.

1854

A considerable restoration in progress: the pues replaced by open benches.

Brislington

50/59–60 St. Luke 22 April, 1850

A Somersetshire church of a character frequent in the county. It consists of nave and chancel, with aisles to the former and south aisles only to the latter, a west tower and south porch. There is no clerestory and the whole is Third Pointed. The tower is the most remarkable feature and is really a fine one of the type prevalent near Bristol. It is of 3 stages, embattled, with an octagonal corner turret crowned by an octagonal pyramid, ribbed at the angles, surrounded by small pinnacles and enriched by a panelled band. The battlement is also panelled and there are 4 corner pinnacles of diagonal form, having small battlements.

In the centrepiece of the battlement, on each side, is an ogee niche, containing [a] statue. The belfry window on each side, is of 2 lights. Below it, on the south side, is a small niche of flattened ogee form, containing figures of

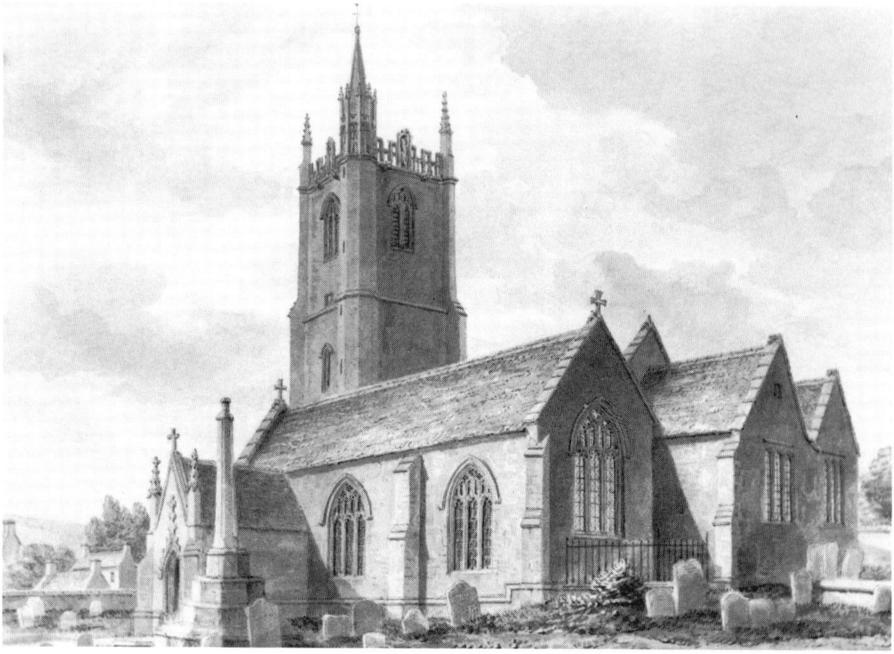

South east view of Brislington Church, 1828, by J. Buckler

a man and a woman. In the 2d stage, is a single window, cinquefoiled, moulded and labeled. The buttresses are diagonal. The west window is of 3 lights with ogee canopy and damaged mouldings. The canopy upon angel corbels. The material is chiefly reddish stone with dressings of a finer quality of grey colour. The chancel extends one bay eastward of the aisle.

The roofs are coved, with ribs, simply crossing and bosses. The windows are pretty, uniform of 3 lights. The arcades of the nave are each of 5 Third-Pointed arches with mouldings, the piers light, of clustered 8 shafts, alternately large and small, and moulded capitals, the bases stilted. The capitals have almost a Mid-Pointed character. The north aisle is wider than the southern. The chancel arch is plainer than the others, but springs from shafts somewhat similar. Between the chancel and south aisle is one moulded arch, springing from awkward shafts and one somewhat similar between the south aisle of the nave and that of the chancel.

There is a stone reredos erected about 20 years ago and not very bad. The church is pued and has a western gallery with an organ. The tower arch is continuous. The south porch is flanked by crocketed pinnacles set on angular buttresses. The outer door is ogee and crocketed. Over the inner door, is a niche.

The north wall is rough cast. A vestry is added on the north of the chancel. The churchyard is pretty. In it, is the shaft of a cross raised upon lofty, octagonal steps.

(The south chancel arch is made double and spandreled as if for covering [?] a tomb.)

Brockley

51/89–90 St. Nicholas 15 November, 1870

This church has nave with north and south transepted chapels, chancel and western tower. There is a porch appended to the west side of the south transept.

The church has been lately smartened up and put in good condition. The north transept looks as if it were modern and each transept opens to the nave by a pointed arch of continuous order. There is no chancel arch. The chancel has 2 single light windows on the south. One, with square head, is Perpendicular. One is a wide lancet. On the north, is another lancet and at the east end, a Decorated 2 light window. Most of them have modern coloured glass. The chancel roof is coved and panelled with ribs and bosses and an ornamental cornice of Tudor flowers, etc.

The windows in nave and transept, are Perpendicular, some square-headed. The organ is in the north transept and the chancel has stall-like seats with poppy heads. The tower is Perpendicular, has 2 string courses and corner buttresses and embattled parapet with 4 crocketed pinnacles, belfry windows of 2 lights, west doorway and 3 light window over it. At the north-east angle, is a square turret for stairs, rising into an octagonal form and surmounted by a battlement.

The pulpit is a fine one of stone, apparently new.

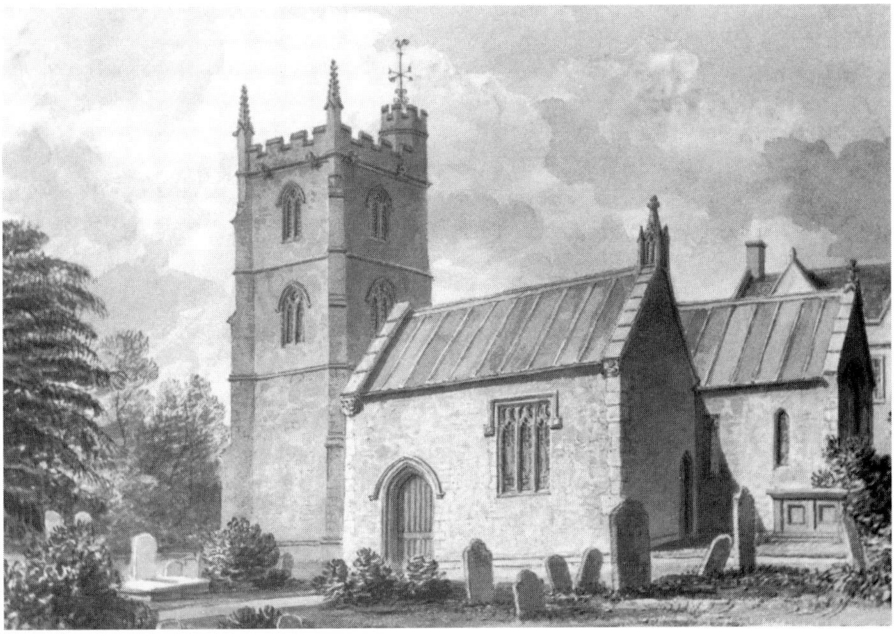

South east view of Brockley Church, 1829, by J. Buckler

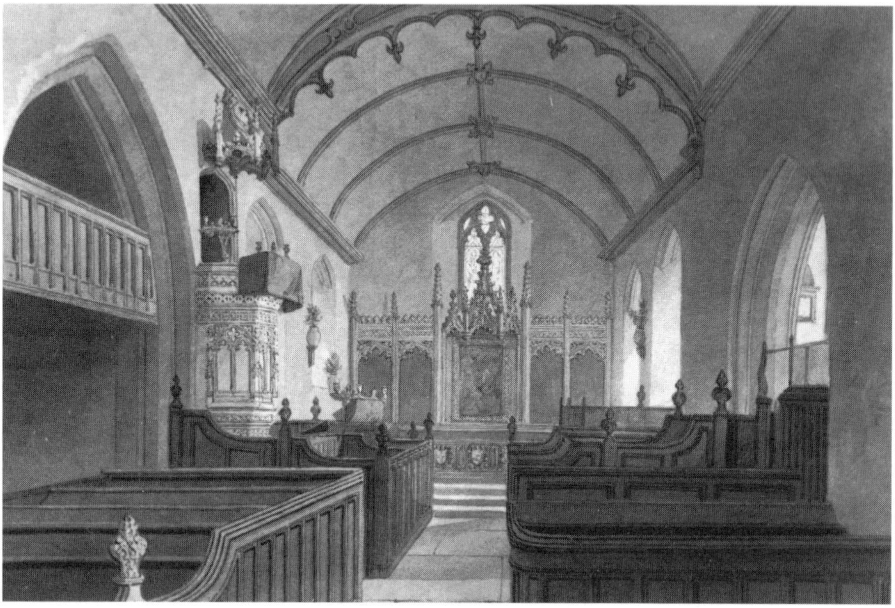

Interior view of Brockley Church, 1829, by J.C. Buckler

Brompton Ralph

50/89–90 St. Mary 7 May, 1855

A neat church both Decorated and Perpendicular in character and having recently undergone much improvement. The plan is a nave with north aisle, chancel, north transept chapel, west tower and south porch.

The arcade of the nave is Decorated with 4 good pointed arches having clustered piers of 4 shafts. The wall of the north aisle has been rebuilt and has Decorated windows of 2 lights. Those on the south of the nave, are Perpendicular, chiefly square-headed. On the south of the chancel, they are of similar character and one has its glass on an inclined plane. There is a horizontal band of stone panelling inserted in the outer wall, beneath one of the windows. The east window is rather small and high in the wall at the first sight, looking like Decorated tracery, whereas it is clearly Perpendicular.

The chancel arch is very wide and springs straight from the wall, and there is a wooden screen for the roodloft. The roofs are of lead. The interior is neat and pleasing, has neither pues nor galleries, but all the benches open with standards, having square tops. The font exactly resembles that of Ash Priors. The inner door of the porch has 2 plain orders. The outer door arch springs straight from the wall. The tower is plain but lofty and covered with rough cast, of 3 stages and embattled with square turret at the north-east. The belfry windows of 2 lights as also the west windows.

The churchyard is very extensive. In it is the shaft of a cross.

(In the churchyard on a tombstone: Isatt wife of Daniel Dibble.)

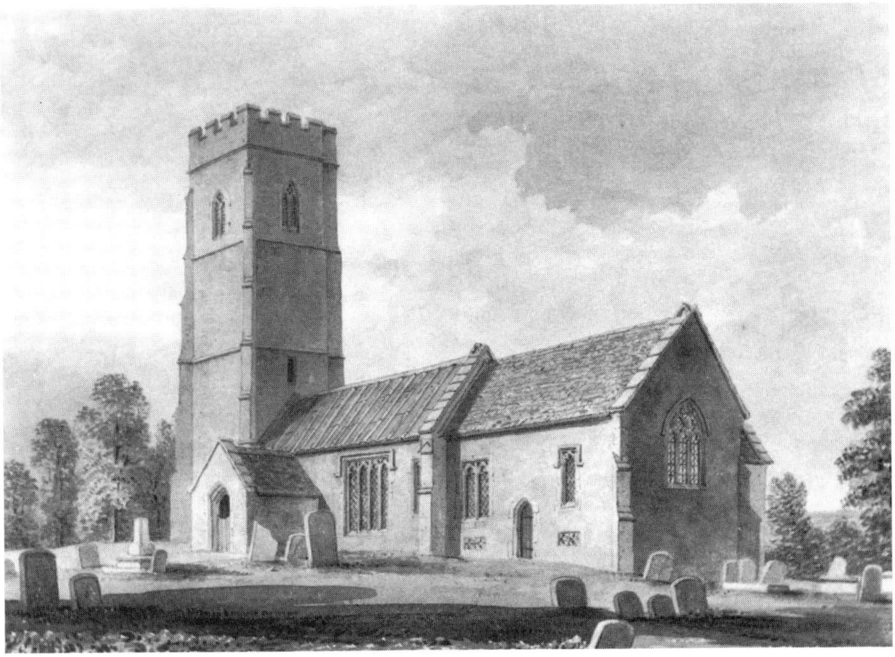

South east view of Brompton Ralph Church, 1841, by J. Buckler

Bruton

19/59–61 [St. Mary] 27 October, 1825

A neat town, surrounded by pleasing scenery and containing numerous ancient houses of about the age of Elizabeth, especially an Almshouse of very handsome appearance. Here is also a very fine church with a singularly elegant and beautiful tower of Perpendicular character. It has a most beautiful, pierced, panelled battlement and is crowned by 4 fine crocketed pinnacles at the angles. Beneath the battlement, is a band of quatrefoils. The belfry windows are three in number on each side. They are very long and beautifully enriched with very fine lattice work. Between them are small false buttresses with pinnacles.

The tower also has some fine niches and crocketed pinnacles set on the set-offs of the buttresses, which have a very beautiful effect. At the west side, is a Tudor arch doorway with spandrels filled with foliage, and a fine Perpendicular window.

(The tower is a very elegant one and of beautiful masonry: divided by 3 string courses, has rich panelled battlement enriched with shields, etc. The west doorway is labeled, has fine arch mouldings and panelled spandrels. Above it, a window of fine proportions of 6 lights subriculated with transom. Above it, are 3 fine canopied niches. There is a 2 light window, with open stone lattice work in the stage above this, set between 2 canopied niches. The belfry storey has 3 windows, each of 2 lights with Somersetshire lattice work

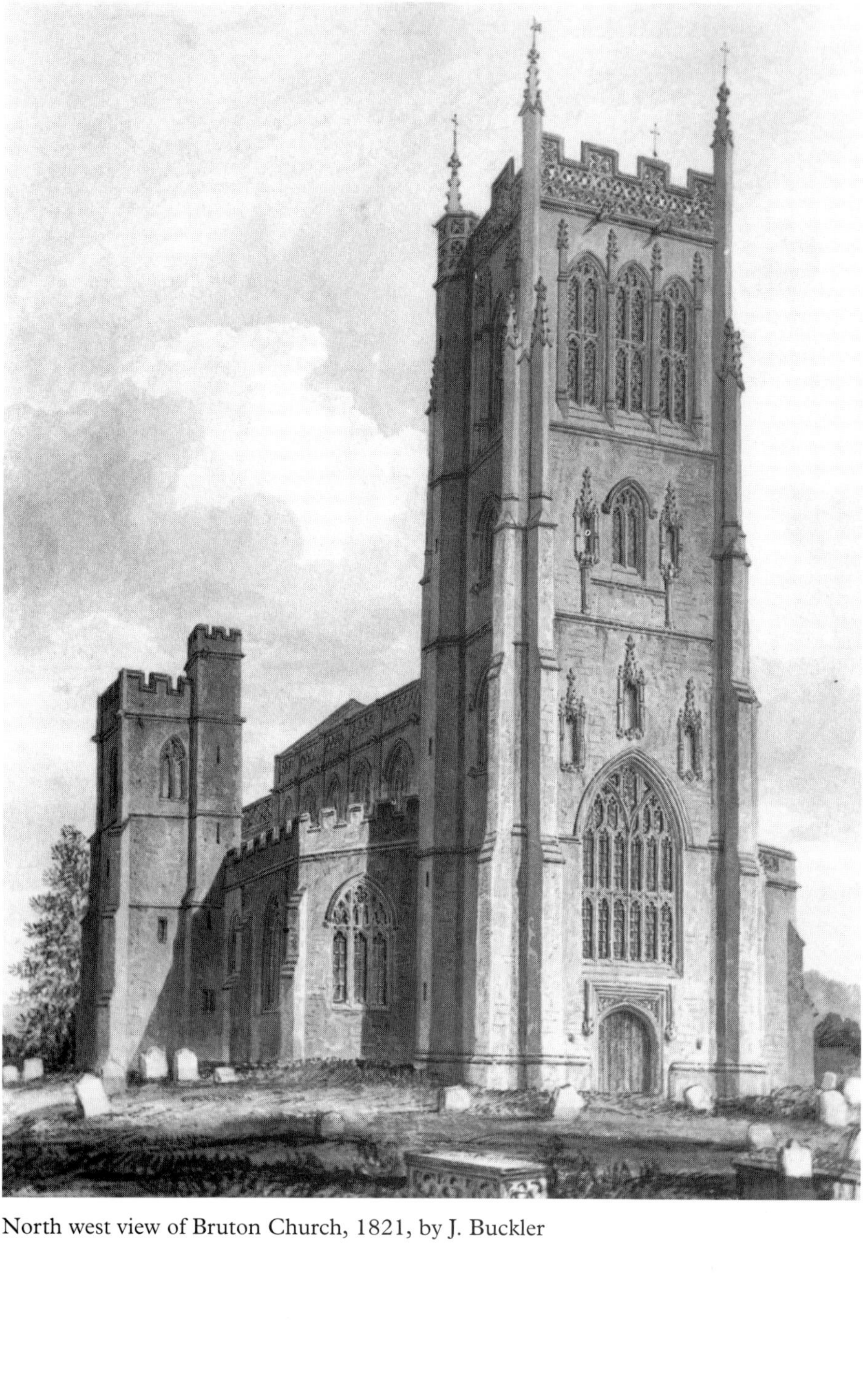

North west view of Bruton Church, 1821, by J. Buckler

very long and effective. Between them, are crocketed pinnacles. There are also light pinnacles set on the buttresses and others at the angles of the transept. Within the tower is fine stone groining.)

A large portion of the church has a very elegant parapet of open work. On the north side is a smaller tower of plain Perpendicular work forming a porch. The interior is spacious and grand, the nave being very broad and much enriched. There are 5 arches dividing it from each aisle acutely pointed with slight curvature. The piers are of ye common Perpendicular form. The clerestory has very broad windows of 4 lights between each of which is a very fine niche with very light and beautiful crocketed canopies, which add considerably to the magnificence of this portion of the church. The roof of the nave is a very fine, timber one with beautiful pierced work, panels, square flower and figures of angels.

The windows are mostly of 3 lights and Perpendicular work but not of particularly elegant tracery. The west window of the tower is, however, a very fine one and is open to the church, as the tower arch is not closed up. The font is an octagon, entirely plain. The chancel has some earlier work and windows of early Decorated character of 2 lights with a circle between the heads. The interior of the chancel is wholly fitted up with modern wainscotting which is much at variance with the general character of this beautiful church. At the west end of the nave is a gallery with an organ. The gallery has Jacobean wood carving. The east window of the chancel is closed.

(The parapet of the nave and aisles, is of elegant pierced panelling; that of the chancel is somewhat inferior.)

(The tower arch is lofty and pointed, with continuous mouldings.

The roofs of the aisles are of flat pitch.

The windows of the north aisle are of 3 lights with transoms.

The tower porch, on the north, is a curious feature, and of 2 stages in height, has battlements and square turret at the inner west angle. It is divided by a floor and the upper part has a 2 light window like that of a belfry.)

June 1871

Bruton church was in course of restoration and the roofs taken off for renovation and all the interior gutted.

Brympton D'Evercy

50/53–54 St. Andrew 7 August, 1849

A small but curious church, situated close to the fine old manor house. It is on a kind of cruciform plan, the transepts being more properly chapels, but the regularity of the plan is disturbed by the dissimilar size of the transepts and the existence of a small aisle on the north of the chancel. There is no tower, but a stone bellcote set over the west end. There are good portions of Middle-Pointed work, both early and advanced, and some of Third-Pointed. The south transept is early Middle-Pointed, has on the east side a 3 light window without foliations, but a hood externally upon corbel heads.

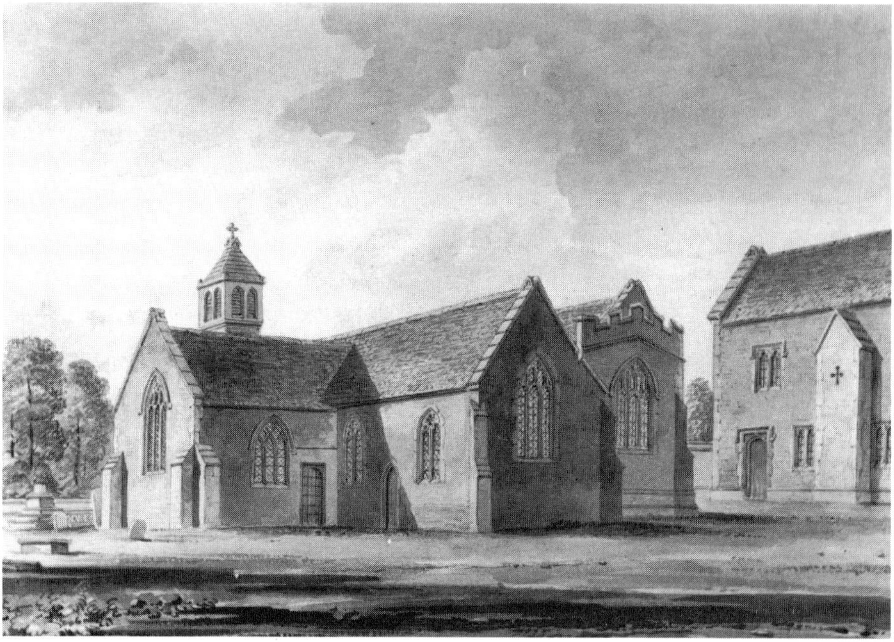

South east view of Brympton Church, 1837, by J. Buckler

On the north side is a peculiarly elegant one of 3 lights, having in the uppermost part, a circle sub-divided into 3 smaller ones, which are trefoiled and filled with good coeval, stained glass. This window has shafts to the rear arch. The arch opening from this chapel to the nave, is a small, odd-looking one. The nave has a shallow porch on the south, the inner door of which has a trefoiled head. The windows of the nave are Third-Pointed, some square-headed.

The north chapel or transept, is advanced Middle-Pointed and forms one uniform plan with the chancel side, both under one roof and embattled, opening to the chancel aisle and to the nave by small pointed arches, which are rather contracted in form. In the pier against the nave is a closed hagioscope and an octagonal piscina under a cinquefoiled fenestella. There are some 3 light windows of late Middle-Pointed tracery in this chapel but in the chancel aisle, the windows are Third-Pointed.

On the west side is a Third-Pointed door. In this transept is a slab with the damaged matric of a brass with legend and another with a cross with the date 1525. There is a curious stone rood screen of transitional character from Middle to Third-Pointed. The chancel has, on the south, 2 Third-Pointed windows of 2 lights and a door. On the north, a Tudor arch with small shafts, opens to the chapel in which there is a fine canopied niche, alongside of its east window. The font has a large octagonal bowl, a stem of like shape having shafts at the angles. There is a wooden Jacobean pulpit on a stone stem.

The bellcote is not inelegant, of square form set over the gable, pierced on each side with 2 open arches and surmounted by a stone pyramidical roof.

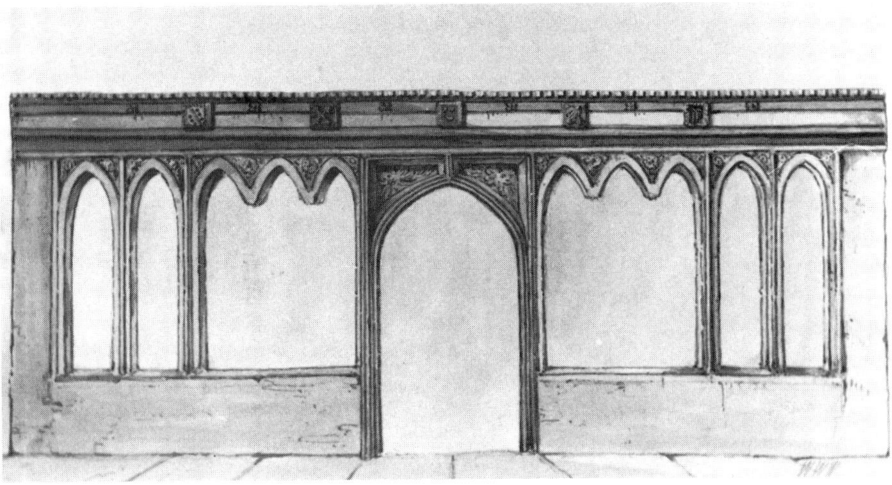

Brympton Church, 1847, by W.W. Wheatley

There are some open benches and . . . the churchyard is full of curious ancient tombs, cruelly exposed to the weather. One on the south side is panelled and there is the effigy of a lady on the same side. On the north side, are two effigies of a cross legged knight and lady. The north chapel of the chancel, has some gorgeous Elizabethan monuments. There is the shaft of a cross on the south side of the churchyard. The roofs, as usual, are flagged.

Buckland, West

50/67–68 St. Mary 24 January, 1854

A fair church, much of the same type as [Bradford-on-Tone] and quite local. The plan: church and nave, each with north and south aisles, a western tower and south porch. The aisles of the chancel are more in the nature of chapels, the chancel extending beyond them. The nave is rather short in proportion. The whole is Perpendicular. The aisles are embattled, the roof tiled. The walls partially stuccoed.

The tower is a very good one, of 3 stages divided by strings, with embattled parapet and 8 small crocketed pinnacles. There is a large polygonal turret in the centre of the south face of ye tower and rising above the parapet. The belfry windows are of 2 lights and have the ornamented stone lattice work of this county. There is a west door with bold, continuous mouldings; over it, a 3 light window. The buttresses are at the angles. The porch, plain.

The windows almost all of 3 lights and of the prevailing character. The eastern one has 4 lights and the rear arch upon shafts. The nave is only of 2 bays. The arches spring from octagonal piers with plain capitals and are of considerable width. There are also arches crossing and aisles. The chancel arch springs from brackets set high on the piers of the arcade, which is

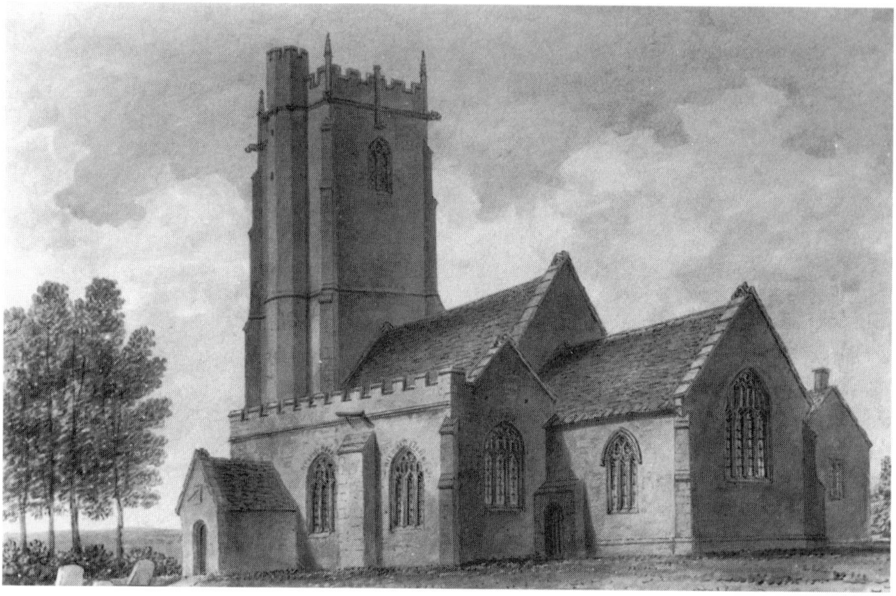

South east view of West Buckland Church, 1837, by J. Buckler

continued with very little intermission according to the Somersetshire fashion.

The chancel roof is coved and boarded with ribs and bosses. The north chapel is not carried so far eastward as the southern, and its arch is cut short against the wall. On the north side, appears a closed trefoil-headed lancet window, which seems to belong to an earlier period. There is a square-headed, labeled, 3 light window in the aisle. The arches from the chancel to the aisles, are of Tudor form and continuous. There is a quasi-chantry on the north side of the nave, with slabby, flat-topped windows. A vestry is added to the east of the north arch.

Burnett

52/18 St. Michael 3 February, 1872

A very small church, not easily found; has only nave and chancel and south porch. Over the west end, is a bellcote. The chancel arch is pointed and very rude. The chancel has some single lancets with trefoil heads. All other windows are late and square-headed or else modern. There is a pointed arch on the south of the chancel which may perhaps have opened into a chapel, now destroyed. Over the south door, within the porch, is a canopied niche.

In the church is a brass of the 16th century to one Cutts, Mayor of Bristol.

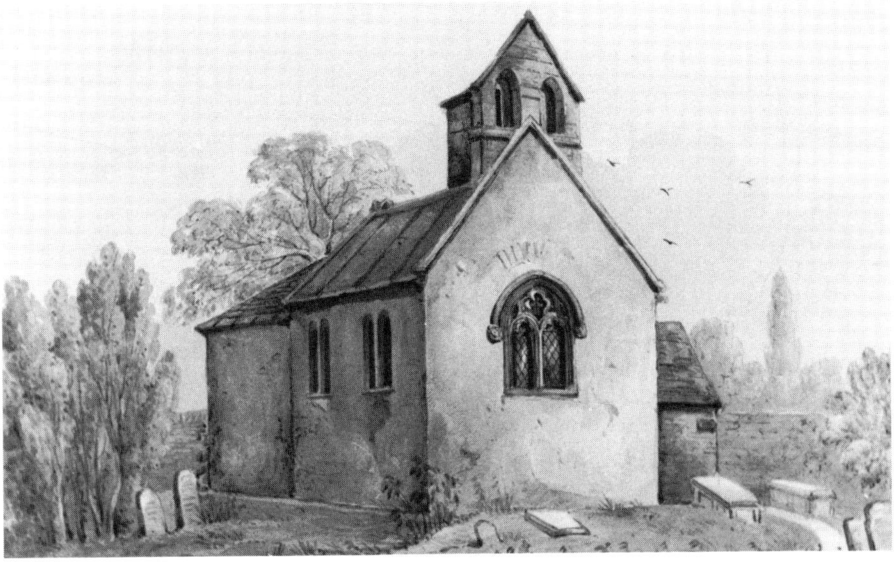

Burnett Church, 1843, by W.W. Wheatley

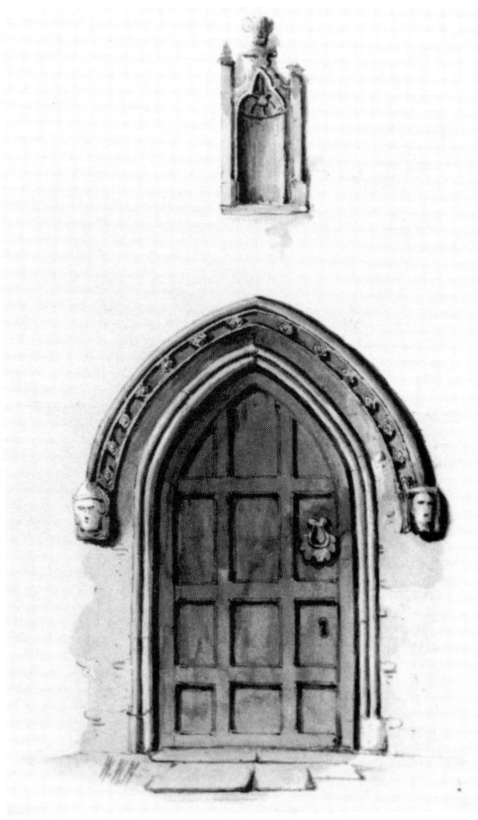

Burnett, 1843, by W.W. Wheatley

Burnham

50/63–64 St. Andrew 27 February, 1852

A long church, the nave at least exceeding the usual proportion in length, having a south transepted chapel and a modern, north aisle. There is a south porch and a west tower. *Almost wholly* Third-Pointed except perhaps the window of the transept which, though the tracery is Third-Pointed of 2 lights, has the Somersetshire feathering to the rear arch, which marks an earlier period. The other windows, on the south of the nave, are of 3 lights and the parapet moulded.

The roof of the nave is a steep, leaden one, coved and ribbed with bosses internally. The south porch has good, continuous mouldings to the inner door: the outer one is modernized. Over the inner door, is a canopied niche and near it an ogeed stoup. The transept opens to the nave by a pretty fair arch of Third-Pointed character on stilted shafts. In the transept, beneath the window, are 2 separate, sepulchral recesses, with bold feathering and finials.

The north aisle is modern and separated by an ugly arcade of depressed arches. The chancel seems to be later than the nave. The chancel arch is four-centred, springing from shafts. The east window is closed by an absurd, modern reredos. On the south of the chancel is a poor, square-headed late window. The tower is large, late Third-Pointed, rather plain and bald. It has a battlement, is of 3 stages with octagonal turret at the south-west and buttresses not at the angles.

The belfry windows, of 2 lights and mutilated. On the west face, a large window of 4 lights and a continuous moulded door, set within a square.

There is much blank wall in this tower.

The gables of chancel and nave have crosses.

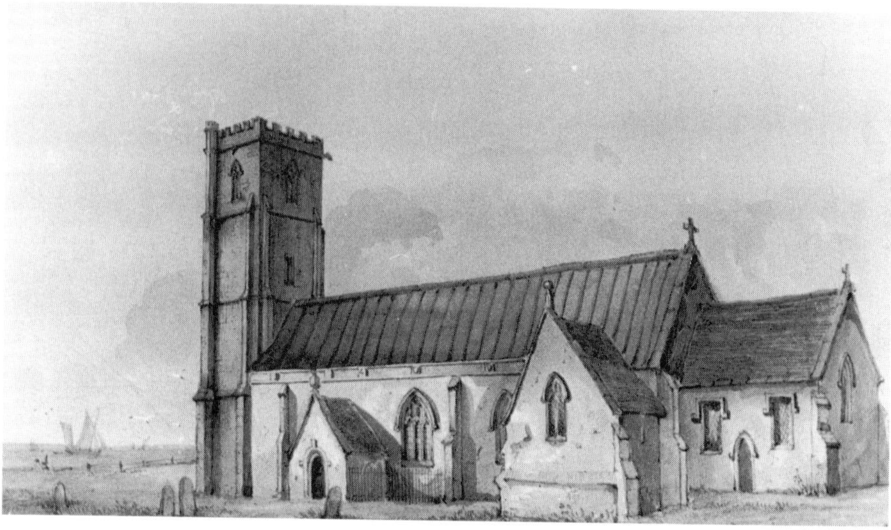

South east view of Burnham Church, 1843, by W.W. Wheatley

Burrington

51/47–48 Holy Trinity 25 January, 1861

Plan: nave with aisles, chancel with aisles, south porch and west tower. A small church, wholly Perpendicular. The roofs coved and ribbed in the usual way, but partly new and flatter in the chapels of the chancel, which are merely continuations of the aisles along the chancel. There is, on each side, an arcade of 4 arches in the nave and one in the chancel. The arches and piers of the usual Perpendicular. The northern piers have plain capitals, the southern sculptured ones to the shafts and there is no clerestory.

The chancel arch resembles the others and there is little, or no, break in the arcade. The east respond on the south, has the sculptured figure of a man recumbent and supporting an octagonal ledge or impost. The tower arch is on concave, octagonal shafts. The windows are generally of 3 lights and one is set over the north door. Between the windows are shafts, with angel capitals, which seem once to have carried the timbers of the roof.

The interior is very neat and decent. There are new uniform seats, but with doors, a new stone pulpit and font. The sacrarium is laid with new tiles and some windows have new stained glass, rather mediocre, but in one north window is some ancient glass of good character. The chancel has an ogee, cinquefoiled piscina on the south and the cill of the south-east window, is extended as a sedile.

The south porch has a fine, pierced parapet of the local type, and the buttresses on each side, have bold gargoyles and are crowned by crocketed pinnacles. (The south porch has a parvise and an octagonal stair turret in the

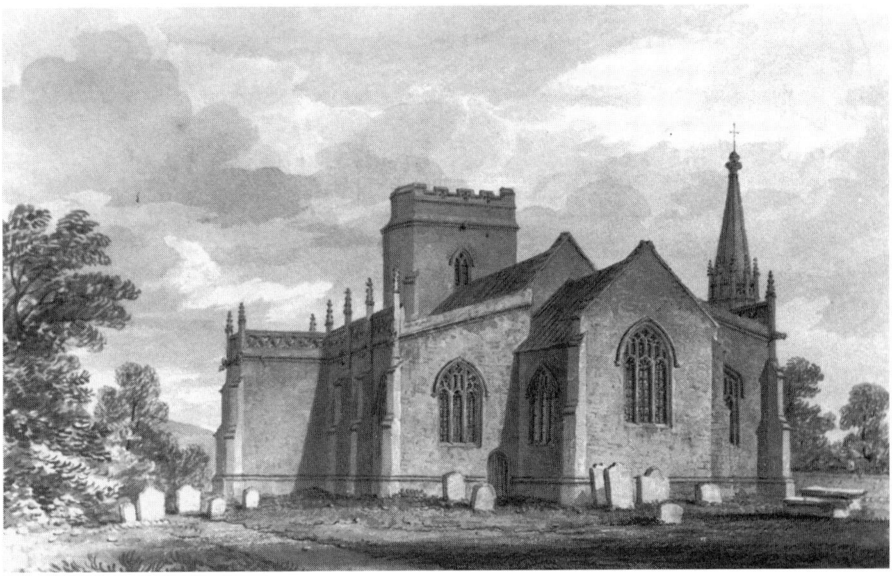

South east view of Burrington Church, 1828, by J. Buckler

angle; the parapet, pierced and pinnacled). There is a large, octagonal rood turret on the north, finely panelled, capped by a lofty pyramid and having a parapet and small pinnacles.

The north doorway has flowered mouldings and the door very good wood carving of Perpendicular character.

The tower is low and unfinished, of plain and poor appearance; has corner buttresses, a west window of 3 lights and a belfry window of 2 lights.

There is a barrel organ.

Butleigh

19/55–57 St. Leonard Before 1840

The church of Butleigh consists of a nave and chancel, with a tower standing between the nave and chancel. On the north side of the nave, is a small chapel, containing the pew and vault belonging to the House. The tower is large and of plain, Perpendicular work in its upper part, with good belfry windows and battlement. The lower part, may possibly be of earlier date, having some plain, trefoiled windows with sloped sides within.

The nave has a very fine and large Perpendicular window at the west end, of 6 lights and very delicate tracery. Its soffit within, is enriched with panelling and shafts. (Of this window, the arch is continued internally down to the ground and the soffit panelled.) A plain, pointed doorway (probably

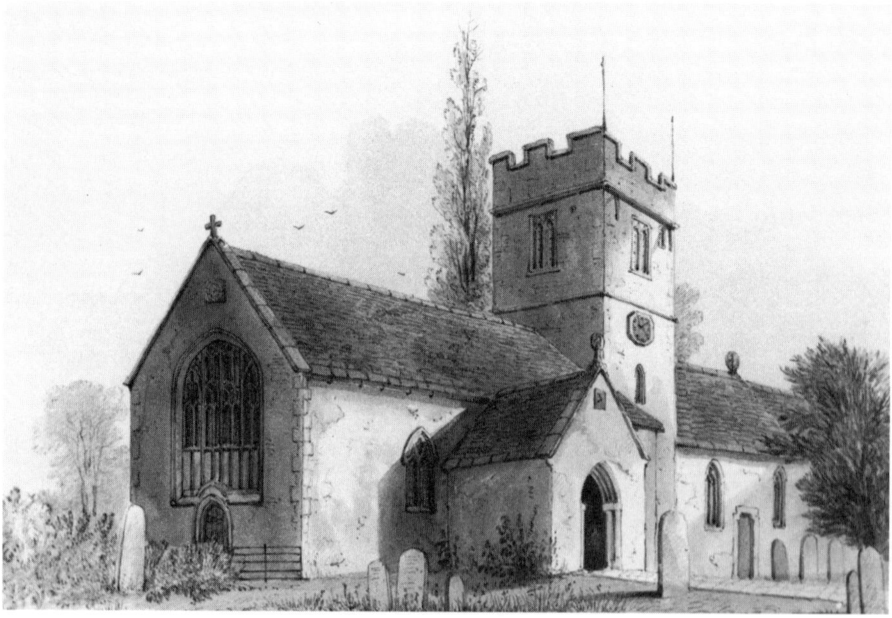

Butleigh, 1846, by W.W. Wheatley

Decorated), with good mouldings, rises just above the sill of the great west window. In the nave and chancel, on the north and south sides, are some very elegant, Decorated windows of 2 lights, the rear arch of which (opening to the interior of the church) is enriched with hanging feathering, which has a rich and beautiful effect (a Somersetshire feature).

On the south side of the nave, there is one square-headed window of 4 lights with a transom of the period of Elizabeth. The outward doorway of the south porch, has imposts with rude shafts on each side. The porch is simple and rustic and crowned with a small cross. The ceiling under the tower, is stone with strong ribs . . . The east window has a good Decorated one, with hanging feathering, but it is now stopped up. In the nave, there are several handsome, carved pew ends. The font is octagonal and handsome, having each of its sides charged with a quatrefoil. Some of the quatrefoils contain, within them, shields some roses, some holy lambs, some doves. The font is, as is often the case, absurdly painted to imitate marble.

The arches of the tower opening to the nave and chancel, are plain and painted. The tower has a clock and 5 bells. There are no monuments of a good period. The dimensions are as follows:-

Length of the nave 56¾ by 22 in breadth
Square of the tower 16¾
Length of the chancel 29¼
Whole length of the church 102¾

An ugly excrescence with a pue has been most improperly tacked on to the east end of this church.

1844

A new roof, open to the interior, has just been put on the nave and is of higher pitch than the former one.

1851

Great changes have been effected. August 7 the church was re-opened with solemn services after the restoration and enlargement. Transepts are added; making the church now cruciform in addition to the chapel added in 1830, on the north side of the nave, of which the floor is now lowered and communication opened into the transept.

The ugly eastern excrescence has vanished and a good eastern window, inserted with fine, stained glass.

1860

North aisle added to the nave.

The Elizabethan window on the south of the nave, has given place to a better. An organ set up in the north transept.

Cadbury, North

52/7–9 St. Michael 10 June 1871

A very fine specimen of the larger sort of Somersetshire church, and wholly of Perpendicular character.

The plan is a clerestoried nave, with north and south aisles, chancel, north and south porches and a western tower. The whole of excellent stone masonry and the parapets have good moulding. The windows of the aisles are of 3 lights, of uniform type and set closely. The interior of the nave is lofty and grand. It has uniform arcades, each of 5 bays with pointed arches on light piers, each of 4 shafts set in lozenge form with hollow mouldings in the intervals and stilted bases.

The clerestory windows are each of 3 lights, simply cinquefoiled. The roof of the nave is a good one, with panelling and bosses and flowered cornice. The aisles are lofty, but their roofs are plainer. Amidst the open seats are several ancient, carved bench ends, with poppy heads. The east end of each aisle, has panelling in the roof and in the south aisle, the south-east window has parts of its cill extended for a seat.

The tower arch to the nave is lofty, upon octagonal shafts, with flowered capitals and the tower has internal buttresses projecting into the nave. The chancel arch is a lofty, pointed one, resembling those of the arcades but has a kind of joint or bead, ranging on level with the capitals of the nave arcade. The chancel is rather plainer than the nave, but of good proportions, has on each side, fair windows of 3 lights. At the east end, a fine one of 5 lights, flanked by rich canopied niches having much colour on them. On the south of the chancel is a small priest's door. On the north is a large, low vestry having square-headed windows and set under the cill of the chancel windows.

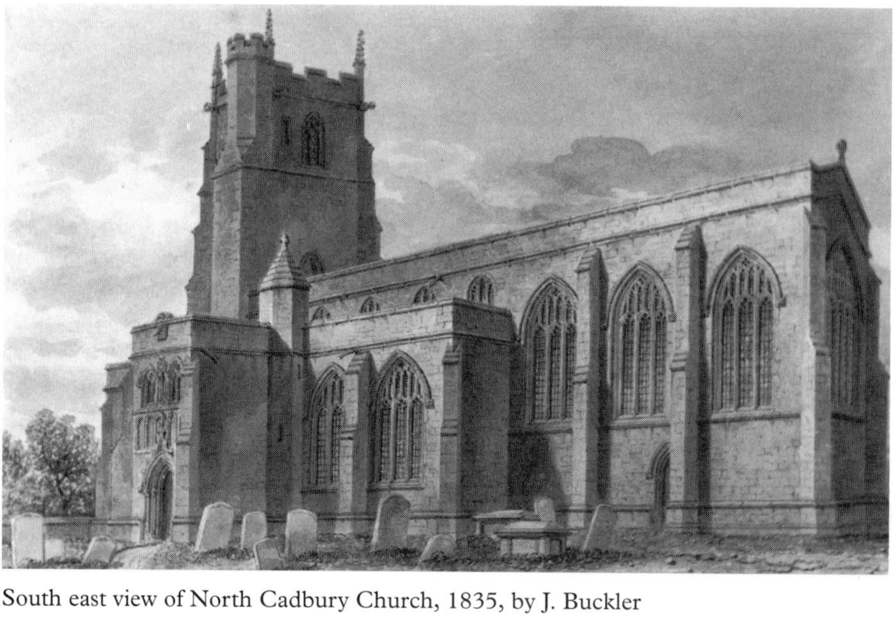

South east view of North Cadbury Church, 1835, by J. Buckler

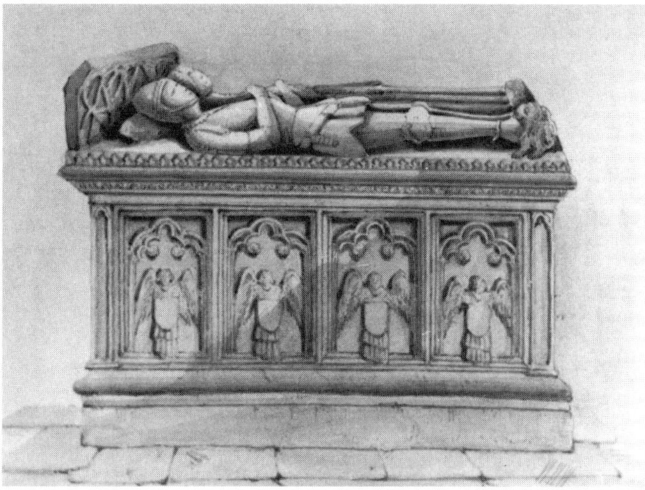

In North Cadbury Church, 1846, by W.W. Wheatley

The roof of the chancel is good, the beams embattled and on corbeled shafts with spandrels. There are, on the south of the sacrarium, 3 equal sedilia with ogee, crocketed canopies, having double feathering, crockets and finials and intermediate pinnacles. There is a new reredos with figures of marble and a cross in the centre. The floor of the chancel is laid with new tiles and the fittings are stall wise. The organ is at the east end of the north aisle. The font is coeval, the bowl octagonal with shields and flowers in panelling. The stem has 4 corner shafts and flowers.

The tower is lofty but not rich – of 3 stages – with corner buttresses and a square turret at the south-east ending in an octagon, rising above the parapet. There is a labeled west door, over it a 3 light, ordinary window; in next stage a slit light, the belfry windows of 2 lights. The north porch has a parvise and fine groining with elegant bosses. The outer doorway has an ogee canopy with finial and crockets and panelling over it. The parvise has 2 windows of 2 lights, between which is a canopied niche. The door within the porch, is plainer.

The south porch is almost exactly similar to the northern and both have their turrets of octagonal form.

Some fine, sepulchral monuments are now set within the tower, having formerly been in the chancel. There are 2 altar tombs, the earlier of which has good panelling and niches containing saints and angels, with scrolls and bearing 2 effigies, of a knight and lady, rather smaller than usual. The lady has the horned head-dress and necklace and the canopies above the heads, have groining. These are probably Sir William and Lady Bottreaux, the founders of the church. The other tomb is Elizabethan (1596) and represents Sir Francis Hastings and Magdalene his wife.

This church is in excellent condition, fitted with open benches and all in good repair and nothing overdone, though handsome.

The church was built c. 1427 by Lady Bottreaux and is remarkably uniform in its style with no trace of earlier work.

The aisles have no west windows.

Cadbury, South

52/10–11 St. Thomas à Becket 10 June, 1871

A Perpendicular church, much inferior to the last mentioned in size and general character. It has nave and chancel, each with south aisle, a north porch and western tower. The roofs are all coved with ribs and bosses after the fashion of the neighbourhood. The nave arcade has 3 pointed, chamfered arches on piers of 4, closely clustered shafts having rather a Decorated character. There is no clerestory. The tower arch a lofty, pointed one, upon shafts. The windows throughout, are Perpendicular, some square-headed of 2 lights.

There is a projecting stair turret on the north, corresponding with the roodloft's place and containing a small window with mutlifoil feathering. The nave is fitted with open benches, A.D. 1835. The chancel arch is panelled as often in the south-west country. On the north of it, is a niche which may have been a hagioscope, having cinquefoil feathering and elegant groining; also panelled spandrels. Across the chancel arch are indications of a low screen.

The chancel is rather short, but divided from the south aisle by 2 narrow, pointed arches of small dimensions, having panelled soffits and jambs with small shafts set in the lower part. There is a similar arch between the south aisle of the nave and that of the chancel. The east window of the chancel is of 3 lights, most others of 2. The font is a new one and not bad. The parapets of the body are plain. The porch is late Perpendicular with the outer arch of Tudor form with panelled spandrels. The door within it has also spandrels, ornamented with foliage.

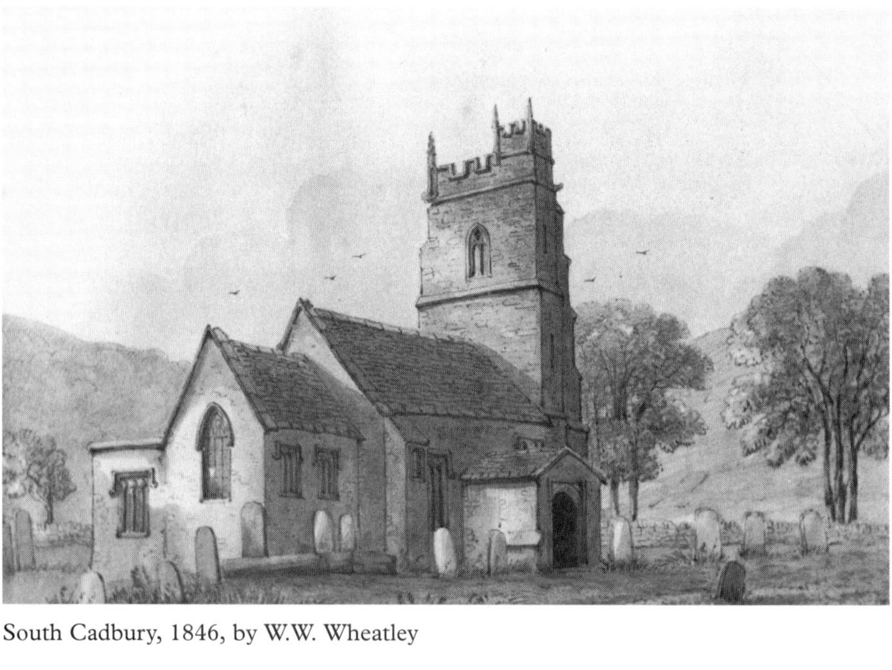

South Cadbury, 1846, by W.W. Wheatley

The tower is divided by 2 string courses, has embattled parapet, 4 small pinnacles, and gargoyles, corner buttresses and a large, square turret; the belfry windows of 2 lights. The west door, plain with arch mouldings and hood on grotesque corbel heads, one crowned. Over it, is a mutilated window.

(The east respond of the nave arcade is a stilted shaft. That at the west, is a shaft with circular capital and joint having somewhat of an Early English character.)

(There is a small Tudor shaped door in the south chancel aisle.)

(The public path to the church is to the north.)

Camerton

51/93 St. Peter June, 1871

This church has nave with a south chapel, chancel with north chapel, north porch and western tower, all apparently Perpendicular. The nave is embattled and has square-headed windows of 3 lights. Those of the chancel are also Perpendicular, mostly square-headed. The chancel arch is pointed and plain. The south transept is disproportionate in extent and modernized; has square-headed windows as has the north aisle of the chancel. The chancel and aisle are embattled and the latter divided from the chancel by 2 pointed arches with mouldings, continued down the pier, poor and apparently modern.

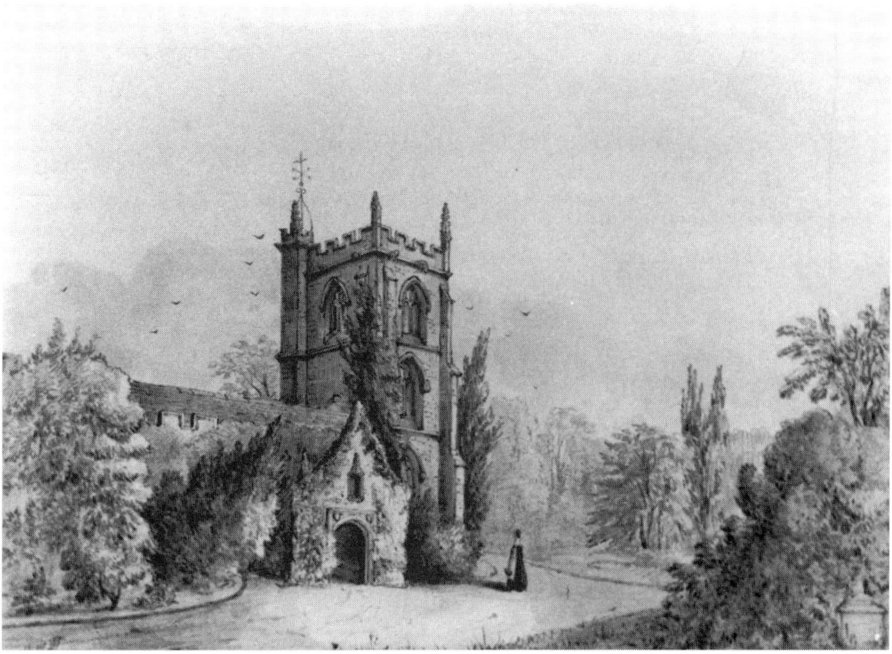

Camerton Church, 1844, by W.W. Wheatley

The tower arch is a good one with continuous mouldings. There is a west gallery and one in the south transept. The porch has an outer door with panelled spandrels. Within is a pointed doorway with continuous mouldings, over which is a canopied niche and the door has good wood carving. There are good gargoyles on the north of the nave. The tower is fair, Perpendicular of a local type, has battlement and octagonal turret at the south-east, is of 3 stages with string courses and has gargoyles at the angles; buttresses set square. On the west side, a 3 light window with hood having corbel heads, one a female. The west doorway has continued arch mouldings. The roofs have new slates.

Carhampton

51/10–11 St. John the Baptist 9 May 1855

The plan of this church: a nave and chancel, each with south aisle, west tower and south porch; church wholly Perpendicular.

There is no architectural division of chancel. The arcade has 6 arches of Perpendicular character, of which 2 are in the chancel and of Tudor shape; the piers light, of the usual lozenge form, with 4 shafts, having capitals, those in the chancel, octagonal. There is a fine rood screen across both nave and aisle, having arched compartments filled with tracery, fan groining and 6 cornices of elegant foliage and shafts supporting the ribs of the groining. The nave is wide. Both nave and aisle have coved roofs with ribs and bosses.

On the north, is a Decorated window of 2 lights and north of the chancel, a square-headed one of 2 lights of Decorated character. At the east of the aisle is

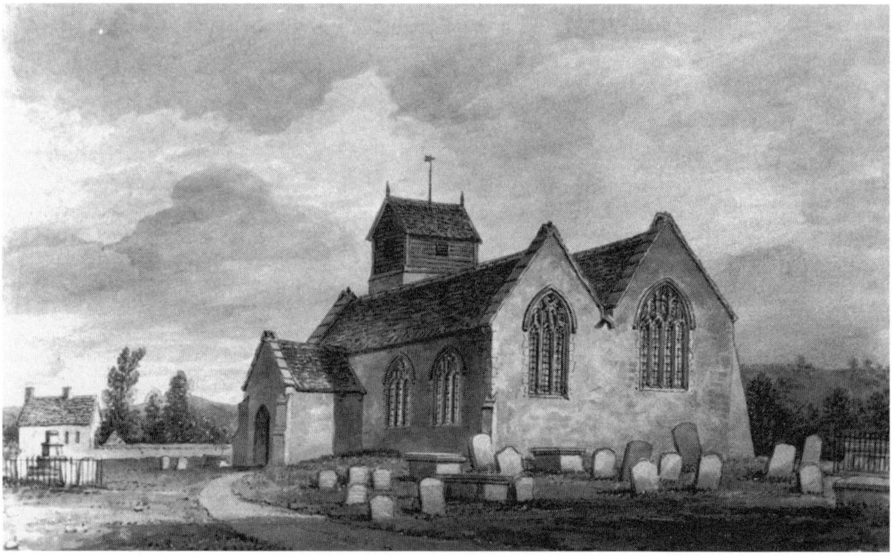

South east view of Carhampton Church, 1839, by J. Buckler

one of 3 lights with transom and Perpendicular as are the other windows. The last window of 4 lights, much mutilated. On the south of the altar is a small piscina; another at the east end of the south aisle of good Perpendicular character with open and pierced spandrels. The font has a round bowl upon cylindrical stem. The tower arch is pointed and coarse, the tower low and plain, with slits only for lights and corner buttresses to the lower part. The upper part is of wood and pointed.

Castle Cary

19/57–58 [All Saints] 27 October, 1825

Castle Cary [is] a small, neat town, situated in very pleasant country. Its church, although not spacious, has a very neat and elegant appearance and stands in a churchyard in which there are some fine, large yew trees.

It consists of a nave, side aisles, south porch and tower at the western extremity. The tower is low and embattled and surmounted by a stone spire, worked with ribs and panelling. At the angles are pinnacles and on the north side, an octangular turret. On the west side is a door of Tudor form with label.

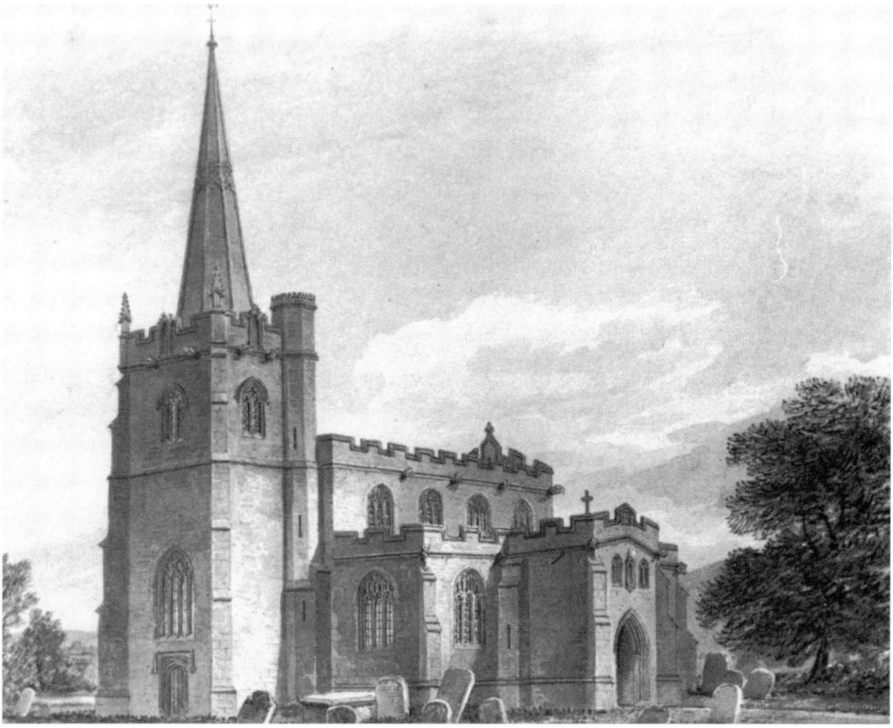

South west view of Castle Cary Church, 1833, by J. Buckler

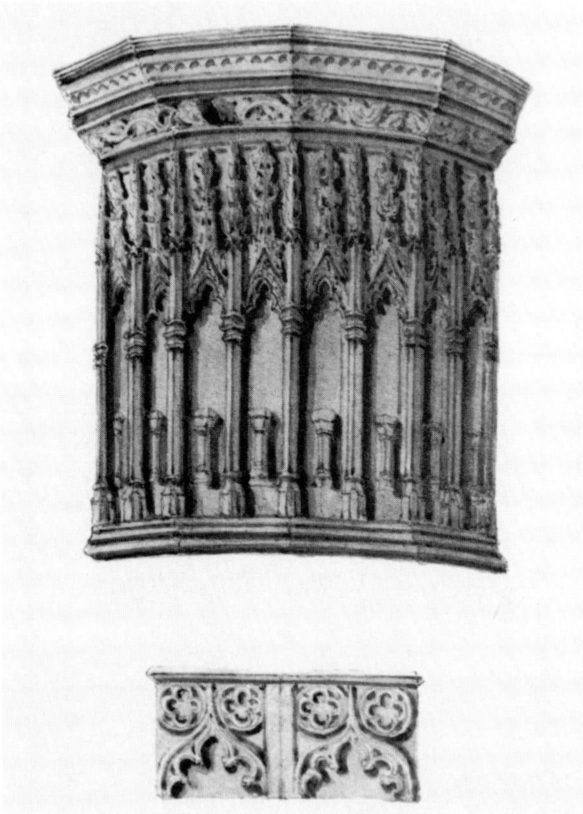

Pulpit and part of rood loft, Castle Cary Church, 1851, by W.W. Wheatley

The whole church has a battlement, excepting the chancel. The south porch is of good Perpendicular work, ornamented with a battlement and good canopied niches. Within it is a fine, stone groined ceiling.

There is no vestige about the church of any work earlier than Perpendicular. The interior has an air of neatness and respectability. The nave is divided from the side aisles by pointed arches with lozenge, Perpendicular piers. The clerestory has good, Perpendicular windows of which character are all the windows in the church. The pulpit is of very fine, carved woodwork, of rich Perpendicular character, having pierced panelling and niches with crocketed canopies.

There is a small gate between the nave and the chancel of the same character. The chancel is divided from the nave by a pointed arch. The font is octagonal, on an octagonal pedestal and is panelled with square flowers. At the west end of the nave is a gallery containing a neat organ. The exterior of the nave and aisles is enriched with large heads of animals for water spouts.

1870

Castle Cary church has been, in great measure, rebuilt and has a new tower and lofty spire.

Catcott

51/86–87 [St. Peter] 17 November, 1868

A poor church, comprising low nave and chancel, with south porch and west tower. The roofs, as usual, coved with bosses and ribs. There is no chancel arch. On the north of the chancel is a single lancet. The east window, Perpendicular of 2 lights. On the south of the chancel, are 2 square-headed windows of 2 lights, Perpendicular, and one on the south of the nave. The porch is plain and has an open wood roof. The font has an octagonal bowl, plain. On the north is a modern excrescence. The tower, low, divided by one string course, has embattled parapet and small corner buttresses, a pointed, tiled roof, on which is a vane. The west door is plain. Over it, a mutilated window. Those of the belfry, simple and trefoliated. On the north, is a small projection. The external walls are mostly whitewashed.

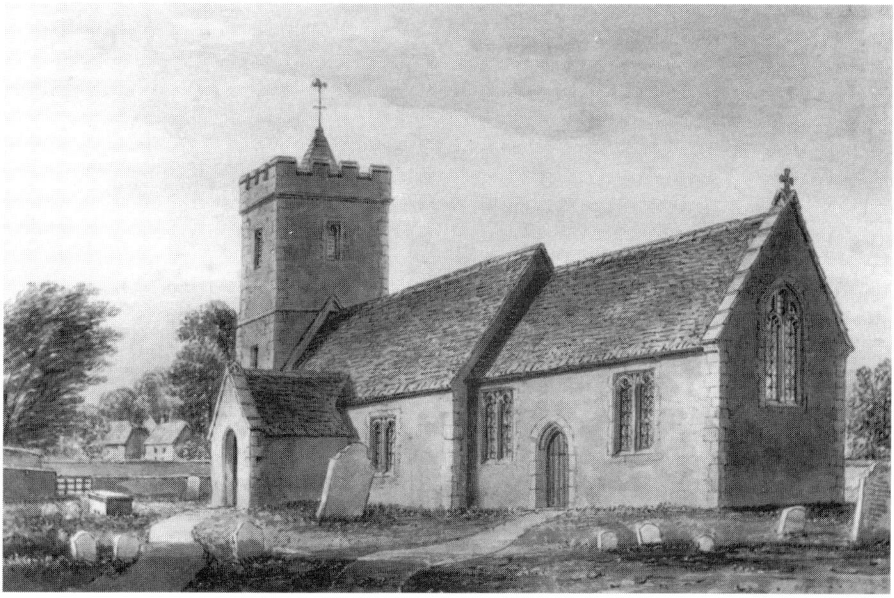

South east view of Catcott Church, 1839, by J. Buckler

Chard

19/37–38 St. Mary 18 October, 1825

. . . The immediate environs of Chard are bare and dreary. The town has many old houses and has a dull and dreary appearance.

The church is a good and handsome structure, consisting of a nave, chancel, side aisles, a transept situate much eastward of its usual place being very near

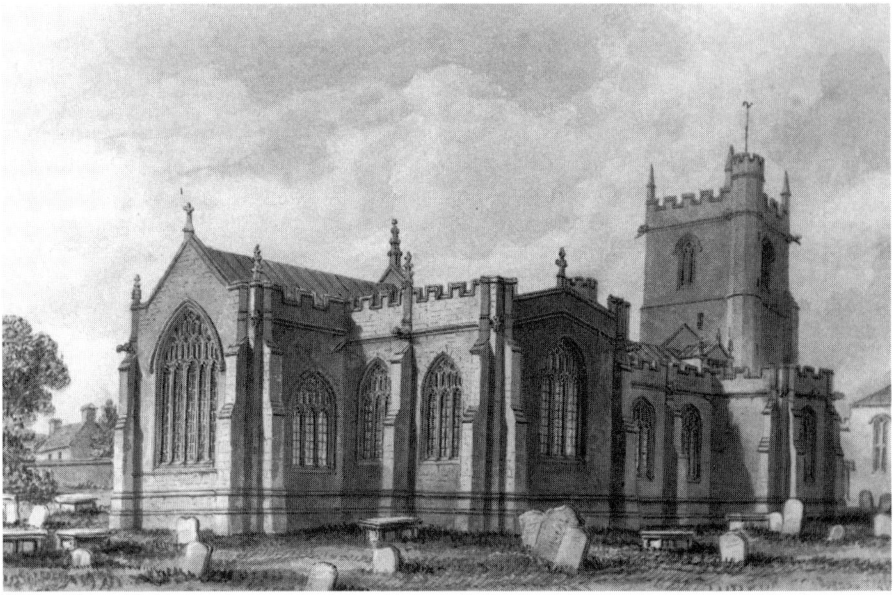

North east view of Chard Church, 1831, by J. Buckler

the east end of the chancel, a north and south porch and a tower at the west end. The tower is of plain, Perpendicular work, but tolerably handsome. It has a battlement and an octagonal staircase turret on the north side. The whole church appears to be of Perpendicular work of very good character.

The whole church has an embattled parapet and large, projecting heads for spouts. The end of the north transept is flanked by an octagonal turret and the south transept end has pinnacles. The porches are of good and elegant composition. The northern is the richest, which has large water spouts and a niche with fine, crocketed canopy over the doorway. There is a small, Tudor arch doorway on the south side of the south transept with spandrels enriched with foliage.

The arches which divide the nave from the aisles, are pointed and spring from the common, Perpendicular piers of lozenge form, with shafts at the corners. There is no clerestory. The arches from the chancel to the transepts have soffits enriched with panelling. The transepts seem to be private chapels and contain some good screen work. Between the nave and chancel is a carved, Perpendicular wooden screen which probably supported the roodloft.

The windows of the church are mostly large and handsome. The east window is of 5 lights and has some good, painted glass. The roof is covered with panels. The font is an octagon, ornamented with quatrefoils, filled with foliage. The church is well and conveniently fitted up for receiving a large congregation. At the west end, is a handsome organ in a Gothic case.

Charlcombe

50/44–45 St. Mary 2 October, 1848

A very small church, though so near to Bath. It has only a nave and chancel, south porch and a small, square tower, engaged in the west end and set upon arches opening to the interior. It appears to be chiefly Third-Pointed. The tower is embattled and is small, square-headed openings on each side. It is of better stone and masonry than the rest of the church. The west window is of 2 lights, the hood having foliated corbels. The east window a very fair one of 3 lights. Almost all the other windows are square-headed, that on the south-east of the chancel has the cill extended for sedile.

In another window south of the chancel, is some stained glass. Some of the windows have trefoiled lights, some cinquefoiled. At the south east corner of the nave, is a projection with stairs lighted by a single cinquefoil window, which may have led to the pulpit or roodloft. The chancel arch is a very clumsy, pointed one. In its northern pier, is an opening, probably a hagioscope. The font has a circular bowl of early character with some flowered ornament upon a cylindrical stem. The interior is much encumbered with pues.

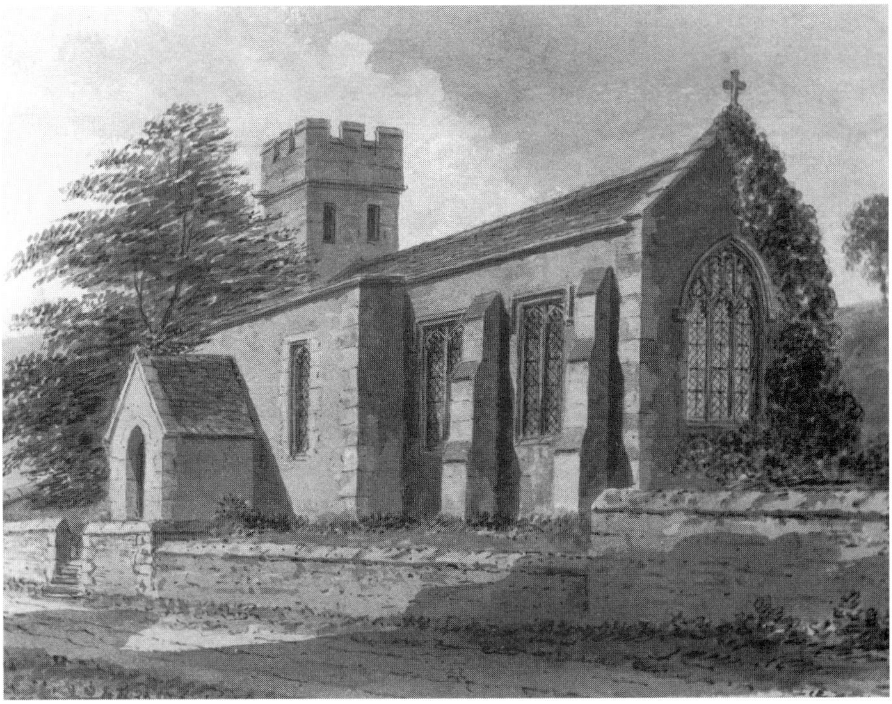

South east view of Charlcombe Church, 1847, by J. Buckler

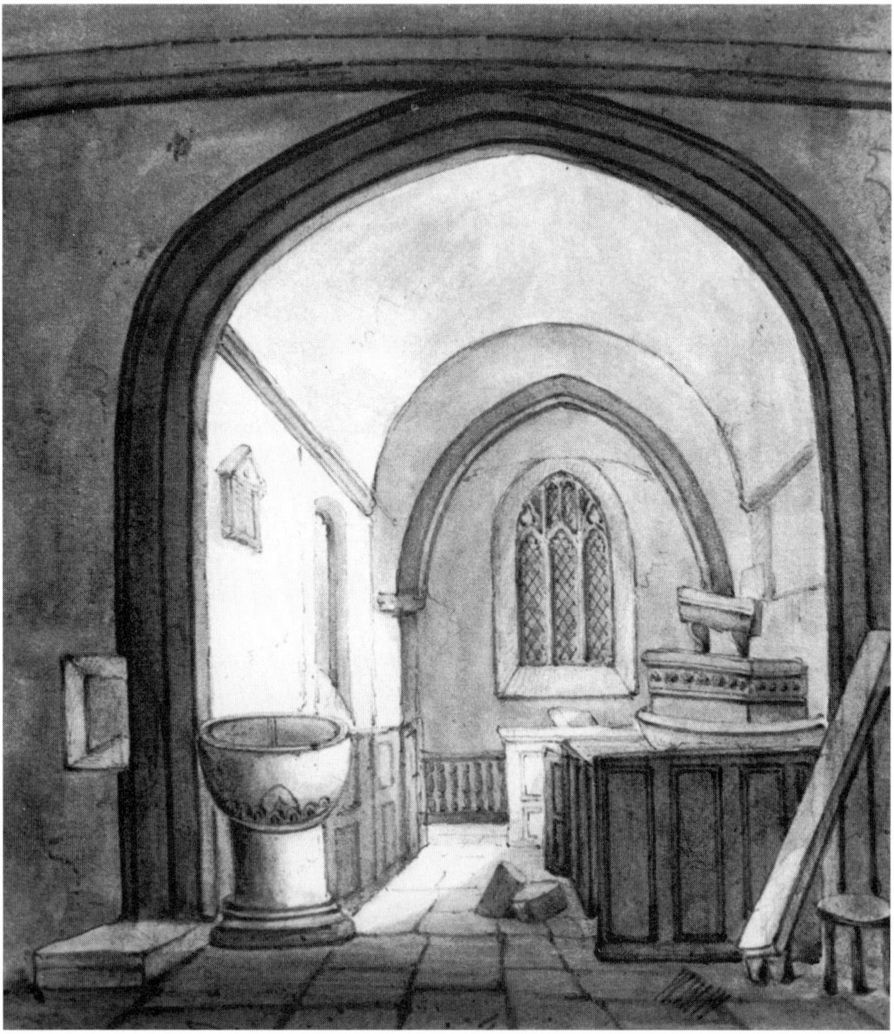

Church interior, Charlcombe, 1857, by W.W. Wheatley

Charlinch

51/74–75 St. Mary 19 January, 1864

This church has a nave and a chancel; without aisles but a south transept, a western tower and south porch. The whole has been lately repaired and partially reconstructed. Within the porch is an early doorway with segmented arch upon shafts, which have square abaci and seem semi-Norman. The aisle is stilted and altogether of rather odd character. The chancel arch is pointed on imposts. The chancel has a Decorated window of 3 lights, apparently new.

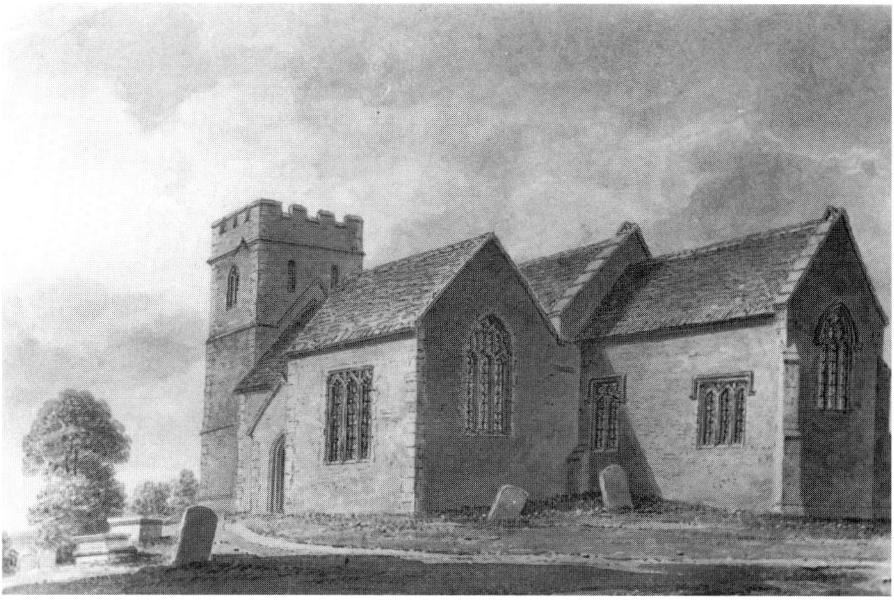

South east view of Charlinch Church, 1840, by J. Buckler

On the south is a Decorated window of 2 lights and one square-headed, Elizabethan, of 3 lights. The other windows throughout the church are late Perpendicular, or debased.

There is a pointed arch on shafts opening to the transept which contains the organ. On the north of the chancel is a vestry, apparently modern. The tower arch is pointed and panelled. The tower, Perpendicular and restored, has battlement and 4 crocketed pinnacles; corner buttresses, belfry windows of 2 lights and an octagonal stair turret at the south-east. The west window of 3 lights. The transept is scarcely of true, transeptal character.

The walls are denuded of stucco and come out a fine red stone.

(The roof is coved and panelled in ribs.)

Charlton Adam

49/18–19 [St. Peter and St. Paul] Before 1840

This church is an uninteresting structure, consisting of a west tower, a nave with a south chapel and a chancel, all of Rectilinear work. The tower is embattled and has a west window of 3 lights. The windows are some with square heads and some pointed. In the [inkblot] porch is a niche in a square compartment. The arches to the tower and chancel, are plain without shafts.

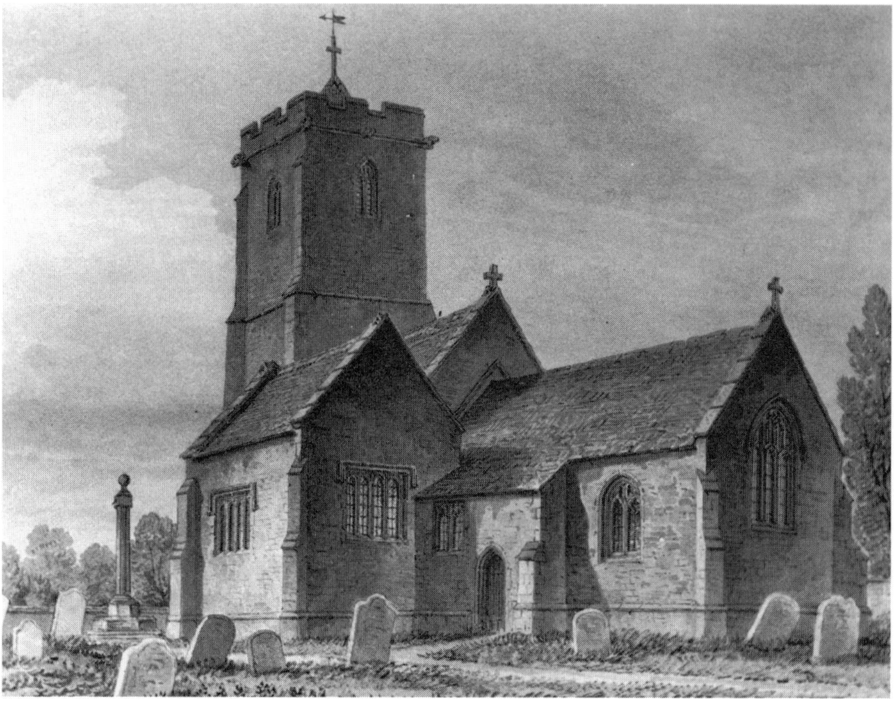

South east view of Charlton Adam Church, 1834, by J. Buckler

Charlton Horethorne

52/23–25 St. Peter and St. Paul 2 July, 1873

An interesting church consisting of nave with north and south aisles, chancel, west tower and south porch. There has been lately, much restoration and renovation, the south aisle being almost wholly new. The nave arcades are each of 3 bays. The main features of the church, Decorated with some later portions. The arches in the nave are pointed – chamfered – the pillars, octagonal with moulded capitals, those on the north having the ballflower ornament, those on the south are new and have flowered capitals.

The responds have corbels of octagonal form with ballflower mouldings upon head corbels representing a king and queen. The windows of the north aisle are Edwardian at the east and west, of 3 lights, the other of 2 lights, some containing coloured glass. In the north aisle is seen the rood door high up and under it a cinquefoiled niche, probably a piscina. On the north are 2 large canopied niches of Perpendicular character set in the angle, the canopies ogee with crocketed pinnacles, one set on a bracket with a rich band of foliage, set upon a head, the other wider and with flatter, arched canopy, bearing traces of colour.

Near them, in the wall, are 2 sepulchral recesses having ogee arches, deeply cusped and with rich finials. The west window of the south aisle is

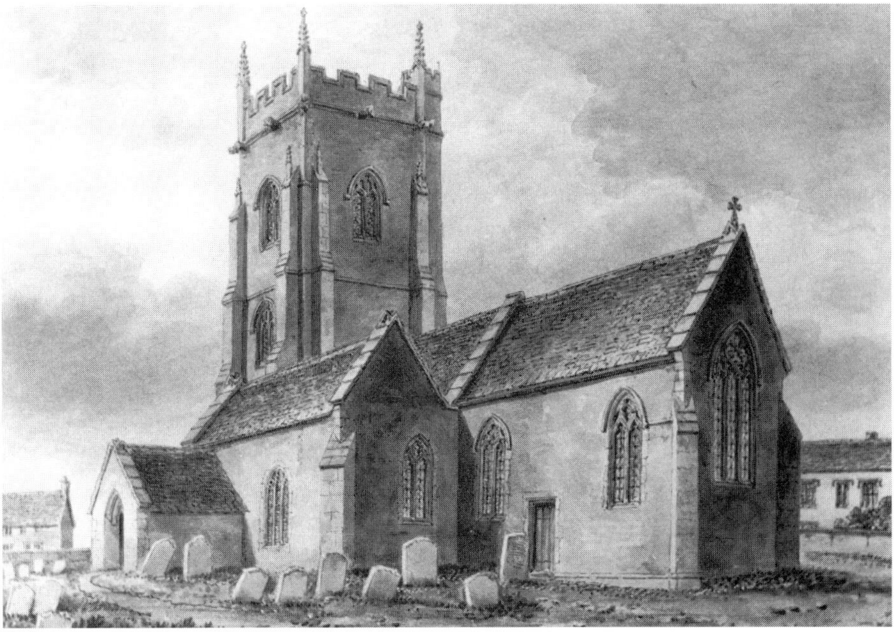

South east view of Charlton Horethorne Church, 1839, by J. Buckler

Perpendicular, of 3 lights; the other windows of this aisle are apparently new but present 2 lights of plate tracery with trefoiled heads and a quatrefoil above, the whole having, internally, a cusped arch like other Somersetshire specimens. In this arch is a sepulchral arch under the cill of a window with double feathering and finial; beneath it a slab of flory cross.

The roof of the nave is coved with ribs and bosses, partially coloured blue. The tower arch to the nave, is lofty but plain and flanked by internal buttresses seen within. The chancel arch is pointed, on short corbeled shafts of octagonal form set on heads.

The chancel is Decorated; the east window of 3 lights, those on the north and south of 2 lights (except a single light trefoiled at the south-west), not exactly similar. On the south of the sacrarium is an ogee, trefoiled piscina with shelf. The chancel is stalled; there is a reredos and candlesticks on the altar.

The font is early and has a circular bowl. The tower is wholly Perpendicular; has strong buttresses set square with flagged slopes. It is of 3 stages, has embattled parapet and 4 crocketed pinnacles. The west doorway is labeled with foliage spandrels and Tudor arch. Over it a 3 light window and in the next stage, a canopied niche. The belfry windows of 2 lights, with stone lattice work. At the north-west is a large, square stair turret rising above the parapet.

The west end of each aisle is gabled and there is a bell niche in the centre of that on the north.

The porch is new. The roof is covered with stone tiles.

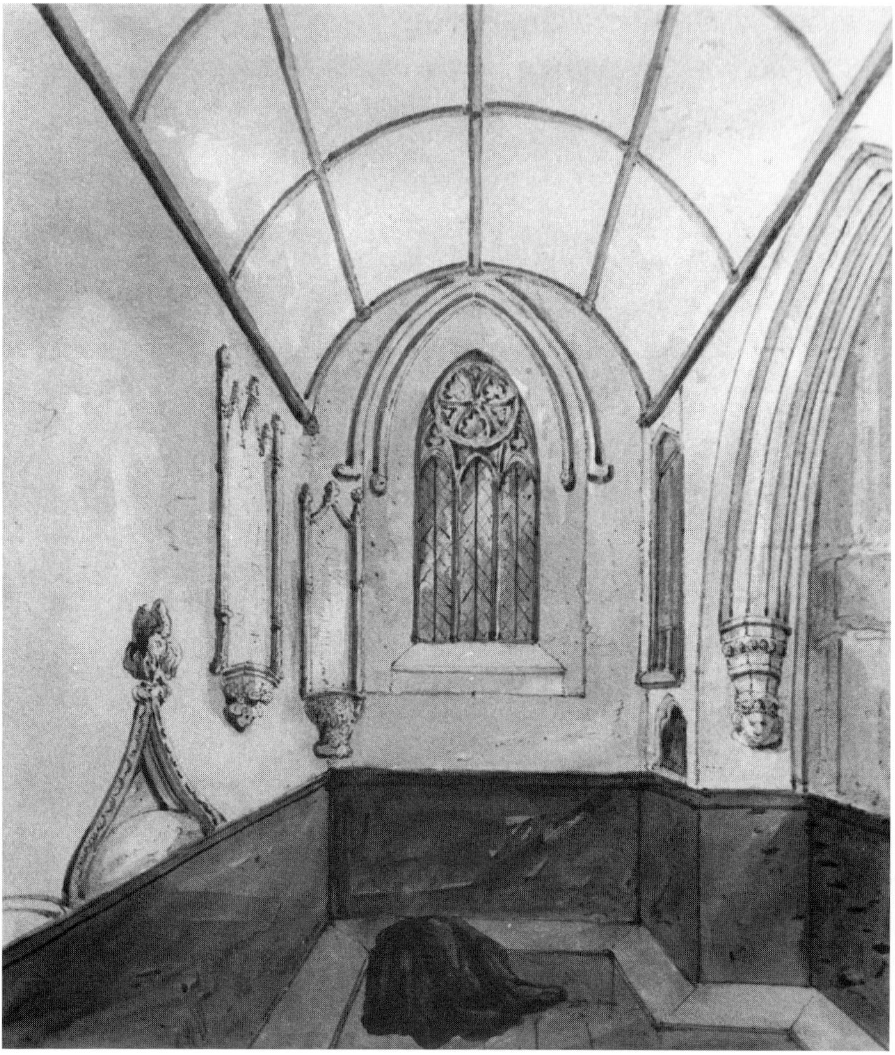

Charlton Horethorne, chantry north side, 1843, by W.W. Wheatley

Charlton Mackrell

49/19–21 [St. Mary] Before 1840

This is a neat cruciform church, with an embattled tower rising from the centre. There are no side aisles, but the chancel has a chapel on the south side. The nave and transepts have a good deal of Curvilinear work; the chancel and the upper part of the tower, are Rectilinear. The latter has crocketed pinnacles at the angles and an octagonal turret to the south-west.

There is a niche over the south porch and the gables of every portion of the

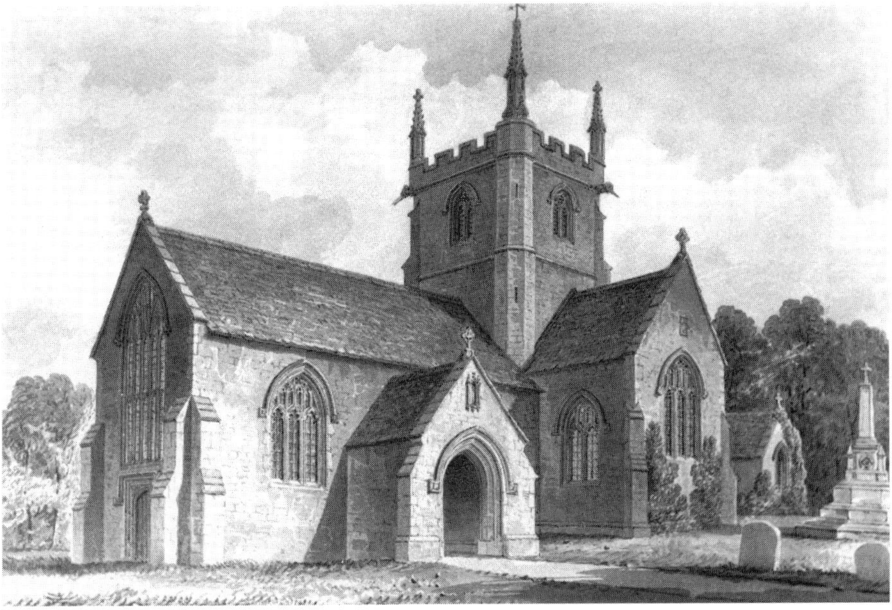

South west view of Charlton Mackrell Church, 1834, by J. Buckler

church, are finished with very rich and beautiful stone crosses. The west window is a fine Rectilinear one of 5 lights with a transom. The other windows of the nave, are chiefly Rectilinear of 3 lights. The interior is very neatly fitted up and its ornamental parts preserved with great care. The whole of the seats in the nave, are open and the ends enriched with fine, sculpture and panelling.

The transepts have each at the end, a Curvilinear window; that on the north is a magnificent one of 5 lights, the interior arch mouldings very fine, enriched with a band of ball flower and supported on shafts. The window of the south transept is small of 2 lights, but beneath it is a rich ogee arch, crowned with a finial, within which was probably once a tomb; near it is another ogee arch in the wall of similar character. Some other windows in the south transept are Rectilinear.

In the north transept is a fine altar tomb, panelled with quatrefoils and shields; upon it are two figures beneath triangular crocketed canopies, which are apparently of Curvilinear character. The arches beneath the tower are pointed and spring from piers of clustered shafts, which seem to be of Curvilinear period.

The chancel has good windows of Rectilinear character and the roof coved and divided by ribs into panelled compartments. The interior of the chancel is fitted up with Gothic wainscotting and good, modern seats. The south chapel is also of good Rectilinear work. The font is of Norman character, being a circular basin upon a banded shaft.

The good condition of this church both within and without reflect great credit on the present rector, who has restored and refitted it at his own charge and added a barrel organ and a very handsome, stone pulpit (1836).

The churchyard is beautifully shaded with trees and contains a very elegant cross.

Charlton Musgrove

50/45 St. Stephen 1 August, 1849

A small church of no great interest, having a nave, chancel without aisles, a western tower and south porch, mostly of rough stone. It is chiefly Third-Pointed but with earlier indications in the chancel, which is lower than the nave. The tower is of 3 stages, embattled, with corner buttresses and a large, square turret at the north-east, which is surmounted by 4 little pinnacles and there are crocketed pinnacles and gargoyles at the angles of the tower. The battlement is of a finer stone.

The west window is of 2 lights and there is a plain door; the belfry windows of 2 lights. The nave has late square-headed windows, some quite Elizabethan. The porch has a coved roof, the inner door a flattened trefoil. The chancel has, on the south, a triplet which may be First-Pointed; the other windows small, Third-Pointed of 2 lights. The east window is debased. On the south of the chancel is a priest's door. The chancel arch is panelled and continuous. On the north-east of the nave is a projection, probably for the rood stairs. The font a poor, plain octagon. The north door is labeled and closed.

(On the south of the chancel arch is a cinquefoiled piscina.)

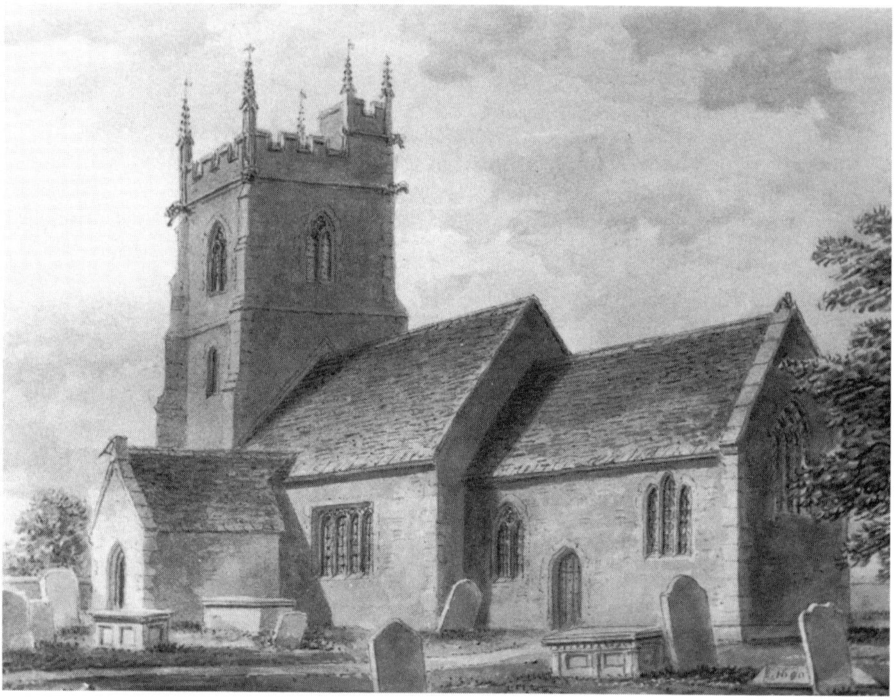

South east view of Charlton Musgrove Church, 1842, by J. Buckler

Cheddar

50/9–12 St. Andrew October, 1830

A fine Perpendicular church, consisting of a lofty west tower, nave and chancel with side aisles, south chapel, north and south porches. The whole of excellent stone. The tower is divided into 4 stages and has a rich, open parapet of pierced panelling. At the north angle is an octagonal turret, covered by a large pyramid with finial. At the other angles are crocketed pinnacles. The buttresses also are enriched with pinnacles. The west window is of 4 lights and set between 2 canopied niches, containing statues. The belfry story has 3 windows divided by pinnacles. In the other stages are single windows of 2 lights.

The north side of the church, aisles and clerestory has a rich parapet of pierced panelling with pinnacles, surmounting the buttresses between the windows. The north porch has a similar parapet and panels, a niche over the door which has panelled spandrels, and the ceiling is panelled. The south aisle has not any parapet. The south porch and chapel adjoin and are of equal height; there is a niche over the south door. The windows are closely set, mostly of 4 lights, some of 3 lights. The clerestory windows are of 2 lights.

There is an octagonal stair turret in the north aisle. The interior is spacious and majestic. The nave very wide, divided from each aisle by 6 pointed arches, springing from octagonal columns, the whole of the nave fitted up with ancient open seats and elegant carved ends. The ceiling of wood with plain panelling,

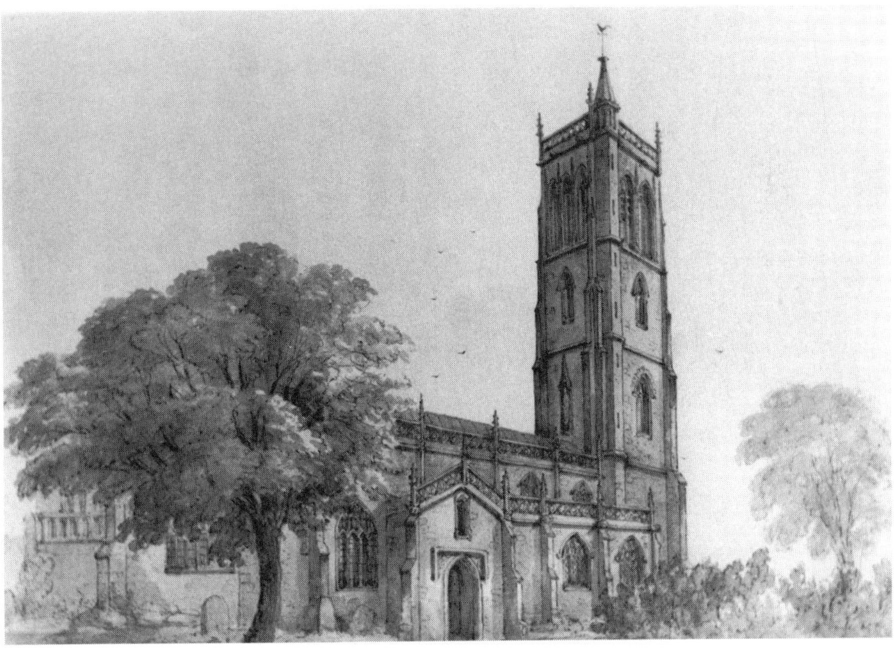

Cheddar, 1844, by W.W. Wheatley

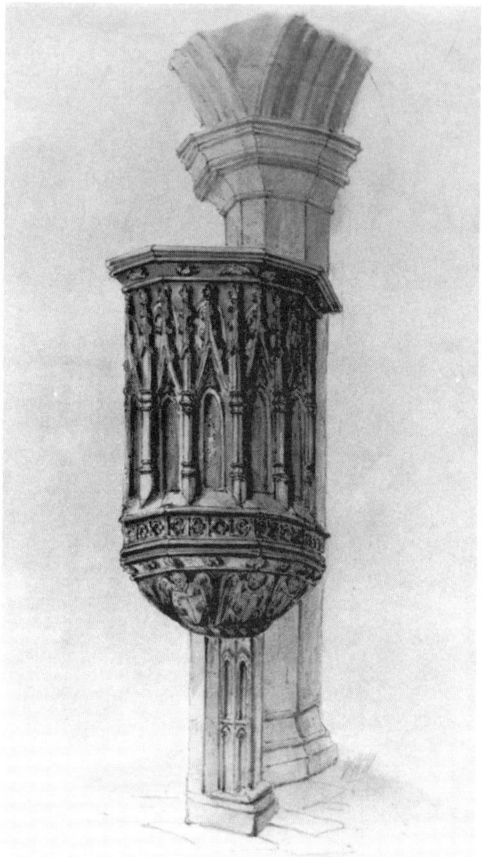

Pulpit in Cheddar Church, 1848, by W.W. Wheatley

the beams on half length figures of angels bearing shields and the bosses gilt in the eastern part of the nave. The pulpit is of stone, painted and gilt with fine, canopied niches and a band of animals and flowers. In the lower part, are angels bearing shields and the shaft panelled.

The tower arch is open and lofty. The ceiling under the tower has stone groining. The south chapel is very rich and late Perpendicular; it opens to the nave by a Tudor arch with panelled soffits and small, slender shafts and rich canopied niches on the piers. There is a large, fine window in this chapel set in a square compartment in 2 divisions, each of 3 lights and quatrefoils in the spandrels. On the east side is one of 3 lights of similar character. In the large one are pieces of fine stained glass. In its moulding also is a canopied niche, having the Tudor flower and containing a large statue.

The chancel is of lower elevation than the nave and extends a little beyond the aisles; its ceiling is coved with ribbed compartments and bosses. There is a plain arch to the nave and a single moulded one on each side, opening to the side aisles. There are beautiful wood screens between the aisles of the nave and those of the chancel. There are very large windows of 6 lights in the chapels of

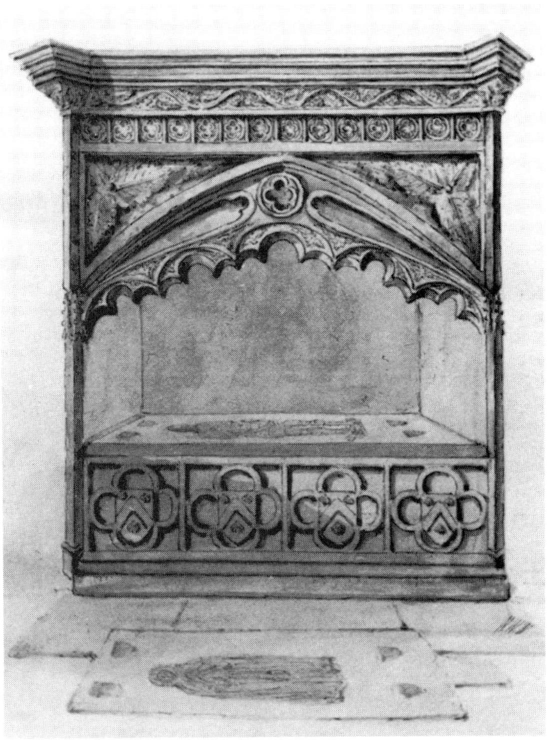

Cheddar Church, north side of the chancel, 1844, by W.W. Wheatley

the chancel with some stained glass. The window at the east end of the south aisle has, internally, some fine, double feathering over it.

In the north aisle, at the east end, is one of 4 and one of 2 lights. On the north side of the chancel, beyond the aisle, is a square-headed window with a hard moulding, forming a contracted arch and filled with square flowers beneath which is the very fine, Perpendicular tomb of Sir Thomas Cheddar, the founder of the church; the figure in brass in armour and near it on a slab, a female figure, also of brass, of his lady Isabella. The canopy of this tomb has a depressed arch with double feathering and very bold foliage in the spandrel above which are horizontal cornices of panelling and vine leaves. The sides of the tomb are panelled with shields and the arms of Cheddar, chevron *entre* 3 shells.

On the south side of the altar is a niche of trefoil form, with very fine mouldings and a double piscina, each drain on a circular shaft. The vestry on the north side of the chancel, has a panelled carpet and is entered by a small door with flowered mouldings. There is a sculptured stone, found in a vault with 4 panelled compartments, containing the arms of Cheddar and others and also the representation of the 5 wounds of Our Lord surmounted by a band of Tudor flower. The reading desk is formed of parts of the roodloft and exhibits rich wood carving. The font is modern, an octagonal bowl moulded with trefoil arches on a cylindrical shaft in imitation of the former one. The churchyard is planted with yews and laurels.

Cheddon Fitzpaine

51/37–38 St. Mary 30 January, 1861

This church has a nave and chancel with north and south aisles to the former, west tower and south porch. The north aisle is either a new addition or a reconstruction of the former, not finished when the church was visited and the chancel in course of restoration. Only the south aisle and part of the nave were used for service. The arcades of 3 Tudor shaped arches with the usual clustered, Perpendicular piers having 4 shafts. The capitals of the south arcade, which are original, have sculpture of angel figures; the others are not yet completed.

The whole of the body and chancel are Perpendicular, the windows of both 2 and 3 lights or ordinary, local type. The chancel has an east window of 3 lights, the roof in course of renovation. The font a plain octagon on stem of like form. The tower is plain and odd, possibly of earlier date than the rest, slender and without buttresses with simple lancet openings and belfry. The belfry windows of 2 trefoil-headed lights and no west door.

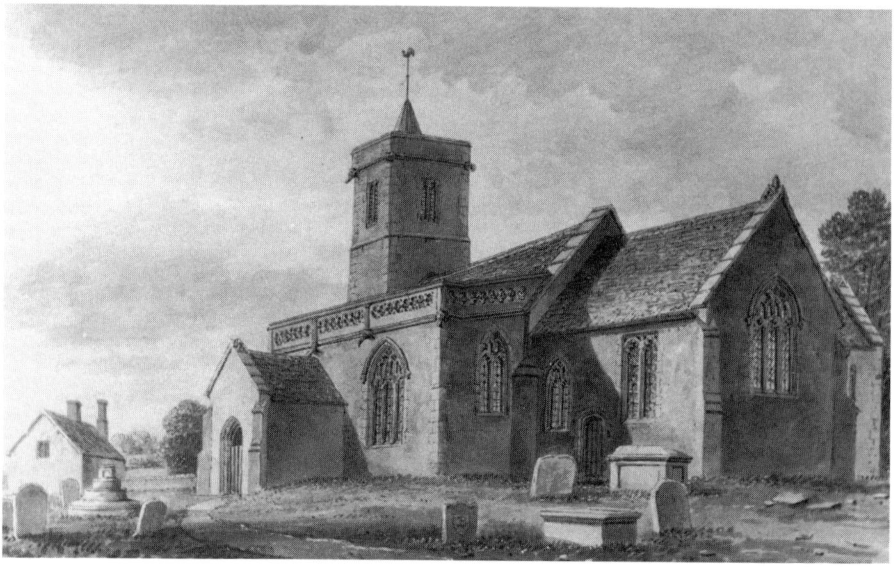

South east view of Cheddon Fitzpaine Church, 1839, by J. Buckler

Chedzoy

50/14–15 St. Mary 2 September, 1843

An interesting church, having a west tower, nave with side aisles and south porch, north and south transepts and chancel. There are good specimens of all the 3 later styles. The tower is of good stone and of Perpendicular character

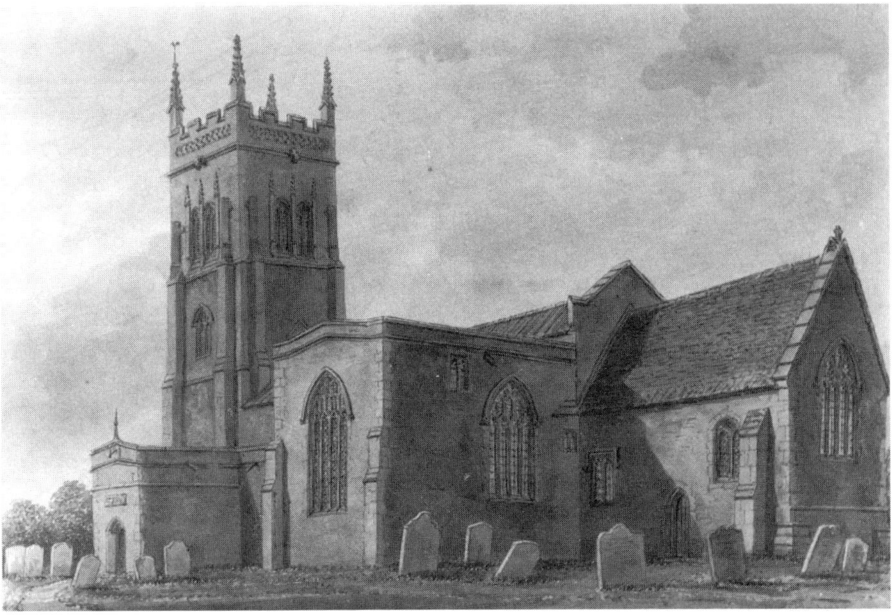

South east view of Chedzoy Church, 1838, by J. Buckler

having an embattled parapet, an octagonal turret on the north side, 4 crocketed pinnacles and a panelled band under the parapet. The buttresses [are] well grouped and pinnacles intended on the upper set-offs. The belfry windows double and large and between them a small pinnacle. The storey below the belfry has 2 light window with stone lattice work. On the west side, a large window of 4 lights and a door with foliage in the spandrels.

The body of the church is all rough cast and the roof has been lowered. There are crosses terminating the gables which have been lately restored. The parapets are all plain. The south porch bears the date 1579 inscribed within a square panel, together with some cyphers, apparently initials.

The nave is divided from each aisle by 4 Early English arches, springing from circular columns with moulded capitals and a fifth arch of like character, opens to each transept. The nave is rather narrow and has a clerestory of square-headed windows of 3 lights. The windows of the north aisle, are square-headed and Perpendicular. In the south aisle, the windows are also Perpendicular except one of Decorated character. The nave is entirely fitted with ancient open seats; the ends have carving of late date and square tops. The roofs are plain. The tower arch is a fine lofty one, with continued panelling in the soffit and small shafts at the angles.

The north aisle is narrower than the southern. The north transept is smaller than the southern, and has a fine stone arch thrown across it, having very rich foliage in the spandrels and mouldings filled with vine leaves and grapes. In the north transept is a Perpendicular window of 4 lights and one nearly similar in the southern in which is also a hagioscope. The south transept has a chantry of square-headed windows.

The chancel arch springs abruptly from the wall: within it is a wooden screen. The chancel is not in a straight line with the nave and exhibits much of Early English work. On its north side, are 2 lancet windows, opening internally by trefoil arches and one Perpendicular one with square-head. On the south, one Perpendicular and one consisting of 2 lancets, externally quite plain but within included under one wide trefoil arch, without mouldings. Beneath, the windows have a string course.

The east window is Decorated of 4 lights. On the south side of the altar are 2 unequal trefoil arches upon circular columns with moulded capitals; one contains a sedile; one a double piscina, eastward of which is a square recess containing a half hexagonal stone projection, apparently a credence, and between this and the niche is a bracket with a hole in it. Over the east end of the chancel the roof is panelled, painted blue with gilt stars and bosses. In the chancel is the brass of a knight with a dog at his feet.

There is a lectern of the 17th century of wood, gilt, but rather plain. The pulpit and reading pue are composed of wood carving, of various dates, apparently collected from various quarters. The font is an octangular bowl on a cylindrical shaft. The west gallery is also composed of ancient wood carving. There are 5 bells. The church very neat and well done by.

(In the south wall externally, is a sculptured stone . . .)

Chelvey

51/90–92 St. Bridget 15 November, 1870

A small church, not without interest, having nave with south aisle or chapel, running to the east end of the chancel, west tower and south porch which latter is set at the west end of the aisle. The chancel has, on the north, 2 trefoil headed lancets. Its east window is Perpendicular of 3 lights. There is no chancel arch. The porch has a panelled parapet and corner buttresses. Within it is a Norman doorway with cylinder in the arch mouldings and shafts with cushion capitals.

Near it internally, is a stoup with a trefoil headed niche. The nave has some Perpendicular windows of 3 lights on the north and south of the porch with some fragments of good, old, coloured glass. The south chapel opens to the nave by 2 wide pointed arches of Perpendicular character with the usual lozenge piers with 4 shafts and concave intervals and eastward, near the chancel, is a small pointed arch. This aisle seems to have been a private chapel; has a ribbed, coved roof and 3 Perpendicular windows of 2 lights. Set closely under each window is an ogee sepulchral arch with crocketed pinnacles and rich feathering, having foliage at the points also flanked by crocketed pinnacles, set diagonally. Beneath these are altar tombs with panelling and flowered bands, of Perpendicular character but without effigies.

The east window is of 3 lights, rather debased, and all have portions of ancient coloured glass. Beneath the east window is an oblong recess with moulded border and flanking it are 2 open niches with continuous jamb mouldings. On the south is a small ogee trefoiled niche and a ledge over it. The chancel has some open, old seats and there is the mark of the base of the

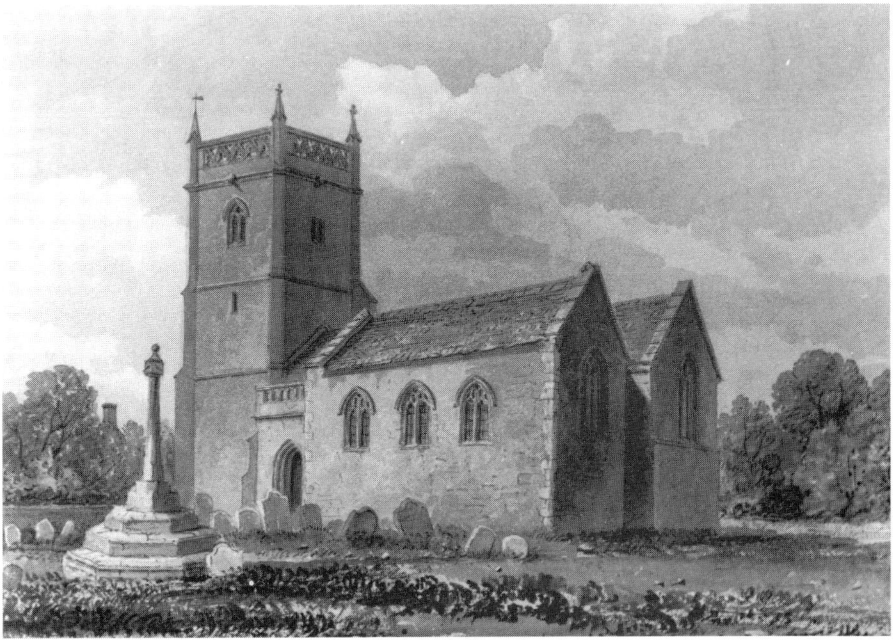

South east view of Chelvey Church, 1827, by J. Buckler

chancel screen, in stone. In the aisle, is a fine piece of Jacobean woodcarving. The font has a plain, octagonal bowl, rounded below.

The tower arch is pointed, with continuous mouldings. The tower is Perpendicular, has an open, panelled parapet and 4 pinnacles, corner buttresses and 2 string courses, an octagonal turret on square base rising at the north-east part of the tower [?] and lighted by slits. There is a west window of 3 lights and belfry windows of 2 and a single opening in the intermediate stage. On the west side is a doorway with continuous moulding and above it a head.

In the churchyard is the shaft of a cross upon high steps.

Cheriton, North

50/45–46	St. John	1 August, 1849

A small Third-Pointed church, consisting of nave and chancel, south porch and west tower. The tower is embattled with 4 pinnacles and varying belfry windows: the north and east are pointed of 2 lights, the south square-headed, the west single, and there is no west door. At the north-east is a projecting turret, reaching up to the belfry storey, divided into stages by strings and surmounted by a pedimental canopy. The buttresses are at the angles.

The tower arch to the nave is a plain, low, pointed one, springing from the

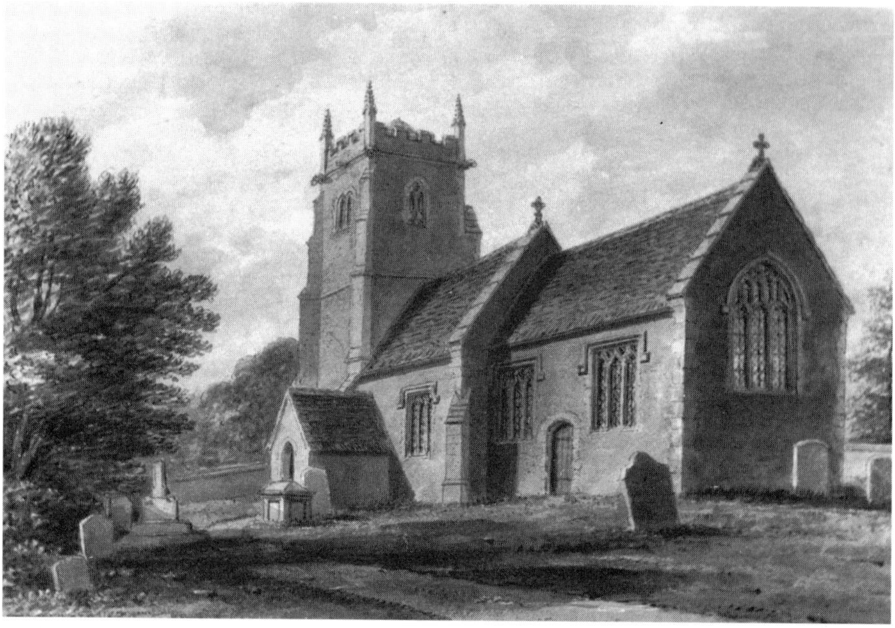

South east view of North Cheriton Church, 1843, by J. Buckler

wall. The porch has been modernized. The nave and chancel [ceilings] are coved with ribs and there is the usual projection in the wall at the north-east. The chancel arch is pointed, upon circular shafts of Third-Pointed character. The windows on the south are square-headed and labeled. On the north they are pointed and the tracery somewhat unusual. There is a niche north of the chancel arch facing west and a bracket on the north wall of the chancel. The font is a plain cylinder diminishing. The pulpit is of carved wood with the date 1633.

Chew Magna

51/69–71 St. Andrew 21 May, 1863

A fine church, chiefly Perpendicular consisting of a nave with north and south aisles, chancel with north and south chapels, western tower and north and south porches. The whole in very good condition and having undergone some recent improvement.

The exterior is of very good stone masonry. There is no clerestory but a steep leaded roof. The south chapel of the chancel has a pierced parapet. The tower a large and fine Perpendicular one having an open panelled parapet and 4 pinnacles and an octagonal stair turret at the north-east angle rising above the parapet with a pointed top. The tower has 3 string courses and very strong buttresses. The west doorway has deep arch mouldings and over it is a 4 light

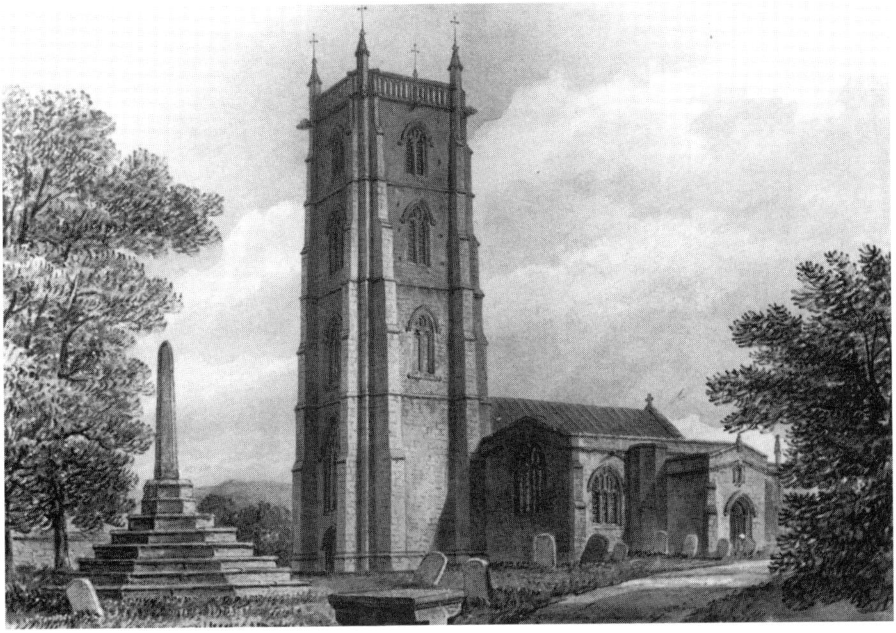

South west view of Chew Magna Church, 1834, by J. Buckler

window. The other windows in each stage, are of 2 lights, some having the pierced lattice work.

The tower arch opening to the nave, is a very fine and lofty one. The porches are good, the southern the largest; the northern has pierced parapet and pinnacles and a doorway with Tudor shaped arch, label and shafts. The interior is striking; the nave has, on each side, 4 pointed arches of which the southern are on octagonal pillars with capitals and appear to be of Decorated date. The northern are Perpendicular and have the usual light piers of shafts with intermediate cavettos.

The roof is open and seems to have been renovated. The chancel arch springs, as frequently in Somersetshire, from corbels above the capitals of the pillars of the arcades and without any break in the arcades. The windows throughout the church are Perpendicular of 3 and 4 lights. Across the entrance to the chancel and both aisles extends a fine wood screen of Perpendicular character.

The chancel has, on each side, a pointed arch opening to the chapels and there are also pointed arches between the aisles of the nave and those of the chancel; that on the south is on corbels of fine execution, one representing a very beautiful head, the other of foliage. The south aisle is very wide in the nave but narrower in the chancel. The north aisle is much narrower. The chancel has a piscina on the south side and there is another in the north chapel. The seats are all low and open. The organ is placed on the north of the chancel, which extends somewhat eastward of the aisles.

In the north chapel is a fine, large altar tomb temp. Henry VI, panelled with

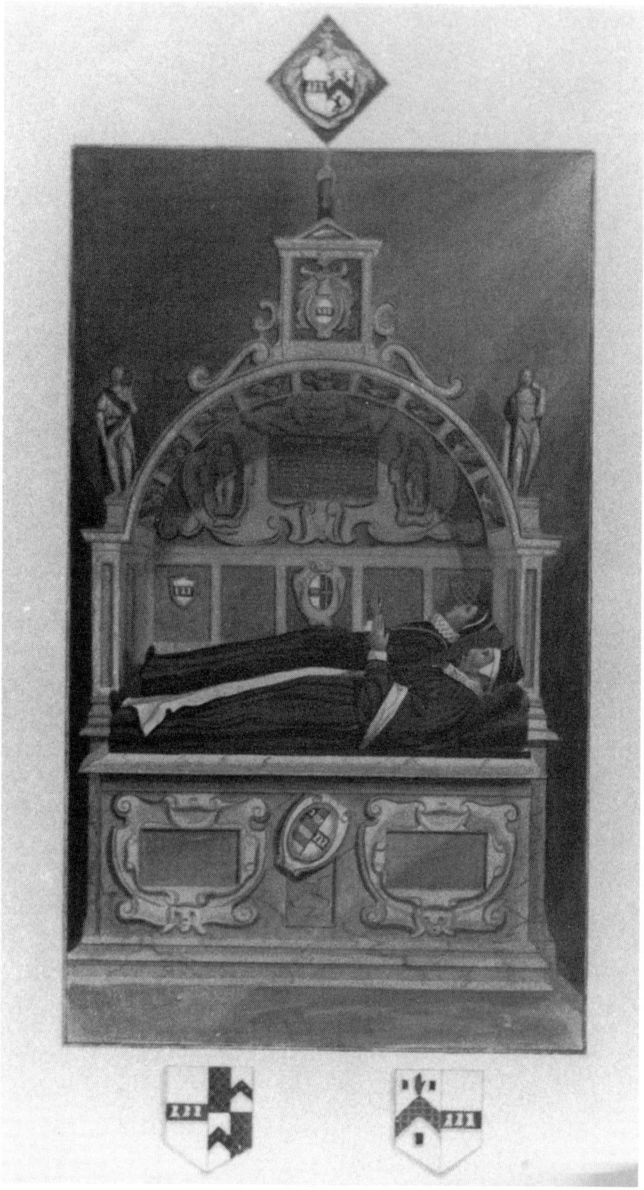

Monument of Baber in Chew Magna Church, by W.W. Wheatley

quatrefoils containing heraldic shields and niches upon which are the effigies of Sir John St. Loe and his lady. His figure is gigantic in armour and cross legged. The effigy of the lady is much injured. She is said to have died 1443.

The south chapel of the chancel has 2 tiers of windows of late Perpendicular character and contains a large tomb with monumental effigies of Edward Baber and Catherine, his wife, 1578 and 1601, in the rich, impure style of that period. The south aisle of the nave has, near its east end, a round arched piscina with continuous arched mouldings and under a window is a restored sepulchral arch (or perhaps quite new) with crocketed canopy, under which is the recumbent effigy in wood, of Sir John Hautville, said to have been removed from Norton church. The figure is curiously carved out of a solid piece of Irish Oak, in armour, leaning on the left side and reclining on his left hip and left elbow. He lived in the reign of Henry III and is said to have been a man of prodigious strength and to have performed various, wonderful feats according to vulgar tradition.

The font has a circular bowl with some fluting on it and upon a cylinder.

Near the church, on the south side, is a very pretty ancient house temp. Henry VI, now used by paupers and said to have been built by one of the St. Loes in 15th century.

In the churchyard is the shaft of a cross on a very high base of 6 steps.

(There is an octagonal pier on the north side, marking the interval between the nave and chancel, perhaps of the same date and character as the south piers.)

(A loose cloak over the armour and the left foot placed against a lion.)

Chinnock, East

51/32–33 St. Mary May 1860

The plan is nave and chancel without aisles and western tower. The nave has been rebuilt in a vile manner, imitating Gothic, wide and sprawling, and the

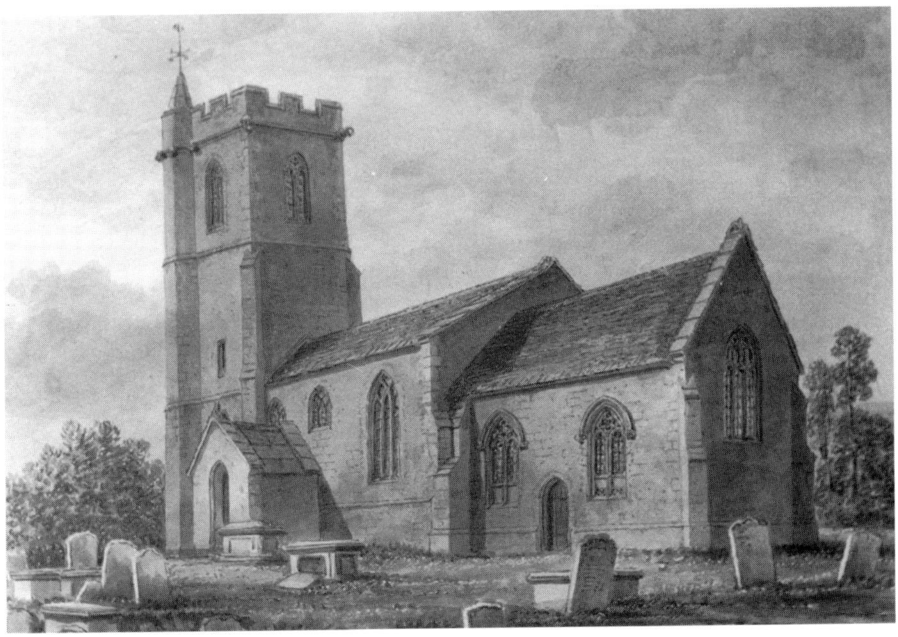

South east view of East Chinnock Church, 1838, by J. Buckler

interior singularly naked and dreary. The chancel arch is a plain, pointed one. The chancel and tower are Perpendicular. The former has a small east window of 3 lights set very high up. On the north and south, are 2 windows similar to the one opposite. The two eastern are square-headed of 2 lights and the southern has its cill extended. The 2 western are pointed, of 2 lights and have the lower part enriched with stone panelling in quatrefoils (not glazed) which is a common Somersetshire feature. There are some pretty pieces of ancient stained glass in the chancel windows. There is a priest's door.

The tower is good Perpendicular, embattled with gargoyles and a high octagonal turret embattled to the south-west. The belfry windows of 2 lights have the local frety [?] pierced stone work in quatrefoils. The west window [is] of 3 lights and below it [is] a plain doorway.

Churchill

51/45–46	St. John	25 January, 1862

This church is wholly Perpendicular but not one of the most spacious kind of Somersetshire churches, though consisting of nave with north and south aisles, chancel, west tower and south porch. The porch has a pierced parapet; the outer doorway has continuous arch mouldings and hood on angel corbels.

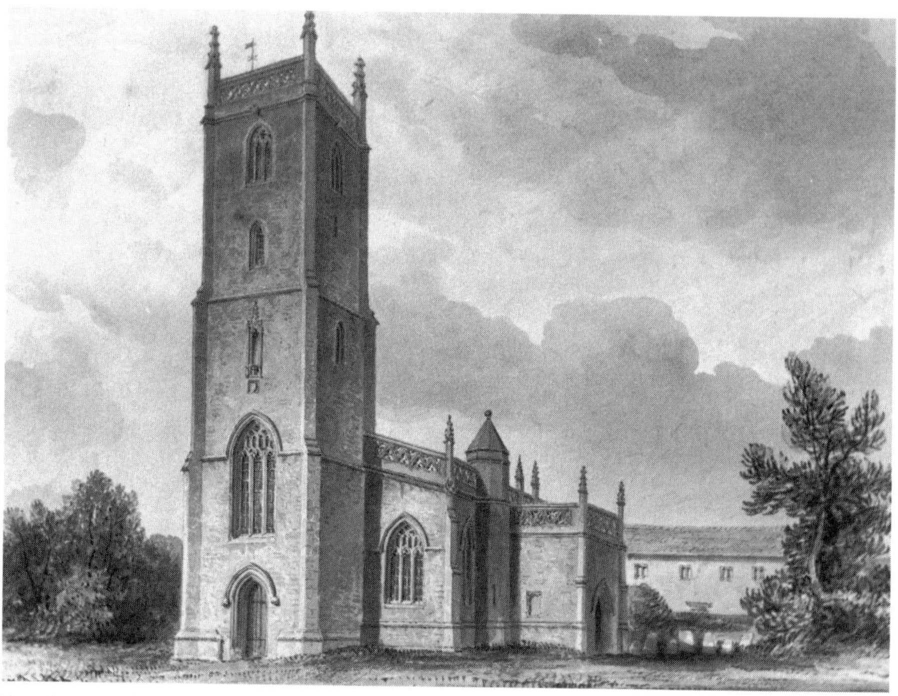

South west view of Churchill Church, 1827, by J.C. Buckler

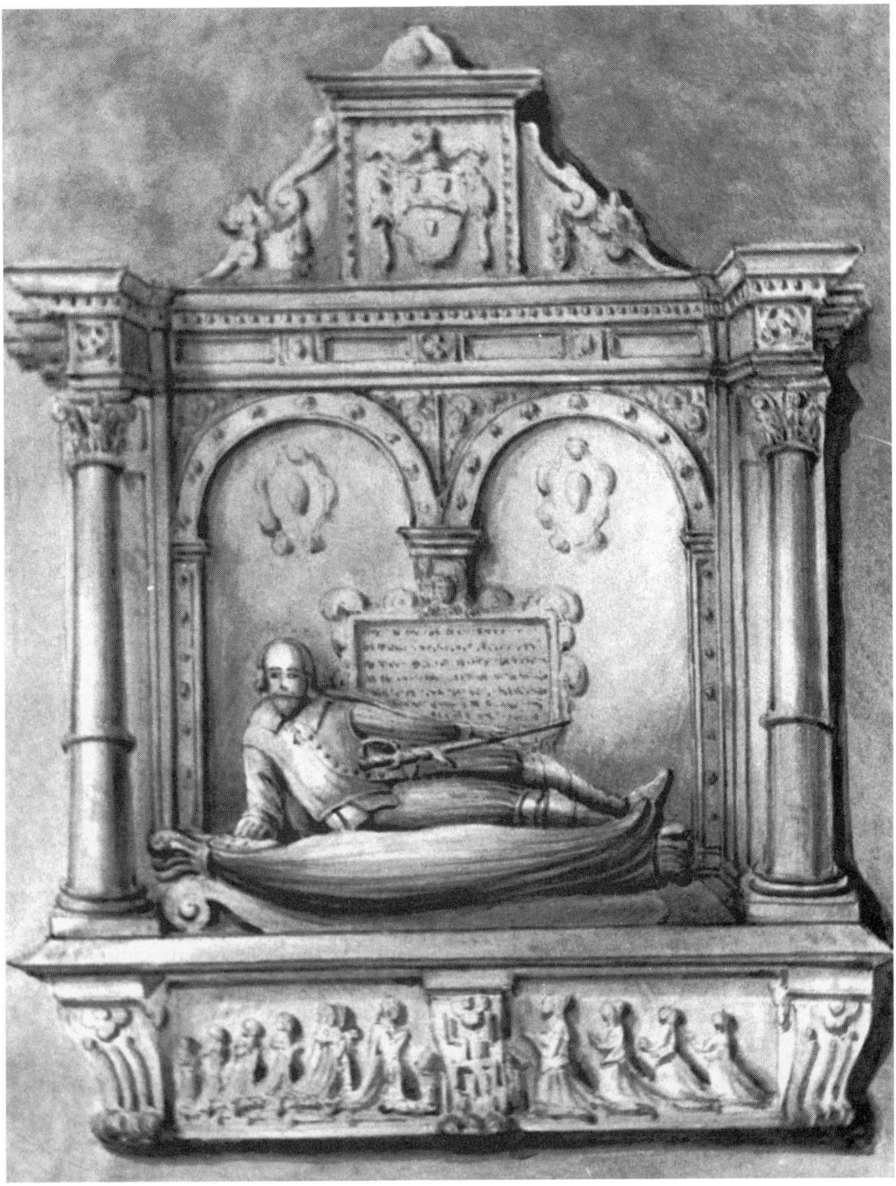

Monument of Sir John Latch and Sara his wife, Churchill Church, 1842, by W.W. Wheatley

There is an octagonal stair turret in the angle of the porch. The aisles and chancel have fine pierced panelled parapets and crocketed pinnacles on the buttresses. There is no clerestory: the roofs are coved and ribbed in a plain way.

The north arcade is superior to the southern and has the usual light pillars of 4 stilted shafts and good arch mouldings. The south is less good in the

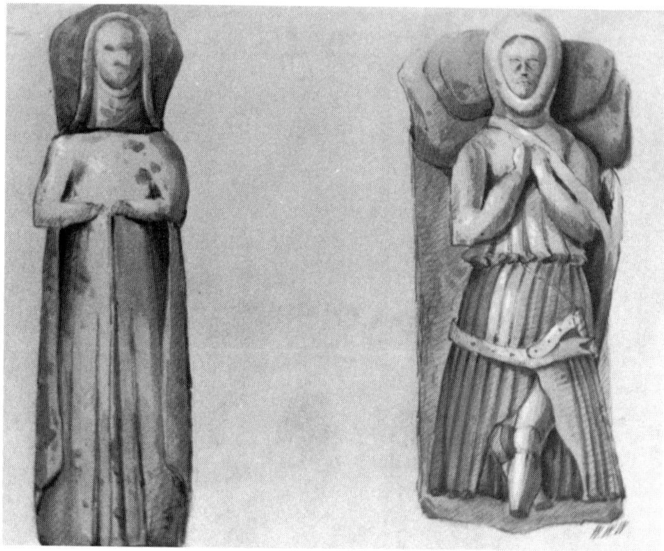

Churchill Church, 1842, by W.W. Wheatley

mouldings and has octagonal columns. The tower arch is lofty and upon shafts and within the tower is some nice stone groining. The windows of the aisles are chiefly of 3 lights. There is a hagioscope from the south aisle into the chancel carried through a window jamb. The angle of the north aisle is curiously cut by a passage for the rood door and lighted by quatrefoil openings.

The chancel is small, has side windows of 2 lights and square-headed and, at the east, one of 3 lights. There is a plain ogee piscina with a round bowl. There is, on the north side, a monument of Sarah Latch with 2 figures, one a lady in a winding sheet and a man bewailing her, another composition of the 17th century. The nave has ancient open seats with poppy heads. There is some new, stained glass in the east window of the south aisle. There is an organ. The font has an early cylindrical bowl with cable moulding. There is an octagonal rood turret at the north-east of the nave. There is a brass of late date, 1572. The tower is plain and rough cast; has a plain, pierced parapet and 4 crocketed pinnacles and an octagonal turret on the north. The buttresses are angular. There is a west doorway and a west window of 3 lights over which is a canopied niche. The belfry windows of 2 lights.

In the churchyard are 2 fine sepulchral effigies of a cross-legged knight and lady. (As usual in Somersetshire, the angel gargoyles are very abundant.)

Cleeve, Old

50/92–94 St. Andrew 10 May, 1855

The plan: nave with south aisle, chancel and western tower, south transept and south porch. The whole Perpendicular.

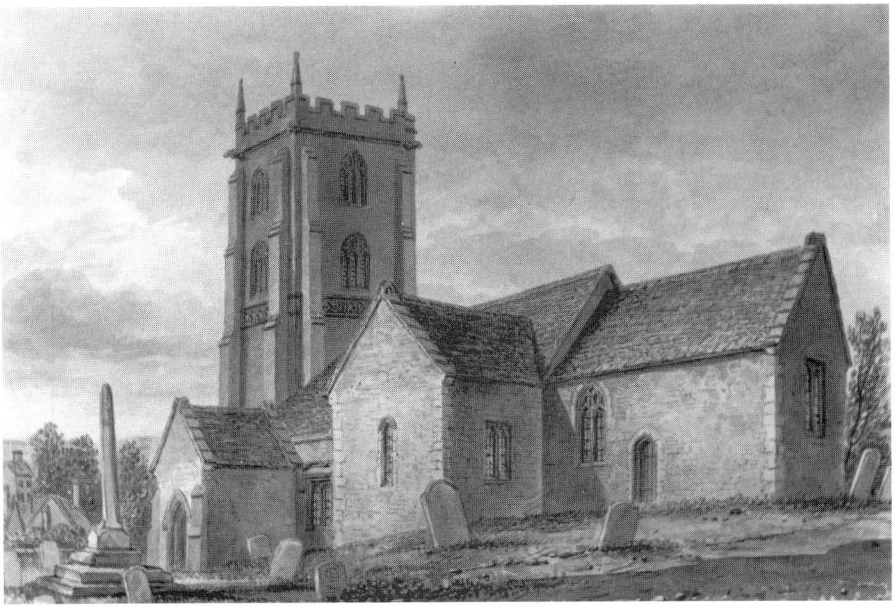

South east view of Old Cleeve Church, 1836, by J. Buckler

The tower is a fine one of the local type, embattled with small pinnacles and an octagonal stair turret at the north-east angle rising high. The buttresses are set near the angles. The west doorway has Tudor arch and label; over it are five horizontal bands of panelling with shields. Above this is a good 4 light window subarcuated and 3 heights of windows, those of the belfry having stone lattice work. The north side the plainest; on the south a canopied niche. The tower arch to the nave lofty and continuous with good mouldings.

The parapets of the body are plain. On the north side, which is as usual the plainest, are 2 windows, one poor and of 2 lights, one of 3 with shafts to the rear arch. In the south aisle the windows are mostly square-headed of 3 lights except that at the west end which has a transom.

The nave is very wide; there is a considerable ascent towards the east, the ground being very sloping and the chancel quite on an inclined plain. The interior in fair condition and has signs of recent improvement, a new prayer desk and pulpit and stained glass in the west window and one of those on the north. The gallery is within the tower. The arcade to the aisle is of 4 Tudor-shaped arches, having but slight curvature, on light, stilted piers of lozenge form with 4 shafts at the angles with moulded capitals and mouldings down the intermediate spaces. The roof of the nave is coved with ribs, bosses and foliated cornice. The east end of the aisle is extended as if a kind of chapel. In the north wall is an ogee arched recess beneath which is the figure of a civilian with hands joined in prayer and his feet on an animal.

The chancel arch is moulded, springing from shafts arranged as in the piers of the nave. To the south of it is a hagioscope with trefoil feathering. The east window of the chancel and one on the south are of 3 lights, the

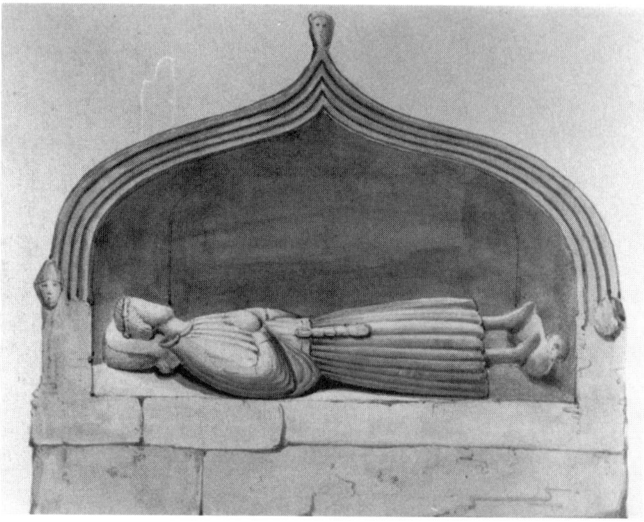

In Old Cleeve Church, north aisle, 1845, by W.W. Wheatley

others of 2 lights, not remarkable. There is a modern Gothic reredos of no great beauty.

The font has a panelled octagonal bowl beneath which, on the slope, are figures of angels bearing shields; the stem octagonal with panelling and shields. There are some fine ancient carved bench ends. All the seats of the nave open, but some closed in the aisle and chancel, and a gallery in the transept. The porch is coved and ribbed; a niche and a flowered band over the interior doorway. There is a projecting turret on the north for the rood stairs. In the churchyard is a fine cross raised upon many high steps. The churchyard is on high and uneven ground and commands a delightful view over Minehead and the channel, etc.

Clevedon

49/55–57 [St. Andrew] 1842

This church in a lonely situation near the sea, is a cruciform building with some early original portions and features of all the styles. It consists of a nave with south aisle and south porch, north and south transepts, a chancel and a central tower. The latter is of transition style from Norman to Early English at least the two stages immediately above the church roof; the upper of these has small obtuse headed windows and an overhanging corbel table beneath what was probably the crowning parapet and of a very Norman character, there being between each corbel 2 small round arches. The upper part of the tower is quite modern and has a battlement and 4 mean pinnacles.

The chancel has, on the south side, an early corbel table of grotesque heads. The roof of the chancel is high and tiled; the whole exterior walls are stuccoed.

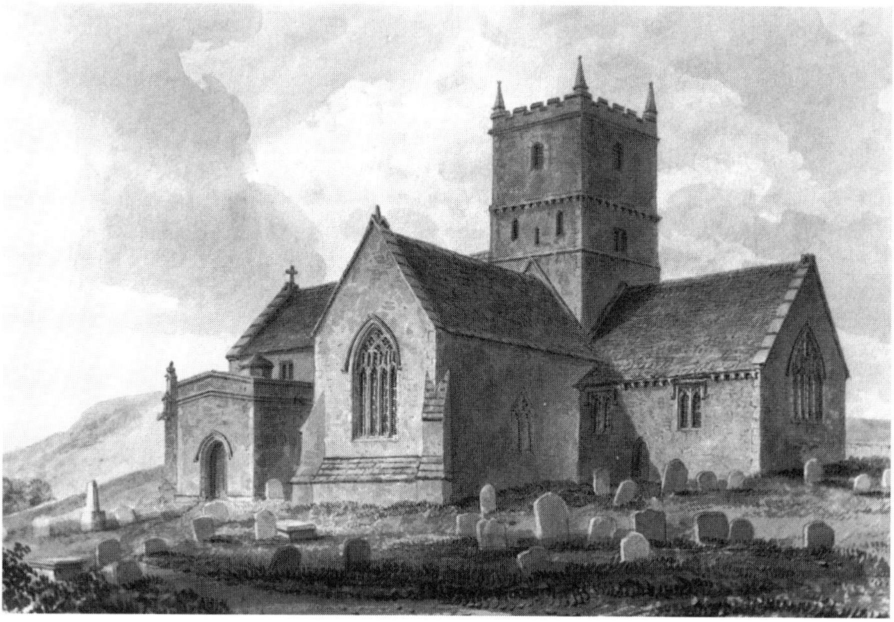

South east view of Clevedon Church, 1828, by J. Buckler

The south porch is large and plain with good moulded parapet of Perpendicular character. The south aisle has also a moulded parapet, the nave a slated roof. At the south-west angle of the nave is a rich, crocketed pinnacle. The west window is Decorated of 3 lights, but mutilated. On the north side, is one square-headed, Perpendicular window of 3 lights and one more resembling Decorated tracery. There is a Decorated window of 2 lights in the south aisle.

The south transept is larger than the northern and has a Perpendicular window of 4 lights beneath which externally, is a sloping plinth and the buttresses are set at the angles. The north transept has a Decorated window rather mutilated. The nave is divided from the aisle by 4 plain pointed arches with dripstones united; the piers extremely simple, and without capitals; probably the work is of early Decorated period. The 4 arches under the tower are pointed and very plain. The chantry of the nave has square-headed Perpendicular windows of 2 lights. The chancel has an east window of 4 lights with Perpendicular tracery, the dripstones having head corbels which appear earlier.

The side windows of the chancel are late and square-headed with labels. In the south transept is a mark in the wall for a tomb with feathering and an effigy of a female much smaller than is usually found. The church is fitted up principally with open seats and rather primitive. The north door is closed as usual. The font is a plain octagon upon a shaft. The population has increased in the village of Clevedon at a distance from the parish church, where a new church has been erected in the Decorated style by Rickman, rather bald in its general effect and the tower very plain.

Closworth

51/34–35 | All Saints | 5 May, 1860

A small church having chancel and nave without aisles, a western tower and north porch, the public path being on that side. The whole appears to be Perpendicular, except a part of the chancel which has, on the north-east, a closed lancet and on the south-east, a trefoiled one. The windows are of 3 lights in the nave but there are smaller projecting ones both north and south, at the east end of the nave, which are square-headed and of 2 lights, the projecting bays having separate roofs. These, perhaps, were connected with the roodloft. On the south side of the chancel arch, is also a little window looking east. The arrangement is curious and quite uncommon.

The tower arch to the nave, is open and continuous with panelling all down the arch and jambs. The roof is coved and whitewashed. There are several ancient, open benches. The chancel arch is small, pointed and continuous and set in the midst of much solid walling rather indicating an earlier period, though the form has been altered. The east window of the chancel is Perpendicular, of 3 lights. In the south wall, internally, appears a bold corbel. The church is stalled.

The font has an octagonal bowl on stem of like form and is cleaned of whitewash. The sides have quatrefoils containing roses, except the western, which has a shield charged with 3 mitres. The north porch is wholly of stone, the roof having strong arched ribs, without bosses, the front flanked with pinnacles.

The tower is handsome Perpendicular, embattled with 4 crocketed pinnacles

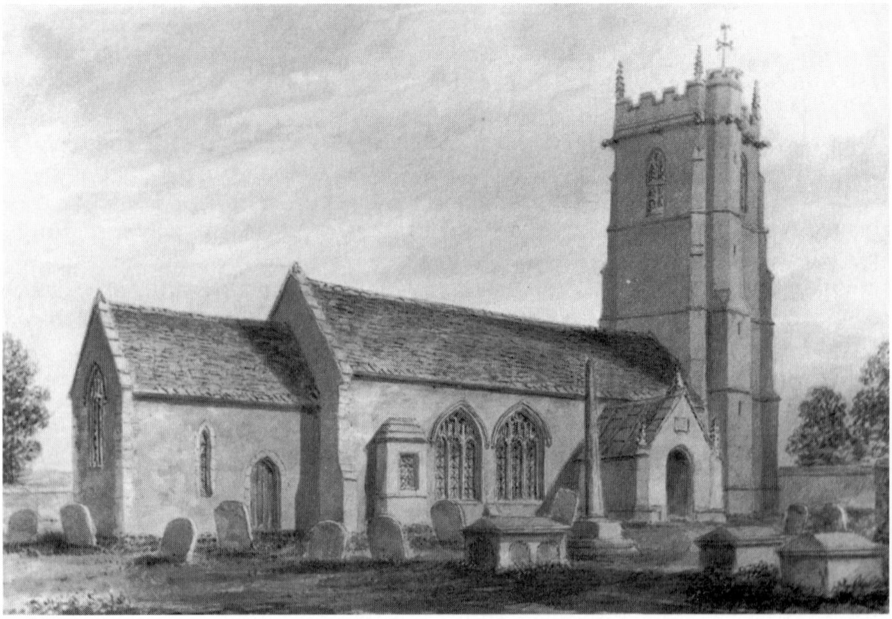

North east view of Closworth Church, 1846, by J. Buckler

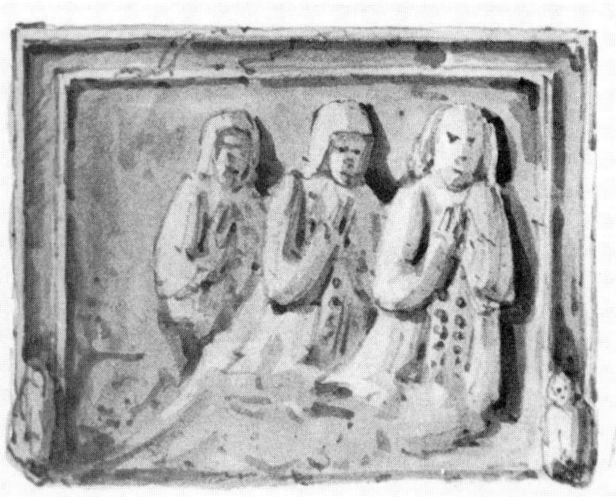

On the third stage of the tower of Closworth Church, 1848, by W.W. Wheatley

and divided into stages by 3 strings; at the north-east a stair turret, octagonal and embattled. On the west side, is a labeled doorway over which [is] a 4 light subarcuated window and above this a pretty, canopied niche, under groined, having label and spandrels containing figures of angels. The belfry windows are of 2 lights, transomed, and containing the pretty pierced stone panelling not uncommon in Somersetshire. The buttresses are at the angles and there are good gargoyles.

On the south side, in the second stage, are 3 sculptured figures in attitude of prayer under a label.

In the churchyard is the shaft of a cross.

Clutton

52/30–31 St. Augustine 16 May, 1874

This church has lately been entirely rebuilt except the tower, but a good doorway has been preserved on the south side of excellent semi-Norman character. It has [a] semi-circular arch, the outer moulding cylindrical and continuous, the inner upon shafts with abaci and foliaged capitals. The tower is curious from having been built in 1728 as recorded in a tablet. Its outline is not bad; it has an embattled parapet and 4 crocketed pinnacles, corner buttresses and projecting stair turret at the south-east. On the upper set off of the buttresses, are set crocketed pinnacles. The tower is divided by 2 string courses and there is a curious mixture of grey and red stone which gives a peculiar character.

The west window has square head and 3 unfoiled lights. The west door is of debased character; the belfry windows of 2 lights, square-headed, labeled, having some of the pierced stone work so frequent in Somersetshire. There is on the whole, a good contour to this tower, generally recalling Perpendicular towers of this county and not bad for the time of its erection, but the details will not bear inspection. The body of the church is rebuilt in no bad way and has Edwardian windows with plate tracery.

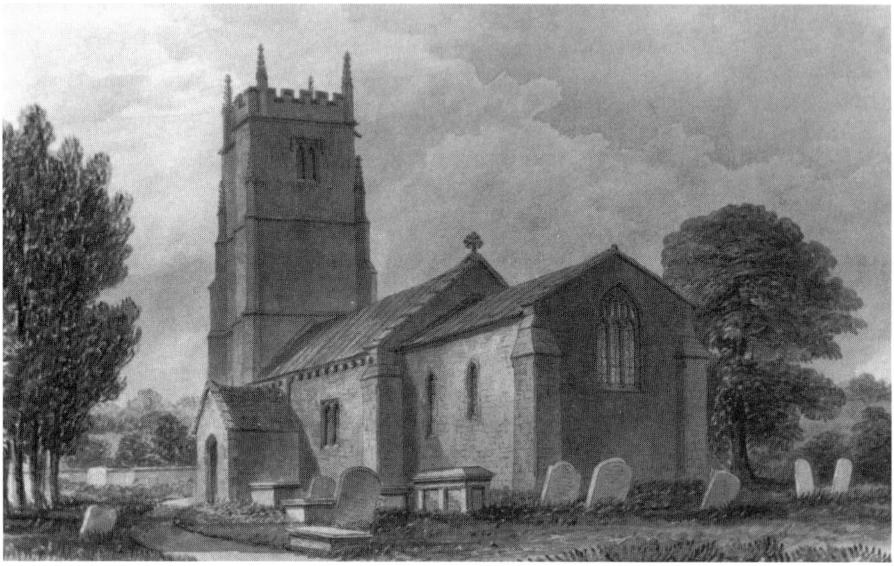

South east view of Clutton Church, 1834, by J. Buckler

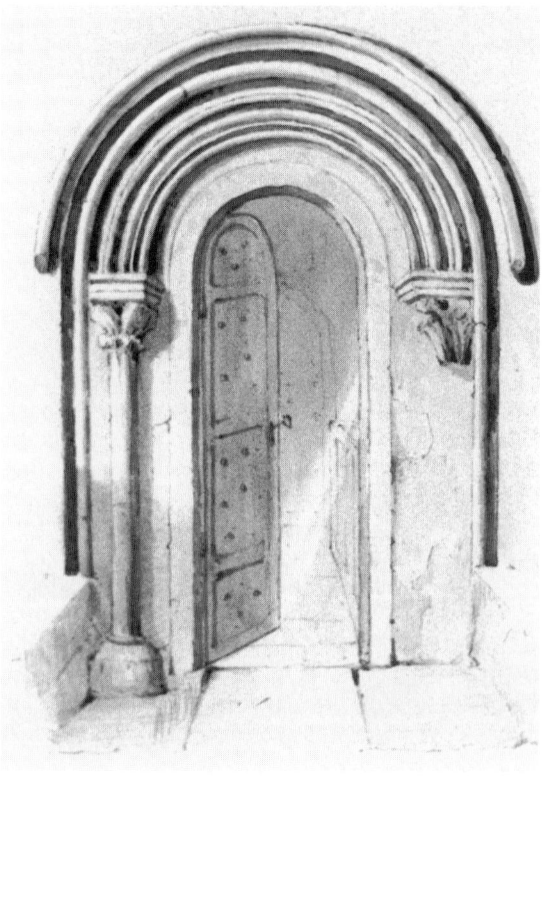

Clutton Church, 1843, by W.W. Wheatley

Coker, West

51/31–32 St. Martin May, 1860

This church has nave and chancel each with north and south aisles and a western tower. There was originally, no south aisle, the present one both in chancel and nave having been added in 1834. The east end presents 3 equal gables and, as the chief approach to the church is from that side, a porch has unhappily been added to the east end of the south aisle. The north aisle of the nave is very narrow; its arcade is Early English and has 3 low pointed arches with circular columns having moulded capitals.

The south aisle being wider and loftier, the new arcade is also loftier, but similar in character to the opposite one. The roofs are of the cradle form with ribs and bosses. The windows throughout the church are Perpendicular; on the north square-headed and labeled and those on the south are, of course, modern but of like character. The chancel arch is Perpendicular, on shafts. The north aisle of the chancel is wider than that of the nave and between them is a pointed arch of division, of narrow proportions. There are 2 brackets flanking the east window and in the chancel an ogee trefoiled piscina having octagonal projecting bowl. There are also traces of a hagioscope.

In the nave are some pretty, ancient carved bench ends. There is a large, Jacobean monument to 2 sisters of the Portman family, the 2 figures kneeling. The font has a circular bowl, but is probably modern. The 3 east gables are surmounted by crosses. The nave has a lead roof and parapet; the chancel a

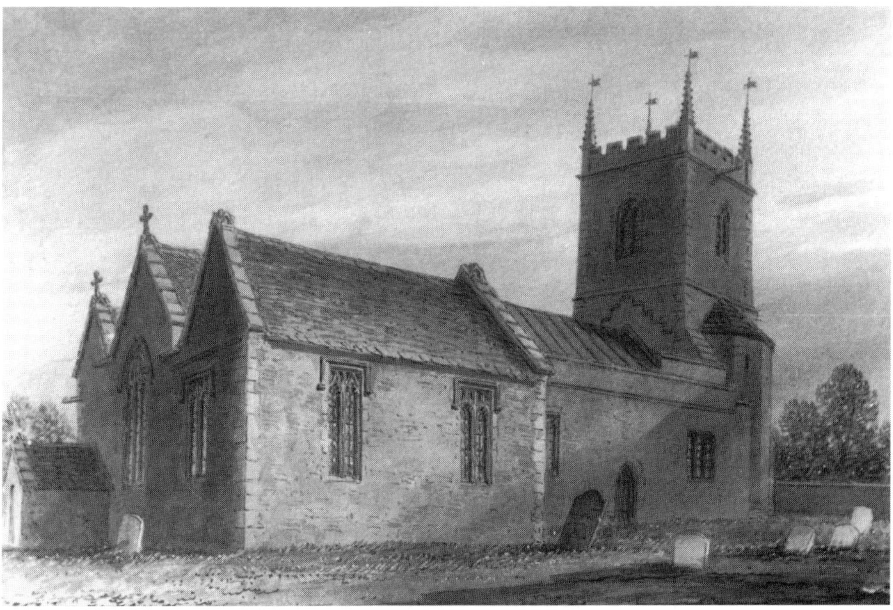

North east view of West Coker Church, 1837, by J. Buckler

high tiled roof. The north aisle does not begin quite at the west end. The tower has a debased look, is embattled with 4 pinnacles and an odd-looking round stair turret on the north, which has slits and is surmounted by a tiled, pointed roof.

Compton Dando

52/19 St. Mary 3 February, 1872

This church has nave with north aisle, chancel with north aisle or chapel (now excluded from the church), a western tower. The tower is a good one of the Somersetshire type and Perpendicular; has embattled parapet and an octagonal stone turret, rising above the parapet. The buttresses are set square in pairs at each angle; the belfry windows of 2 lights with the pierced stone lattice work, a good west window and doorway with label, panelled, and spandrels. The nave is short and divided from the aisle by 2 Perpendicular arches with piers of clustered shafts which have capitals of foliage, not quite of the usual kind. The chancel arch is pointed.

The windows in the nave are mostly square-headed and Perpendicular. On the south side, they are arranged in 2 tiers, the lower has one 3 light and 2 one light windows, square-headed; the upper have pointed arches of 2 lights. There is no east window to the chancel. The buttress at the north-east angle has a rude sculptured figure. The organ is in the north aisle. The font has a circular cup-shaped bowl which looks early.

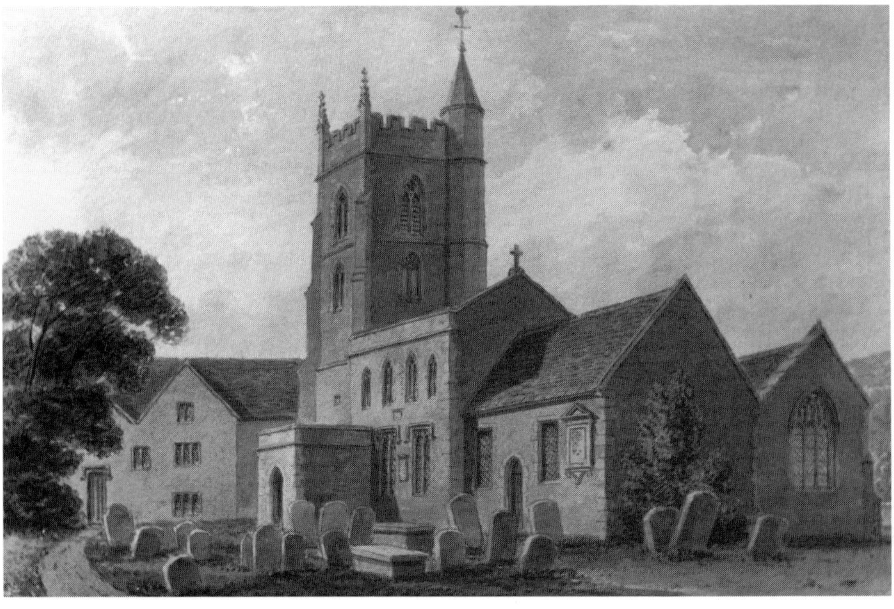

South east view of Compton Dando Church, 1847, by J. Buckler

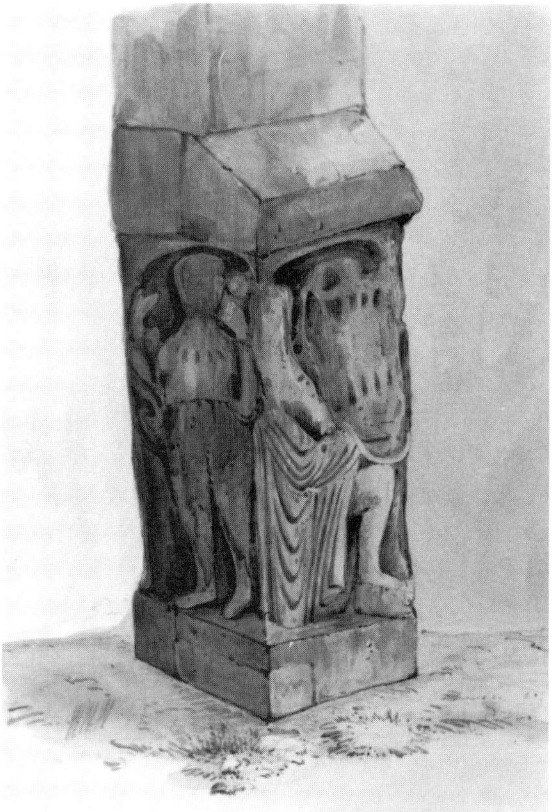

Roman altar, lately dug up and affixed to Compton Dando Church, 1845, by W.W. Wheatley

Compton Dundon

49/52 St. Andrew Before 1840

This is a rather pretty church consisting of a west tower, a nave, and a chancel without aisles. The tower and the nave are Perpendicular; the former is not lofty and is of plain work with a good battlement and bold gargoyles and the belfry window square-headed. The windows of the nave are of 3 lights and without drip stones. The south porch is plain. Over the east gable of the nave is a fine cross.

The nave has a coved roof divided by ribs into panels with fine bosses. The chancel arch is very plain. There is within it, the stone basement of a screen with traces of the hinges of the door in the centre. The pulpit is of woodwork temp. James I and approached by ancient stone steps. North and south are square-headed windows, set high for lighting the roodloft. There are some old, plain open seats and portions of roodscreen work. The chancel has 2 windows on each side, three of which are Decorated of 2 lights, one square-headed and later.

The east window is a singular and rather elegant Decorated one of 5 lights, the arch having corbels internally. There are in it, some fine pieces of stained

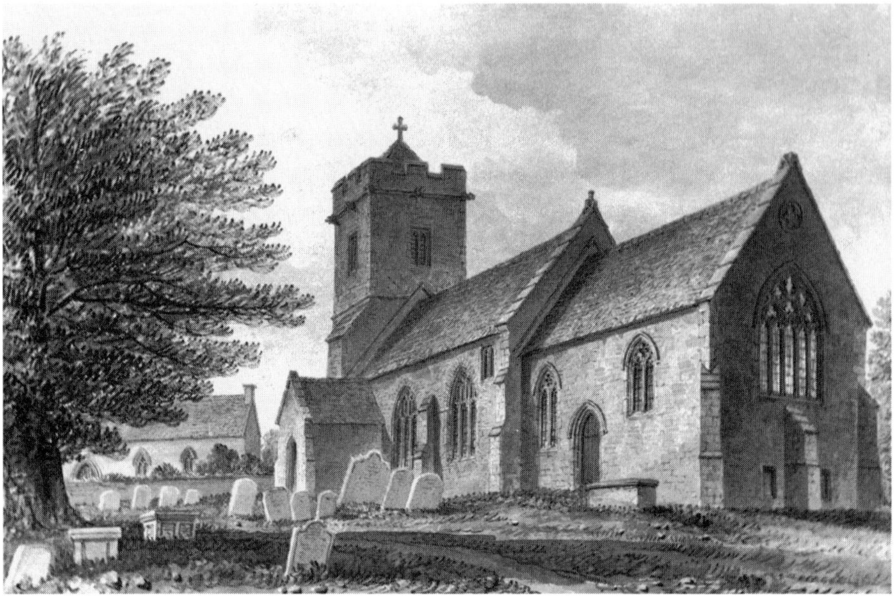

South east view of Compton Dundon Church, 1834, by J. Buckler

glass. South of the altar were 3 sedilia with ogee heads and good mouldings, but one is cut away to make room for a more modern window. There is also a niche with trefoil head with a piscina. The font is an octagonal basin on a stem of like form. There are 5 bells. In the churchyard is a fine yew tree and a delightful view.

The villages of Compton Dundon contain some very picturesque, ancient stone houses with windows and doors of excellent design.

Compton Martin

50/23–24 [St. Michael] April 1845

A curious church with much Norman work and some of later date. The plan comprises a nave with aisles, a chancel with south chapel, a north porch and a handsome western tower. The original features are Norman but the tower and some windows are much later. The former is a fine, Perpendicular one of the true Somerset kind and built of excellent stone; divided into 4 stages and having a fine parapet of pierced panelling with four pinnacles at the angles. There is an octagonal stair turret on the north side near the east corner. The buttresses are at the angles and the pinnacles are set diagonally upon them.

The belfry windows are obtuse headed, of 2 lights with transoms and each set between 2 canopied niches. In the second stage from the bottom, are 2 small crocketed pinnacles, set upon the string and a canopied niche between them. The west window of 3 lights and below it a good doorway, labeled, and

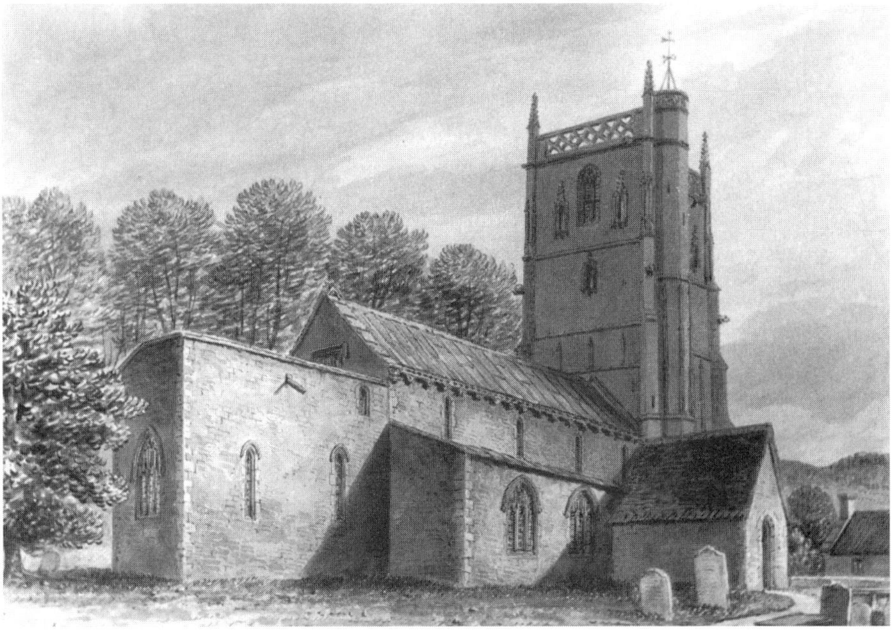

North east view of Compton Martin Church, 1835, by J. Buckler

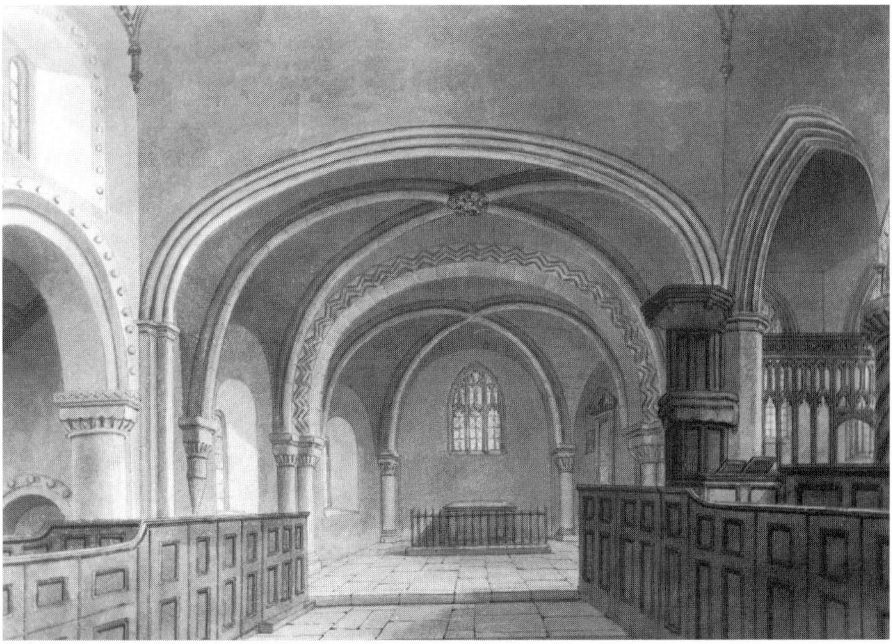

Interior view of Compton Martin Church, 1835, by J. Buckler

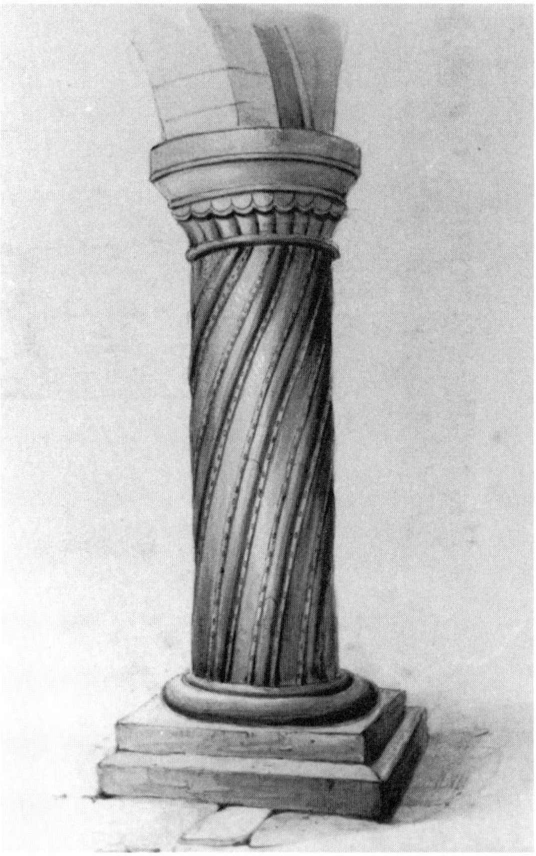

Compton Martin Church, 1844, by W.W. Wheatley

having roses and foliage in the spandrels. The tower arch to the nave is lofty and open having the soffit panelled continuously.

The clerestory on the north side of the nave has a Norman corbel table of heads, etc., below the parapet and also a course of chevron ornament. The roof is high and leaded. The north porch has a stone seat on each side; the door within has good mouldings and hood with corbels of square-form containing quatrefoils. The south side and all the chancel has plain, moulded parapets.

The nave is divided from the north aisle by 4 semi-circular arches springing from circular columns with round capitals, but the eastern respond, is square. On the south are 3 semi-circular arches with circular columns and the 4th, or eastern one, is pointed. The eastern pier is most curious having spiral channeled mouldings with courses of beads, the capital and bases square. On the north, are 3 Norman clerestory windows, narrow but much splayed. The 4th is a later insertion. The clerestory on the south, much resembles that on the north but is closed. The roof is coved having ribs and large bosses and corbels as at West Harptree.

The chancel is Norman and open to the nave by a very odd, flattened arch, the mouldings of which appear to be Perpendicular. Above it is a window modernized. The chapel has a stone groined roof with very strong ribs forming rather a segmental arch. One boss represents 4 figures of beasts, the heads uniting in the centre. The arch between the 2 compartments of groining has some chevron ornament and springs from clustered shafts against the wall with a kind of cushion capital with hatched abacus.

On the north of the chancel are 2 trefoil-headed lancets and one on the south. On the north and south of the east end, are square apertures in the wall. The east window is Perpendicular of 3 lights. Between the chancel and its south chapel is a pointed arch of Perpendicular character rising from half octagonal shafts with small battlements on the capital. There is a good wood screen for the roodloft across the entrance to the chancel and also across the south chapel having vine leaf hands. There are Perpendicular windows of 3 lights in the south chapel, one containing some tolerable pieces of stained glass. The north aisle has strong wood ribs in the roof with bosses.

The font has a circular bowl chevroned round the top, the stem and base also circular. The south doorway has small shafts.

Congresbury

50/69–71 St. Andrew 16 January, 1854

A nice church whose well-proportioned spire forms a pleasing object within the surrounding country. The plan is nave with aisles, chancel with north and south chapels, a western tower with spire and south porch. The exterior is principally, but not wholly, Perpendicular: in the interior appears a good deal of earlier work.

The arcades of the nave are Early English, but they do not exactly correspond. Each arcade is of 4 arches. On the north, they are acute and rather plain and the piers circular with round moulded capitals. On the north, the arches are of superior work and better cut, later in character and verging to Decorated, the pillars still more approaching that style: clustered of 4 shafts with the intermediate spaces well moulded and capitals also moulded; the bases raised. (The bases of the piers on the south shew the traces of the bases of 4 surrounding shafts.)

The clerestory of the nave has the windows set close with a light appearance, each window being of 2 lights and having something of a Decorated character. The roof of the nave is a good one of wood, coved, and with ornamental ribs and bosses; the cornice and the spandrels above the clerestory enriched with elegant open panelling. The windows of the aisles are Perpendicular of 3 lights; that at the west end of the north aisle, has the rear arch and shafts.

The chancel arch has been altered and is partly continuous, partly on shafts. Across it is a good rood screen of plain open panelling with beautiful cornices of vine leaf carving. Across the south aisle is a richer screen which does not match it, having the compartments arched and with fine tracery and foliaged spandrels. There are continuous arches from the aisles of the nave to those of the chancel. The tower arch is very plain.

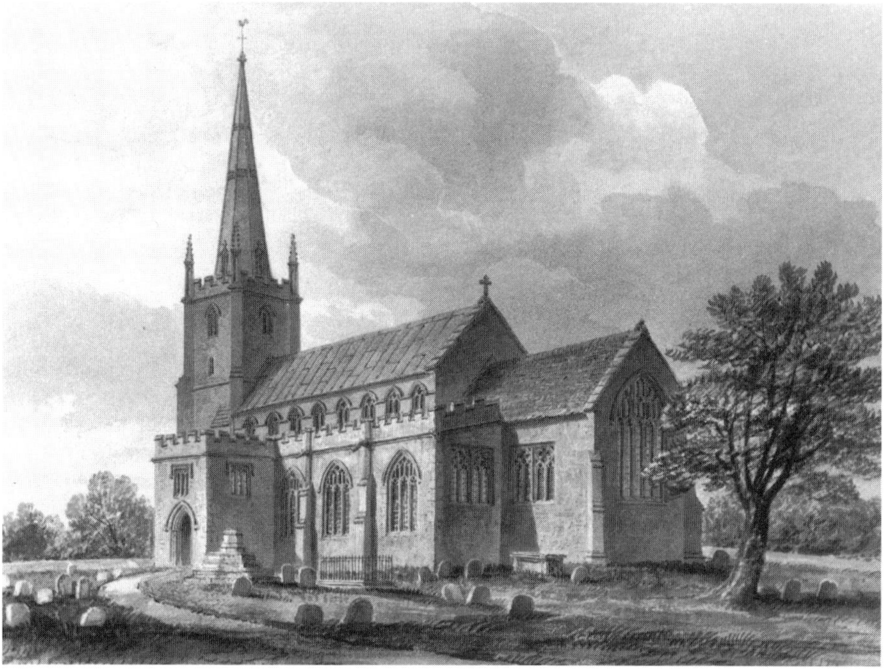

South east view of Congresbury Church, 1827, by J. Buckler

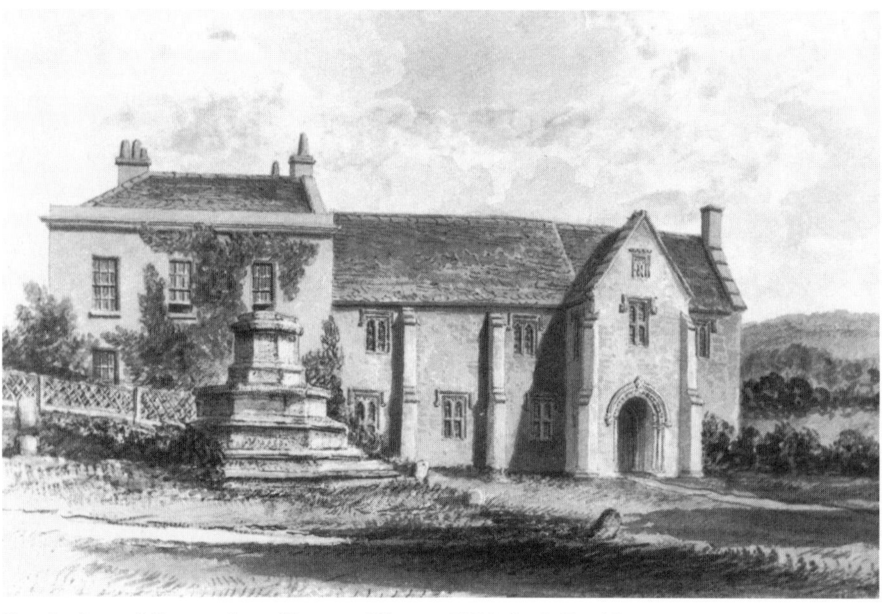

South view of Congresbury Rectory House, 1828, by J. Buckler

The chancel opens to its chapels by late, continuous arches in the southern of which is a piece of good stone screen with battlement and in this chapel is a curious square-headed window in two divisions, each of which is of 2 lights with a quatrefoil in the head, apparently of Decorated character. The chancel has a Perpendicular, east window of 5 lights and square-headed ones on the north and south of the sacrarium.

On the south is a very good double piscina, transitional from Early English to Decorated, with trefoil heads very well moulded and hood mouldings following the like form, the shaft detached with moulded capital. There is a reredos of tolerable design in stone with open panelling and a band of vine foliage. The north chapel has a Decorated window of 3 lights at the east end containing some fragments of stained glass; also a Perpendicular niche with pedimented canopy.

The font is Early English, the bowl circular diminishing downwards with cable moulding round it, set upon a cylindrical stem surrounded by 4 marble shafts with capitals and bases, standing upon a square plinth. The interior is light, neat and cheerful, but pued, though in a uniform style, and there is a gallery at the west end containing a finger organ.

The tower is plain and of rather poor detail with battlement and 4 crocketed pinnacles set diagonally on the buttresses and panelled. The spire is octagonal and of very good proportion, probably the most elegant and satisfactory in the county. The west doorway is moulded and rather obtuse, having niches and panelling in the jambs; over it a small 3 light window. The tower is of late character; it has a clock and 6 bells, the porch embattled and has a square window.

The churchyard is unusually large, but part of the area is railed off and not so applied. It contains a cross upon steps and on the north side is the vicarage, a pretty, picturesque building of the late Gothic, of true Somersetshire character. There is another cross, raised high on steps, in the village.

Corfe

50/75 [Unknown] 11 May, 1855

A small church recently rebuilt, except the tower, which is low and plain without buttresses; with moulded parapet and gargoyles. Belfry windows simple, trefoiled and west window Perpendicular of 2 lights. The tower arch is plain, pointed, straight from the wall.

The church has chancel, nave and small north aisle. The whole has been rebuilt in the Norman style and, however little one may approve the adoption of that style, with laudable regard for ecclesiastical propriety and all the work well done and good of its kind. The arcade of the nave is good, the doors enriched and the windows filled with stained glass. The benches all open. The front old and Norman, of cylindrical form with interesting arches, on a stem with shafts attached.

In the churchyard are some very good new gravestones with crosses and coped.

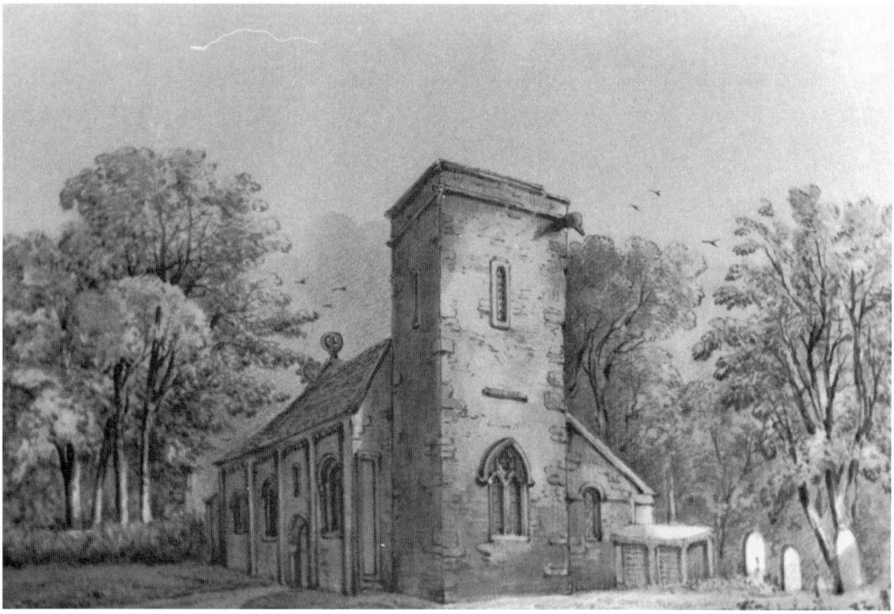

Corfe, 1848, by W.W. Wheatley

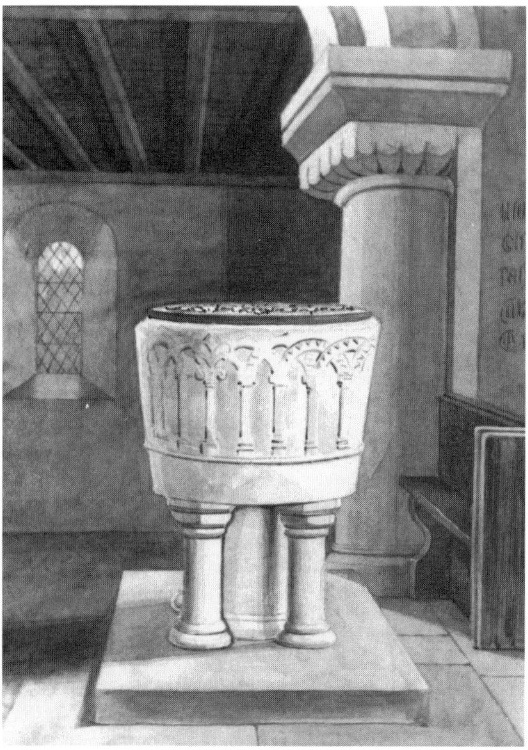

Corfe Church, 1848, by S.G. Tovey

Corston

52/21 All Saints 3 February, 1872

The church has nave, to which a new north aisle has lately been added, chancel, north porch and west tower. The chancel has, on the north and south, some single lancets with trefoil heads. There is also a piscina on the south side of the chancel and a trefoil-headed recess in the east wall. The arcade of the nave is new and in Early English character with 3 pointed arches rising from circular columns with capitals. The chancel arch is a new one upon circular shafts with square abaci and capitals of foliage. The font is new. The tower is late Perpendicular or debased; its west window of the lattice [type]. It carries a short stone spire of octagonal form.

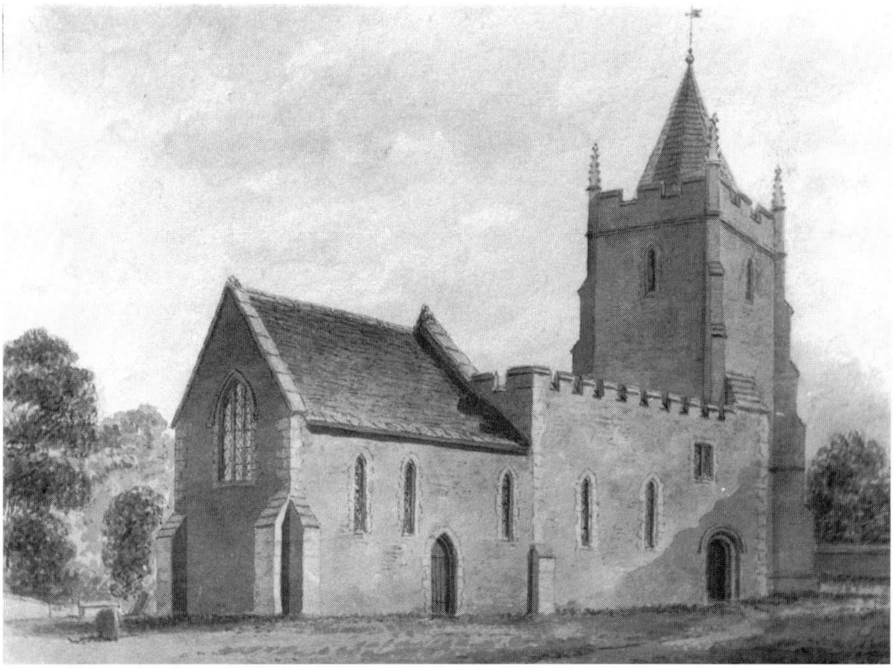

North east view of Corston Church, 1847, by J. Buckler

Cossington

51/85–86 St. Mary 17 November, 1868

A neat church, consisting of nave and chancel without aisles, south porch and west tower. The porch has the outer doorway with continuous arch mouldings. The roofs are as usual, coved and panelled with ribs and bosses. The chancel arch is pointed and from foliaged corbels. The windows of the nave,

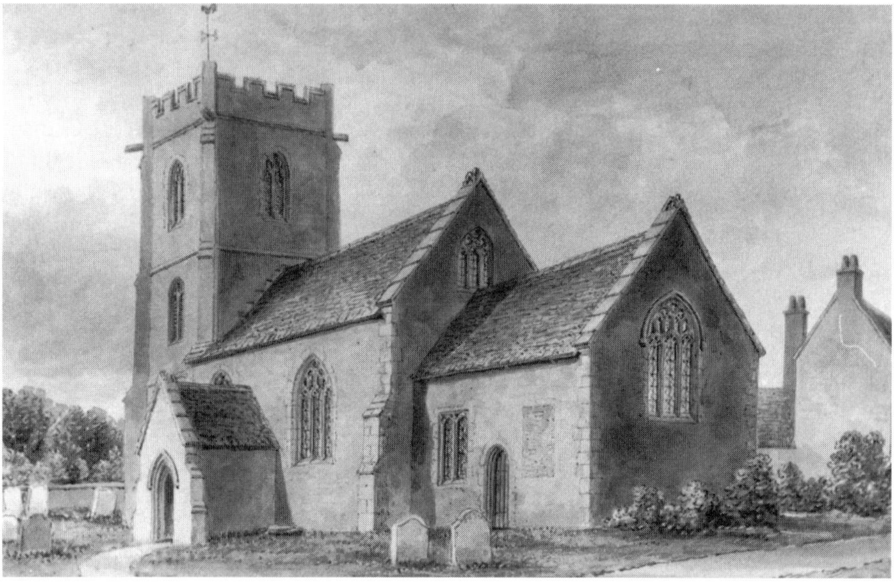

South east view of Cossington Church, 1839, by J. Buckler

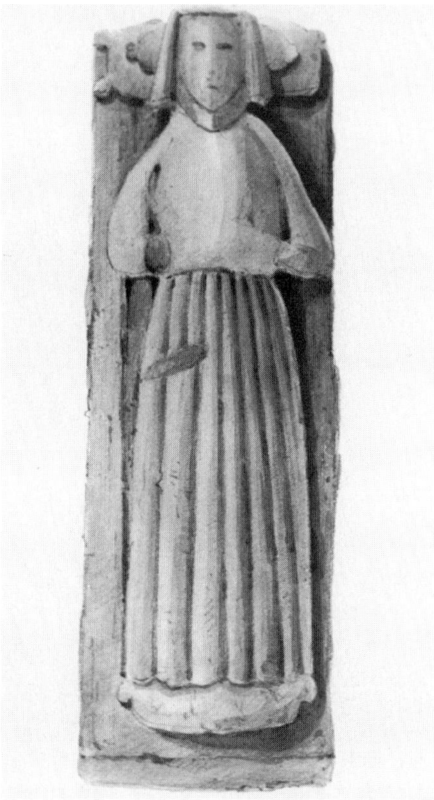

Claricia de la Ford, lately discovered, Cossington, 1851, by W.W. Wheatley

Perpendicular of 3 lights. In the chancel, the east window is similar. On the south are windows of 2 lancet lights, doubtful if original.

The tower is Perpendicular, embattled and divided into 2 stages. The buttresses at the angles are shallow; at the north-east is an octagonal turret. The west doorway is good; has foliage in the spandrels and label on corbels. At the apex is a figure of an angel bearing a shield. Above is a 3 light window; the belfry windows of 2 lights. Over the chancel arch in the gable, is a 3 light, Perpendicular window and one buttress on the north has panelling. In the chancel is a brass with figures of a man and woman of the 15th century and in the churchyard the effigy of a lady of large size, but much defaced.

Crewkerne

19/69–71 [St. Bartholomew] Before 1840

Crewkerne is a neat and pleasant town, situated in a valley and has a convenient market place in the centre of ye town. The church is a noble structure of most beautiful Perpendicular architecture and built in the form of a cross. It consists of a lofty nave with side aisles, a chancel with a north aisle, a north and south transept and a handsome tower in ye centre, containing a clock and 6 bells. The church itself has a very fine exterior and is much loftier than the other parts of ye church.

The windows are mostly of large size; the great western one is of 7 lights and

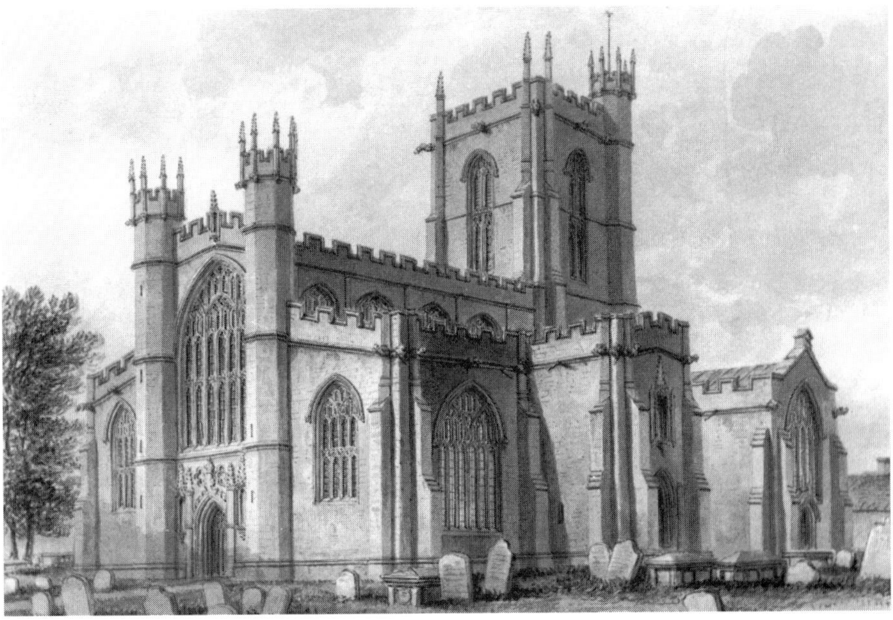

South west view of Crewkerne Church, 1831, by J. Buckler

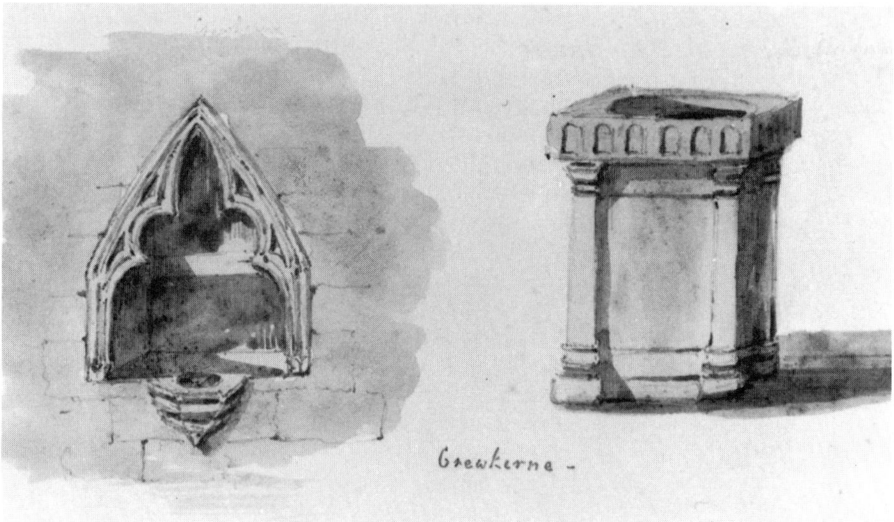

Crewkerne, by W.F. Elliot

many of the others are of 6 lights; that in the north transept has some good panelling over its head. There is a band of quatrefoils running under ye windows and ye greater part of ye church has an embattled parapet. The tower is simple but elegant; has a staircase turret on one side and is crowned by 8 crocketed pinnacles. The south porch has a niche over the doorway. The west front of the nave is flanked by 2 octagonal turrets and has a very fine doorway, enriched with a band of square flowers and a rich, crocketed ogee canopy flanked on each side, by 2 small buttresses ending in crocketed pinnacles. Above each of these pinnacles is a rich niche containing a statue and ye whole has a very fine effect.

Some of the doors of the church are fine specimens of carved woodwork and are enriched with elegant, Perpendicular tracery. The interior of the nave is very fine from its loftiness and lightness. The ceiling is of recent workmanship, and plaster, very beautifully worked. The clerestory windows are of Perpendicular work and have between each of them, a figure in stone. The arches which divide the nave from the aisles, are high and of pointed form with architrave mouldings and spring from piers of lozenge form, having shafts at the angles and the intermediate spaces fitted with plain mouldings.

The nave is very handsomely pewed, has a fine pulpit and a good organ at the west end. The tower is supported by 4 pointed arches with piers of clustered shafts. It was intended to form a stone groined ceiling under ye tower and the beginning of the groins may be seen but they have not been finished. The north aisle runs past ye tower and is continued along ye chancel, but not quite to ye east end. The chancel is divided from this aisle by arches of Tudor form. The north transept has a fine old wood roof and there is a small chapel on its east side.

At the east end of the chancel, on either side of the altar, is a doorway of Tudor form with the spandrels enriched with carved figures. These formerly led to a small chapel, now destroyed, which was probably used as a penitentiary. Chapels of the same description may be seen in Ilminster and Langport churches. On the south side of the altar, is a feathered niche and water drain, and in ye same wall a brass bearing the date 1525 with a black letter inscription and the popish part of the inscription cut out; this is a rare instance.

The font appears to be of Norman character. It is of square form moulded with rude semi-circular arches and supported upon a circular shaft at each corner. Much praise is due to the parishioners for the care they have taken in improving and restoring this beautiful church.

(The nave arcades are of 3 Tudor shaped arches which are unusually wide. The chancel is very low in proportion to the rest. The windows are generally very large. In the north transept is one which has its arch nearly round. In the south transept the east wall has indications of earlier work and there is a piscina at the south-east.)

Dimensions of Crewkerne Church

	Feet		Feet
Length of nave	59	Length of transept	100
Area of tower	17	Breadth of nave with aisles	59
Chancel	48	Breadth of chancel	20–9
Whole length	124	Breadth of aisle of chancel	16–9

Croscombe

49/49–50 St. Mary 1842

This is a handsome church, in high preservation and consisting of a nave and chancel, each with side aisles, and a tower crowned by a stone spire at the west end. The tower has a panelled battlement, the central piece of which, on each side, is crowned by a niche. At each angle is a crocketed pinnacle set diamond wise. The spire has a band of panelling, but does not rise beyond 108 feet in height. The steeple is clearly Rectilinear. There is a south porch with a panelled parapet not rising into a gable, with a doorway having mouldings and shafts which appear to be Decorated. The exterior is chiefly Rectilinear in its character. The clerestory and chancel are embattled and the eastern portion enriched with pinnacles. The aisles have fine panelled parapets.

The interior has a very rich appearance from the quantity of carved work with which it is adorned, it being full of screens and sculptured bench ends. There are 3 pointed arches on each side of the nave and 2 in the chancel, all of which seem to be of Decorated character, the piers formed of clustered shafts, 4 large and 4 smaller. The roof of the nave is coved, divided by ribs into square compartments with rich bosses of foliage. The windows throughout the

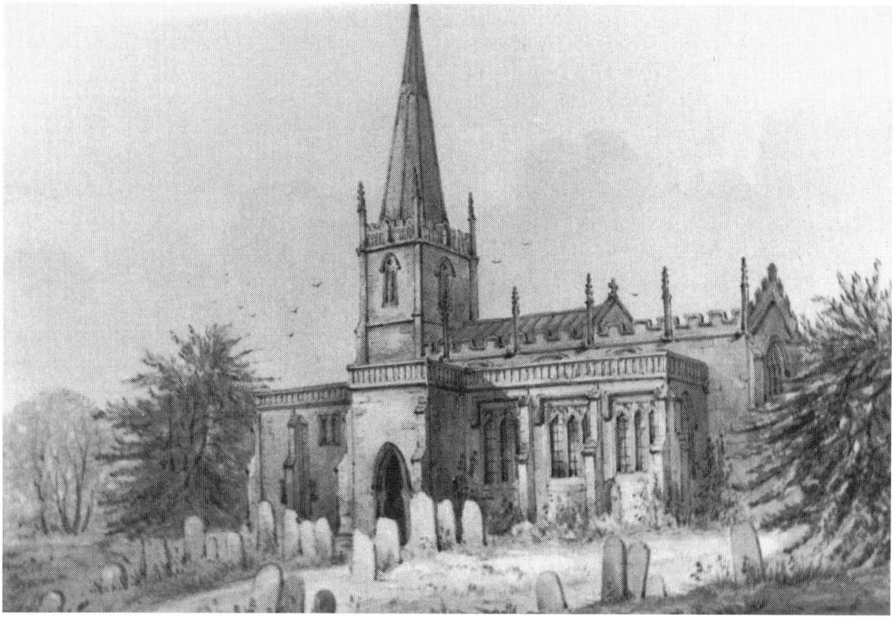

South east view of Croscombe Church, ? 1844, by W.W. Wheatley

church are Rectilinear, those at the east of the chancel and the south aisle are of 5 lights. Most of the others are square-headed. The clerestory is continued over the arches both of the nave and of the chancel.

The chancel arch rises upon brackets. The side aisles are continuous without divisions, but the chancel extends eastward of them and there is a vestry on the north. The roof of the chancel differs from that of the nave and is high pitched with pierced panelling above the tie-beams. The nave is fitted up with open seats, the ends of which display a variety of rich wood carving. Some are ancient and of good design; others are modern imitations and some of the period of James I: though on a minute examination there appears to be much mixture, the general effect is fine. At the entrance to the chancel, a large open screen runs across the church and there are others enclosing the chancel of the date 1616: the design incongruous yet tending to produce a fine *coup d'oeil*. The colour is very dark and the whole is sculptured in Arabesque patterns and adorned with armorial bearings, amongst which appear those of Fortescue; also with scripture texts.

The pulpit is in the same style. The arrangement of the seats in the chancel, is particularly happy. There are fragments of stained glass in the east window. The vestry has a curious stone vaulted roof with strong arched ribs and small, narrow window. There is an octagonal chapel on the north side, with a door for the steps to the roodloft. The font is a plain octagon. In a western gallery is a handsome organ. The churchyard is planted with evergreens. The village, or town, is very picturesque in its situation and contains several fine specimens of domestic architecture.

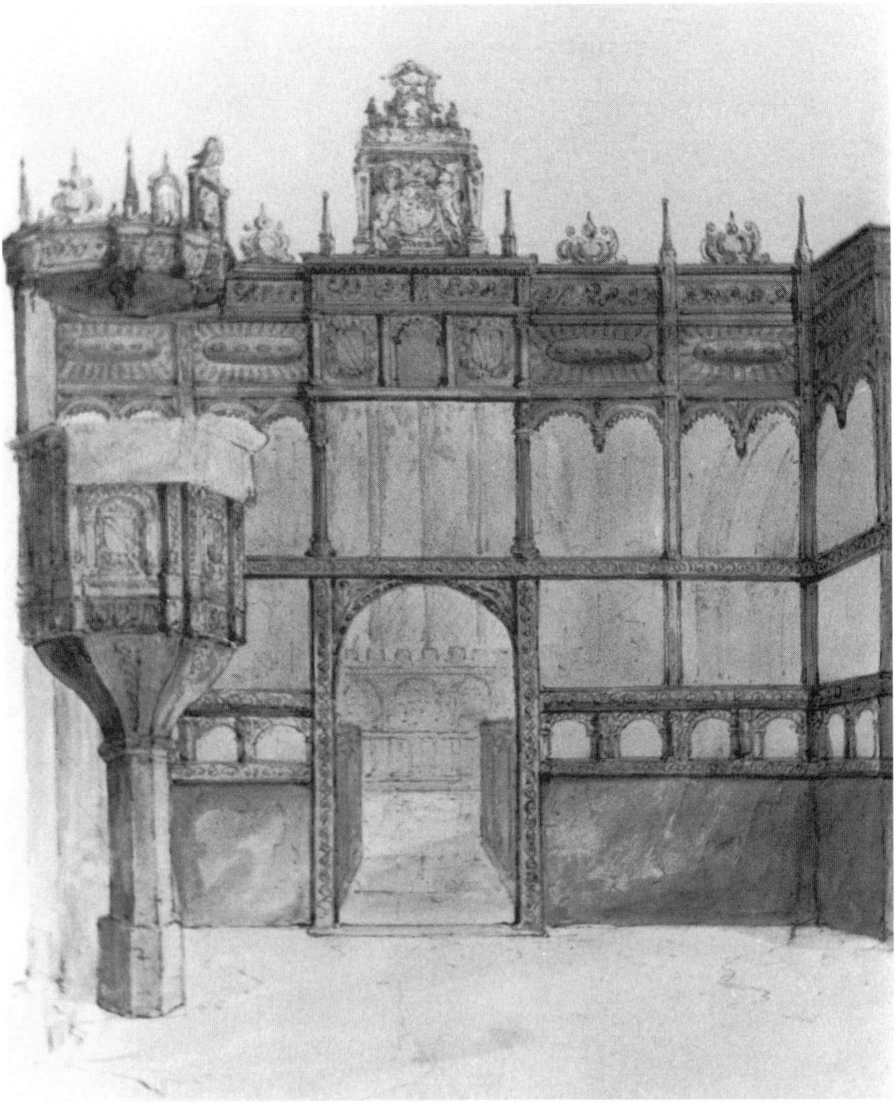

Croscombe Church, 1844, by W.W. Wheatley

Crowcombe

49/72–74 [Holy Cross] 1843

This church is in a delightful situation on a slope, shaded by fine trees, adjoining the grounds of the mansion house. It is a Perpendicular structure consisting of a west tower, a nave, chancel, south aisle, north transept and a very fine, south porch. There is much of the usual Somersetshire character.

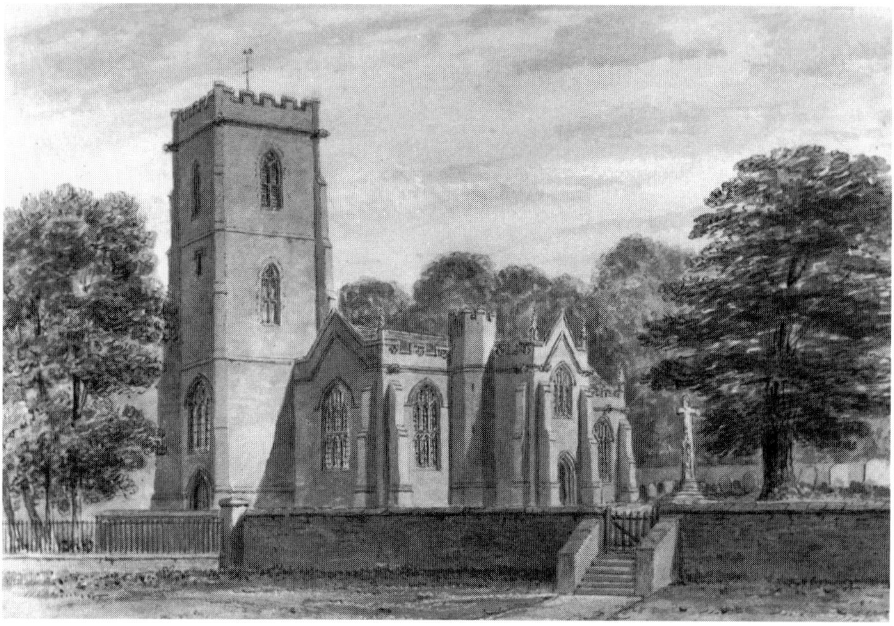

South west view of Crowcombe Church, 1842, by J. Buckler

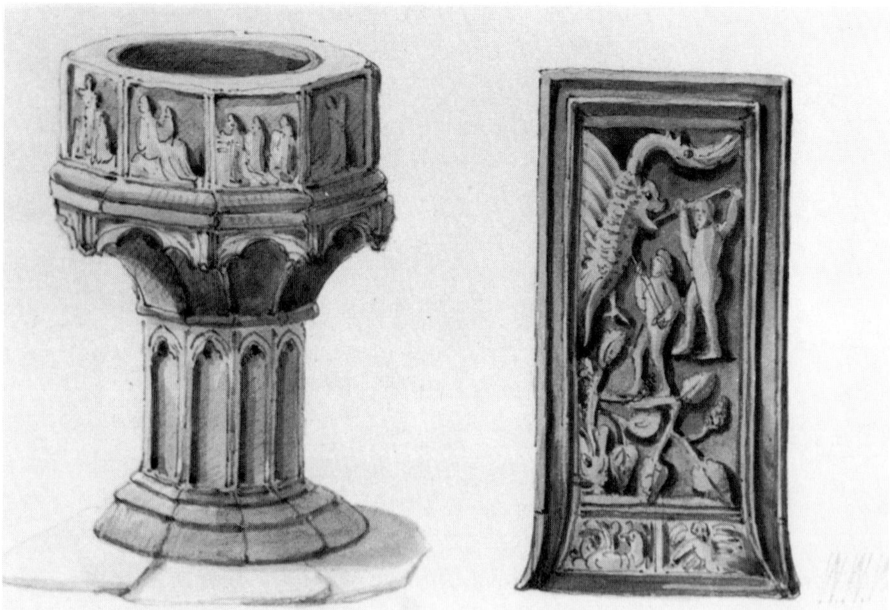

In Crowcombe Church, 1850, by W.W. Wheatley

The south aisle has a rich battlement, panelled with quatrefoils containing shields, and also crocketed pinnacles. The southern windows are large and fine, of 3 lights with transoms. The south porch is large, having a gable, flanked by pinnacles and a parvise in the upper part. There is, in the north-west angle of the porch, an octagonal embattled stair turret. The ceiling is beautifully groined in stone with a pendant. The parvise has a 3 light window, the arches of the doorways resembling those of Bishop's Lydeard.

The tower is embattled and has a large turret on the north side, which is square in its lower part and octagonal above, terminating in a small pinnacle. The belfry window is of 2 lights with transom. The tower is of 3 stages in height, has angular buttresses and no pinnacles. On the west side a 3 light window and plain doorway. The tower and nave are of good red stone, the chancel stuccoed and the north side is much plainer than the south. The north transept has square-headed windows. The interior is solemn, the nave divided from the aisle by 5 good pointed arches with mouldings and piers like those of Wellington, the capitals of the shafts being gilt.

The chancel arch is wide, rising from cluster shafts. The aisle is continued one arch beyond the chancel arch. The transept opens to the nave by a pointed arch on clustered shafts with foliated capitals. There are several open benches with carved ends which present very elegant tracery and sculpture. On one is the date 1533. There is a later screen at the entrance to the chancel and within its south aisle, apparently temp. Elizabeth. The east window is a good one of 4 lights. The font is an octagonal one with ordinary panelling. In the churchyard is a fine stone cross on 3 octagonal steps with a canopied niche containing the image of a Bishop. The village is beautifully situated and all built of stone.

Culbone

51/2–3 St. Culbone 9 May, 1855

A very small church, among the smallest in England and further remarkable for its very beautiful and sequestered situation amidst the woods of Lord Lovelace, but commanding a sea view down a beautiful combe.

It comprises merely chancel and nave and the architectural features are plain and rude. There is a plain pointed chancel arch. There are Perpendicular windows with square heads, of 2 lights, and one at the east end of 3, the light merely trefoiled. South of the chancel is a sort of oblong window and on the north 2 obtuse headed lights. The roof is coved and ribbed. There is part of the roodscreen remaining and the upper part of the arch closed. In the north wall is a small recess. The font has a circular bowl upon a banded stem. Some very rude open benches remain. There is a south porch. At the west end no window but a pointed bell turret slated. In the churchyard is the base of a cross with high steps.

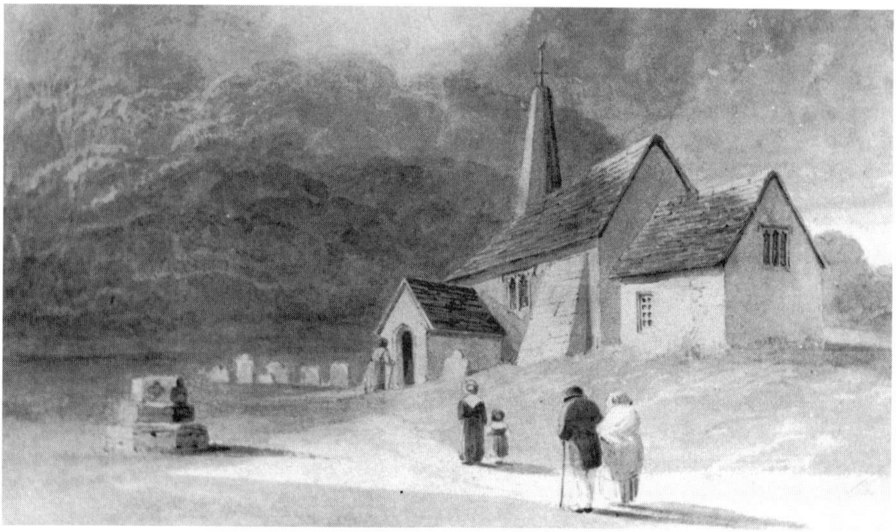

Culbone, by S.G. Tovey

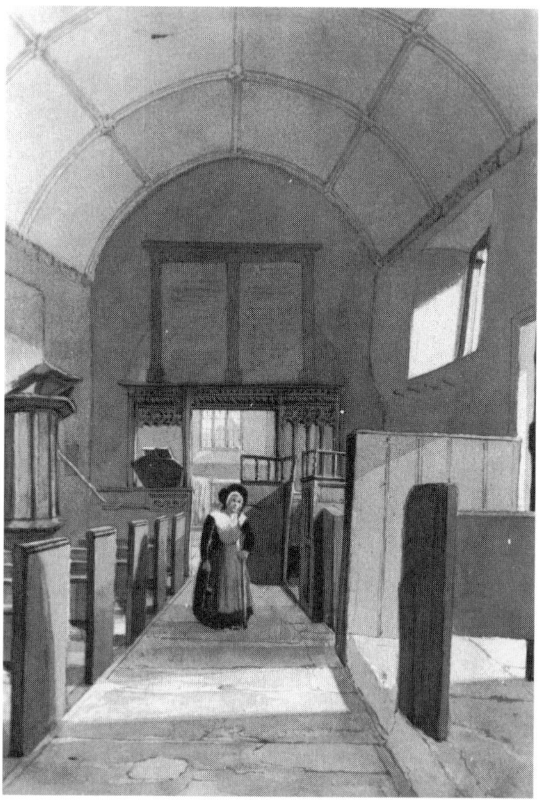

Culbone, by S.G. Tovey

Curry Mallet

50/96 All Saints 13 February, 1857

This church seems to be wholly Perpendicular and has a nave with north aisle, a south transeptal chapel, chancel and western tower and south porch.

The chancel seems to have been rebuilt and has poor windows. The arcade on the north of the nave has 3 arches with the usual Perpendicular, clustered piers with moulded capitals. The chancel arch is panelled. The arch opening into the south transept is a rich one, of obtruse and rather late form, but finely panelled. This chapel has a panelled roof and there is the trace of an altar on its east side. All the windows are of 3 lights, of fair Perpendicular character. Some have been rather mutilated; in others are pieces of stained glass. The porch is of a shed-like form, adjoining the west side of the transept into which a door from it opens. The nave has a leaded roof.

The font is Perpendicular, the bowl octagonal and panelled with quatrefoils containing shields; the stem panelled. The tower is a good one of 3 stages with a battlement and an octagonal turret at the north-east, which is embattled and panelled at the top. The west doorway [moulding] is continuous, over it a window of 4 lights. The belfry windows are of 2 lights with the pierced stone lattice work often seen in the towers of this county.

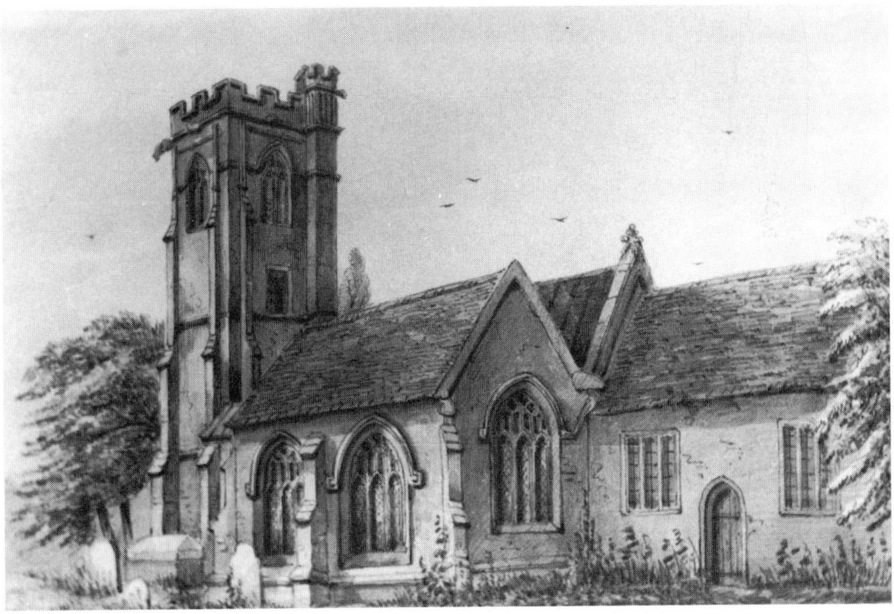

Curry Mallet, 1850, by W.W. Wheatley

Curry Rivel

49/29–30 [St. Andrew] 1839

A fine, spacious church, consisting of a handsome west tower, a nave with side aisles and a chancel with side chapels; the whole, save a small portion, is good Rectilinear. The tower, lofty with a fine battlement and unfinished pinnacles (stair turret on north); large belfry windows with transoms and over that, on the south side, a canopied niche containing a statue. The west doorway is fine: the arch Tudor, with panelled spandrels and fine mouldings and clustered shafts. There is also, on the west side, a panelled band.

The whole of the church has a rich battlement, the north side, contrary to custom, being equally well finished with the south. The windows are large, chiefly of 4 lights with transoms and set very closely. The south porch is of 2 stories with a groined ceiling and a window of 3 lights to the upper chamber below which is a rich band of quatrefoils, intermixed with the portcullis, the rose, etc. The corbel table has figures of animals. Near the outer door is a stoup. There is no clerestory. The nave has, on each side, 4 elegantly formed arches, the piers of the usual Rectilinear form, the shafts being large.

The side aisles have good, panelled ceilings of wood. Across the body and aisles, on entering the chancel, is an elegant wood screen with band of vine leaves. The chancel opens to its side chapel by one wide arch. In this portion, the windows are without transoms and there is a small, trefoiled niche. To the north chapel, the chancel opens by 2 arches resembling those of the nave. The

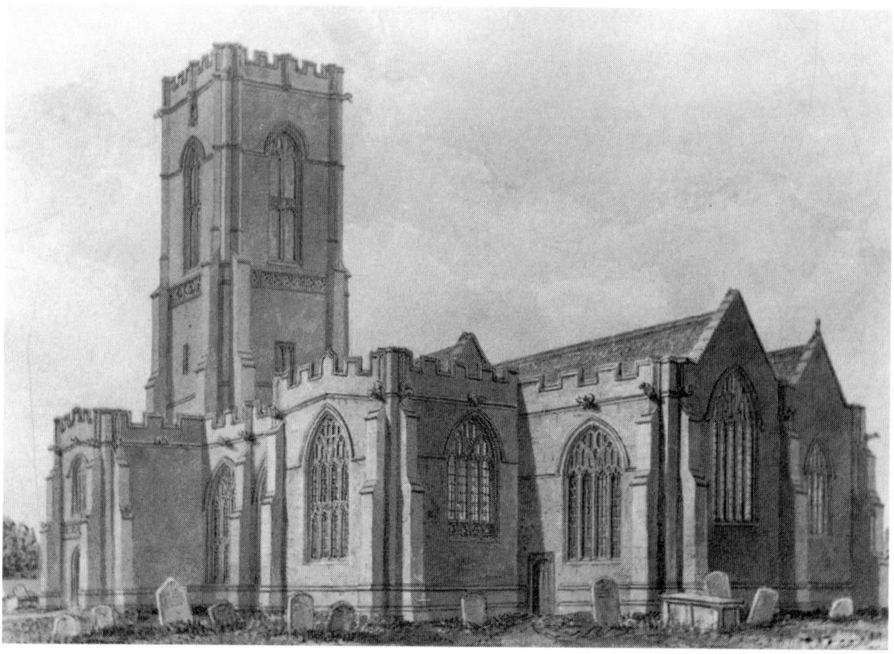

South east view of Curry Rivel Church, 1830, by J. Buckler

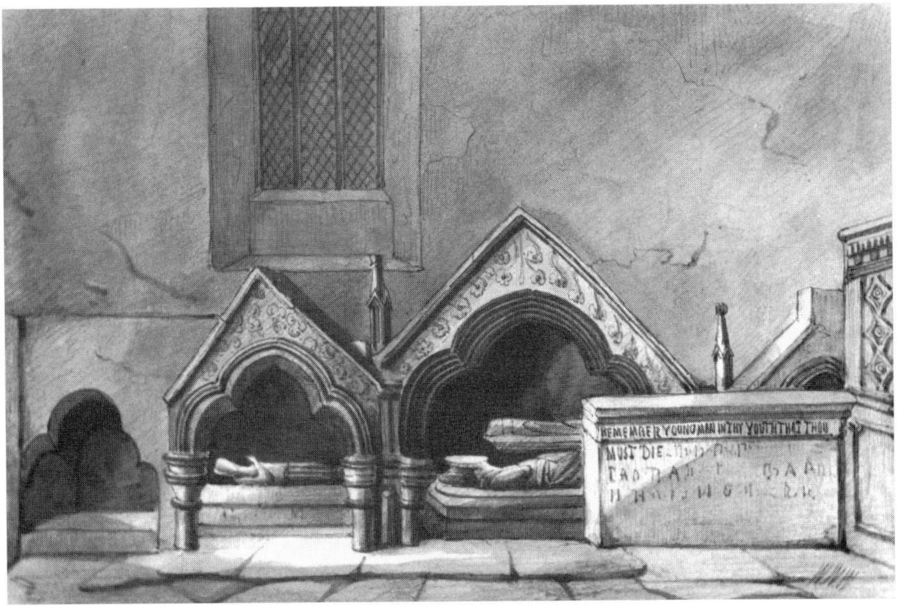

In Curry Rivel Church, north chantry, 1850, by W.W. Wheatley

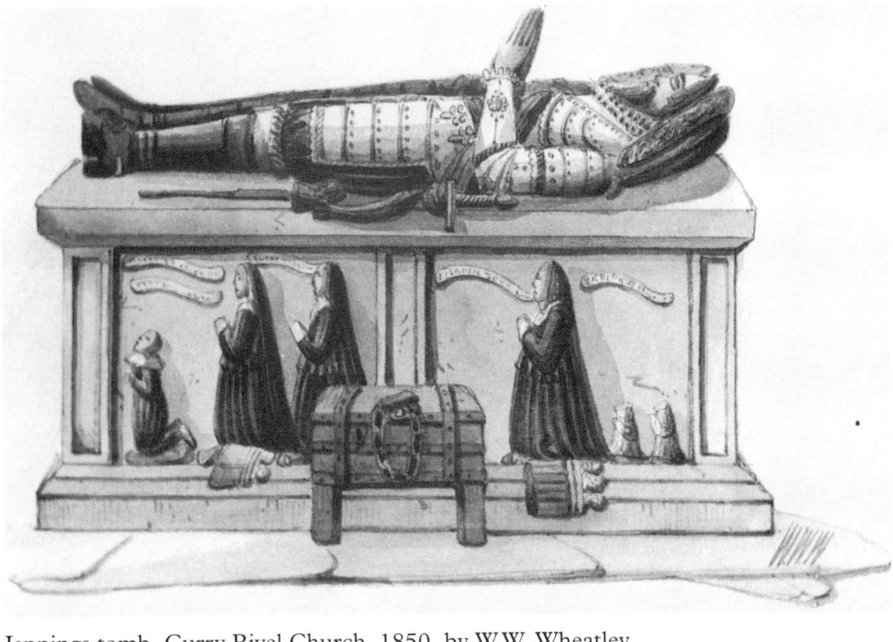

Jennings tomb, Curry Rivel Church, 1850, by W.W. Wheatley

north chapel is of Decorated character, at least was so originally. Its east window has had Rectilinear tracery inserted, but the arch moulding within, has the ballflower and rises upon shafts in the capitals of which is seen the nail head ornament so that the character is early. Near it is the large pedestal of a niche.

The north windows are also Decorated in their mouldings and the arch in the interior, has cusps as at Butleigh, but Rectilinear tracery is inserted. On the south side of the east end of this arch is a fine cinquefoiled niche with the shelf and piscina having elegant mouldings and shafts and surmounted by a triangular, crocketed canopy.

In the north wall are several arches for tombs of decidedly early Decorated work, with feathering and triangular pediments and otherwise enriched with foliage of very excellent character. One of small size rises upon shafts and has the pediments, crocketed, and within it *a monumental effigy of very small size.* Another of these tomb arches is unluckily hidden by an ugly modern monument to Peter Jennings Esqr. Within one of the arches opening to the chancel is a large monument, temp. 1680, to some of the Jennings family with numerous figures and some representing children in swaddling clothes as lying dead outside the monument. The chancel has a coved roof, ribbed in squares.

The font is octagonal and panelled. There are several, ancient carved ends of seats, some with open work and there is a good deal of fine, ancient, stained glass. There is an altar picture representing the Entombment.

Cutcombe

51/7–8 St. John 8 May, 1855

A plain church with chancel and nave undivided, north aisle to both, west tower, (also south porch), chiefly Perpendicular but with some rough, plain portions which may be of any age. The windows are of 3 lights on the south and sometimes of 2. The arcade is of 3 very rude, pointed arches, of which the eastern is tallest, with plain, narrow piers having no capitals, but the mouldings continued down them. In the chancel are 2 small pointed arches, lower than the others, having clustered piers with octagonal capitals.

The east window has modern, stained glass; the chancel and aisle have modern ceilings, the nave [a] coved roof with ribs and bosses. There is a pointed arch across the aisle, dividing its eastern from the western part. There are some very high pues in the chancel and the interior is glaring with whitewash. In a west gallery, a barrel organ. The tower arch is quite plain without mouldings. The font is attached to a pier and is of early character, the bowl, square upon a cylindrical stem and 4 shafts set upon a square base.

The tower is plain, with small buttresses (to the lower part only) and an embattled parapet. On the east face the central piece of battlement is graduated. The belfry windows, square and small, marked by louvre boards. On the west side, a window of 2 cinquefoiled lights and a door.

The walls are all externally covered with rough cast. The east end seems to be new. The chancel extends a little beyond the aisle.

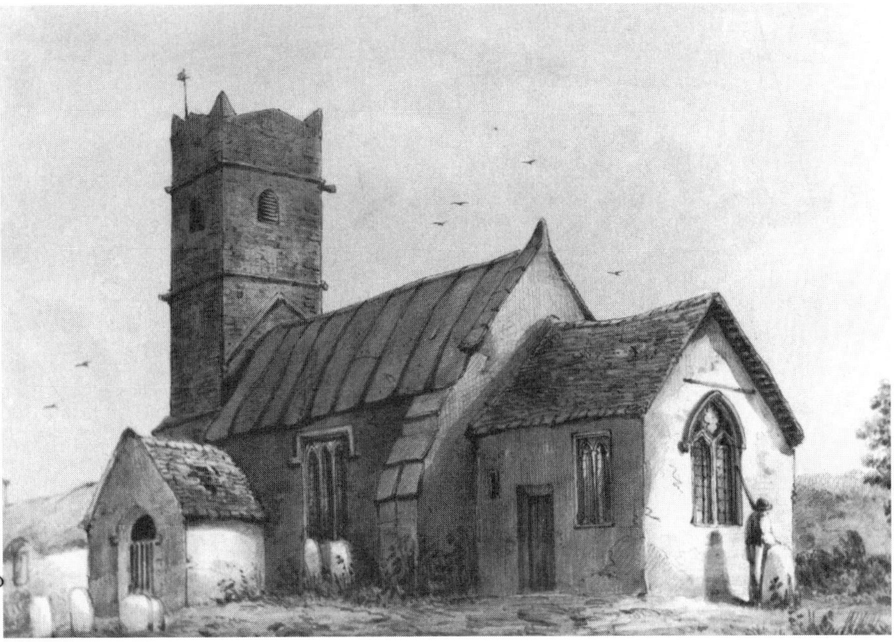

Cutcombe, 1849, by W.W. Wheatley

Dinder

49/50–51 St. Michael Before 1840

This is a small church, consisting of a nave with north aisle and a chancel, with a tower 60 feet high at the west end, which is of fine, grey stone with a battlement and octagonal turret on the north side, and belfry windows on the north side, adorned with stone lattice work in pierced lozenges. The whole is Rectilinear and the west window of 3 lights. The nave has a panelled battlement and pinnacles to the gable. The chancel has a high, pitched, leaded roof with a cross at the apex of the gable. The aisle is low and plain externally. The whole church is of Rectilinear character, except a few early indications in the chancel.

The interior is particularly neat and light and has been lately fitted up with some taste. The nave is separated from the aisle by 3 pointed arches with the usual Rectilinear piers of this county; above the piers are some enriched corbels. The tower arch is open and within it is placed the gallery, a far better arrangement than when it intrudes upon the nave, destroying its appearance and contracting the space. Many of the windows are square-headed. The chancel arch is acute. Two side windows appear to be of plain, early Decorated character. There is also a plain niche south of the altar with shelf and piscina.

Another window in the chancel is a trefoiled, single light in a square and on each side, above the windows, is a singular piece of sculpture, apparently Early English, a kind of spiral band ending upon it. There is a small vestry on the

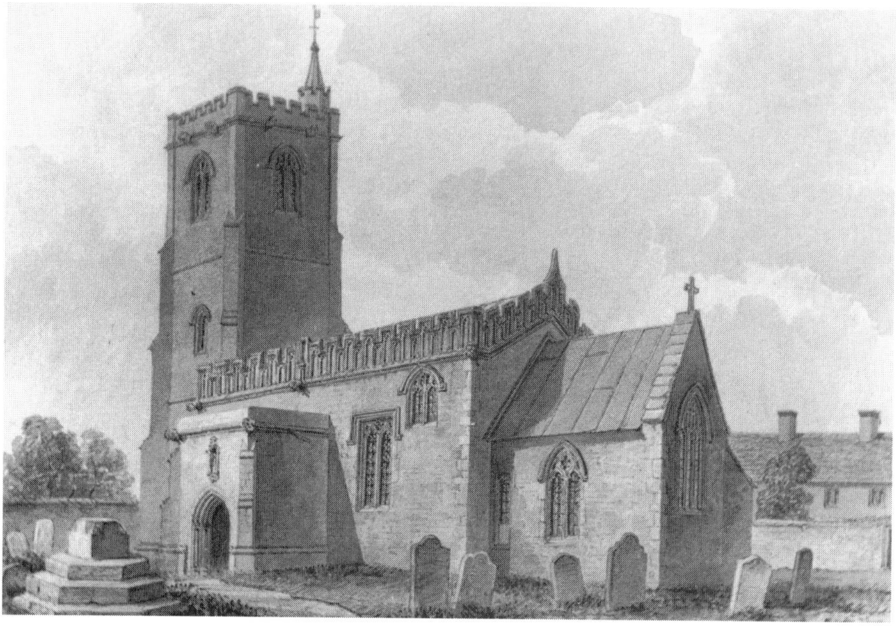

South east view of Dinder Church, 1833, by J. Buckler

north side. The east window is Rectilinear of 3 lights containing some stained glass with figures of saints and inscriptions.

The pulpit is of stone but of debased character with arabesque and other ugly ornaments bearing date 1621. The south porch has a panelled ceiling and the arch of the outer door, upon shafts. The font is octagonal with quatrefoils. In the pretty, sequestered churchyard, is the shaft of a cross upon steps. The village has many neat buildings in stone.

Ditcheat

49/23–24 St. Mary 1835, revisited 1855

This is a handsome, spacious cruciform church with a tower, rising from the centre. The whole has a fine stone battlement with buttresses crowned by crocketed pinnacles. The windows are chiefly of 3 lights, those at the extremities in the transepts of 4. The north side is, as frequently, rather less enriched than the south but the whole is handsome. The nave has a clerestory and is divided from each aisle by a range of well-formed pointed arches on light, clustered piers. The tower has an octagonal turret at the north-west angle and 4 corner pinnacles. On its west side are two canopied niches in one of which is the Virgin Mary on a pedestal. The west window has a label on corbels of grotesque heads, one with the tongue out.

The church is of Rectilinear period, save the chancel, in which are two tiers

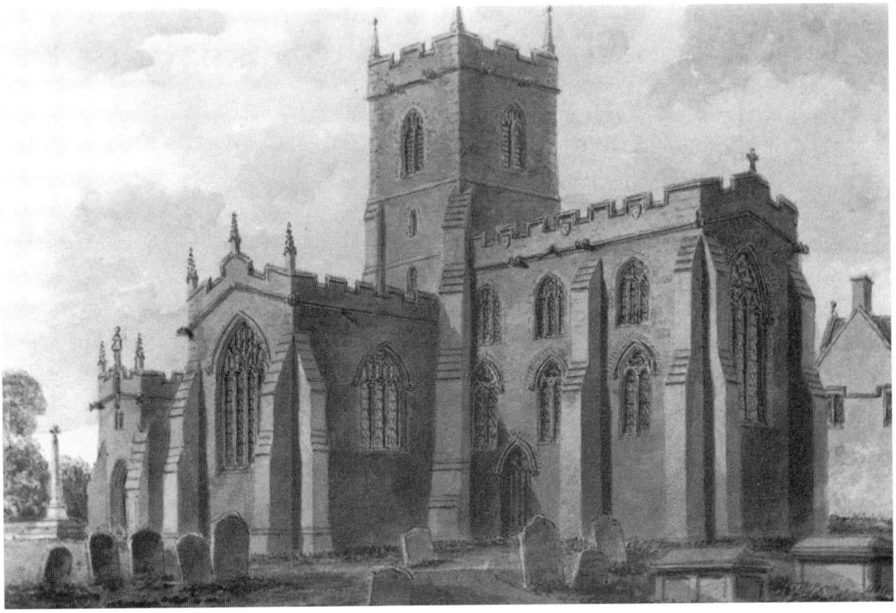

South east view of Ditcheat Church, 1844, by J. Buckler

of windows, the lower being Curvilinear of 2 lights and the eastern one of 3 lights of like character with a spherical triangle in the tracery of the upper part. These windows internally, present trefoil feathering in the arch as at Butleigh. Beneath the window is a string course and there is a small doorway with feathered arch. There is a large south porch of two storeys. Near the church is a fine manor house of stone temp. James I.

1855

The nave has aisles but not the chancel; the whole Perpendicular, except the chancel which is Decorated. The arcades of the nave of good, Western Perpendicular character. The roof of the nave is good with tracery over the beams and the beams foliated with angel figures carrying emblems of the Passion, etc., supporting the brackets, all in fine preservation. The south transept roof resembles that of the nave, and the north transept very similar. The tower rises on 4 large, plain pointed arches with continuous mouldings which may be earlier.

The nave has a clerestory; the piers have stilted bases. There is a hagioscope on each side of the chancel. The eastern part of the roof of the nave is panelled more intricately than the rest. The eastern window of the north clerestory has been altered with a late debased form. The tower has a good, groined stone roof open to the interior.

There is a curious post-Reformation screen between the nave and chancel having round arches and double doors. The chancel has been fitted with wainscotting and stalls of the same date and has a ceiled roof. The lower windows of the chancel all Decorated, on both sides of 2 lights, at the east end of 3 (arch and foil). Above them, a clerestory of 3 light Perpendicular windows. The pulpit and desk, Jacobean. The Decorated windows have feathering to the rear arch as often seen in early Decorated work in Somesetshire.

In the south aisle is an ogee cinquefoiled piscina. The font has a plain, octagonal bowl on stem of like form. The organ in the north transept. The west door is good; [the moulding] is continuous, the hood has corbels of mitred and crowned heads. The west window of 3 lights. There is an entrance on the north of the steeple by a staircase.

This is a handsome, dignified church.

Doulting

19/77–78 [St. Aldhelm] Before 1840

Doulting is a village 2 miles from Shepton Mallet on the Frome road. The church is a very elegant structure in the form of a cross, consisting of nave, chancel and transepts. From the middle, rises an octagonal tower crowned by a neat stone spire. The nave and chancel have a plain parapet. The south transept has a bold and handsome parapet and the north transept a beautiful, pierced parapet of quatrefoils enriched with crocketed pinnacles. The tower has some handsome belfry windows with lattice work.

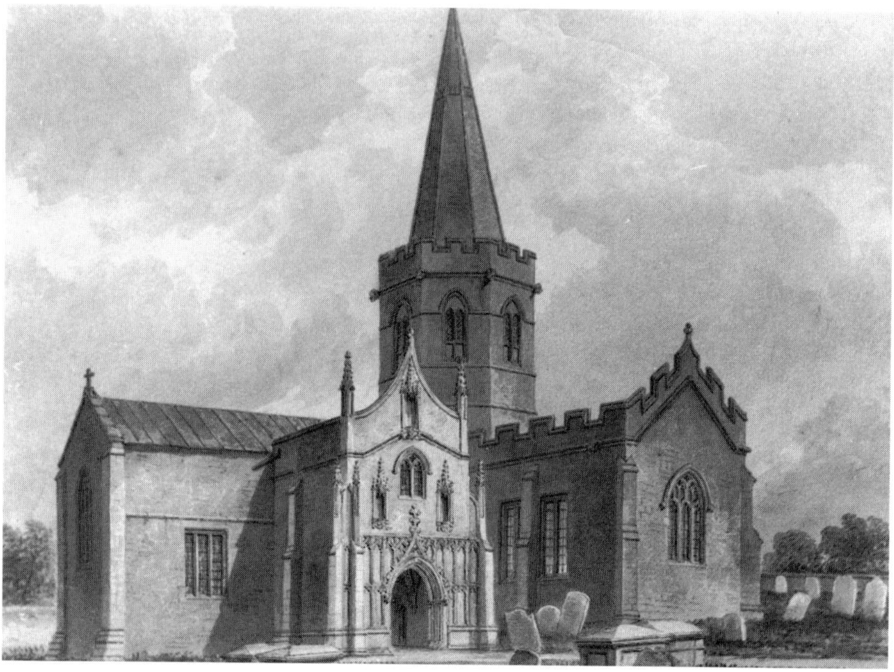

South west view of Doulting Church, 1833, by J. Buckler

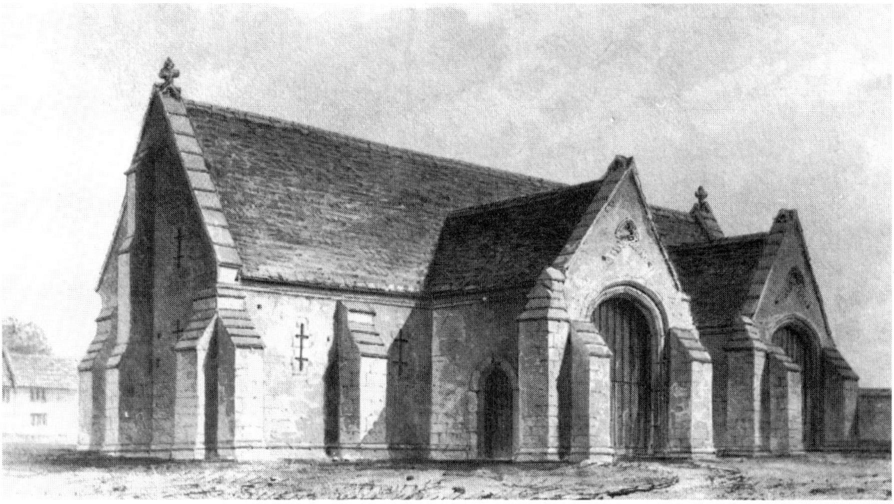

Doulting Barn, 1833, by J. Buckler

The nave has 2 very fine porches. The southern one very rich and forming one of the finest specimens of a Rectilinear porch that can be met with. The outer doorway is beneath an elegant ogee canopy with crockets and finial and the spaces on each side of the doorway, are enriched with very elegant panelling. Over the door are 2 fine large niches with very rich, crocketed canopies. In the gable of the porch is another niche, equally fine. The buttresses are crowned with rich, crocketed pinnacles which have a very fine effect. The ceiling within, is of stone, richly groined with pendants.

The north porch is less rich; has a Tudor doorway with niche over it. The inner doorway is of singular form being a wide obtruse arch, springing from shafts with Norman capitals. Over it is a rude niche. The interior is very neat. The arches supporting the tower are high and bold, pointed and springing from clustered shafts, some having plain, round capitals, some early Gothic, foliated, and some Norman. Under the tower is a stone ceiling with plain, cross ribs. The windows are of ordinary Rectilinear tracery.

There is a small chapel on the south side of the chancel, now made into a large pew. The font is very elegant, of Rectilinear design, octagonal form, each side being worked with quatrefoils beneath which is a large band of bold foliage and an octagonal pedestal panelled.

There is, at Doulting, a very ancient barn, much resembling that at Pilton.

Dulverton

49/5–8 All Saints Before 1840

This church is a plain, Rectilinear structure, consisting of a nave, chancel and side aisles and a square tower and a corner turret at the west end of the nave.

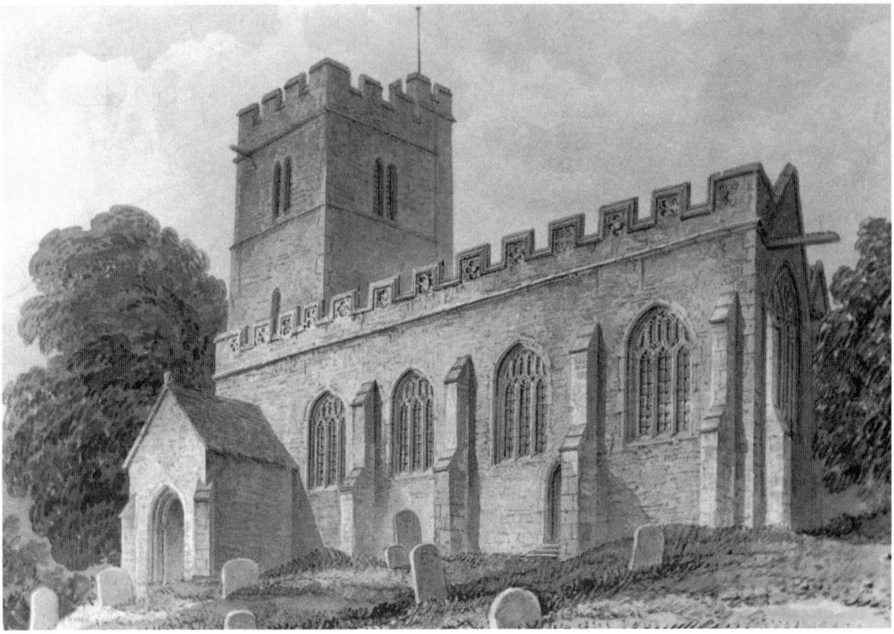

South east view of Dulverton Church, 1833, by J.C. Buckler

There is also a porch on the south side, within which is a doorway having square flowers in its mouldings. The chancel has a panelled battlement. The windows are all of 3 lights, the tracery of a character very common to Somersetshire and Devonshire. There is no clerestory and the nave is divided from each aisle, by 3 pointed arches, the piers formed each of 4 shafts with mouldings down the intervals.

The chancel has, on each side, 2 Tudor arches with similar shafts. Between the nave and chancel is a fine roodscreen with roodloft, richly painted and gilt. In the west gallery is an organ. The exterior walls are covered with stucco as is often the case in the neighbourhood. The situation is pleasing, the churchyard occupying the slope of a steep hill commanding a lovely prospect.

Dundry

50/64–65 St. Michael 15 February, 1853

This church is well-known from its conspicuous situation on the summit of a lofty hill, 4 miles from Bristol. Its tower, too, is of peculiar elegance and an excellent specimen of the enriched type for which Somersetshire is distinguished.

The church consists of chancel, nave and north aisle to each, south porch and west tower. The latter is Perpendicular, but the church has earlier features. The whole of the body and porch of the church has an Early English block

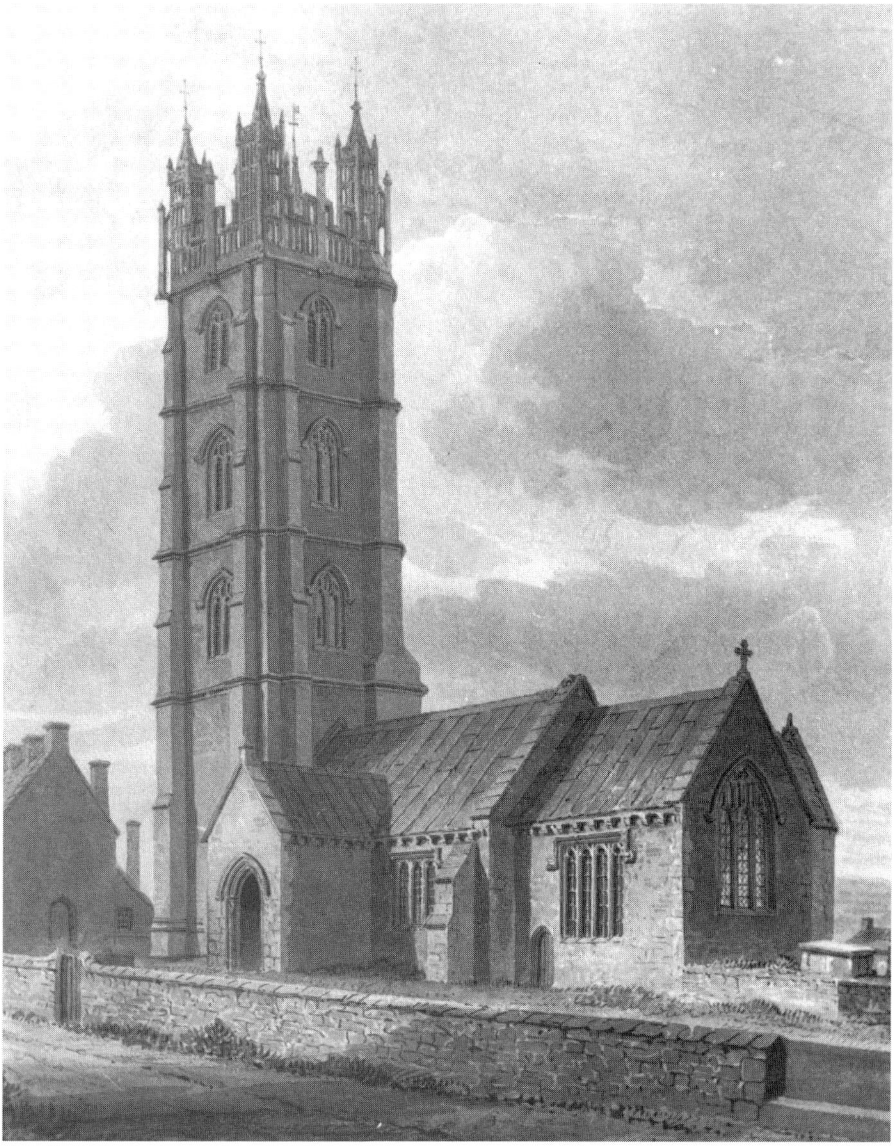

South east view of Dundry Church, 1827, by J. Buckler

corbel table, just beneath the roof. The roofs are steep and leaded, the chancel somewhat lower than the nave. The outer door of the porch is Early English with a cylindrical moulding on horn-shaped corbels. The inner door is Perpendicular with continuous moulding.

There is a trefoil headed lancet at the west end of the aisle and also another on the north. The other windows are chiefly Perpendicular, mostly square-headed, but that at the east of the north aisle, has, to its rear, arch shafts. The

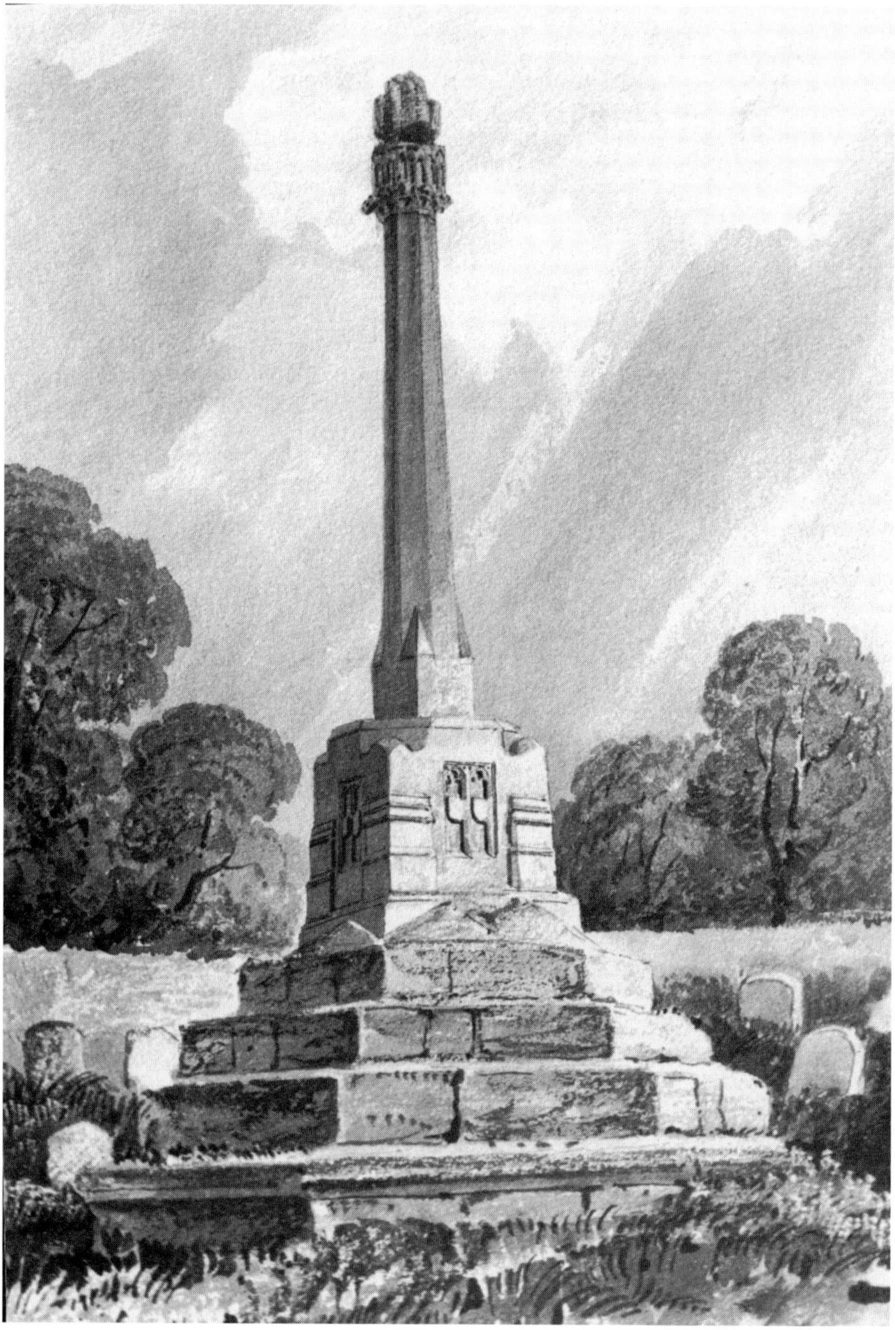

Cross in Dundry churchyard, 1827, by J.C. Buckler

arcade is Early English. In the nave, there are 3 rather low pointed arches with mouldings and circular columns of large size with moulded capitals. The chancel arch is pointed and springs from the capital of the eastern pier of the nave and on the south, straight from the wall. Between the chancel and the north chapel is one arch issuing from Early English shafts attached to the pier and between the north aisle of the nave and the north chancel is another pointed arch.

There is a piscina in the north chapel with trefoiled arch and expending in the wall. The roof of the chancel has good bosses and an enriched cornice. The south window of the chancel has 4 lights, is Perpendicular and has a stone seat below it. The church is pewed and possesses a harmonium. The tower is said to have been erected in 1482 and is something of the same type as Taunton, St. Stephen, Bristol, and others, and certainly ranks high. It has 4 stages, is of excellent masonry with graduated buttresses, not at the angles, and a fine, panelled battlement with large, pierced pinnacles of square form at the angles and smaller diagonal ones in the intermediate spaces. There is an octagonal stair turret at the north-east and in all the stages 2 light windows except the first on the west side, where the window hath 5 lights and below it is a good door with continuous mouldings.

The font is Perpendicular, octagonal and panelled with quatrefoils. In the churchyard is the shaft of a cross adorned with niches and panelling, upon 4 very high steps.

(The roofs are coved and ribbed. On one pier appears a shallow niche. The square, angular turrets have small pinnacles, attached to them by minute flying buttresses.)

Dunster

49/9–11 St. George 1828

This is a very large and handsome church, consisting of a nave with aisles, transepts, a tower rising from the centre and a large chancel with side chapels, almost wholly of Rectilinear character, but with indications of an earlier period. The tower is lofty and embattled, but plain, the pinnacles being broken. The belfry windows are each of 2 lights. In the tower are 8 bells and a clock. There is no clerestory, the aisles are of equal height and the south aisle has an embattled parapet.

The windows are all Rectilinear and mostly of 3 lights. That in the south transept is of 4 lights with a transom and that at [the] west end has a transom and the east window of the chancel is of 5 lights. In the south transept, on each side of the window externally, is a canopied niche. There is a south porch of plain character with a battlement and, about the middle of the south aisle, an octagonal staircase turret.

The western portion comprising the nave and aisles is fitted up neatly for the celebration of divine service being divided from the eastern part entirely by a partition. The eastern portion, including the chancel with its chapels, presents, internally, such an appearance of neglect, dirt and ruin as must be lamented by all who witness it and is highly disgraceful to the representatives of those whose tombs are here, suffered to fall into decay.

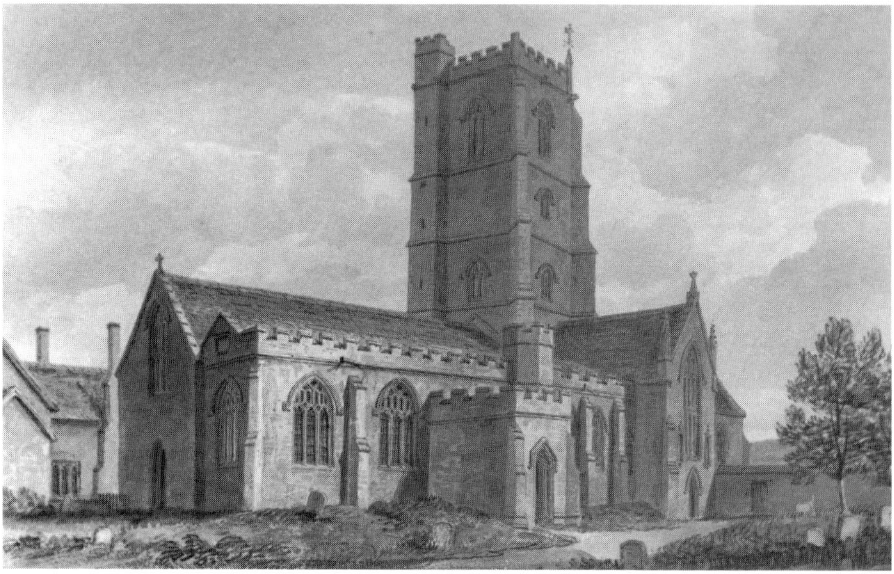

South west view of Dunster Church, 1828, by J. Buckler

The nave is spacious but the north aisle is not continued to the west end. To the south aisle there are 6 pointed arches; to the north only 4; the piers of lozenge form with shafts and mouldings carried down them. The roof of the centre aisle is coved and divided by ribs into panelled compartments. The south aisle has a richer panelled ceiling. At the west end is a large gallery and across the east end of the nave, is a beautiful wood screen with rich tracery, fan groining and cornices of vine leaves and other foliage. Over the altar is a painting of not much merit representing the crucifixion.

The tower is supported upon 4 large, pointed arches with plain piers in the western of which, facing the nave, are shafts with capitals of decidedly Norman character, remnants of an earlier structure.

It is painful to describe the state of the chancel, which is falling rapidly into decay, the ornamental parts much injured and the pavement entirely taken up. The side chapels do not extend to the east end, but open each to the chancel by 2 arches of Tudor form with lozenge piers. Opening from the south chapel to the south transept is an arch of most singular form, the age of which it is very difficult to determine. It is formed into a kind of trefoil shape with good mouldings, the shafts being bent in a most curious manner so as to follow the curve of the mouldings. Within the arches of the chapels are remnants of rich wood screen work.

The tombs in the chancel are chiefly to the Mohun and Luttrell family. In the south wall is a fine, crocketed ogee arch, with a rich finial beneath which is the effigy of a female. Within one of the arches, to the north, is a monumental chapel having a feathered arch and enriched spandrels and containing a tomb with the alabaster figures of a knight and lady of the Mohun family, greatly mutilated.

There are some other memorials to the Luttrells and on a flat stone, is sculptured the figure of a lady under a canopy with this inscription: *orate queso*

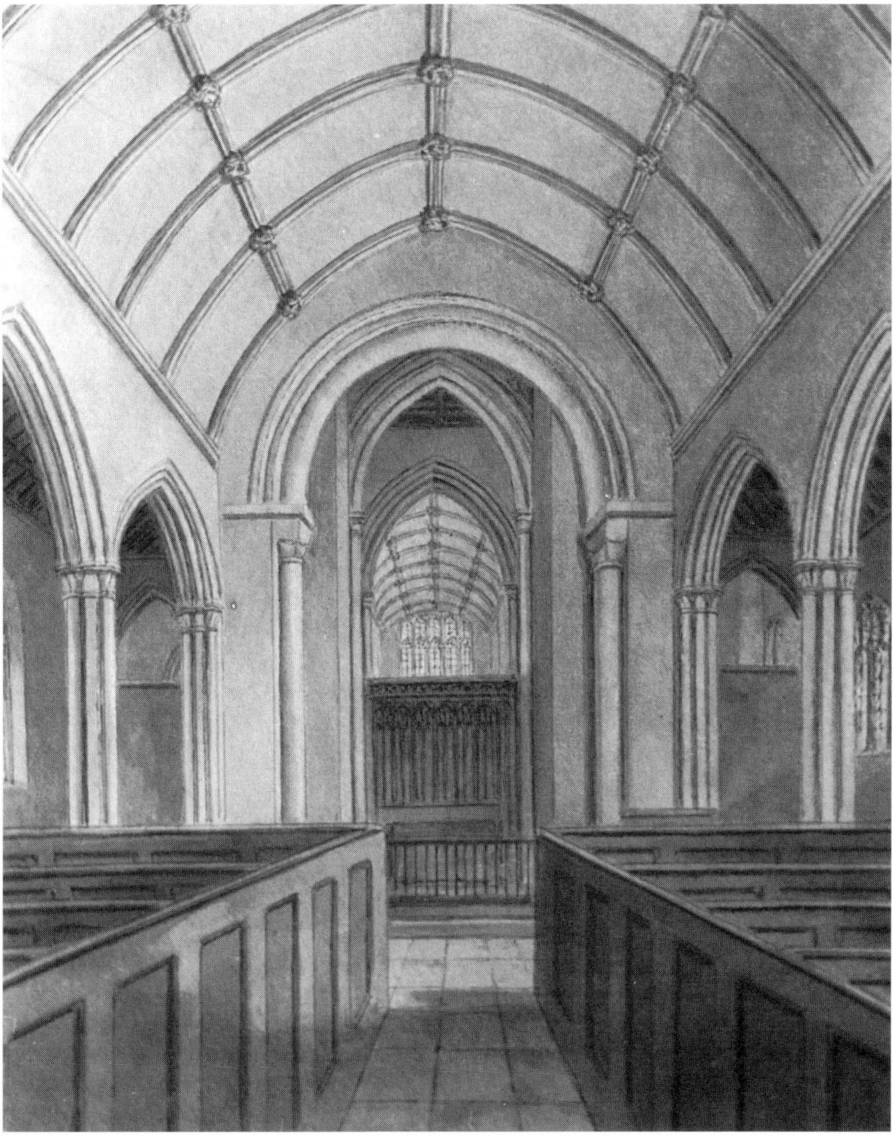

Interior view of Dunster Church, 1842, by J. Buckler

pro ai 'a d'ne Elizabeth Luttrell que obiit primus die mensis Septembris anno d'ni MCCCC nonagesima tertio nunc xpe te petimus miserer qs qui veisti redeme pditos noli dampnare redemptos. This lady was of the Courtenay family. There are some glazed tiles in the pavement bearing various figures. There are also some ancient slabs bearing crosses and some few brasses, one in the nave to John Wyther and Agnes his wife, 1487. The font is an octagon, panelled and painted, bearing shields charged with I.H.S. and emblems of the crucifixion.

Durleigh

51/75–76 [Unknown] 19 January, 1864

A small church, comprising chancel and nave only, with western tower and south porch, the whole covered with white stucco. On the north of the nave is a small projection for stairs opposite the place of the roodloft. On the north of the nave is a Decorated, 2 light window and a 2 light, Perpendicular window, set high up. On the south, are 2 Decorated windows of 2 lights. The chancel arch is of rather clumsy form, pointed and continuous.

The chancel has, on the north, a single lancet and a simple Perpendicular one, square-headed and with trefoiled arch. On the south are 2 lancets with heads cut off and one 2 light, Decorated. There is also a priest's door. The east window Decorated of 2 lights. On the south of the sacrarium is a shaft in the wall and mutilated piscina. On the north of the nave, internally, is a plain door to the roodstairs.

The tower arch is moulded issuing at once, from the wall. The font has an octagonal bowl with quatrefoil panelling and stem of the same character. It has a fine, pyramidical wood cover. The pulpit is of wood with the linen pattern. There are ugly pues and a west gallery with paintings of David, Absolom and the 4 Evangelists. There is also some modern painted glass.

The tower has a battlement on the east and west and a gabled roof rising in the middle. There are no buttresses; one string of division under the belfry. There is a 2 light, Decorated window on the west side and no door; 4 bells. The belfry windows square-headed.

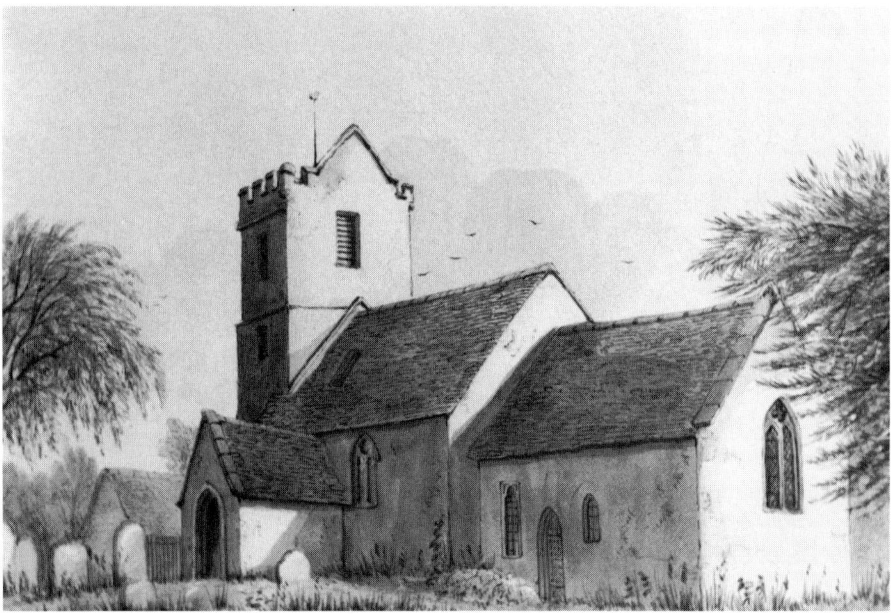

Durleigh, 1845, by W.W. Wheatley

Durston

51/88–89 St. John 28 January, 1870

This church seems to have been wholly rebuilt, save the tower. The body consists of nave, north and south transepts and chancel and has been reconstructed in the Decorated style and is fairly carried out. The seats all open. The chancel arch may possibly be original, is pointed and springing at once from the wall. There are no arches to the transepts, which is a mistake.

The tower is of fair Perpendicular; not large but opening to the nave by a good, panelled arch. It has embattled parapet and 4 crocketed pinnacles and an octagonal stair turret on the north, but not at the angle and all the way up. There are good base mouldings, a west doorway with continuous mouldings and label returned; the west window of 3 lights. Those of the belfry are square-headed, of 2 trefoiled lights and having the stone lattice work of the country. Below them is a string course and under that, an oblong trefoiled window. The buttresses are rather withdrawn from the angles.

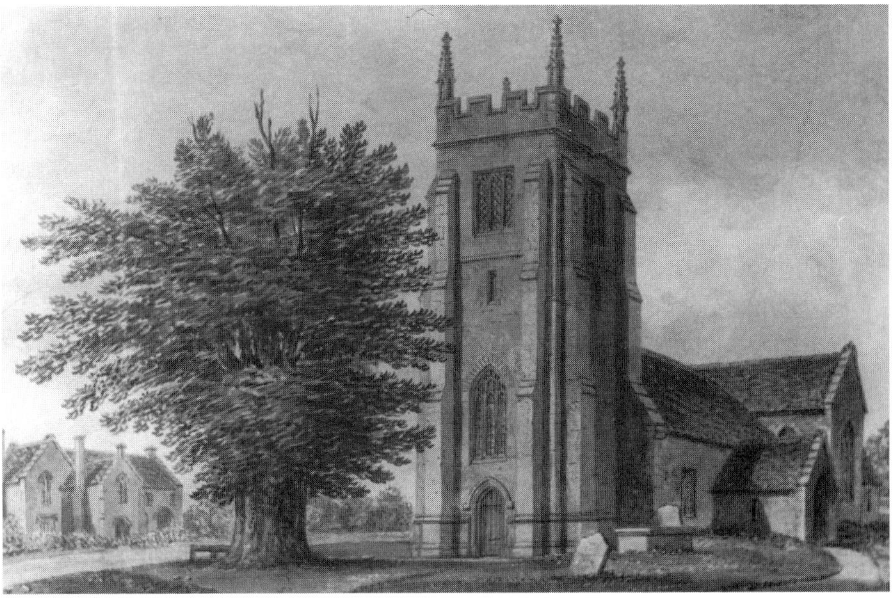

South west view of Durston Church, 1838, by J. Buckler

Elworthy

50/90–91 St. Martin 10 May, 1855

A small church of no architectural beauty, but lately improved and kept in excellent order. The plan is chancel, nave, south transept, chapel and west

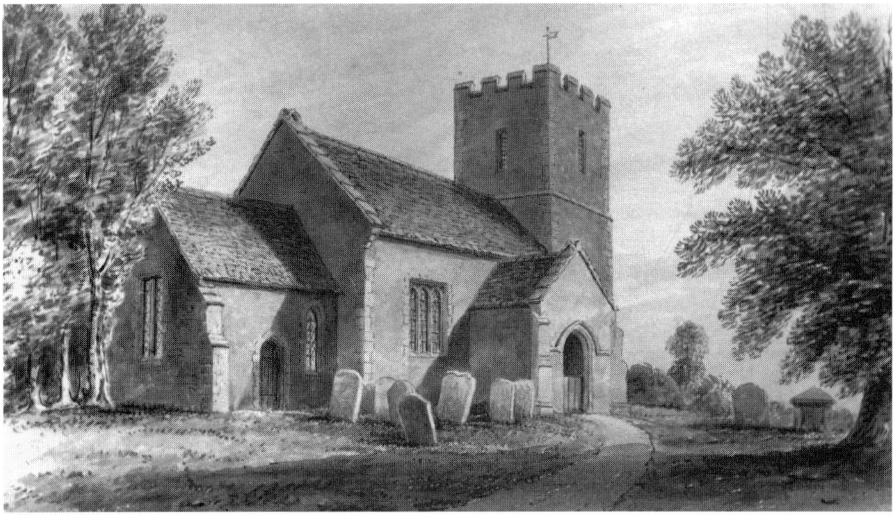

North east view of Elworthy Church, 1839, by J. Buckler

tower and south porch. Most of the windows are Perpendicular, some square-headed, but not that at the east end, which has 3 lights, but there is one Decorated window on the south of the chancel and one small lancet on the north. The tower arch is very small and pointed; that to the south transept also pointed and plain, springing from octagonal imposts.

The chancel arch has neither moulding nor imposts. There is a roodscreen, painted and gilt, with Perpendicular tracery. The chancel is but small, but contains stalls and lectern and a credence. The roof of the chancel is coved and coloured blue. That of the nave is ribbed. The pulpit has good wood carving on a stone base and there is, on the north, the accustomed projection for the roodstairs. The east window has inferior stained glass. The tower is small with a poor battlement and without character, possibly modern. The belfry window square. There are steps outside to the belfry.

The seats are all open but seem to be new. The font is rather small, the bowl octagonal and panelled; the stem has shafts at the angles; the cover has [a] wood canopy. There are some fine yew trees in the churchyard and the situation very pretty. The outer door of the porch is continuous. Over the inner door is written: Lord prepare our hearts to praye A.D. 1632. The public path and entrance being on the north, there are no graves on the south. The roughcast has been removed from the outer wall.

Englishcombe

51/81–83 [St. Peter] 27 April, 1865

This church has nave with south chapel and south porch, chancel and a tower placed between the chancel and nave. (The nave is short and narrow; the

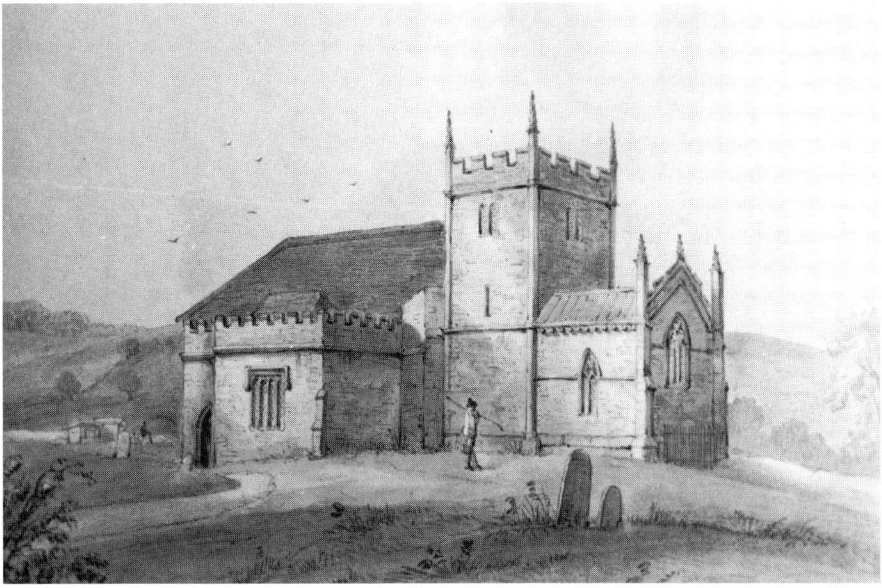

Englishcombe Church, 1843, by W.W. Wheatley

porch closely adjoins the south chapel.) There are several curious features. The south doorway of the nave is of Norman origin altered and has a tympanum. Over it is an ogee canopied niche. At the west end of the nave, in the centre is a flat buttress having also an early character.

The nave has a flat, modern ceiling and is partly pewed and partly furnished with open seats. The west window is Perpendicular, of 3 lights, with transom and jambs filled with fine, continuous panelling in which are shields charged with shields bearing the arms of the Archbishop of Canterbury and other emblems: as a horn, a bow, etc. On the north are 2 good, Perpendicular windows. There is, on the south, a pointed arch opening to the chapel set upon octagonal corbels. (Over the arch opening to the south chapel, is a 2 light clerestory window.) The chapel has a Perpendicular window of 4 lights with jambs, panelled and ornamented as the west window. In the north wall of the nave is an octagonal corbel.

The tower rises on 2 pointed arches, opening to the nave and chancel, of Early English character, acutely pointed and of 2 orders on massive shafts with abaci and Norman capitals. The arches are facing west and on the north side only, some additional shafts upon square bases having tongue-like figures at the angles. On the north side of the tower, in the wall, are 2 fine semi-circular arches with rich, beaded, chevron mouldings upon shafts of which the capitals have varied sculpture, cushion and animals heads. The eastern face of each arch is plain.

The chancel is Early English and transitional. Externally on the south, there is a corbel table and a 2 light, early Decorated window with hood returned. The east window is Decorated, of 3 lights and has shafts internally. The south-east window has its cill extended for a sedile. On the north is a trefoil-headed lancet window with moulded inner arch. On the south of the altar is a piscina with quatrefoil orifice and ogee canopy, double feathered. Near it is an oblong recess in the wall.

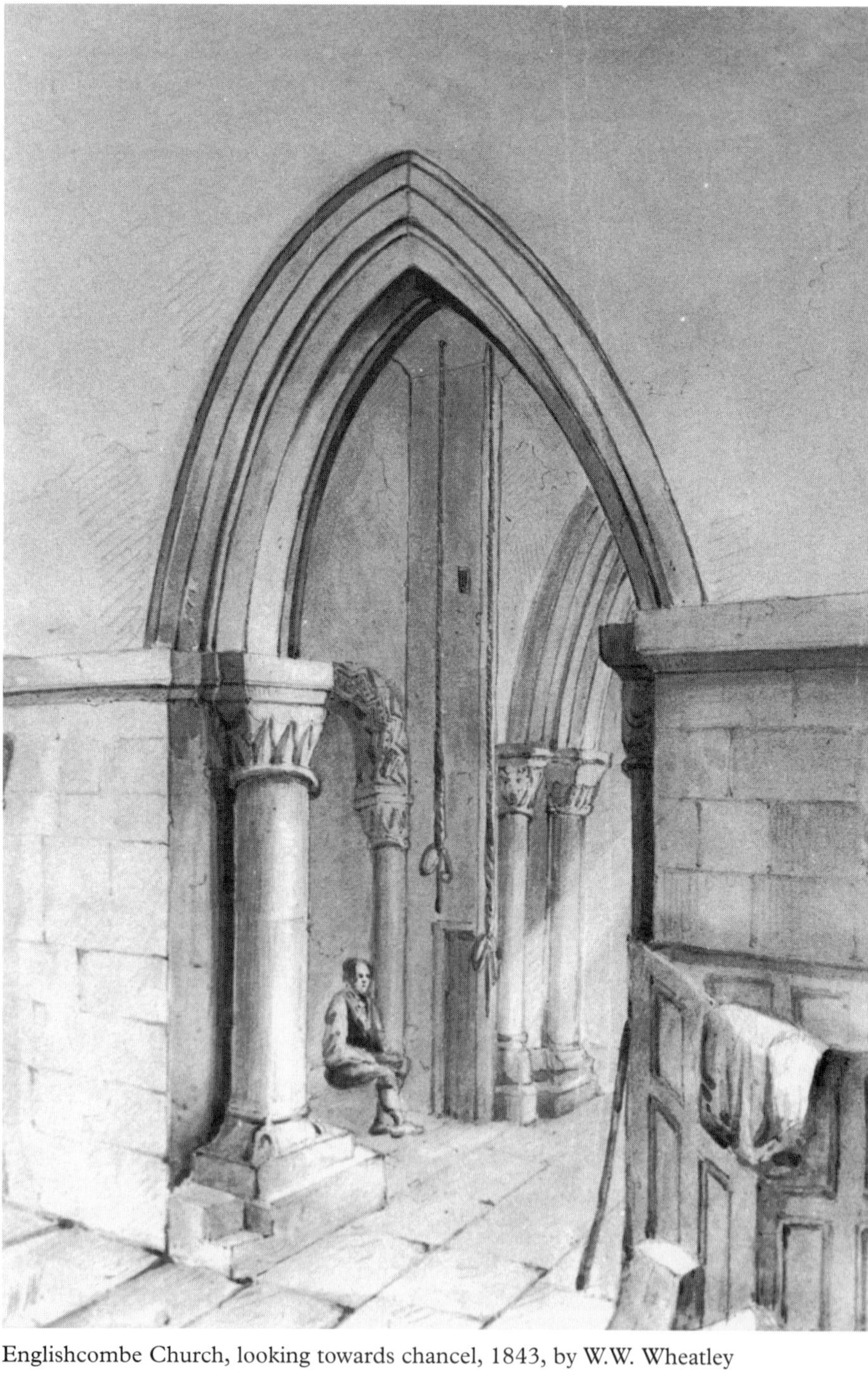

Englishcombe Church, looking towards chancel, 1843, by W.W. Wheatley

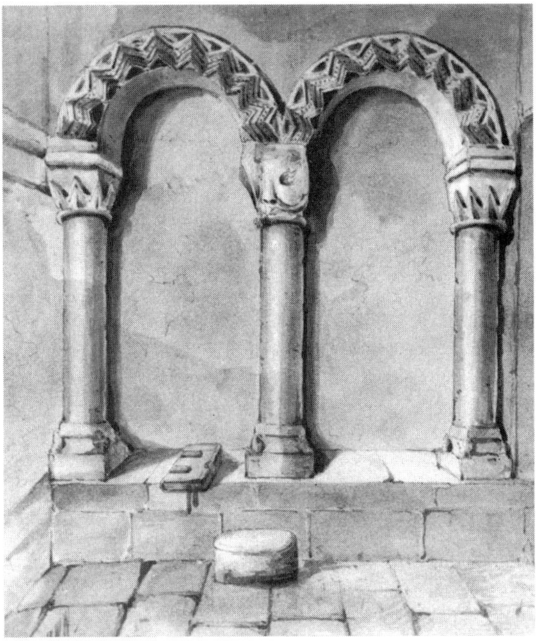

Englishcombe Church, interior under tower, 1843, by W.W. Wheatley

The east end has the gable flanked by octagonal, pinnacled turrets. The north side of the chancel has externally, a corbel table and battlement over it. The roof of the chancel is leaded; that of the nave higher and tiled.

The tower is low and plain; has battlement and 4 poor pinnacles, debased belfry window of 2 lights but having some pretty stone lattice work, after the way of Somersetshire; the walls bald and without buttress, but on the south side is a trefoil-headed lancet. At the north-east of the tower is a projection as if for the roodstairs. The roof of the nave encroaches on the tower. The north side of the nave is very bald. The font is small, ugly and of doubtful age, a square bowl on an octagon. (5 bells.)

The churchyard is very pretty; steep and broken ground with view over woody slopes and orchards full of blossom.

Enmore

51/77–78 St. Michael 19 January, 1864

This church has a nave, chancel, west tower, a sort of a transeptal chapel on the south of the nave, and a modern, south porch. Here is some earlier work than found generally hereabouts. The south doorway is Norman, has a rich cornice of double chevron ornament and a moulded hood, shafts with abaci and capitals of rude foliage. The chancel has, on the north and south, 2 small single lancets. The east window is incipient Middle-Pointed, of 3 lights, each trefoil-headed and the central highest and quatrefoils above. The chancel arch

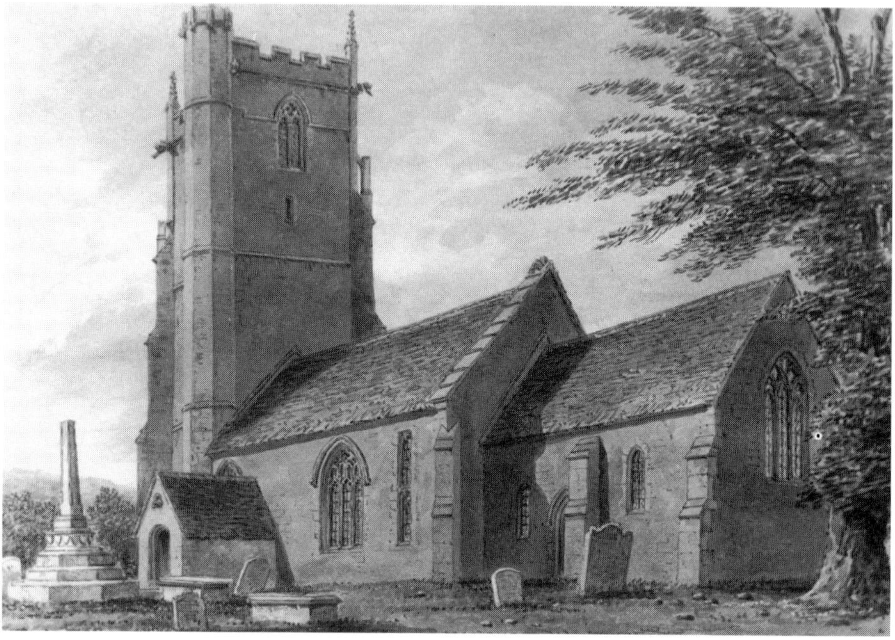

South east view of Enmore Church, 1838, by J. Buckler

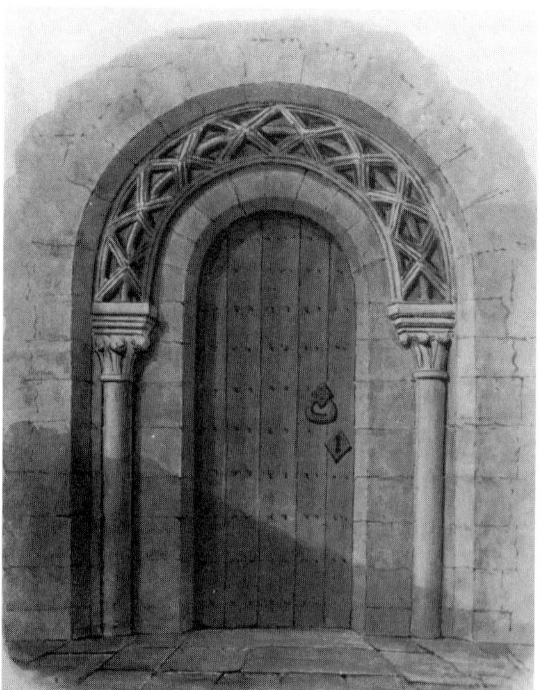

South door way, Enmore Church, 1838, by J. Buckler

is pointed and Perpendicular having a panelled soffit; part of the rood-screen remains within it. (There are shafts set in a chancel arch.)

In the nave, the windows are Perpendicular, some of 3 lights, one on the south consists of a long, narrow window, divided by a transom and, as it were, 2 single trefoil-headed windows, one placed over the other and set near the east end of the nave. The seats are chiefly open. The external walls of the body are covered with stucco but not of the tower which has the original stone untouched. It is good Perpendicular with corner buttresses, embattled and having small pinnacles at the angles, an octagonal stair turret at the south-east and gargoyles, 2 string courses. West window good, of 4 lights and subarcuated, and doorway of 2 orders; belfry windows of 2 lights with pierced boards.

In the churchyard is the shaft of a cross on a base, panelled with shields, raised on several steps. (There is a gallery and organ.)

Evercreech

49/47–48 St. Peter Before 1840

This church has a nave with north aisle, a south chapel with porch adjoining, a chancel and a very fine tower at the west end. There are elegant parapets with pierced quatrefoils and crocketed pinnacles to the greater part of the body. The tower is of great richness and of the character peculiar to Somersetshire,

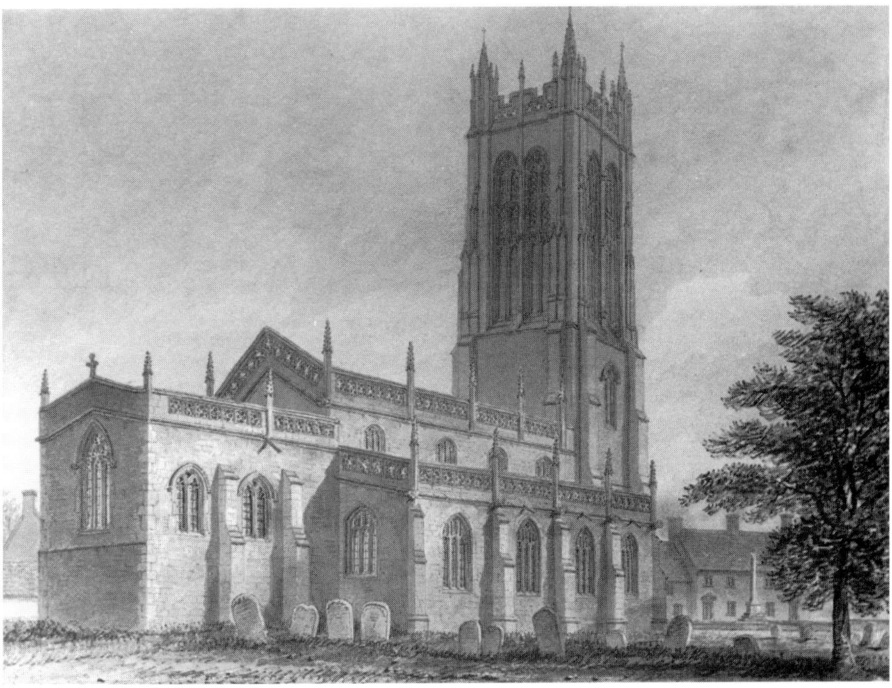

North east view of Evercreech Church, 1833, by J. Buckler

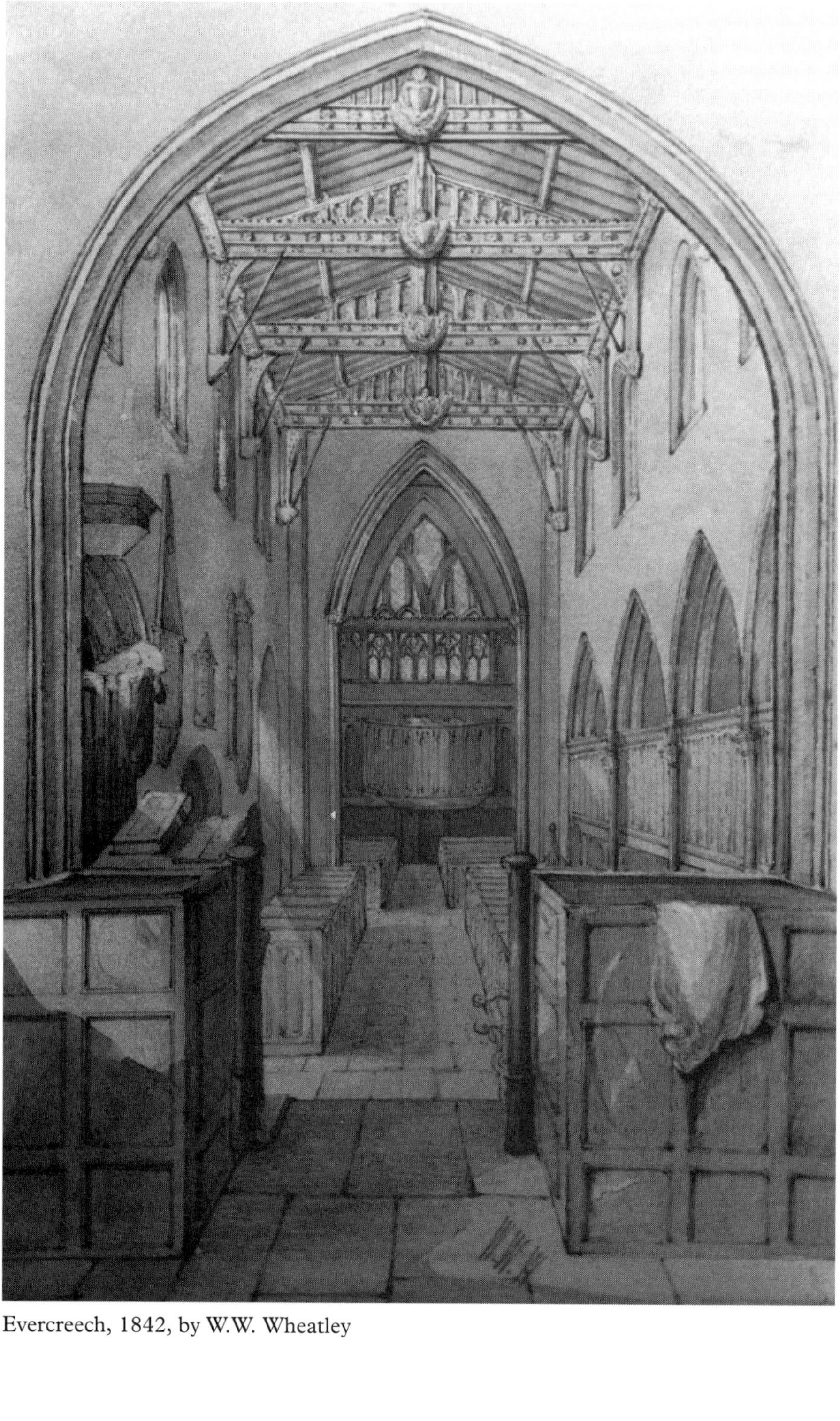

Evercreech, 1842, by W.W. Wheatley

resembling those at North Petherton, Huish, etc. The battlement is pierced in quatrefoils and there are, at the angles, 4 large crocketed pinnacles, set diagonally and with points attached to them, as at Huish, and in the intermediate spaces smaller pinnacles, also crocketed, set upon buttresses. The tower is 3 stages in height; the belfry windows are double and very long with beautiful stone lattice work. The buttresses are enriched with pinnacles in the set offs. The west doorway has a label and quatrefoils in the spandrels and in the stage above, is a niche containing the statue of a saint.

The tower opens to the nave by a very fine, lofty arch with elegant mouldings and slender shafts. The interior is lofty and elegant, in neat condition, but too much of modern pews, etc. Between the nave and the north aisle are 5 elegant, pointed arches upon light piers, having 4 shafts and hollow mouldings running between them. Upon the piers are half length figures of angels bearing shields. There is a clerestory with 3 light windows on both sides, though no arches on the south, but the tracery is gone. The roof is a fine one of timber, the tie-beams flowered and good, pierced tracery above them in the pitch of the roof. The south chapel, or transept, opens to the nave by a flat arch with panelled soffit and has late Rectilinear square-headed windows.

The chancel has a Decorated window of 3 lights at the east end and some of late and plain Rectilinear on the side; also one low side single window on the south, with a single light and trefoil head. On the south side of the altar is a niche with a piscina which is a half octagon in form and ornamented with the ballflower.

The font is a circular cup upon a cylinder. The gallery has a neat, modern pattern of carving in front, which diminishes the evil of its existence in some degree. The south porch joins the transept and is a plain and rather coarse piece of work having a very large arch for the outer door, springing upon shafts and containing a smaller arch within it. It is rather more in the domestic than in the ecclesiastical style of architecture.

The exterior of the chancel is plain, but the nave has an elegant pierced parapet and pinnacles.

Farmborough

52/3–4 All Saints 8 June, 1871

This church has been greatly renovated and enlarged; originally without aisles, but an aisle has been added on the north, both of nave and chancel. The tower is late Perpendicular with embattled parapet and an octagonal turret rising above it at the north-east. There are 4 small pinnacles and 2 string courses divide the tower into 3 portions. The west doorway is labeled with shields in the spandrels and over it is a 3 light window. The tower arch to the nave, is pointed and continuous. The chancel arch is pointed with very plain soffit.

The east window is Decorated, apparently restored and contains good, new coloured glass. On the south of the chancel are trefoil-headed lancets. The chancel roof is coved and ribbed. On the south is a piscina with ogee canopy. A low stone screen separates the chancel from the nave – which is new. The stone masonry within the church is all bare and freed from plaster. The seats

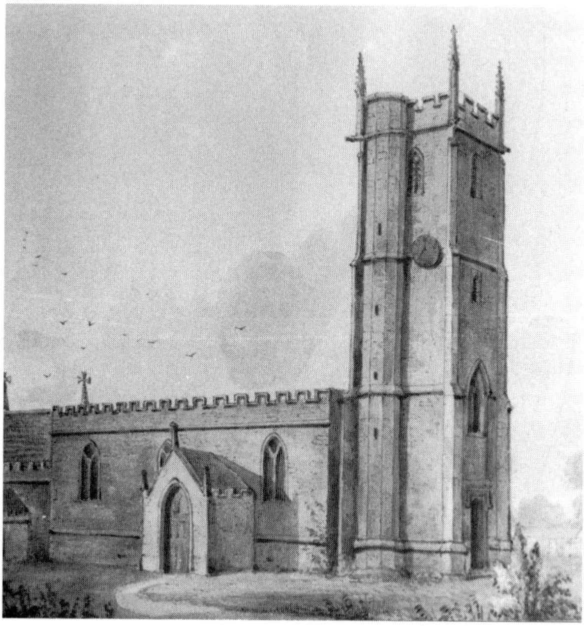

Farmborough, 1843, by W.W. Wheatley

are open; the whole expensively restored and in High Church style. The arcade of the nave, which, of course, is new, has 4 pointed arches on circular columns.

The north aisle, or chapel, contains the organ and vestry. The south side of the nave has debased, square-headed windows of 2 lights with obtuse arches and labels over them. In this wall is an ancient piscina, doubtful if *in situ*. The font is ancient; the bowl octagonal with quatrefoil panelling on a pedestal which is panelled. (6 bells.)

Fivehead

50/33–34 St. Martin April, 1845

This church has a nave with south chapel and porch, a chancel and west tower. The chancel is of Early English origin. The tower and the nave Perpendicular. The former is rather large and a good specimen of the plainer Somersetshire kind. The parapet is embattled and there are corner buttresses and an octagonal stair turret on the north, rising above the parapet. On the west side is a flat, ogee doorway with leaves and shields in the spandrels and a label above it. The west window is of 5 lights, large and fine, with a transom and shafts internally. In the second storey is a 3 light window. In the belfry, the windows are of 2 lights with elegant stone lattice work having pierced quatrefoils.

The material of this church is chiefly blue lias, but most of the south side is yellow washed. The windows of the nave and its chapel are mostly Perpendicular, of 3 lights. The tower arch is lofty and springs on small shafts.

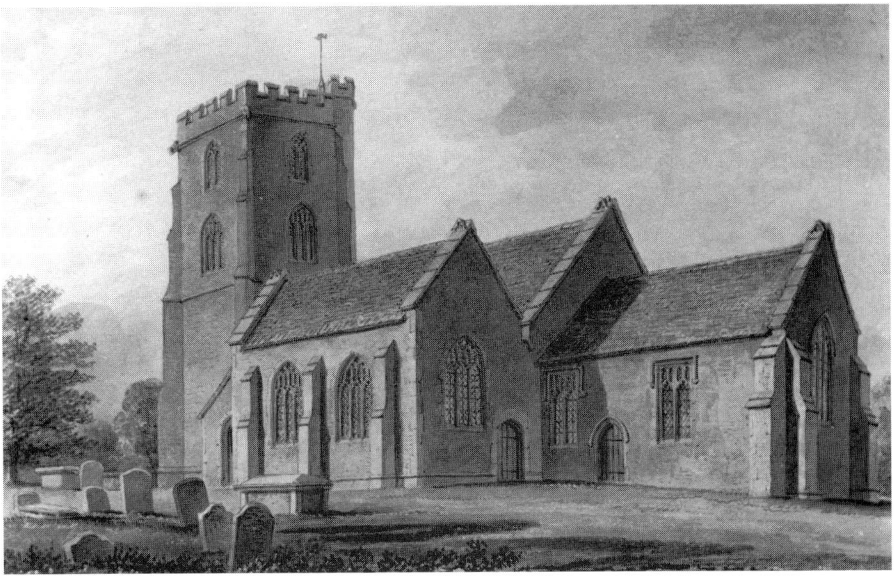

South east view of Fivehead Church, 1841, by J. Buckler

The south chapel is divided from the nave by 2 rather elegant, Perpendicular arches, the piers light with clustered slender shafts upon stilted base. The nave has a coved roof of wood. At the east end of the chapel is a piscina with obtuse arch and canopy clogged with wash. The chancel arch springs on small shafts as the tower arch. The chancel presents some curious work of Early English character, not very uncommon in Somersetshire.

The east window has 3 trefoil-headed lancets which are contained (internally only) under a curiously shaped arch approaching to the cinquefoil form. On the north of the chancel are 2 single lancets, also trefoil-headed, opening internally with considerable splay, the interior opening not exactly resembling that of the east window, nor corresponding with each other, one being something of a cinquefoil form, the other flattened but somewhat invected. The 2 windows on the south of the chancel are Perpendicular and square-headed. There are fragments of ancient stained glass in some of the windows.

The font is early, the bowl circular with a rope moulding round the lower part, upon a cylindrical stem raised on a square plinth. The tower contains a clock and 5 bells.

Freshford

51/26–27 St. Peter 20 April, 1860

An uninteresting church, much modernized; has nave and chancel, each with north aisle, and a western tower. The latter is almost the only original portion which is untouched and is of good Perpendicular, embattled with 4 crocketed

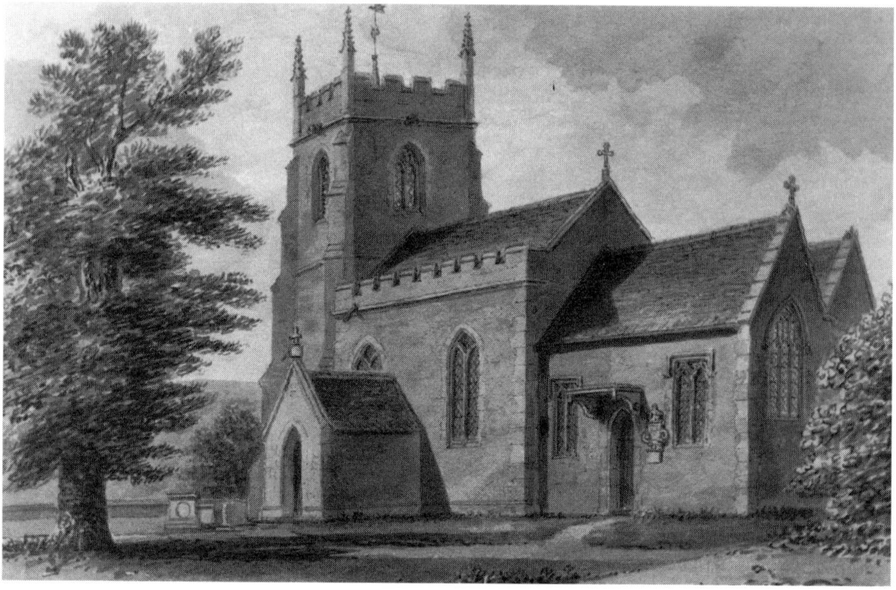

South east view of Freshford Church, 1847, by J. Buckler

pinnacles and divided into 2 stages. The buttresses are set at the angles. There is an octagonal stair turret on the north, displacing the belfry window. The west window [is] of 3 lights and below it a good, labeled doorway on angel corbels and with foliage in the spandrels. The whole of excellent stone masonry.

The tower arch has continuous mouldings and is opened to the interior. As to the rest of the church, it is difficult to say whether any of the work is original. There are ugly windows in the nave and better, Perpendicular ones in the chancel; 2 new flat arches dividing the aisle with a new marble column and what looks like a hagioscope, but which is a modern invention. The font a plain octagonal.

Frome

49/3–4 St. Peter Before 1840

This is a spacious church consisting of a nave with side aisles, a chancel with side chapels, a north transept, and a tower, surmounted by a stone spire, singularly situated on the south side and standing between the aisle of the nave and that of the chancel. The tower in its lower portions, seems to be Early English, but the upper part is Rectilinear and has a pierced, panelled battlement and a crocketed pinnacle at each angle. The spire is ornamented by bands running round it. The steeple, though good in itself, is not sufficiently lofty or important for the extent of the body which is of very considerable length.

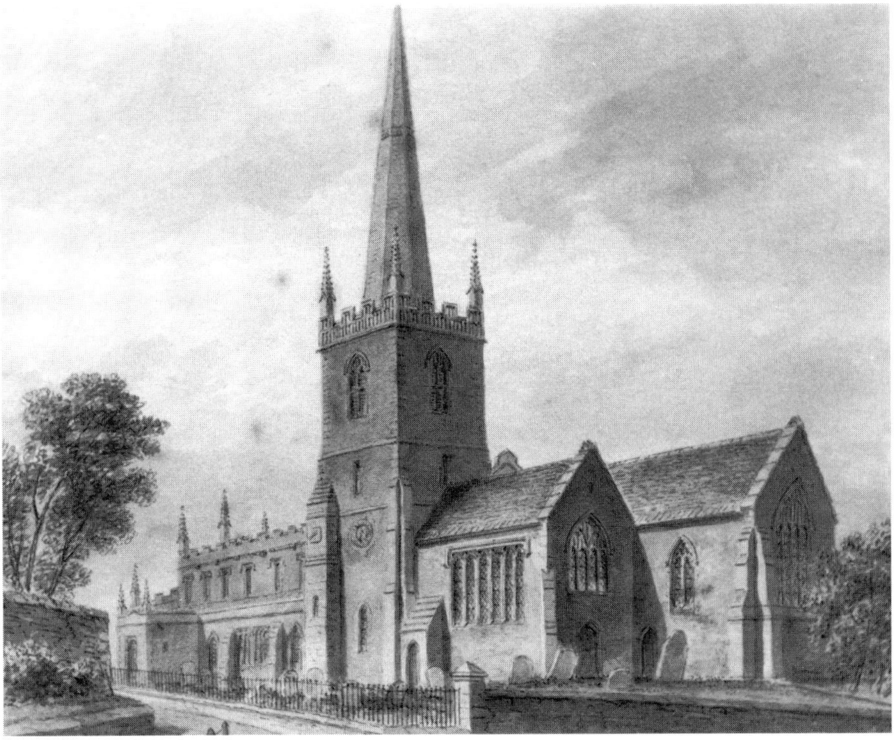

South east view of Frome Church, 1845, by J. Buckler

The nave has a clerestory which is embattled, but the rest of the church has the parapet plain. The chancel has a tiled roof and no clerestory. The west end has been rebuilt in the Gothic style, of which character is also a gateway into the churchyard. Many of the windows in the nave have been mutilated, but there are some of Rectilinear character with square-heads. The clerestory windows have lost their tracery; there is a plain, south porch. The nave has 7 pointed arches on each side of which the 4 western ones have piers without capitals, the arch mouldings being carried down the sides of the piers. The 3 other arches are loftier and more acute and having their piers formed each of 4 clustered, octagonal shafts and altogether better finished than the western arches.

The interior wants height and is much crowded with pews and galleries. At the west end is an organ of considerable size. The chancel extends considerably eastwards of its side chapels and has an east window of 5 lights with very early Curvilinear tracery without feathering. The side chapels have Curvilinear east windows of 2 lights, stopped up, and some square-headed Rectilinear ones. The chancel has been very much modernized within. The font is a fine, Early English one, of square form resting upon an octagonal shaft in the centre and a circular one at each angle.

This church, though large, is plain and poor in good work of which it seems never to have had a large share, and much mischief has been done by modern alterations.

Glastonbury

19/45–6 20 October, 1825

Went to Glastonbury where there are several objects well deserving attention. On a steep hill of some height rising abruptly, is situated the Tor, or St. Michael's Tower, which is said to have belonged to a chapel dedicated to St. Michael, long destroyed. The tower, however, is in good preservation and from its elevated situation, is a fine and conspicuous object. It is in early Perpendicular style and has some good windows and canopied niches of very fine work. It is hollow within. From it, there is a delightful and extensive prospect over rich country.

The ruins of the once magnificent abbey are most highly interesting and present fine architectural features. There is not much remaining of the church but sufficient to show that it was a most spacious and splendid structure. The eastern arch of the central tower, with a small portion of the choir, still remains. These are of Early English work of an early period, the arches being pointed and moulded with the Norman chevron work. The arch of the tower is very bold and lofty. The principal part of the ruin is a chapel dedicated to St. Joseph of Arimathia, which was at the west end of the church.

This presents a specimen of the architecture of about the 12th century, when Norman was giving way to the pointed arch. Of this period, this is a specimen perhaps unrivall'd in richness and minute ornament. There are rich ranges of intersecting Norman arches with chevron mouldings, windows with bold and splendid herringbone mouldings and some ranges of trefoiled arches and features of decidedly Early English character, while others are as decidedly Norman. There are 2 semi-circular doorways of uncommon richness having 4 bands of mouldings, charged with rich scroll work, medallions, etc. At the west end are 2 square turrets of fine Norman work. The ornament of the whole is so intricate and profuse that it would be very laborious to describe it minutely.

The Abbot's Kitchen is a specimen of Perpendicular work. It is an extraordinary and curious building of octagonal form, with a stone, groined, pyramidical roof with plain, strong ribs springing between the windows. There are 4 fireplaces with chimneys communicating with one common chimney at the summit of the pyramid, which is octagonal also. This is a wonderful work and has kept entire to this day. There is an effigy of an abbot in this kitchen, removed from the church, and a curious old chopping block.

The town of Glastonbury has 2 churches of which that dedicated to St. John is by far the handsomest. This church is a very spacious and beautiful fabric of excellent Perpendicular work but is chiefly remarkable for the extreme lightness and magnificence of its tower which somewhat resembles that of Huish and, from its great height, is seen at some distance. The tower has in its 2 lower stages some very rich, canopied niches; the third stage is enriched with much panelling and tracery and the upper has 2 fine long belfry windows. The whole is crowned with an elaborate, pierced battlement with pierced turrets at the corners (as Gloucester Cathedral) to which are attached, by small, flying

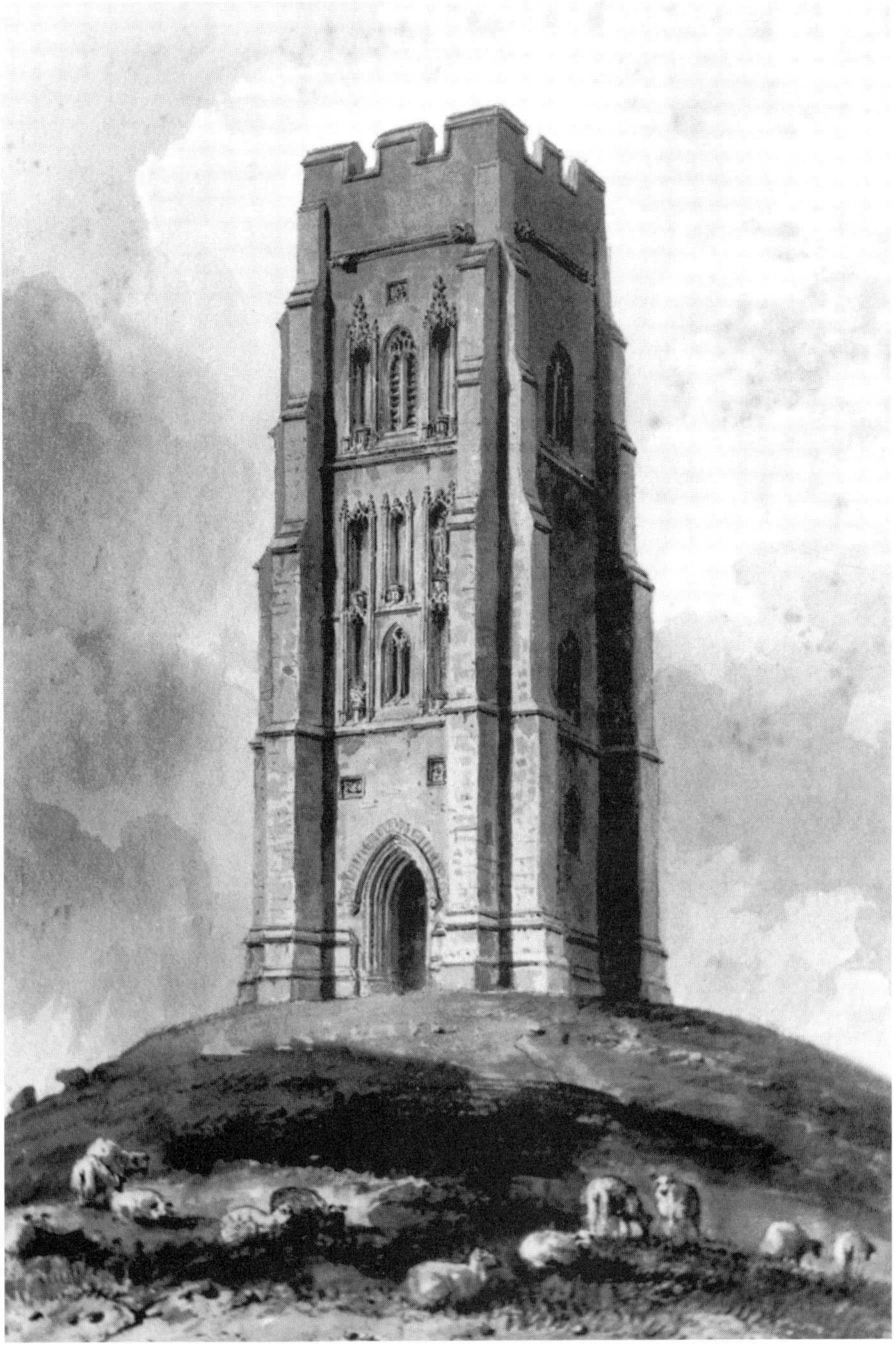

St. Michael's Tower on Glastonbury Tor, 1822, by J. Buckler

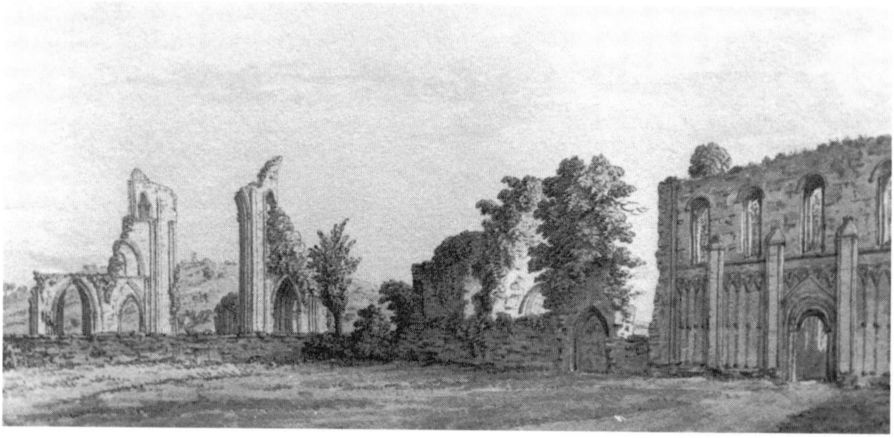

Glastonbury Abbey ruins, 1786, by S.H. Grimm

buttresses, very light, small pinnacles. The buttresses have upon each, set-off elegant crocketed pinnacles with flying buttresses, which give to the whole, a great air of lightness and richness. The west door of the tower is very fine, is placed between two richly wrought niches. It has a pointed head and is moulded with a rich band of foliage. The label is continued over the buttresses and the spandrels have quatrefoils.

The church is lofty, fine, consisting of a nave, chancel, side aisles, transept and fine, large south porch. The south porch (has a groined ceiling), is equal

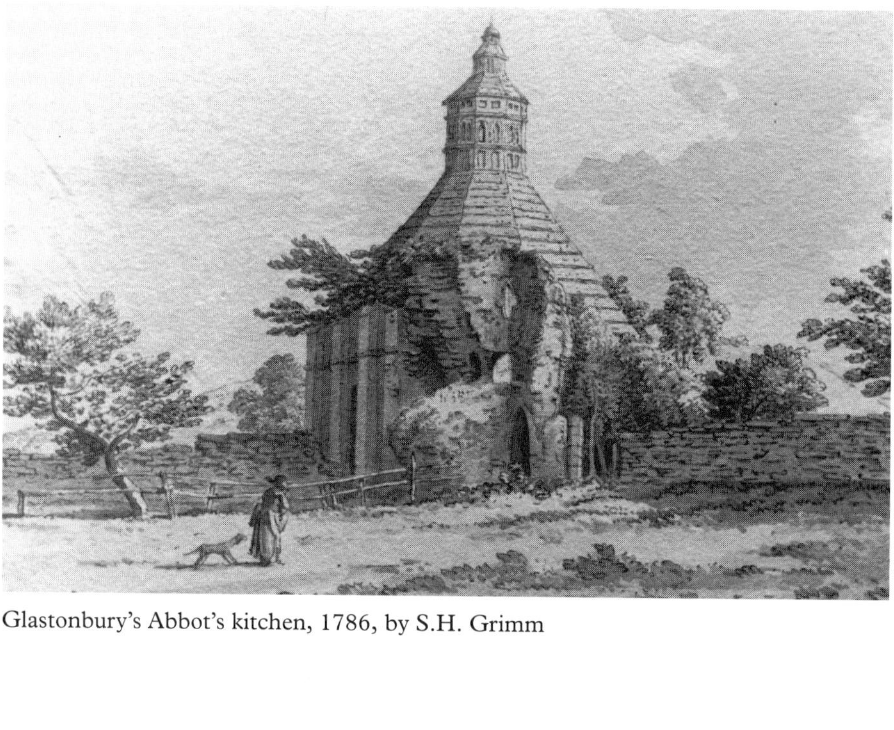

Glastonbury's Abbot's kitchen, 1786, by S.H. Grimm

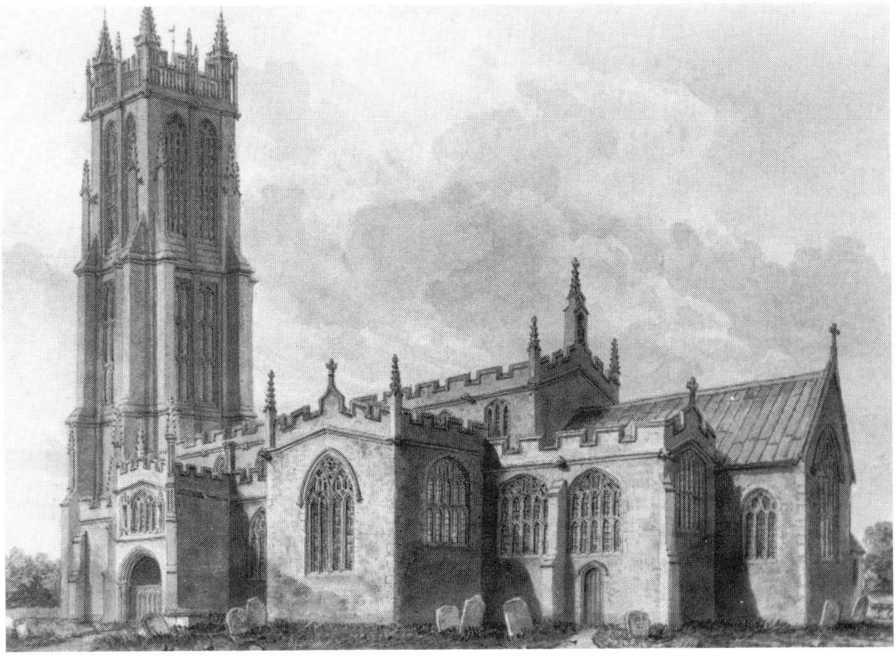

South east view of St. John Baptist, Glastonbury, 1825, by J. Buckler

to the aisle in height and is enriched with pinnacles and niches. The nave and aisles have a battlement, but the chancel a plain parapet. The interior is very fine and light from its loftiness, breadth and length and the size and number of the windows. The arches which divide the nave from the aisles, are very lofty and spring from lozenge piers with shafts at the angles. The clerestory has fine windows with rather flat arches. Above the clerestory windows are stone figures bearing shields supporting the roof.

The nave is of 7 arches and has its symmetry injured by clumsy galleries. The south aisle has a tolerable panelled ceiling. The south transept is much larger than the north and has a fine window of 4 lights, resembling that in the north transept of Ilminster Church. The chancel seems to be much later than the nave from the arches being entirely of Tudor form, both those which divide the aisles and those of the windows. The east window is, however, a very fine one of 7 lights and contains some painted glass of very bright colours. The aisles of the chancel have fine, panelled ceilings painted blue and covered with gilt stars. A neat Gothic stone altar screen has been erected in tolerably correct style. In the south aisle of the chancel, is a tomb panelled and ornamented with figures of angels and camels with scrolls with monkish verse nearly unintelligible. There is a figure somewhat mutilated.

At the west end of the nave is a good organ beneath which has been erected a very handsome stone screen of correct Perpendicular open work, within which is enclosed the vestry. In the churchyard and near the east end, is an altar tomb richly charged with panelling and quatrefoils but rather weather beaten.

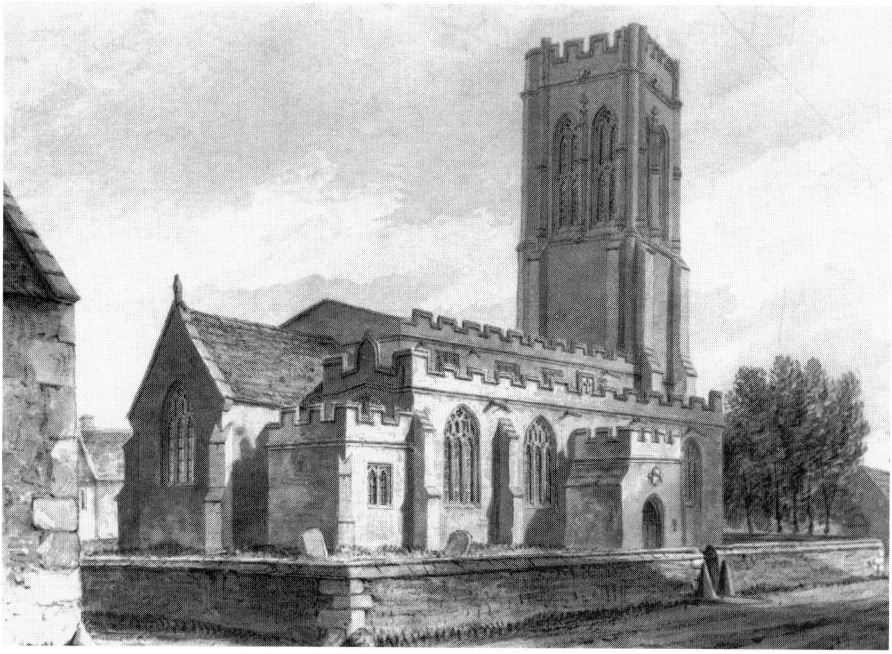

North east view of St. Benedict, Glastonbury, 1825, by J. Buckler

Dimensions of St. John's Church

Length of nave	97 ¾	Breadth of body with aisles	47 ½
Length of chancel	34 ¾	Breadth of transept	about 60
Total length	132 ½		

1858

The interior of the church undergoing a thorough cleaning and being fitted with open seats. The organ moved to the north aisle of the chancel.

St. Benedict's Church is entirely of Perpendicular work but is worked plainer and is far inferior in every respect to St. John's. It consists of a nave, chancel, north aisle and porch with a good tower of handsome but not rich Perpendicular work. Its western side is worked richer than the other sides having a good doorway above which is a good window between two fine canopied niches. The belfry windows are fine and long, 2 on each side, and enriched with lattice work and pinnacles between them. The battlement is plain. The tower opens to the church by an arch with panelled soffit and has a good groined ceiling, open to the lower storey. The north side of the church has a battlement but the south, a plain parapet.

The north porch is embattled and of good Perpendicular workmanship. The nave is divided from the north aisle by a row of Tudor arches with lozenge piers and shafts. There is a clerestory on both sides although there is no south aisle. The clerestory windows are square and the other windows in the church, of good Perpendicular work. The chancel has one arch to the north aisle. South of the altar is a good niche and water drain. The pulpit is of stone, ornamented with panel work and band of square flowers. In the north aisle is a good, flowered bracket for a niche. The roof is supported by figures bearing shields. The font, octagonal on a pedestal, panelled elegantly and lined with lead. This church is much neglected and the interior out of repair, there being rarely divine service performed in it.

The town of Glastonbury contains many handsome old houses, especially the George Inn, the front of which is very rich, Perpendicular work with fine panelling, tracery and oriel windows.

[Sir Stephen may have considered that he had not done justice to St. Joseph's Chapel in his original note, so he added a longer and more detailed account.]

The present remains (of Glastonbury Abbey) consist of St. Joseph's Chapel at the west end of the nave, which is pretty entire, a portion of the south wall of the nave, part of the magnificent and lofty eastern arch which supported the tower, the arches leading to the choir aisles, and a good portion of the south side of the choir. St. Joseph's Chapel is very rich; it has, at opposite corners, 2 fine, square turrets richly worked with intersecting arches, etc. The windows have semi-circular arches with herringbone, chevron and other very rich ornaments in their architraves, both externally and internally. Beneath them runs a rich range of intersecting arches with very fine enrichments. The western window is triple, the central [light] being the highest.

The groining of the roof has been very fine. Beneath it is a crypt of fine workmanship now left quite open to view, as the chapel floor has fallen in. The arch of the crypt is of singular contracted form. The doorways are rich beyond conception having several bands of semi-circular mouldings, filled with very rich ornaments, medallions containing a variety of figures with rude early foliage, etc. Each doorway has a pyramidical pediment. The windows on the south side of ye nave have semi-circular heads, but are rather less rich than those of St. Joseph's Chapel. The arches forming entrance to the choir aisles, and a small chapel north of the choir, are pointed with rich chevron mouldings. The eastern arch of the tower has been of a most magnificent height; the pillars to it remain perfect and the breadth from pillar to pillar is 28 feet. The pillars are 70 feet high to the capitals. The choir windows are pointed with rich chevron mouldings and shafts with elegant, foliated capitals. Some fine sepulchral effigies of abbots, have been found, which retain traces of gorgeous painting and gilding.

Goathurst

51/76–77 St. Edward 19 January, 1864

This church has nave, chancel and north and south transepts with a west tower and south porch. There are no aisles. There has been much modernising but the original portions are Perpendicular. The walls of all parts are covered with

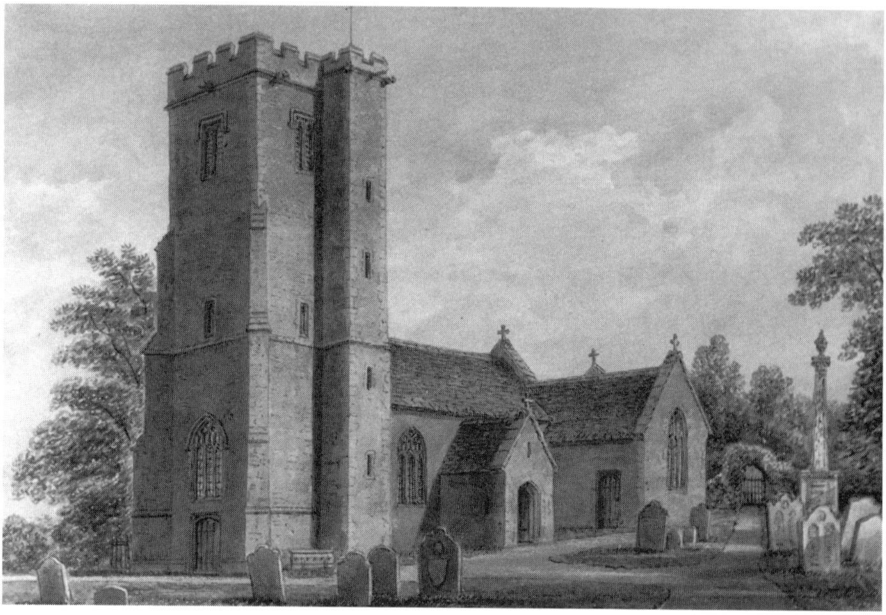

South west view of Goathurst Church, 1838, by J. Buckler

yellow wash. The tower is embattled, has a square turret at the south-east, also embattled. There is a 3 light west window, belfry windows of 2 lights, labeled, and having some of the pierced stone lattice work prevalent in Somersetshire. The west doorway has a flat arch and spandrels.

The windows throughout the church are Perpendicular of 3 lights. The tower arch is pointed, rising from the wall. The chancel is lower than the nave and much modernised in the style of 70 years ago. The arches to the transept are somewhat metamorphosed and the south transept has its ceiling decorated with heraldic shields and is made into a family pue of the Tyntes of Halswell.

The nave has a coved roof of plaster with ribs and roses. The pues have some rather respectable old Italian wood carving. The chancel arch is wide and appears debased. The chancel may have been wholly rebuilt, has a low, coved roof with plastering of Italian character, the eastern part boarded and ribbed, coloured blue and gold. The chancel has heavy, modern wainscoting and there are 2 pictures and several costly, modern monuments to the Tyntes. The font is small, has a panelled octagonal bowl on stem. The porch has coved, ribbed roof; the inner doorway has a hood, the outer continuous arch mouldings. On the porch gable is a cross.

There are 6 bells; a west gallery and organ. One monument. Both Goathurst and Enmore and most neighbouring churches had the evergreen decorations, very beautiful.

Greinton

50/65–66 [St. Michael] 23 January, 1854

A small church comprising only chancel and nave with west tower, the whole Perpendicular except part of the south side of the chancel. The latter has been lately restored and in great measure rebuilt and the interior is altogether in good care and likely to receive further improvement. The roof of the nave is coved with ribs, forming panels and a quatrefoil panelled cornice. The windows of the nave Perpendicular of 2 lights. One on the north, near the pulpit, is set in a projection and is of rather odd character having 2 trefoil-headed lights with a kind of triangle in the head between them.

The tower arch is open and has continuous, plain mouldings. The chancel arch is late and rather misshapen, of somewhat obtuse form and with continuous mouldings. The nave has a number of good, old, open seats with carved standards. The chancel has, on the south, 3 trefoil-headed lancets, rather wide, the eastern one of which has, in the angle of its cill, a piscina having a quatrefoiled orifice. The north windows of the chancel are Perpendicular of 2 lights, the eastern one of 3, and having its lower part occupied externally by quatrefoil panelling not pierced.

There is a new stone reredos of fair Perpendicular work. The sacrarium is laid with encaustic tiles and all the chancel windows are filled with stained glass, executed at Exeter. That at the east end has representations of the Crucifixion, the Resurrection and the Ascension. The chancel has plain stalls. The south porch is used as a vestry; the north porch modern and poor. All

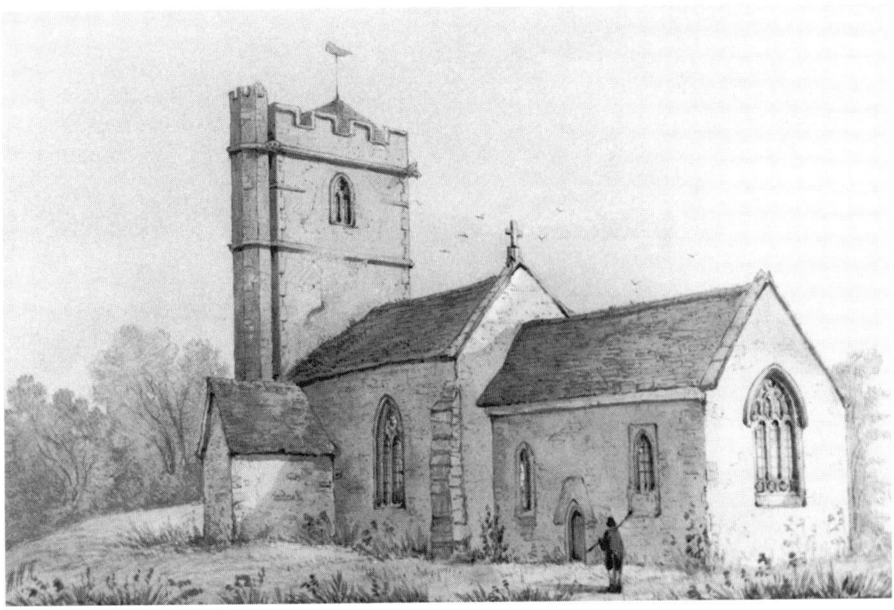

Greinton, 1843, by W.W. Wheatley

pues have disappeared. The font is small, shallow and modern, of octagonal form. The tower is low and embattled with a corner turret at the south-west. The belfry windows of 2 lights, the west window of 3 lights, the buttresses at the angles. The west door small: 4 bells. There is a barrel organ in the tower. The chancel inclined to the south. Parts of the walls are rough cast.

Ham, High

49/27–28 [St. Andrew] 1839

This handsome church was built in 1476 by Abbot Selwood with contributions from Lord Poulett and others and the chancel, it is supposed, by the Revd. John Dyer, Rector, who lies buried therein under a flat stone with brass plate inscribed thus: 'Hic jacet Johannes Dyer, A.M., rector istius ecclesie in utroque jure Baccalaurius qui obiit vicesino die Septembris A.D. MCCCCXCIX cuius animae propicietur Deus.'

The church consists of a nave with side aisles and clerestory, a western tower and a chancel. The buttresses are enriched with canopies and those of the chancel with crocketed pinnacles; the chief portion of the walls of rough lias stone, the corners and more ornamental portions finer. The south porch has enriched buttresses and a niche over its doorway; also a stoup in a niche. The tower is plainer than the body and not lofty, the battlement strong and plain and the pinnacles small. The belfry windows have the stone lattice work not uncommon in the county and there is a square stair turret on the north side.

The interior is light, spacious and lofty, the nave separated from each aisle by 5

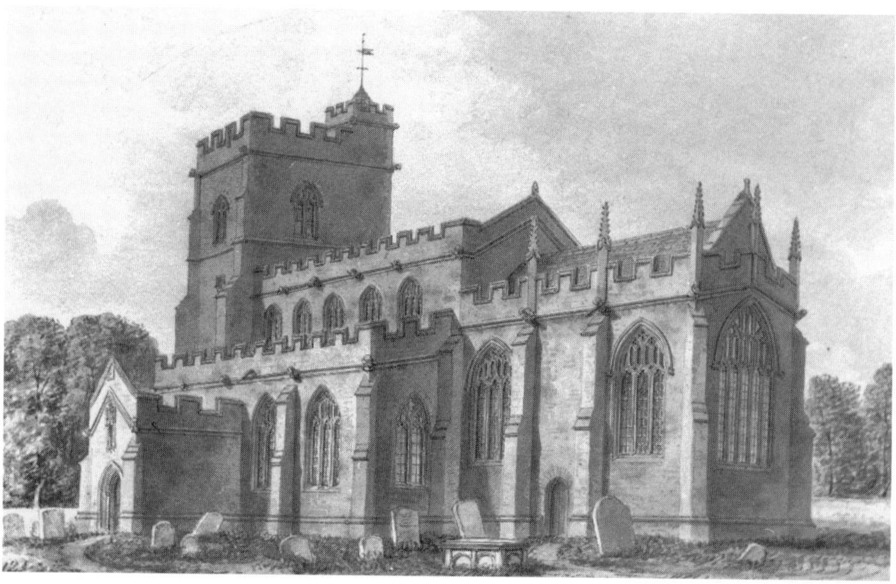

South east view of High Ham Church, 1830, by J. Buckler

fine arches with the usual light piers. The clerestory windows of 3 lights and the side aisle windows very similar. The roof is high-pitched and open, the space above the tie-beams filled with flowered and open tracery and the beams not on stone corbels. The east end of the side aisles has [a] rich, panelled ceiling. Between the nave and chancel is a very fine rood screen with the roodloft enriched with 4 bands of vine leaves, grapes and various foliage, fan groining under the loft and the arches filled with excellent tracery, the centre arch containing double doors. There are also several original, open seats with carved ends.

The chancel arch has no shafts but entirely filled with panelling. The chancel has a large, east window of 5 lights with small shafts. The side windows of 3 lights. On the south of the altar is a niche with piscina. The roof of the chancel is rather richer than that of the nave and has corbels and angels with shields. There are some old stalls in the chancel. In the nave an ancient, wooden lectern and stone steps lead to the pulpit. The font is much earlier than the church: a circular cup upon a cylinder and surrounded by a band of rope moulding.

Ham, Low

49/28–29 1839

This was formerly a domestic chapel appended to the mansion built by Sir Edward Hext, Knight of the Shire, 1 James I. This chapel was also erected by him (who died 1624) and though the work of that period is of much better architecture than could be possibly expected being wholly in the Gothic style though with some indication of debasement. It is a kind of miniature church, consisting of a nave with aisles, a clerestory, a small tower and a chancel on a small scale.

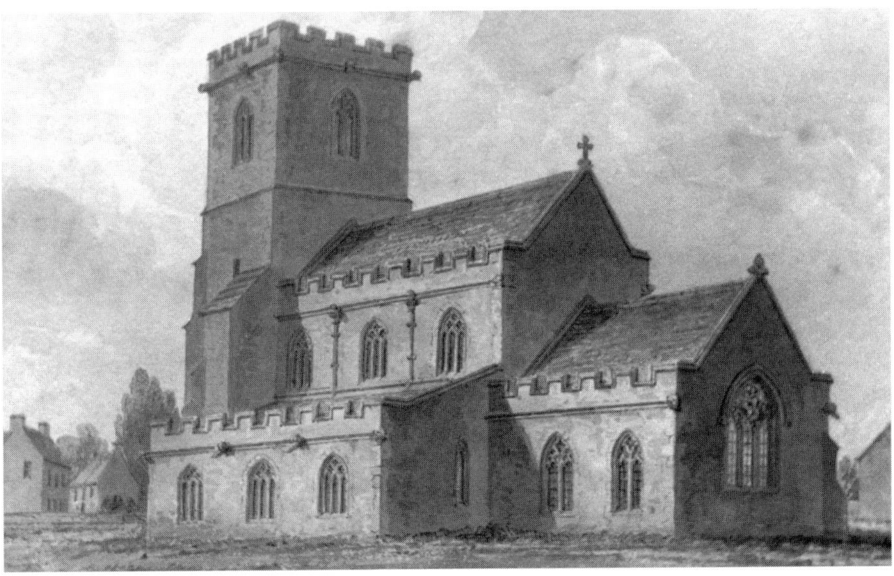

South east view of Low Ham Chapel, 1830, by J. Buckler

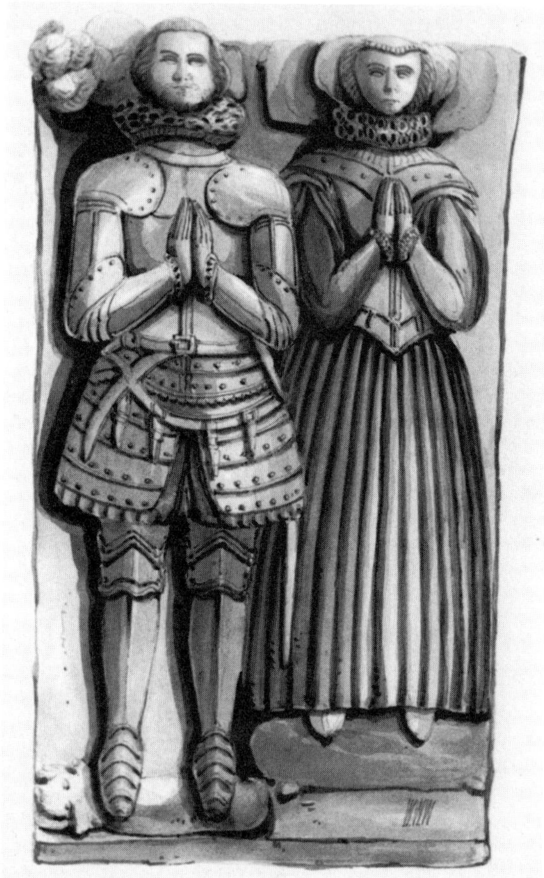

Low Ham, north aisle, 1847, by W.W. Wheatley

The exterior is embattled. The nave has 3 arches on each side, with light piers as at High Ham. The windows both of aisles and clerestory are of rather debased tracery. The ceiling of the nave is groined in plaster, the ribs resting on shafts set on angel corbels. Between the nave and chancel is an elegant, wood screen enriched with vine leaves, Tudor flower and tracery, painted and gilt and inscribed 'My sonne [feare God and the Kinge and meddle not with them that are given to change'].

At the extremity of the aisles, are odd, single light windows. The arch to the tower is open. The chancel has an odd, east window with a circle in the tracery and of 3 lights, the side windows of 2 lights. The roof of the chancel coved and painted with stars. The pulpit carved and gilt. There is an altar tomb of freestone to Sir Edward Hext (the founder) and Dionysia his wife, with effigies in the costume of the day. He died 1624 and she 1633. Also a tomb to Ralph, Lord Stawel, grandson of the above, the son of whom began another sumptuous mansion in place of the former which was afterward sold and the greater part has now been pulled down, but there are some remains still visible.

Harptree, West

50/21–22 St. Mary 30 April, 1845

A curious church of mixed styles with some early features. The plan consists of a nave and chancel with south aisle, a vestry south of the chancel and a tower at the west end, crowned by a spire of wood, covered with lead.

There are curious portions of Norman and Early English character. The north door partakes of the former, but is very singular from the very flattened or depressed form of the arch. The inner member, or door, has no shafts but an impost moulding. The outer arch springs from octagonal, Norman shafts with cushion [?] capitals. On the north side under the roof, both in nave and chancel, is a corbel table of Early English character. The tower is plain, Early English and has a similar corbel table. The buttresses are very flat; the belfry windows double, long and narrow with square heads. On the north side, in a lower stage is a plain slit; on the south a high lancet; below the belfry windows a string course.

There is no arch between the tower and the nave, only a flattened doorway. There is a south porch with a good moulded parapet of later date and the western part of the south aisle has an embattled parapet. Most of the windows are Perpendicular, but on the north side of the nave, near the pulpit, is a small, rough [?] obtuse headed one, which seems to be Norman. On the north side of the chancel is a round-headed doorway and a window which has Perpendicular tracery of 2 lights inserted, but presenting to the interior, a trefoil lancet arch much splayed, which seems to be of transitional from Early English to Decorated. The east window is a questionable one of 3 lights without foils.

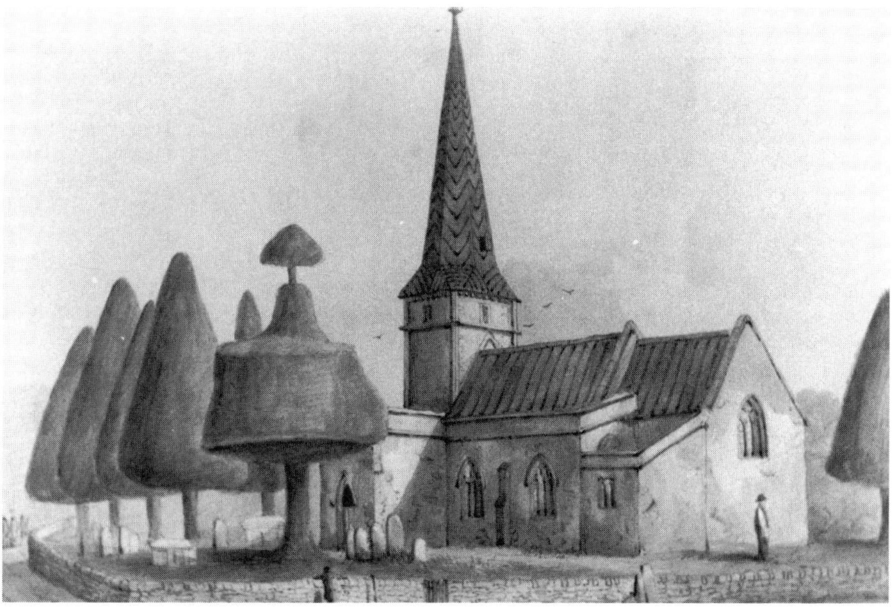

West Harptree, 1843, by W.W. Wheatley

The nave is divided from the south aisle by 3 pointed arches, springing from octagonal pillars. The chancel arch is a very curious feature of segmental form, the two sides being quite unequal and whether intended to be so, appears doubtful; perhaps it may arise from a faulty calculation originally or else is the result of subsequent alteration. The impost on the north side has a Norman appearance and near it, in a recess, is a Norman capital. There is some Perpendicular panelling with traces of painting and gilding in the lower part of the north pier. The roof of the nave is coved with ribs and bosses; the ribs upon small shafts rising from well sculptured head corbels. The chancel has a boarded, plain roof.

The chancel opens to the south aisle by a pointed arch and the chancel aisle to that of the nave by a similar one, there being between the two, an octagonal pier whence also is sprung the chancel arch. The vestry is eastward of the aisle and attached to the south aisle of the east part of the chancel, which there retains its original breadth. On the wall of the vestry, next to the chancel, is a canopied, ogee arch. The font is a [?] modern one.

Haselbury Plucknett

51/33 St. Michael May 1860

This church seems to have been wholly rebuilt save the tower, retaining perhaps the original battlements. The style is quasi-Perpendicular and not satisfactory.

The tower is good Perpendicular, embattled with pinnacles, has 2 strings of division, gargoyles and corner buttresses, the belfry windows of 2 lights. The west window of 3 lights, the west doorway is labeled with foliage in the spandrels. There is an octagonal stair turret at the south-east.

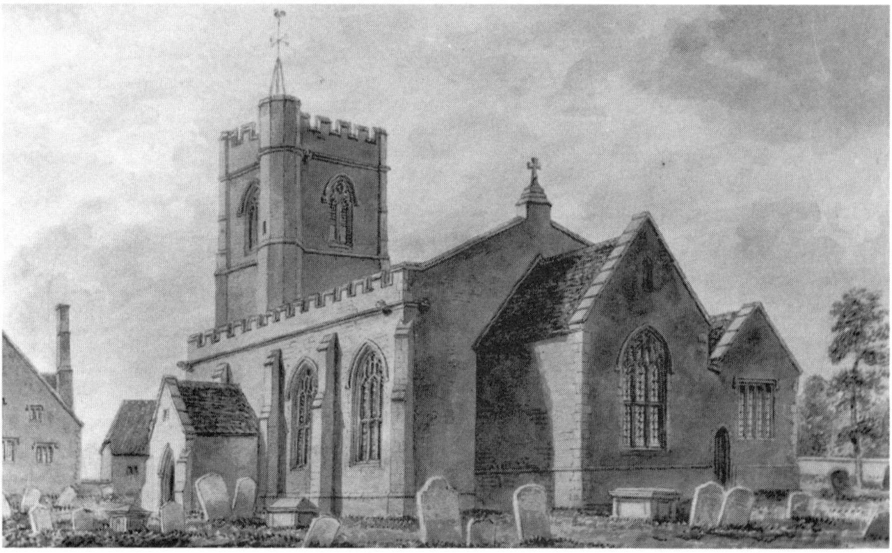

South east view of Haselbury Plucknett Church, 1839, by J. Buckler

Hatch Beauchamp

51/17–18 [St. John the Baptist] 12 February, 1857

This church has nave with north and south aisles, chancel and transeptal chapels, and west tower, wholly Perpendicular.

The arcades are not quite regular. On each side are 3 good Perpendicular arches of Tudor form with the light clustered piers of 4 stilted shafts, which have general capitals of foliage. The eastern (4th) arch on each side is very small, that on the south resembles the 3 others; that on the north is much plainer, but may have been tampered with. The south side has been much renovated and has 3 light windows with panelled soffits. The north side has not been touched and has 3 light windows within square heads, the spandrels being panelled. That at the west of this aisle contains some new obituary glass, those at the east end of the same, are bad. This aisle is incumbered by pues.

The chancel arch is plain and appears modern; [that] between the chancel and north aisle is pointed. On the south a modern vestry has been built transept fashion. The east window of 3 lights has been closed and against it within is a modern picture. Some windows have pieces of old stained glass. In the western part of the nave are some ancient seats and remarkably fine carved bench ends in which appear various subjects and figures: the Resurrection, St. John, St. George with the Dragon. There is an organ played with keys. The tower arch is open with continuous mouldings and there is incipient groining in the tower.

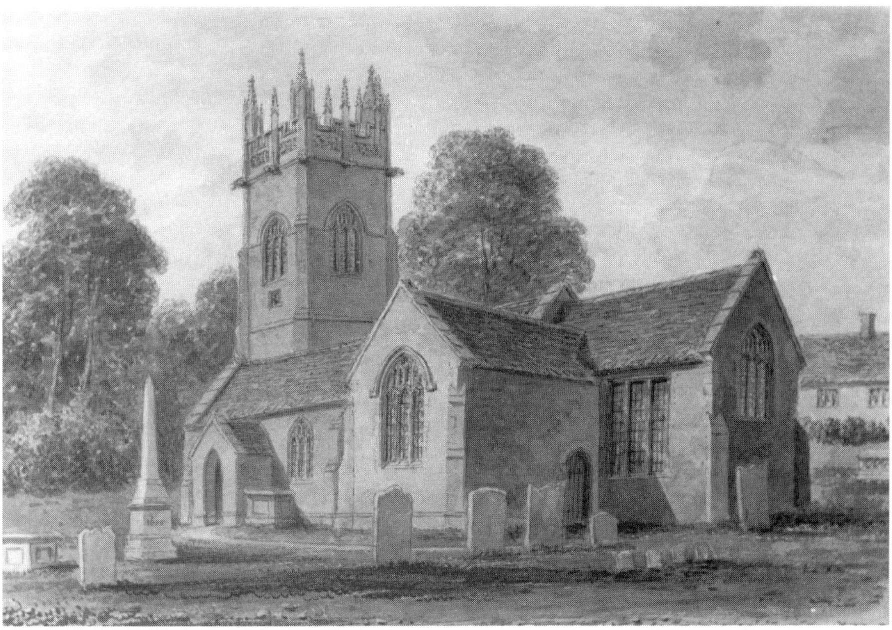

South east view of Hatch Beauchamp Church, 1842, by J. Buckler

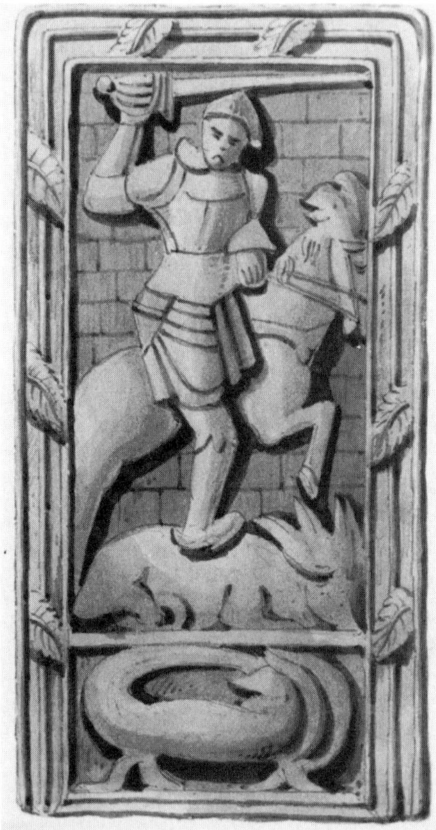

Hatch Beauchamp Church, 1849,
by W.W. Wheatley

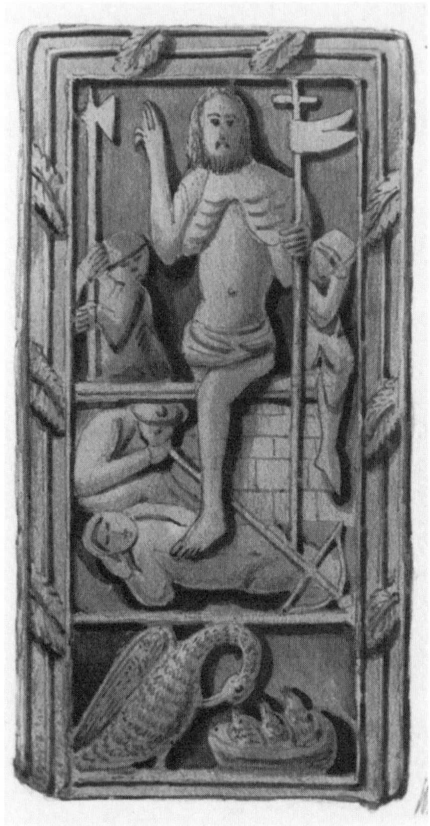

Hatch Beauchamp Church, 1849,
by W.W. Wheatley

The font is Perpendicular, the bowl octagonal, panelled with shields as also the stem. The tower is a fine Perpendicular one, buttressed at the angles and having a fine, pierced, panelled battlement with 8 large pinnacles to which smaller ones are attached (Somersetshire fashion) and all crocketed. The belfry window large, of 3 lights, having pierced stonework in the quatrefoils instead of louvre boards. The west window a good one of 4 lights. At the north-east is a corner turret of octagonal form. The west doorway [is] beneath a label carried to the ground.

Heathfield

51/53–54 St. John 1 February, 1862

A small church, having nave with south aisle, chancel, west tower and south porch. The aisle is rather a chapel than an aisle, being very short and bounded

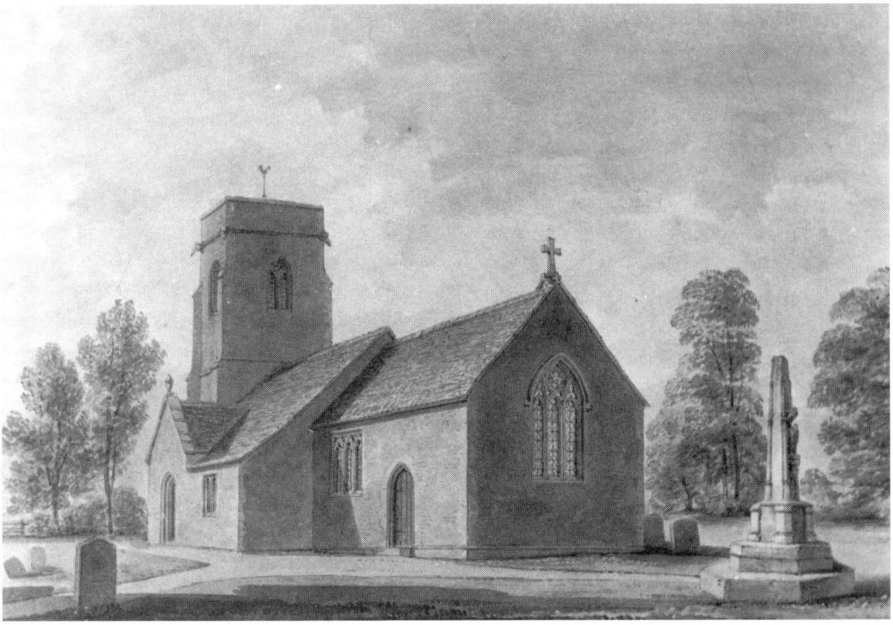

South east view of Heathfield Church, 1841, by J. Buckler

on the west by the porch. The arch dividing it from the nave is wide, flat and debased-looking. There is no chancel arch. The northern window square-headed of 4 lights, late Perpendicular. The roofs are coved with the usual ribs and bosses. The chancel is long and Decorated in character. The east window a very good one of 3 lights, early in the style. On the south is a square-headed, Decorated window of 3 lights. On the north is a square-headed single window.

The interior unimproved: has pues and gallery and an organ. The tower is low, has a moulded parapet, corner buttresses, west window Perpendicular of 3 lights and those of the belfry of 2. There is a flory cross built into the south wall of the chapel. In the churchyard the shaft of a cross, once apparently fine and charged with canopied niches, one of which has a statue, and set upon a square base on high steps.

Henstridge

50/46–47 St. Nicholas 1 August, 1849

The plan, nave and chancel, each with a north aisle, a western tower and south porch and a south chapel, or sacristy, very curiously added at the south-east angle of the chancel. The church is chiefly Third-Pointed and of no great excellence. The arcade of the nave has 4 moulded arches with lozenge clustered piers of the usual western kind and banded capitals and there is the

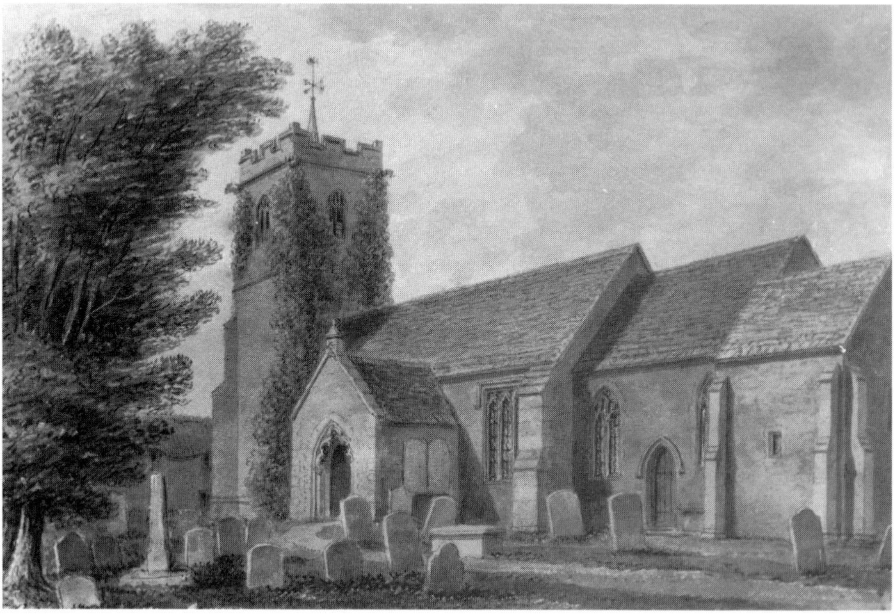

South east view of Henstridge Church, 1843, by J. Buckler

segment of a 5th arch abutting against the eastern pier. The chancel arch is a bold pointed one, springing straight from the walls.

There is an arcade of 2 pointed arches with octagonal piers on the north of the chancel. The south wall of the nave and that of the chancel are not quite in a line. On the south side of the nave are square-headed, labeled windows with tracery varying from Middle to Third-Pointed. The 2 east windows are of 3 lights and Third-Pointed. Those of the north aisle are similar and some on the south of the chancel have no hoods. The south porch is plain, but its outer door is not inelegant and remarkable for double feathering. The roofs are coved except in the aisle of the chancel, which has a flat ceiling.

In the eastern arch of the chancel is inserted a fine Third-Pointed tomb, with considerable traces of gilding and colour, bearing 2 mutilated effigies and an inscription in which occur the well-known line 'Sic testis Xte' etc. Adjacent to the tomb is an elegant door with flowered moulding. This has evidently been a chantry chapel. The canopy is flat and foliated with some niche panelling and small shafts.

In the north aisle of the chancel is a marble table set in the angle. Some of the windows retain pieces of stained glass. The font is a plain octagonal bowl on stem of like shape. There is a small barrel organ. The eastern chapel was closed but seems to be used as a vestry. The tower is a poor one with Third-Pointed battlement, 2 light belfry window, a square-headed west window and no west door. It is partly covered with ivy.

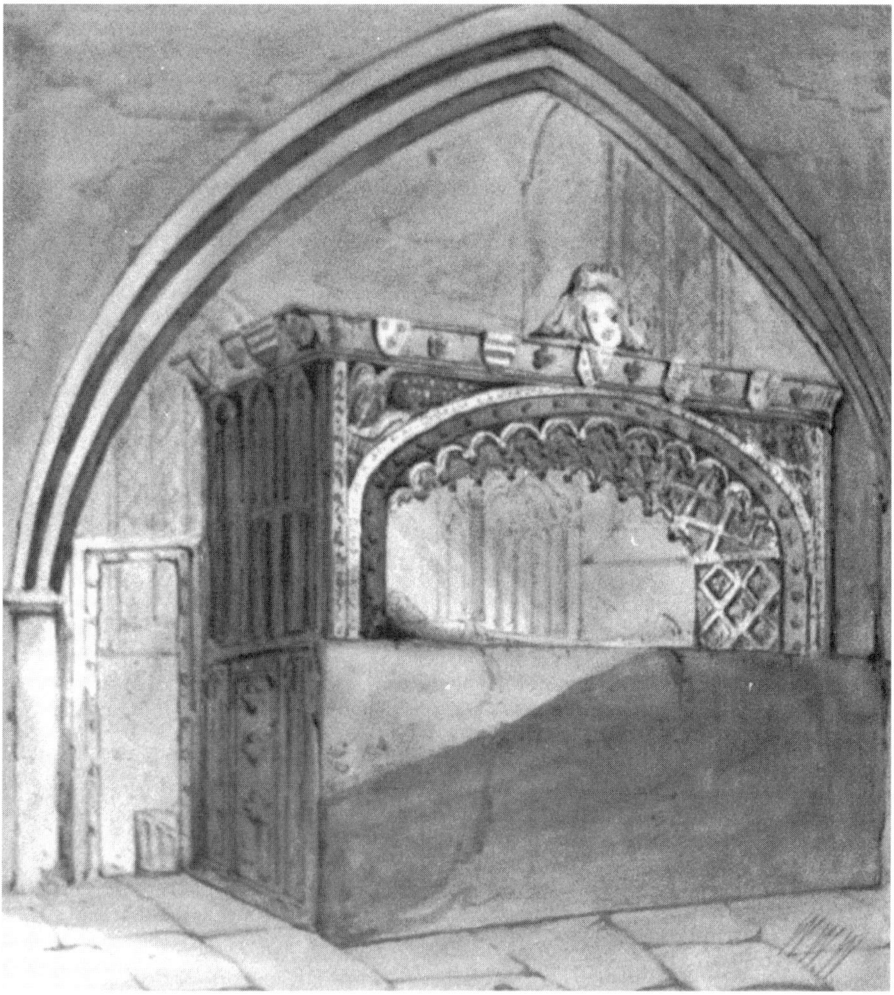

Monument in Henstridge Church to Sir William & Alice Carent, 1846, by W.W. Wheatley

Hinton St. George

52/16–18 St. George 19 February, 1852

The church has a wide nave with south aisle, chancel with north chapel and south aisle or chapel, a north transeptal chapel, west tower and south porch, all Perpendicular, but excepting the tower, the church does not quite rank among the fine churches of Somersetshire.

The tower is a very good one, divided by string courses; has buttresses set square near the angles, pierced battlement with panelled band below it, crocketed pinnacles at the angles and a stair turret at the south-east rising above the parapet and crowned by small pinnacles. There are good gargoyles,

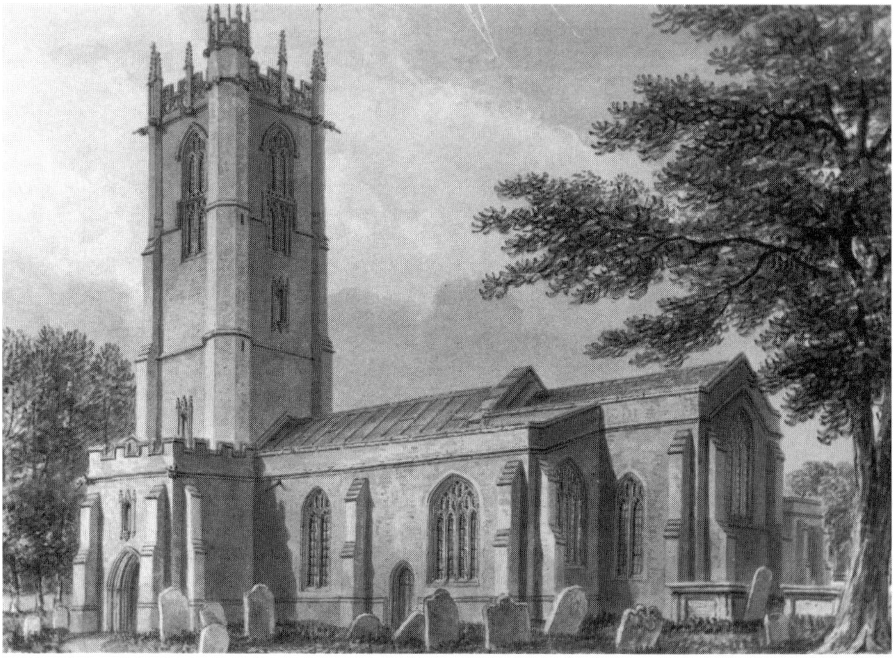

South east view of Hinton St. George Church, 1831, by J. Buckler

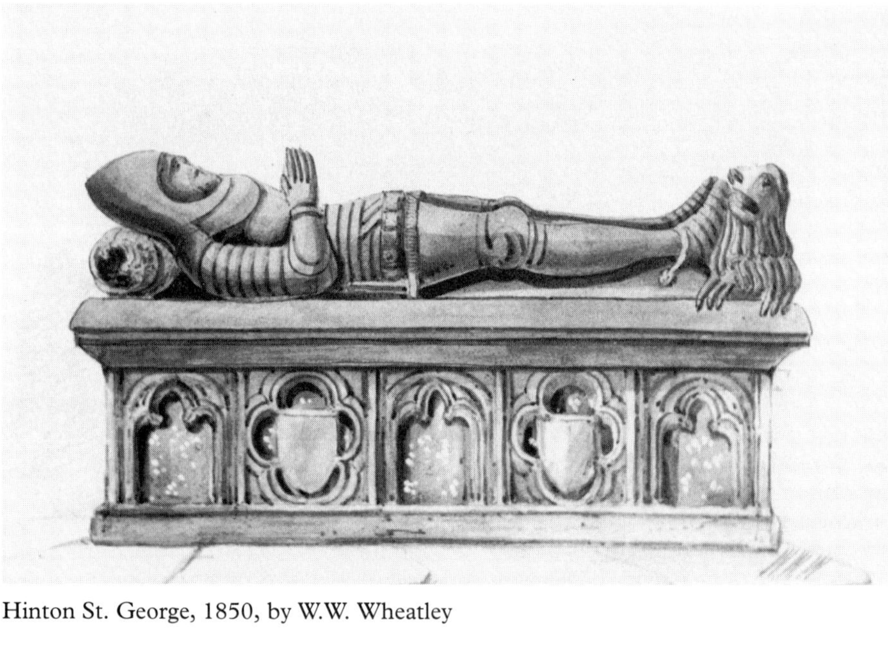

Hinton St. George, 1850, by W.W. Wheatley

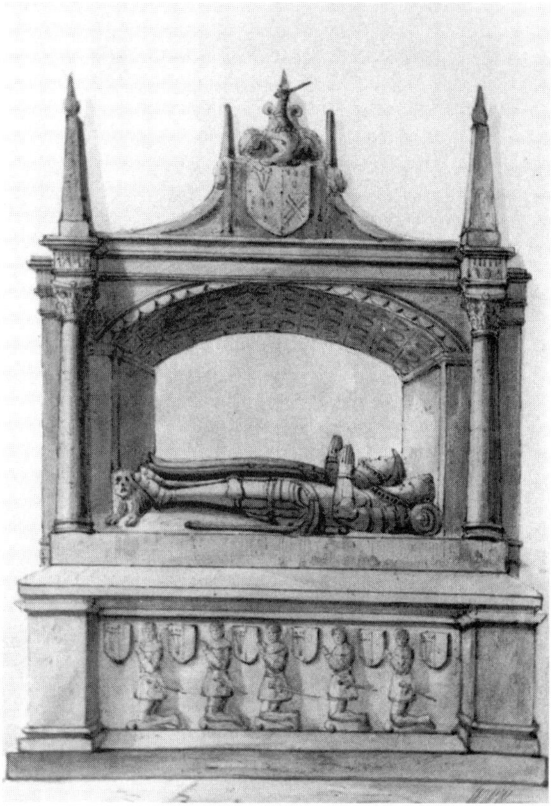

Sir Anthony Poulet & Katherine Poulet, Hinton St. George, by W.W. Wheatley

long belfry windows of 2 lights, and transomed, with the stone lattice work; canopied niches on the south and east, a 4 light window on the west below which is a door with label and panelled spandrels.

There is no battlement to the rest of the church, save the porch of which the outer door arch is on shafts and over it is a canopied niche. The inner door has continuous arch moulding and wood tracery of Perpendicular character. The nave is unusually wide. The arcade of the nave has 3 Perpendicular arches on the usual clustered piers with octagonal stilted bases and a 4th small arch next to the east, set askance. The tower arch is a good one entirely panelled. The windows are all Perpendicular, some of poor kind without foliations, but those at the east of the chancel and south aisle are better, the former of 3, the latter of 4, lights.

The nave roof is of flat pitch, panelled with figures of winged angels under the wallplate and tie-beams. The arch to the north transept has small shafts set at intervals.

The chancel arch is lofty, resembling the others. The chancel has, on the south, a 2 light window and piscina of plain character: extending beyond the south aisle to which the chancel opens by a panelled arch lower than the others. The north chapel, or transept, belongs to the Pouletts and abounds with sepulchral memorials of the family. There is, on the north of the nave, an altar tomb of the 15th century, panelled with trefoiled niches and with traces of colour, bearing the effigies of a knight in attitude of prayer and a band of square flowers.

A panelled arch opens from the transept on the east to the north chapel of the chancel, now a vestry. In the transept are 2 altar tombs, each with the effigies of a knight and lady, of mixed Gothic and Italian character, with debased canopies. On one are figures kneeling. There is one stately monument to Sir Anthony Poulett and Katherine his wife with effigies, 1600 and 1601. Others are of later date. A modern appendage has been made on the west for a family vault. The font is Perpendicular, has octagonal bowl panelled with shields bearing the arms of Poulett and others; a foliage band under the bowl and a panelled stem.

(The aisle to the west of the porch has battlement and good gargoyles.)

Hornblotton

51/28–29 St. Peter 2 September, 1862

A small, mean church consisting of nave and chancel, south porch and a quasi tower at the west end. The east window is Decorated, of 2 lights, containing portions of ancient stained glass and there are other similar Decorated windows north and south of the nave, one of which has been renovated. The west window Perpendicular of 2 lights and square-headed and one, also square-headed, of a single light is in the nave. The chancel arch is obtuse and ugly, apparently modern.

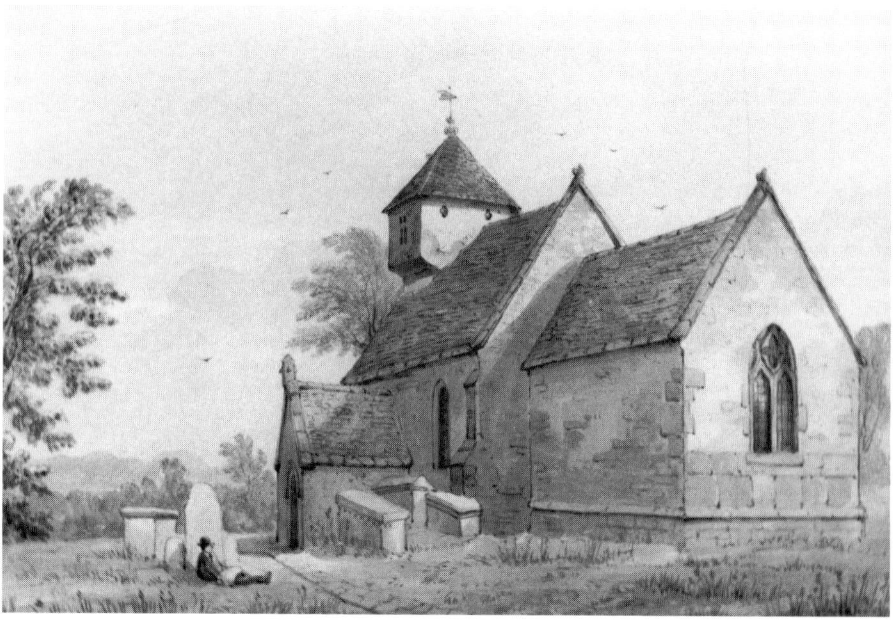

Hornblotton, 1845, by W.W. Wheatley

South of the altar is a piscina with quatrefoil orifice and pointed niche. Near the south door is a stoup. The font is Norman, circular and cup-shaped without a stem. The chancel arch is not central, there being much more of the chancel on the north than on the south. The walls lean outwards and the church is generally out of repair. The seats are open but very plain. The walls of blue lias covered with stucco; the roofs flagged. The belfry has a pointed roof and is an odd composition altered from the original plan. The chancel has a north door; the roof is ribbed and coved without bosses; that of the chancel is lower.

Horsington

51/80 St. John 8 February, 1864

This church is scarcely worth notice having been wholly rebuilt in very poor style except part of the tower, but retaining its former arrangement of nave and chancel, north porch and west tower. The chancel arch is round; there is an ogee-headed priest's door. The lower part of the tower may be old and has corner buttresses and stair turret on the north. The upper part has no character but 4 ugly pinnacles. The font is Perpendicular, bowl octagonal with quatrefoil panelling round the top, finishing in cup shape on octagonal stem and having figures of angels displayed. (5 bells, harmonium, pues, north and west galleries.)

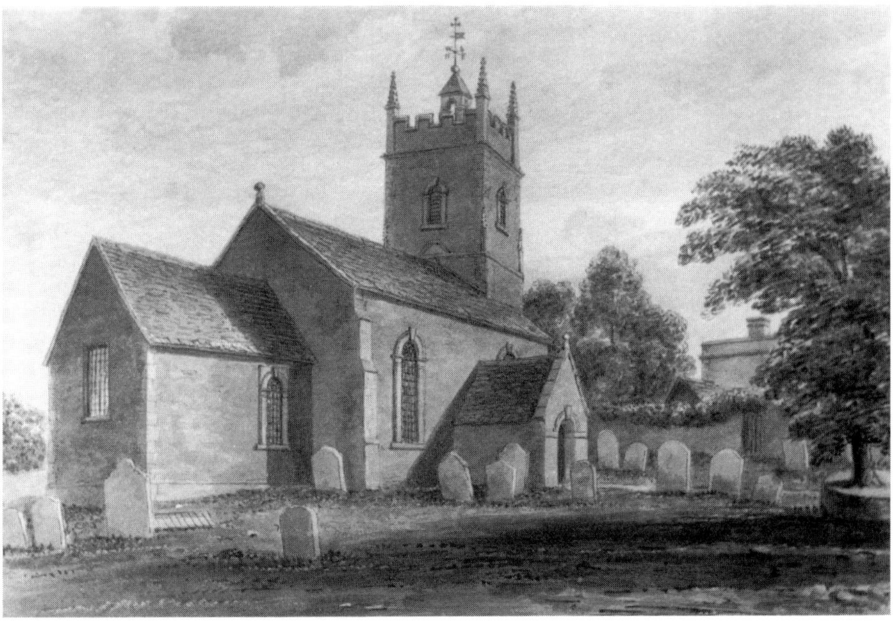

North east view of Horsington Church, 1842, by J. Buckler

Huish Episcopi

19/43–44 [St. Mary] 19 October, 1825

About half a mile from Langport is the village of Huish which has also a fine church with a tower of extreme richness and beauty which is hardly to be equalled. The tower is very lofty and forms a fine object in the surrounding country. It consists of 3 ornamented stages between each of which is a rich band of quatrefoils. The lowest stage has 2 fine niches with very rich, crocketed canopies, the next a large window with Perpendicular tracery filled with very rich stone lattice work. On either side of this window is an extremely rich niche with elaborate crocketed canopy. The highest stage has 2 large double belfry windows with most exquisite lattice work having between them small buttresses with pinnacles.

The whole is crowned with a battlement of most delicate open work and 8 rich crocketed pinnacles each having 2 small light pinnacles attached to them by slender flying buttresses, which give a most light and delicate appearance to the whole. The buttresses of the tower have springing from each of the set-offs, a delicate, crocketed pinnacle which has a fine effect. On the west side is a large Perpendicular window and below it is a handsome doorway flanked by false buttresses with pinnacles. Above it is a band of quatrefoils filled with lozenge shaped pieces of foilage. The spandrels of the doorway are filled with foliage. On the north side is an octagonal staircase turret.

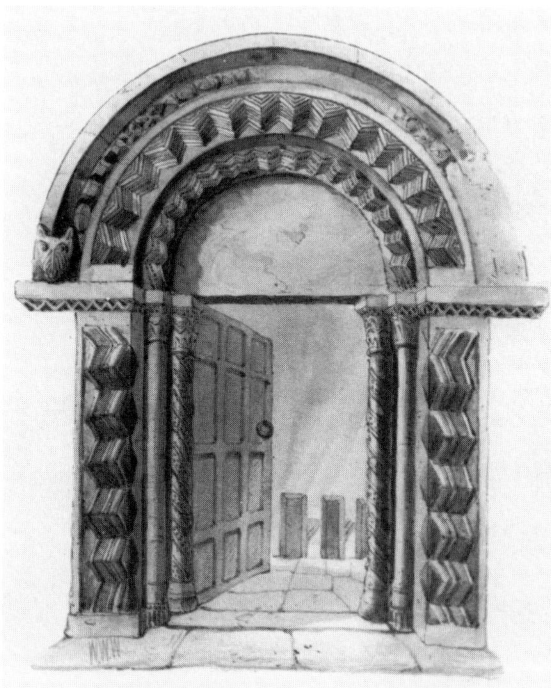

In Huish Episcopi Church, south door within porch, 1850, by W.W. Wheatley

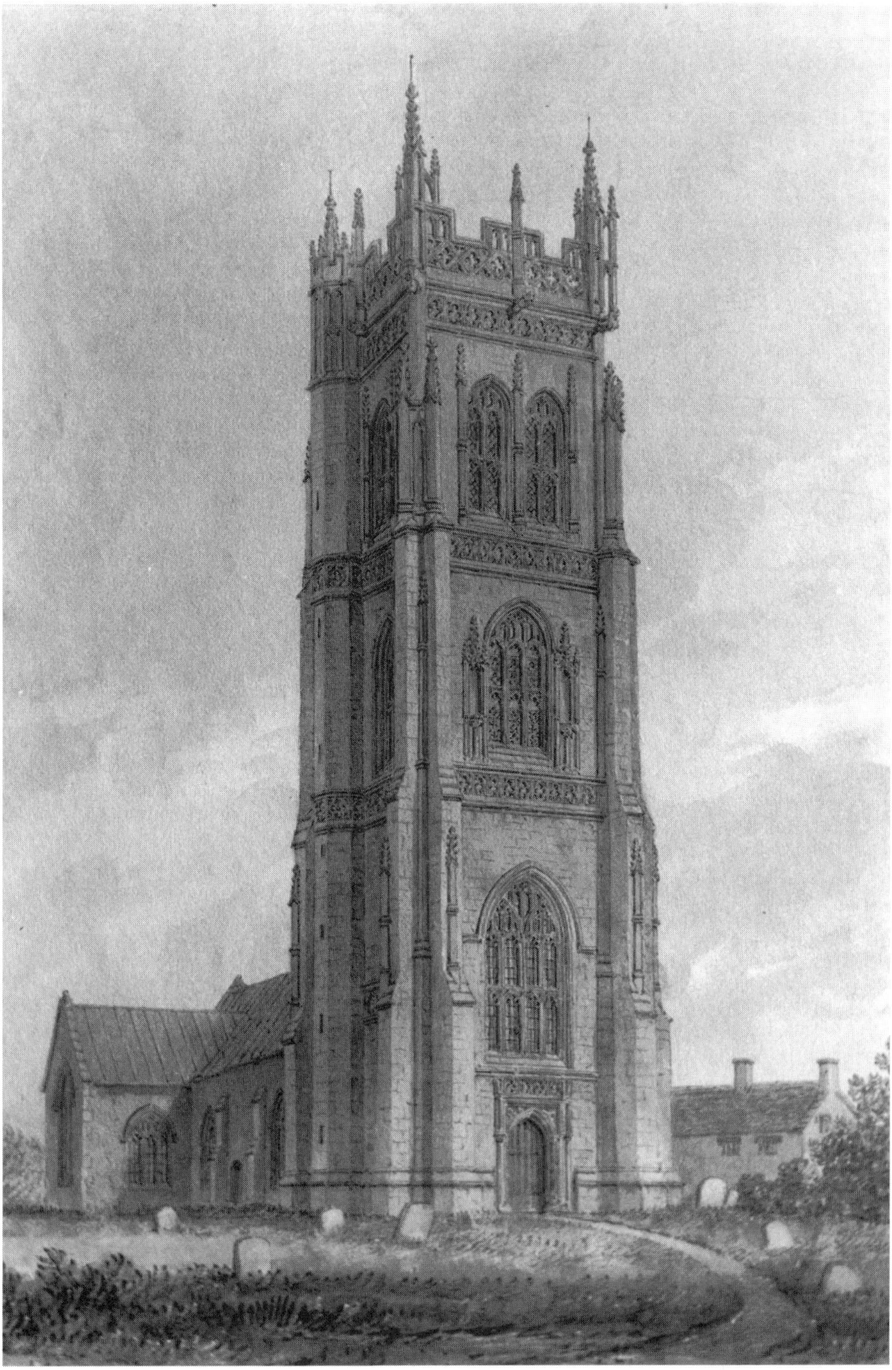

North west view of Huish Episcopi Church, 1830, by J.C. Buckler

The church is not equal to the exquistely rich and splendid tower but is not devoid of interest and has some early portions. It has a single nave, a north transept and a chancel which has a side aisle. The parapets are plain except in the aisle of the chancel which has a fine battlement. Within the south porch is a very good Norman doorway with two orders of moulding containing the chevron and other ornaments springing from shafts. The porch ranges with the chapel of the chancel. There is a Decorated window in the transept; the other windows are Rectilinear and one in the south chapel is handsome and of 4 lights. The tower arch is quite open to the interior and very handsome with panelled soffit. The chancel is divided from its south chapel by 2 arches slightly curved on a diamond shaped pier with 4 shafts, probably of Rectilinear period. The font is a panelled octagon. The interior is neatly kept.

Huntspill, West

50/61–63 All Saints 27 February, 1852

A large Third-Pointed church, having aisles to both chancel and nave, a western tower and south porch. There is no clerestory; the chancel aisles are embattled, but not those of the nave.

The interior spacious and handsome and unencumbered with galleries. The tower arch is lofty and open, the moulded orders upon shafts. The arcade of the nave has 5 good, moulded arches with good piers of the usual western arrangement, with 4 shafts which are but slightly stilted and have round

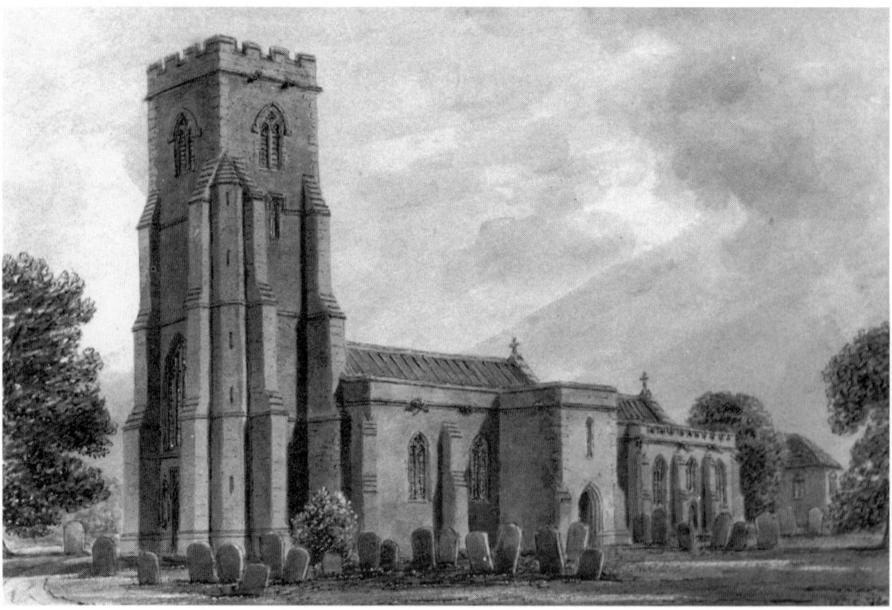

South west view of Huntspill Church, 1843, by J. Buckler

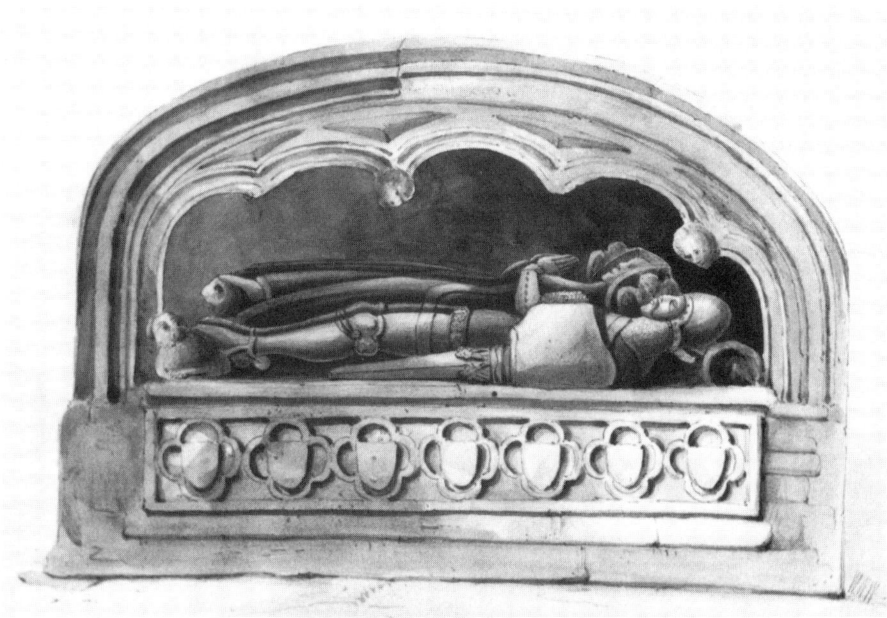

In Huntspill Church, 1843, by W.W. Wheatley

capitals. The chancel arch springs from a short shaft set up high above the pier which intervenes between the two lines of arcade, the interval being very small, does not allow space for more.

The chancel arcade, which is of 2 bays, on each side, very much resembles that of the nave, but the shafts are more stilted. The chancel extends one bay beyond the aisles and has on the north, a vestry with apartment over it, having one slit window and one square-headed of 3 lights with label. The nave has a modern ceiling; in the aisles are the original flat roofs with ribs, bosses and brackets. The windows of the aisles of the nave are chiefly of 2 lights; in those of the chancel of 3 lights, and those at the east of 4; the east window of the chancel of 5. Those on the north and south of it are of 3.

The south-east window is continued downward so as to form 3 seats divided by stone elbows. The chancel has a new open roof. There is a very small arched recess (a piscina?) between the arcade [and] the sedilia. The sacrarium is laid with fine coloured, encaustic tiles. There is an Italian reredos and candlesticks on the altar. There are arches of division between the aisles of the nave and those of the chancel. There are parclose screens in the chancel, which is fitted with modern stalls and has a marble pavement.

In the south aisle of the chancel, is a deep sepulchral arch which extends beyond the wall, so as to form an external projection. It is of somewhat flat form, has mouldings and good feathering with heads at the points of the latter. Under it is a low tomb panelled with a line of quatrefoils filled with shields. On the tomb, the effigies of a knight and lady in very good preservation, the lady has the square head dress and cherubs supporting her head; at her feet a dog; at the feet of the knight, a lion. Over the point of the arch is an angel bearing a shield.

In the south aisle of the chancel, under a window, is an ogee trefoiled niche with projecting, octagonal piscina. One of the south windows is filled with memorial stained glass to John and Edith Cripps. The font appears Third-Pointed, the bowl plain, octagonal with Perpendicular mouldings at the angles, the stem octagonal with shafts at angles having neither bases nor capitals. The cover is Jacobean.

The nave presents, externally, a steep lead roof. The porch is large, but has never had an upper floor. The outer and inner doors both have continuous mouldings and there are stone benches. The east gables, both of chancel and nave, have plain crosses. There are labeled priests' doors in the north and south chancel aisles. On the north side, corresponding to the roodloft place, an octagonal stair turret. The whole of the exterior is white with roughcast.

The tower is large and plain, embattled and divided into 3 stages with large buttresses not set at the angles. At the south-west is a stair turret rising not so high as the belfry window and connecting with the buttresses by flagged stop. The belfry windows are of 2 lights with hood. Below them a square-headed opening, labeled. On the west side is a 5 light window damaged by the top of the foils and tracery. Beneath it a pointed door with good mouldings set within a square with shields in the spandrels and flanked by panelled spaces containing niches with pedestals.

The churchyard is pretty, planted with trees and open to the fields. On the north side an ancient, pleasant-looking Rectory.

Ilchester

19/35–36 St. Mary 18 October, 1825

Ilchester is now a small poor place containing for the most part mean houses ranged in 3 short streets meeting at the centre in the market place. The church is dedicated to St. Mary and is a small building consisting of a nave and

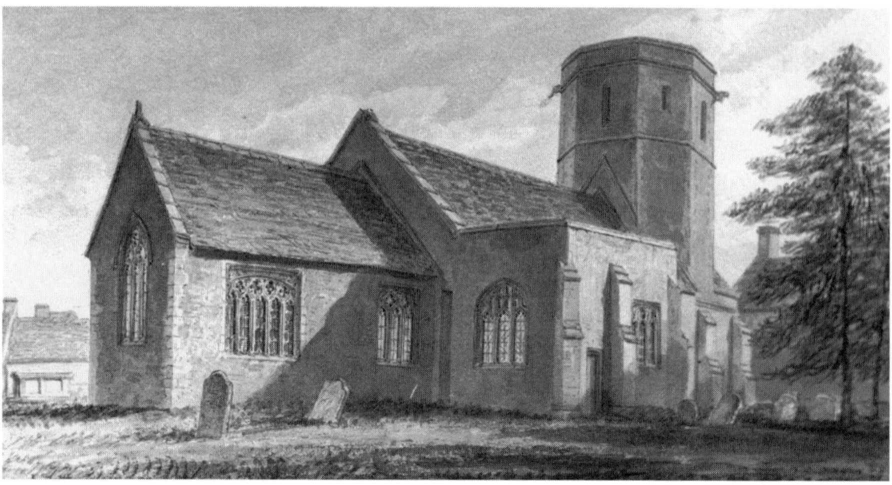

North east view of Ilchester Church, 1832, by J. Buckler

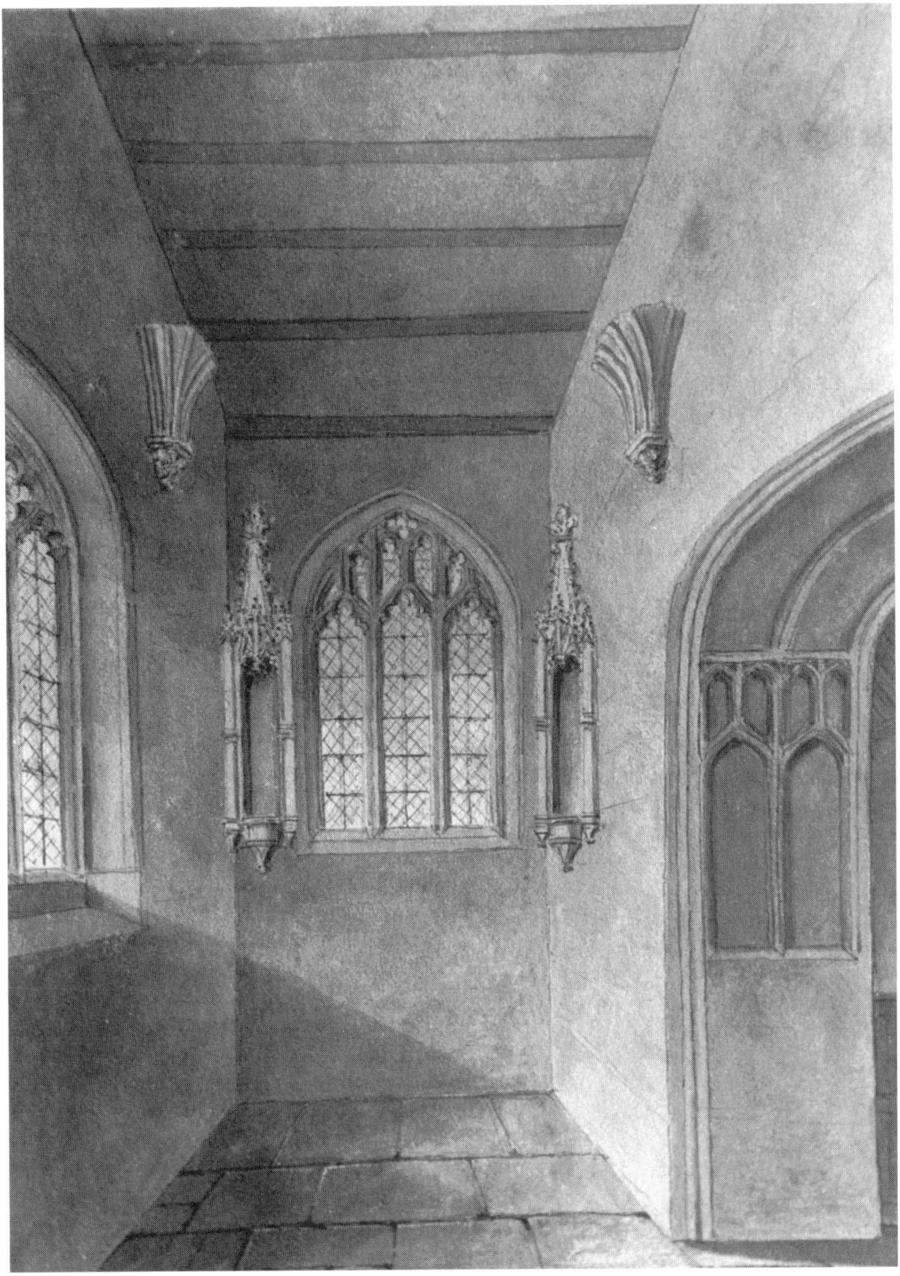

Interior view of chapel on north side of Ilchester Church, 1843, by J. Buckler

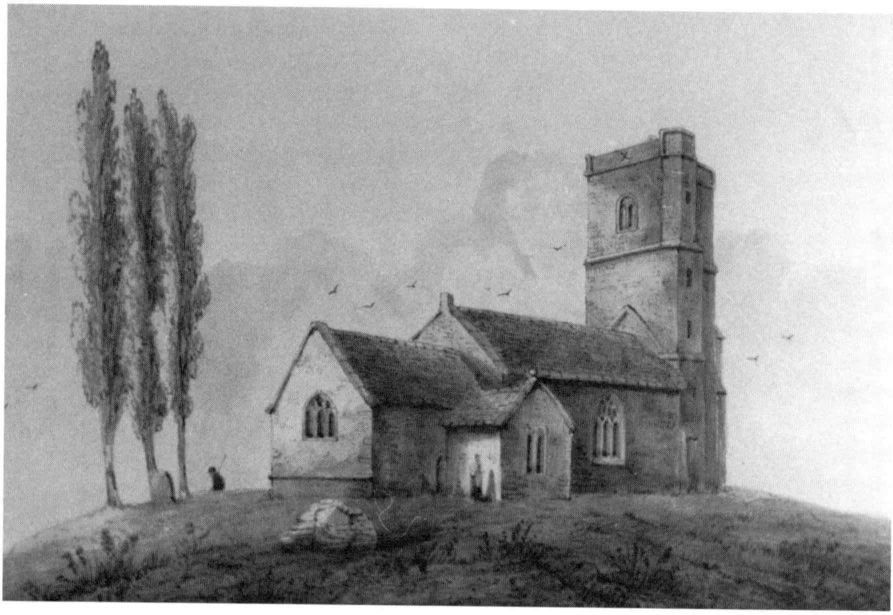

Northover, 1847, by W.W. Wheatley

chancel with a small chapel on the north side of the nave. At the west end is a low octagonal tower containing a clock and 5 bells. The tower (together with the whole church) is built of an ugly brown stone and has some plain lancet windows.

The arch from the tower to the church is Early Gothic: pointed and springing from brown moulded brackets having the nail head ornament. The windows of the church are mainly of Rectilinear character, but not elegant. On the north side of the chancel are some [windows] having a very contracted flat arch set in a square compartment and having the spandrels filled with foliage. The arch from the nave to the chancel is plain and pointed. The north chapel has some very good features of late Rectilinear work. The arch opening to it is contracted with panelled soffit and the windows of 3 lights with rather flat arches.

The ceiling is plain but it was originally intended to be groined in stone as may be seen from the springing of the ribs of the groining at the angles of the chapel. There are in this chapel 4 fine Rectilinear niches with very rich canopies of stone tabernacle work with fine crockets and pinnacles. The font is a plain octagon. At the west end is a gallery for singers.

The small village of Northover is over the river, opposite to Ilchester. The church is a small uninteresting fabric consisting of a nave, chancel and tower at the west end. The whole is very plain. The tower has a plain top and a square turret on the north side and 4 bells. The windows are chiefly of 3 lights and Rectilinear tracery of good work, without dripstones. The tower has on ye west side a plain niche. The chancel is divided from ye nave by a pointed arch. On the north side of the chancel is a small chapel belonging to the Chichester family. There are some carved wooden pew ends. The font is a plain octagon. The east window of 3 lights with an arch of slight curvature and a quatrefoil in the head.

Ilminster

19/39–41 [St. Mary] October, 1825

Ilminster Church is a very spacious and handsome structure in the form of a cross and consisting of a nave with aisles, a transept, chancel and tower in the centre. The style of the church is, as most others in this country, wholly Perpendicular of rich character. The tower is of rather late work but is very rich and magnificent. It is lofty and has 2 stages above the roof of the church, each of which is divided into 3 square compartments which are filled with Perpendicular tracery within large pointed arches and which, in the upper storey, is of open work in order to light the belfry.

Between the compartments are small flat buttresses with very rich crocketed canopies for set-offs. The whole is crowned with an embattled parapet and 12 large crocketed pinnacles. On the north side is a staircase turret. The nave of the church has lately been taken down and rebuilt in the original style and extremely earnestly. The west end has a fine large Perpendicular window of 5 lights. The south porch is also very good Perpendicular being much ornamented with panelling and having a beautiful doorway with rich ogee crocketed canopy.

The clerestory windows are broad and the arches which divide the nave from the aisles have been rebuilt in the Tudor form and are only 3 in number being much wider than the original ones which were 5 in number. The piers are of the common Perpendicular form. The nave has been newly pewed and fitted up in an extremely neat and respectable style with handsome galleries.

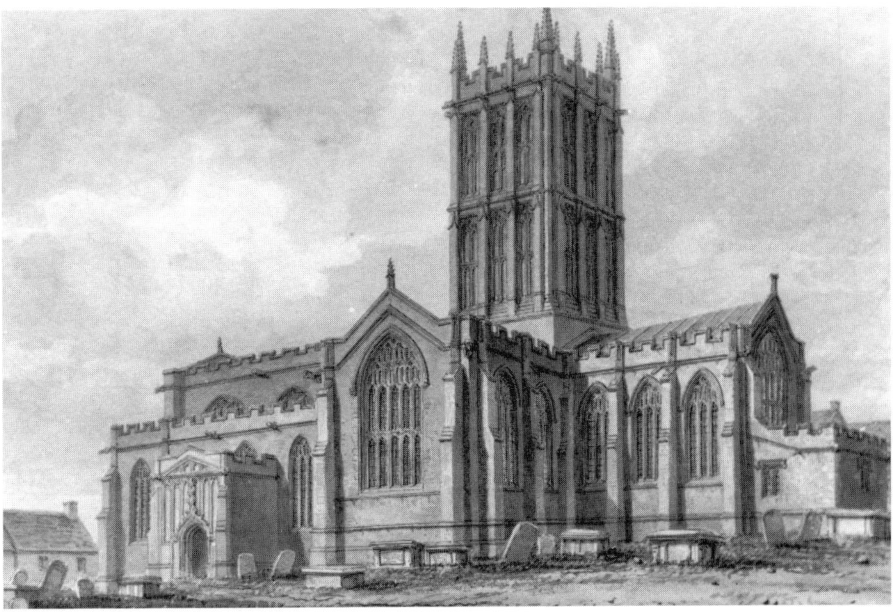

South east view of Ilminster Church, 1831, by J. Buckler

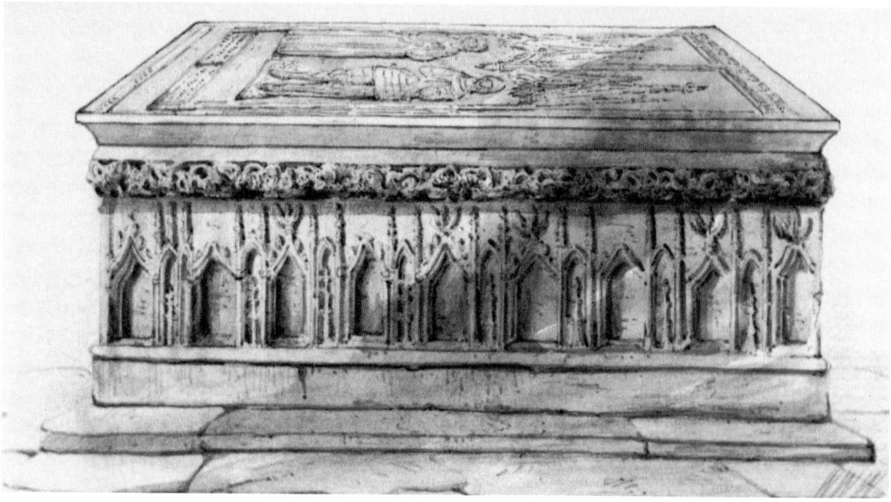

In Ilminster Church, 1850, by W.W. Wheatley

The exterior of the north transept is of extremely rich and handsome work. The window at the north end is of very elegant early Perpendicular work, having 5 lights and a cinquefoil above the head of the central light.

The north end of this transept is divided into three divisions of which the central gable is enriched with crockets and pinnacles and has the fine window before mentioned. The eastern side of the transept has a very beautiful parapet enriched with quatrefoils having fine crocketed ogee canopies. Beneath this is a band of square flowers and large water-spouts. The windows on this side have rather flat arches and are within square compartments. They are of 3 lights and have transoms and of long form. The spandrels have panelling and the dripstones are enriched with square flowers. The buttresses are richly panelled and have crocketed canopies. The side divisions of the north end and the west side have the same parapet as the east.

The west side has windows of the same form and a small Tudor door. The south transept is far less enriched and is in all its parts worked plainer. The south window is of 5 lights. The north transept has within an old roof with good pierced beams. The nave has a new wooden groined roof of very good execution. The ceiling under the tower is of stone and groined and the arches supporting the tower have their soffits panelled and piers of clustered shafts. On either side of the eastern arch of the tower is a small arched opening in the wall to the chancel and ornamented with panelling.

The chancel is worked plainer than the north transept, has an embattled parapet and 3 good windows on each side with a larger eastern one of 5 lights. The eastern gable has no battlement. East of the chancel is a small, low chapel now used as a vestry and opening to the interior by a pointed doorway. It is embattled and has water spouts and of the same character as the church but plainer. There are several instances of this small chapel in this country. What its use was appears to be uncertain. (A vestry.)

On the north side of the chancel is a small Tudor arched doorway with label and spandrels filled with shields. The font is at the west end of the nave; is octagonal with quatrefoils, a band of foliage and panelled pedestal. In the north transept are 2 fine tombs with brasses in excellent preservation. One is an altar tomb with the sides enriched with niches, canopies, etc., and on it are the brass figures of a knight and lady of the Wadham family beneath elegant canopies. Round them is an inscription on brass of which a great part is gone and beneath is a brass with some monkish verse. The figures are very perfect. The date 1410.

There is also another altar tomb to Nicholas Wadham and Dorothy his wife, founders of Wadham College, Oxford. The tomb is of black marble and Italian work has on it the figures of them in brass in most excellent preservation and of beautiful workmanship . . .

There are the following inscriptions on 2 brass plates in black letter:

Here lyeth interred the body of
Nicholas Wadham whiles he lived of
Merefield in ye county of Somersett
Esquire ffounder of Wadham Colledge
in Oxforde who depted this lyfe ye XX
day of Octob. 1609.

Here lieth also ye body of Dorothie
Wadham widow late the wife of
Nicholas Wadham Esqr foundresse of
Wadham Colledge in Oxforde who
died the 16th of May 1618 In the
yeare of her age 84.

Against the wall is a heavy marble monument with Corinthian pillars bearing a long inscription in monkish verse (vide Collinson).

The dimensions of the church are as follows:–

Length of the nave	60 feet by 46 in breadth
Square of the tower	21 ½
Length of the chancel	32 by 20 broad
Total length	113 ½ Transept 78 in length, 20 ½ broad.

Ilton

50/97–98 St. Peter 13 February, 1857

A pretty church in course of partial restoration, the progress of which, however, seems to be suspended. The plan includes a nave with north aisle, a south transept, chancel, and a tower with shingled spire on the south side of the nave.

The chancel is Decorated and has 2 windows on each side of 2 lights; the east window Perpendicular of 3 lights. On the south side of the chancel is a slight projection lighted by a small slit-like opening with a door to the chancel and communicating with the present pulpit, formerly, no doubt, with roodloft. The chancel arch is plain, pointed and continuous. An incongruous dormer window has been inserted on the south near the roodloft's place for giving light.

The nave is Perpendicular with an arcade on the north side of 3 arches of the usual kind with the western clustered pier of shafts and mouldings. The south transept also opens by a pointed arch. The windows are mostly of 2

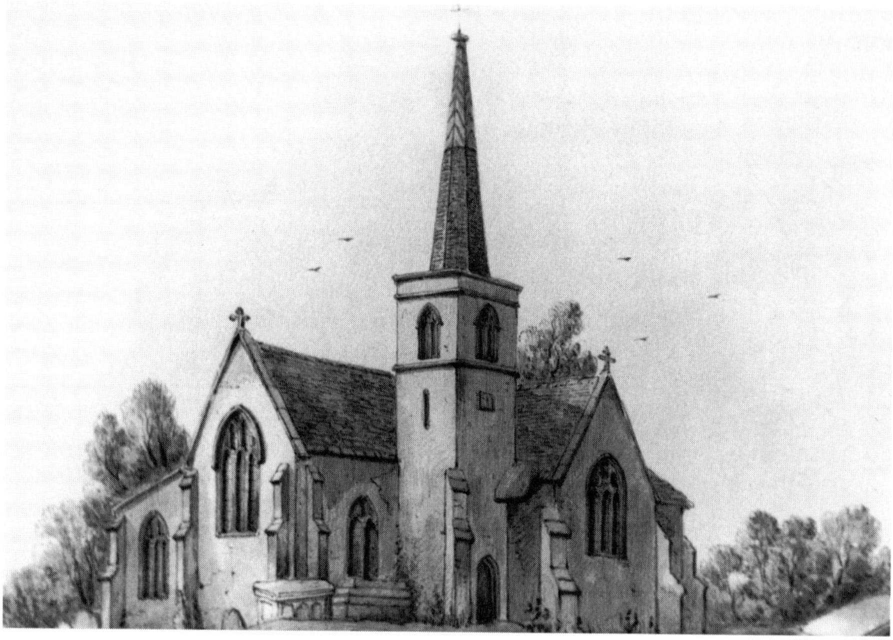

Ilton, 1850, by W.W. Wheatley

lights but that at the west of the nave and at the east end of the aisle are of 3 lights. The transept has a 3 light Perpendicular window on its east side filled with poor stained glass. This transept seems to be a private chapel and has inserted on its east side a modern door, the hood of which has a skull and hour glass for corbels, and over it the inscription Psalm 26.8.

There is an octagonal piscina at the east end of the aisle. In the nave are several pretty good carved ends of benches. There is also a squint in the aisle to the chancel. The font has an octagonal panelled bowl. The chancel contains a small organ. The altar is vested and on it are 2 candelsticks.

The roof of the aisle is leaded, the chancel slated, the nave tiled. The tower, which forms in its lower part a porch, is plain and may be earlier than the nave. It has one string, a moulded parapet without batttlement, corner buttresses, 2 light belfry windows and, within the square of the tower, an octagonal shingled spire. The door has good mouldings, the hood corbels are a crowned and mitred head. The gables are crowned by crosses.

Isle Abbots

50/99–101 St. Mary 13 February, 1857

A fine church of considerable interest. It comprises a nave with north aisle, chancel, west tower and south porch. The tower and north aisle are

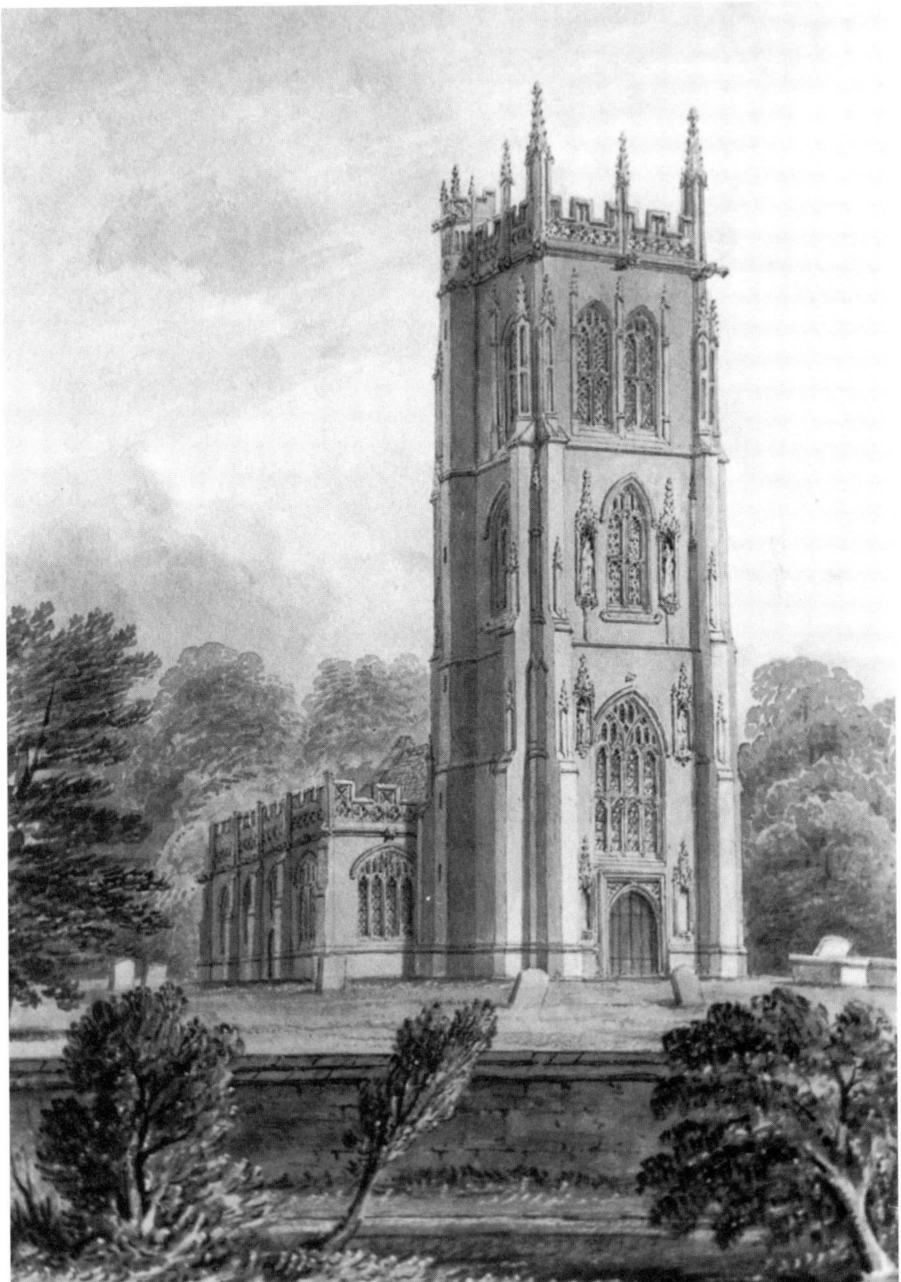

North west view of Isle Abbots Church, 1841, by J. Buckler

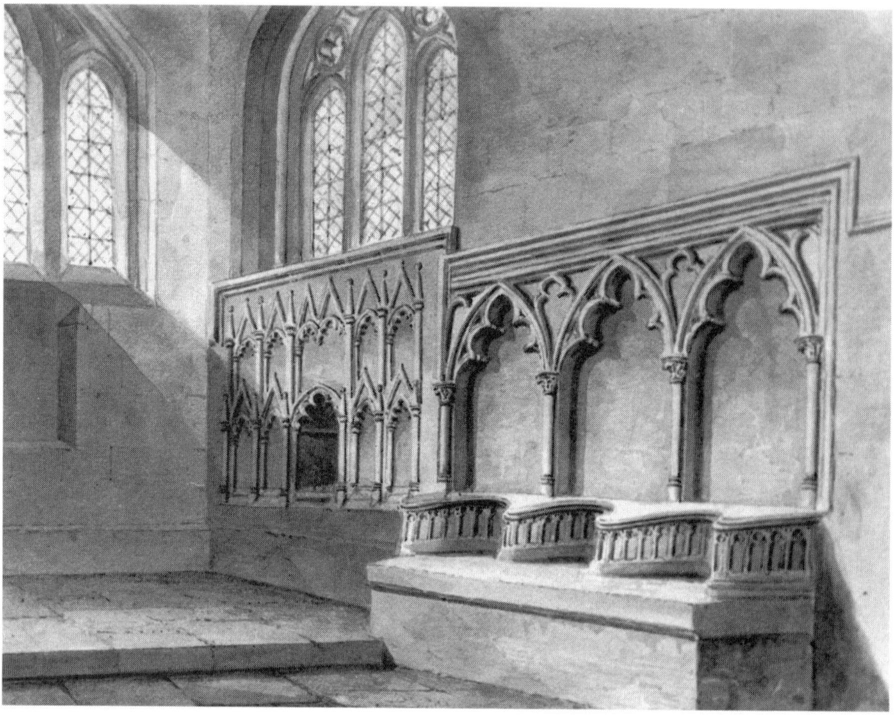

Priests' stalls on the south side of the chancel of Isle Abbots Church, 1840, by J. Buckler

Perpendicular, the former a fine specimen of the grand Somersetshire sort, the latter very late in the style. The chancel Decorated with some excellent and curious features.

The tower is divided into stages by 3 strings one of which is on a level with hood of the west window. The battlement pinnacles; the larger ones at the angles have small ones attached to them; the smaller ones in the centre of each side are set diagonally. Under the parapet is a fine panelled band of quatrefoils. The buttresses have at each stage crocketed pinnacles. The belfry windows are double on each side, of 2 lights, with transoms and the stone work pierced with quatrefoils in lieu of buffer boards which is almost peculiar to Somersetshire and has so fine an effect.

Between the belfry windows are also crocketed pinnacles. In a second stage is a single window set between fine canopied niches containing statues. On the west side is a large 4 light window with transom between 2 magnificent canopied niches containing respectively figures of the Blessed Virgin crowned and of St. Michael with angels. The west doorway is labeled and enriched with a panelled band and on each side of it a canopied niche but without statues. At the north-west angle is an octagonal turret running to the parapet and panelled at the top. The tower is built of beautiful stone.

Part of the body of the church has the stonework covered with stucco. The roof of the nave is partly covered with tiles, partly with lead. The north aisle has a rich panelled pierced parapet. The south porch has also a panelled battlement and gargoyles and a fine groined roof of late Perpendicular character with fan work and pendants: on the side, single trefoil windows and near the inner doorway a mutilated stoup.

The nave is divided from its aisle by an arcade of 4 very late arches of flattened form on light stilted piers of lozenge form having 4 slender shafts attached, intermediate hollows and general capitals of foliage. The nave has a coved roof, that of the aisle flat with ribs and bosses. The tower arch is continuous. On the south of the nave are 2 Decorated windows one of 3 lights trefoiled and one of 2 lights. In the aisle the windows are Perpendicular of 4 lights, subarcuated. The chancel arch is panelled in the Somersetshire fashion: part of the roodscreen remains and over the arch is the Decalogue, etc. The benches are mostly ancient and open, the ends presenting some fine wood carving.

The chancel is entirely Decorated of rather early character. Its roof coved and ribbed. The east window rather singular and plain having 5 plain lights without tracery or foils under rather a flat arch and set high in the wall with indications of a reredos beneath it. On the north and south are good 3 light windows the light trefoiled and 3 quatrefoiled circles in the tracery. On the south of the sacrarium 3 shallow sedilia without canopies though they perhaps were intended. Instead of canopies appears an arcade in the wall corresponding with the seats, each arch cinquefoiled, with foliage at the points springing from shafts and trefoils in the spandrels. This is a remarkable arrangement and the work is very good.

To the eastward of the sedilia is another remarkable arrangement in 2 compartments of which the eastern has a piscina with feathered arch, shelf at the back and sexfoil orifice, surmounted by a quasi-canopy consisting of 3 arches with feathering and crocketed pediments over the 2 extremities, both the piscina and the canopy upon shafts standing on bases of foliage and having fine capitals. The western compartment has 2 pedimental, crocketed and cinquefoiled niches, one over the other, flanked by octagonal shafts terminated by crocketed pinnacles. All this series of work is very curious and ranges under the window cills.

The font is early, the bowl square and Norman, the stem cylindrical with 4 shafts at the angles set upon a square base. On the bowl are small rude arches on one side containing foliage. On the other side grotesque sculpture much defaced.

On the north of the chancel arch is seen the rood door.

Isle Brewers

50/98 All Saints 13 February, 1857

A mean, small church, neglected and uninteresting. It has merely a nave and chancel with west tower and south porch. On the south side of the chancel is a 2 light Decorated window with square head; also a Decorated window on the south of the nave. The east window is Perpendicular of 3 lights and some other windows are single and Perpendicular. The chancel arch, if it ever existed, has disappeared; the ceilings plastered.

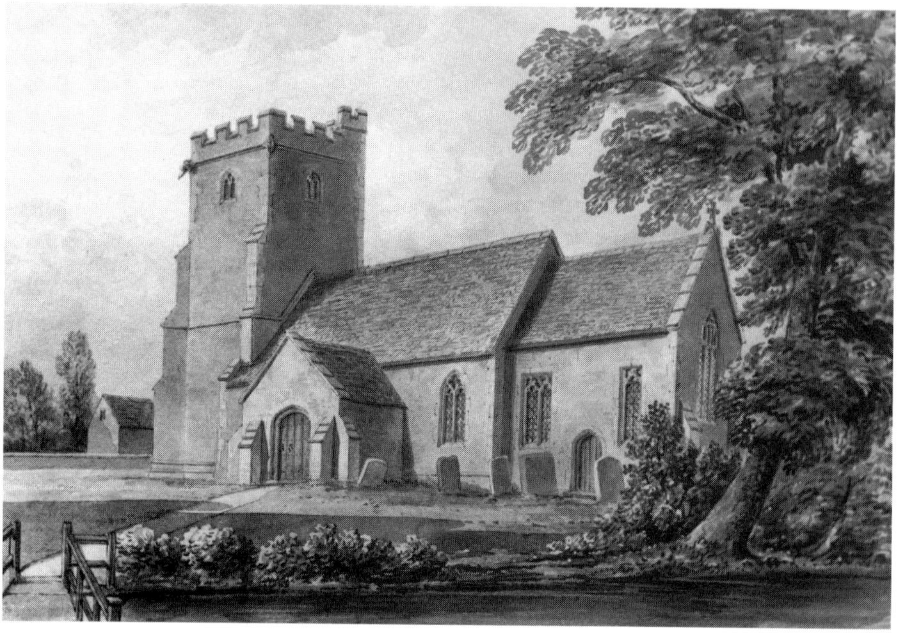

South east view of Isle Brewers Church, 1841, by J. Buckler

The interior is poorly pewed and much needs improvement. A few plain old benches remain. The tower is a plain Perpendicular one divided from the nave by a pointed arch on shafts. It is embattled and has an octagonal turret at the north-east. The belfry windows of 2 lights. There are gargoyles but the tower is stuccoed. The font is early, a circular bowl on a stem of similar form with a rope moulding. There are 4 bells. The churchyard is close to the river, damp and muddy.

Keinton Mandeville

49/26 St. Mary Magdalene Before 1840

A small church partly rebuilt and comprising a nave and chancel without aisles and newly built western tower of blue stone and rather bad design. The original tower stood on the north side of the nave and was of octagonal form with a conical top and it is much to be lamented that so curious a specimen should have been destroyed. The nave seems also to be all modern, but there are crosses on the gables both of nave and chancel.

The chancel arch is pointed but very rude, without mouldings and probably early. On its north side are two lancet windows and one at the east end which, to the interior, are set within wide arches of trefoil form. The font is apparently Norman: a circular basin on a cylindrical pedestal standing upon an octagonal base.

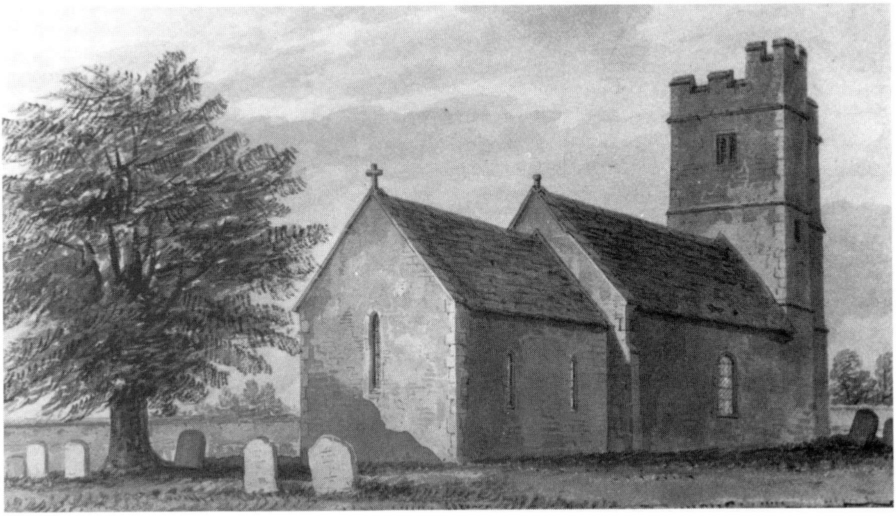

North east view of Keinton Mandeville Church, 1834, by J. Buckler

Kelston

52/1 St. Nicholas 9 June, 1871

This church has a nave with south aisle, chancel, west tower and north porch. The arcade of the nave is semi-Norman having 3 pointed arches on circular columns having foliage in the capitals. The chancel arch is Early English, pointed, on corbeled shafts which have capitals of foliage. The roof of the nave

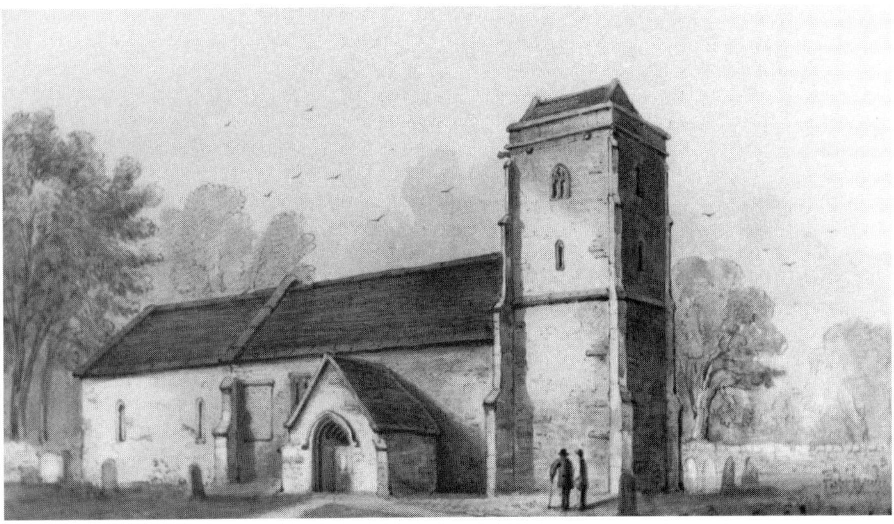

Kelston, 1843, by W.W. Wheatley

is new. The windows on the north side are new, of Decorated character, of 3 lights with segmental arches. The southern windows are similar, also renovated or wholly new, but of 2 lights.

The chancel has on the north and south 2 single lancets cinquefoiled and a priests' door. The east window Decorated, geometrical, of 3 lights. The north porch is Perpendicular; the doorway within it has ogee head. The tower arch is low and pointed. The tower is so much mantled in ivy as to cover its details. It is of plain Perpendicular work with corner buttresses, 2 light belfry windows; the parapet has a low, pointed gable on the east and west so as to form a saddle roof. The pinnacles are unfinished. There is a small 2 light window on the west and gargoyles at the angles of the parapet. The roof of the nave is slated. The public way is on the north. The churchyard is very pretty and planted with flowers.

Near the church is an ancient barn.

Kenn

51/60 [Unknown] 16 August, 1862

This small church has recently been almost wholly rebuilt. It consists of a nave and chancel without division, south porch and small western tower. The latter is ancient but very plain and devoid of architectural character having neither buttresses nor string courses, plain lancet openings and surmounted by a whimsical quasi-spire recently added which is stepped and surmounted by a cross. The roof of the church is ridged, the eastern part of richer character and

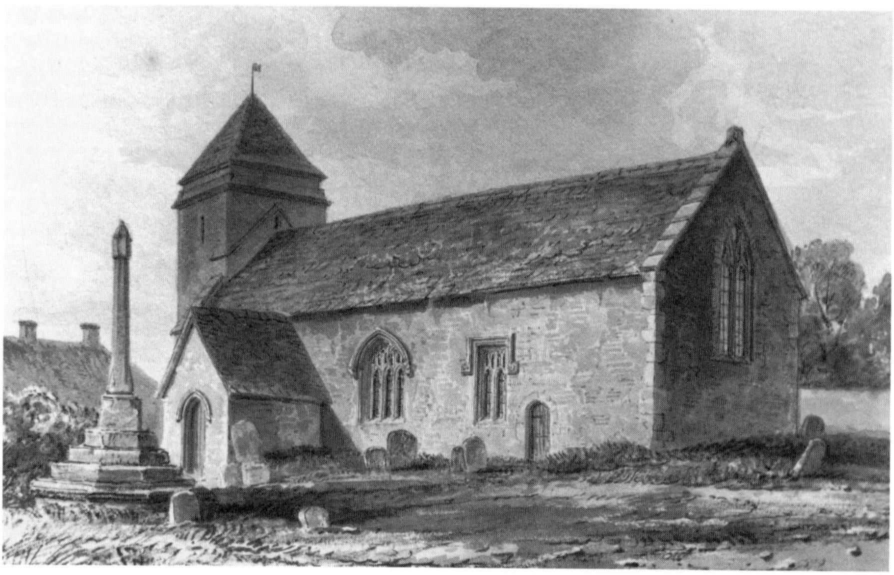

South east view of Kenn Church, 1828, by J.C. Buckler

ironwork. The south porch has the outer doorway with obtuse arch having continuous mouldings and hood upon corbel heads.

The tower arch is low, pointed, very plain. The walls of the body are all new, the windows Perpendicular of 2 lights in the nave. The east window Decorated, of 2 lights. The roof of the cradle form. On the north of the chancel is a vestry. The chancel stalled. The nave has open benches of oak. The pulpit a new one of stone. The sacrarium laid with tiles. There is a stone reredos and marble steps to the altar.

The font has [an] octagonal bowl on a stem surrounded by shafts with small capitals and moulded bases. In the churchyard the tall shaft of an ancient cross upon 4 high steps.

(The tower has some of its openings with square heads. The church was opened 29 April, 1862.)

Kewstoke

51/57–59 St. Paul 16 August, 1862

This church has nave with south chapel and porch, chancel and western tower. It is of early origin and retains some early portions with much of late date. The south doorway within the porch is fine Norman surmounted by a pediment and having 3 courses of arch mouldings, all ornamented, the outer with the

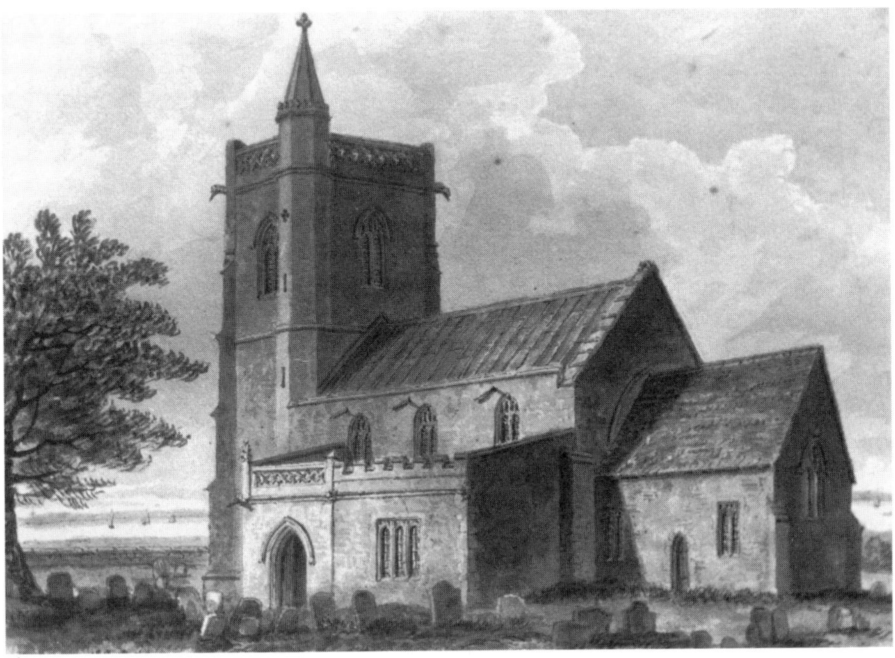

South east view of Kewstoke Church, 1828, by J. Buckler

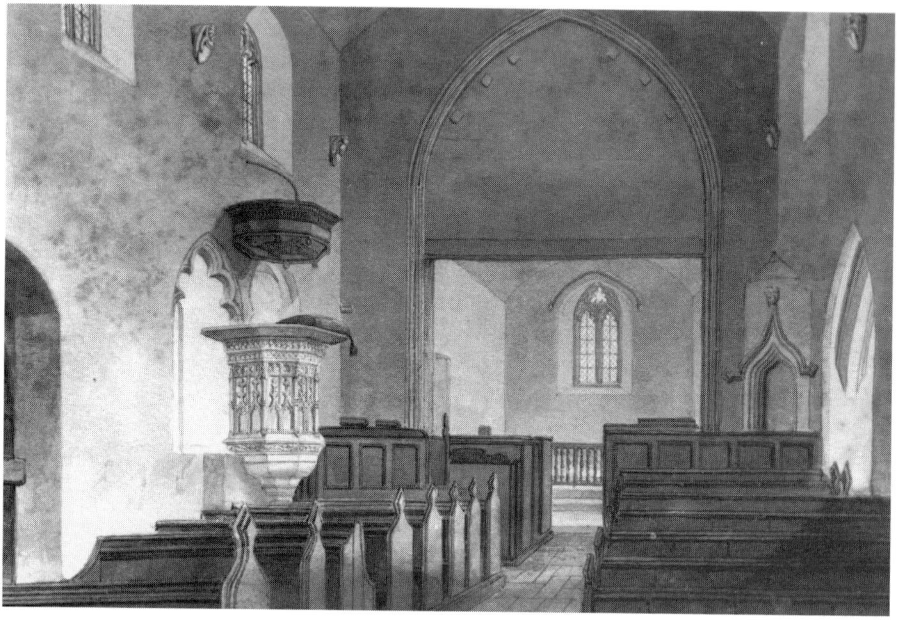

Interior view of Kewstoke Church, 1829, by J.C. Buckler

billet and indented work, the second with the beaded embattled, the inner with studded lozenges or frettes. (The hood has indented ornament.) The second member has shafts with spiral mouldings and capitals, the others are upon imposts.

On the north side of the nave are 2 Decorated windows of 2 lights with the feathering to the rear arch after the Somersetshire use. The nave has a clerestory on each side though there are no regular aisles, the windows being Perpendicular of 2 lights. The porch is large and modernised but has a pierced panelled parapet. The chapel adjoins the porch on the east and is low and Perpendicular with square-headed windows of 3 lights. It opens to the nave by a pointed arch springing at one from the wall. Some other windows in the nave are Perpendicular. The roof of the nave is new and is fitted with neat new open seats.

The tower arch is Perpendicular and continuous and the chancel arch is similar. The pulpit is a fine ancient one of stone with much ornamental panelling and niches with ogee canopies, a band of vine leaves and grapes and a Tudor flower cornice, all upon an octagonal stem. The prayer desk is modern. The font has a plain octagonal bowl on a circular stem with base mouldings.

The chancel has a lancet on the north; on the south 2 Perpendicular square-headed windows of 2 lights and a new porch, rather inappropriate. The east window of 2 lights and over it a rose window. There is a new reredos and the sacrarium is laid with new encaustic tiles. On the north side is a square aumbrye. South of the chancel is an odd doorway with ogee head with finial. There is an organ in the nave. On the north of the nave is a Decorated doorway with cinquefoil feathering. The clerestory on the north has a good parapet. The roof leaded; the south chapel has a small battlement.

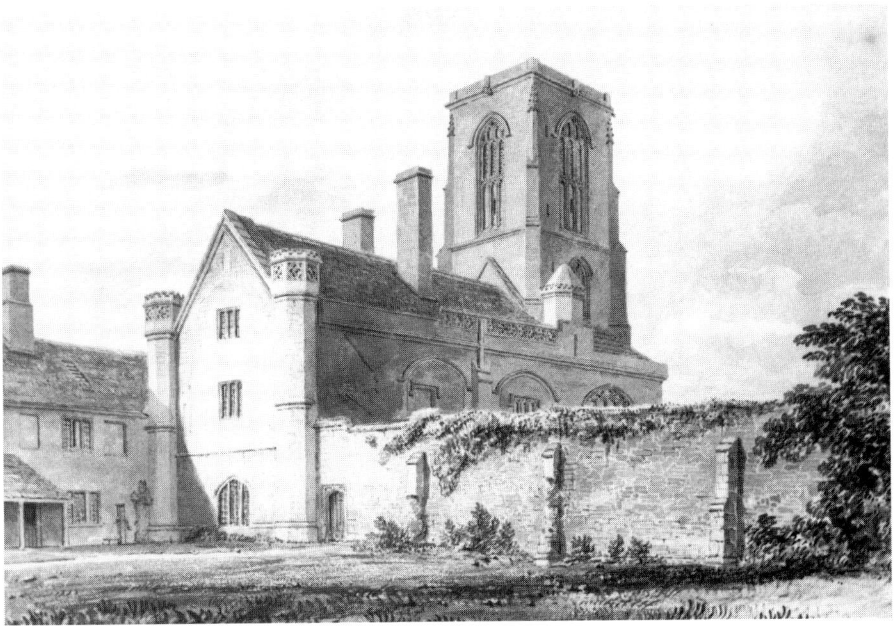

South west view of Woodspring Priory, 1827, by J. Buckler

The tower is good Perpendicular of a local character divided by one string course, having a fine parapet of pierced lozenge panelling, corner buttresses and at the south-east an octagonal stair turret surmounted by a lofty pyramid. The west window and those of the belfry are of 2 lights. The site of the church is striking: on an eminence bounded on one side by beautiful woody hills and on the other commanding an extensive view over a flat plain extending to the sea.

In this parish 3 miles distant, in rather a secluded site on the plain are the remains of Woodspring Priory which are imposing as seen at a distance. The lofty Perpendicular tower remains perfect which probably once rose from the centre of the church, but it is now surrounded by buildings which, though partly original, have been altered and modernised so as to form a dwelling house for the adjacent farm and it is not easy to trace the exact arrangement of the monastic buildings and church.

The tower has the local pierced parapet and latticed belfry windows of 3 lights. All the work which can be seen appears to be Perpendicular. There is a very fine base in the form of a cross, the buttresses of which have heraldic shields. There are also 2 shields on each side of the gateway, one armorial, one with the 5 wounds borne by angels.

(The tower was probably central; certainly at the east end of the nave which is now formed into the family house and is inacessible.

There are elegant, small octagonal turrets at ye west end of the nave with pierced quatrefoils. The 2 shields, now upon the gateway, were once on pillars within the church.

The refectory remains with its fine open wood roof but is now a cart house.

Illustrations in Rutter's Somersetshire.)

Keynsham

50/7–9 St. John the Baptist 9 September, 1843

This is a large church, Perpendicular in its general appearance but with an earlier chancel and some features in other parts of an earlier character and some singularity. The plan at the present embraces a lofty west tower, nave with side aisles and south porch, chancel with south chapel. On the north side, eastward of the aisle, stood the original tower which fell down in 1632, but the lower portion remains and is used as a vestry. Perhaps the present tower was built subsequent to that date for though its general outline is good and in imitation of Perpendicular work, there are strong indications of debased style.

It is 3 stages in height, the parapet pierced in a style common in the vicinity of Bristol and there are 4 square band pinnacles at the angles. The belfry windows are of poor character. The next stage has rather fine panelling in squared compartments. There are octagonal stair turrets at the angles of the west side of the aisles.

The south aisle has indications of early Decorated work externally: under the parapet is a cornice of ballflower continued round the turret. The parapet itself is moulded. At the west of the south aisle is a small door now closed. The north door also is closed and south porch, an elegant Perpendicular specimen, made into a coalhole! It has a good battlement and niche in front and a cornice of 4 leaf flowers. Within, the stone roof has beautiful groining, but the whole is in a wretched state.

The north aisle is embattled and also its western turret. It has some good gargoyles. It seems to be entirely Perpendicular of which character are all the

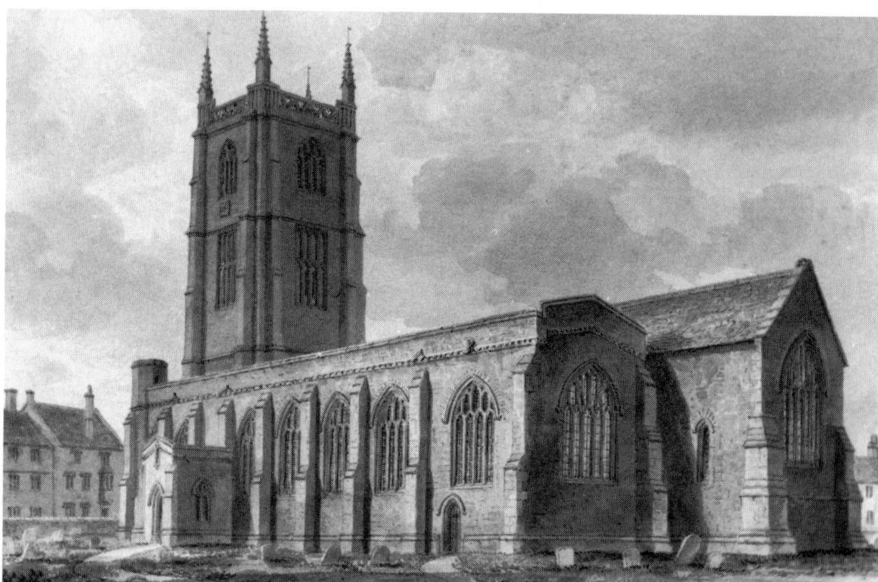

South east view of Keynsham Church, 1828, by J. Buckler

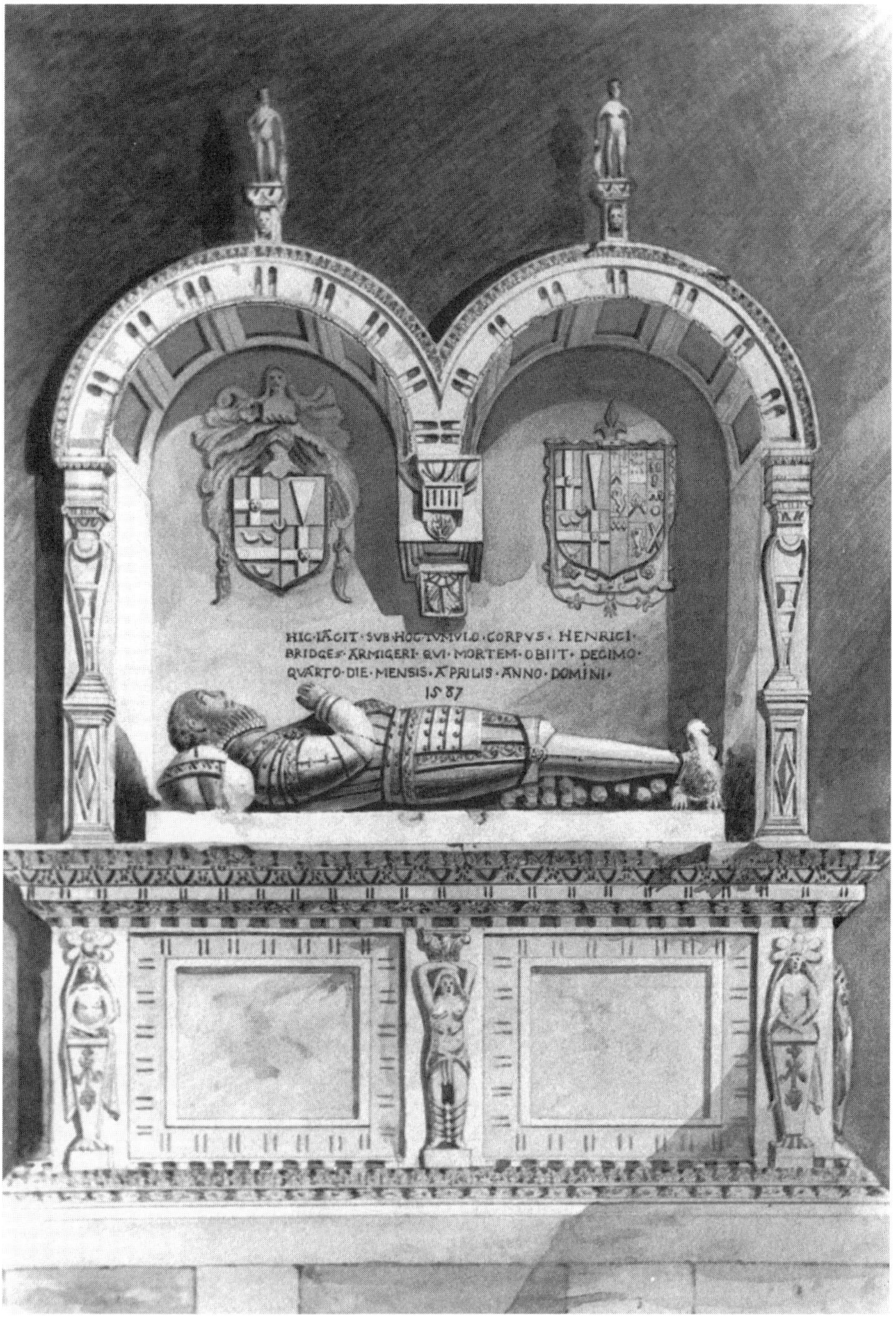

In Keynsham Church, ? by W.W. Wheatley

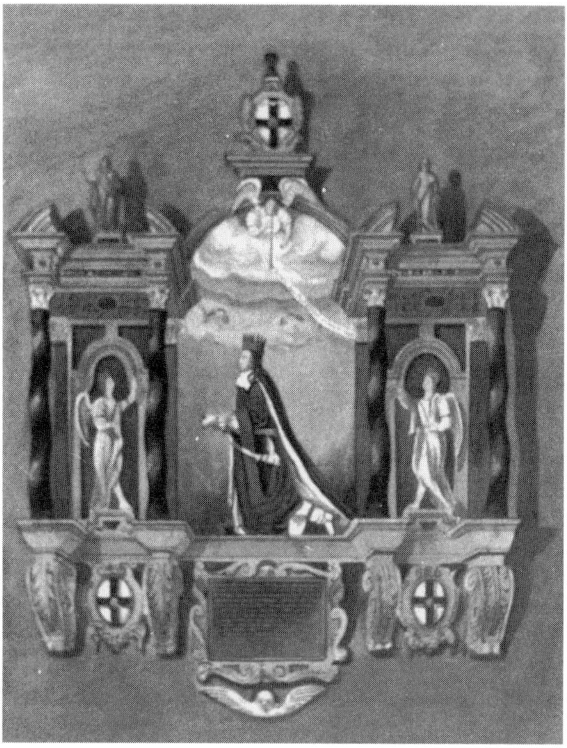

In Keynsham Church, ? by W.W. Wheatley

windows in the aisles of the nave. The interior is very spacious, of great length but too low in comparison and, unfortunately much out of order and disfigured by modern arrangements. There are 8 arches on the south side of the nave and 7 on the north but there is a gallery across it at a distance of 3 arches from the tower, the space westward of it being quite open, that eastward incumbered with frightful white pues and used for divine service.

The arches on the south side are tall and pointed, with octagonal piers having square bases. The northern have better mouldings, the piers light and lozenge form of Perpendicular character, 4 small shafts attached and octagonal capitals and bases. There is no clerestory. The south aisle has a beautiful panelled ceiling of wood, sub-divided into many small compartments and the ribs on brackets. That of the north aisle is perhaps still better in its panelling and tracery and pierced spandrels, but both are unfortunately much out of order. The nave has a coved roof with plaster ceiling probably of the 17th century. The north aisle is narrower than the southern.

The nave is divided from the chancel by a wide pointed arch springing straight from the wall and deformed in its appearance from the two sides being unequal. This arises from the alteration on the south side of the chancel by the addition of a chapel when this arch was extended on the south side beyond the original pier. There is a roodscreen, of late and debased character and now painted white and bearing arms of Brydges, within the chancel arch. There is between the south aisle of the nave and the south chapel of the chancel a very elegant roodscreen of Perpendicular character with fine tracery, vine cornice and roodloft.

The chancel has Early English walls in which appear several lancet windows now closed. It seems also to have had a small chapel on the north and the original string occurs in the exterior of the east end stopped by the present inserted window of Perpendicular character and of 5 lights. An arch has been opened in the original thick wall communicating with the south chapel, the whole of the soffit elegantly panelled in the Perpendicular style. The south chapel has fine Perpendicular windows, the eastern of 5, the southern of 4 lights. The chancel and south chapel have plastered ceilings as the nave.

The space enclosed for the altar is large and there are 2 large monuments opposite each other, that on the north to Sir Henry Bridges, 1587, in debased style, that on the south to Sir Thomas Bridges, a very large one full of confused sculpture in the usual gorgeous and pompous style of the 17th century. There is also a slab in the chancel with a cross in relief, apparently of the 15th century. The base of the former tower, now the vestry, opens to the body by a low pointed arch, eastward of the north aisle. The tower opens to the nave by a high pointed arch on half octagonal shafts.

The pulpit has some tolerable woodwork but, like everything in the church, painted white. It bears this inscription: 'Blessed are they that have the word of God and kepe it 1634.' The font is modern. The only entrance is now by the west door of the tower. There are 8 bells. The interior is altogether in a bad state; the arches lean very much outwards, especially so on the north; the fine roofs greatly out of repair and daily getting worse and the horrible arrangement of whitewashed pues and gallery across the nave cannot fail to disgust all who appreciate ecclesiastical propriety.

(The windows of the aisles are of 3 lights except those at the west end which have 4. In the vestry is a copy of a brief for the repair of the church recording that the tower fell in 1632.)

Kingsbury Episcopi

49/33–35 St. Martin 1842

A fine church, wholly Rectilinear. The plan consists of a west tower, a nave with side aisles and a chancel with side chapels, that on the north of a kind of transeptal form. The tower is of singular beauty and richness, but has experienced injury from want of repair, though all its ornamental portions, including the statues, seem to have passed safely through the ordeal of the days of Puritanism. The battlements are with pierced panelling and there are 8 crocketed pinnacles, like those of Huish, with small ones attached to those at the angles, but these have been somewhat mutilated.

There are two large belfry windows on each side with small buttresses and pinnacles between them and fitted with fine lattice work in stone. The second stage is also very fine having on each face windows also enriched with lattice work and set between 2 rich niches containing statues, many of which are in fine preservation. The west doorway is of contracted form with foliated spandrels set between canopied niches in which are statues the heads of which

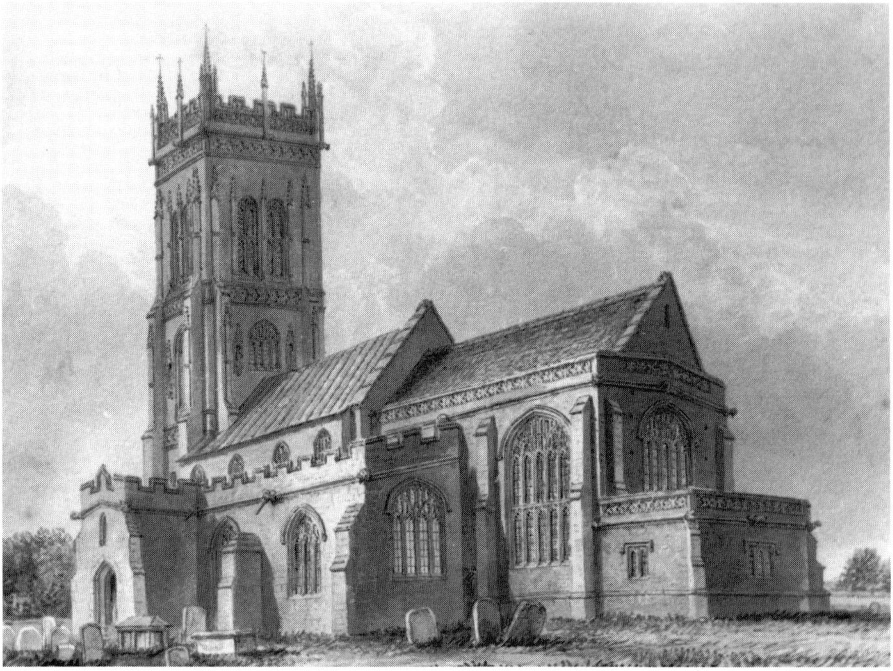

South east view of Kingsbury Episcopi Church, 1832, by J. Buckler

have disappeared. Above is a 5 light window. There is an octagonal stair turret on the north side rising above the battlement and 4 rich bands of panelling are carried completely round the tower and turret forming the divisions of different stages. In the south wall of the tower are seen some shields; the buttresses are adorned with small pinnacles.

There is a large south porch of 2 stages, embattled. In the battlement forming the apex of the gable is a crucifix in bas relief. In the exterior wall near the south porch is an arched tomb surmounted by a sloping stone roof. The effigy is destroyed. The clerestory has a high-pitched lead roof. The south aisle is embattled, but the north is plain.

The nave is lofty and is divided from each aisle by 4 rather plain pointed arches upon octagonal piers, inferior to the general style of the church, and from the tower by an extremely fine lofty double arch, ie. one within another, both having the soffits panelled. This arrangement is very singular. On each side of this arch the piers are charged with two tiers of niches with fine triangular canopies, but clogged in white wash and partially concealed by a hideous painted singing gallery.

The clerestory windows are set high, each of 2 lights and very long. Between them are wooden shafts upon angel corbels whence spring arches bearing the beams of the roof and having a kind of plain feathering. Between the nave and chancel a fine wood screen with the roodloft having bands of vine leaf, etc., but inferior to that at Long Sutton and covered with coarse paint. Immediately above it the roof is boarded, a feature not very uncommon. The head of the

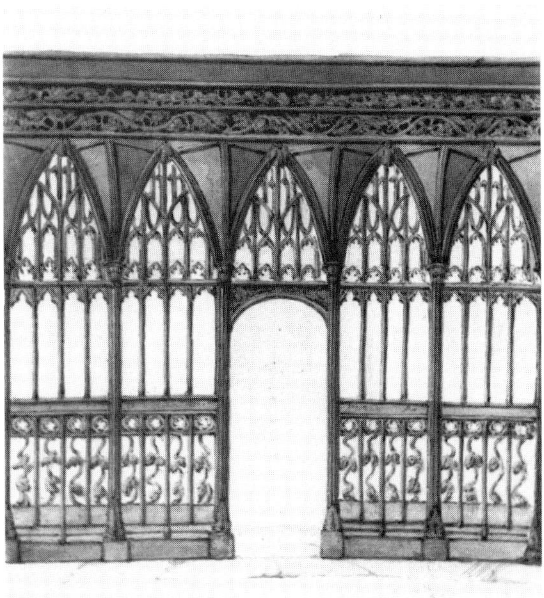

Chancel screen, Kingsbury Episcopi, 1850, by W.W. Wheatley

chancel arch above the roofloft is filled with a wretched painting on wood representing a curtain.

In the nave are several original open seats with carved buds, some with the linen pattern, some with pierced panelling. The font is a plain octagon. The windows of the side aisles are of 3 lights. The chancel is probably of later date than the nave and is more highly finished with larger and finer windows. The north aisle was evidently a chantry chapel and extends, transept-like, considerably beyond the breadth of [the] aisle of the nave. It has externally an octagon staircase turret. Part of the chancel has a fine pierced parapet and, at the east end, beneath the window sill, is the vestry, placed as at Ilminster and elsewhere and having a fine parapet of pierced quatrefoils.

The chancel extends beyond the aisles from each of which it is divided by two elegantly moulded Tudor arches, but much depressed with light lozenge piers with a band of foliage round the capitals. Over the south arches is a clerestory with a 3 light square-headed window. There are wood screens enclosing the chancel and the roof is of plaster and coved. The east window is of 5 lights and those north and south of the chancel are fine and large with transoms, all with depressed arches marking a late period. In the east wall is a small doorway with depressed arch, label and foliated spandrels, opening into the vestry.

The north chapel has two fine windows: that on the north of 5 lights, that on the east of 4, both with transoms and containing large portions of original stained glass in which appear several figures of saints and the Virgin Mary and canopies of a sort of flamboyant character; also several armorial bearings. The arch mouldings of these windows are good and the mullions are adorned with shafts. The south chapel has an east window of 4 lights with some stained glass and part of an inscription. Its ceiling (as also that of the south aisle of the nave) is of wood and flat, divided into panels with pieced quatrefoils and foliated bosses, all of considerable elegance. There is a niche with a stone shelf but no piscina. The arch between this chapel and the aisle of the nave is panelled.

This fine church requires much repair and church rates are not easily obtained. The vicarage has some good domestic architecture and a pointed window with a transom, probably early Rectilinear. In the village are several ancient houses.

Kingsdon

19/62–63 [All Saints] Before 1840

Kingsdon church consists of a nave, transepts and chancel, and a handsome tower at the west end, built of blue stone and of Rectilinear character, 4 stages in height. The west door has a Tudor arch and label. The belfry windows are double and each of 2 lights. There is an embattled parapet and between the belfry windows rises the beginning of a pinnacle, stopped by the string of the battlement. On the north side is an octagonal turret. The west window is of 4 lights. The south porch is of the same period and the doorway arch springs from shafts. The tower arch has the soffit panelled. The windows of the nave are of 2 lights. The north transept is larger than the south and has 2 fine

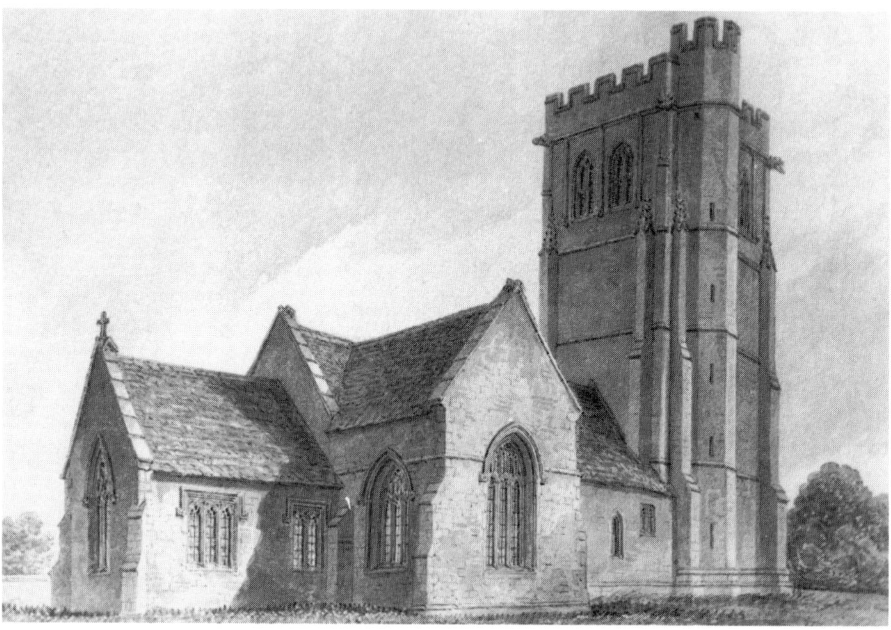

North east view of Kingsdon Church, 1832, by J.C. Buckler

windows of 3 lights with shafts and good stained glass. The south transept windows are modern. Near the south door is a small niche. The interior has some good carved seats. The chancel opens by a pointed arch upon shafts. The east window is Curvilinear of 3 lights; the side windows are square-headed and Curvilinear. South of the altar is a niche, feathered, with a drain and a square recess. The pews are all open. The font is circular upon a cylindrical shaft with a square base.

Kingston Seymour

51/59–60 All Saints 16 August, 1862

A Perpendicular church of local Somerset type. The plan: nave with south aisle, chancel, western tower with spire, and south porch. The north side has a good parapet of pierced trefoil panelling but the parapet on the south is plainer. There is at the north-east of the nave a projecting stair turret with slit windows and lead roof. The porch is very large and has over the outer door a Perpendicular window of 2 lights; the inner doorway continuous; over it a niche with groined canopy and near it an ogee recess, probably a stoup. The chancel is tiled, the nave leaded. The tower has a fine open parapet and 4 crocketed pinnacles and from the centre rises an octagonal spire of fair proportions. There are corner buttresses, belfry windows and on the west side

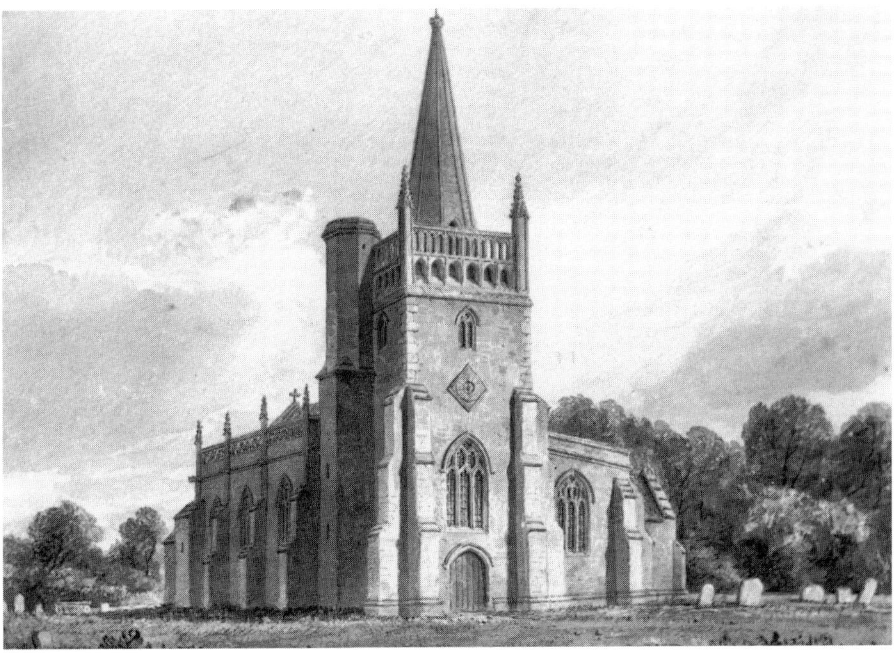

North west view of Kingston Seymour Church, 1829, by J. Buckler

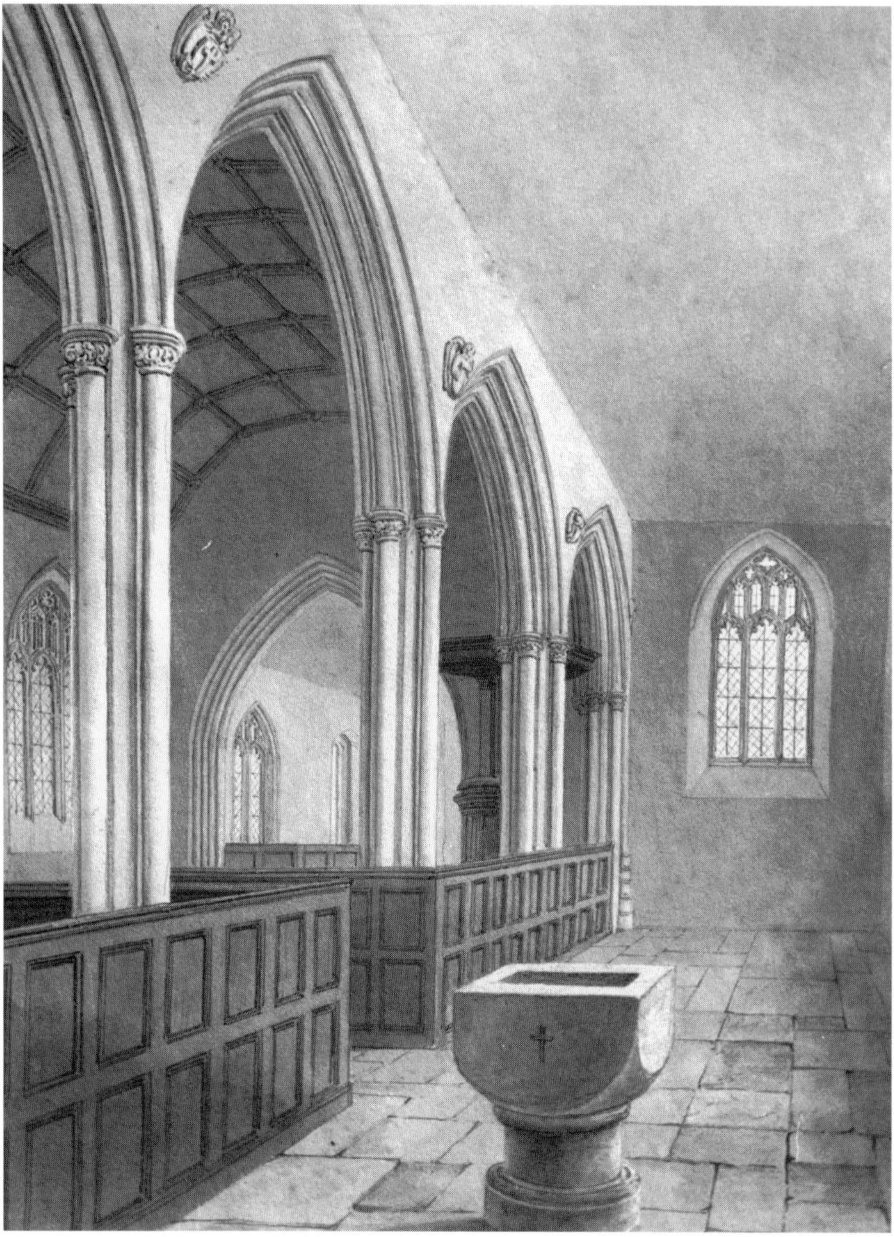

Interior view of Kingston Seymour Church, 1829, by J.C. Buckler

a continuous arched doorway and 3 light window. The tower arch is open, has continuous cylindrical mouldings on an octagonal base.

The nave has a coved roof with ribs and bosses. The arcade of the nave is of 4 arches with fair mouldings and the usual piers of 4 shafts in lozenges with foliated capitals and octagonal bases. The windows are all uniform of 3 lights. The chancel arch is clumsily shaped with continuous mouldings. The east window is closed. There are 2 windows of 2 lights on each side, the south-east has the cill extended for a sedile. On the north is a squint; on the south a trefoil-headed piscina, perhaps of earlier date, and opposite is a rude oblong aumbrye. The chancel is fitted stall-wise. In the south aisle is an ogee-headed piscina with a shelf. The font has a new square bowl on an old circular stem.

(5 bells. The south aisle has angel figures bearing shields which seem once to have carried the timbers of the roof. The walls are chiefly whitewashed externally and there is a harmonium in the chancel).

Langford Budville

51/49–51 St. James 1 February, 1862

An elegant church though not spacious, wholly of the best Somersetshire type and in excellent condition. It comprises a nave and chancel, a south aisle to the nave, west tower and south porch, the whole Perpendicular. The south side, including the porch, has a fine parapet of pierced panelling presenting

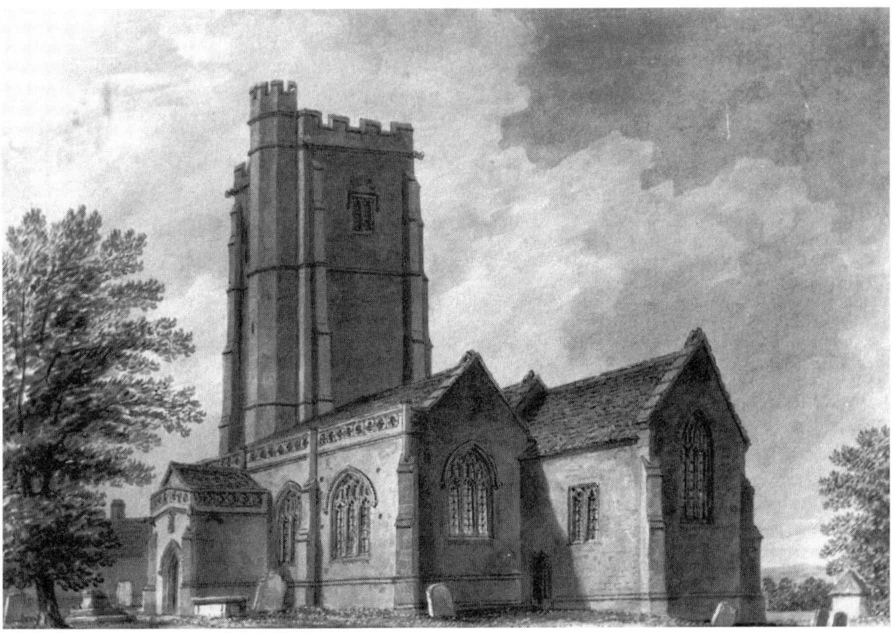

South east view of Langford Budville Church, 1837, by J. Buckler

quatrefoils, and roses and crocketed pinnacles surmounting the buttresses. The porch has a niche over the door with a canopy rising above the parapet. The outer doorway has jamb mouldings with foliage with shafts and hood. There is also a niche over the inner doorway.

The windows of the south aisle are of 3 lights; on the north are windows of 3 and 4 shafts internally. The roofs are coved with ribs and bosses, both in nave and aisle with a somewhat richer portion over the east end of the nave. There are illuminated angel figures bearing shields under the timbers. The tower arch is pointed and quite plain. The nave has an arcade on the south of 3 arches with the usual piers with stilted shafts having capitals. The chancel arch is similar, but the capitals are square and have a doubtful look. On the north is a rood door.

The aisle is carried along part of the chancel to which it opens by one narrow arch on shafts. The chancel has at the east a 3 light window; north and south are square-headed of 2 lights. The altar is well veiled. The roof of the chancel is coved and ribbed. There is an octagonal stoup near the south door. The font has an octagonal bowl on a stem of like form which is surrounded by pillars having something of a cinquecento look. The seats are all open and there is an organ.

The tower is rather a plain one of red stone, is embattled and has a 3 light west window and Tudor arch doorway below it. There is an octagonal turret on the south, buttresses removed from the angles and square-headed belfry windows. In the churchyard are the steps on which once stood a cross.

Langport

19/41–43 [All Saints] 19 October, 1825

A dreadfully wet day which prevented us from enjoying the country. We went to Langport, 10 miles distant [from Ilminster], a small ancient town with an ancient gateway. It also contains a very large and magnificent church of Perpendicular work of great elegance.

The church is of great length and breadth and consists of a nave with side aisles, a small transept on the north, and a chapel on the south, a chancel with small chapel at its east end, and a fine lofty tower at the west end. The tower, though not as rich as some others in the county, is very beautiful. It is embattled and crowned with 4 pinnacles. The buttresses have fine canopied set-offs. The belfry windows are double, large and fine, and worked with fine stone lattice work. There are also some very beautiful canopied niches on the tower and at the west side a Tudor doorway and fine window.

The church has a battlement over every part, but has no clerestory. The nave is divided from the side aisles by 6 pointed arches with the common lozenge Perpendicular piers. the south chapel is divided from the south aisle by two arches with a lozenge pier having shafts with flowered capitals. The ceiling in this chapel is of timber and most elegantly ornamented with panelling. The windows are mostly large and fine: one at the east end of the south aisle has some very brilliant painted glass. The north transept has also a very fine large window.

The chancel has a very fine timber roof ornamented with vine leaves and square flowers. The east window is large, of 5 lights, and is entirely filled with

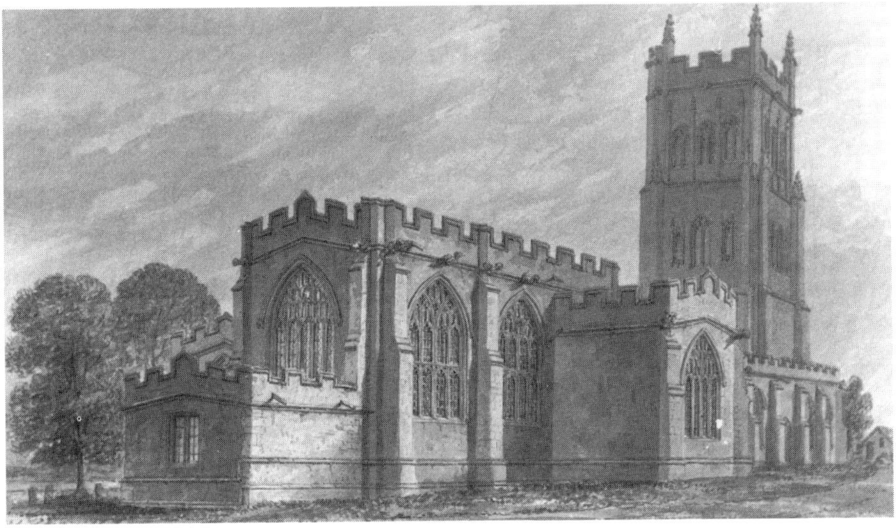

North east view of Langport Church, 1830, by J. Buckler

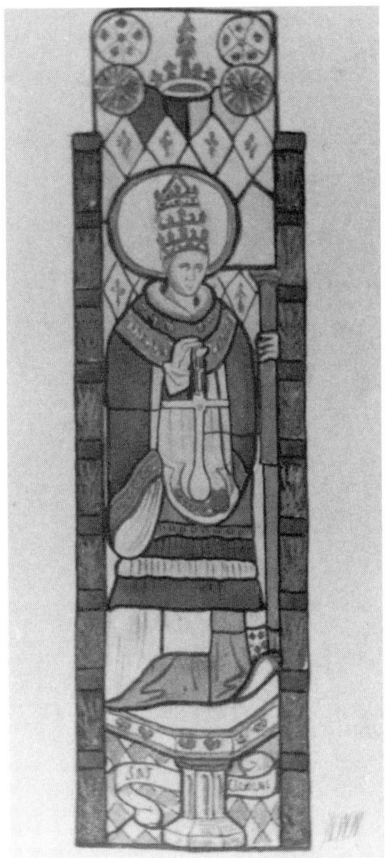

In chancel window, Langport Church, 1850, by W.W. Wheatley

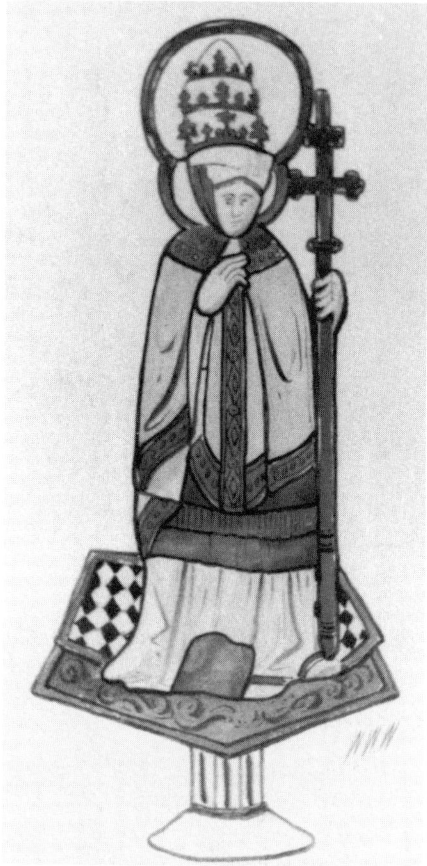

In chancel window, Langport Church, 1850, by W.W. Wheatley

very rich painted glass in a very perfect state, representing saints, etc., which has a very fine effect in looking up the church. The other windows of the chancel are very large and handsome, mostly of 4 lights and rather peculiar tracery. The chapel behind the altar exactly resembles that at Ilminster; it is low, being below the sill of the east window, and has an opening both from within and from without. There is a fine canopied niche against one of the piers on the south side of the nave. The font is an octagon on a pedestal and is ornamented with quatrefoils. The pewing, etc., in the interior of this beautiful church are not quite as neat and decent as they should be.

Langridge

52/1–2 St. Mary 9 June, 1871

A small church having only chancel and nave with western tower and south porch and a vestry added on the south of the chancel. The south doorway

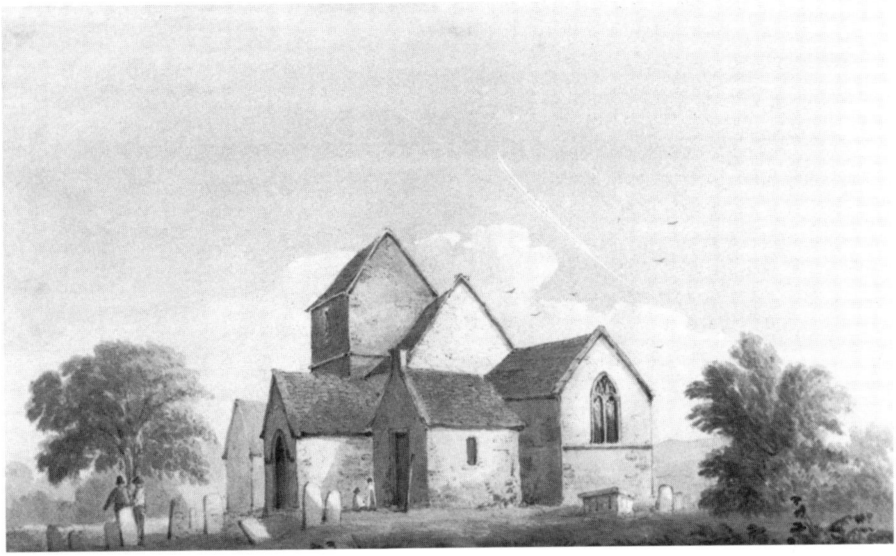

Langridge, ? 1850, by W.W. Wheatley

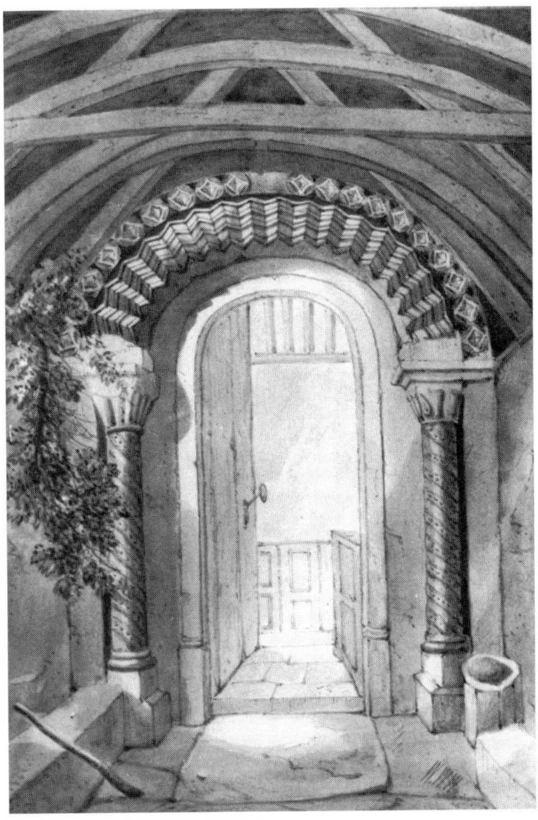

Langridge, south porch, 1850, by W.W. Wheatley

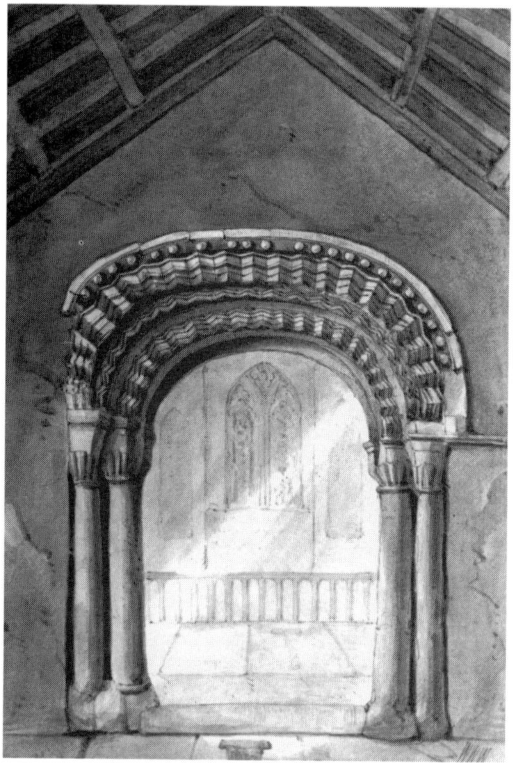

Langridge, chancel arch, 1850, by W.W. Wheatley

within the porch is good Norman and the church is evidently originally of that style. The doorway has 3 orders of moulding, the outer having chevron ornament with shafts having abaci and one with spiral mouldings round the shaft. There is a small Norman window on the south of the nave and the chancel arch is of the same character with plain outer moulding on simple imposts, and inner one with chevron ornament and shafts.

The chancel has no windows on the north. Those on the south are apparently modern imitations of Norman with shafts. Other windows are of 2 lights and Decorated but one doubtful without foliation: another set high near the pulpit is square divided by a mullion. The tower is small and low, has no buttresses but one string course. On the west a 2 light Decorated [window] and 2 other openings are lancets, one trefoil-headed. The porch window seems to be Perpendicular. The seats open. The situation is lonely, but pretty.

Limington

50/57–58 St. Mary 11 August, 1849

This church has a nave with north transeptal chapel, chancel, west tower and south porch. The nave and transept are Middle-Pointed (the latter of very

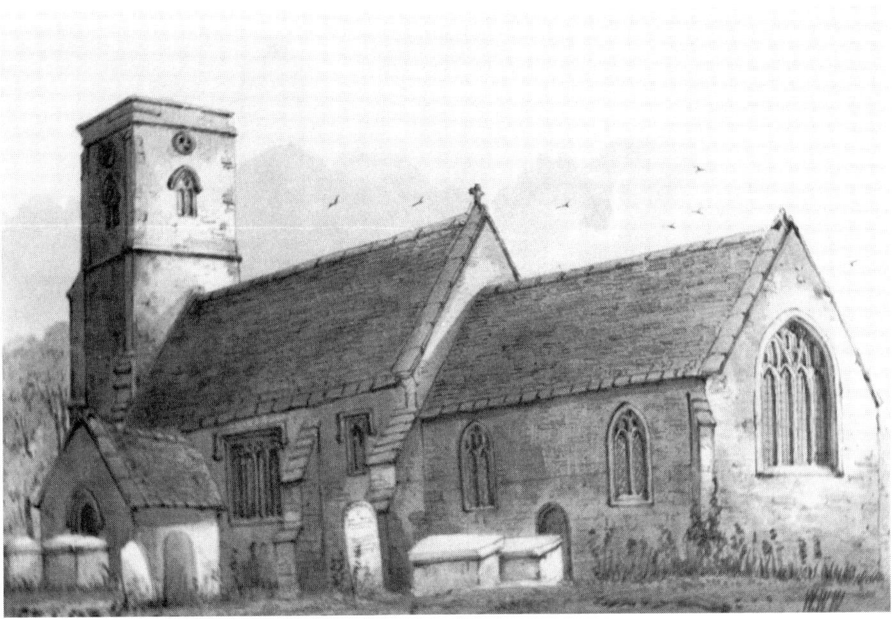

Limington Church, 1847, by W.W. Wheatley

excellent character), the chancel and tower are Third-Pointed. The nave has some 2 light windows of Middle-Pointed work, one of which has feathering to the rear arch. On the south a square-headed Third-Pointed window and a single cinquefoiled one near the pulpit.

In the arch opening from the nave to the transept is an altar tomb with the effigies of a knight and lady, the knight, not in armour, cross-legged, the lady in a wimple or kind of veil. Another effigy, also cross-legged, remains of the knight in armour . . . having on his shield armorial bearings, a bend between 3 escallop shells with considerable traces of colour and a dog at his feet. On the floor of the chapel is the figure of a lady in a wimple. These are supposed to be of the family of Gyvernay.

The chapel is a very elegant and interesting Middle-Pointed specimen having a steep pitched roof of stone covered externally with flags. Within the roof has fine stone arched ribs. The window at the north end is of 3 lights, the tracery varying to a flamboyant character and below it, under a fine arched recess with bold featuring which has knobs at the points and shafts with moulded capitals and bases, is the effigy of the cross-legged knight before mentioned, no doubt the founder of the chapel.

On the east and west sides are 2 light windows, the latter having the wavy circle in the tracery and indicating an advanced period of the style. The chancel arch is pointed springing straight from the wall. In the transept in an angle is a piscina with quatrefoil orifice. On the north of the chancel arch beyond the chancel wall is a pointed arch recess in the wall. The east window of the chancel is of 4 lights. On each side of it are 2 windows of 2 lights. On the south is a priests' door and a piscina having quatrefoiled ogee arch and with panelled spandrels. The orifice is deep and quatrefoiled.

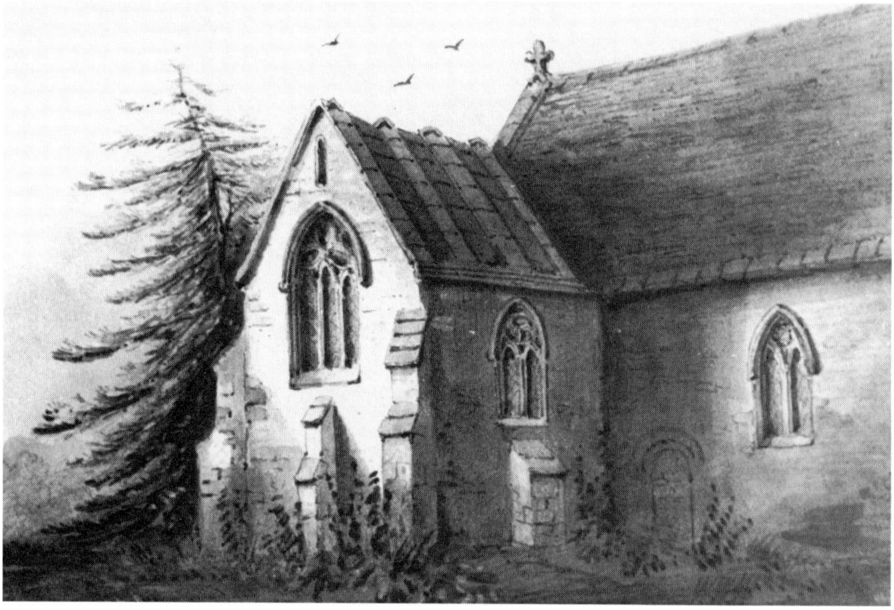

Chapel on north side of Limington Church, 1847, by W.W. Wheatley

There is a little Jacobean wood sculpture among the pewing. The font is octagonal with quatrefoil panelling containing shields, diminishing gradually to a panelled stem. The south porch has stone benches; its outer door has mouldings dying into the wall and a hood upon corbels. The inner door has continuous mouldings. The tower is of 3 stages with a plain parapet having an unfinished appearance without battlement. The buttresses are at the angles and on the north side is an octagonal stair turret reaching up the whole way. The belfry window and that below it are of 2 lights and over the belfry window a wavy circle in a tablet. The west door is plain and over it a 3 light Third-Pointed window.

(View in Gent Mag. 1825 pt. 1, p. 9.

Sir Richard Gyvernay A.D. 1329 gave lands for the maintenance of a service for the souls of himself and wife and of his father and mother. One of them must have been the founder of the chapel.

There is a small 3-foiled niche in the gable of the transept, over the window externally.)

Locking

51/44–45 St. Augustine 25 January, 1862

This church has an ancient tower, but the body has been rebuilt in a pointed Perpendicular style imitating the prevailing character of the county. The chancel is developed and open to the nave by a continuous pointed arch, doubtful if original.

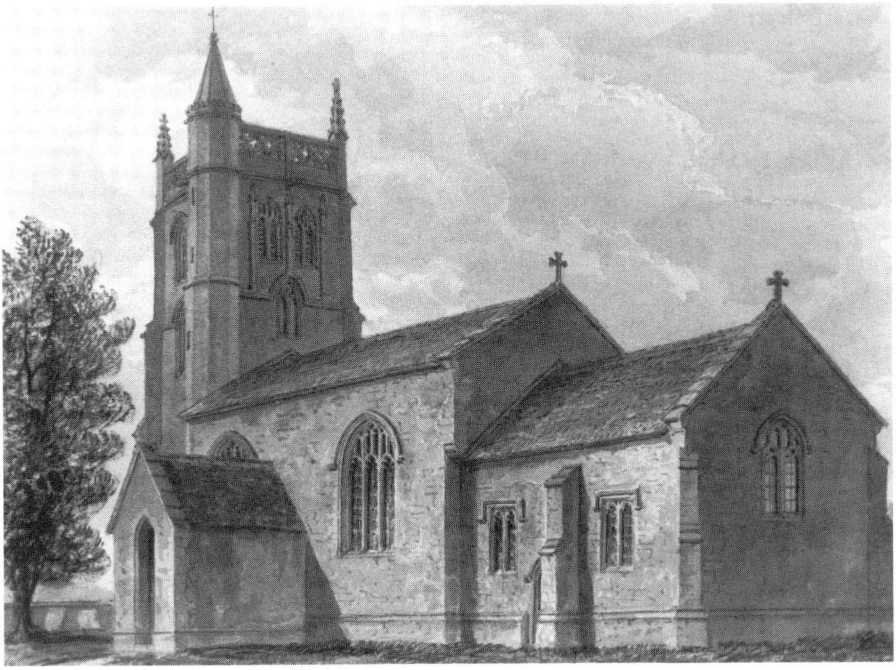

South east view of Locking Church, 1828, by J. Buckler

The tower arch is pointed and continuous. The tower is certainly a good one of the local character having corner buttresses and a pretty pierced parapet with 4 crocketed pinnacles. There is an octagonal turret at the south-east of some size and crowned by a lofty pyramid with small battlement. The west doorway has an ogee arch with rude crockets and flanking pinnacles. The arch mouldings are fair. The west window is of 3 lights, the hood moulding continued in string course. The belfry windows double, each of 2 lights flanked by pinnacles and having some pretty stone lattice work.

Within the only interesting object is the ancient Norman font, the bowl square and rudely sculptured with spiral mouldings, scrolls and beads. At each angle is a figure extending its arms so that they meet along the bowl and at each angle a shaft with octagonal capital. The church has a nave with north aisle and chancel.

Lopen

52/11–12 All Saints 19 February, 1872

A mean church much modernised comprising a nave and chancel and a modern transept on the north, a south porch and a bellcote on the west end with 2 open arches for bells.

The chancel arch is a plain pointed one. The chancel has single lancets on

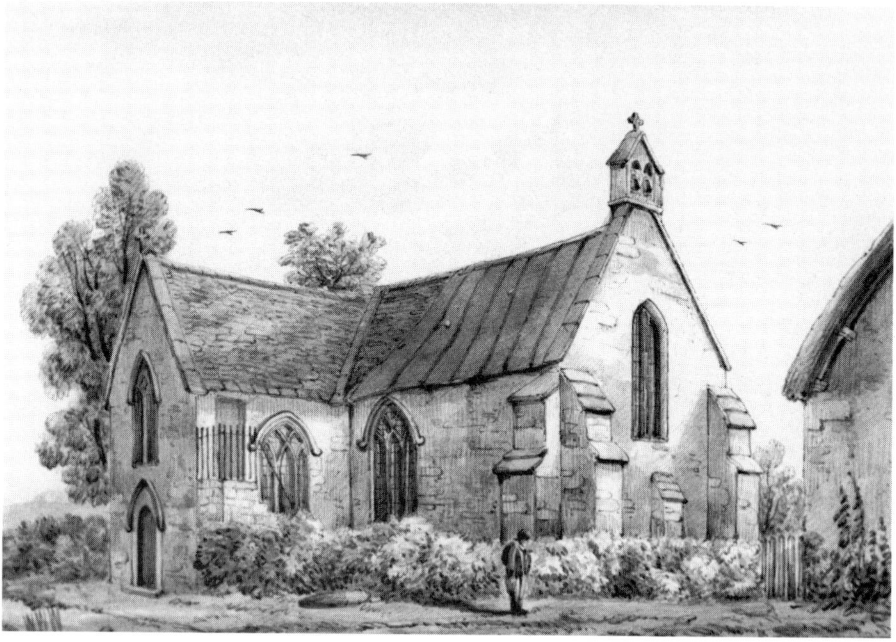

Lopen Church, 1850, by W.W. Wheatley

the north and south, one with obtuse head and one other, north-west, set low. The east window is poor Perpendicular, of 2 lights. There are 2 shallow niches in the east wall and on the south side a piscina of rather rude kind. The chancel has [a] coved roof; the nave is ceiled. On the south of the nave are some poor 3 light windows without foliation, but with hoods on corbels. Other windows are modern.

The porch is plain with pointed doorway. The church is pewed and in a very unimproved state. The font has a plain octagonal bowl.

Lovington

51/13–14 St. Thomas 6 February, 1858

A small church having a narrow nave and a chancel properly distinguished, a western tower and south porch. The roof partly of slates, partly of stone flags. The whole is Perpendicular; the nave has some windows of 3 lights on the south, the others of 2. In the chancel the east window of 3 lights, those north and south of 2. The western part of the nave is occupied by some very fine ancient open seats, the ends of which have poppy heads and varied carvings a little too high for so small a church and causing rather a crowded look.

The chancel arch has mouldings and springs from circular shafts having moulded capitals. On the western face are arched recesses on each side of the chancel arch and also some odd recesses in the angle of the eastern end of the

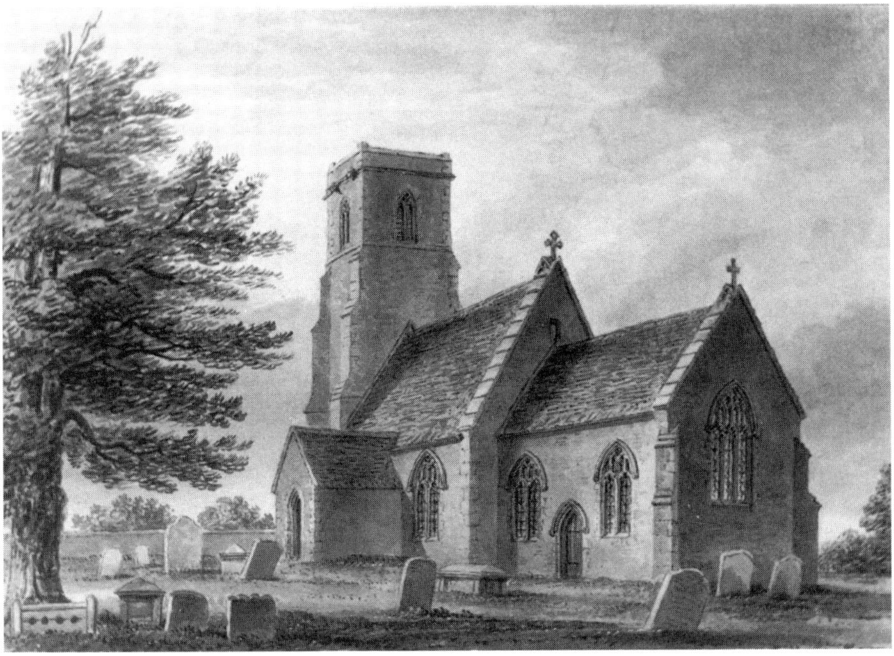

South east view of Lovington Church, 1840, by J. Buckler

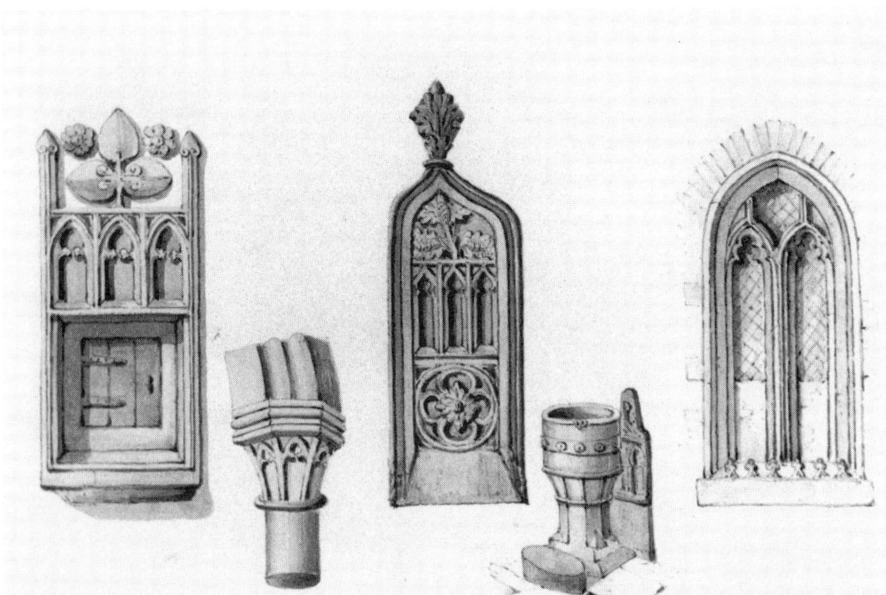

Lovington Church, 1845, by W.W. Wheatley

nave. There is also a piscina under one of the windows south of the nave and there is a little ancient painted glass. There is a plain roodscreen of rather late date.

In the church a priest's door on the south and a plain piscina with shelf. On the north side of the sacrarium is a curious aumbrye with some enriched stone panelling exhibiting roses and fleurs de lys in 2 tiers. In the third tier is a wooden square door opening to the aumbrye.

The tower arch to the nave is narrow and springs from panelled octagonal capitals which are much concealed by the gallery. The font has a circular bowl upon an octagonal stem having round it a band of roses and wedged at the base on alternate sides. The tower is small but divided into 3 stages, has a parapet, but no battlement. The belfry windows of 2 lights on each side, one of them almost destroyed. The west window of 2 lights and has a range of Tudor flowers along the cill and buttresses at the angles.

The porch has the inner doorway of good character with continuous flowered mouldings. Over it a niche and a stoup by the side.

Luccombe

51/1–2 St. Mary 8 May, 1855

This church is wholly Perpendicular and comprises a body and south aisle without distinction of chancel, a north porch and west tower.

The windows are almost all of 3 lights without foliation. That at the east of

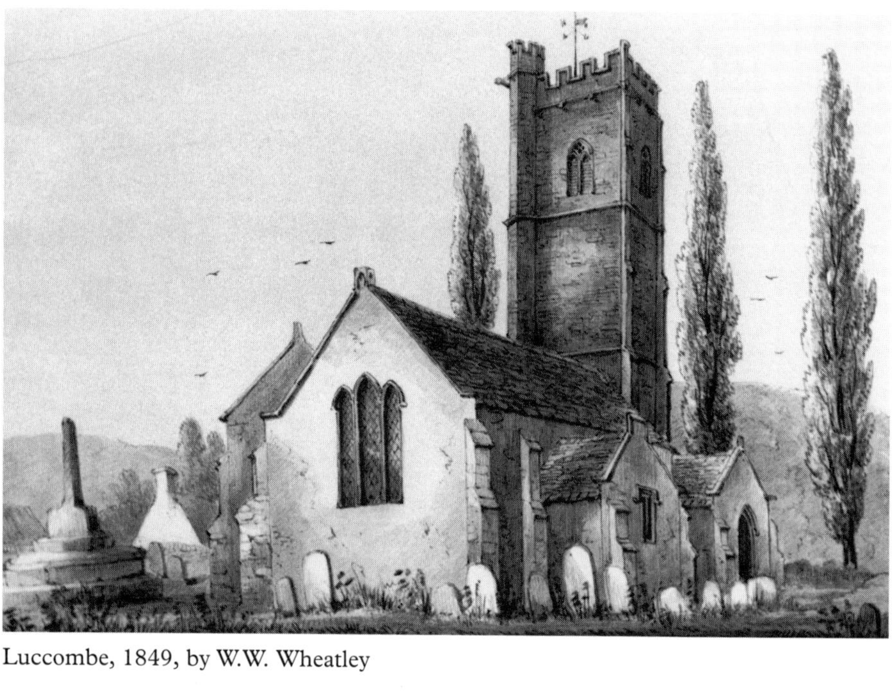

Luccombe, 1849, by W.W. Wheatley

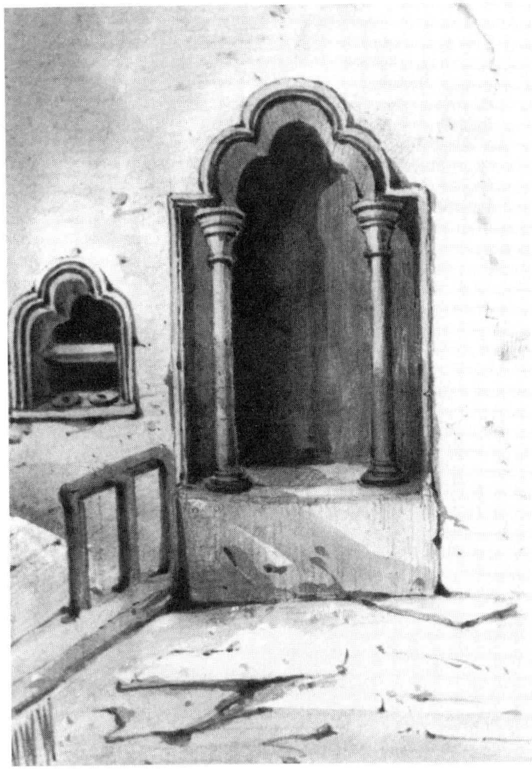

Luccombe Church chancel,
by W.W. Wheatley

the aisle is of 4 lights with a transom and subarcuated. The arcade is good of 4 well moulded arches with light clustered piers of shafts of which some of the capitals are enriched with sculpture of shields and vine leaves; but some are plain and with simple octagonal capitals. The roofs are coved with ribs and bosses. In the chancel, the ribs are more intricate and ornamental and in the aisle they are more so than in the nave.

The east window seems to be modern. On the south of it an early portion, an Early English sedile and piscina, both [of] which have an obtuse trefoil head; the former shafts with capitals, the latter has a stone shelf and double water drain. At the east end of the south aisle are 2 brackets and a fine Perpendicular piscina with good mouldings and quatrefoil orifice. The interior was repaired and refitted 12 or 14 years ago and is on the whole neat and decorous but not particularly ecclesiastical character in the arrangements.

The tower arch is lofty upon shafts but has a gallery inserted. The font of octagonal form panelled – of the usual kind – with a Gothic cover. The tower is handsome and not covered with whitewash; has 3 stages and a battlement panelled, 4 small pinnacles and gargoyles. The west window of 3 lights and west doorway has continuous moulding, corner buttresses, belfry windows of 2 lights. The north porch is large. In the churchyard is the shaft of a cross on 4 high steps. The graves are chiefly to the east.

Luxborough

51/8 St. Mary 8 May, 1855

A small church in a beautiful romantic situation but itself of no beauty. It has a nave with north aisle, chancel and west tower. The nave and aisle seem to have been rebuilt and is in poor Gothic style. The chancel is ancient, opening to the nave by a rude arch. The roof coved and ribbed. On the north and south are single lancets. On the south a priest's door. The east window Perpendicular of 3 lights. Below the south window is a square-headed piscina. On the north a bit of stone cornice embattled with a black cornice under it. The font has an octagonal bowl upon a pedestal. The tower arch is rude. The tower small and without much character with a saddle roof; the belfry windows double and obtuse-headed. The west window Perpendicular of 2 lights.

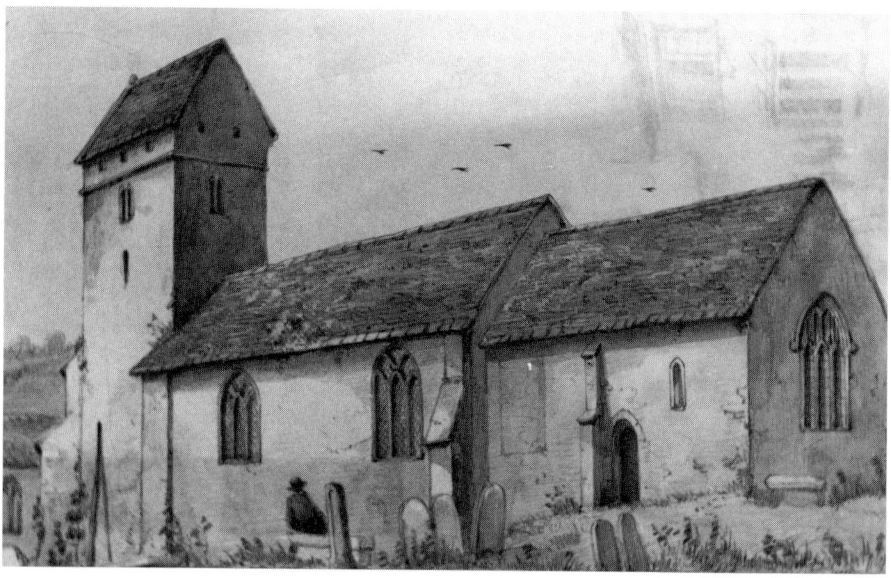

Luxborough, 1849, by W.W. Wheatley

Lydeard St. Lawrence

50/87–88 [St. Lawrence] 10 May, 1855

This church is much superior to [Ash Priors] though the chancel and nave have only a north aisle but it is longer and loftier and altogether of far better architectural character. It has also north and south porches and a western tower, all Perpendicular except the chancel.

The north aisle is externally better finished than the south side and has a fine pierced embattled parapet with quatrefoils and pinnacles. The 2 porches

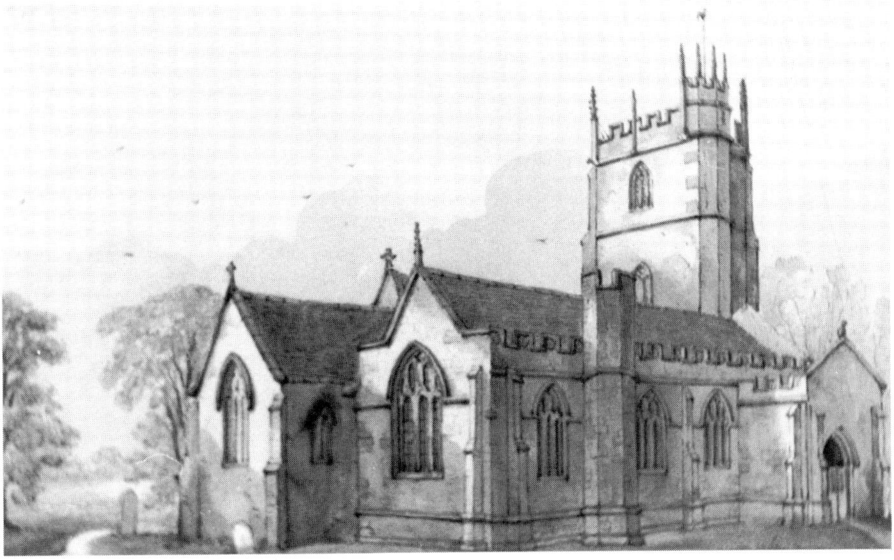

Lydeard St. Lawrence, 1845, by W.W. Wheatley

are both very large. The southern has 2 storeys with a parvise and a pierced quatrefoil parapet and fine gargoyles. The outer doorway continuous. The north porch is very similar but has the pierced parapet on the sides only, the other on the gable as well. There is an octagonal rood turret on the north. The windows, both north and south of the nave, seem to have for the most part, lost their foliations and are of 3 and 4 lights.

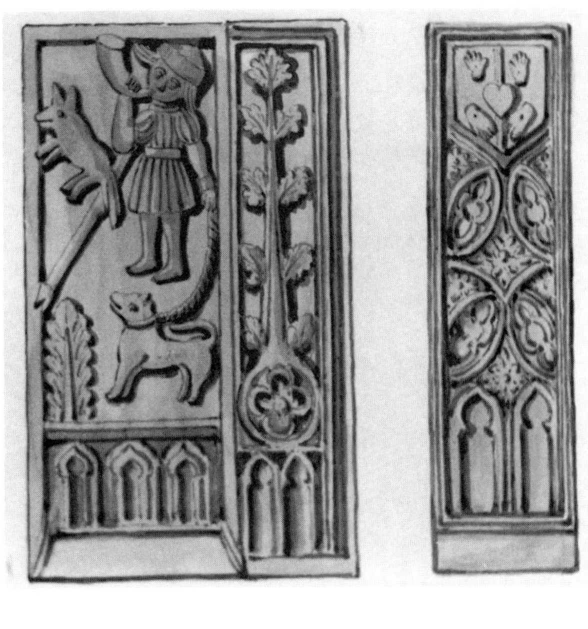

Lydeard St. Lawrence Church, 1845, by W.W. Wheatley

The arcade of the nave is good south-western Perpendicular, the piers of clustered shafts and mouldings with general capitals of fine foliage. The roofs are coved; the chancel arch wide and plain and a fine roodscreen across the chancel and the aisle having tracery in arched compartments. The chancel is Decorated, has on the south one regularly Flamboyant window of 2 lights and one labeled, square-headed, of Perpendicular character. The east window Decorated, of 3 lights reticulated.

The chancel extends a little eastward of the aisle, the east end of which has a pierced parapet to its gable, and flanking pinnacles. Its east window has lost its foliations. The chancel opens to the north aisle or chapel by a fine arch resembling those noticed at Ash Priors, but more elaborate, apparently once over a tomb, and on both faces having pretty shafts with angels bearing shields in the capitals. There is a priest's door on the south of the chancel. The pulpit is Jacobean.

The nave abounds with beautiful old standards exhibiting a variety of beautiful tracery and wood carving. The font has a plain octagonal bowl. The tower is fine, embattled, with 8 pinnacles and an octagonal turret at the north-east angle which has small pinnacles at its angles. The belfry windows of 3 lights with ornamental lattice work, and, in the second stage, [a] 2 light window also with stone lattice work. The west window of 3 lights and no west door. The churchyard is very pretty and quiet with large trees. In it, on the south, is the stump of a cross on a square base. The gables are crowned by crosses.

Lydford, East

51/11–12 St. Peter 6 February, 1858

A small church rather mean in architecture and in a lonely situation on low, marshy ground. It has only chancel and nave without aisles but of pretty good height. A wooden belfry on the west and a porch on the south of the nave. The porch is very large and reaches high up in the roof of the nave thereby much improving the outline of the otherwise uninteresting exterior.

The chancel is lower than the nave but of the right proportion, though apparently rebuilt and with ugly debased windows. The chancel arch is pointed but extremely small in the midst of a large proportion of dead wall. On each side of it a square recess, one of which (on the south) is walled up. The other has a squint through it. There is part of the roodscreen – panelled.

On the south of the nave one Decorated window of 2 lights with remnants of painted glass. The other windows of the nave are modernised. The church is poorly pewed. At the west end, no windows, but 2 buttresses. The porch has slit-like lateral openings and stone seats. Over the door is a trefoiled stoup. The woodwork of the door is old. The old font stem is in the churchyard, of cylindrical form. The bowl of the same form still remains in the church.

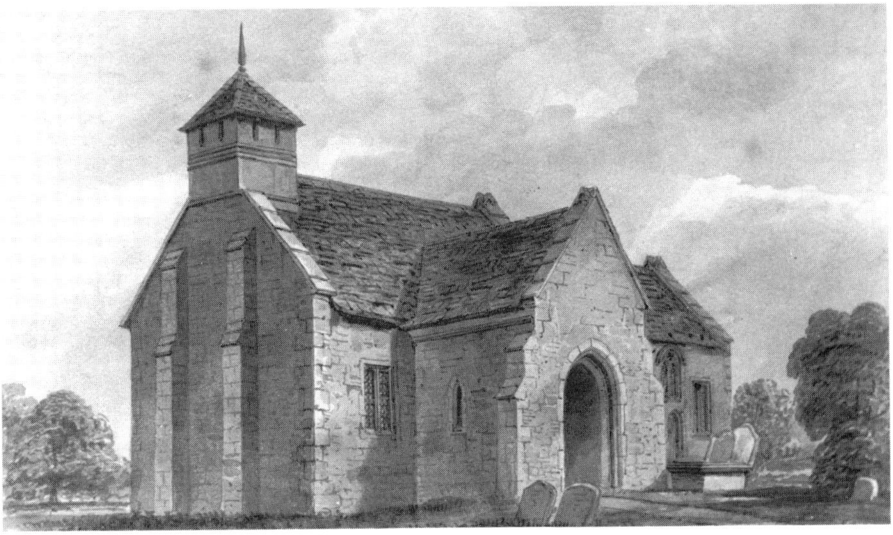

South west view of East Lydford Church, 1833, by J. Buckler

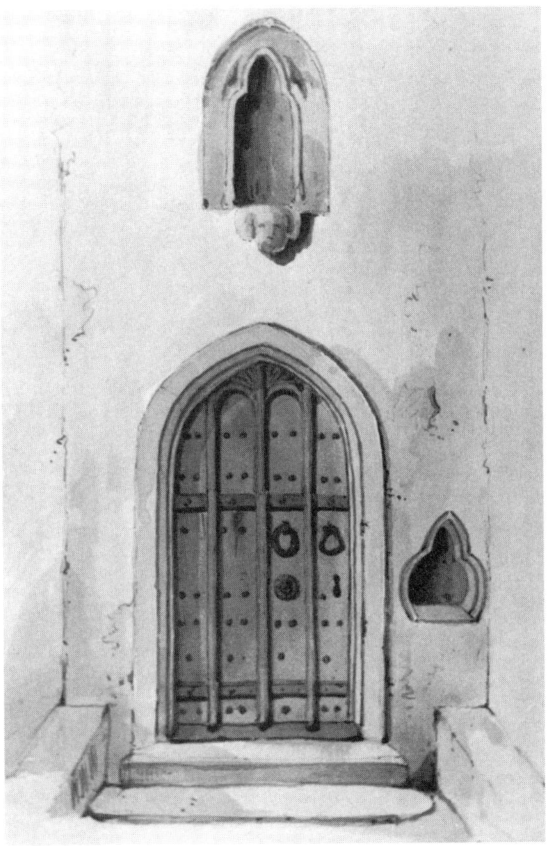

East Lydford Church, 1846,
by W.W. Wheatley

Lydford, West

19/61–62 [St. Peter] Before 1840

The church of West Lydford is situated close to the River Brue and near the road between Ilchester and Shepton Mallet. It contains little remarkable and consists of a nave, north aisle, chancel and tower at the west end. The tower is embattled and surmounted by 4 pinnacles and a pyramidical penthouse roof. The whole church is of Rectilinear work. The nave has a tiled roof, the north aisle a flat roof and a good battlement with small pinnacles.

The nave is divided from the aisle by a row of 4 pointed arches springing from lozenge piers with shafts at the angles. These arches lean very much outwards. The windows are of good Rectilinear tracery, especially those of the north aisle. The chancel is divided from the nave by a pointed arch and lies lower than the nave. The wooden ribs in the roof are ornamented with square flower, etc. The font is a plain octagon on a pedestal of the same form with a little plain panelling. The south porch has a doorway with the soffit filled with square flowers and a dripstone supported by heads. Over it is a niche with crocketed canopy containing an image.

West Lydford Church was rebuilt in 1843 in the Perpendicular style. *Ferrey architect.* The new building occupies exactly the site and coincides with the plan of the old church and is an excellent church-like specimen.

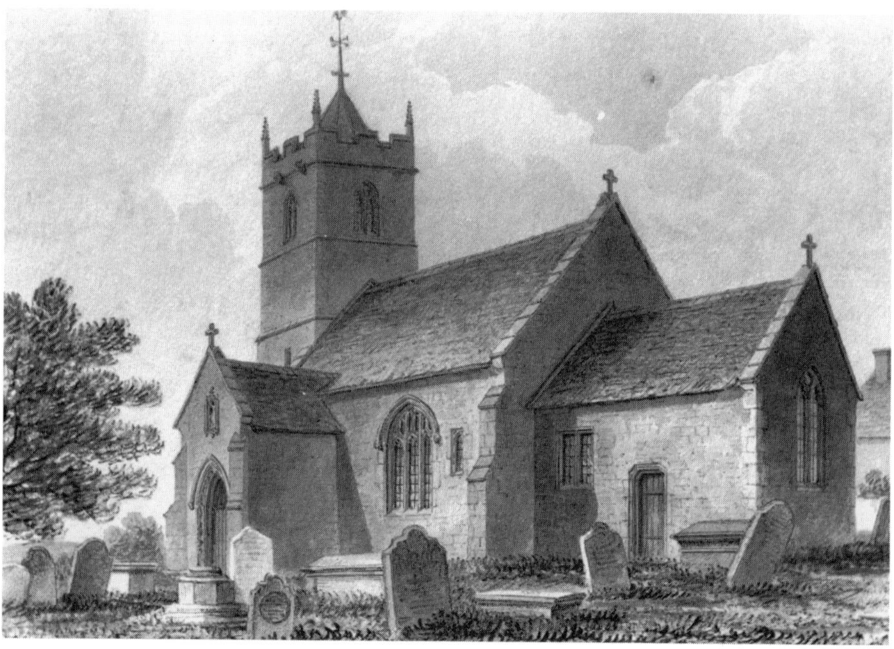

South east view of West Lydford Church, 1833, by J. Buckler

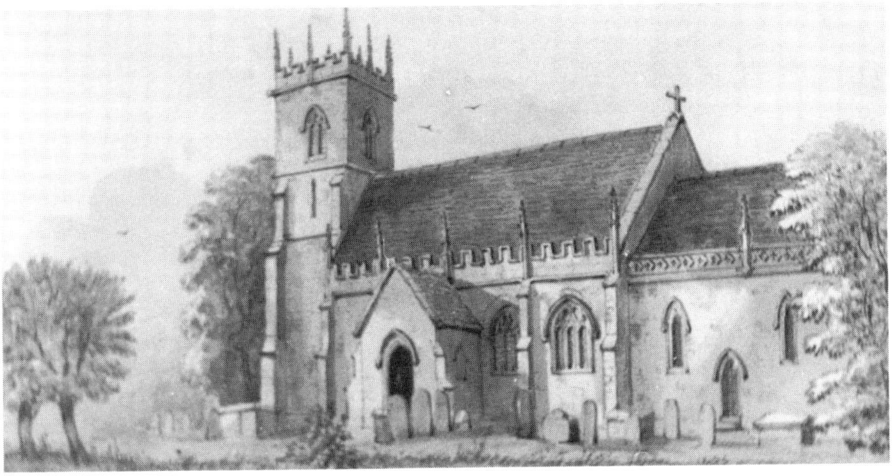

West Lydford, 1846, by W.W. Wheatley

Marksbury

52/20 St. Peter 3 February, 1872

A very uninteresting church consisting of nave, chancel with north porch and west tower. The whole seems to be poor and plain Perpendicular. The chancel arch is pointed, extremely rude and coarse. The windows are mostly square-headed and labeled. In the chancel is a piscina under a trefoiled arch. The tower is plain, coarse Perpendicular in its lower part; the upper storey seems to be debased, with battlement and 4 ugly pinnacles.

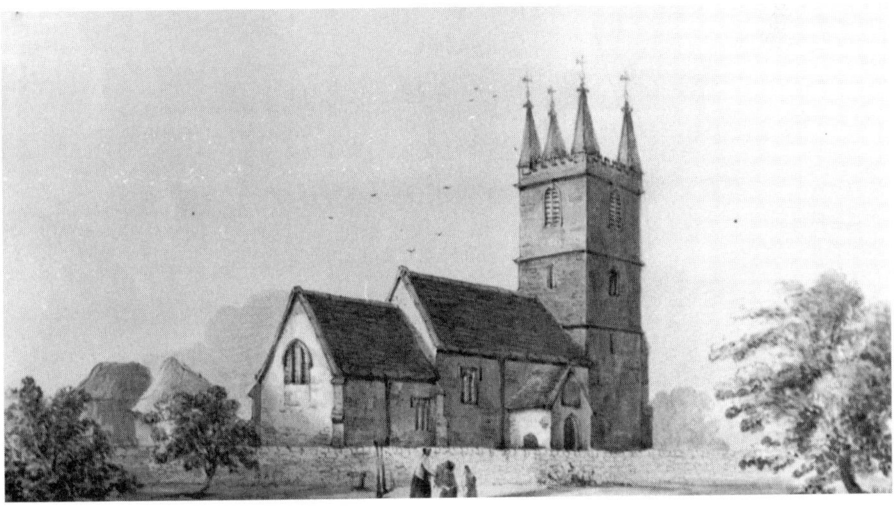

Marksbury, 1843, by W.W. Wheatley

Marston Magna

52/5–6 St. Mary 10 June, 1871

This church has a nave with north aisle, chancel, west tower and south porch. The chancel has some Early English work, the rest mainly Perpendicular. The east window of the chancel has 2 equal lancets; a north-east window is of lancet form with the top square; the rear arch has a Norman character. The north-west window is square-headed, of 2 lights and Perpendicular and there are other Perpendicular windows of 2 lights north and south of the chancel. The chancel arch is pointed with continuous mouldings stilted, looking as if once connected with a screen.

The north aisle is evidently a chantry chapel and opens to the nave by one wide Perpendicular arch on clustered shafts and a pointed doorway opened in the wall. At the west side of this chapel is a turret staircase. The windows both of the chapel and on the south of the nave are Perpendicular, all of 3 lights. The chapel does not extend entirely to the west of the nave. In its east wall is a fine canopied niche and a stone seat on the north side; also some good wood screen work. The roofs are of ordinary character but covered with stone slate. There is a western gallery much interfering with the tower arch which is pointed and chamfered.

The tower is plain Perpendicular of the Somersetshire type; has an embattled parapet and octagonal stair turret at the south-east rising above the battlement. In each central pierce of the battlement is a rose. The tower has corner buttresses and is of 3 stages divided by string courses. There are small pinnacles. On the west side a plain pointed door. Over it a 3 light window; belfry windows of 2 lights. The aisle has a plain parapet. In the chancel on the south is a buttress on a gargoyle. The font is Norman having some indented ornament surrounding the bowl and some foliage and curious figures.

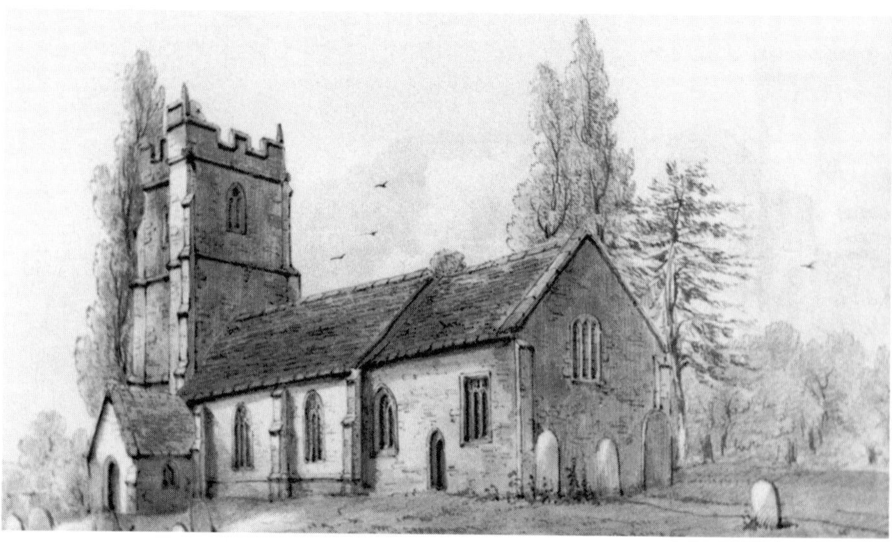

Marston Magna, 1847, by W.W. Wheatley

Martock

49/39–41 [All Saints] Before 1840

This is one of the largest and most beautiful churches in the county and consists of a lofty and spacious nave with aisles a chancel with side chapels and a tower at the west end. The chancel has some Early English work, but all the rest of the church is of the fine Rectilinear character so prevalent in this county. The tower is inferior in richness to the nave and by no means equals those of some of the neighbouring churches, but it has panelled battlements with unfinished pinnacles; double belfry windows with transoms but no dripstones; a west window of 5 lights with transom and, below it, a doorway set between buttresses with unfinished pinnacles. At the north-west corner is a staircase turret.

The church is wholly built of fine grey stone. The clerestory has a rich open battlement of pierced quatrefoils with shields and a niche in its east gable. The south aisle has a good battlement without panelling and the south porch is large and plain with a parvise over it and a groined ceiling and semi-circular turret at one angle. In the south chancel [chapel] there are rich crocketed pinnacles on the buttresses. The windows of the aisles of the nave and of the clerestory are of 4 lights without dripstones. In the chancel they are of 3 lights.

The north aisle is plainer than the south and the tracery of its windows appears to be [of] earlier character. A small doorway rises above the sill of one of the northern windows and there is a large, embattled octagonal turret near the chancel arch on the north side which contains the staircase which led to

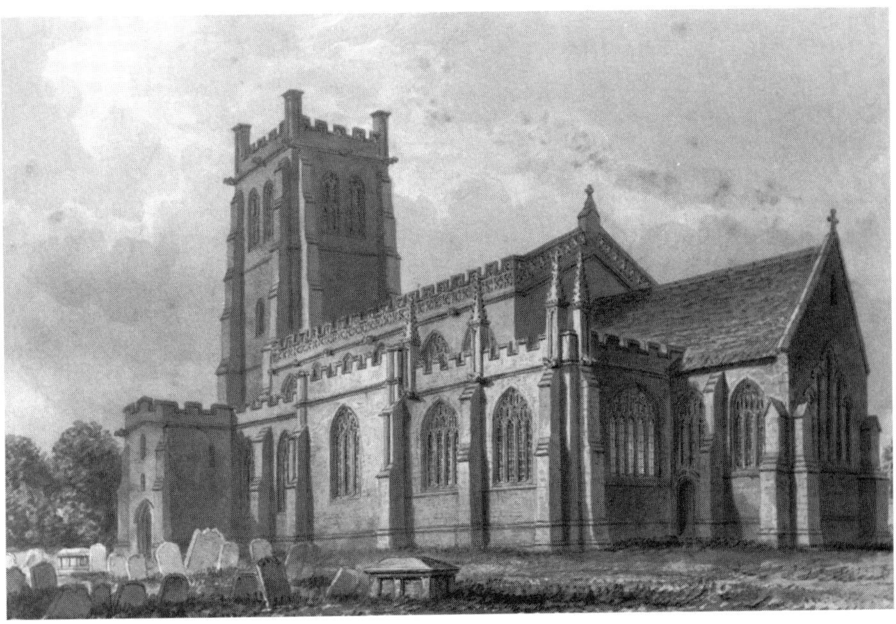

South east view of Martock Church, 1832, by J. Buckler

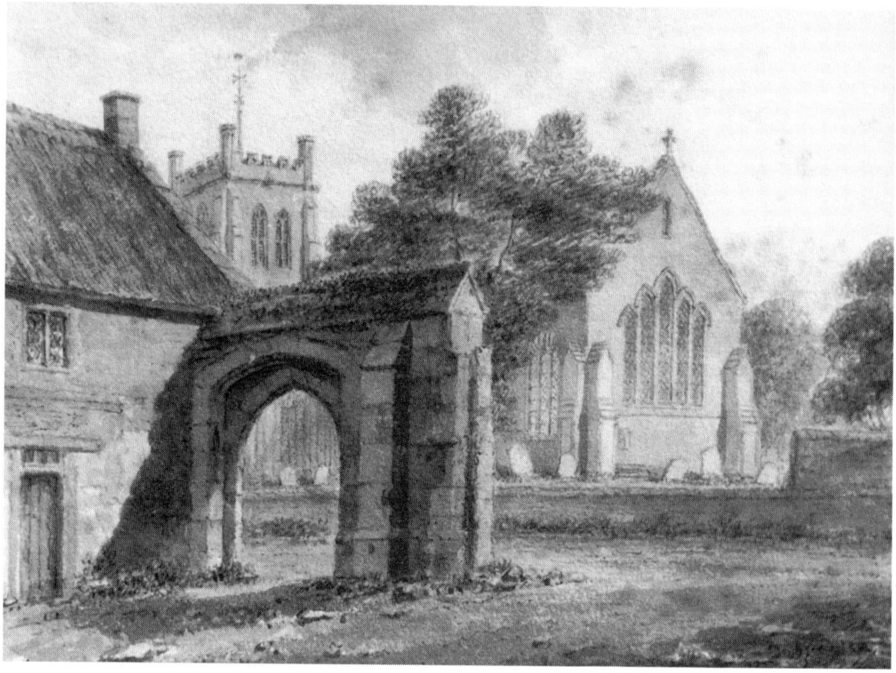

Remains of ancient gateway, Martock, 1848, by J. Buckler

the roodloft. The east windows of the north and south aisles are Rectilinear of 5 lights. The east window of the chancel has 5 Early English lancets, now walled up and unfortunately obscured by the incongruous modern altar screen. Beneath this window externally are two slabs in the wall, one with the effigy of a female, one with a head only sculptured.

The interior has a grand appearance from its loftiness and breadth. The nave has 6 pointed arches on each side with light piers having fine mouldings down them and shafts set at equal intervals. The spandrels of the arches are panelled with quatrefoils and there are small shafts set above each pier upon angel corbels. Between the clerestory windows are fine canopied niches. The tower arch is lofty and panelled and on either side of it is a niche as in the clerestory. The west window has, internally, shafts.

The roof of the nave is one of the finest specimens of an open roof that can be seen: its sides are enriched with panelled compartments containing quatrefoils, the tie-beams are sculptured with bands of foliage and figures of angels bearing shields and the space above within the pitch of the roof is filled with beautiful pierced tracery. There are rich pendants of foliage hanging from the point of the roof at the intervals between the beams. The north aisle has a flat, panelled wood ceiling; that in the south aisle is unfinished. The base of the roodloft screen remains between the nave and chancel and has some good wood panelling and on the north side is the staircase door. The chancel arch is wide and panelled and those between the aisles of the nave and those of the chancel are finely moulded upon shafts. The chancel has on either side 2 pointed arches with piers as in the nave, but there is no clerestory. The chancel has the plain coved roof with ribs forming square compartments and below it a cornice of square flower. In the south aisle the ceiling is panelled and flat; in the north plain.

The font is octagonal upon a shaft of like form. The church is too glaring with whitewash and has a considerable quantity of pews and galleries though less obtrusive than sometimes is the case. There is a large organ. The altar screen a strange Italian composition with wreathed columns blocking the east window.

The churchyard is approached through 2 open stone arches, one on each side of the church temp. James I, the effect of which is not bad. In the town are various good specimens of domestic architecture of the 15th and 16th century, the stone very fine.

Meare

49/53–54 [St. Mary] Before 1840

The church consists of a low western tower, a nave with side aisles and a chancel. The tower has no buttresses but a large embattled parapet, belfry windows of 2 lights and a considerable polygonal turret on the south side rising a good deal above the parapet and encroaching on the belfry window. This is of Perpendicular character, as is the nave, but the chancel is principally Decorated and much lower than the nave. The nave and aisles have good

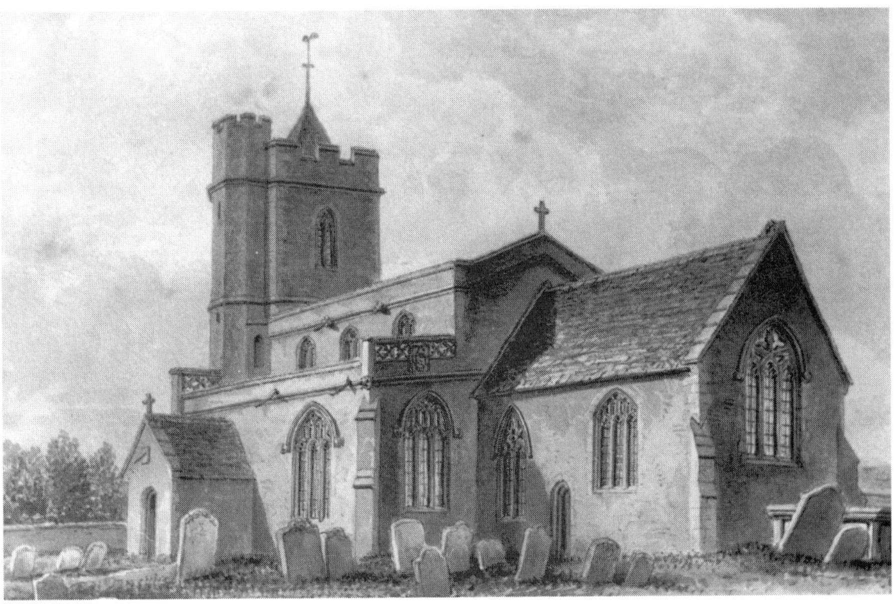

South east view of Meare Church, 1831, by J. Buckler

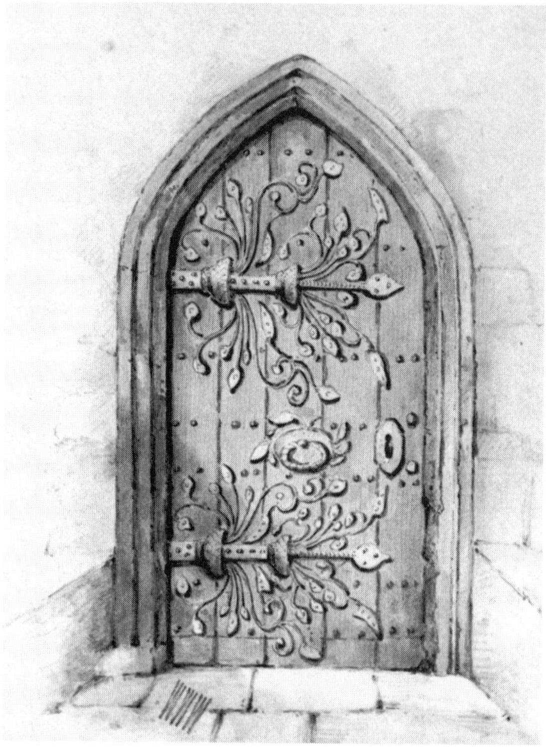

Meare, by W.W. Wheatley

moulded parapets and the east and west ends of the south aisle have them enriched with pierced panelling. Over the east gable of the nave is a cross.

The door within the south porch presents some fine iron work. The chancel is slated. The nave is wide and lofty and divided from each aisle by 3 large pointed arches upon lozenge piers of shafts with individual capitals. The clerestory windows are of 3 lights with depressed arches. The aisle windows are also of 3 lights. The roof is boarded and panelled with sculptured bosses, a cornice of flowers and brackets upon stone angel figures. The south aisle roof has smaller compartments than the nave and more work about it.

The chancel arch is Decorated in style and its windows are of the same style. The east window, of 3 lights, is poor. Those at the side are of 2 lights with very acute arches and rather peculiar tracery and one is Perpendicular. The roof of the chancel is open, the spaces between the queen posts arched and trefoiled. In the chancel is a trefoil niche with piscina. There is also a low side window or lychnoscope. On the place where stood the roodloft there is a boarded ceiling, panelled and painted, representing scripture subjects. The font is an octagon with several courses of horizontal mouldings diminishing towards the stem which is of like form. At the west end of the church is a fresco painting representing the Last Judgment. In the pulpit is the stand for the hour glass.

In the parapet of the south aisle occurs a tablet sculptured with a mitre and the cypher A.S.

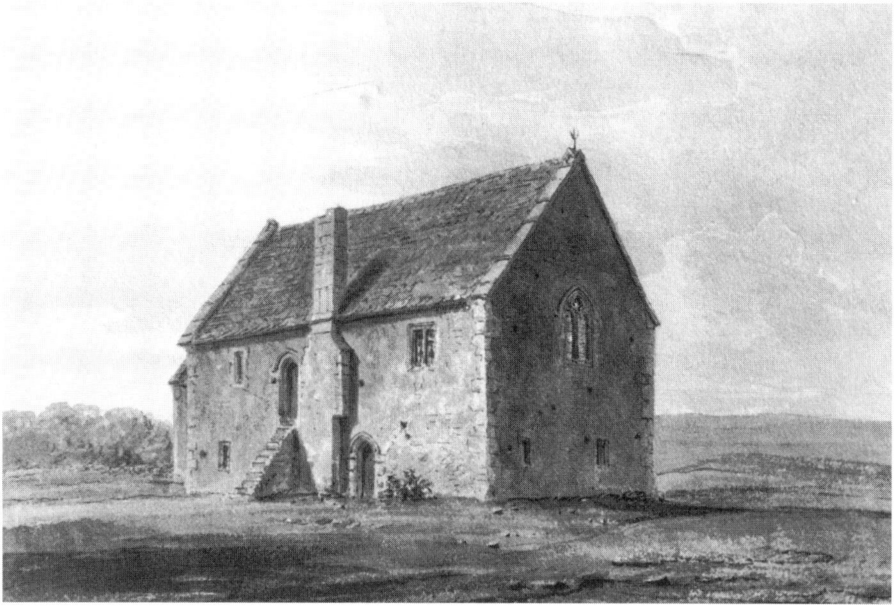

South east view of fisherman's house, Meare, 1828, by J.C. Buckler

Near the church is the Abbot of Glastonbury's house, now a farm. The porch has its gable surmounted by the figure of an abbot. The hall has Decorated windows resembling those in the chancel of Butleigh church, having foils in the interior arch. Some other windows with like tracery have transoms. There is also a very fine fireplace and a great extent of ancient walls and outbuildings.

There is also a fishing house which has some Decorated windows and a fine, large room approached by steps from without, having an open roof of fine framework much resembling that in the chancel of the church.

Mells

50/49–50 St. Andrew 31 July, 1849

A fine church, wholly Third-Pointed, consisting of nave with aisles, chancel with lateral chapels, west tower and south porch. The whole of fine stone with battlement; buttresses, and windows for the most part of 3 lights. At the east end of the clerestory of the nave is the sancte-bell in a niche. There is on the south side of the nave a curious semi-octagonal sacristy with battlements and pinnacles and 2 tiers of windows which are square-headed; also some canopied niches and armorial bearings, apparently later than the rest of the church.

The tower is a very fine one of 3 stages, of which the 2 highest are much enriched each having 3 windows of 2 lights with intermediate pinnacles and elegant stone lattice work. The lowest of these are not pierced. The buttresses

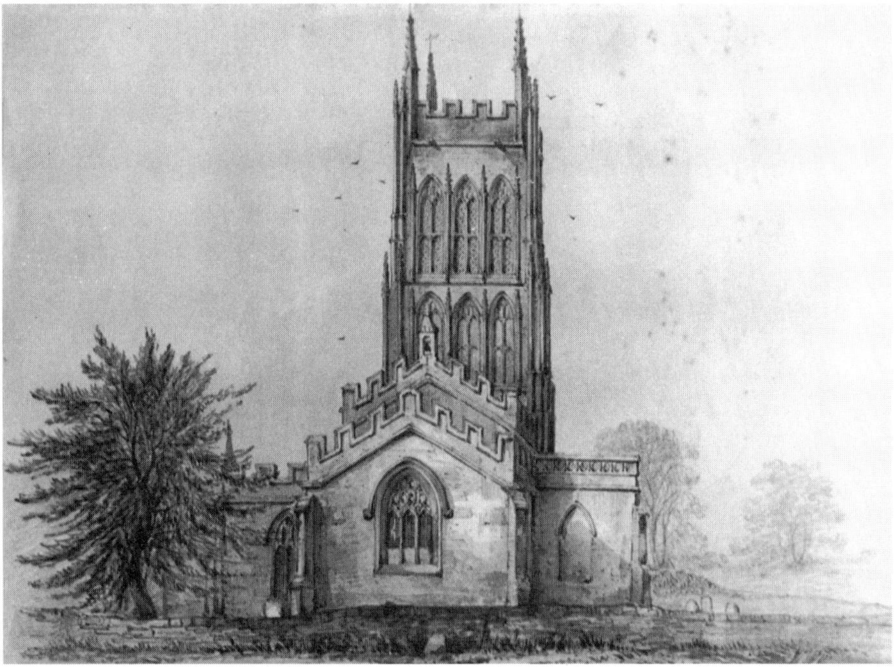

Mells, 1843, by W.W. Wheatley

are fine with pinnacled set-offs and there are 4 large pinnacles at the angles of the tower. The west window is of 5 lights. The west door has very good deep continuous mouldings.

There are no windows at the west ends of the aisles and the aisles do not extend quite to the west of the nave. The porch is a very handsome one with a curious ogee gable flanked by crocketed pinnacles and the apex crowned by a fine high canopied niche. The buttresses are also pinnacled. The outer door is ogee with finial and a band of panelling above it. The parvise is lighted by a 2 light window in front which is flanked by a canopied niche. The porch has elegant fan groining, the ribs of which lie upon shafts.

The nave has on each side an arcade of 4 good Third-Pointed arches with light clustered piers of the usual sort, the shafts having moulded capitals. There is a considerable space of wall between the western arch and the tower. The clerestory windows are of 3 lights. The tower arch is a very grand and lofty one and in the tower is some very good stone groining. The roof of the nave is a poor plain one A.D. 1736. Those of the aisles and chancel have been plastered after an incongruous ornamental fashion being a benefaction of a native of the parish within the last 50 years. The chancel arch is similar to the others. The pues are curious as of the age of James I.

There are some nice wood screens enclosing the chantry chapels which flank the chancel, retaining considerable traces of colour and gilding. These chapels seem to be additions, but not quite similar. Between the chancel and each of

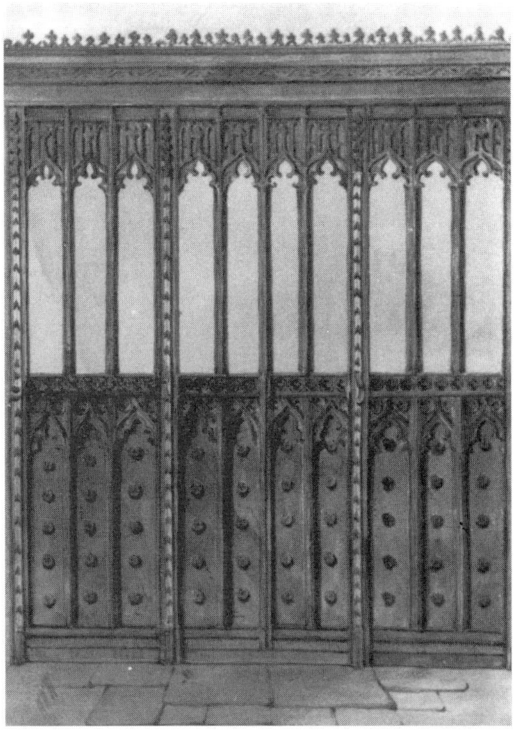

Screen, south aisle of Mells Church, 1845, by W.W. Wheatley

them is one Third-Pointed arch on shafts (as in the nave) and a small one eastward of it. The east window is wide, of 3 lights, with tracery somewhat Flamboyant. The south chapel has its roof panelled, but not finished, but is in some respects better finished than the northern.

The latter has a very good panelled ceiling with elegant bosses and moulded ribs. The east window is obituary with stained glass by Ward & Nixon. In this chapel may be seen the original altar stone with crosses. On the chancel walls is some trace of colour and figures. The chancel extends a little eastward of the aisles and under the southeast windows are 3 sedilia without canopies, divided by stone elbows; also a trefoil-headed piscina.

There are altar candlesticks and 3 coronae lucis; an organ in the south chapel. The font is of cylindrical form with a cornice of rope moulding and a square chamfered base.

Merriott

52/12–13 [All Saints] 19 February, 1872

A fair church mostly Perpendicular and in good condition consisting of a nave with aisles, chancel with aisles, south porch and western tower. The chancel has been recently rebuilt and in Decorated style of which character at least are

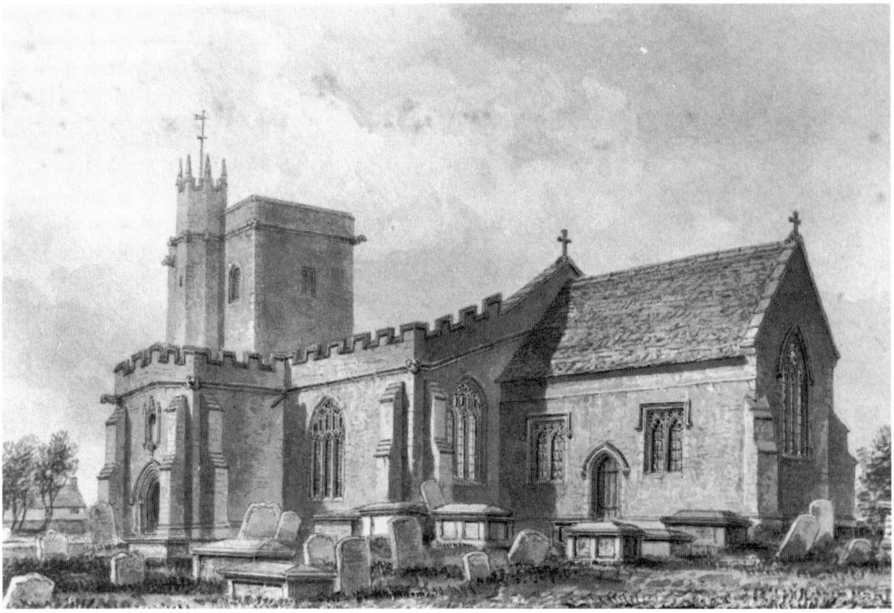

South east view of Merriott Church, 1831, by J. Buckler

all its windows. The eastern of 3, the others of 2 lights. The chancel arch is new and more of Early English character with shafts having foliaged capitals. There are also 2 arches dividing the chancel from the aisles with piers formed of detached marble shafts ranged round a circular pier. The floor of the chancel is laid with good tiles, that of the sacrarium is richer with marble steps. The chancel is fitted stall-wise. There is a sedile south of the sacrarium with triangular canopy. The roof of the chancel is panelled.

The arcades of the nave are each of 4 Perpendicular arches; the piers of a common arrangement with 4 shafts and alternate hollow mouldings; the bases octagonal and stilted. There is no clerestory; the windows of the aisles are Perpendicular of 3 lights. The roof has been renovated. The seats all open of pitch pine. The font is new and of Perpendicular character. The tower arch is pointed, of strong make and on circular shafts with moulded capitals. The tower is low with parapet not embattled. In the centre of the south side is an octagonal stair turret. There are no string courses. The western belfry window is plain, square-headed, of 2 lights; that on the south has the pierced stone lattice work.

The west doorway has panelled spandrels; the window over it of 3 lights. In the stage over there is a single light. There are gargoyles at the angles. The south porch has a pointed arch of entrance with shafts over which is a canopied niche and a band of foliage. The porch has embattled parapet and buttresses between the windows; also some gargoyles. There is also a niche over the door within the porch.

(The stair turret has an exterior doorway.)

Milborne Port

50/1–2 St. John Evangelist 30 October, 1842

This is a spacious church possessing several early and curious features. The plan cruciform. The chancel has a north chapel and the nave a north aisle which last is a modern addition. The tower rises from the centre. The whole church is of early Norman origin and much of the work is of a rude and curious character. In the west front are some single stone ribs (these are peculiarities of very early work and resemble the style of the tower at Barton St. Peter [Northants.]) and straight sided arches upon impost mouldings, but these are partly obscured by more modern work.

The west doorway is good Perpendicular with quatrefoils in the arch mouldings and foliage in the spandrels. On each side is a niche. There is a very fine south doorway of Norman work (also very early in the style), the arch tall and narrow with shafts having sculptured capitals and the nail-head ornament on the abacus. In the head of the arch above the doorway is a sculpture representing animals. In the west wall of the north transept is a Norman arch upon shafts.

The tower in its lower part is early Norman and rests upon 4 arches opening to the nave, chancel and transepts. Those on the north and south are semi-circular with extremely bold mouldings on a large scale. The eastern and

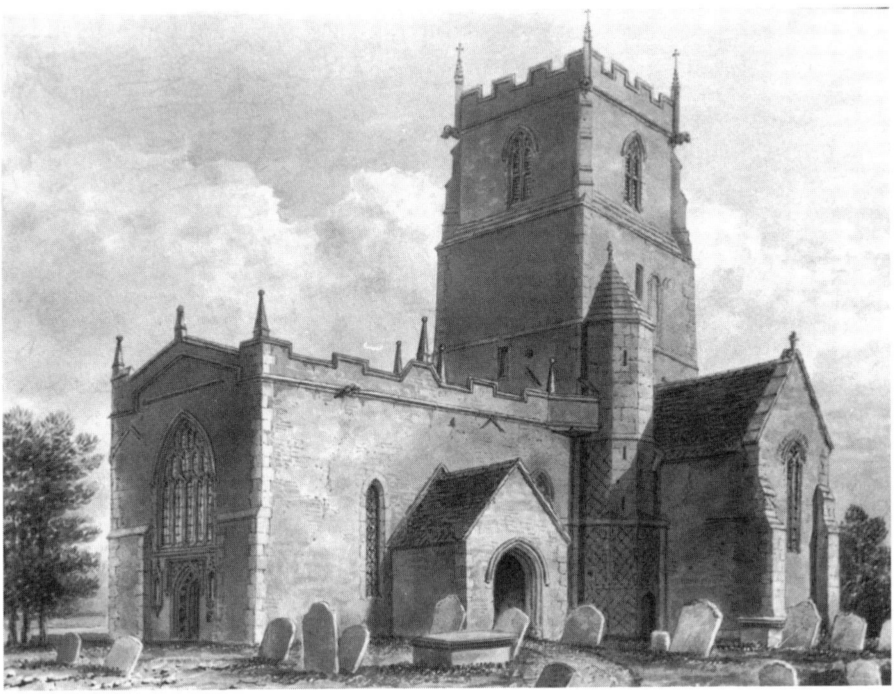

South west view of Milborne Port Church, 1839, by J. Buckler

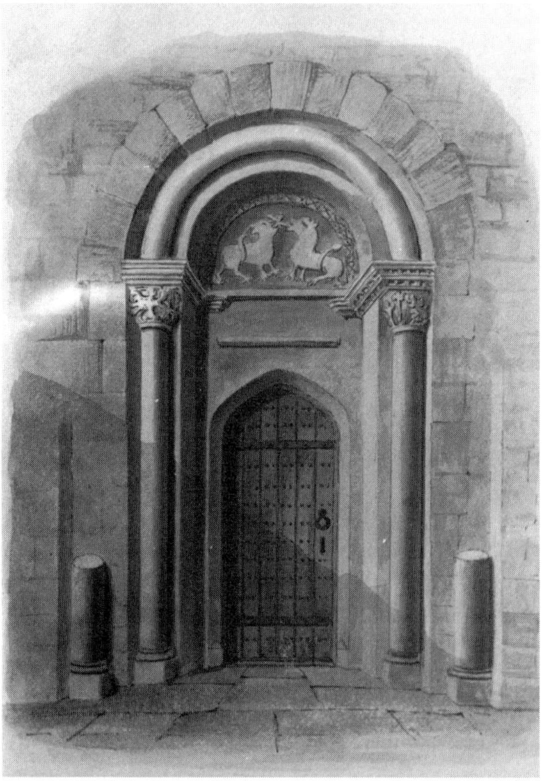

South door way, Milborne Port Church, 1839, by J. Buckler

western are pointed but in all the piers are similar shafts of unusually large size, the capitals also very large with the abacus and rude sculpture of scroll work, etc. and fleur de lys.

The tower has one stage above the roof of Norman work, but the arches are obliterated except on the north side. The upper part of the tower is Perpendicular, as at Sherborne, and being considerably less in diameter than the part below. It is connected with it by a bold, graduated slope. It has an embattled parapet and 4 small pinnacles. The belfry windows of 2 lights and plain character. There is a large octagonal turret at the south-west angle of the tower, but only extending along part of the lower stage.

On the south side of the chancel are indications externally of early work: string courses, ribs, and capitals are partially visible and two very narrow, plain lancet windows. At the east end of the north chapel are also 2 very narrow lancet windows with mouldings. The interior is encumbered with pues and the north aisle which is a modern addition only extends along part of the nave, opening to it by 2 plain pointed arches with a poor octagonal pier. The south transept has 2 early Decorated windows, almost Early English, the inner arch being trefoiled. In the south wall of this transept is a trefoil niche with drain, also a tomb arch. The cornice of the roof in this part has square flower.

The north transept contains monuments to the Medlycotts. The chancel

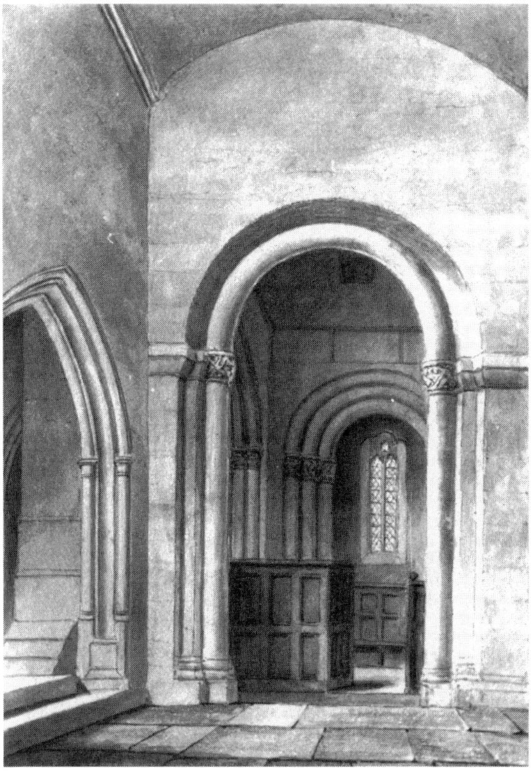

Interior view of Milborne Port Church, 1843, by J. Buckler

and its aisle are ceiled and the former fitted up with stalls. In the chancel arch is the screen of the roodloft, of elegant Perpendicular woodwork with tracery and band of vine leaves. The chapel is divided from the north aisle by 2 well-moulded Perpendicular arches upon a light pier with 4 shafts attached to it. This aisle is raised. In the chancel are some Perpendicular windows and one on the north of lancet form, the inner end being cinquefoiled.

On the south side of the chancel is a plain niche and drain. There is an Early English font of marble and an octagon in form, panelled, with plain pointed arches. The pedestal is square with circular shafts at the angles.

The north aisle of the chancel has a battlement and incipient pinnacles. The roof of the chancel is high-pitched. There is a good organ in a west gallery.

Milverton

51/51–53 St. Michael 1 February, 1852

This spacious and striking church is now in excellent condition. It stands within a very large churchyard and is seen to great advantage on all sides. The whole is Perpendicular but of a less ornate kind than many other churches of

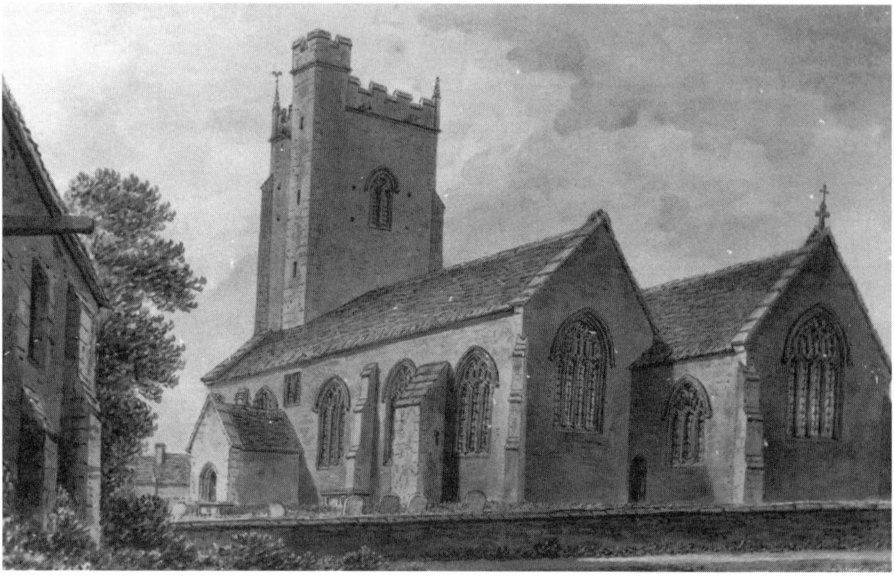

South east view of Milverton Church, 1837, by J. Buckler

Somersetshire and on the whole it has more of severe grandeur than richness.

The plan is a nave with north and south aisles, chancel with north and south chapels, western tower and south porch set at the west end of the aisle. The interior is remarkably solemn. The nave is of unusual width and separated from each aisle by an arcade of 4 large pointed arches on octagonal piers with capitals. There is no clerestory. The roofs are all coved with moulded ribs. All the seats are open with good carved bench ends, some of which may be ancient, but many are of varied wood carving, some rather cinquecento in character.

The tower arch, open to the nave, is a strong one with 2 orders, the inner member on short corbeled shafts with capitals. The chancel arch is wide upon octagonal pilasters set according to Somersetshire fashion in the very small interval between the aisles of the nave and the chapels of the chancel.

The windows of the aisles are mostly of 3 lights, but not all alike in tracery. Some of the south aisle are of 4 lights and one over the porch is square-headed. The east windows of the aisles are both of 4 lights. The roofs of the aisles coved and ribbed. The chancel is nicely arranged; has stalls of fair wood carving, the sacrarium laid with ornamental tiles and a very fair illuminated reredos. The chancel has one arch to each chapel, lower than those of the nave, on octagonal corbels. The east window of the chancel is of 4 lights; those north and south are of 2. The chancel extends beyond the aisles, has a priest's door on the south and vestry on the north. On the north of the altar is a new tomb of altar shape charged with a cross in brass. There are illuminated scrolls over the doors and windows of the chancel. The organ is in the north chapel. Many of the windows are filled with new stained glass. The pulpit is of stone, also new. The font is Norman, the bowl circular on a stem of like form with cable moulding just under the bowl. The exterior is plain, the material all red stone. The aisles have parapets; the roofs are new. The tower is a plain one with battlement and 4 small pinnacles crocketed; buttresses at the angles and no string courses. At the north-east a square stair turret embattled. On the west a small 3 light window; belfry windows of 2 lights having quatrefoil pierced lattice work.

This is a good specimen of more severe Somerset Perpendicular in a large church.

(In Somersetshire, where there is a chancel arch, it usually reaches nearly up to the roof and is set on shafts which sometimes stand upon the very capitals of the adjacent piers of the unbroken arcade which often runs along both nave and chancel. The chancel is generally equal in height to the nave and its separation by no means so complete as in other parts of the country where the chancel is usually lower and narrower than the nave. In Devonshire and Cornwall the chancel arch is generally altogether wanting, but the division marked by screens.)

Minehead

51/3–6 St. Michael 9 May, 1855

A large church in a fine elevated situation and having an imposing outward appearance, but the interior not corresponding in beauty and chiefly from the pues and general fill up being so very bad. The whole is Perpendicular and the plan comprises a nave and chancel, each with a north aisle and a south porch and a lofty, handsome western tower.

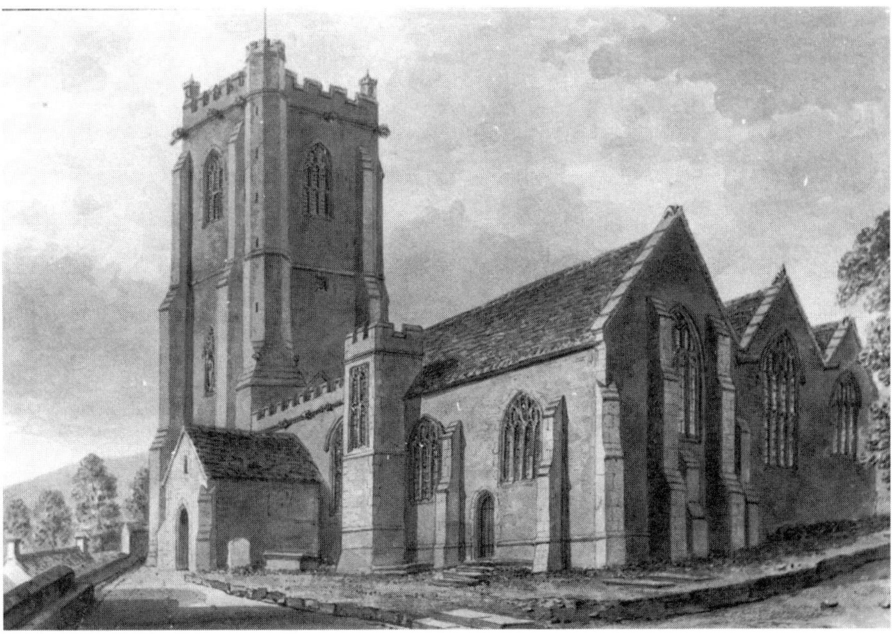

South east view of Minehead Church, 1839, by J. Buckler

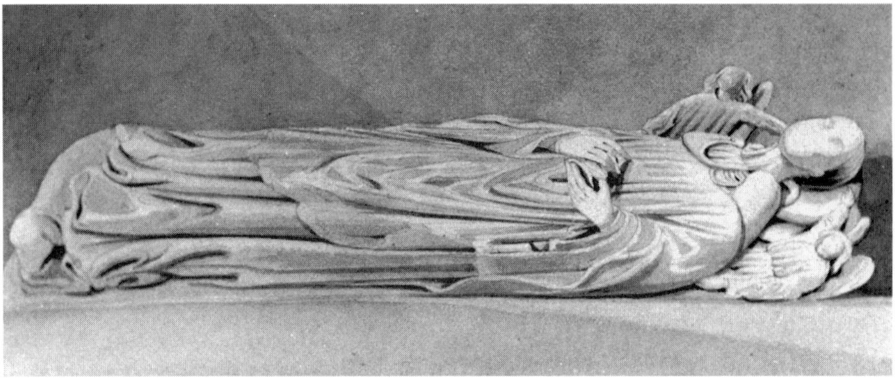

Effigy of Henry de Bracton in Minehad Church, 1844, by S.G. Tovey

The south side of the nave is embattled. The north side is not. There is a rood turret on the south, also embattled, containing the stairs and lighted by small windows. The tower is a very fine one, though not of the highly enriched type and has embattled parapet with unfinished pinnacles, an octagonal stair turret at the south-east, a large west window and doorway, belfry windows of 3 lights with transoms and in the second stage a statue of St. Michael within a square tablet. The tower arch to the nave is lofty and fine with good mouldings and imposts but no shafts.

The nave and chancel are undivided by any arch but the roodscreen remains and runs across both body and aisle having vine leaf cornices and fan groining. Upon it an ugly gallery has been erected. There is an arcade of 5 [*sic*] arches of which 5 are in the nave and 3 in the chancel, rather plain and ordinary, with octagonal columns having capitals. The arcade leans out of the Perpendicular and is strengthened by wooden framework. There is a west gallery containing an organ and most irregular, unsightly pues. The roof coved and plastered.

On the south side is one fine large window of 4 lights with transom and shafts to the rear arch. Many of the other windows have been mutilated. That at the west of the aisle is of 3 lights; the east window of the chancel of 5 lights: ordinary Perpendicular. In the north chancel aisle is a square-headed one of 2 lights and a good east window (bearing the date 1529) which has a soffit with groining either in stone or plaster. Within the most easterly niche is a fine Perpendicular tomb, supposed to be that of Henry de Bracton, the celebrated lawyer. This tomb has its sides enriched with canopied niches. The effigy is robed, apparently in judicial robes and the hand holds what resembles a chalice but it is mutilated. There is a high canopy with groining but the whole is now clogged with whitewash.

Chained to the desk, fixed against this tomb, is a black letter Bible printed 1639 and an edition of Jewell's Sermons. Within this north chapel, enclosed by iron railings, is a fine statue of Queen Anne in white marble; the sculpture of the lace, collar, sleeves and very elegant [*sic*], presented in 1719 by Sir Jacob Banks, M.P. for the Borough. Adjoining at the north is a vestry to which opened formerly an arch. In the vestry is a small 3 light window at the east end and a 2 light square-headed one with some remains of stained glass. Its roof is panelled and ribbed, boarded over the east end. There are traces of a piscina on the south. The

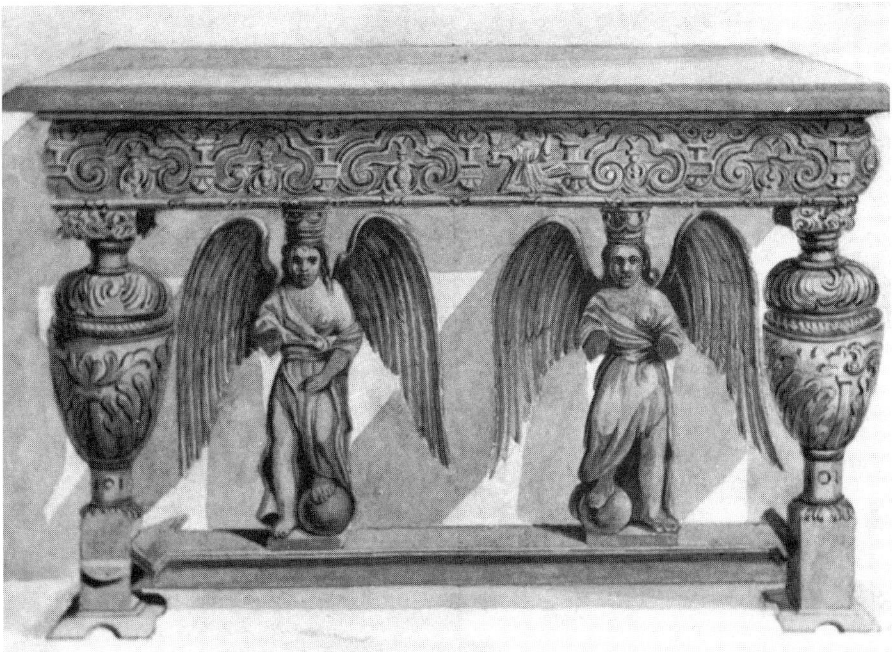

In Minehead Church, 1844, by S.G. Tovey

pavement has several encaustic tiles and there is a fine ancient chest with excellent wood carving shewing the arms of England and France.

The south wall of the church seems to incline towards the east. The font is a good one, the bowl octagonal, sculptured with figures of saints in a kind of sitting posture. The stem has ogee canopies with niches and statues. There is a flat stone near the altar with the brass figure of a lady and the remains of an inscription. The head dress is high and the remains of the inscription qu . nd Justiciarii Anglie que . . . quart Virginis anno dom Mill CCCCXL cui etc.

The Decalogue bears the date 1634. The altar is rather handsome, well-carved with 4 swelling legs and angel figures.

There is a fine cross on the south side of the churchyard. The ground on the north is very uneven.

(Length 116; width 42; tower 90 feet high; has clock, chimes and 5 bells.)

Monksilver

50/91–92 All Saints 10 May, 1855

A pretty little church which underwent a most satisfactory restoration about 1844. The plan is chancel and nave, each with a south aisle, a west tower and a south porch ranging with it and forming a part of the south aisle. The whole is Perpendicular. The south aisle has a rich battlement with pierced quatrefoils

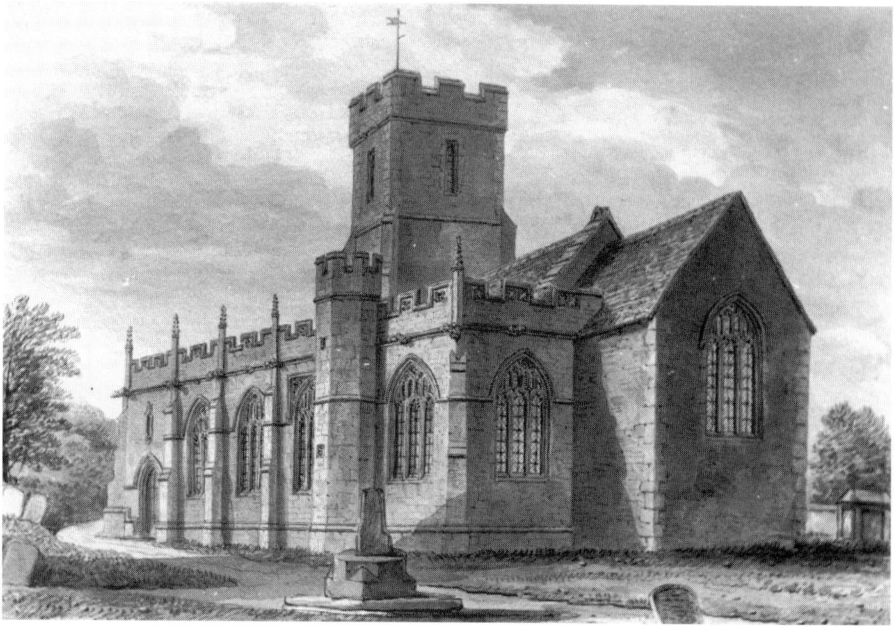

South east view of Monksilver Church, 1836, by J. Buckler

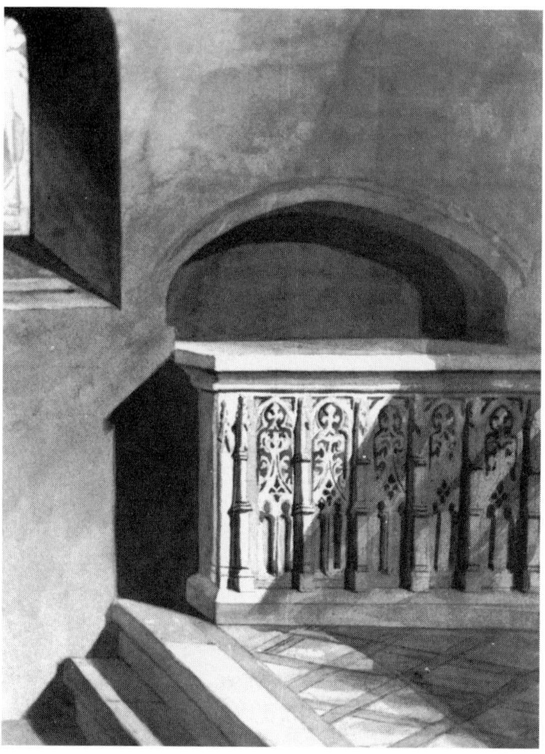

In the chancel of Monksilver Church, 1845, by S.G. Tovey

and pinnacles and some curious gargoyles representing toads and other beasts. On the south side is an octagonal rood stair turret which is embattled.

The windows are mostly square-headed; one on the south has pierced spandrels. On the north of the chancel is one small window apparently Norman, the only remains of the original building. Most of the windows are filled with very fair stained glass. The arcade is elegant, the arches small and in proportion to the church. The nave has 3, the chancel 1 opening to the aisle, the chancel extending eastward of the latter. The piers are light and elegant, of the usual Somerset Perpendicular make. The roofs of the nave and aisles are coved with ribs and bosses and cornice. The chancel is also coved and coloured blue.

The chancel arch as usual is wide, from wall to wall, the tower arch very narrow. The interior is very beautiful and in true ecclesiastical order. All the pues and galleries are gone and the whole of the seats open with finely carved ends some of which may be original, but the new ones admirably imitated. The roodscreen has been very well restored and has 5 compartments with door and good tracery and the prayers are read from stalls in the chancel. For the lessons an ancient eagle lectern is used.

To the north of the altar is a fine panelled tomb below a flat arch, probably that of the Founder. The altar is stone and raised, the space about it paved with encaustic tiles. The font has an octagonal bowl with quatrefoil panelling upon a stem. The porch has a canopied niche over the door. The tower, small, embattled, with single, square-headed belfry window and corner buttresses. The west window of 2 lights. There is a piscina on the south of the chancel. All the stone work has been cleaned and repaired. The churchyard very steep and romantic. In it is the stump of a cross.

Monkton, West

51/39–41 St. Augustine 30 January, 1861

A handsome and spacious Perpendicular church of the Somerset type in a secluded churchyard shaded by fine trees and near an ancient family mansion. In the churchyard, both here and at Thurloxton, are seen the stocks.

The church consists of a nave with north and south aisles, chancel, west tower and south porch, the nave having a clerestory. The whole is of the normal local Perpendicular except perhaps a small 2 light window at the north end of the south aisle which may be early Decorated. Both aisles and porch are embattled. The clerestory has rather a high pitched roof. The chancel is lower, the walls externally covered with stucco.

The windows of the south aisle are chiefly of 2 lights; those of the north aisle of 3, except a 2 light one at its west end. The arcades are lofty and good, each of 4 well-shaped arches with the usual light Perpendicular piers of 4 clustered shafts having intermediate hollows. The clerestory has 3 light windows. The roof of the nave is coved with ribs and bosses. The church is pewed and hath a western gallery with an organ. The chancel arch is pointed rising directly from the wall. The east window is Decorated, of 4 lights and subarcuated, filled with modern stained glass. The other windows of the chancel are large

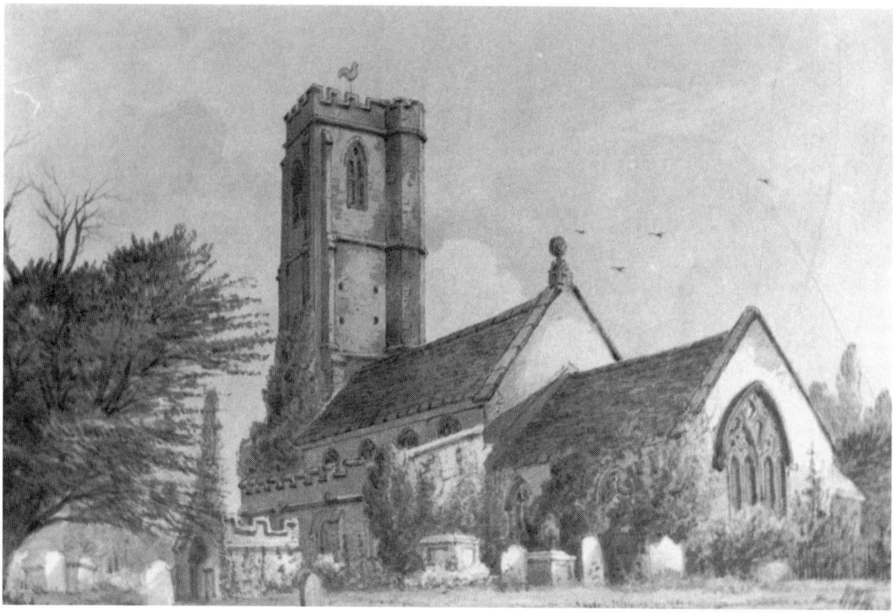

South east view of West Monkton Church, 1848, by W.W. Wheatley

Perpendicular ones of 2 and 3 lights. The chancel is full of modern monuments. Its south doorway is labeled with foliage in the spandrels.

The east gable of the clerestory has a very small bellcote. The tower is lofty, embattled, and not covered with stucco like the other parts. On its west side is a fine continuous doorway with excellent mouldings. The west window of 3 lights and transomed. The buttresses are not at the angles. There are 2 strings and an octagonal turret at the north-east; the belfry windows of 2 lights. The porch has battlement and gargoyles; the outer doorway on shafts with capitals of foliage; the inner door with continuous mouldings and over it a bracket with sculpture representing an angel.

Montacute

49/41–43 [St. Catherine] Before 1840

This is an interesting church with varied architecture, cruciform in its plan and without aisles and having at the west end a lofty, embattled tower which, together with the greater part of the nave, is Rectilinear. The transepts are of Early English origin with later additions and in the chancel are traces of Norman with later additions and much modern alteration.

The tower is a very handsome Rectilinear specimen constructed of the finest stone, divided into stages by rich panelled bands of quatrefoils with another just below the battlement. At the north-east angle is an octagonal staircase turret. The buttresses are charged with unfinished pinnacles; the belfry

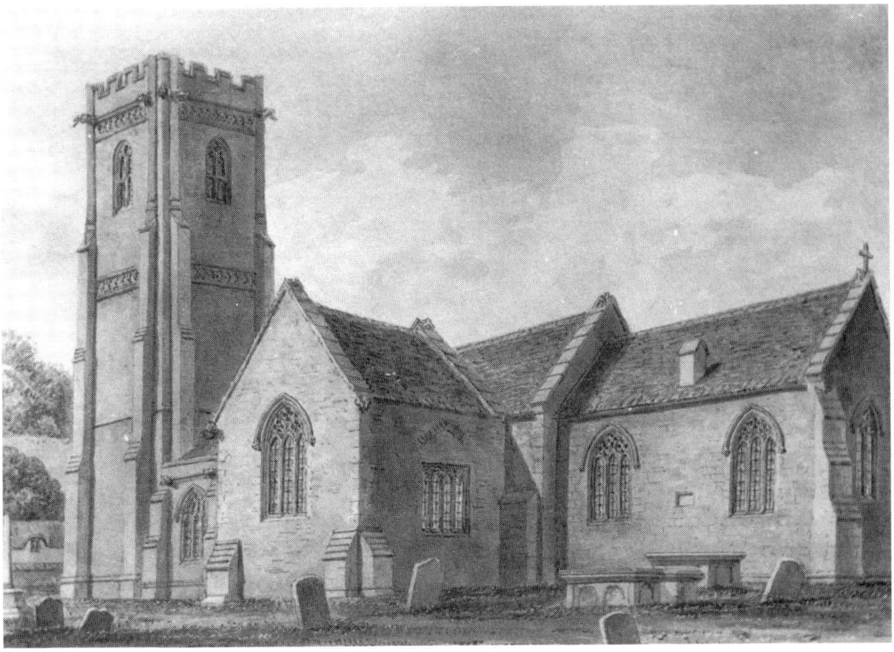

South east view of Montacute Church, 1836, by J. Buckler

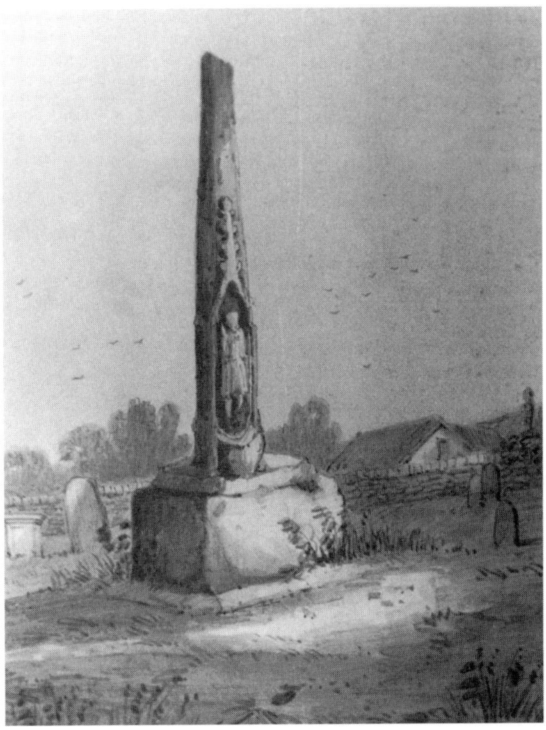

Old cross in Montacute churchyard, 1848, by W.W. Wheatley

windows each of two lights with transom and fine pierced lattice work in stone. The west doorway has fine mouldings, panelled spandrels and set between pinnacles. Above it, as usual, a large 4 light window with transom.

The north porch is large and of plain Decorated character having a fine canopied niche over the doorway and in the head of the gable a small 2 light window. The ceiling is groined, the ribs upon shafts, and above it is the parvise storey. The windows of the nave are chiefly Rectilinear of 3 lights. The parapets are plain and the roofs covered in the stone slates used in this district.

The arches opening to the transepts are pointed with a very slight curve, upon shafts which on the south side have some of the nail-head in their capitals while the others appear to be of Decorated period. There are a few lancet windows in the transept and others with Decorated tracery of 3 lights, and one with 4 lights having a square head. In the south transept is a trefoil niche on shafts with a piscina and a shelf. The arch to the chancel is Norman upon shafts of plain character. Near it is part of a chevroned string course and the door which led into the roodloft.

On each side of the altar is a rich niche with beautiful canopy having groining on the underside and set between buttresses, the pedestals richly panelled and standing on the ground. These seem to be Rectilinear. The greater part of the chancel is sadly modernized.

The arch to the tower is lofty and finely panelled; through it the west window appears to much advantage. There are several open seats and carved ends. In the north transept a late monument to one of the Phelips's A.D. 1508. The font is an octagon panelled.

In the churchyard is an ancient cross and a gateway formed by a Tudor arch. Near it, an ancient house with a fine battlement and porch with gable and a kind of embattled tower in which is a beautiful oriel window and bands of panelling, evidently about 1480.

The magnificent mansion, Montacute Hall, is one of the finest specimens in the country of an Elizabethan house and retains a good deal of Gothic forms and ornament, especially a rich, pierced parapet which runs upon the porch, the front of which has also some rich panelling. In place of pinnacles are some pedestals having spiral mouldings and crowned by human figures.

Moorlinch

51/18–19 St. Mary 3 February, 1858

This church has chancel and nave only, west tower and south porch. The outer doorway of the porch is obtuse and rather singular from having one cylindrical moulding and one studded at intervals with lozenges, having a semblance of Norman work. The porch itself is later, has stone benches and a coved, ribbed roof. The inner door has fine wood work with tracery of a Decorated character. The chancel arch is pointed, on octagonal columns. The chancel has a north and south window, Decorated, of 2 lights, one square-headed on the south of 2 lights, Perpendicular as is also

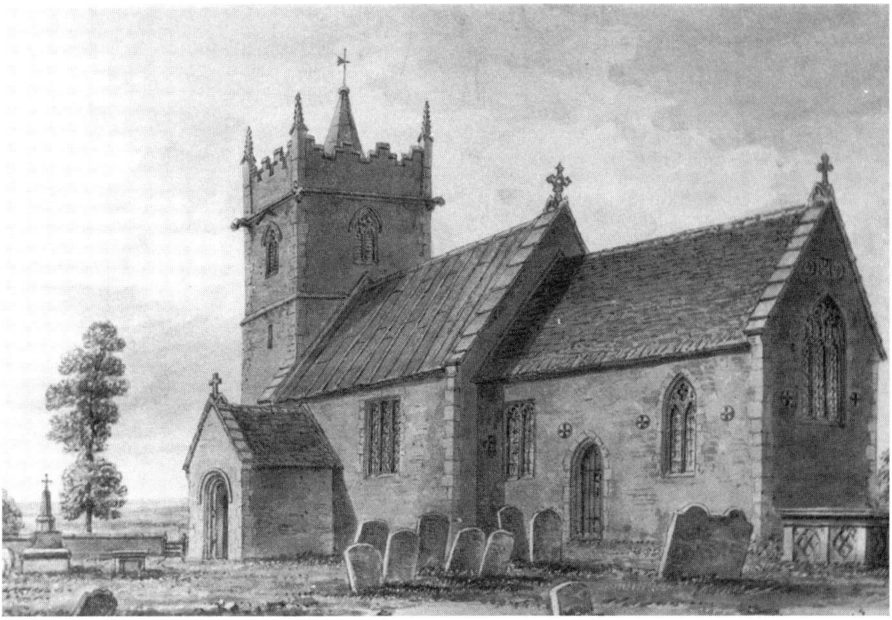

South east view of Moorlinch Church, 1838, by J. Buckler

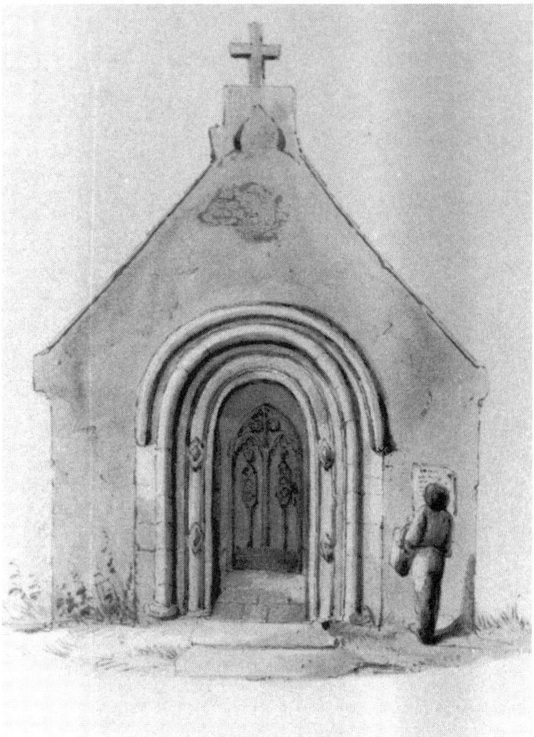

South porch, Moorlinch Church, 1843, by W.W. Wheatley

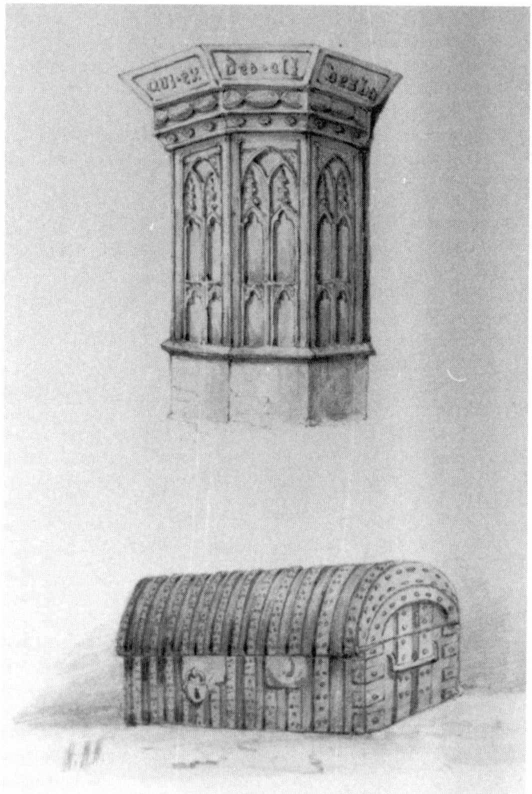

Pulpit and chest in Moorlinch Church, 1843, by W.W. Wheatley

the east window of 3 lights. The south-west window (Perpendicular) is surmounted internally by an arch which is shouldered in an odd way. On the south of the altar is an octagonal bracket with round bases of columns attached.

In the south wall of the nave appears an arch as if there had been once a transeptal chapel. The tower arch is pointed and plain on imposts. The tower is low without buttresses, in its lower portions Decorated having a west window of 3 lights, simple trefoiled, and its rear arch has cinquefoil cusping. The belfry storey is Perpendicular with 2 light windows and battlement and 4 small crocketed pinnacles. There are gargoyles at the angles.

The font has a circular bowl on square base with rope moulding round it. On the south side of the nave remain some ancient benches with wood carving representing roses, armorial bearings and tracery. The windows of the nave have been badly altered. Under a north window is a fine effigy of a lady on a panelled tomb, the head dress square and netted; the hands are destroyed. The south side of the church has been much renewed. The chancel covered with slate; crosses on both the east gables.

(There are 5 bells and a fine old chest having iron work on it. The situation is elevated and striking, commanding an extensive view.)

Muchelney

49/21–23 [St. Peter and St. Paul] 1830

The church is a very neat Rectilinear structure consisting of a handsome tower and nave with aisles, a south transept, and a chancel. The tower is 4 stages in height having a west doorway with a label and panelled spandrels and on its south side a very beautiful stoup enriched with quatrefoil panelling and having a bracket with fan work. Over the window [*sic* – doorway?] is a large window of 4 lights. The next stage has on the west side a 2 light window between two niches and the belfry storey has on each side 2 windows of 2 lights upon a string. The parapet is embattled and the corner buttresses are terminated by small crocketed pinnacles, two at each corner. There is also a crocketed pinnacle in the centre of each side, set diagonally and crowning a small buttress between the belfry windows. At the south-east angle is an octagonal turret.

The south aisle has a plain parapet and the north aisle a rich panelled battlement. There is a south porch of two stages with a panelled battlement and pinnacles, the lower stage having a groined roof. The nave is divided from each aisle by 3 pointed arches springing from light piers each having 4 shafts. Over the east end of the nave is a fine wood roof; that in the chancel is plainer. The south chapel, or transept, opens to the nave by an arch with panelled soffit without shafts. In the chapel is a fine panelled ceiling painted and enriched with figures of angels bearing scrolls.

The windows are mostly of 2 and 3 lights, but the east window is of 5 lights

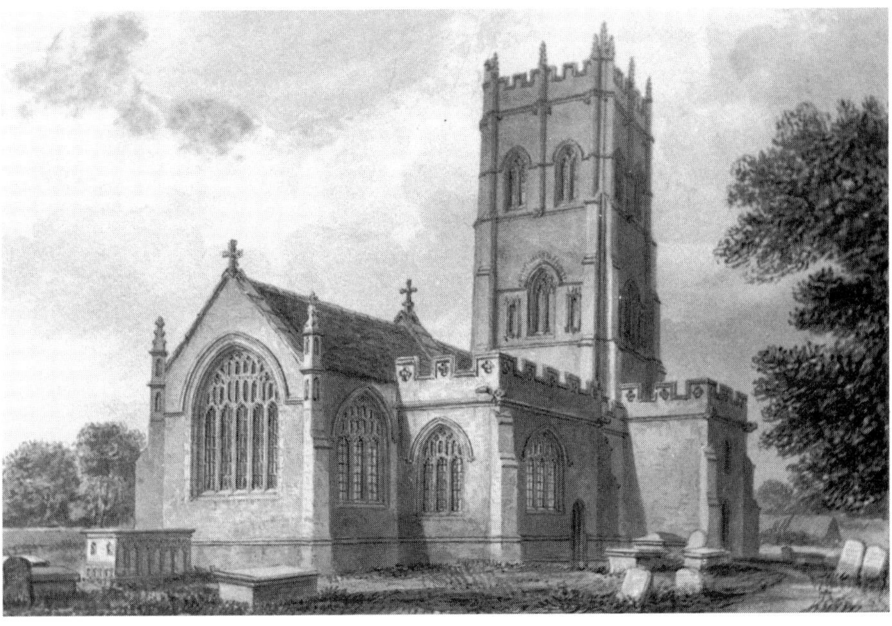

North east view of Muchelney Church, 1830, by J. Buckler

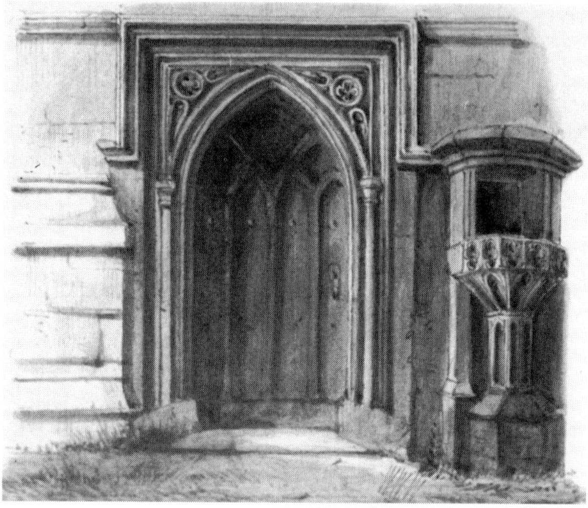

West door of Muchelney Church, 1850, by W.W. Wheatley

and filled with good stained glass. The other windows of the chancel are small and square-headed. The tower opens to the nave by a lofty arch with panelled soffit and has a good stone groined ceiling. The font is an octagon, panelled with quatrefoils containing figures. There is a small square shaft attached to the alternate angles; the pedestal octangular.

In the churchyard near the east end is an altar tomb of Rectilinear work with good panelling.

The remains of the abbey seem to be of wholly Rectilinear work of good character and the greater part of the buildings occupied as a farm. The

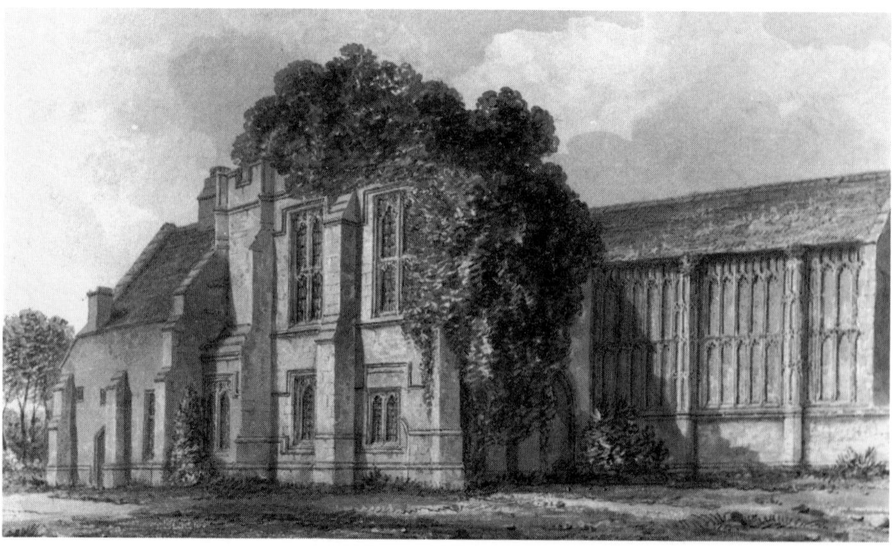

South view of Muchelney Abbey, 1830, by J. Buckler

windows are chiefly square-headed and there are several doorways with labels and very fine bands of foliage and panelling. There is one splendid chimneypiece enriched with a band of quatrefoil panelling and a beautiful cornice of vine leaves with grapes. The chimneys are octagonal. The chapel had once a stone groined ceiling of which the springs remain and some rich windows with square-heads resembling those in the cloisters of Christchurch, Oxford. In some are pieces of fine stained glass.

Mudford

51/79–80 St. Mary 1 February, 1864

A nice Perpendicular church with good and well-finished work, consisting of nave and chancel without aisles, a north transeptal chapel and a south porch and a western tower. The nave and porch have embattled parapets, but not the chancel. There are good gargoyles and the roof is covered with stone flags. The tower is a good one, embattled, with 8 small crocketed pinnacles and an octagonal stair turret at the north-east, also embattled. Belfry windows of 2 lights and under them a good panelled band. The buttresses are somewhat withdrawn from the angles. On the west side is a good doorway with label, and foliage in the spandrels, the label upon corbels; also a 3 light window. There is on this side also the trace of a rood in relief, now defaced and surmounted by a label; part of the figure on the cross may be seen.

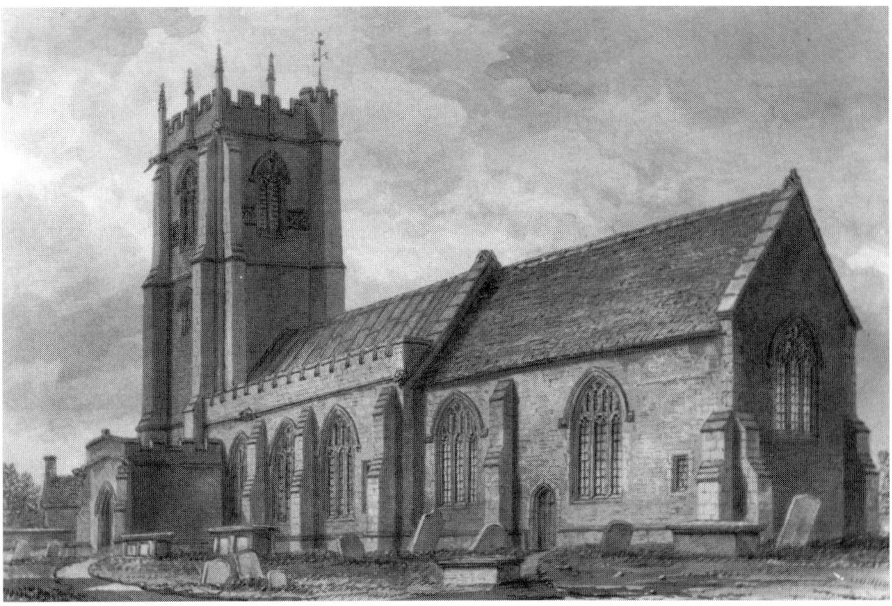

South east view of Mudford Church, 1835, by J. Buckler

The south porch has the outer doorway with continuous arch mouldings and within it is a niche. The tower arch to the nave is a fine and lofty one enriched with panelling. The nave is long, well-proportioned and in neat condition; the windows uniform, of 3 lights and set close. In some are the remains of stained glass. There is a plain north doorway. The roofs are coved with ribs and bosses; that of the chancel lower than that of the nave. The nave is fitted in very uniform manner with pewing and pulpit of the Caroline pattern, quite regular.

The north chapel seems to have been added about the same time for a family seat, opening with a round arch and having debased square-headed windows. There is a Perpendicular bracket in the east jamb of a south window with figure of archangel bearing a shield. The chancel arch is round and appears to have been tampered with when the other alterations were made. The east window of the chancel is a Decorated one of 3 lights; those on the sides are Perpendicular of 3 lights. The font has an octagonal bowl diminishing downwards enriched with panelling and Tudor flower, on a panelled stem. Near the east and on the south appears outwardly a small, oblong opening or slit with grating. (In the chancel is some old stained glass in fragments. There are 5 bells.)

Nailsea

50/37–39 Holy Trinity 28 September, 1848

This church is entirely Third-Pointed and consists of a nave and chancel each with a south aisle, a north chapel to the chancel, a south porch and western tower. The latter is of genuine Somersetshire cast as is the prevailing character of the church. The tower is of 4 stages divided by string courses, has corner buttresses and an elegant parapet of pierced panelling. There are 3 stages of 2 light windows of which 2 have the stone lattice work and one is closed, but all similar in tracery. The west doorway has continuous mouldings and a hood on square block corbels. The west window of 3 lights, the hood having for corbels a crowned and mitred head. The stone is varied, the dressings being of a finer quality. At the north-east is an octagonal stair turret continued to the top. The pinnacles are unfinished. In the centre of each side is a large gargoyle of the head of a beast.

The parapets of the body are moulded. Some ugly large buttresses have been added on the south and the south porch bears the date 1712. Within the porch is a doorway with continuous mouldings, the hood returned and a bracket over it. The outer walls are much covered with rough cast. The north doorway resembles the western. The windows are generally of a very uniform western character of 3 lights; that at the east end somewhat differs and its corbels externally remain unfinished. The north-east and south-east windows of the chancel are square-headed of 2 lights; those in the north chapel also square-headed, of 3 lights having discharging arches. That at the east end of the south aisle is of 4 lights, the western of 2 lights and square-headed.

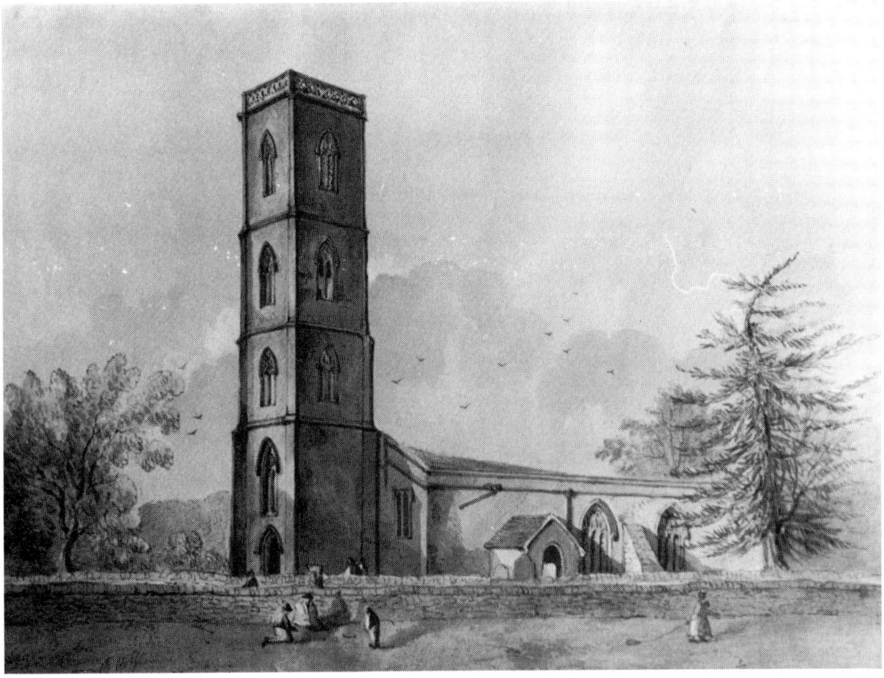

Nailsea, 1843, by W.W. Wheatley

There is an arcade on the south of 5 Third-Pointed arches, one of which is within the chancel. The piers are rather rich, of lozenge form, having each 4 shafts whose capitals are separate and foliated. The intermediate spaces between the shafts are fluted and somewhat varied occasionally with diminutive shafts. The pier has also a general octagonal capital. On the 4th pier, adjacent to the entrance of the chancel, is inserted a square shelf, or ledge, beneath which are sculptured figures of a man and a winged ox, probably the emblems of Saints Matthew and Luke. On the corresponding side on the north appears the winged lion of St. Mark.

The tower arch has continuous moulding. There is no chancel arch, but the roof of the chancel is rather lower than that of the nave. In the angle, to the north of the entrance into the chancel, are two pointed small doors. One communicates with the steps leading both to the pulpit and roodloft, the other with the north chapel of the chancel. The pulpit is a fine one of stone, 5 sides enriched with tracery and shields with crocketed pinnacles at the angles. The upper part has a projecting moulded cornice, the lower part has fan groining running to a slender octagonal shaft which has a sort of crown of foliage.

The shaft of the pier, entering the chancel, has been cut away evidently for the purpose of inserting the roodloft. The chancel extends one bay beyond the aisles and on its south side is an ogee crocketed piscina with trefoil feathering. The north chapel is now formed into a pue and opens to the chancel by a Third-Pointed arch resembling the others. It has some stained glass and a

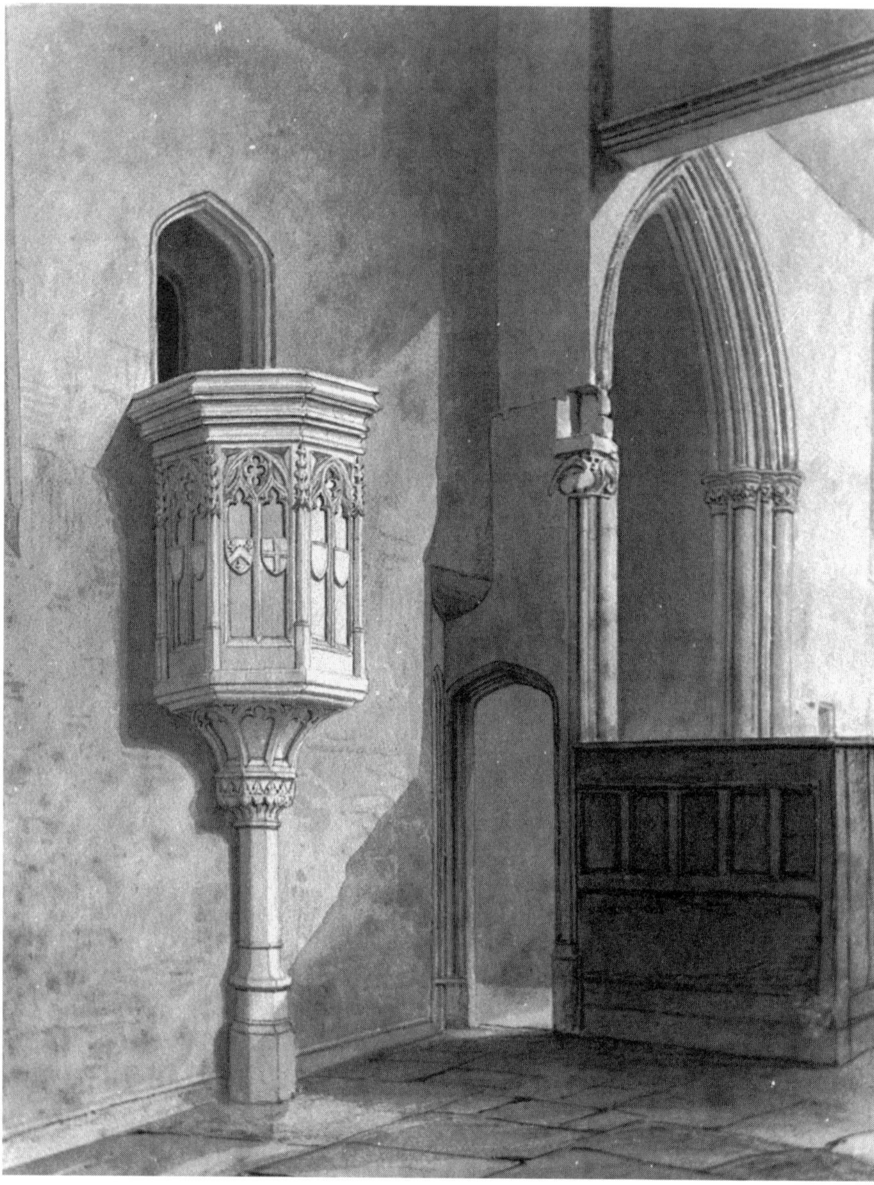

The pulpit in Nailsea Church, 1828, by J.C. Buckler

hagioscope into the chancel. The south aisle has a head bracket in its east wall and a square recess in the south wall.

The font is attached to a southern pier, the bowl octagonal with 4 leaf flower panelling on an octagonal panelled stem. The roofs have been ceiled. Some old open benches still remain towards the west end, but the church is chiefly pued, even the chancel and there are west and south galleries.

Nempnett Thrubwell

50/24–25 St. Mary April, 1845

A small church consisting of nave and chancel, south porch and west tower, the whole Perpendicular.

The tower is 3 stages in height with a panelled parapet and 4 pinnacles; an octagonal turret at the south-east corner. The belfry window of 2 lights with stone lattice work in lozenge forms. The west window of 3 lights; the door has continuous mouldings and foliated corbels to the dripstone. The windows are some of 3 lights, others of 2 lights and square-headed and there is a little painted glass. The chancel arch has continuous mouldings. The porch has its outer entrance also with continuous mouldings; the inner door square-headed. The nave is leaded. The chancel tiled and less lofty. In the churchyard are the steps of a cross.

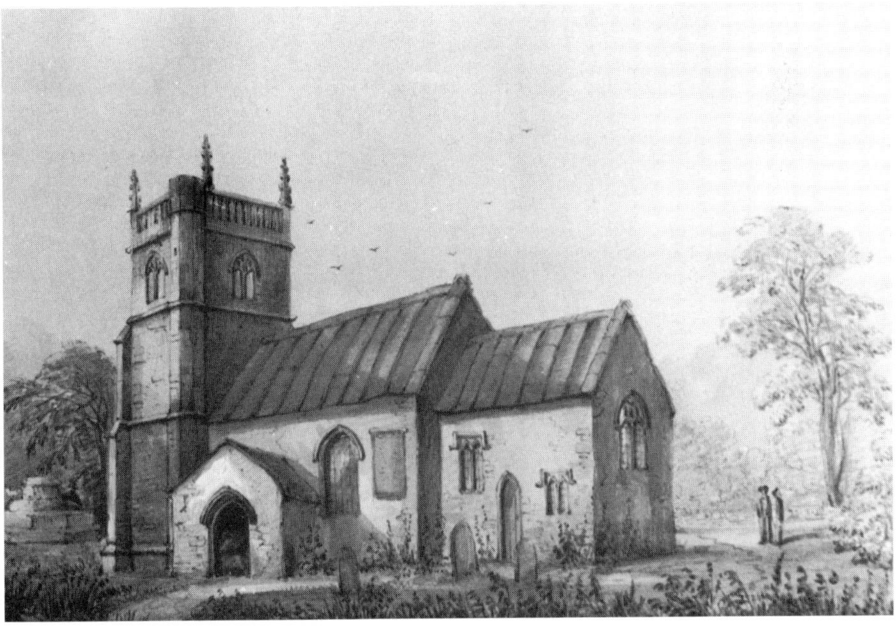

Nempnett Thrubwell, 1843, by W.W. Wheatley

Newton St. Loe

49/65–66 [Holy Trinity] Before 1840

This church has a west tower, a nave with south aisle and a chancel. The tower is Perpendicular, embattled, with 4 crocketed pinnacles, all of good masonry and finely mantled with ivy. On its north side is a turret. The west window of 3 lights, the belfry windows dissimilar. The nave and its aisle are embattled. The

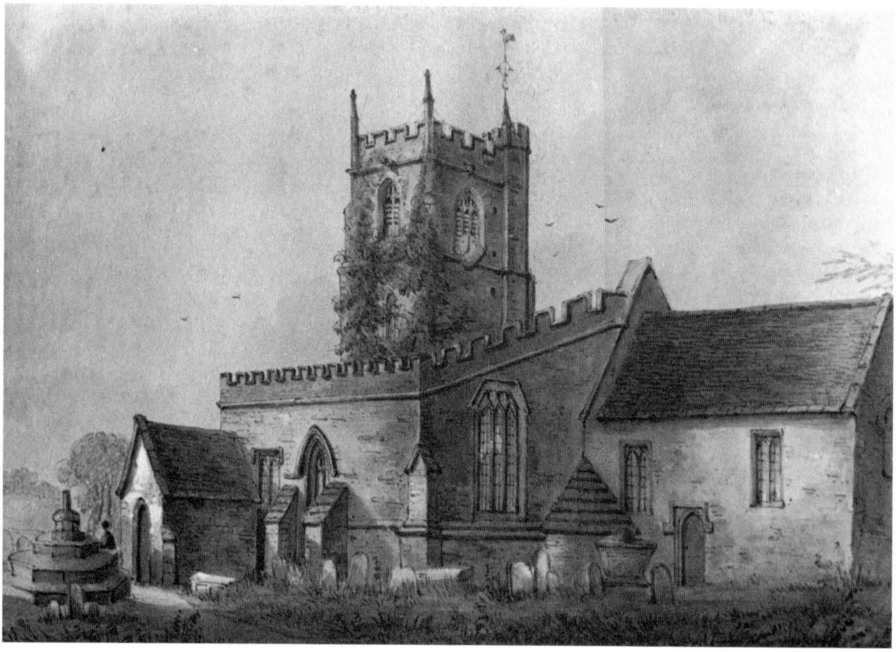

Newton St. Loe, 1843, by W.W. Wheatley

chancel has a tiled roof. There is a small window lighting the pulpit and, at the east end of the aisle, a Decorated window of 3 lights, the top of which is cut off.

The other windows are Perpendicular, those in the chancel square-headed with labels. On the north side of the nave are two large square-headed windows of 4 lights of which the interior mouldings are all panelled with shields and emblems inserted. The nave is divided from the aisle by 4 pointed arches and a segment of a 5th; the piers clustered of 4 large and 4 small shafts. The chancel arch is pointed. The font is octagonal on a cylindrical stem with square base. At the west end of the south aisle is a gorgeous marble monument A.D. 1701 and the burying place of the Langtons.

Norton Fitzwarren

50/31–32 All Saints April, 1845

This church has a nave and chancel each with north aisle, a south porch and a western tower; of mixed Decorated and Perpendicular character.

The tower is a good Perpendicular one, divided into 3 stages, having a good embattled parapet and buttresses at the angles, well-finished, and animal figures for gargoyles. The belfry windows of 2 lights with transom. In the next stage on the south a fine canopied niche with panelling and label above it. On

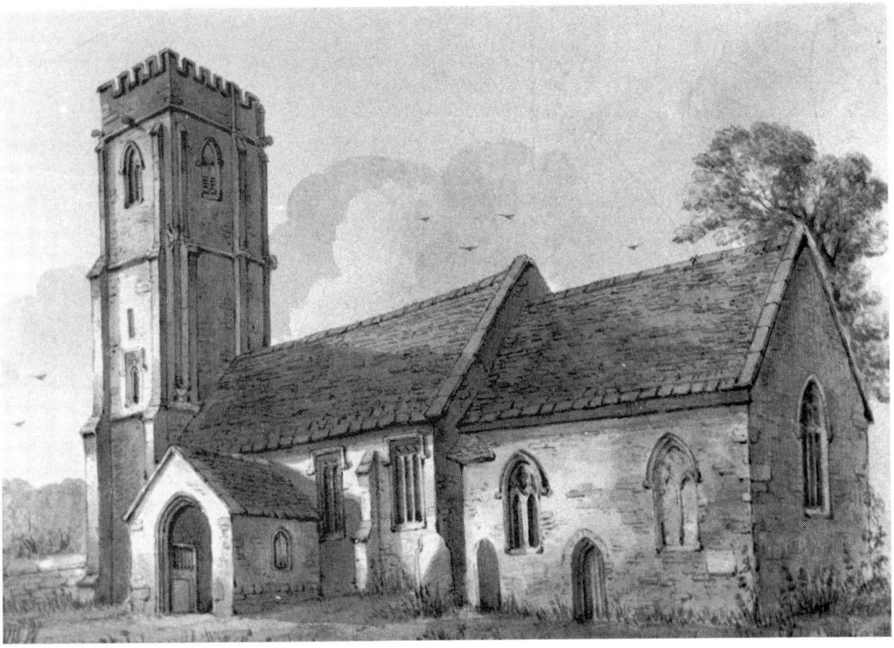

Norton Fitzwarren, 1848, by W.W. Wheatley

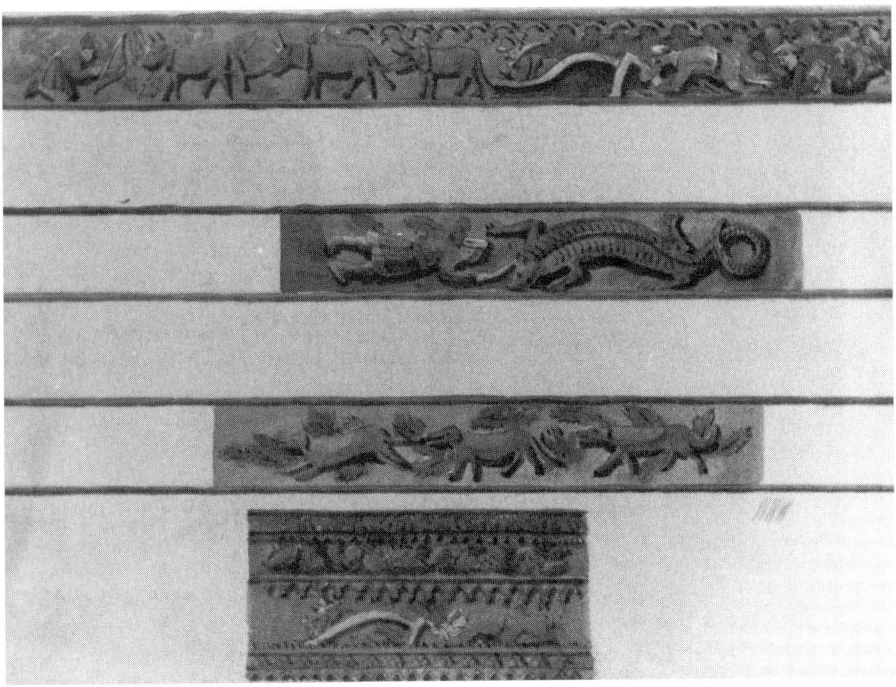

Screen, Norton Fitzwarren, by W.W. Wheatley

the west side a 3 light window and door with arch mouldings. On the east angle an octagonal turret rising high and embattled.

There is a plain parapet on the north side of the nave; the windows of the nave Perpendicular, that at the west of the north aisle of 3 lights; those on the south are square-headed and labeled. The south porch is entered by a large moulded arch and has stone benches and on its east side a single 3-foiled window. Within the porch is a plain moulded doorway. The nave is divided from its aisle by 3 wide pointed arches with octagonal pillars. The west respond is Early English, a short shaft on corbel.

The tower arch springs straight from the wall. In the nave are several fine, richly carved, bench ends and between the nave and chancel a very fine roodloft screen, much mutilated. It is of 5 pieces, each compartment ogeed, with groining under the loft and the usual rich cornice of vine leaves and grapes with the addition of another frieze in which appear oxen ploughing and various monstrous figures, both human and bestial and an inscription. The whole painted and gilt and varying from the usual character of those in Devonshire. The loft is unluckily surmounted by a hideous gallery.

The chancel arch has been cut away and that between the north aisle and north chancel partially so. The chancel has a coved roof. Its east window is of 3 lights of Decorated character as also is one on the north, eastward of the arch. On the south are 2 windows of 2 lights, of doubtful Decorated character. The north chapel has square-headed labeled windows. The roof of the north aisle is ribbed. There are several inscribed monumental slabs of the 16th century, one remarkably bold and large with a cross, A.D. 1529. The font has an octagonal bowl of large size on short massive base. In the tower arch is part of a wood screen. There are 6 bells.

(The tower is of stone and masonry far superior to the body which is much covered with yellow wash.)

Norton St. Philip

50/39–40 [St. Philip] October, 1848

This church was undergoing extensive restoration and the interior laid bare, except the chancel. It consists of a nave, chancel and aisles, south porch and western tower, principally Third-Pointed, but with some Middle-Pointed features. The tower is a remarkably rich one of true Somersetshire kind, but some singularities. It is full of ornamental panelling, has octagonal stair turret at the south-east, buttresses not at the angles and a battlement and 4 crocketed pinnacles.

The belfry windows large, of 3 lights with transom. The stage below the belfry has much blank panelling of 3 light tracery, some small part of which is glazed, and 3 ogee niches, below which are 3 other ogee niches, trefoiled and a 3 light window on each side, that on the east having a pediment and a transom. On the west side is a shallow porch with stone groining, over which is a 3 light window. The tower arch to the nave is remarkable for being double; the east face has one order of shafts, the western has 2 and stone groining between them.

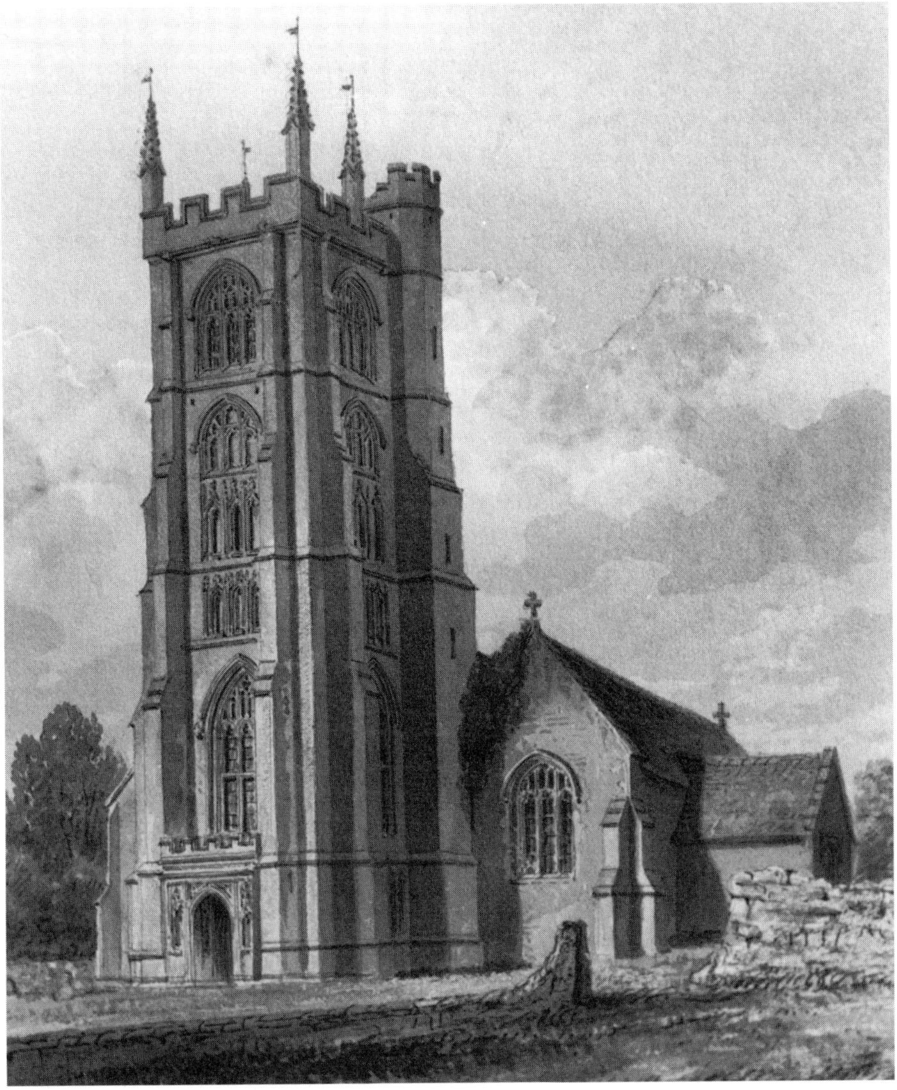

West view of Norton St. Philip Church, 1828, by J.C. Buckler

The walls of the aisles of the nave seem to have been rebuilt, the windows mostly Third-Pointed in style with square heads, but pointed at the extremities. The arcades of the nave are irregular. On each side are 3 arches. On the north the first from the west is of Tudor form with panelled soffit and large wall pier; the second is pointed, upon imposts against the pier; the third is a smaller flat arch entirely panelled. On the south the 2 western arches appears to be Middle-Pointed with clustered piers of 4 large shafts. The eastern has only a slight curve springing from octagonal shafts attached to the piers. But these are of somewhat doubtful date. There is no clerestory.

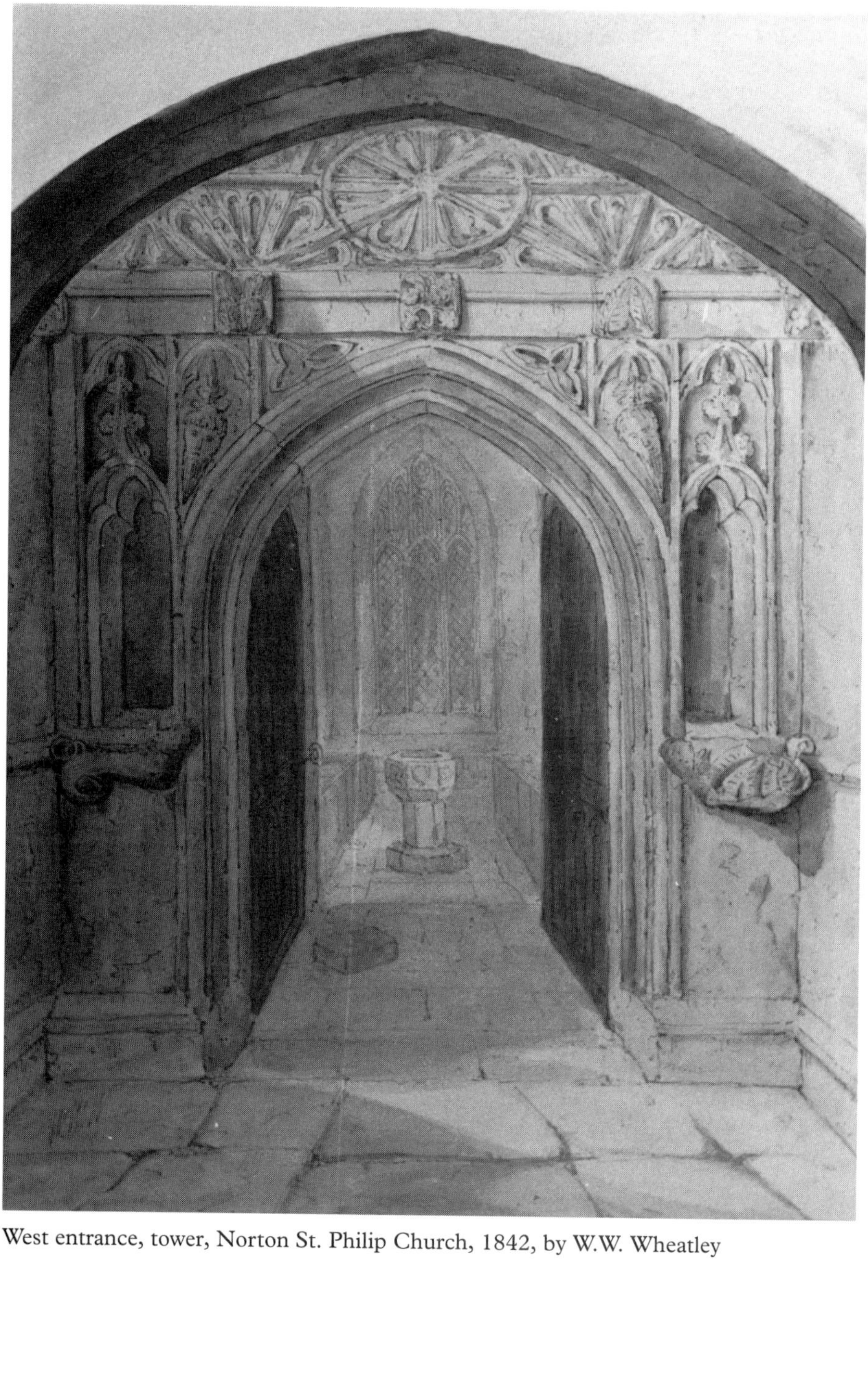

West entrance, tower, Norton St. Philip Church, 1842, by W.W. Wheatley

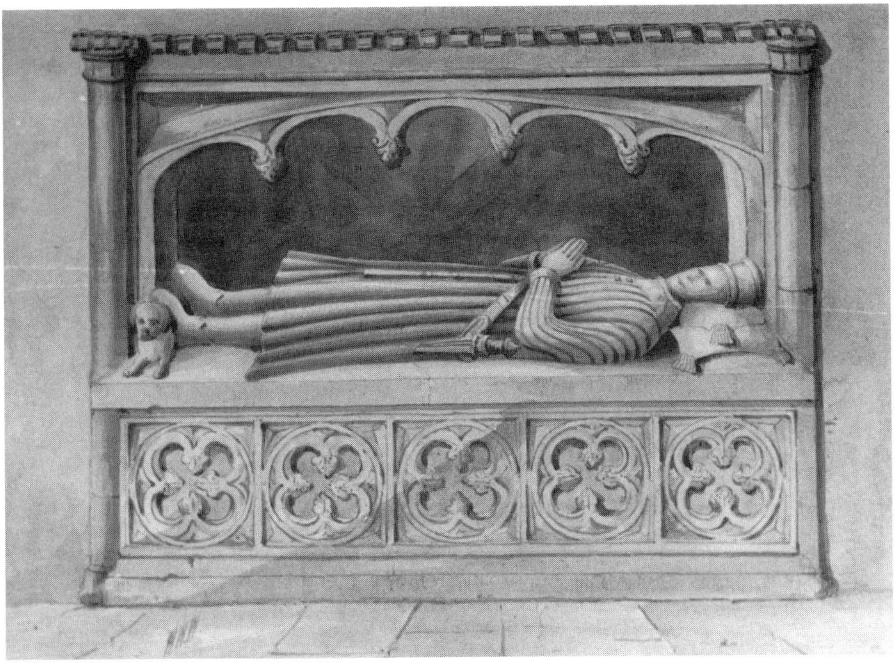

Norton St. Philip Church, 1843, by W.W. Wheatley

The chancel arch is pointed, springing from short shafts which are set upon brackets. The roof of the nave is open, of fair pitch and without tie-beams. In the south pier of the chancel arch is a hagioscope of large size with trefoil feathering; also the roodsteps. The chancel roof is coved and boarded. It has to the south aisle a panelled Third-Pointed arch, rather straight sided with small shafts. A similar one on the north but without shafts. The east window is of 3 lights having on each side a long niche.

The chancel, extending one bay beyond the aisles, has north-east and south-east windows, the rear arches of which have shafts of Middle-Pointed appearance, but the tracery is Third-Pointed. The north aisle has a fine east window of 4 lights, though the arch is too obtuse, but the tracery is late Middle-Pointed, verging towards the next style. There is some tolerable late woodscreen work in the north chancel aisle. In the south aisle at the east end are 2 niches with pedestals upon shafts and an ogee piscina. Under one of the south windows is a late Third-Pointed tomb with flat arch with cornice and flat foliations. The figure seems to represent a merchant with dog at his feet.

The font is ordinary Third-Pointed, an octagonal bowl with quatrefoil panelling and similar stem. The organ is in the north aisle of the chancel. The south porch is large, has a labeled outer doorway with panelled spandrels.

Nunney

50/51–52 St. Peter 31 July, 1849

A cruciform church with west tower engaged and aisles to the nave. The transepts are more in the nature of chapels there being no central steeple. There is a mixture of Middle and Third-Pointed features. The arcades of the nave are inelegant, each of 3 wide pointed arches with continuous chamfers down the piers which have no capitals. These may possibly be Middle-Pointed. The roof has been modernised and the clerestory, if ever there was one, abolished.

The tower arch is continuous and there are arches of a similar kind across the aisles opening to the transepts. The windows of the aisles are Middle-Pointed of 2 lights. The transepts have a good deal of Middle-Pointed work; each has a 3 light window at the end and a later, square-headed one, on the east side. The north transept has 3 large tombs of the Delamares, one Italian, the others Third-Pointed, panelled with shields containing heraldic bearings. On one the effigies of a knight and lady.

The chancel arch is pointed and continuous. In one of its jambs is a kind of stone pedestal which may have been connected either with the pulpit or the screen. In this arch is a wood screen which has been removed from the transept. There are also 2 hagioscopes flanking the chancel arch, that on the south having iron bars; that on the north is square-headed of 3 lights. Both transepts have doors. The chancel has a ribbed roof with cornice of small

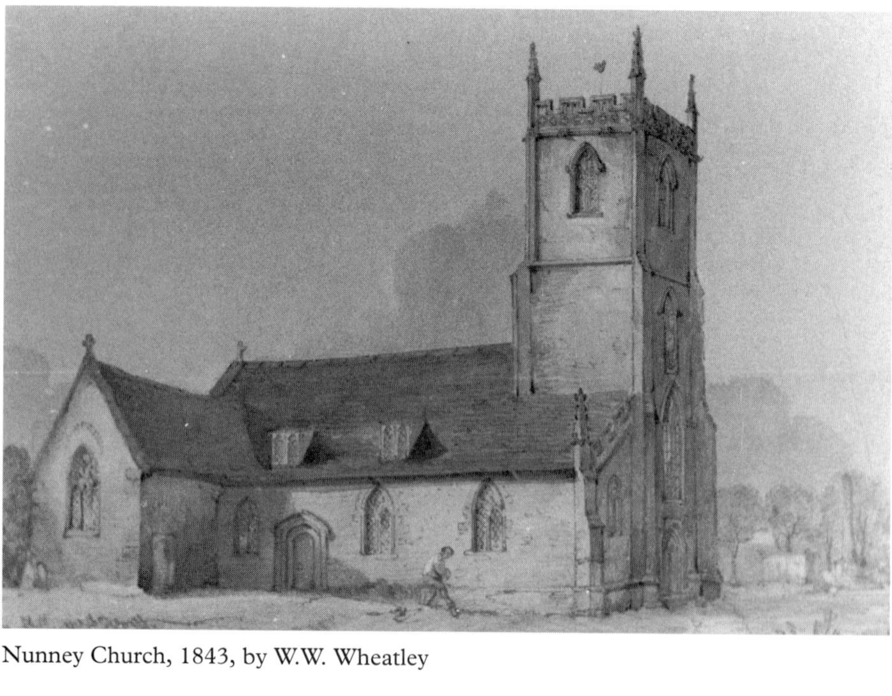

Nunney Church, 1843, by W.W. Wheatley

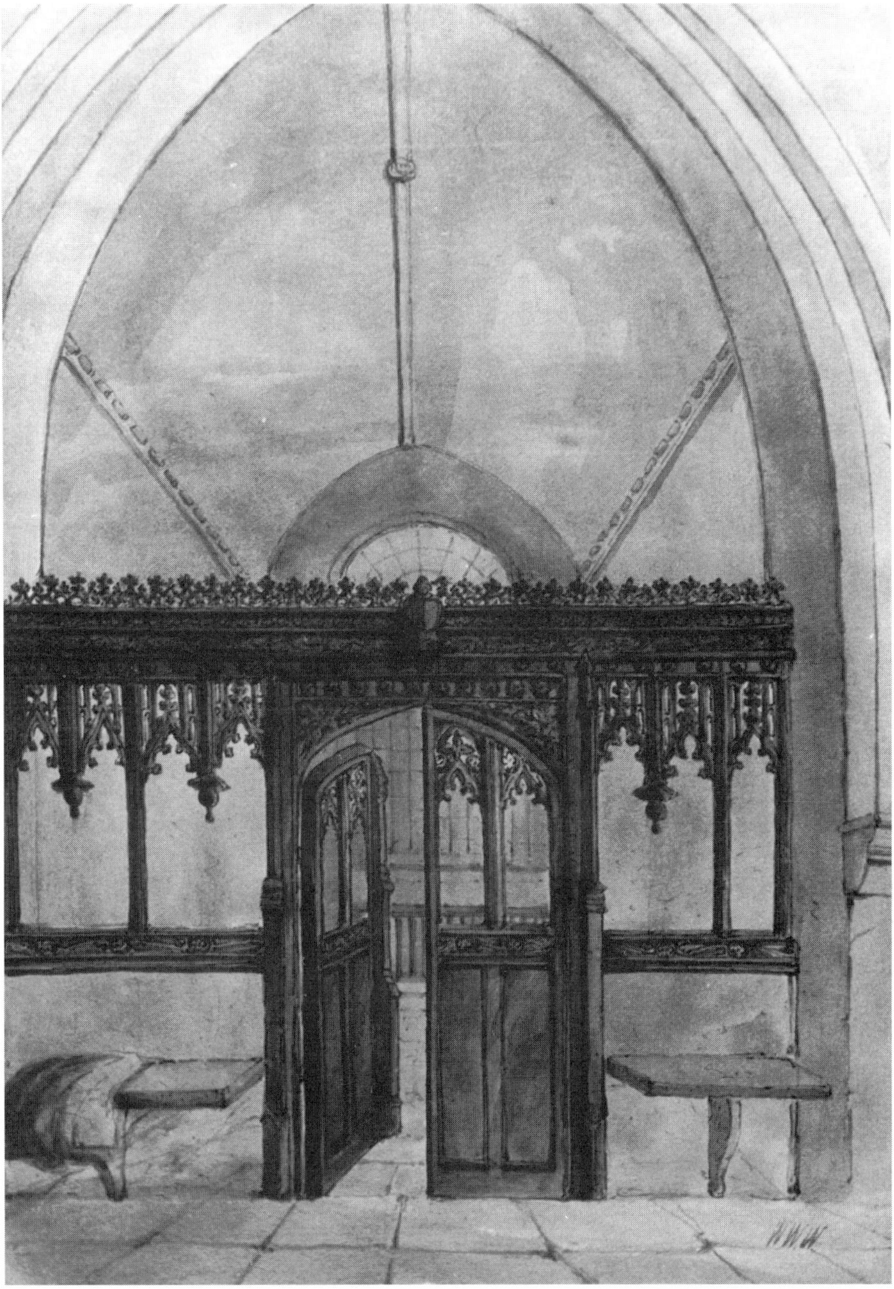

In Nunney Church, 1844, by W.W. Wheatley

battlements. On the north side of the chancel are 2 lancet windows. At the south an incipient Middle-Pointed one of a kind often seen in Somersetshire, the rear arch of which has cinquefoil feathering, the window consisting of 2 trefoil-headed lancets and above them a splendid triangle cinquefoil.

Another southern window nearer the west has a flat rear arch quatrefoiled and no foliations. There is part of a stone reredos. The font has a circular bowl, scalloped, on a square base. The south porch is plain. The tower is a good Third-Pointed one with an open panelled battlement and 4 crocketed pinnacles and an octagonal stair turret on the south. The west door is labeled; the window over it is a bad one. The 2 higher stages have 2 light windows of which those of the belfry have stone lattice work and transoms. Over the west window is a canopied niche with cord enclosing the Key, part of the arms of the Delamares. There is an organ in the west gallery and in the churchyard an ancient cross.

(There is a piscina in the east wall of the transept.)

Nynehead

51/87–88 All Saints January, 1870

This church has a nave with south aisle, chancel, south porch and western tower and a kind of transeptal chapel on the north and an aisle north of the chancel which appears to be modern. The church seems to be principally Perpendicular but with some modern alterations. The nave has a Perpendicular arcade of 4 arches with the common piers of shafts and cavettos. The windows on the south of the nave are Perpendicular of 3 lights; that at its east end of 4 lights.

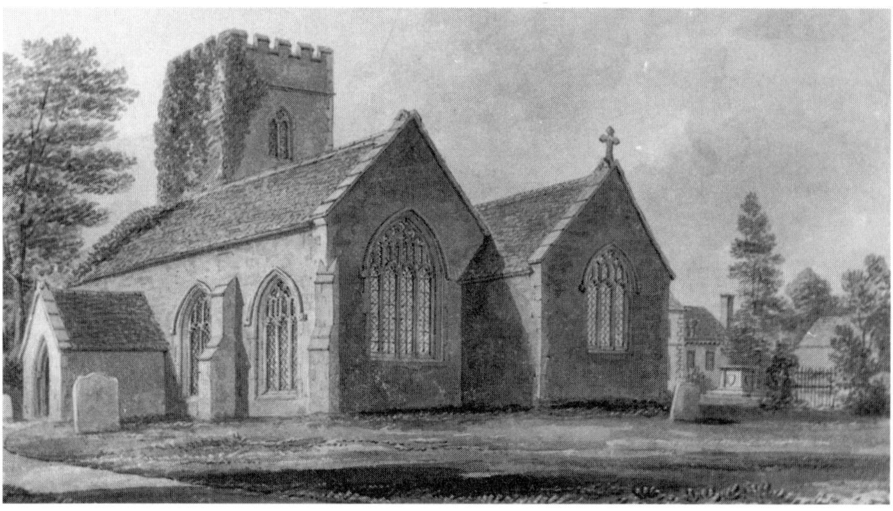

South east view of Nynehead Church, 1841, by J. Buckler

The nave and aisles have waggon roofs with ribs and bosses. The tower arch is a plain one without imposts. The windows north of the nave have 3 lights simply cinquefoiled. The nave is fitted with open seats. The chancel arch is pointed on shafts and there is a good roodscreen across it; also the rood staircase on the north.

The transept has a new rose window and seems to be a private chapel. The chancel has a single light window trefoiled on the north of the sacrarium. The east window Perpendicular, of 4 lights, its hoods having head corbels. There is a narrow pointed arch between the chancel and north chapel. The south-east window is square-headed, of 2 lights and late Perpendicular. There is a vestry at the east of the north chapel. The font has an octagonal bowl panelled. The porch is very large; has a coved roof ribbed; the outer doorway on shafts, the inner continuous.

The tower is rather plain, has battlement and projecting turret on the south part of the way up. The west doorway has continuous arch mouldings; over it a small 3 light Perpendicular window. The belfry windows of 2 lights. Some of the windows have modern coloured glass. In the churchyard is the shaft of a large cross and double octagonal base.

Oake

51/48–49 St. Bartholomew 1 February, 1862

A small church consisting of a nave and chancel with a porch tower and chantry chapel all ranging on the south side and giving the whole an unusual outline. The walls are externally whitewashed. The porch is set at the extreme

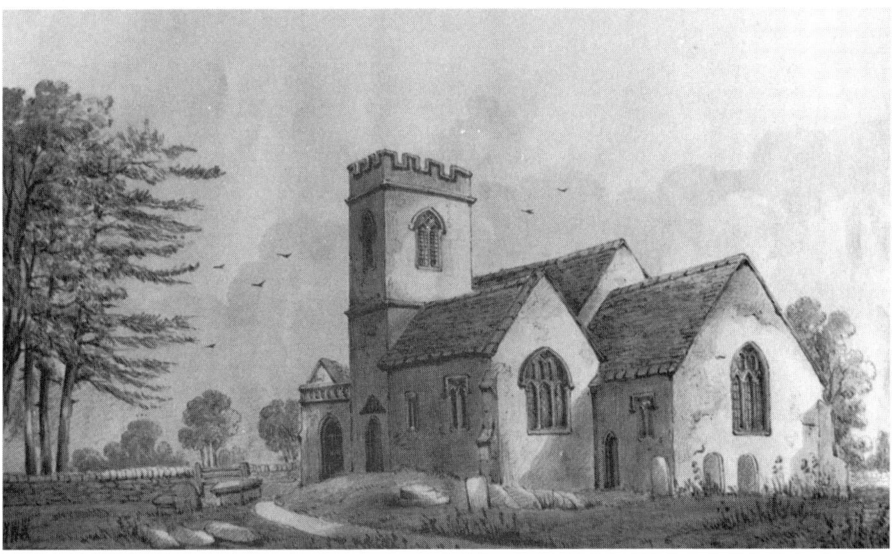

Oake Church, 1848, by W.W. Wheatley

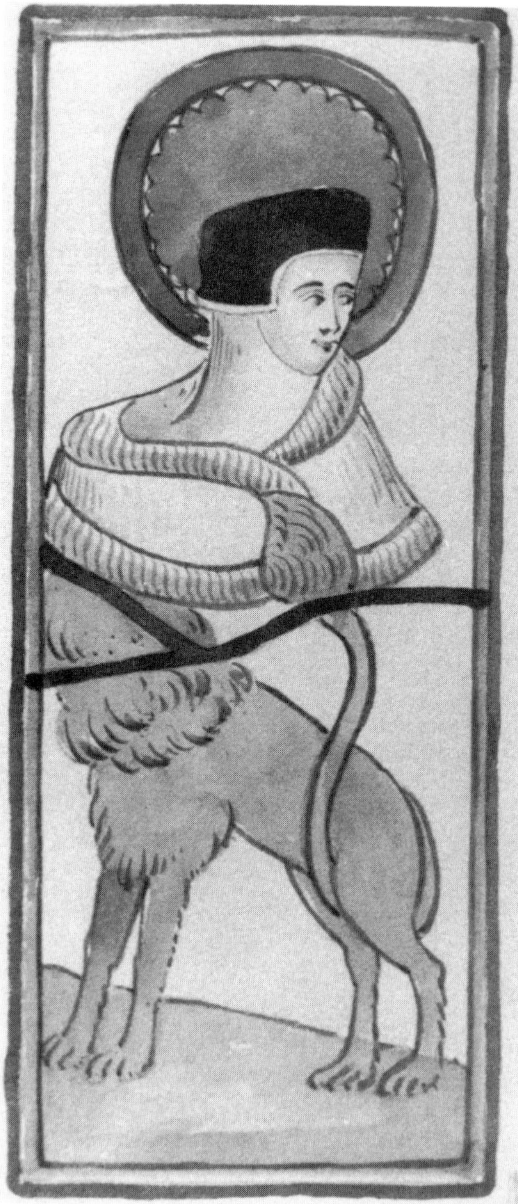

Glass in Oake Church, 1848, by W.W. Wheatley

west on the south side of the nave and has the Somersetshire Perpendicular pierced parapet of quatrefoils containing flowers. The outer doorway is good Perpendicular with small shafts to the arch mouldings. The inner doorway has a plain arch of small curve.

The tower is plain and embattled and without buttresses. The belfry windows Perpendicular, of 2 lights, and a plainish doorway on its south side.

The tower has a pointed arch, now closed, on its east side next to the chantry chapel. The upper storey of the tower seems rather to overhung. The west window of the nave is Perpendicular of 3 lights. On the north side of the nave is a window of remarkable size, at least disproportionate to the small size of the church. It is Perpendicular, of 6 lights subarcuated, and externally has shafts with capitals on which are sculptured heads. The chapel opens to the nave by 2 pointed arches with octagonal pillar having a capital. This chapel has 2 square-headed windows on the south of 2 lights, one of which is Perpendicular, the other looks Decorated. At its east end is also a Perpendicular window of 3 lights.

There is no chancel arch. The chancel is Perpendicular, the east window of 3 lights those north and south square-headed and labeled. The chapel extends a little beyond the beginning of the chancel but does not open into it by any arch. There are some pieces of ancient stained glass. The roofs have modern ceiling. The chantry has a tiled roof. The font has a circular bowl. There are some pews and some new open seats and a barrel organ.

Odcombe

50/54–55 St. Peter and St. Paul 7 August, 1849

The plan a chancel and nave without aisles and a square tower situated between them, a south porch and an Elizabethan vestry added on the south

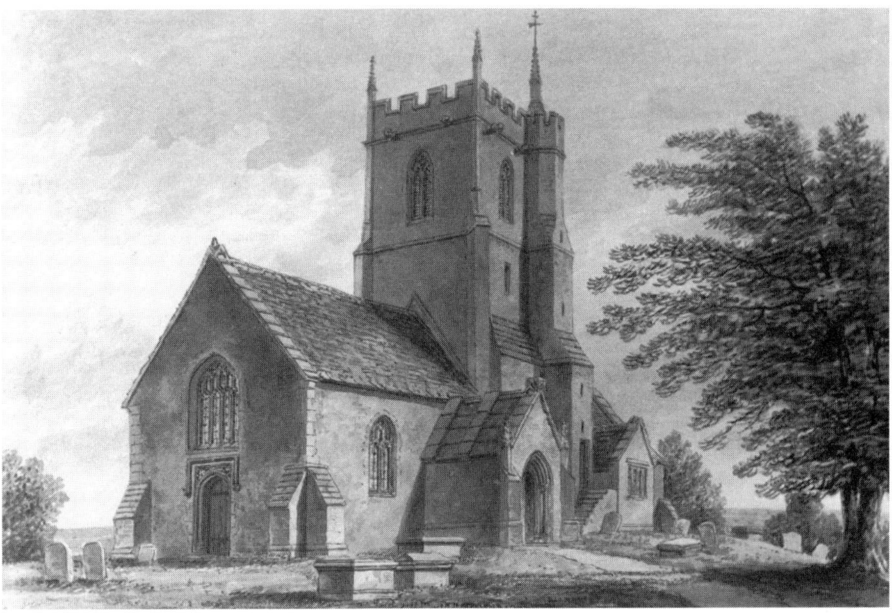

South west view of Odcombe Church, 1836, by J. Buckler

side of the chancel. Most of the actual work is Third-Pointed but the form suggests an earlier origin and indeed there is one trefoil-headed lancet on the north side of the nave. All other windows are Third-Pointed. The west door is closed, has label and foliated spandrels. The window over it is of 4 lights. The south porch is flanked by pinnacles set on the buttresses; its outer door has shafts.

The tower is of good masonry with a battlement and 4 crocketed pinnacles and a stair turret at the south-east angle. The belfry windows of 2 lights have the western stone lattice work. On the north and south are 3 light windows, slightly projecting from the wall and surmounted with flagged roof. The vestry has square-headed windows and a gable. The nave and porch have stone tiles on the roof. The nave roof is coved, having ribs with bosses and a good double cornice with square flower. The open benches are Jacobean exhibiting figures of animals and other carvings.

There is some approach to a cruciform plan by the slight projections north and south of the tower. The east and west arches of the tower are Third-Pointed with small shafts and intermediate mouldings, all nicely cleared from whitewash. There is a Third-Pointed wooden roodscreen set on a stone basement. On the south side of the chancel is a large piscina with polygonal drain having a rose orifice the fenestella trefoiled with knobs at the points and going deeply into the wall and surmounted by an ogee canopy at the apex of which is a finial in the form of a small cross.

There is a course of quatrefoil panelling on the north side of the chancel beneath the windows. (Underneath the east window is a slab with cross flory externally.) The font has a square bowl with a plain First-Pointed arcade set on a square stem which exhibits Third-Pointed panelling.

Orchard Portman

50/76–77 St. Michael 11 May, 1855

A small Perpendicular church in good order consisting only of nave and chancel with a west tower and south porch. Within the porch is a new doorway in Norman style with rich chevron and other mouldings which may be possibly the reproduction of a former old one. The windows on the south side are mostly square-headed and fair Perpendicular. The east window pointed of 3 lights. On the north they are also square-headed but later and without foliations, but have labels. The chancel arch is pointed, springing straight from the wall.

There is an eagle lectern and the seats all open. The tower arch is continuous. The tower of 3 stages, divided by strings, embattled and with an octagonal turret at the north-east rising above the parapet, but square in its lower part and having pinnacles at its angles. The belfry windows of 2 lights and a similar one on the south below the belfry. The west window of 3 lights and a small, continuous door beneath it.

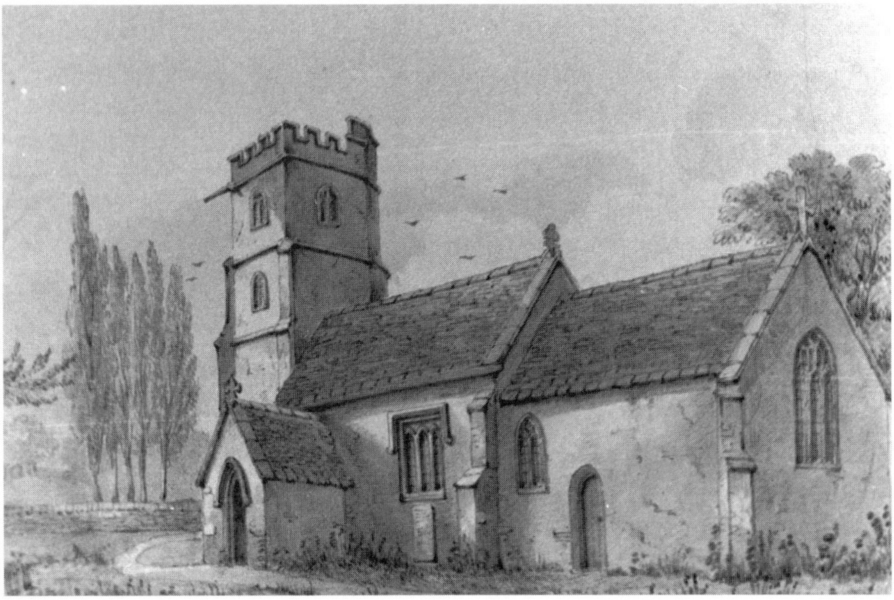

Orchard Portman Church, 1848, by W.W. Wheatley

Pawlett

50/60–61 St. John 27 February, 1852

A small church of cruciform plan, without aisles, with a west tower. The whole of the exterior is roughcast and of such a glaring white as to be almost spectral. The church is coarse and uninteresting. In the transepts are some indications of First-Pointed work; in the south transept a triple lancet window; in the north transept one with trefoiled head which may be later. On the east side of the north transept is a square-headed slit, in the south a single Third-Pointed window, trefoiled with square-head.

The arches opening from the nave to the transepts are pointed and very coarse. That on the north is irregular in form and both spring straight from the wall. The roofs are coved with the usual ribs and bosses. The chancel arch is depressed and late Third-Pointed, springing from shafts. Within it is the roodscreen having fair wood tracery and a cornice with band of foliage and grapes and surmounted by Tudor flowers. It retains some traces of colour. The chancel windows of 3 lights, that at the east without tracery seems a spurious First-Pointed one, that on the south has lost the tracery of the head.

The chancel is wainscoted; the whole church pewed, though neat. The windows of the nave are ordinary Third-Pointed, some with good square heads and set high in the wall. The font has a cylindrical bowl, a stem of like form. The tower arch rises straight from the wall. The tower Third-Pointed, has a battlement and some buttresses and is divided by one string course just under

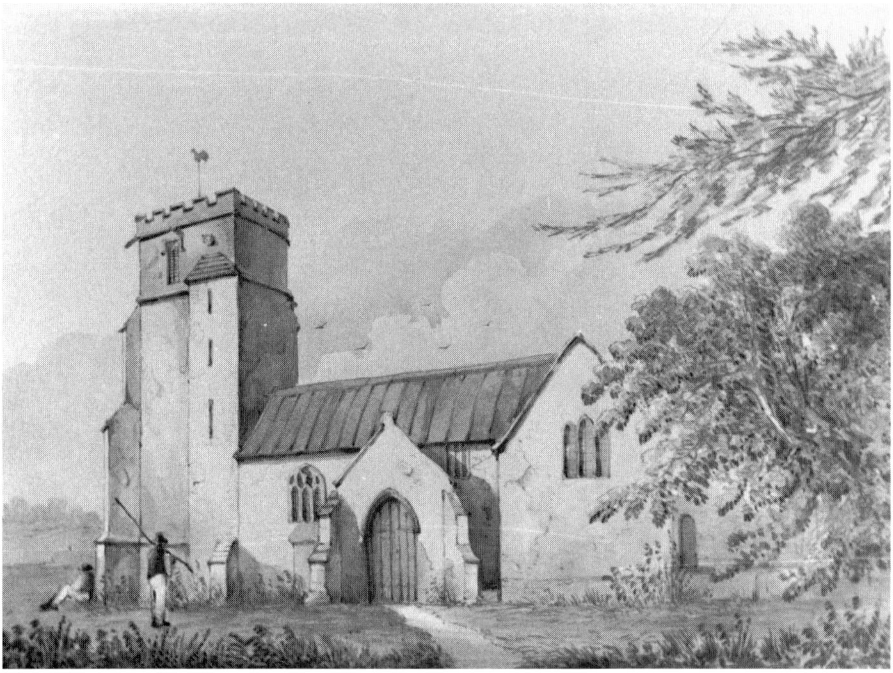

Pawlett Church, 1843, by W.W. Wheatley

the belfry windows. The latter are of 2 lights and labelled. There is a square turret at the north-east and a west window of 3 lights and a late, flat-arched doorway. The porch on the south is large. The nave and chancel have steep, leaded roofs; those of the transepts modern and slated. On the north of the chancel is an original vestry with one slit window and one square-headed with label. The churchyard very neat and nicely kept. There are 5 bells.

Pennard, East

49/25–26 [All Saints] 1835

This church wholly Rectilinear and consists of a nave with side aisles, a chancel and a square tower at the west end which has a plain parapet and is low and devoid of ornament, except a stone worked into the form of a rose on the north side. The parapets of the body are plain, the chancel is tiled and the gables are crowned with crosses. There is a plain south porch and no buttresses.

The interior of the nave is light and lofty. The nave has on each side 4 pointed arches with lozenge piers having shafts at the points. The arch to the tower is not in the centre. The clerestory windows are square-headed; those in the aisles are fair ones of 3 lights. The roof of the nave is open, the tie-beams sculptured and above them open tracery filling the space. This sort of roof has

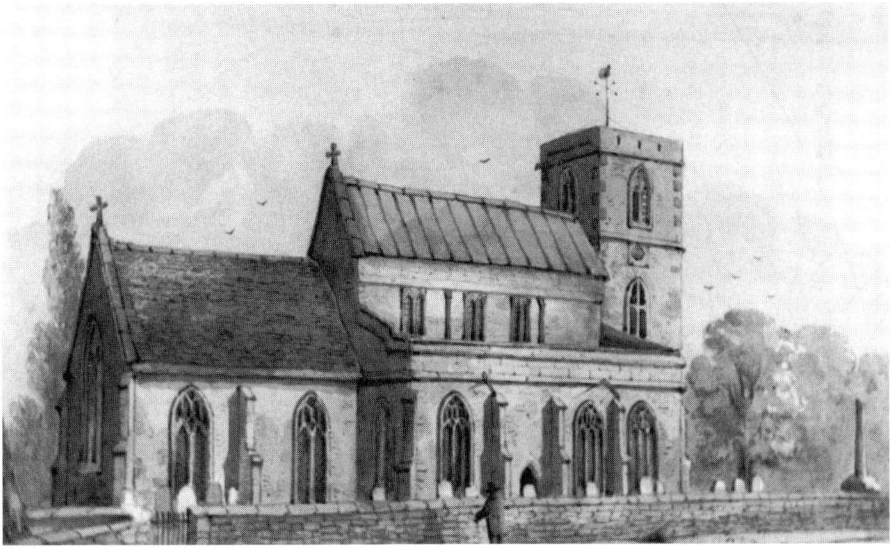

East Pennard, 1845, by W.W. Wheatley

always a good effect. The chancel arches filled with barbarous paintings on wood representing Adam and Eve, Abraham and Isaac.

The chancel has very good Rectilinear windows, the east of 4 lights with some ancient stained glass, the others of 2 lights. The font is Early English, the basin square, moulded with trefoil arches with heads of Bishops mixed with foliage under it; the pedestal circular on a square base. This church is a good specimen of a very simple, unadorned Rectilinear church, and of fair dimensions, contrasting with some of its richer neighbours. There are fine ilexes and other evergreens bordering on the churchyard and the village is pleasing and picturesque.

Pennard, West

19/71–73 [St. Nicholas] Before 1840

West Pennard church is pleasantly seated on the side of a finely wooded hill 3 miles from Glastonbury and near the road from thence to Shepton Mallet. It is a large and very handsome structure wholly of Rectilinear character and consisting of a nave with side aisles, a chancel, and tower at the west end. The body is covered with lead. The stone is in tolerable preservation. The tower is of very elegant workmanship and is crowned by a beautiful panelled battlement and 4 crocketed pinnacles. Midway between each pinnacle is a very rich niche with lofty crocketed canopy rising much above the battlement and giving a fine effect. There is also a small, low, shingled spire. On the west side

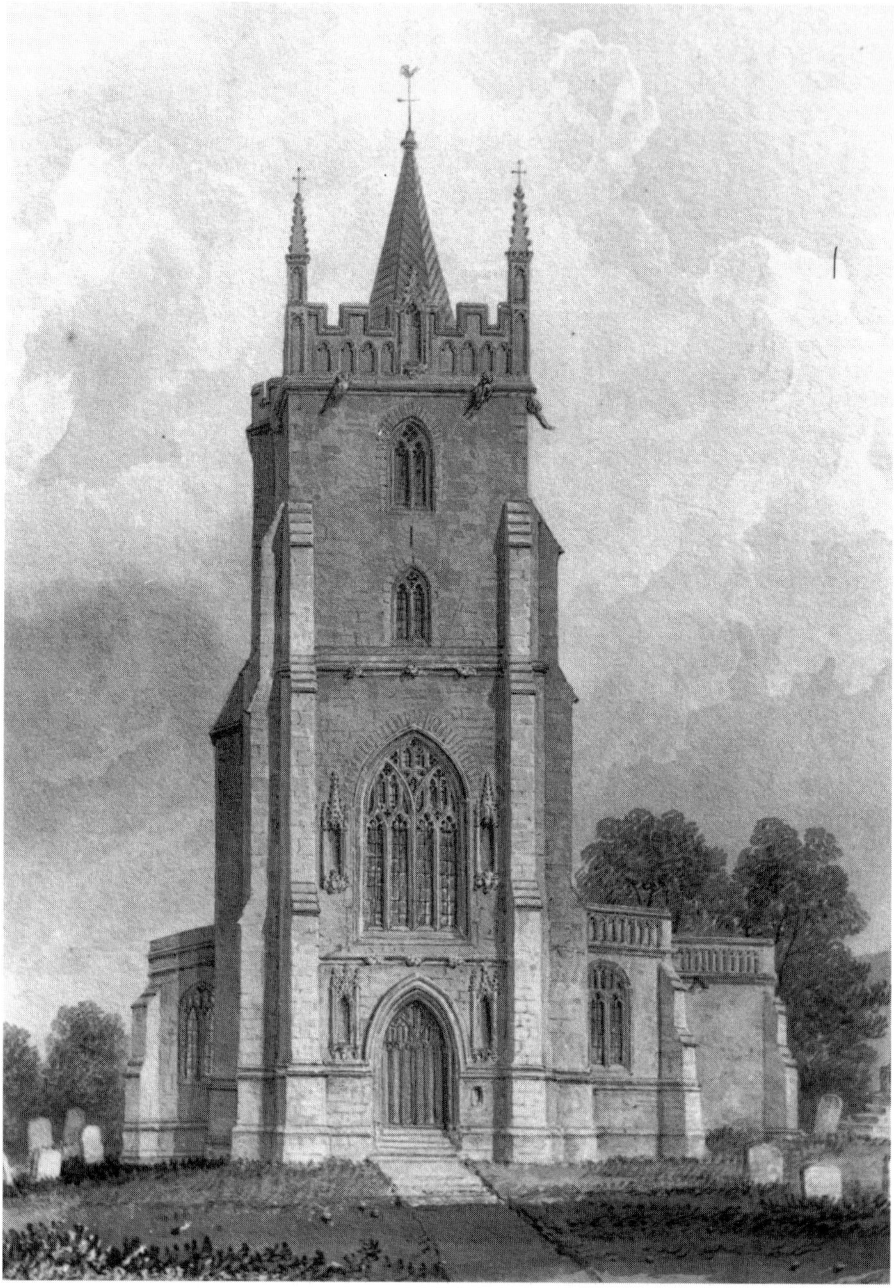

West view of West Pennard Church, 1833, by J. Buckler

of the tower is a good plain doorway with dripstone returned between 2 niches with elegant crocketed canopies. Over this door runs a fine band filled with figures of angels with shields above which is a good Rectilinear window of 4 lights between 2 very fine niches with crocket canopies much more elaborate than those of the lower niches and bases ornamented with figures of angels. This window has no dripstone. Of the west door the woodwork has Rectilinear tracery. The tower has within a stone groined ceiling.

The clerestory and the chancel are enriched with a beautiful parapet of pierced quatrefoils and crocketed pinnacles rising from between the windows. The south aisle and porch have a panelled parapet not pierced and that of ye north aisle is plain. The south porch is good but plain and has a niche over the doorway. There is an octagonal turret between the south aisle and the chancel. On [the] south side of the chancel is a small Tudor arch door with label and spandrels enriched with foliation. There is a similar door on the north side of the nave rising above the sill of a window.

There are several fine large heads, etc. for water spouts. The windows have some good tracery, several of them are without dripstones. The interior is light and handsome. The nave is divided from the side aisles by arches of Tudor form springing from lozenge piers with shafts set at the angles. The clerestory windows have also contracted arches and are each of 3 lights. The side aisles have handsome wood roofs divided into panels. That of the north aisle is much the most perfect and most ornamented, having large flowers for bosses and much enriched with small square flowers, etc.

Between the nave and the chancel is a handsome wooden screen with elegant open tracery and a cornice of vine leaves with grapes. The chancel has a good wooden ceiling, resembling that of the north aisle. There is a large aperture in the wall from the chancel to the south aisle of the nave. The east window has a contracted arch and is of 5 lights; the side windows of the chancel have 3 lights and good tracery.

Many of the windows in this church contain fragments of painted glass. The font is of octagonal form, upon an octagonal shaft which seems to have been surrounded by 4 detached small shafts placed at equal distances, the capitals and bases of which remain and are of circular form. There are 5 bells.

Petherton, North

49/16–18 [St. Mary] Before 1840

This is a beautiful church of Rectilinear character, particularly remarkable for its magnificent tower standing at the west end and which is among the finest in the county. It somewhat resembles that of Glastonbury and Huish and is 3 stages in height. The summit has a rich battlement pierced with quatrefoils and 8 crocketed pinnacles, the angular ones being the largest, all having smaller ones attached to them.

The belfry windows are double on each side, of 3 lights with transoms and entirely enriched with exquisite sone lattice work. The second stage has on each side a single window of similar character with lattice work. The lowest has a 4 light window on the west side and below it a doorway with label and

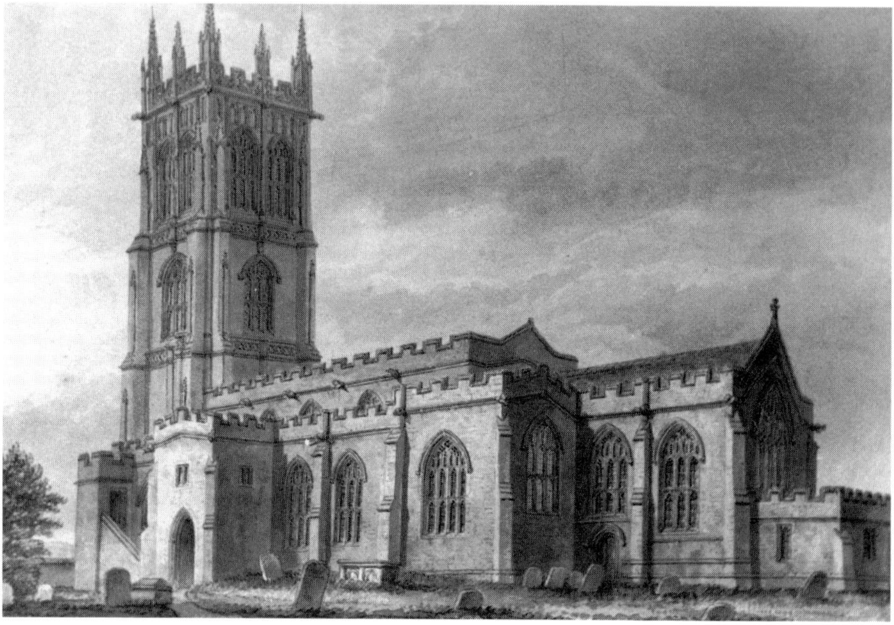

South east view of North Petherton Church, 1832, by J. Buckler

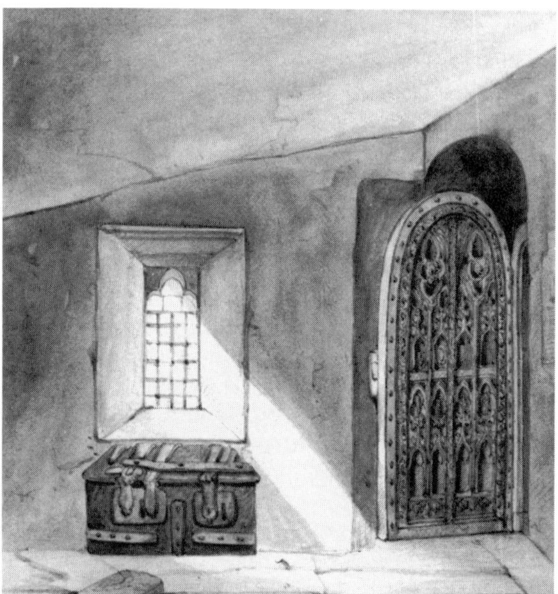

The confessional and vestry in North Petherton Church, at the end of the chancel, 1850, by W.W. Wheatley

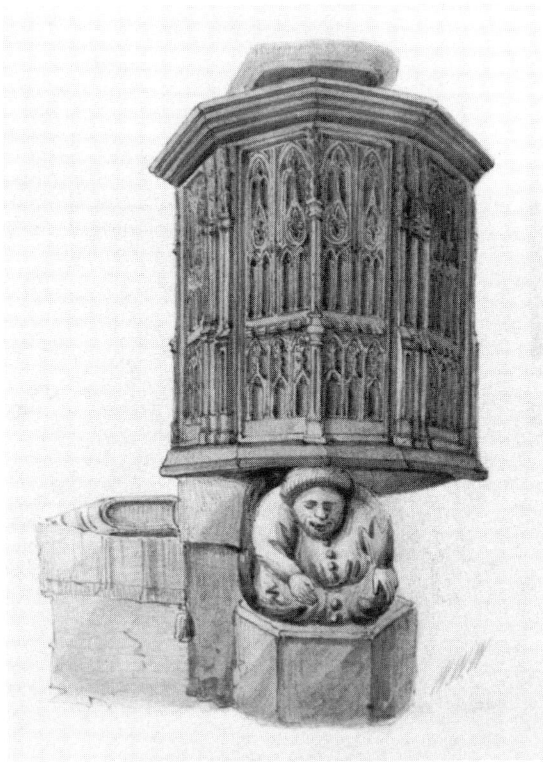

North Petherton Church: oak pulpit, by W.W. Wheatley

panelled spandrels above which is a fine band of quatrefoils and on each side of it a fine canopied niche containing a statue. Between each stage is a rich panelled band and the buttresses at each stage are enriched with crocketed pinnacles.

The church consists of a nave with side aisles and clerestory, north and south transepts and a chancel. The whole has an embattled parapet except the east end of the chancel, the gable of which is crowned by a stone cross. There are large north and south porches, the latter of which has a doorway with shafts and panelled soffit. At the angle of the west end of each aisle is an octagonal turret with a staircase.

The nave is divided from each aisle by 5 pointed arches with light lozenge piers having shafts at the angles with foliated capitals. The clerestory windows are of 3 lights with contracted arches. The windows of the aisles are of 3 lights with transoms. The transepts are rather higher than the aisles and open to the nave and aisles by arches of contracted form. In the transepts are windows of 4 lights.

Part of the ceiling of the aisles has wood panelling, the brackets of the beams resting on stone figures bearing shields. The pulpit has some good wood carving and the upper part of the south porch is occupied by a gallery pew with open arches, twisted columns, arabesque ornament and a figure of Time. The west gallery is also finely carved and supported by pillars enriched with vine leaves, etc. In it is a large organ.

The chancel is very light and handsome; the east window a fine large one of 5 lights. The roof is a very handsome timber one open to the interior divided into panelled compartments by ribs and the whole of the spaces between the beams and the roof itself filled with the richest pierced tracery varying in pattern and having a singularly rich effect. The brackets of the beams rise from stone shafts set between the windows. At the east end of the chancel, below the sill of the east window, is a vestry having a battlement and square-headed windows and opening to the chancel by a doorway enriched with fine wood carving.

The font is an octagon panelled with square flowers. Within the wall of the tower arch is a curious grotesque stone figure in a niche. In the churchyard is the shaft of a cross, of octagonal form, enriched with Rectilinear panelling.

Petherton, South

52/13–16 St. Peter & St. Paul 19 February, 1872

A fine church cruciform in plan with central tower. The nave has aisles but not the chancel. The nave Perpendicular, the north transept and chancel chiefly Decorated. There are also north and south porches. The church has been recently very fairly restored and is in good condition.

The windows of the aisles are of 3 lights and very uniform tracery; that at the west end is of 5 lights with transom. (There are Early English doorways

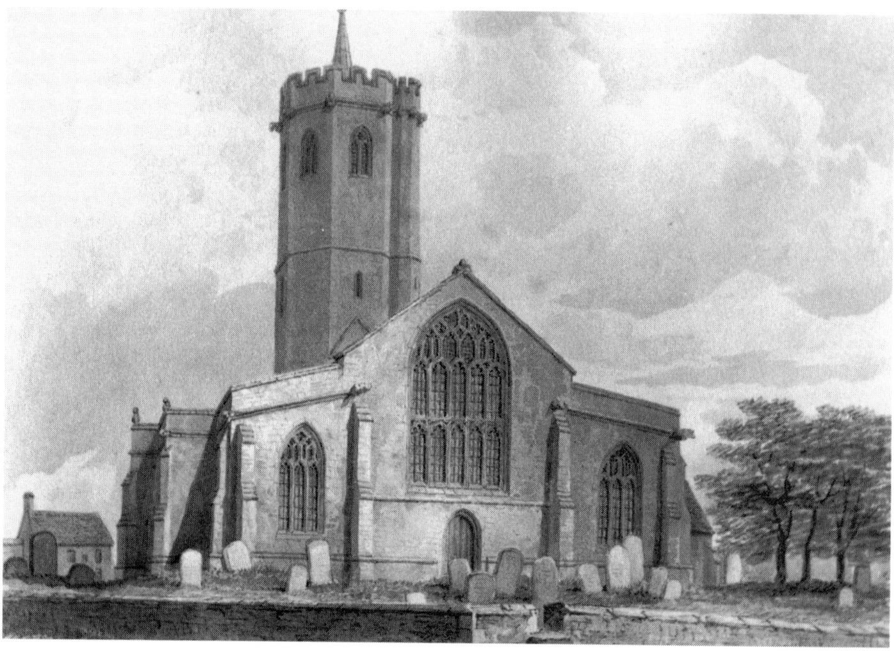

West view of South Petherton Church, 1832, by J.C. Buckler

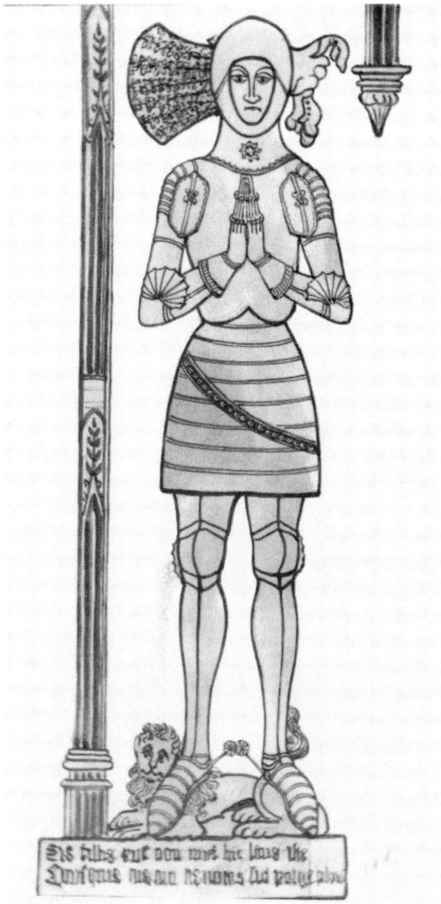

In South Petherton Church, 1850,
by W.W. Wheatley

north and south. Of this character is the lower part of the tower, though the north and south arches supporting it within have been recast in later style. Those, however, on the east and west are original Early English. There is a western doorway, now closed. There is Early English work in the lower part of the tower and doorway of the nave; Transitional to Decorated in the chancel, Decorated in the north transept; the rest is Perpendicular.)

There is an Early English doorway within the north porch having shafts with capitals and bases. Over this door is a niche with trefoiled canopy. The porch is of two storeys, having a parvise and a groined roof with ribs and boss. There are square-headed windows lighting the parvise and the outer doorway has label and panelled spandrels with shafts in the jambs.

The south porch is originally Early English of which character is its outer doorway having a steep roof rising high and covered with flags but no parvise. The nave has the roof covered with lead and the timbers within have been entirely renovated. It has tie-beams and bosses. The aisle roofs are plain and quite low pitched. The north transept is embattled; the rest of the church has

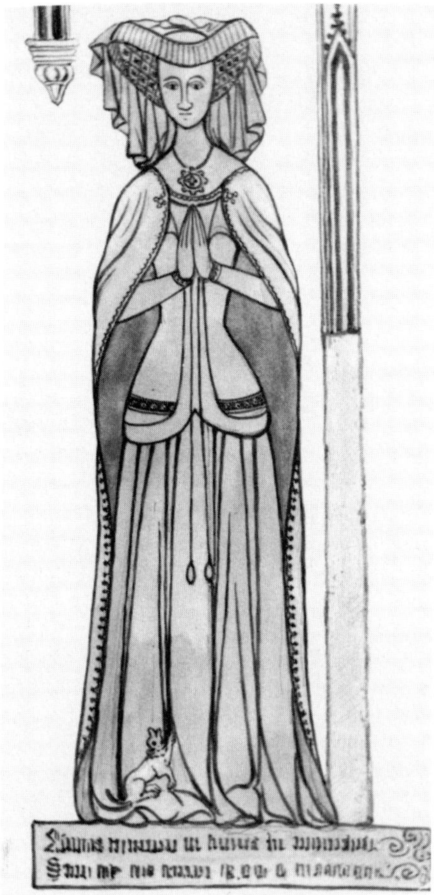

In South Petherton Church, 1850, by W.W. Wheatley

plain parapets. There is no clerestory. The arcades of the nave are of 4 bays and of a common Perpendicular type resembling those at Merriott having stilted bases. The seats are all open.

The tower rises on 4 arches and has stone groining – 8 ribs diverging from a central opening. The north and south arches have been altered into a late form and stilted. The east and west arches are the original Early English, of 3 orders with shafts having round moulded capitals and trefoil chamfering in the intermediate spaces. There is a staircase within at the south-east of the tower. The north transept is Decorated; has a good 5 light reticulated window at the end with hood on corbels. On the east side a square-headed one, also of 5 lights and Decorated, and on this side is a piscina with ogee niche with foliation, finial and pinnacles; also a very large squint opening into the chancel.

There is a Perpendicular opening from this transept into the aisle. The south transept has a Perpendicular 4-light window at the end; at the east one of 3 lights, near which is a piscina with plain arch and stone shelf; also a stone bracket. There also is a fine Perpendicular altar tomb, the sides panelled with quatrefoils and small niches at the ends. It has a marble slab with figures in brass of a knight and lady under an ogee crocketed canopy flanked by pinnacles and somewhat mutilated; of 15th century. The organ is placed under the south arch of the tower. The south transept roof has been renovated.

The chancel has a Perpendicular east window of 4 lights, but some of the lateral windows are earlier and it is evident that the eastern has been altered to its present form as its arch internally is of early Decorated or Transitional date, upon shafts with capitals of foliage. The north-west and south-west windows are Perpendicular, of 3 lights, but those at the north-east and south-east are Transitional from Early English to Decorated, have 2 lights with foliated circle in the heads. They have good rear arches with excellent mouldings on shafts having vained capitals – chiefly of Early English foliage – but one has 3 heads and the bases of the shafts are set on a string.

In the south wall is a piscina rather more decidedly Early English having good foliation and canopy of triangular form with finial and flanking pinnacles rising on shafts with circular capitals and bases. The drain is octagonal with 4-foiled orifice. In the north wall is an oblong aumbrye labeled.

The chancel roof is plain and flat. It contains several ancient seats one of which has pierced panelling with wavy lines and foliation. There are corbels above the windows internally. There is on the south a plain priest's door with moulding in the arch. The tower is lofty and of octagonal form; has 2 storeys above the roof of the nave which have lancet single windows, evidently Early English; one string course of division. The upper part later and Perpendicular; has embattled parapet and 2 light belfry windows exhibiting the pierced stone lattice work of Somersetshire. The tower is lofty and the masonry of the upper part quite different from the lower. There is an octagonal stair turret lighted by slits at the south-west of the tower.

The font has a panelled octagonal bowl and seems new.

Pilton

19/73–75 [St. John the Baptist] Before 1840

Pilton is a village 3 miles from Shepton Mallet on the road to Glastonbury. It is pleasantly seated in a valley and has a most beautiful and spacious church built of excellent stone and in fine preservation. It consists of a large nave with north aisle, a chancel, and a tower at the west end. The exterior is entirely of Rectilinear work.

The tower is not so lofty as that of Pennard but is handsome and has a good, but plain, battlement with 4 very elegant crocketed pinnacles at the angles. On the north side is a large octagonal turret which is crowned by a fifth pinnacle much larger than the others and with small crockets. On the west side is a Tudor doorway with label supported by corbels and foliated spandrels. The whole of the exterior has particularly fine ornaments.

The nave has a clerestory which is much hidden on the north side from the great elevation of the north aisle. The battlement on ye south side of ye nave is plain, but bold, and there are crocketed pinnacles set on buttresses between

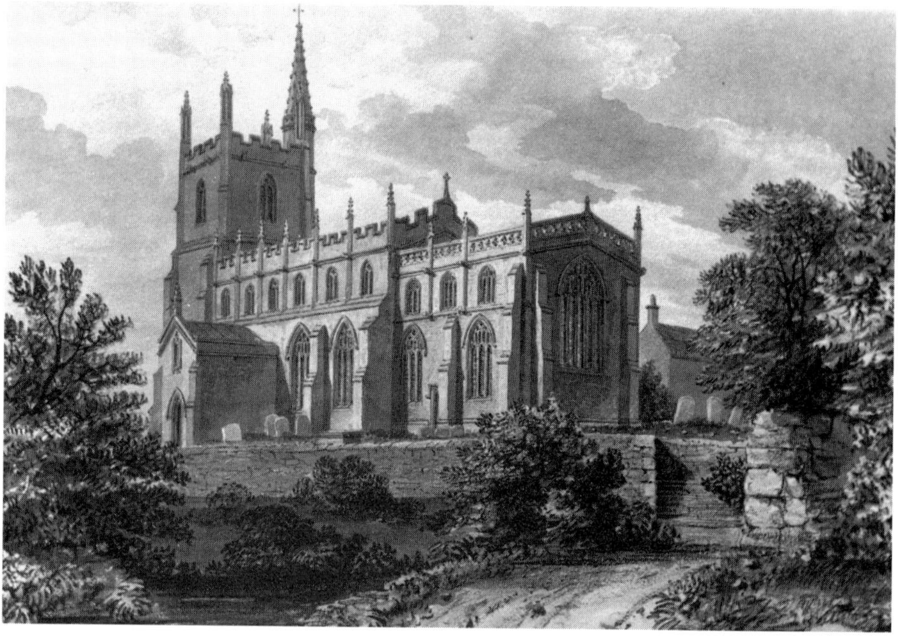

South east view of Pilton Church, 1827, by J. Buckler

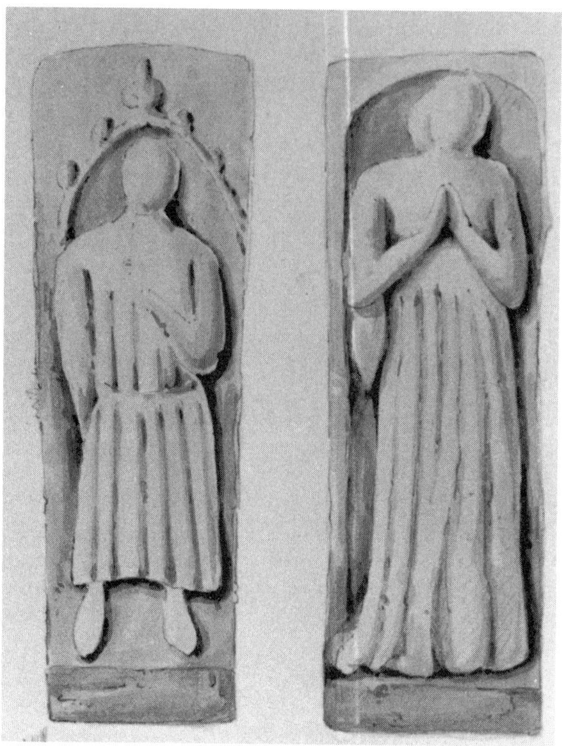

Pilton Church Yard, 1846,
by W.W. Wheatley

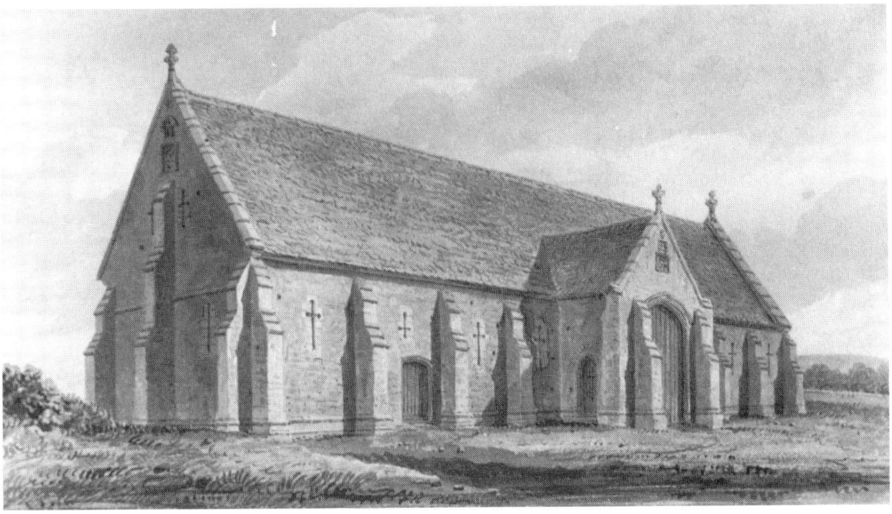

Abbot's barn, Pilton, 1827, by J.C. Buckler

the clerestory windows. The windows have all good Rectilinear tracery. The south porch resembles that of Pennard. The north aisle has a panelled parapet with pinnacles and a string with bold large heads of animals for spouts. The windows have dripstones supported on heads.

The chancel is particularly elegant. It is without aisles, has a fine parapet of pierced quatrefoils with pinnacles in which, over the eastern gable, is fixed a stone charged with a scroll and black letter inscription. The east window is a beautiful Rectilinear one of 5 lights. On each side of the chancel is a double tier of windows, the effect of which is particularly elegant; the upper ones are of smaller size but all have good tracery. On the south side of the chancel is a Tudor door like that of ye tower.

The nave is divided from the north aisle by lofty pointed arches of acute form springing from octagonal piers having capitals of Norman character. The roof of the nave and aisle has been very handsome. It is of wood with pierced tracery above the beams and has been gilt and painted. The eastern end of the north aisle is enclosed by some very fine wood screen work and forms a small chapel. Under its north wall and hidden by a pew is a flat stone sculptured with a cross of singular form with the head of a person in bas relief represented within a portion of the cross. Over it is an arched canopy, the architecture of which is filled with ballflower peculiar to the Curvilinear style. This is said to be the founder. There is also another stone charged with a cross.

Many of the windows in all parts of the church display large and brilliant portions of ancient stained glass. There is ye same aperture in the wall to the chancel as at West Pennard. The arch to the chancel is partly walled up but has a panelled soffit. Part of the roodloft screen remains which has been very rich.

The chancel is particularly elegant from its lightness. The ceiling is of wood and resembles that of West Pennard. Under a window on the south side of the altar is a stone cornice enriched with quatrefoils. There is also a handsome niche in a square frame with spandrels filled with foliage. The altar cloth is of blue silk and very handsome, worked with figures of the Virgin Mary and other Romanish devices. It is of great antiquity and has a black letter inscription worked upon it which shows it to have been the gift of one Richard Pomeroy.

The font is octagonal but does not appear to be genuine. In the churchyard are two fine old sepulchral effigies which are going fast to decay from their exposure to the elements. They are so far gone that it is difficult to say what they are, but they seem to be figures of men and one has over the head an elegant crocketed canopy. In ye vestry are some old Latin black letter Bibles.

There was formerly an Abbey at Pilton. Some of the buildings form now part of a mansion west of the church and there is a great extent of ancient walling now mantled with ivy. At a distance to the south of the church stands the Abbey Barn quite perfect. It is an enormous size and has about the middle a kind of porch on each side (like the transept of a church) making the whole barn of the form of a cross. It has bold buttresses and over the principal door is a piece of sculpture within a quatrefoil representing a winged lamb. This barn is very curious and deserves examination.

Pitcombe

52/26–27 St. Leonard 28 July, 1873

This church has been nearly rebuilt and put into a very good condition. Very little of it, except the tower, is in an original state. It consists of a nave and chancel each with north aisle, a western tower and south porch. The tower is

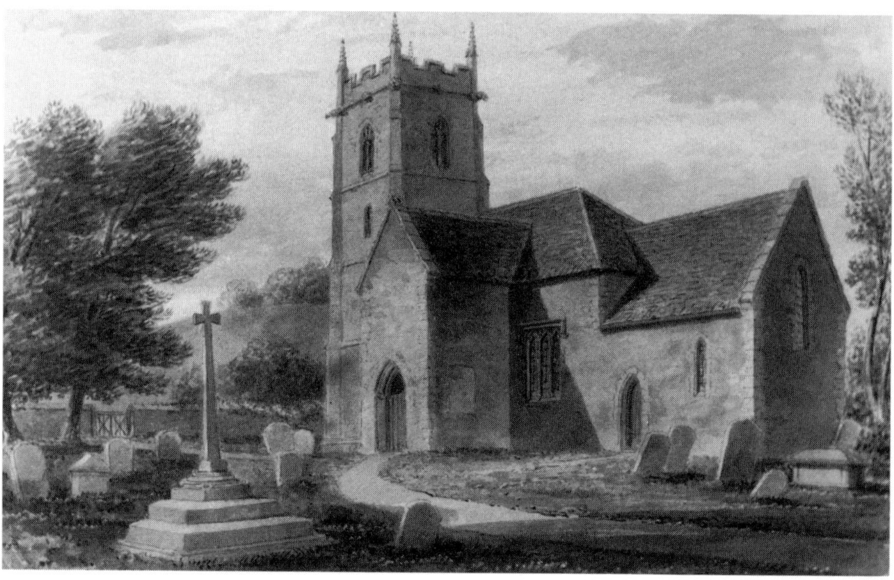

South east view of Pitcombe Church, 1842, by J. Buckler

Perpendicular, low and plain, has embattled parapet and 4 crocketed pinnacles and corner buttresses. The west door has moulded arch; over it is a 3 light window. There are 3 string courses. The belfry windows of 2 lights. In another stage is a single oblong window cinquefoiled. On the north is an octagonal stair turret.

The tower arch to the nave is panelled. The roof of the nave is new and open. There is an arcade in the nave of 3 pointed arches with piers, clustered, of 4 shafts. Between the chancel and aisle is a pointed arch on circular shafts. The windows on the south are of 3 lights trefoiled, of apparently Perpendicular character. The other windows are varied, some lancets, trefoil-headed, some of 2 lights. In the chancel is a piscina with angle shaft. There are several ancient benches with carved ends having good tracery. The font has a circular bowl on square stem chamfered. In the churchyard is a cross on high steps with figures at the angles.

Pitminster

50/73–74 | St. Andrew and St. Mary | 11 May, 1855

A large church in a rural and beautiful locality. The plan, chancel and nave, each with aisles, north and south porches and a tower square below and octagonal above, surmounted by a spire, engaged in the west end of the nave.

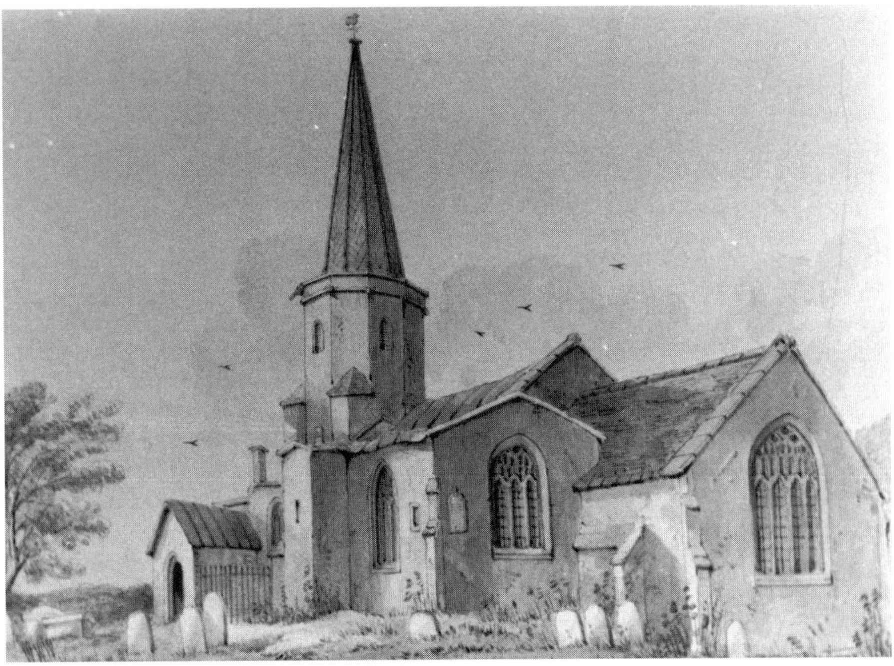

Pitminster Church, 1848, by W.W. Wheatley

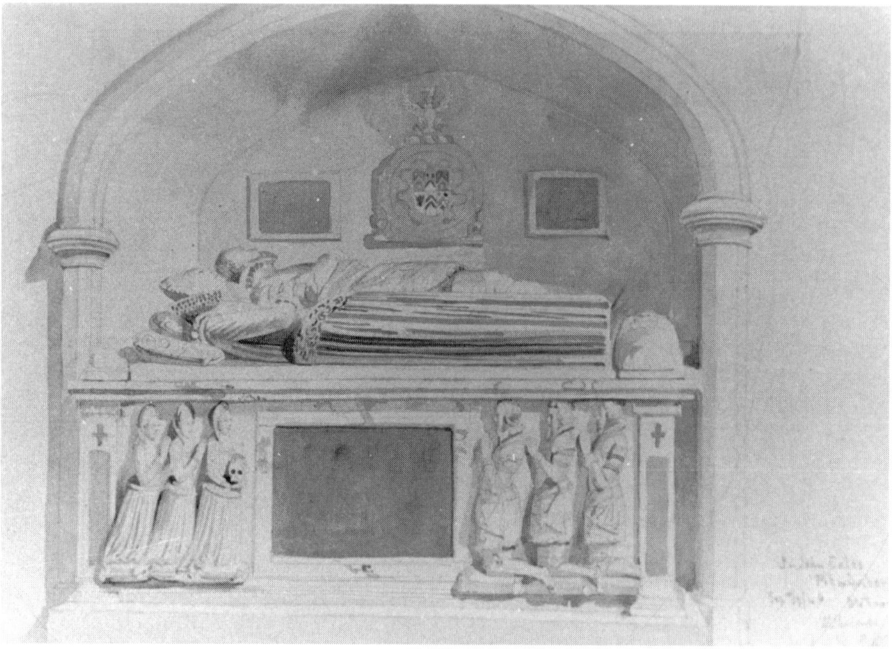

Sir John Coles, Pitminster, 1846, by S.G. Tovey

The church is now chiefly Perpendicular but vestiges of earlier work are to be seen in the western portion and the arrangement is rather irregular from the original arrangement having been changed. The present north aisle is altogether an addition and the original south aisle was very narrow as may be seen by the present western part of it, but it has been altered and much extended, both in height and width, eastward of the porch.

The steeple is plain, perhaps early Decorated, emerging from Early English, opening from the nave by a plain, pointed arch without imposts. The north, south side walls of the tower are not perforated and at the west end of each aisle is a small 2 light Decorated window. The north porch presents two doorways side by side, one large and another small, which last leads to a staircase. Within this porch is an Early English doorway with segmental arch and shafts with moulded capitals.

The south porch is plain and now used as a vestry. Near to it is a small, 2-light Decorated window cut by the porch and in this aisle is a small tier of pointed windows, being a quasi-clerestory. There is a steep, leaded roof to the nave. The aisles have no parapets. The chancel is slated.

There are large and handsome 4 light Perpendicular windows in the north aisle; those to the south of 3 lights, also good, as are those of the chancel. The northern arcade is of 3 very late obtuse arches with lozenge-shaped piers having longitudinal mouldings and capitals. The south arcade is of 3 wide arches with piers of 4 shafts of the frequent Perpendicular kind having general capitals. There is a clerestory over them of square-headed windows.

The chancel arch and that between the north aisle and the north chancel resemble the north arcade. The south chancel opens to the south aisle by one of good Perpendicular character with shafts and the chancel has on each side a very good Perpendicular arch opening to it aisles having shafts with capitals exhibiting figures holding scrolls. The nave and north aisle are ceiled. The south aisle has a panelled roof.

The windows contain several pieces of stained glass but mutilated. In the sacrarium, north and south, are large tombs to the Coles' having effigies of men and women in the ruffs fashionable about 1627. The figures variously coloured. That on the south has on its side 4 kneeling ladies, that on the north 3 men and 3 women, one of whom carries a scull. (There are long quaint inscriptions in verse.)

The pulpit is Jacobean. On the sounding board the date 1614 and 'Blessed are they that heare the work of God.' The font has an octagonal bowl; the sides have quatrefoils containing emblems, figures of saints and roses; the stem octagonal with shafts at the angles. There are small arches across the west end of each aisle ranging with the tower arch. In the cill of the west window of the north aisle is the effigy of a knight.

There is a square rood turret in the south aisle. The organ is on the ground in the tower. The tower is a large square in its lower part with a Perpendicular west window of 3 lights, otherwise very plain. On this rises a smaller octagonal belfry storey with alternate 2 lights Decorated windows upon which is a spire of octagonal form and leaded. The tower has no battlement.

There is a beautiful coped gravestone with cross in the churchyard lately erected.

Pitney

49/32–33 St. John Before 1840

A small church consisting of a west tower, a nave and a chancel without aisles, but a kind of transeptal chapel on the south. The tower is plain with a battlement, a two light belfry window and a window of 3 lights on the west side which is of dubious character between Decorated and Rectilinear tracery. The gables of the nave, chancel and porch have crosses. The nave walls lean outwards. On the whole there is little to attract in this church.

The south windows are Rectilinear of 3 lights; those on the north Curvilinear and of 2 lights. The transept has a panelled battlement externally, a flat panelled ceiling within and is evidently an addition of 1500. The nave has a coved ceiling with ribbed compartments and bosses; the chancel a boarded roof. The arches to tower and chancel plain. On the south of that opening to the chancel is the transverse opening commanding the altar, by no means unfrequent.

The east window of 3 lights . . . there is one lancet and one square-headed window. The font is a plain octagon. The doorway of the south porch has a kind of cinquefoiled arch and near the inner doorway is a plain niche and also in the soffit of the door arch a recess in which is set a singular basin of circular form not unlike a Norman capital.

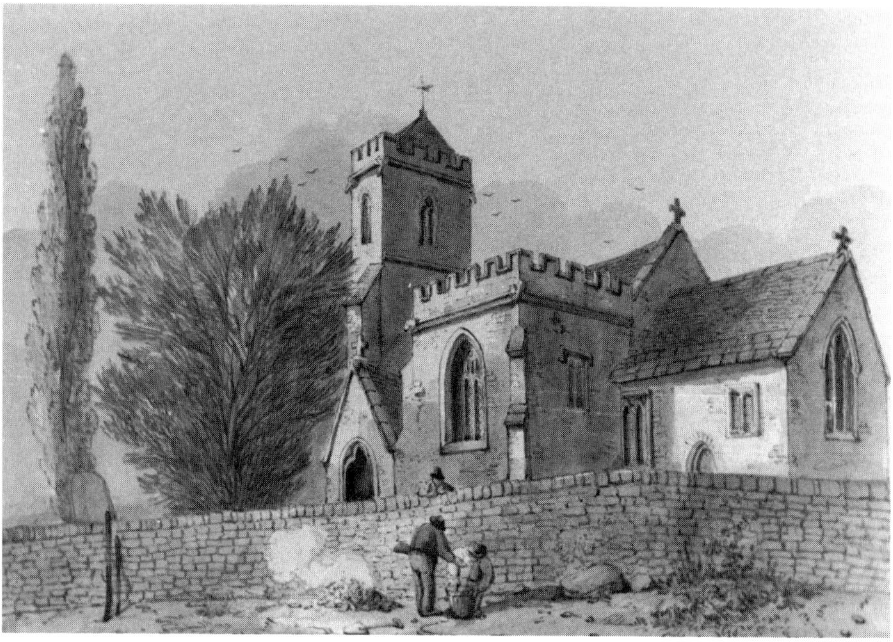

Pitney Church, 1845, by W.W. Wheatley

Podimore Milton

50/2–3 St. Peter 5 September, 1843

This small church consists of a nave and chancel only with a south porch and a low and slender octangular tower at the west end of the nave. The south porch is very plain. The tower in its lowest stage is square, the upper portion octangular and divided into 3 stages by strings and having plain lancet windows except in the belfry stage where they are later. There is no west door. On the north side is a small projecting turret.

The roof of the church is covered with flags of stone. On the stone side near the chancel arch is the usual projection for the rood staircase. The tower is quite open to the nave by an Early English arch having good mouldings on moulded corbels and there is no gallery. The west window of the tower is Decorated of 2 lights. The octagonal portion is very neatly fitted to the square part internally. On the north side of the nave are 2 windows of 2 lights of Decorated character. On the south they are later.

The nave is fitted chiefly with open seats. The chancel arch is pointed, but very plain and rude. The chancel roof is lower than that of the nave. Both are of the coved form with ribs and bosses. The east window of the chancel is Perpendicular of 3 lights. The side windows of the chancel are chiefly Decorated. One on the north is a single light. There are pieces of stained glass. On the south side of the chancel is a square recess. The font is a circular bowl upon a stem of similar form. There are 3 bells.

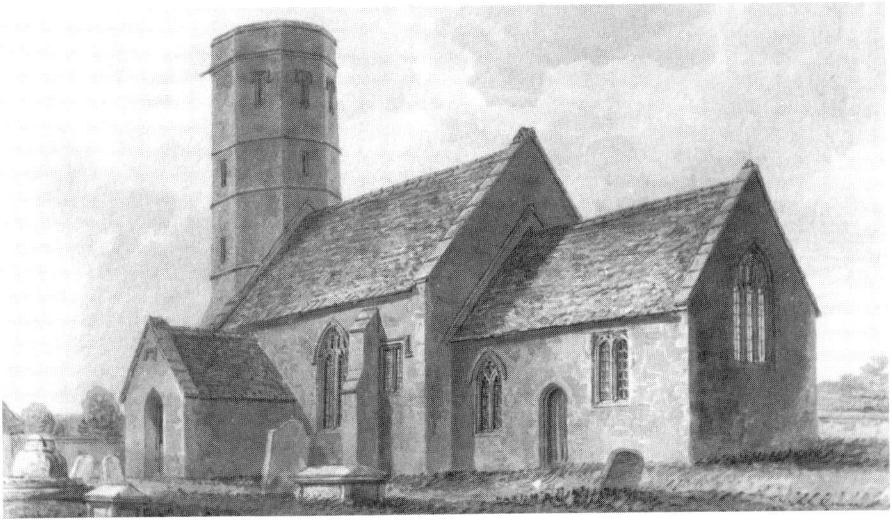

South east view of Podimore Church, 1832, by J. Buckler

Porlock

49/8–9	[St. Dubricius]	1828

This church consists of a nave with south aisle, a chancel and a massive tower at the west end surmounted by a large shingled spire, the upper part of which has been broken off. The tower is massive and very plain having an Early

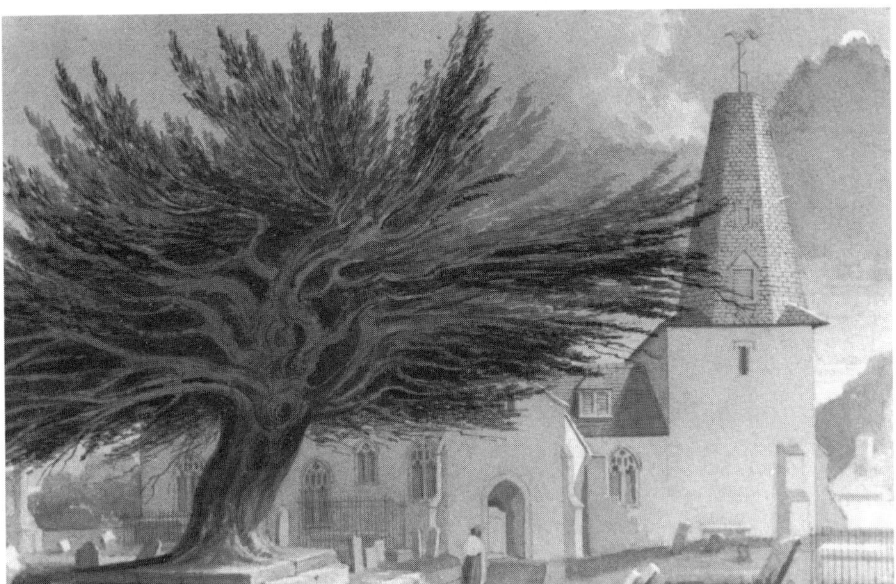

Porlock Church, 1844, by S.G. Tovey

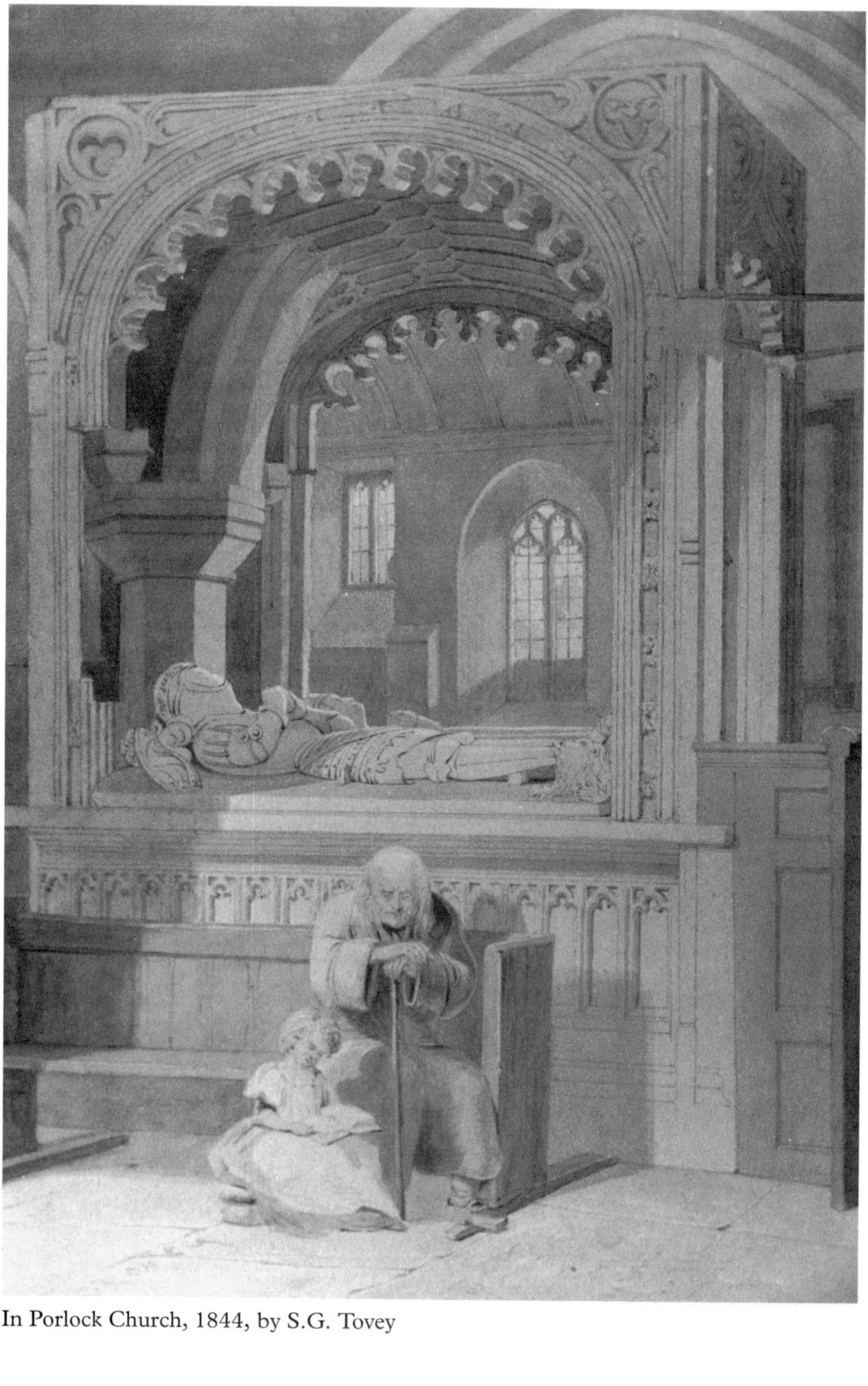

In Porlock Church, 1844, by S.G. Tovey

English lancet window on the west side. The windows of the nave are chiefly Rectilinear of 2 lights. There is a plain north porch.

The nave is divided from the aisle by 5 pointed arches with octagonal piers having overhanging capitals. The roof is coved and divided by ribs into panels. The chancel has an Early English east window of 3 lancets. In the south wall of the chancel under an arch is the effigy of a cross-legged knight with a shield. There is also a large tomb of Rectilinear character beneath a canopy with contracted arch enriched with feathering. There is also an altar tomb within the communion rails. The font is cased in wood. The pews are old and mean.

(The exterior walls are all whitewashed. The north porch is unusually large. At the east end of the chancel is a Perpendicular vestry not in the centre but added under the east window with entrance to the south of it. The churchyard is entered by a very large Church House gate.)

Preston Plucknett

50/55–57 [St. James] 1849

This church is cruciform having transeptal chapels not uncommon in this county, but no central tower. The tower is at the west end. The chancel is well developed but neither chancel nor nave have aisles. The greater part of the church is Middle Pointed. The arches opening to the transepts narrow and small; that on the south has octagonal imposts with corbel heads of good execution. One is that of a female in a wimple, the other has a wig and hands brought up to the ears.

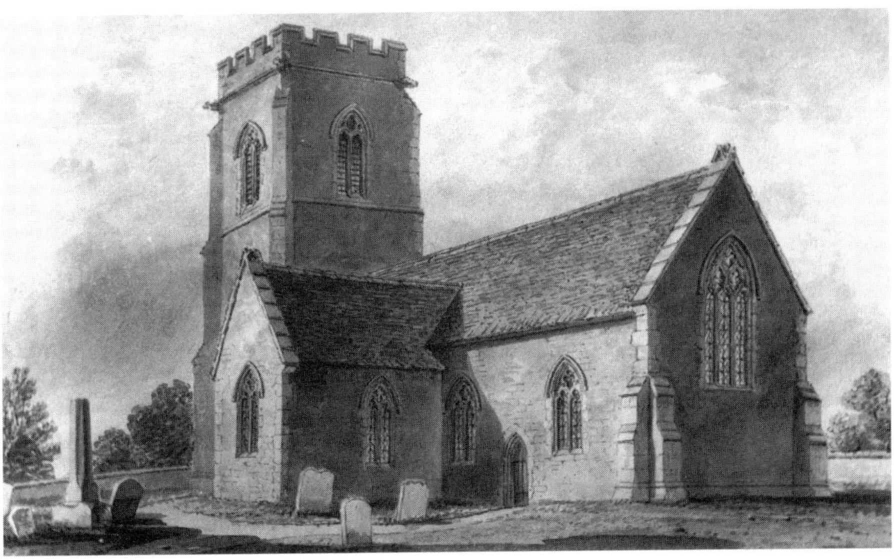

South east view of Preston Plucknett Church, 1839, by J. Buckler

In the south transept are 2 Middle Pointed windows. In its south wall a very deep piscina having a trefoiled fenestella. In the east wall are 2 embattled brackets and a hagioscope opening into the chancel. The arch of the north transept has sculptured capitals which vary; the western has foliage with an animal figure like a rabbit; on the east one like a cat. The windows of the north transept are like those of the south and on this side are the rood door and staircase. The pulpit is Caroline on a stone base.

The roofs are coved with ribs and bosses. The chancel has Middle Pointed windows, the eastern of 3 lights, the lateral ones of 2. In the north wall is the trace of a hagioscope, now closed. On the south is a large piscina resembling that in the transept with octofoil orifice and rose. The nave has one Middle Pointed window on the north: the other windows are late. The porch is plain. The font is Middle Pointed, the bowl octagonal, on each face an ogee arch trefoiled, the stem square with the angles cut off by 4 shafts which have moulded capitals. There are a few open benches.

The tower arch has fair continuous mouldings, hid by a gallery. The tower is of 3 stages diminishing and of late Third Pointed with battlement and corner buttresses, the belfry window of 2 lights. The stage below has a single light. There are large gargoyles and a stair turret on the north up two stages.

Priddy

50/27–28 St. Lawrence April, 1845

A small but rather interesting church consisting of a nave with north aisle and chancel, each with north and south chapels, a south transept and a western tower and south porch.

There are portions of different styles. The tower is Perpendicular, rather low, having corner buttresses and an elegant pierced parapet of trefoiled lozenges and 4 large, crocketed pinnacles. The belfry windows vary, some of

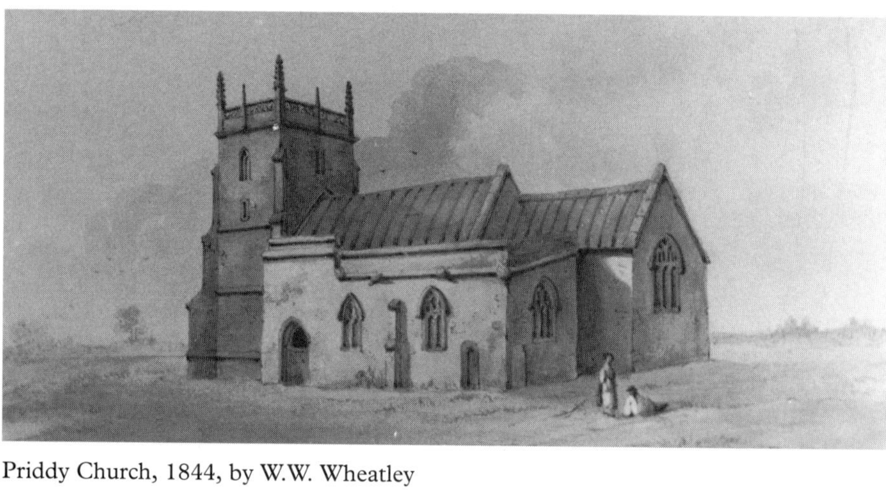

Priddy Church, 1844, by W.W. Wheatley

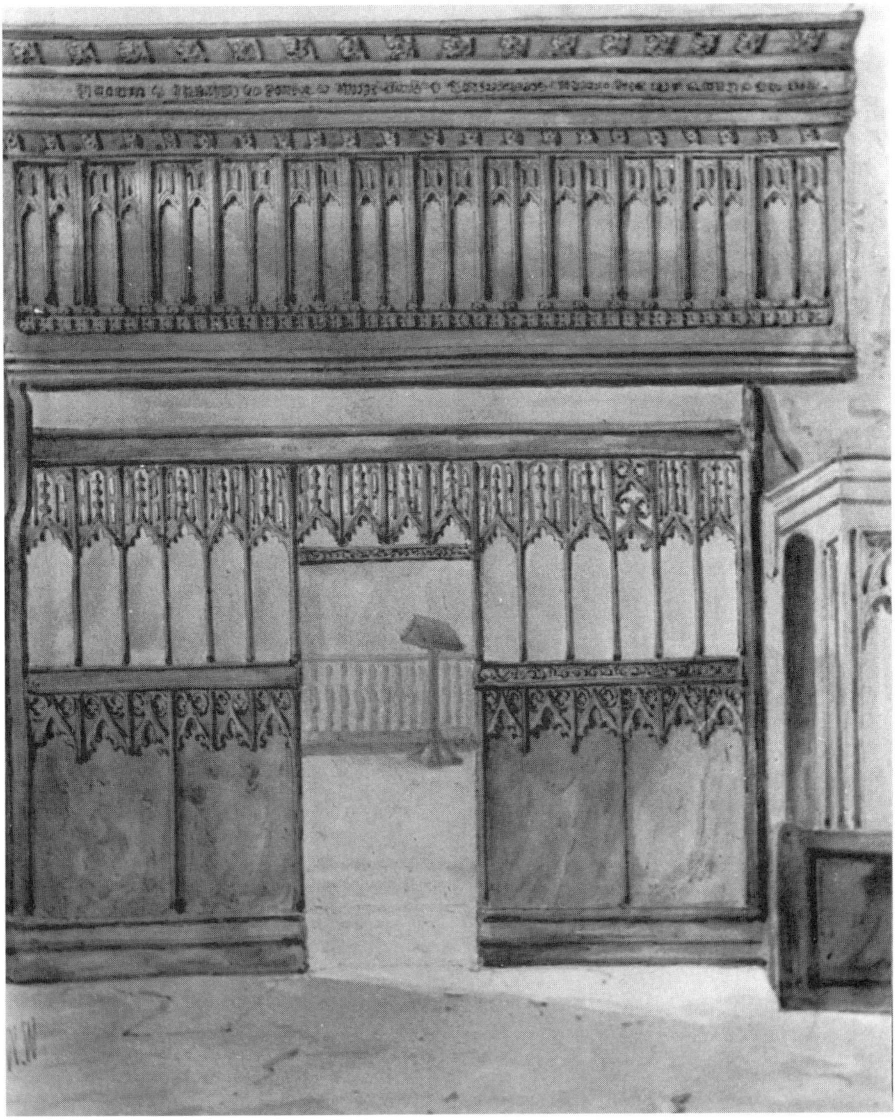

Priddy Church, 1844, by W.W. Wheatley

one, some of 2 lights with square heads. There is an octagonal turret on the north, but not reaching all the way up the tower which is of 3 stages. The west window of 2 lights and the door moulded.

The roofs are leaded. The south porch and transept have moulded parapets. The former is entered from without by a pointed arch with mouldings of Decorated character and shafts with small capitals. There are stone benches within the porch and near the inner door a very good complete benatura having an octagonal bowl upon a shaft which stands upon the stone bench.

The inner doorway has continuous mouldings. On the south side of the nave is a stone bench externally under the windows.

There are several Perpendicular windows, some square-headed, on the north of the chancel large and good of 3 lights with early Perpendicular tracery without labels. The tower arch has continuous mouldings. The nave is divided from its aisle by 3 pointed arches. The first pier is clustered of 4 shafts with moulded round capitals and octagonal bases; the other pier consists of a half octagon and circular shaft whence spring the two arches respectively. The arch to the transept resembles the first. There is a rood door and steps on the north side of the chancel arch. Part of the roodloft and screen remain, of good carved woodwork, painted and gilt.

The chancel arch has a panelled soffit. The chancel has an aisle or chapel on both sides and opens to each by a pointed arch with mouldings. That on the south has small shafts, that on the north has panelling but no shafts. The base of the pier has some stone panelling. There is a stone seat along the wall within a great part of the south chapel, the transept and at the west of the north aisle. In the north chancel is a rood screen and across the north aisle of the nave is a pointed arch upon clustered columns which seems to have divided off a quasi-transept and appears to be Decorated.

The chancel extends a little beyond the aisles and has a Perpendicular east window of 3 lights with label having bold corbel heads and on each side small square-headed single ones closed. The south chancel has an east window of 3 lights. There are some open benches of plain character and, in the south chancel, an old wooden lectern. The south chancel has a small obtuse door. The transept has a Decorated window of 2 lights and opens to the south chancel by a pointed arch of plain character with continuous moulding.

The font has a circular bowl with mouldings upon a cylindrical stem with round base. The churchyard is very large, the situation dreary.

Priston

52/4 St. Luke 8 June, 1871

This church has nave and chancel without aisles and a tower placed between the nave and chancel. There is some early work and the nave has a good corbel table of that character beneath the parapet and 2 long Norman windows on the south. The west window is Perpendicular of 3 lights. The porch is plain.

The tower is of debased character and of 2 stages above the roof of the nave. The arches under it are modern imitations of Norman, opening to the nave and chancel. The chancel is of different masonry superior to that of the nave and of Decorated character, has, north and south, 2 good windows of 2 lights with connecting hoods, the rear arches within having the cusped and foliated work not unfrequent in this county. There is a good open panelled parapet on both sides of the chancel of Perpendicular character. The east window is of 3 lights reticulated. There is on the south a priest's door with ogee canopy and finial. The base mouldings of the chancel are very good.

The churchyard is very pretty. (The Norman windows of the nave are probably modern.)

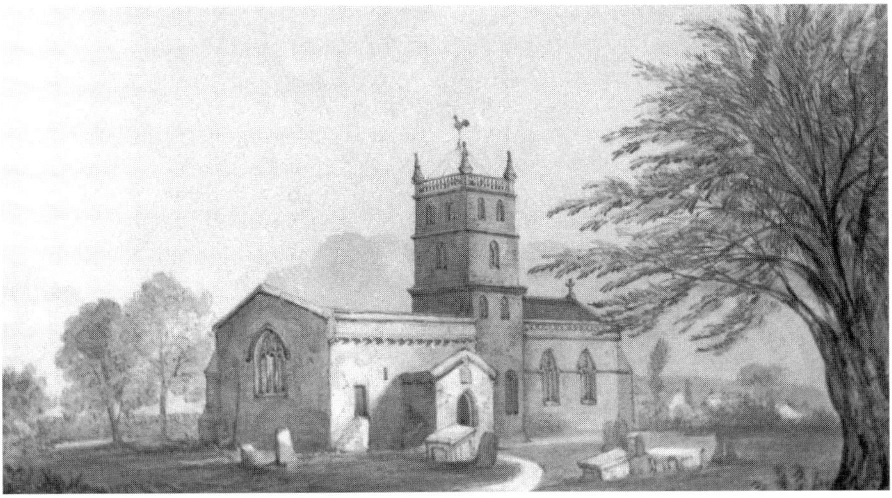

Priston Church, 1843, by W.W. Wheatley

Pylle

50/6–7 St. Thomas Becket 4 September, 1843

This is a small Perpendicular church consisting of a west tower, a nave, north transept, south porch and chancel. The tower is rather handsome with a battlement and 4 crocketed pinnacles and divided into 3 stages. The belfry

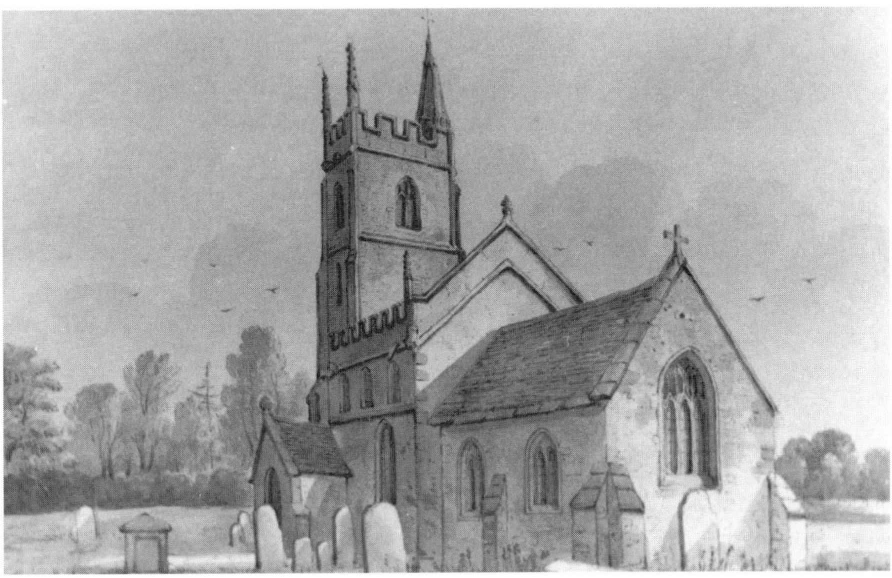

Pylle Church, 1845, by W.W. Wheatley

windows and those of the other stages of 2 lights with stone lattice work with quatrefoils and varying in character. On the north-east side is a polygonal turret crowned by a pyramidical finishing and small battlements. The west door has good mouldings and over it is a window deprived of tracery.

The nave has a fine battlement and pinnacles at the ends. On each side a clerestory or upper tier of windows, though there are no aisles. On the south the windows have lost their tracery. On the north they are of 2 lights. In the chancel the east window of 3 lights, the others of 2. The east gable of the nave has good moulding and crowned by a finial. The chancel arch has plain mouldings and on the north pier of it is a small, arched recess. The arch to the north transept is flat and late. The font is Norman, a circular bowl with inverted moulding on a cylindrical stem. The altar is shabby. The south porch is surmounted by a cross and on its exterior is a small stoup. (The chancel arch is Norman.)

Quantoxhead, West

50/18 St. Ethelred 15 July, 1843

A small church in a lovely situation consisting of a western tower, nave, south porch, south transept and chancel. The tower and nave Perpendicular but plain. The former is embattled and has the common octagonal stair turret at the north-east. The belfry window of 2 lights. The west doorway has plain and good mouldings and over it a 3 light window. The tower, according to a custom not very uncommon but very barbarous, has a sort of piebald look being partially whitewashed, but not the buttresses.

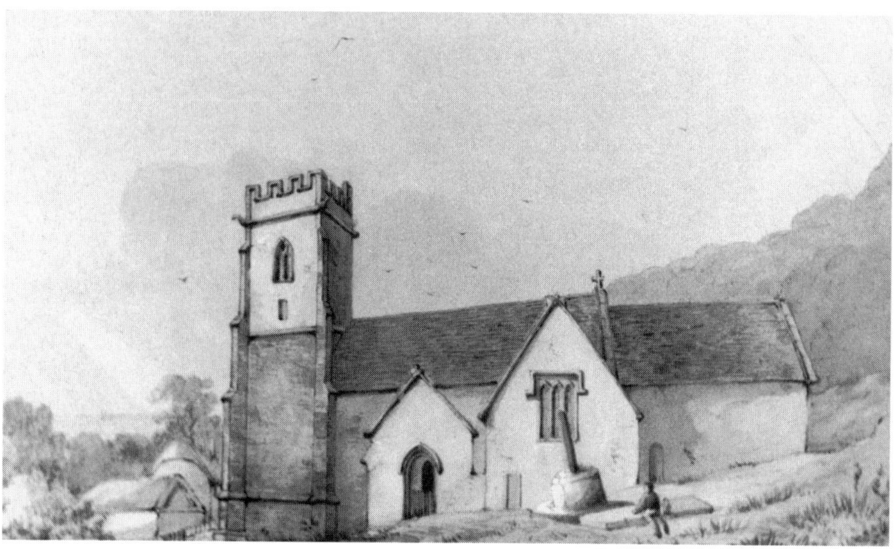

West Quantoxhead, 1845, by W.W. Wheatley

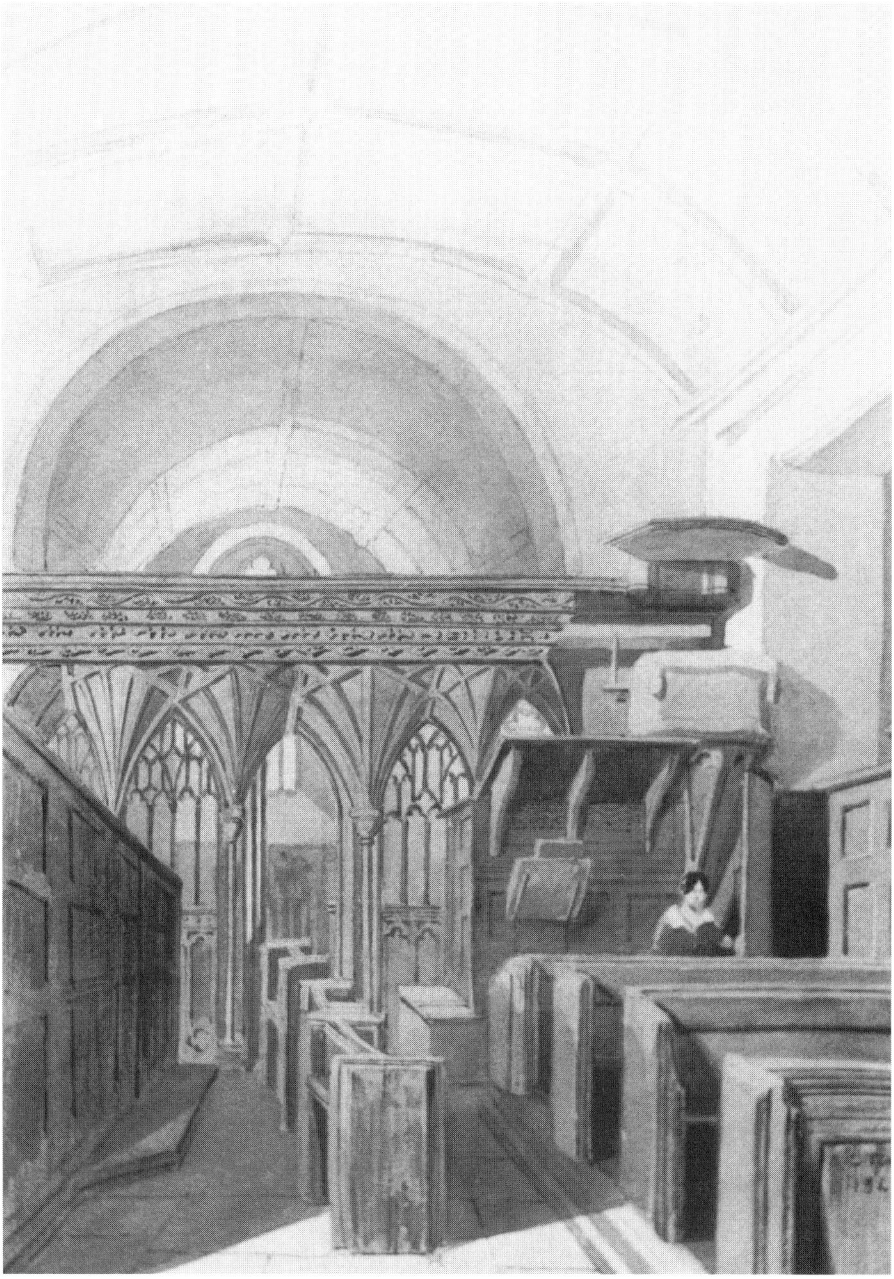

West Quantoxhead, 1845, by S.G. Tovey

The porch is large and plain. The transept communicates with the nave by a flattened aperture without arch and has a ribbed roof. The chancel arch is obtuse and the chancel has some plain lancets on both north and south. The east window early Decorated of 2 lights with circle in the head but no foils. The roodloft is a very fine one in good preservation rich in groining and ornamented cornices especially facing westward. In the north wall of the chancel is a large arched recess, perhaps a credence and on the south side part of a rude stone seat. The ground rises considerably towards the east. There is an organ in the west gallery.

In the churchyard the base of a cross. The parsonage is a picturesque thatched building.

Queen Camel

50/3–5 St. Barnabas 8 September, 1843

A large and handsome church consisting of a west tower, nave, side aisles and chancel, the greater part Perpendicular but with earlier indications. The tower is lofty, very strong and solid, but plain and more of the Dorsetshire than the Somersetshire style. It is divided into 4 stages which are divided by strings at rather short intervals. At the north-west is an octagonal turret embattled and crowned by 2 small pinnacles at each angle. The parapet of the tower is plain and the pinnacles unfinished. The belfry window on each side of 2 lights and on the west side another Perpendicular window of 2 lights with a niche over it. The buttresses are not at the angles. The west door has good arch mouldings and over it a 3 light Perpendicular window.

The parapets of the church are without battlement. The chancel has a flowered cornice. The south door is within an ugly Italian porch and situated very near the middle of the aisle instead of the usual position more to the west. There is an octagonal turret with the rood stairs at the south-east angle of the clerestory which raises high and is finished by a finial. The whole is built of fine dark stone. The windows on the north are Perpendicular of 4 lights and square-headed; those of the clerestory of 3 lights of a plain kind with pointed arches. In the south aisle, 2 are square-headed externally and with depressed arch over them within.

At the east end of the south aisle is a square-headed 4 light window with tracery of transition character from Decorated to Perpendicular. Near to it is one Decorated window of 2 lights with nice arch mouldings. The tower is unusually large and solid and opens to the nave by a moulded pointed arch springing from shafts with foliated capitals. Above this arch a large portion of the solid wall of the tower is open to the nave, the present elevation of which is greater than the original of which the pointed pitch is seen in the well of the tower above the arch. This is not an ordinary, as the new roofs are usually lower than the original ones. Within the tower is placed a good organ in a gallery which exhibits some wood carving.

The interior is handsome. The nave is divided from each aisle by 4 moulded pointed arches springing from octagonal columns of which two on the north have Tudor flowers in the capital and one foliage with roses. The southern

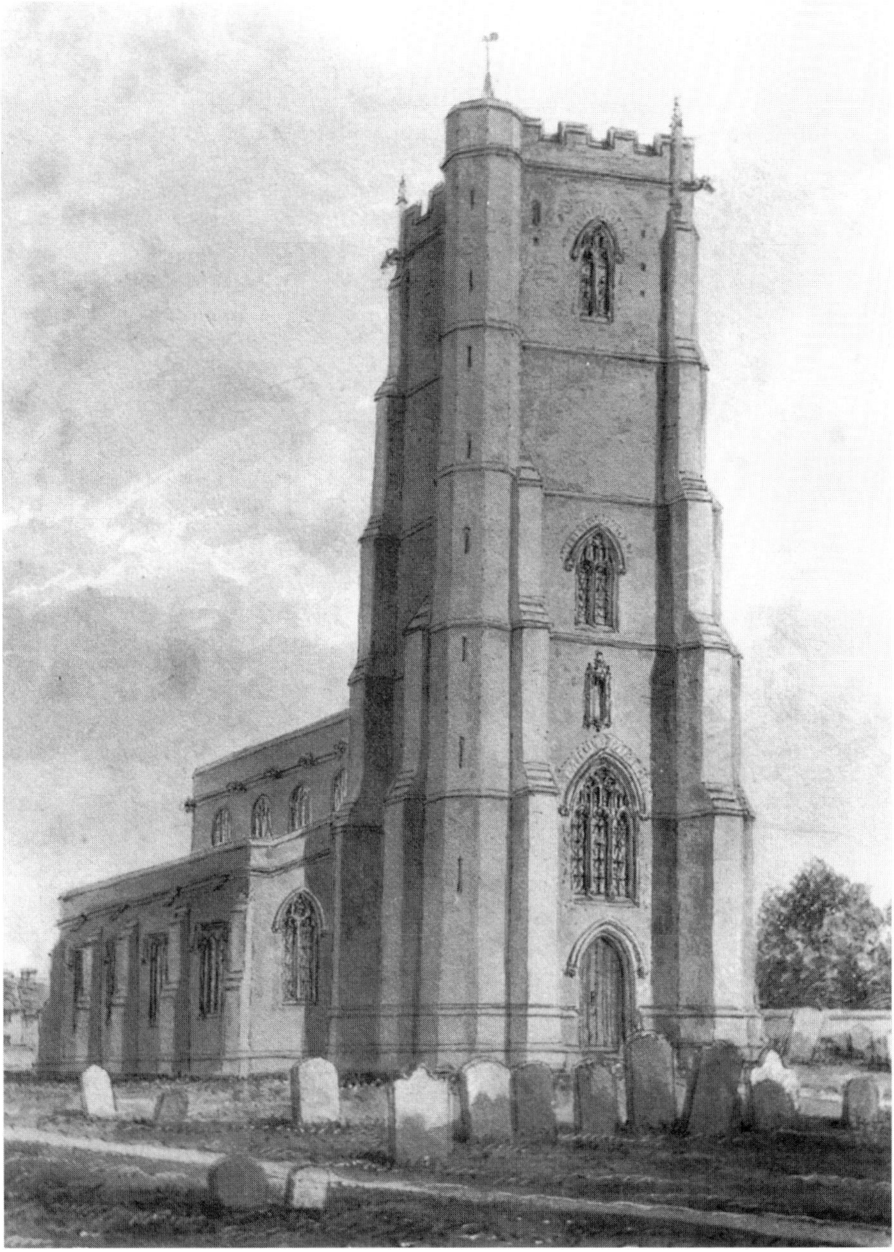

North west view of Queen Camel Church, 1843, by J. Buckler

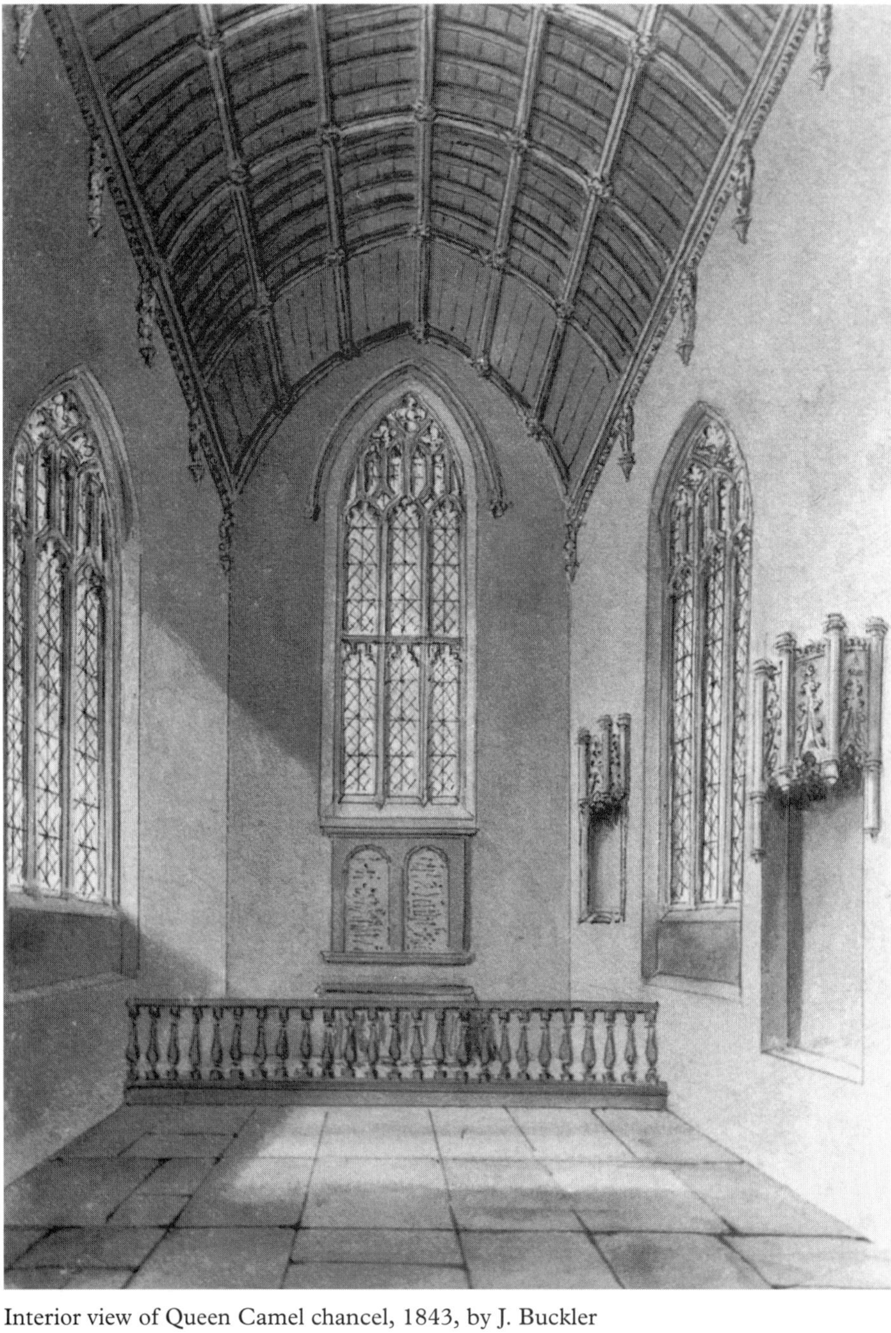

Interior view of Queen Camel chancel, 1843, by J. Buckler

capitals have plain mouldings. The two western arches on each side are much narrower than the others and the north aisle is itself narrow and there is no appearance of a northern door. The roof of the nave is a fine one with flowered beams and pierced tracery above.

Above the eastern portion of the nave corresponding with the roodloft and also over the eastern part of the south aisle is a boarded panelled ceiling having rich foliated bosses. The chancel arch is tall and has a very finely panelled soffit continuous and, of course, of Perpendicular character. On the south side of the chancel arch is a door to the roodloft steps. The roodloft and screen remain in the chancel arch and a very good specimen. There are 5 arched compartments fitted with Perpendicular tracery, fan groining and fine cornices of vine leaves, etc.

The chancel is wholly Perpendicular and has on each side 2 windows and one at the east end, all of 3 lights, the latter with transom. On the south side of the altar is a piscina surmounted by a very rich canopy of tabernacle work upon shafts and there is a single sedile (a window intervening between it and the piscina) with a very elegant triple canopy of tabernacle work much resembling that of the piscina. This arrangement is very uncommon. In the angles of the chancel walls are some small canopies which have a good effect.

The chancel roof is coved, in panels with ribs and fine foliated bosses in which are mixed figures of various animals, fish and especially camels from the name of the place. The cornice has female figures on stone brackets. Over the altar the roof is boarded. There are some old wood seats. The pulpit is very elegant in wood carving of the 16th century with tabernacle work and on an octangular stem. The font an octagonal bowl richly panelled with shields and with octagonal shafts at 4 of the angles charged with niches and statues and a square central pedestal.

Rode

50/43–44 St. Lawrence 3 October, 1848

A Third Pointed church comprising nave with aisles, chancel, western tower and north porch, the principal entrance, contrary to usual custom, being on the north. There is a clerestory to the nave, but no part of the nave or chancel has any moulding or parapet. The tower is of 3 stages and embattled having a stair turret at the north-east, square below and octagonal in its upper part. The west doorway has a label returned upon lozenge-shaped corbels not equal in size. Above it is a 4 light window badly altered. The buttresses are at the angles and the two upper stages have 3 light windows, partly closed with stonework, but which in the belfry has quatrefoil lattice work.

In the north-west buttress of the nave is a niche. The roofs are flagged externally and separate so that the clerestory is scarcely seen from without. The nave has on each side an arcade of 4 arches with the usual piers, the shafts having separate octagonal capitals and Tudor flower in the mouldings. The clerestory windows are square-headed, deprived of tracery. The chancel arch resembles the other arches; the shafts have been partly cut away for the roodloft. The east pier on the north side has a door which must have

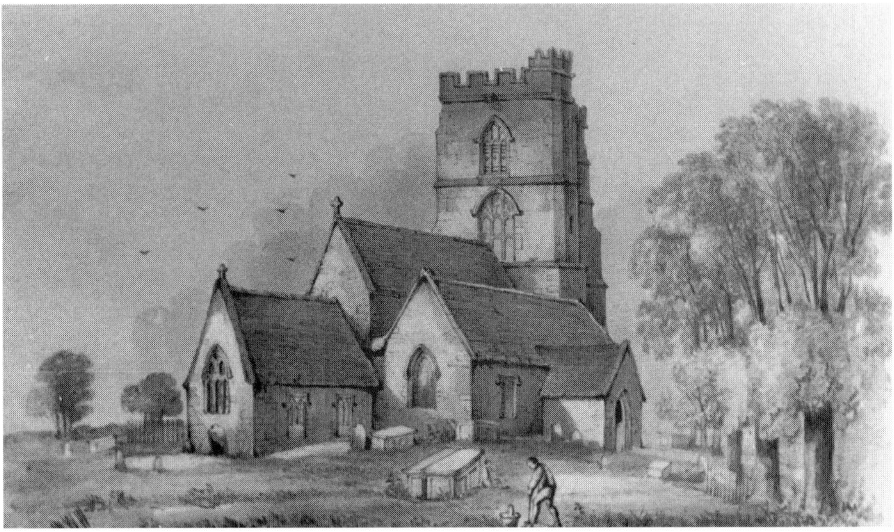

Rode Church, 1843, by W.W. Wheatley

communicated with the roodloft. The aisle windows are square-headed, having labels with corbel heads, but the tracery has been much destroyed except in those at the east.

The chancel is much lower than the nave and its ceiling cuts the arch. Its east window is of 3 lights. There is an ogee piscina, trefoiled and with shelf at the east end of the south aisle. Beneath one of the southern windows is a very late tomb arch with embattled cornice and coarse flat foliation: on the sides of the tomb niches with shields. The font is ordinary: an octagonal bowl panelled with quatrefoils. The nave is pued and galleried. The exterior is plain but the stone good and on the gables are crosses.

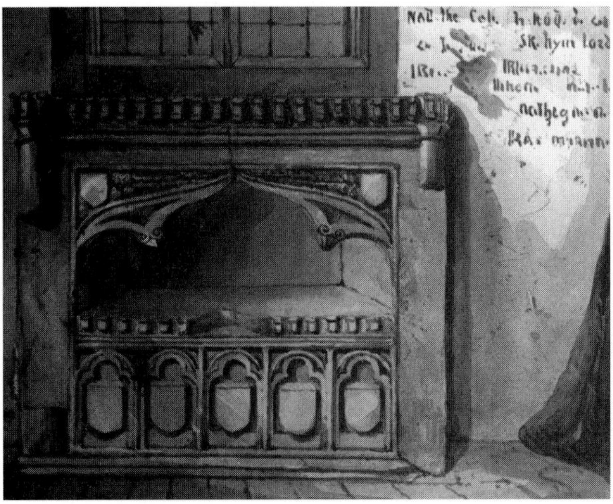

Tomb and writing on the wall lately cleared of whitewash, south aisle of Rode Church, by W.W. Wheatley

Rodney Stoke

51/55–56 St. Leonard 27 January, 1862

A small church; plan: nave and chancel with chapel north of the latter, west tower and north porch. The chancel rebuilt in poorish style. The whole Perpendicular. The parpapet of the nave has pierced panelling and small pinnacles; that of the north chapel is similar, but of richer character. The outer walls are partially covered with rough cast. The tower is fair Perpendicular; its arch to the nave is upon shafts. The tower is embattled without pinnacles, has an octagonal stair turret at the north-east and is of 3 stages divided by string courses. The west doorway has a depressed arch and mouldings. The west window is good, of 4 lights subarcuated. Under it is sculpture of 3 angels bearing shields, the central containing the 5 wounds. There are 2 heights of 2 light windows.

The porch contains a stoup of fair character. The windows of the nave are of 3 lights. The chancel arch pointed and continuous. There is a roodscreen singular from being of renaissance character, A.D. 1619. The roof of the nave is panelled. The north chapel is of later Perpendicular than the rest, is separated from the chancel by an arch in which are 2 fine Perpendicular Tombs of the Rodney family, one of which is very rich, the canopy having double feathering with figures at the points and the sides of the tomb having niches with figures. There are also some later monuments of the Rodneys temp. James I. The chantry has a flat panelled roof and an ogee doorway with finial ending in a niche. There is also a cinquefoiled piscina. The font has a circular cup, plain and doubtful in character.

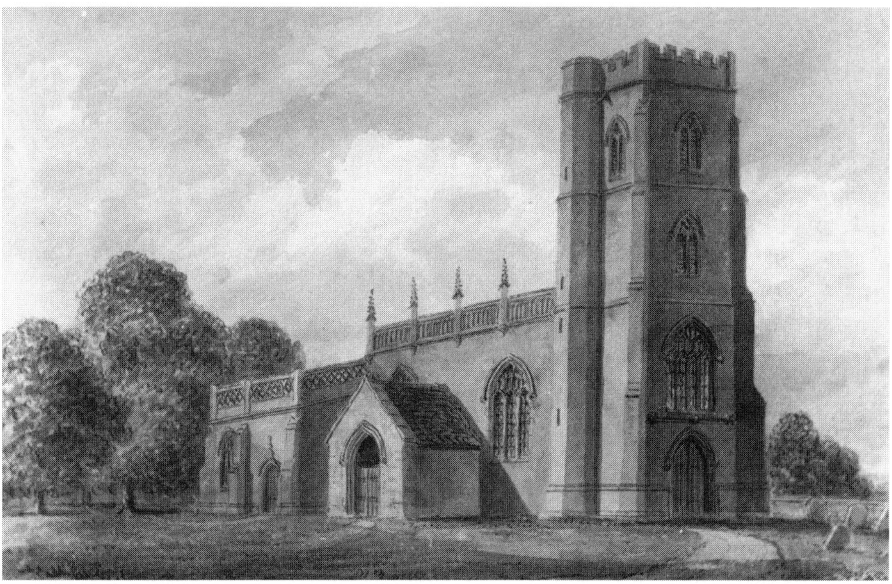

North west view of Rodney Stoke Church, 1844, by J. Buckler

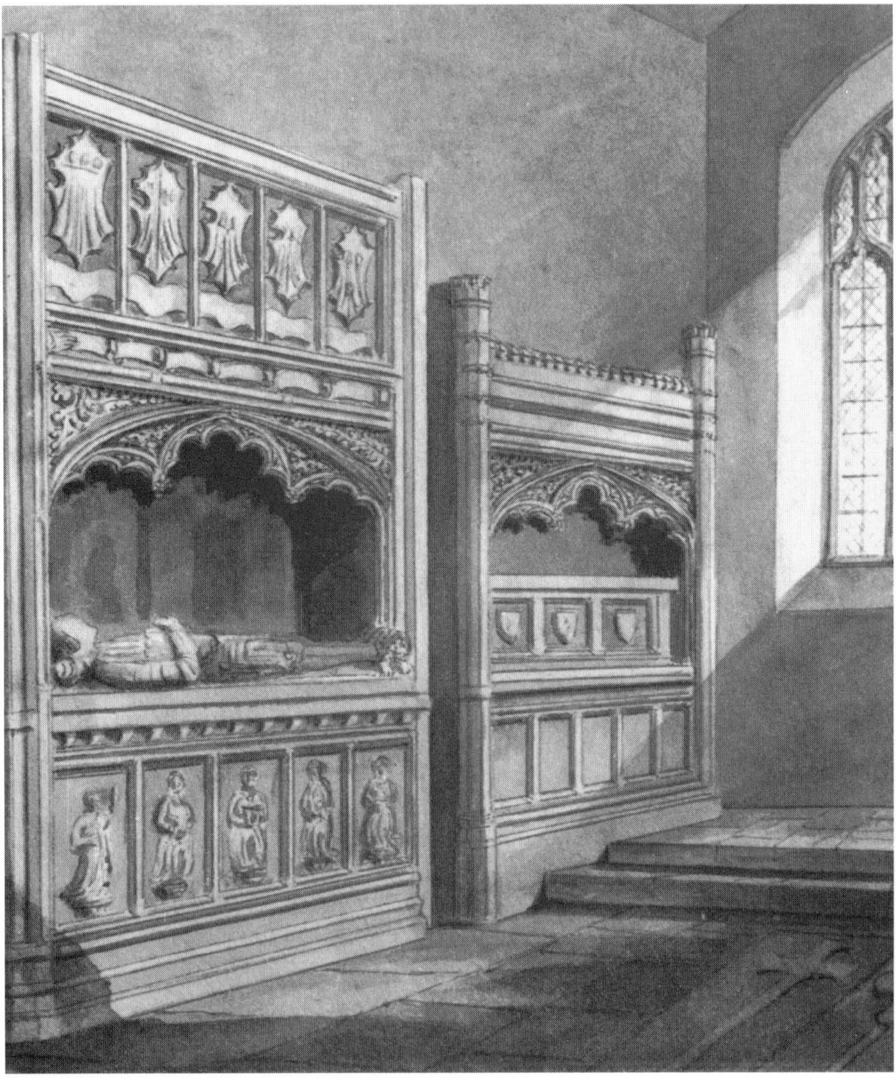

Monuments in Rodney Stoke Church, 1844, by J. Buckler

Rowberrow

51/56–57 St. Michael 25 January, 1862

A small poor church having only chancel and nave with west tower and south porch. The windows south of the nave are Perpendicular of 2 lights. The chancel has a poor east window of 3 lights which may be Decorated and on the south side square-headed late windows of 2 lights. The chancel arch is pointed and ordinary. The tower arch upon imposts. The chancel is small. On its north side is a square

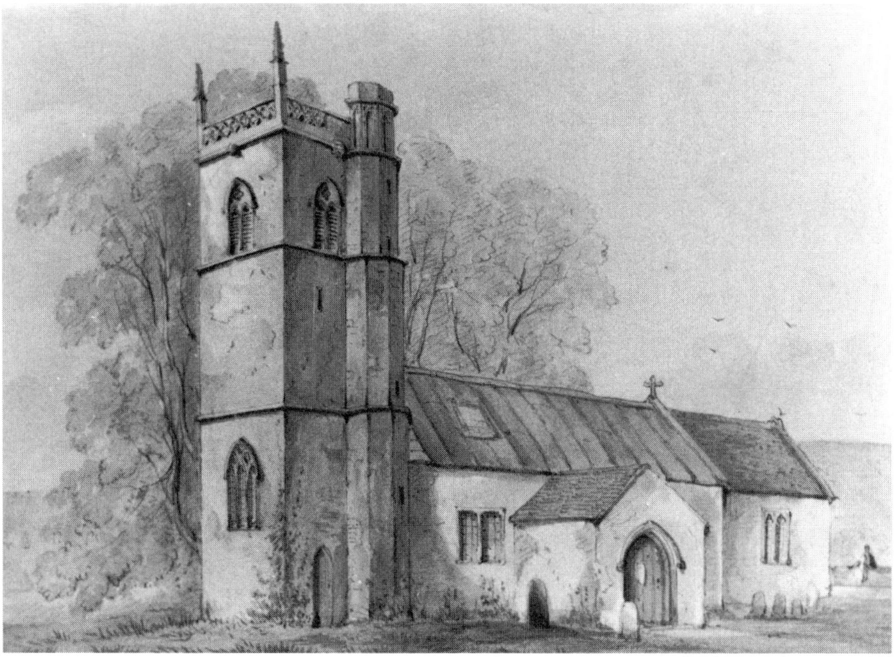

Rowberrow, 1843, by W.W. Wheatley

recess. The font is good Perpendicular, has pretty panelling on an octagonal bowl, set on octagonal stem. The gables have crosses. The porch plain. The tower is low and without buttresses, has parapet of pierced panelling and 4 small pinnacles, is divided by 2 string courses. The west window has an appearance of Decorated character. Belfry windows of 2 lights. At the south-east an octagonal stair turret. Most of the exterior walls are stuccoed.

Ruishton

50/35–36 St. George April, 1845

This church consists of a nave and chancel with a south aisle, south porch and west tower. The prevailing features are as usual Perpendicular but with a few earlier portions especially in the chancel. Within the south porch is the trace of a Norman door, much mutilated, having shafts with stilted bases. The porch itself is Perpendicular. The tower is a fine Perpendicular one though unfinished and of the kind peculiar to Somersetshire.

It is divided by 2 horizontal bands, filled with quatrefoils containing shields and flowers, into 3 stages. The 2 upper ones have each long double windows, each of 2 lights with lattice work of pierced quatrefoils and pinnacles between. On the west side is a labeled doorway with angel corbels and spandrels filled with cyphers. Above the door is a panelled band of quatrefoils and a good

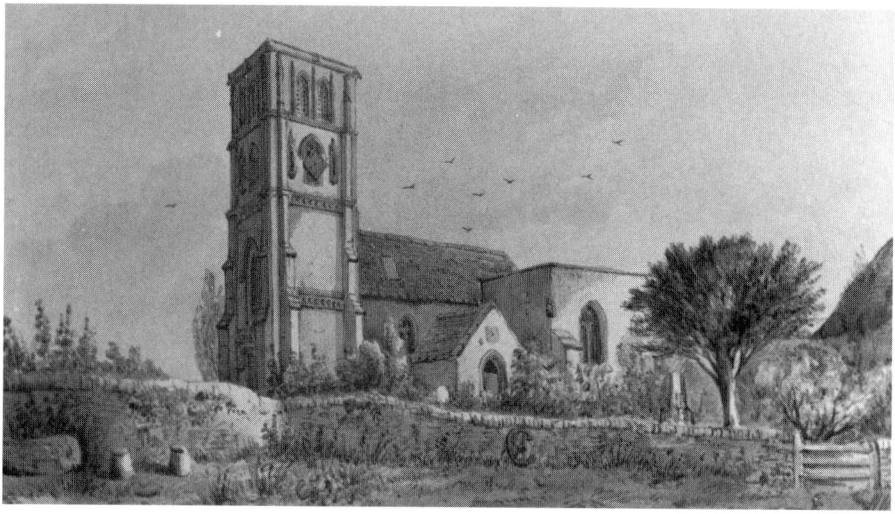

Ruishton, 1848, by W.W. Wheatley

window of 4 lights. On the north and south, the lowest stage has a 2 light window between fine canopied niches having angel brackets. The buttresses are well grouped and surmounted by small pinnacles. On the north is an octagonal stair turret. The parapet of the tower has never been completed.

The tower arch opening to the nave is lofty and handsome with panelled soffit and small shafts. The roofs are coved and the windows in the nave and aisle are mostly of 2 lights. The nave is divided from the aisle by 2 elegant Perpendicular arches springing from a very light small pier of 4 clustered shafts with octagonal capitals and mouldings continued between them. The aisle is not continued westward of the porch. In the south pier of the chancel arch is a hagioscope form divided by a mullion with 2 trefoiled lights, and close to it a small door opening into the aisle.

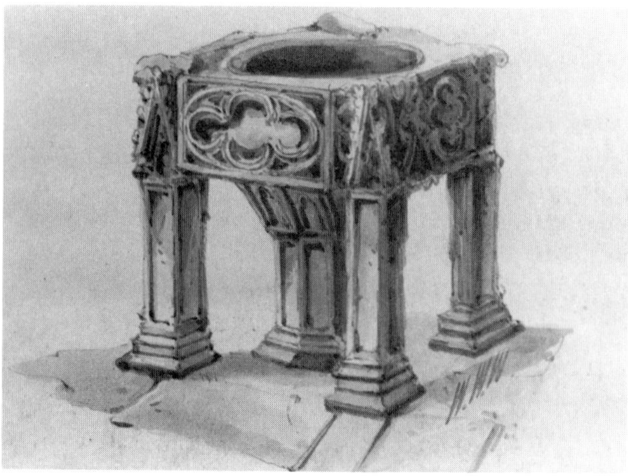

In Ruishton Church, 1848, by W.W. Wheatley

The east window is of transition character from Early English to Decorated having 3 unequal lancets and 3 arches above, within a general pointed arch which presents internally five toothed mouldings and shafts with toothed capitals and moulded bases. On the north and south are similar windows of 2 lights. The altar is neat and there is a Flemish picture in the reredos representing the Adoration of the Magi. There are too many pues, but the interior is on the whole neat.

The font is a fine large Perpendicular one, the bowl octagonal diminishing with quatrefoil panelling and vine leaf band round the upper part an octagonal stem surrounded by 4 large square shafts set against the alternate sides of the bowls crowned by rich crocketed pedimented canopies rising higher than the bowl.

The exterior has been stuccoed; the parapets moulded. In the churchyard is the shaft of a cross with octagonal base surrounded by shafts like those of the font.

Runnington

51/38–39 [St. Peter] 29 January, 1870

A small church having only chancel and nave with south porch and west tower. There is a square chancel and doubtful if original. The windows of the nave are Perpendicular, square-headed of 2 and 3 lights merely foliated. The tower arch pointed and very plain. The roofs are coved with ribs. There is a small projection on the north for stairs connected with the roodloft. The chancel has a poor modern east window. On the north-east is a plain window of 2

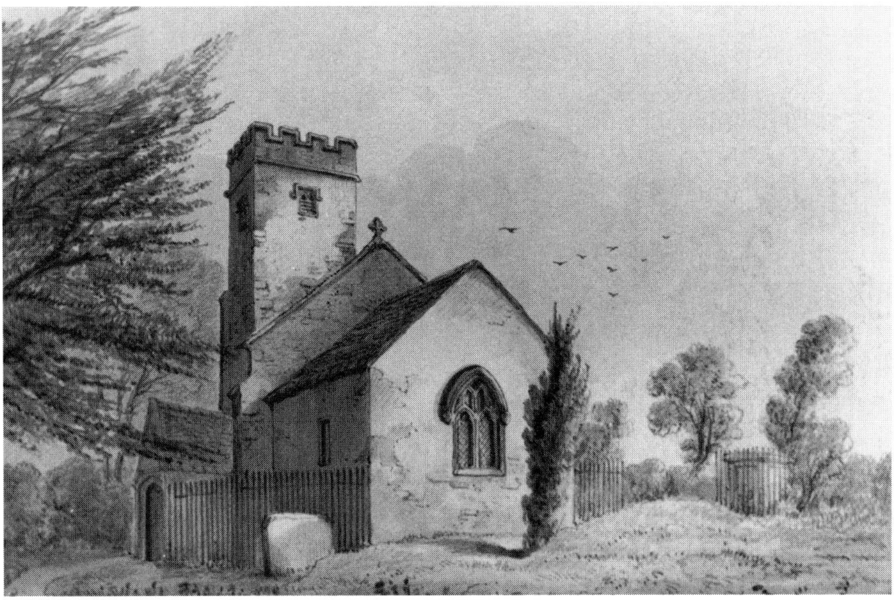

Runnington, 1848, by W.W. Wheatley

unfoliated lights, doubtful if original. The chancel is wainscoted, the nave pued.

The tower is Perpendicular, rather small, with corner buttresses and battlement, built of a red coloured stone. On the west side is a plain doorway with continuous arch mouldings and a small 2 light window. The belfry windows are labeled, of 2 lights. The chancel is covered externally with plaster but not the nave. The porch is modern. The south doorway has a flat arch.

St. Catherine

51/83–85 | 27 April, 1865

A small church amid lovely woody scenery near to a large and picturesque old court house. It has nave and chancel, south porch and west tower. Of good stone masonry and externally of Perpendicular character, but the tower and north wall were rebuilt in 1704. The tower is small and without buttress with battlement and 4 crocketed pinnacles; string and gargoyles, a single obtuse-headed window on the west and belfry windows of 3 lights of really good Somersetshire Perpendicular work having the ornamental lattice work and very well executed if of the above date. The porch is plain, its outer doorway pointed; within it is a fine Perpendicular doorway with continuous mouldings, hood on foliated corbels and above it a plain niche. The nave roof is slated; the chancel has stone tiles. Within the roofs are coved and ribbed.

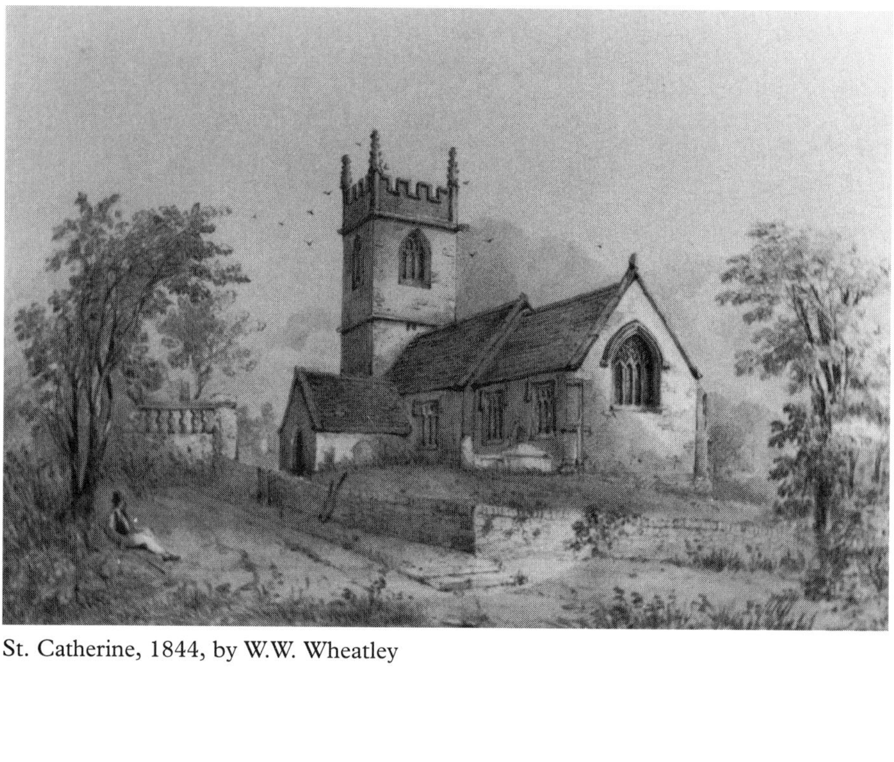

St. Catherine, 1844, by W.W. Wheatley

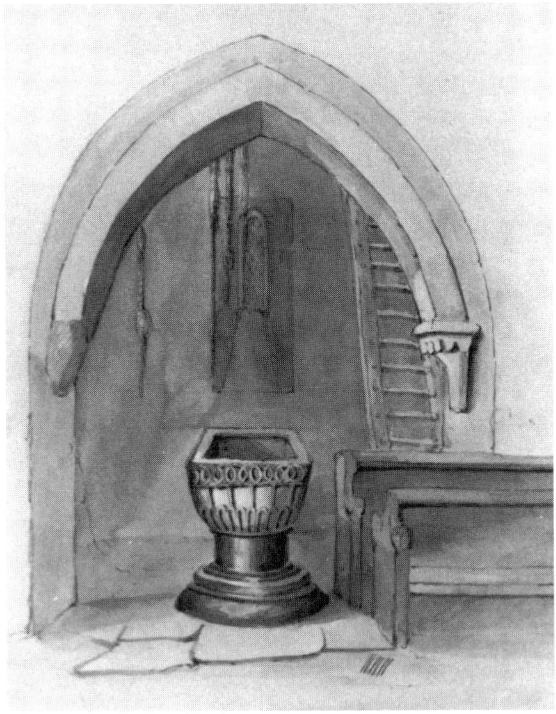

St. Catherine, 1844, by W.W. Wheatley

The interior is in very good condition. The original tower arch remains and is Early English, low and on Early English corbeled shafts which have square abaci and rude foliage. The arch plain of 2 orders. The windows on the south are Perpendicular, square-headed and labeled. Those on the north debased. The chancel arch is Early English, pointed and low – with wall about it – upon recessed Early English shafts which have square abaci. On the north side of this arch is a hagioscope set obliquely. In the windows south of the nave are some good pieces of old stained glass. The pulpit an ancient one of wood with panelled tracery, ogee canopies and pinnacles, coloured and gilt. The seats are all open.

The chancel is small. The east window Perpendicular of 4 lights full of mutilated ancient stained glass. On the north is a 3 light square-headed window hidden in part by a large Blanchard Monument erected 1631. On the south is a good priest's door with continuous moulding and 2 windows of 2 and 3 lights having cill continued for sedile. On the north of the chancel is the rood turret and staircase projecting within and lighted by slits.

The font is a remarkable Norman one, in form of a square with angles cut off. On each side the ornamentation varies. On the south are intesecting arches which are alternatively set on shafts with square abaci. On the east are intersecting circles and scalloping below. On the north are single semi-circular circles on corbels. On the west there is too much mutilation to make out the pattern. The stem is circular.

(4 bells. In the stained glass of the east window appears this inscription . . . dni Johis . . . hanc cacella qui anima . . . 1490.)

St. Decuman's

50/19–21 16 July, 1843

A handsome Perpendicular church, though with earlier portions, as often is the case, about the chancel. It consists of a lofty (but not rich) west tower, nave and chancel, each with side aisles and a south porch, the whole of good stone. The tower has 3 storeys and an embattled parapet with the bases of pinnacles which probably never were finished. The belfry window large, of 2 lights, with transom and the stone lattice work of pierced quatrefoils so common in Somersetshire. The second stage has a single square-headed aperture, labeled, and a small niche on the south. There is a west window of 4 lights with transom and under it a door with obtuse moulded arch and stoup to the north of it. On the north side of the tower is the common octagonal stair turret.

The side of the church is covered with whitewash and on this side are 2 Perpendicular windows of 3 lights, the tracery of which is rather singular. Those of the south aisle of the chancel have transoms. The south porch is large and plain and there is a stone shelf in one of its angles. The north side is much superior in beauty and richness to the south as well as free from whitewash. It has a panelled battlement enriched with quatrefoils, a string course and corbels, and the west gable crowned by a cross. There is also an octagonal stair turret of large size and embattled, corresponding with the

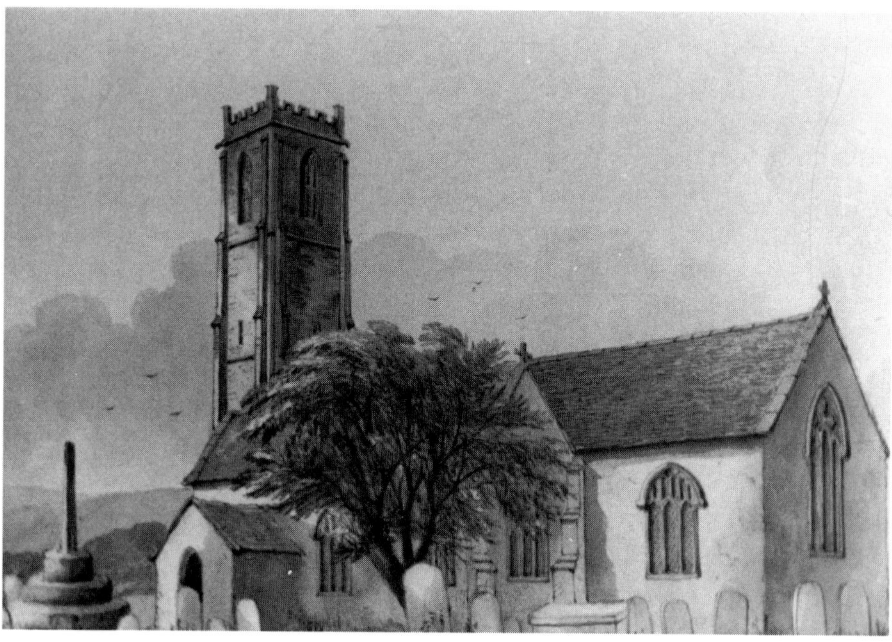

St. Decuman's, 1845, by W.W. Wheatley

place of the roodloft and exactly resembling those of Stogumber and Bishops Lydiard.

There is no clerestory. The nave is divided from each aisle by 4 rather wide arches and the chancel by 1 arch, it extending beyond the aisles. These are all Perpendicular. The piers in the nave are light, of wavy form, with 4 shafts and continued mouldings in the intervals. On the northern piers and responds are some small canopied niches in some of which are images of saints. The eastern pier on the south side has panelling on one face. The eastern arch of the nave is wider than the others and inelegant. The chancel arch is wide and springs from a corbel on the north side, but straight from the wall on the south.

The nave and chancel are quite of even height. The tower arch is lofty and open having continued mouldings. The roofs are very good with ribs and foliated bosses and cornice enriched with vine leaves and angel figures bearing shields and books. There is no distinction between the aisles of the nave and those of the chancel, the latter are chantry chapels and each opens to the chancel by a Tudor shaped arch. There is a large portion of the roodloft screen remaining, but some of it has been barbarously cut away and adapted for the insertion of a reading pue of Italian taste.

On the south side of the chancel is a parclose screen of late character and mutilated. That on the north is entirely gone, and within the northern arch a huge late Perpendicular tomb is inserted, having a high canopy. The chancel has on the north side a trefoil lancet containing some beautiful early painted glass. The inner arch is trefoil-headed and expanded, springing from shafts and having fine mouldings. The east window is early Decorated of 3 lights, just emerging from Early English: the dripstone on head corbels. Internally it has shafts with elegant foliated capitals. The other windows are Perpendicular.

The north chapel belongs to the Wyndhams of Orchard Wyndham to whom it contains some very sumptuous monuments of varied characters, none of the best period, but furnishing an instructive specimen of the gradual decline of monuments into downright paganism. Against the east wall are two slabs which contain late but well executed brasses of a man and woman of the 17th century and there is one still later with the very unusual feature of brass busts in bas relief: the date 1720. There are 2 other large monuments presenting specimens of 2 bad periods, but one has a religious character (the figure kneeling), the other wholly pagan with scrolls and urns.

The large tomb within the north arch has 2 very well executed brasses representing Sir John and Lady Wyndham, 1520. On the south side of the chancel is a huge pue erected by one of the Wyndhams in the later part of the 17th century.

The font is an octagonal bowl on a panelled shaft; under the bowl foliage and angel figures.

The view on the north side of the church is enchanting over the sea and a richly wooded and undulating landscape. The church stands almost alone on a steep hill above the town of Watchet. In the churchyard is a cross on 3 octagonal steps.

Saltford

50/58–59 St. Mary 21 April, 1850

A small poor church, mostly of debased character, consisting only of a chancel and nave with south porch and west tower. The latter is low and plain without buttresses. The chancel is properly developed, its arch semicircular, but having a keystone on the south of the chancel. The east window is a single one labeled. The other windows are square-headed and later. On the south a vestry has been added and there is a square recess in the wall. The porch has a stone seat and a small benatura. Without is a round arched door with hood. The font is plain octagon. There is a west gallery.

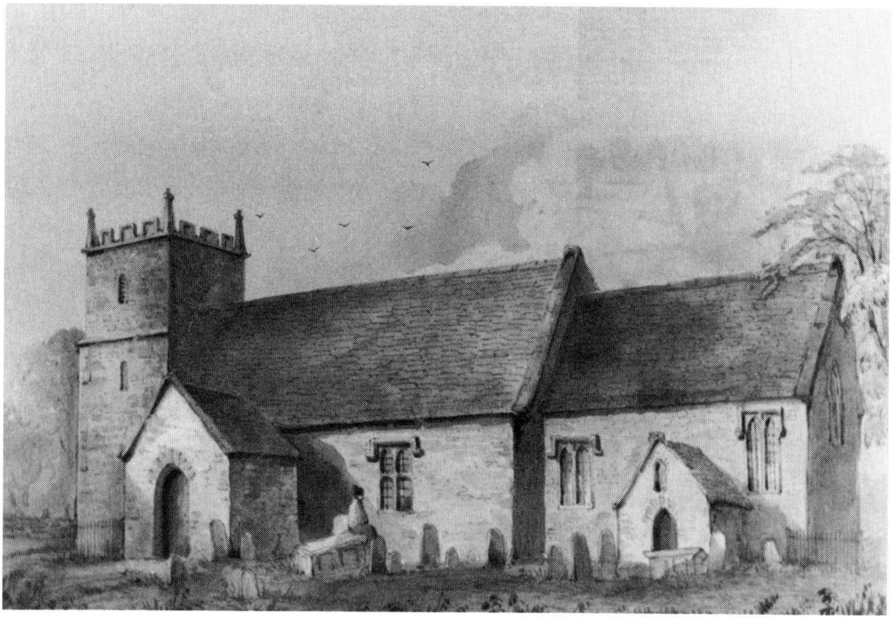

Saltford, 1843, by W.W. Wheatley

Selworthy

49/7–8 All Saints Before 1840

This church has a west tower, a nave with aisles and a chancel with a north aisle. The tower is low and embattled and has a small Curvilinear (or Perpendicular?) window of 2 lights on the west side. There is a south porch of 2 storeys with a door having a Tudor arch and the upper storey made into a pew.

The church is principally Rectilinear and the exterior plain and stuccoed. The windows on the south side are very large, of 4 lights with transoms; those

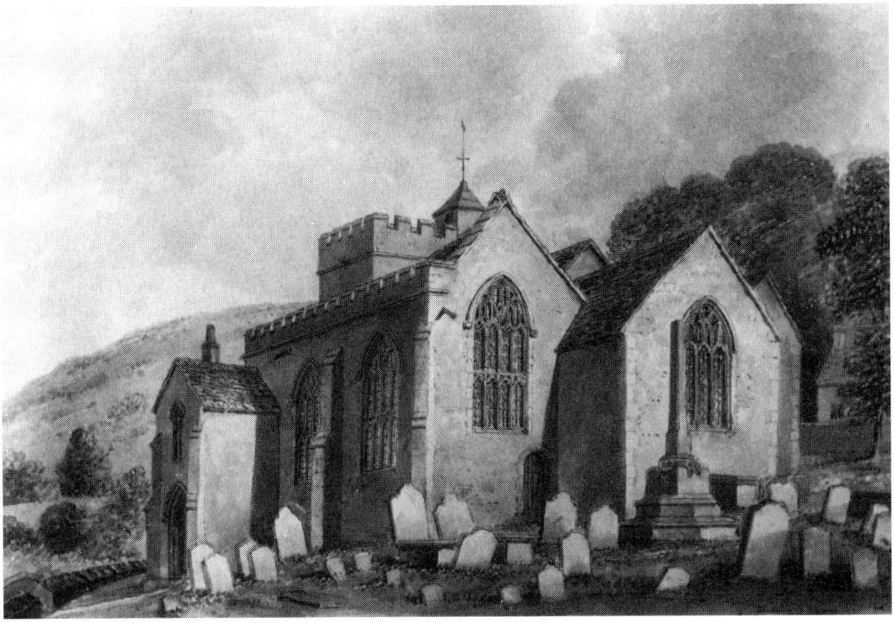

South east view of Selworthy Church, 1839, by J. Buckler

in the north aisle and in the chancel are of 3 lights and smaller. There are 4 pointed arches on each side of the nave, those on the south side having lozenge piers with a shaft at each angle and mouldings carried down the intermediate spaces. The capitals are enriched with fine foliage. The piers on the north side have the capitals very plain. Upon one of the pillars is the following date: Ano dni MVCXXX.

The nave has the roof enriched with wood panelling and bosses and painted blue. That in the south aisle is of richer character with fine panelling and bosses of varied foliage; beneath it runs a cornice with figures of angels bearing shields. The pulpit has Rectilinear carving. In the chancel is a small piscina with a moulded arch. The font is a circular basin standing upon a shaft of the same form.

Shapwick

49/51–52 St. Mary 1842

This church consists of a nave and chancel with a square tower between them which is of plain Perpendicular character with a modern parapet and a stair turret on the north side. The nave is built of the coarse blue stone. The other parts of the church are stuccoed. Most of the windows of the nave are Decorated of 2 lights, but there is one Perpendicular of 3 lights on the south and at the west one of 5 lights. There is a plain south porch. The tower opens

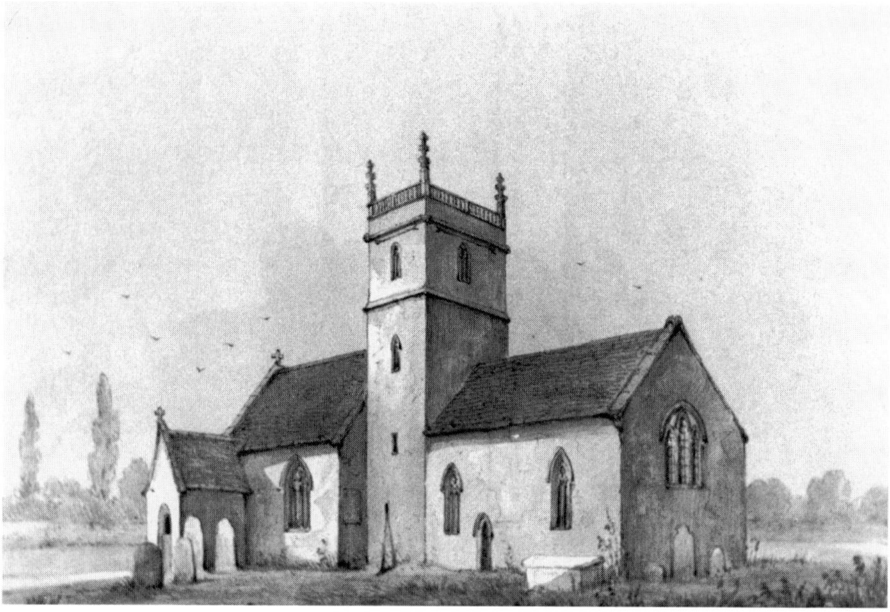

Shapwick, 1843, by W.W. Wheatley

to the nave and chancel by ugly pointed arches and there are small square-headed windows in the lower part of the tower. The roof of both nave and chancel is of waggon form panelled in ribbed compartments. The chancel has side windows of Decorated character and 2 lights. The east window of 3 lights appears Perpendicular. The chancel is full of modern monuments to the family of Strangways. The pulpit is a good plain one of stone with simple panelling and a band with square flowers. The font is a plain octagonal basin on a stem of like form.

Shepton Beauchamp

49/36–37 [St. Michael] 1842

This is an interesting church consisting of a nave with side aisles, a large chancel with a north chapel and a fine tower at the west end. The tower is Rectilinear and of excellent character though not very rich. The battlement is good but the pinnacles are broken. The belfry windows of 2 lights with transom. The west doorway has shields in the spandrels and set between small buttresses with pinnacles. Over it a 4 light window with panelled bands in one of which is a niche containing the statue of a bishop carrying a staff. On the north side is a stair turret.

There are north and south porches; the former is small, but entirely of stone, the roof arched in strong ribs. The south porch is plain with a niche

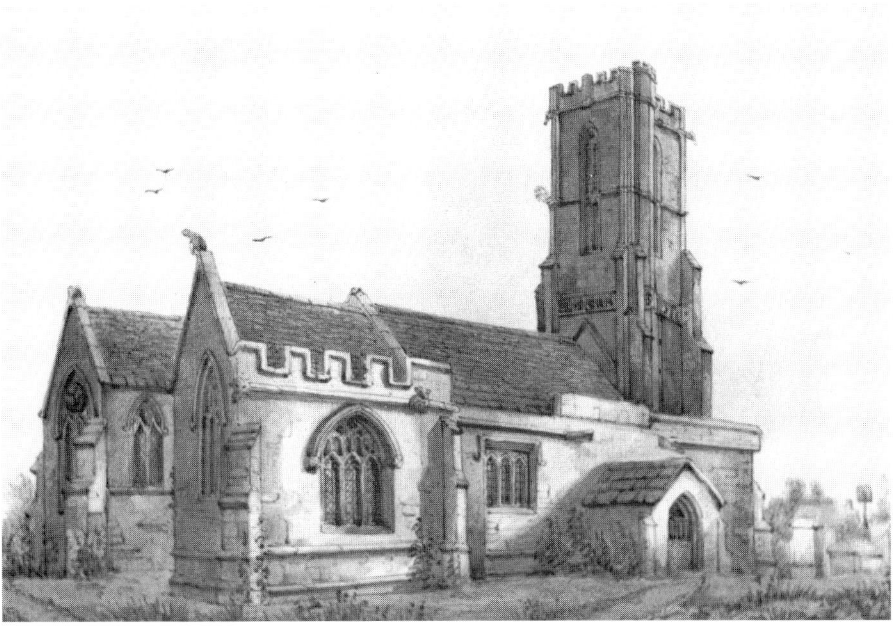

Shepton Beauchamp, 1850, by W.W. Wheatley

over the door containing an image. The body of the church has no battlement except the north chapel of the chancel. The chancel itself has a high tiled roof. The interior of the tower has an extremely fine groined ceiling of stone and is open to the nave by a beautiful lofty arch with panelling and small shafts in the soffit. The effect of this arch, through which the fine groining and west window are seen from the nave is singularly good.

The nave has traces both of Early English and Decorated work. On each side are 3 pointed arches, the piers on the south being octagonal, but the arch nearest the chancel rests upon a half column of circular form. Of the northern piers one is octagonal; one is square with a shaft attached. The south clerestory has square windows of 3 lights. The south aisle is very narrow; the northern is wide and across the south aisle are stone arches. In this aisle the windows are Rectilinear and square-headed. The sills are carried considerably down below the glazing.

The windows at the ends of the aisles are of 2 lights of transition character from Decorated to Rectilinear. The nave has an arched roof ribbed in panels which cuts the chancel arch. In part of the north aisle the ceiling is plain and panelled. The base of the pulpit is of stone and painted. The chancel arch is singularly depressed upon shafts with foliated capitals. The chancel is Decorated of excellent character. The east window of 3 lights, the others of 2, the string course being carried continuously over the south door and sedilia. The sedilia are 3 in number and ascending, the arches with plain mouldings and in the 2 piers between them are small apertures: one in cinquefoil, one in trefoil form. The string is carried over their arches in like form and having

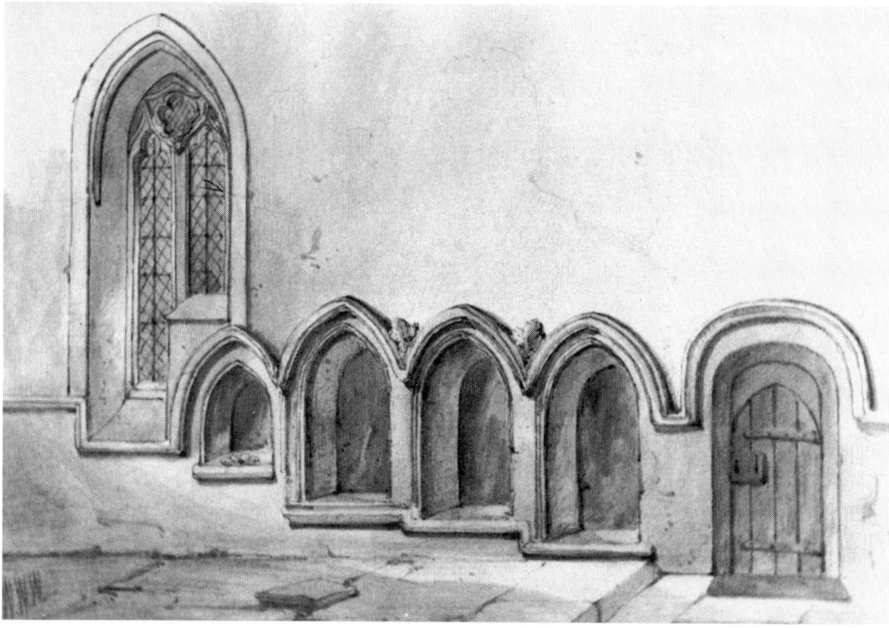

In Shepton Beauchamp Church, 1850, by W.W. Wheatley

small pieces of foliage at the points ranging with the sedilia and eastward of them a smaller niche of like form with a piscina, the orifice of which is in a ballflower set in the centre of a cinquefoil. Part of one of the windows is obscured by the stonework of the sedilia.

The north chapel of the chancel is Rectilinear and opens to the chancel by a panelled arch. Its windows are of 3 lights and that on the east end has considerable portions of stained glass representing late Gothic canopies, etc., as at Kingsbury. There are traces of an altar and on the south side a cinquefoil niche with a piscina. The font is probably Norman; a circular cup with mouldings round the base upon a cylindrical shaft attached to one of the south piers and raised on a step.

(The third arch (next to the chancel) and its pier on the north side are not set in a straight line with the others.)

Shepton Mallet

19/75–77 [St. Peter and St. Paul] Before 1840

The town of Shepton Mallet is 3 miles from [Pilton]. It is populous and ill-built and with narrow streets.

The church is handsome consisting of a nave, side aisles, chancel and transepts equal in height to the aisles, but with a large lofty tower at the west end of good workmanship on which once was a spire, the base of which

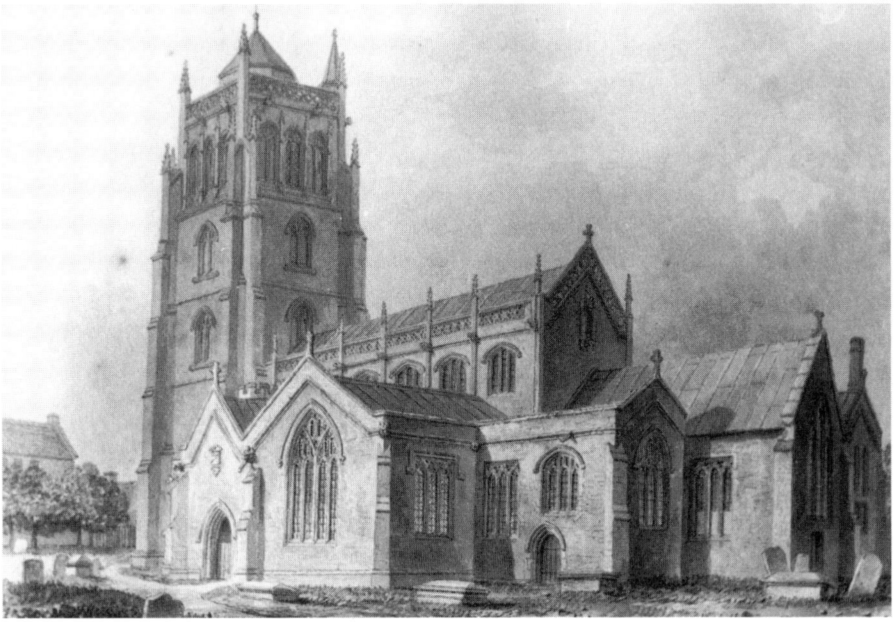

South east view of Shepton Mallet Church, 1833, by J. Buckler

remains. The fault in the external appearance is the large and lofty tower being ill-proportioned to the length of the body. The tower is of good Rectilinear workmanship and divided into 4 stages and crowned by a handsome pierced parapet with 4 crocketed pinnacles at the angles. (On the north side of the tower is an octagonal turret). The upper stages have triple windows with fine stone lattice work. On the west side are 3 niches with rich crocketed canopies containing images of saints. The buttresses are elegantly grouped and their set offs about half way up the tower crowned with large crocketed pinnacles connected to the tower by small flying buttresses which gives the whole a very elegant appearance. The tower has a clock and 8 bells.

The clerestory is high and has a very beautiful open parapet formed of pierced quatrefoils containing pieces of foliage, shields, etc. Between each window in the clerestory is set an elegant crocketed pinnacle. The east gable of the nave is high and enriched with a fine niche with crocketed canopy. The side aisles have a plain parapet with string and heads for spouts. The south porch is good and has a fine groined stone ceiling. The church windows are all Rectilinear: that of the south transept has 4 lights and is very elegant. There are some with square heads and of 3 lights.

The interior of the nave is much disfigured by large galleries. The arches of ye nave are pointed and plain and spring from square piers quite plain, the capitals of which are hidden by ye galleries. The large arches opening to the nave, chancel and transepts are pointed and spring from shafts set at the extremities of plain piers. These shafts have some Early English foliated, some Norman capitals. One shaft rests on a fine bracket. The clerestory windows are of 3 lights but have been mutilated.

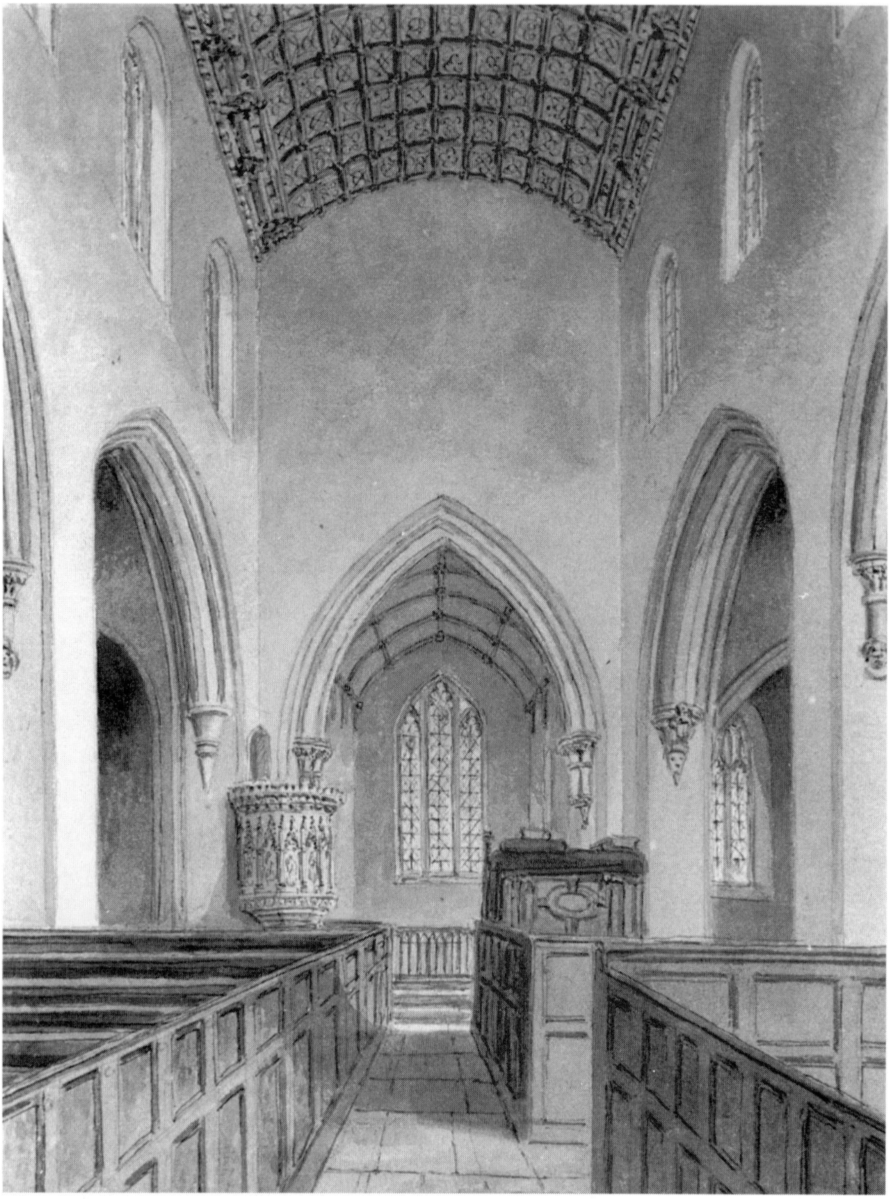

Interior view of Shepton Mallet Church, 1834, by J. Buckler

The ceiling of the nave is a very rich wooden one, finely panelled with beautiful large bosses of foliage and much enriched with figures of angels, etc. The pulpit is of stone and very rich ornamented with a range of fine feathered niches with rich triangular crocketed canopies. Over them, however, is a cornice of Italian work whence it seems probable that it was executed in the 17th century.

The chancel is very much lower than the nave and has side chapels with the ceilings resembling that of the nave. Under 2 windows in the north aisle are placed 2 stone effigies of cross-legged knights in armour, somewhat mutilated. The font is large and plain, of circular form standing on a cylindrical shaft. A large handsome organ is in the western gallery of the nave. The chancel roof is plastered and divided into compartments by wooden ribs having bosses at the intersections.

Somerton

19/45 [St. Michael] 19 October, 1825

From [Huish Episcopi] we went to Somerton, a neat well-built town. The church is a large structure consisting of a nave with side aisles, a north transept, a tower on the south side of the south aisle, which is square below and octagonal above, forming a small south transept, and a chancel. The aisles

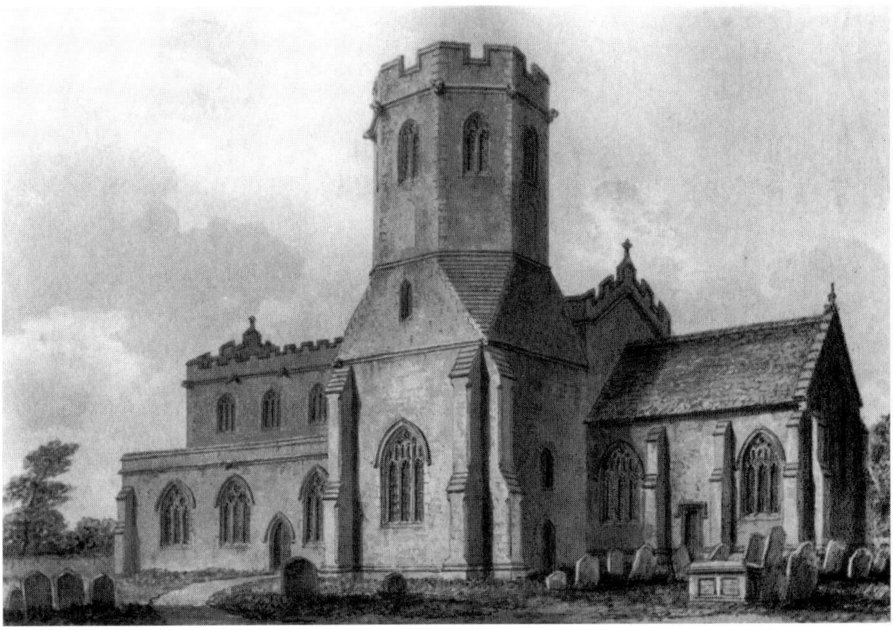

South east view of Somerton Church, 1830, by J. Buckler

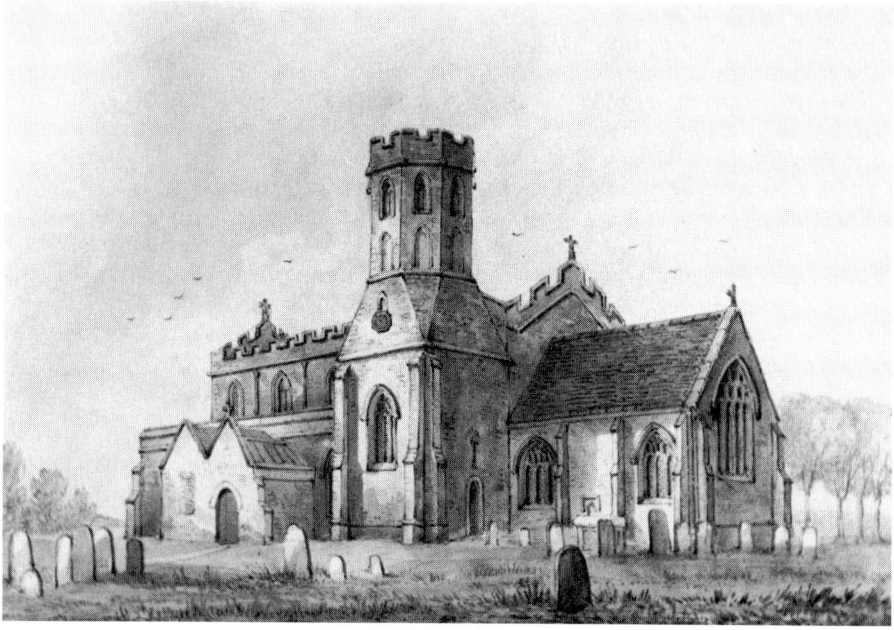

Somerton, 1845, by W.W. Wheatley

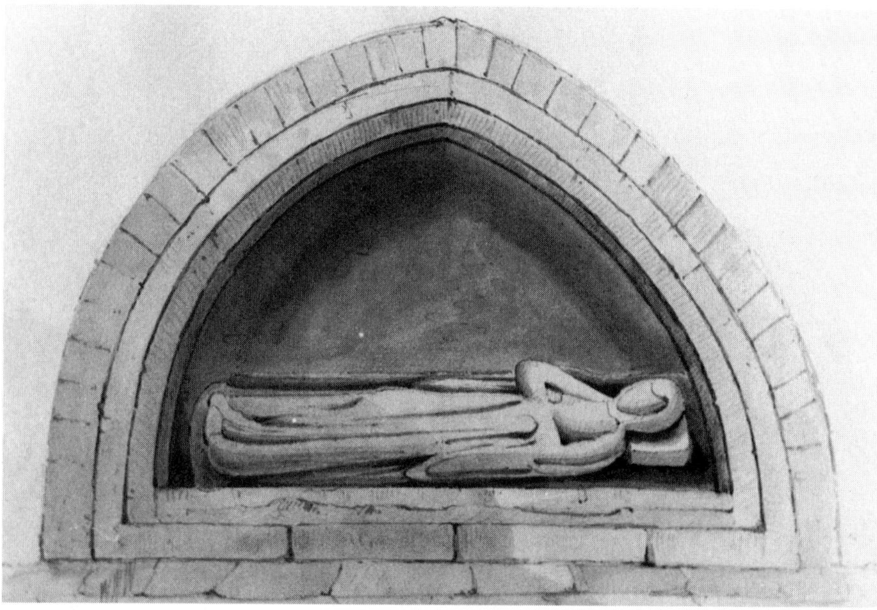

Somerton Church, under the tower, 1845, by W.W. Wheatley

of the nave have some Decorated windows of simple character and 3 lights. The nave is extremely broad; also of considerable height and is divided from the north and south aisles by 4 pointed arches with octagonal piers.

The clerestory has square-headed Perpendicular windows and there are also some of the same description in the aisles of the nave. The roof of the nave is one of the finest that can be seen as a specimen of a timber-roof being richly carved and ornamented with quatrefoils, foliage, grapes, figures and open work. Its effect is singularly rich and beautiful. The tower is octagonal in its upper portion and of plain, early Decorated work. It is divided from the church by a continuous pointed arch. The north transept or chapel has a plain, long Decorated window of 2 lights. The chancel is Perpendicular and has some good windows, the east window of 5 lights. The font is octagonal, panelled and charged with quatrefoils.

(There is one fine specimen of domestic architecture in Somerton of about the age of Henry 7, but only a fragment.)

1849

A fine church, chiefly Decorated with Perpendicular additions. The tower has a lancet on the west side. The south porch very large, but plain. The roof has vineleaf cornices and large dragons above the beams. Some open benches remain with poppyheads. In the tower is the effigy of a female in a whimple. The pulpit has the date 1615 and the altar, which is a fine carved one of wood, with baluster legs, painted and gilt, has the date 1626. Behind it an Italian roodscreen forms now a kind of reredos. There is a western gallery and an organ.

Sparkford

52/6 St. Mary 10 June 1871

This church has a modern nave rebuilt about 1825 in poor modern Gothic style and square transepts have been added north and south. The chancel and tower Perpendicular. The former has an east window of 3 lights. Those north and south have 2 lights and there is a piscina on the south with pointed arch. The chancel arch is Perpendicular on shafts set at intervals. The tower is of the plain Somersetshire kind. Perpendicular with corner buttresses divided by 2 strings into 3 stages; the parapet embattled with 4 pinnacles and gargoyles at the angles. On the north-east is a square turret of some projection, with pinnacles, for the staircase. The west window of 3 lights. In the middle stage is a canopied niche. The belfry window of 2 lights. These in the intermediate stage square-headed and single and cinquefoiled.

(The pulpit is Jacobean. The seats are open. The organ is in the south transept.)

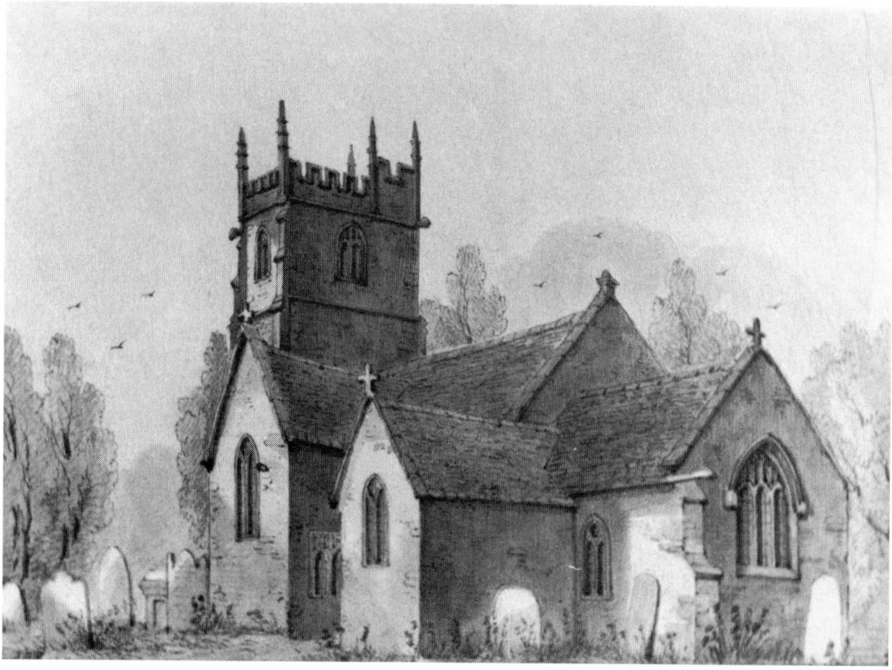

Sparkford, 1847, by W.W. Wheatley

Spaxton

51/73–74 St. Margaret 19 January, 1864

A good church, almost wholly Perpendicular of a fine quality. The plan is nave and chancel each with a south aisle, a lofty west tower and a vestry to the north of the chancel, south porch. The north side, being comparatively little seen, is much plainer than the south being of inferior stone and without parapet.

The whole of the south side has a fine parapet of pierced panelling, each pierced compartment having a shield in the centre. The roof has a ridge crest. The south porch is large and of 2 storeys with battlement and good gable. In the angle is a large embattled turret of octagonal form. The outer doorway has good continuous arch mouldings.

The tower is lofty and of excellent stone masonry with battlement, 4 pinnacles and corner buttresses and an octagonal stair turret at the north-east. It has 2 string courses, belfry windows of 2 lights, square-headed double windows in the next stage and on the west a 3 light window and doorway with deep arch mouldings and hood upon crowned and mitred head corbels.

The tower arch to the nave is lofty upon shafts. The nave is divided

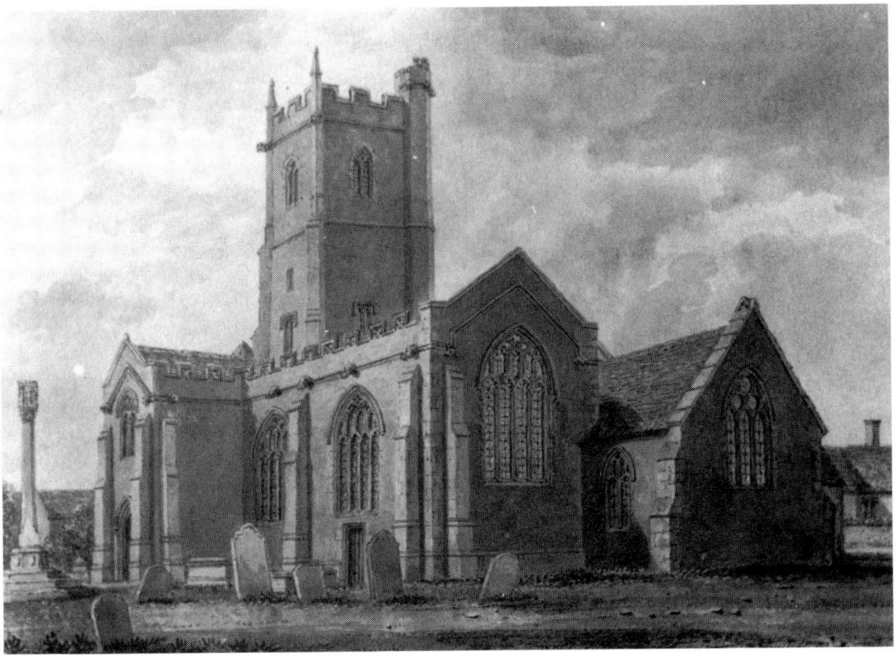

South east view of Spaxton Church, 1840, by J. Buckler

from the aisle by 3 large Perpendicular arches with light piers of the accustomed lozenge form with shafts and intermediate mouldings down the piers. The south aisle is wide and has a coved roof with ribs and bosses. The windows of the nave and aisle are Perpendicular, mostly with shafts and of 3 lights.

There is a pointed arch between the south aisle of the nave and that of the chancel. The chancel arch is wide and pointed upon imposts. The chancel is lower than the nave and has some earlier work. The east window is transitional from Early English to Decorated of 3 lights with 3 circles in the head and on the north is a Perpendicular 2 light window. The aisle opens to the chancel by 2 rather small arches on piers of unusual make, plainer than in the nave and the shafts having octagonal capitals with scrolls.

On the north side is a vestry divided off by a fine Perpendicular tomb having a rich canopy within the thickness of the wall and opening on each side, enriched with foliations and spandrels. The tomb itself is panelled with a range of ogee niches containing shields. It bears the effigies of a knight and lady. The canopy is undergroined and the side next the vestry is richest. There is also a doorway corresponding to the tomb and opening into the vestry. The seats are all open and have good carved ends, partly old, partly new. The font has a plain octagonal bowl. The organ is in the tower.

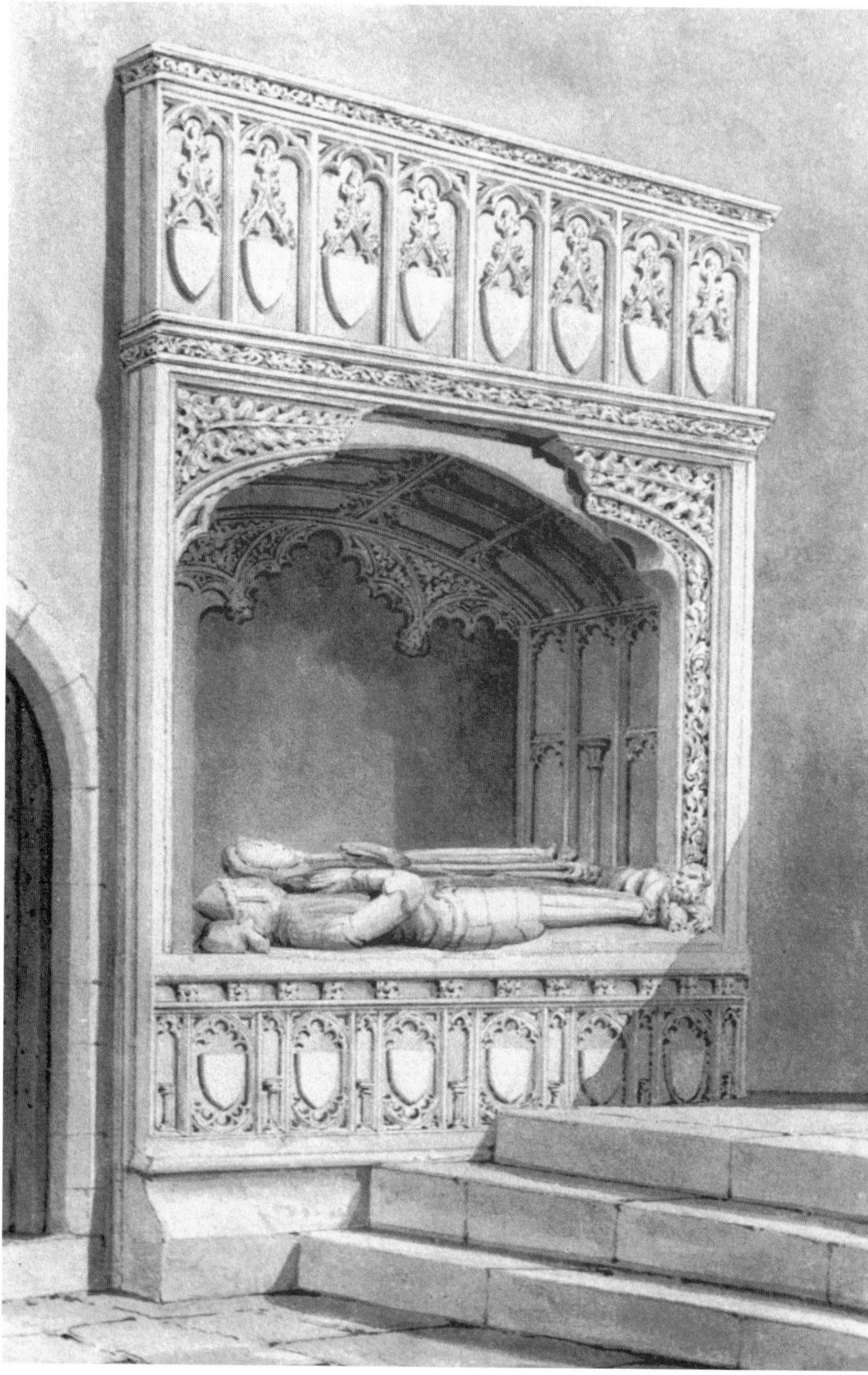

Monument in Spaxton Church, 1840, by J. Buckler

Stanton Drew

51/71–72 St. Mary May 21, 1863

A church of irregular plan with rather poor details mostly late Perpendicular. The plan is nave with south aisle, chancel with south chapel, tower on north of nave forming a porch in its lower part and a chapel or aisle added to the east of the tower. To make the outline still odder a porch is added to the north side of the tower.

The nave has an arcade of 5 Perpendicular arches on piers with octagonal clustered shafts having capitals and bases. There is a pointed arch opening to the tower on the north and one also into the north chapel from the nave. Also one from the chancel to the south chapel and from the latter into the south aisle of the nave. The windows are all Perpendicular, mostly of 3 lights, but some in the south aisle of 4. The east window of the chancel has 4 lights and odd late tracery.

The whole church has a smart modernised air and the roofs seem to have been renewed. The windows on the north of the chancel are closed. There is an organ and new regular pues. There is a piscina and a transomed 2 light window in the north chapel which looks early Edwardian.

The porch has a good inner doorway with ogee arch and fair mouldings; the

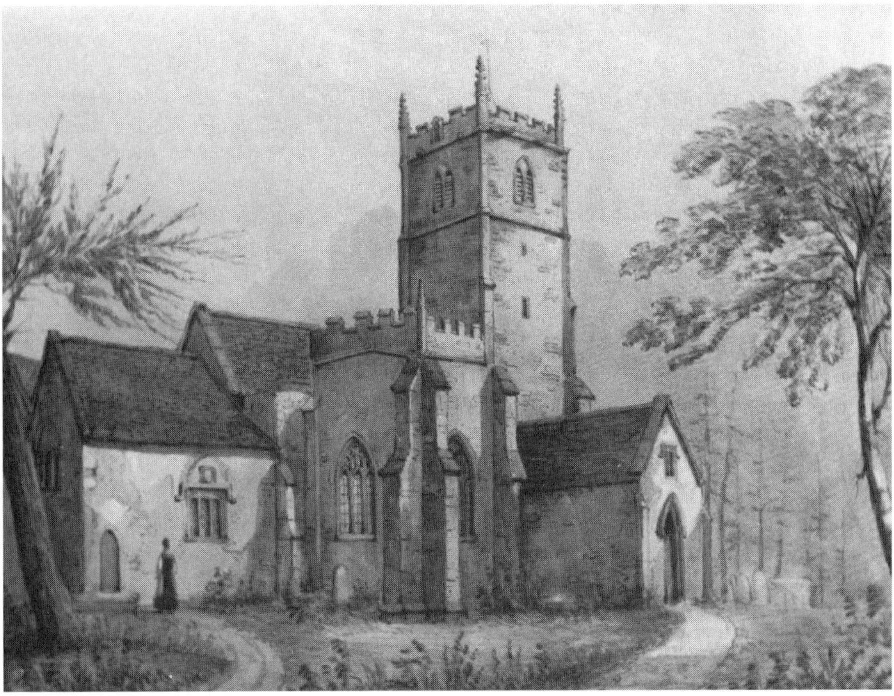

Stanton Drew, 1843, by W.W. Wheatley

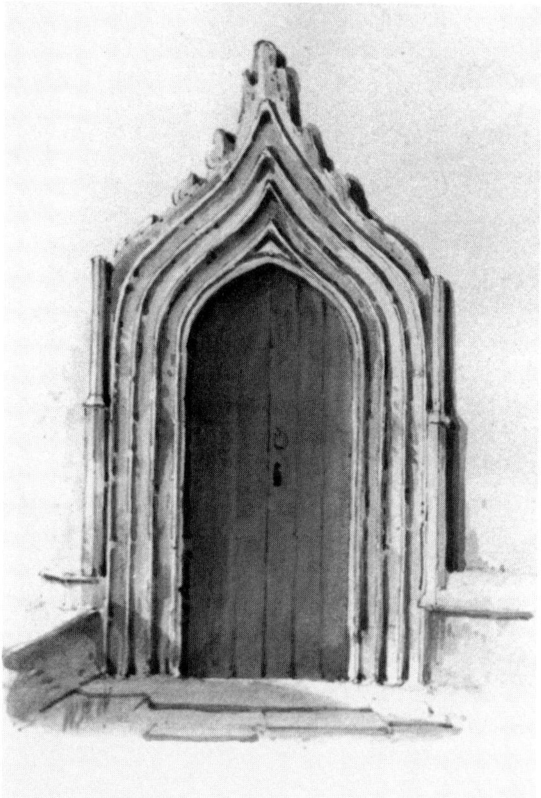

Entrance within the porch, Stanton Drew Church, 1843, by W.W. Wheatley

outer doorway has continuous arch mouldings. The tower is embattled with 4 crocketed pinnacles and buttresses at the angles, gargoyles, belfry windows of 2 lights, very plain. Under the belfry windows a string course. The north chapel of the chancel is embattled and panelled externally. The font has a circular bowl on a stem of like form.

Stanton Prior

52/20 St. Laurence 3 February, 1872

The church has nave and chancel, north porch and west tower, mostly Perpendicular, but the chancel has north and south some lancets with trefoil heads. Most of the other windows are square-headed and labeled. The outer doorway of the porch is rude and pointed. Near the inner door is a stoup and over it a niche. The tower is a good Perpendicular one with embattled parapet and an octagonal stair turret on the north rising above it. The west window is a good one and below it is a door. The belfry windows of 2 lights have the stone pierced lattice work.

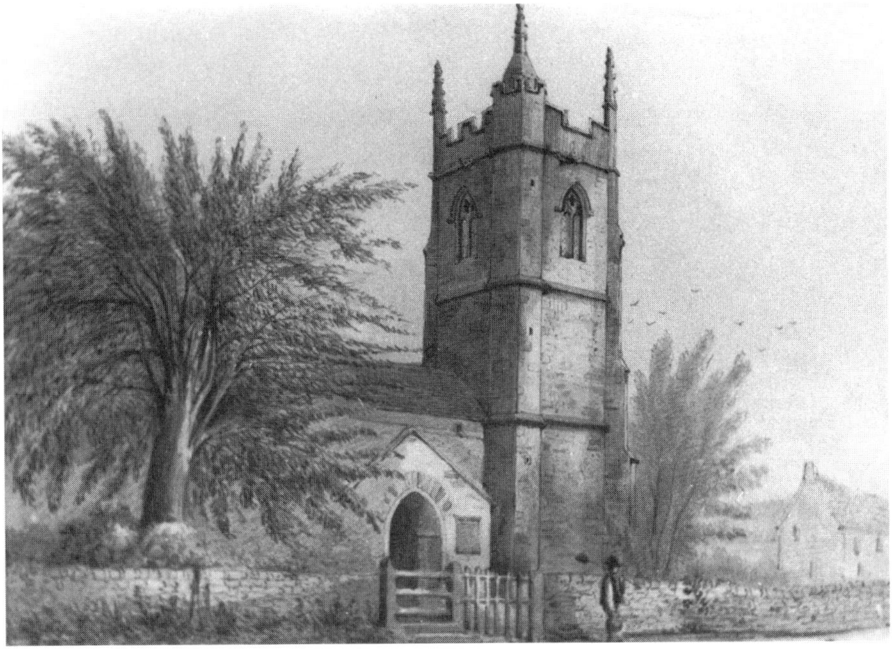

Stanton Prior, 1843, by W.W. Wheatley

Staplegrove

50/32–33 St. John April, 1845

This church has a nave with north aisle, a chancel with south aisle extending along part of the nave and a low tower at the west end of the south aisle and forming in its lower storey a porch. The tower is small and undivided by string courses, of rather indefinite character but having a plain slit on the south side and belfry windows of 2 lights. The parapet is embattled, the buttresses small. The entrance of the porch by a plain pointed doorway and within it is another rather loftier door. A modern addition has been made at the west end and the whole church has suffered in a great degree from bad modern alterations.

Some windows may be Decorated, others Perpendicular, but none of good or remarkable character. The original arches between the nave and north aisle have been removed and replaced by 2 wide ill-shaped modern ones. The chancel is very low and rather mean. The chancel arch is obtuse and very plain and a very similar one opens from the nave to the south chapel. The latter opens to the chancel by a very low obtuse arch with a large and plain pier. This is of uncertain date and may be either very late or very early. The windows of the chancel are very late and square-headed without foils. The font has a small octagonal bowl.

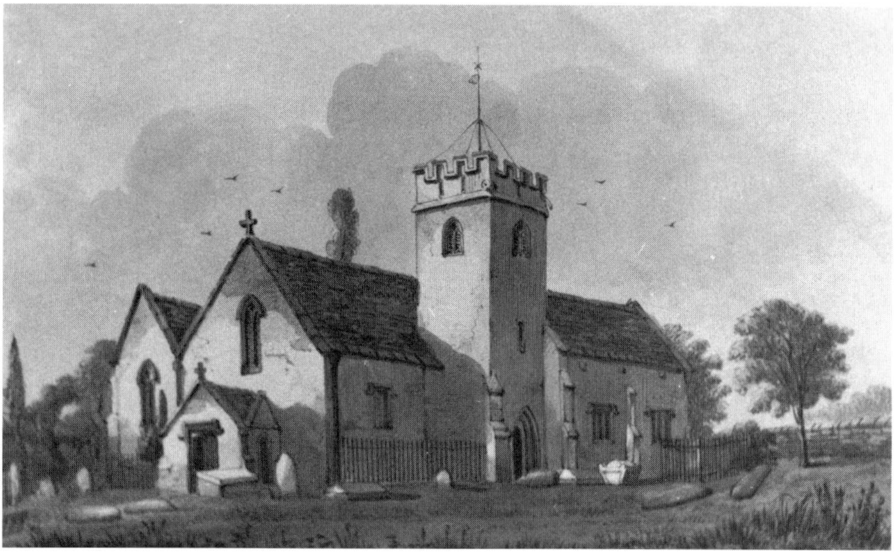

Staplegrove, 1848, by W.W. Wheatley

Stogumber

49/74–75 [St. Mary] 1843

This is a large church, chiefly Perpendicular but with traces of earlier work and consisting of a nave and chancel, each with side aisles, a north porch and south porch and a square tower at the west end of the south aisle. The whole is externally covered with stucco.

The tower is of 3 stages, plain and rather tapering towards the top with a large coarse square turret near the north-west angle. The buttresses angular; the belfry window and another window on the west side of 2 lights and ordinary; the battlement extremely simple. There is at its north-west angle a huge gargoyle in the shape of a fish. The south porch has a battlement and large gargoyles. The north porch is larger but open to the roof undivided by a floor. The outer door has good arch mouldings, the interior doorway with the arch on octagonal shafts.

The north side of the nave is far more enriched than the south and has a battlement panelled with quatrefoils containing shields and small pinnacles. The windows good of 3 lights. The south side of the nave has square-headed windows of 3 lights but no parapet. The south chapel of the chancel has parapet embattled and pierced with quatrefoils and adorned with small pinnacles.

The west gable of the nave and north aisle are pointed and have very good mouldings. The former has a Perpendicular window of 4 lights; the latter one of 3 lights. Part of the north aisle is cleared from stucco. On the north side of the nave is the common octagonal stair turret corresponding with the roodloft.

The interior is spacious. The nave is divided from the north aisle by 5 elegant moulded arches, the piers having 4 shafts and general capitals of foliage mixed with angels bearing shields. On the south of the nave are 4

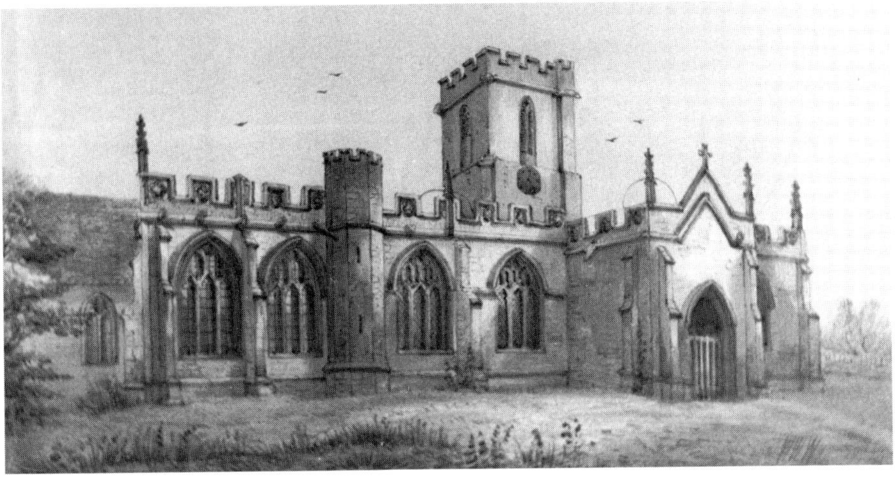

Stogumber Church, 1850, by W.W. Wheatley

arches of which the western most in the tower is very wide but closed; then comes a very wide pier and the next arch is low and ill-formed with an octagonal pillar east of it. The other 2 arches are of good Perpendicular character with light piers of continuous moulding and shafts.

The chancel arch is wide and moulded springing immediately from the wall. The south aisle extends to the east of the chancel and is divided from it by 3

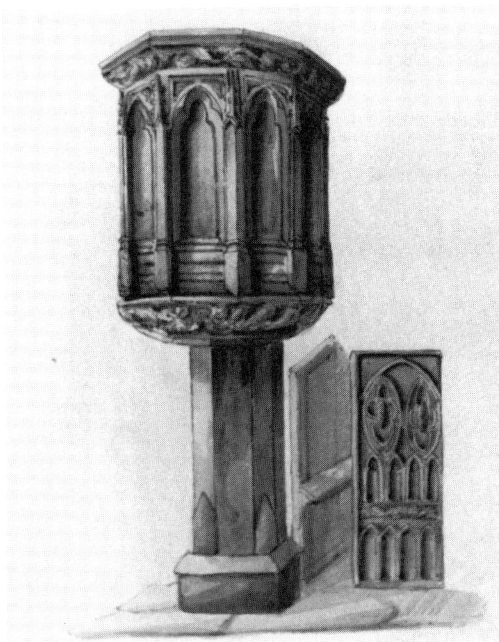

In Stogumber Church, 1850, by W.W. Wheatley

arches similar to the 2 eastern ones of the nave. The north aisle is not continued quite to the east end and opens to the chancel by 2 late pointed arches the pier of which has a general capital of foliage and is cunningly perforated by an arched opening as is also the north pier of the chancel arch.

The east window of the chancel is Perpendicular of 4 lights. In the eastern arch on the south is a large Italian tomb inserted. There is no clerestory. The pulpit is of stone with good panelling and pinnacles at the angles; a fine foliated band. The nave is almost wholly fitted up with ancient open benches, most of which are enriched with fine sculpture, foliage, niches and tracery and the monogram IHC. In the south wall of the nave is a trefoil niche. The font is octagonal panelled with quatrefoils.

Stoke, North

52/2 St. Martin 9 June, 1871

A small, uninteresting church almost wholly debased in style and with scarcely any original features. It has nave and chancel with south porch and west tower. The tower is low with plain parapet and 4 pinnacles. An inscription records it having been built in 1737. The chancel arch is pointed, but rather obtusely and is of doubtful character, very plain and upon simple imposts. The chancel is long in proportion to the nave and, the ground rising considerably towards

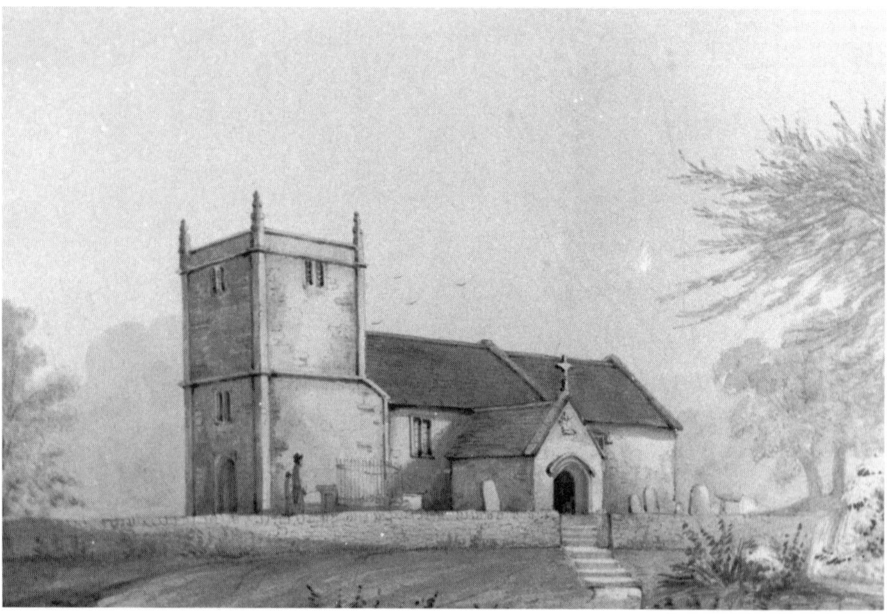

North Stoke Church, 1843, by W.W. Wheatley

the east, there is a great ascent in the chancel. The chancel has some double lancets on the south which look modern and the east window is certainly modern. There are no windows on the north of the nave; on the south they are late, square-headed of 2 lights with arch or foil. (The roof is covered with stone tiles.)

Stoke, South

51/65–66 St. James 26 May, 1863

The church consists of a nave with south aisle, chancel, western tower and north porch. The aisle was added to the original plan in 1845 when the church was otherwise repaired and refitted.

The north wall is old as also the tower. The porch is flagged with stone and within it is a fine and enriched Norman doorway. The door has a square head and the tympanum of the arch has some fret work and flowered mouldings. The outer moulding of the arch has some scroll work. The arch moulding has rich chevron ornament and the shafts have very fine and varied mouldings, one fretty, one with beaded lozenges containing pieces of foliage and the capitals have square abaci.

The windows are mostly new Decorated insertions. The arcade has 3 pointed arches on octagonal columns. The seats low and uniform with poppy heads; a new stone pulpit. The font has octagonal bowl on a stem and there is

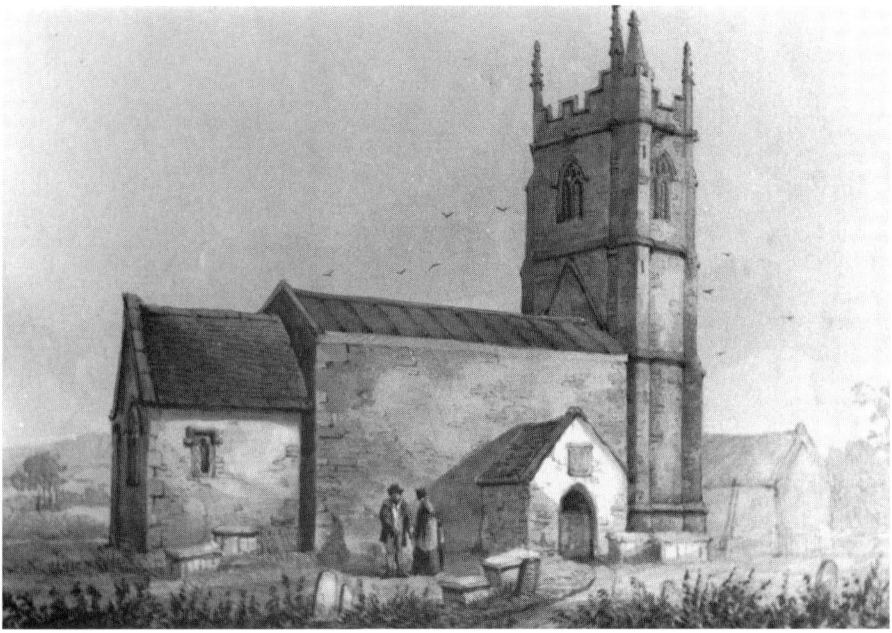

South Stoke, 1843, by W.W. Wheatley

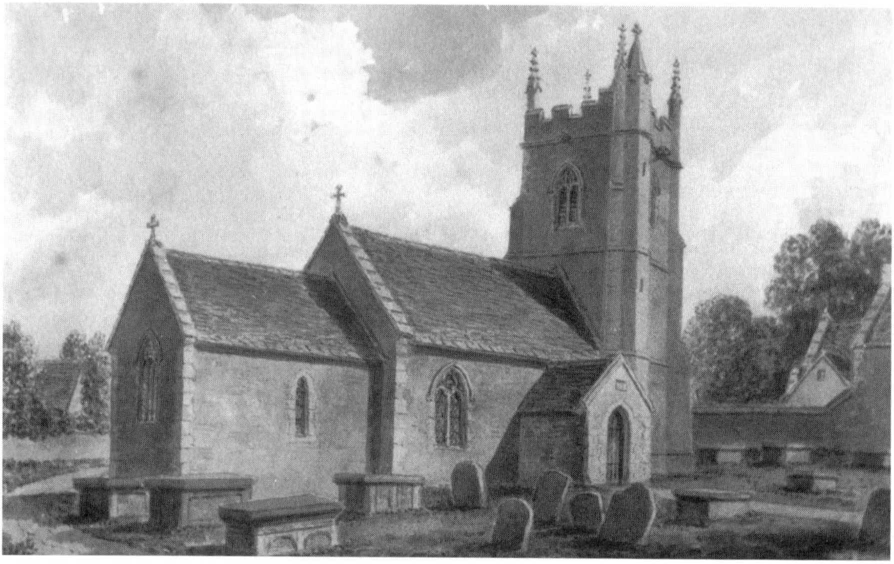

North east view of South Stoke Church, 1847, by J. Buckler

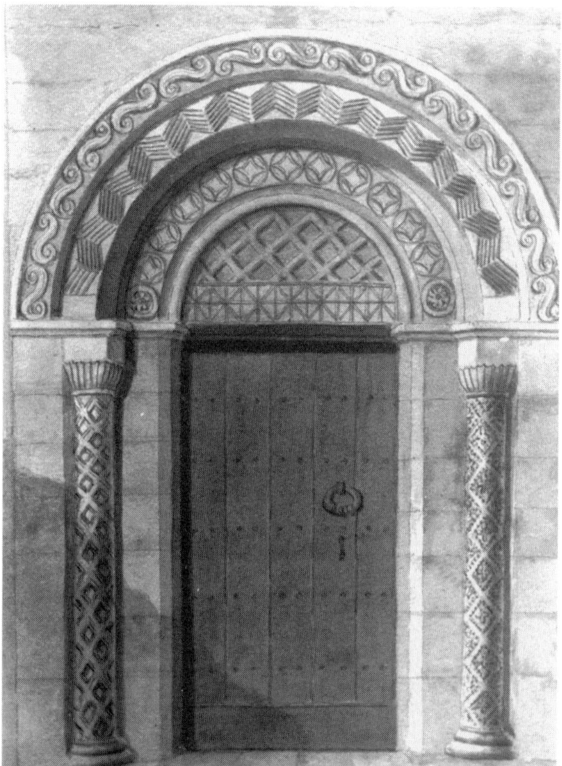

North door way, South Stoke, 1847, by J. Buckler

an organ at the east end of the south aisle. The original flagged roof is retained. The tower is late Perpendicular; its arch to the nave has continuous mouldings. The tower is low, has embattlement and crocketed pinnacles; at one angle the stair turret rises into a higher and ogee-headed top; the buttresses at the angles. There is one string course. The belfry windows of 2 lights have the pierced stone lattice work often seen in Somersetshire. The west window of 2 lights has a Decorated look and there is no doorway.

Stoke St. Mary

50/94–95 12 February, 1857

The church is small and externally uninviting being covered with roughcast and having a very modern look. It has only a chancel and nave with west tower. The whole is chiefly Perpendicular but perhaps the tower may be earlier as it is very plain and low without buttresses and only slit-like, narrow openings. The parapet is embattled.

The north porch is very plain. There is one 2 light Decorated window on the south, the other windows Perpendicular, of 2 lights. There is no chancel arch. To the tower a low, pointed arch over which appears internally the mark showing the original pitch of the roof. The roofs are now coved and modernised with plaster. The interior is neat and the chancel carefully kept. The churchyard is large and in it a large yew tree surrounded by a bench.

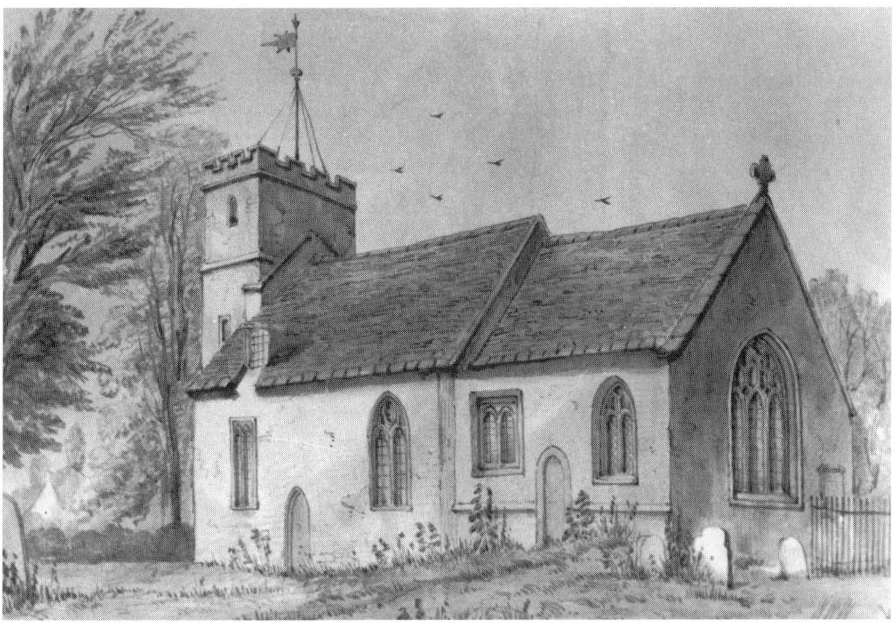

Stoke St. Mary, 1848, by W.W. Wheatley

Stoke sub Hamdon

49/43–45 St. Mary Before 1840

A cruciform church having a tower forming the north transept and a large north porch exhibiting several portions of Norman and Early English work as well as some of later character. There are doorways north and south of the nave of Norman character; that on the south has shafts with spiral mouldings, but the upper part has been mutilated to make way for the insertion of a large Rectilinear window. On the north there are fine shafts of octagonal form, one enriched with a scale ornament, one with a series of small squares charged with a kind of nail-headed pattern but not in relief. One of the capitals has something resembling feathers.

The north porch is large and has a groined stone ceiling so low as to cut off the upper part of the arch of the doorway. The groining has strong plain ribs crossing, springing from grotesque heads as corbels. There is an odd side door in the thickness of the wall leading to the staircase to the parvise which is lighted by a good Decorated window of 3 lights above which is a high peaked gable. There are also various small windows about the porch. In the north wall is seen a piece of rude sculpture representing St. George and the Dragon and under a window on the same side is a singular projection with a piece of foliage and over it a cross. The nave has a good battlement of late date and constructed of fine stone. The tower has a good battlement below which are corbels representing fabulous animals etc. The belfry windows are double Early English lancets with very fine mouldings and on the west side is a

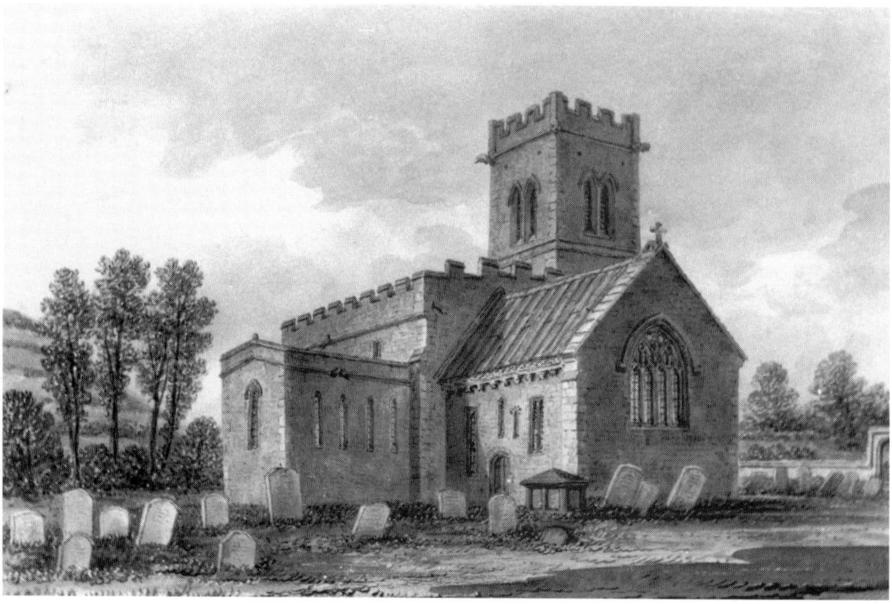

South east view of Stoke sub Hamdon Church, 1835, by J. Buckler

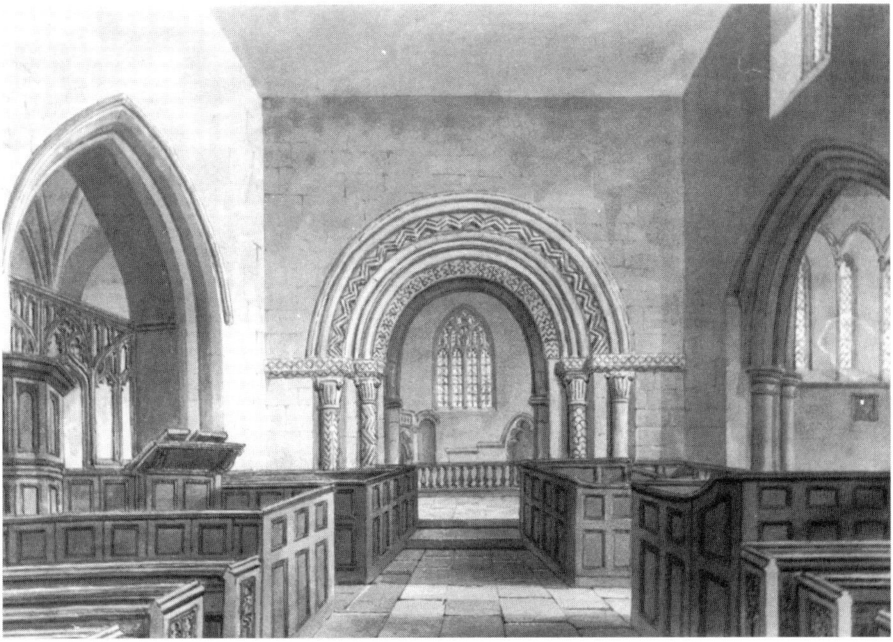

Interior view of Stoke sub Hamdon Church, 1835, by J. Buckler

Rectilinear window of 3 lights. The tower has a staircase turret on the east side but no buttresses. The chancel is covered with stone slate of the country, and below the roof is a corbel table of heads and billets, decidedly Early English in character, set under a band of embattled ornament.

The arch from the body of the tower is Early English upon imposts and across it is a fine stone screen with elegant open panelling and a band of quatrefoils. The tower has a plain stone groined ceiling, apparently Early English, with strong ribs merely crossing, springing from foliated brackets and being without a boss. The west window of the nave is Decorated of 5 lights and rather early tracery. One on the south is Rectilinear and 2 other opposite windows are single lights rather elegantly foiled, perhaps of a transition character from Early English to Decorated. In the nave are several carved open seats. The arch to the south transept springs from shafts which appear almost of Decorated character, but has on its east and west windows a range of 4 lancet windows set so close as to have between them the very smallest intervals and the dripstones upon heads. Within the transept is a large niche with feathering and supported on shafts, containing a projecting shelf. The lower part is hidden by a lumbering pew. In the transept is also a monumental effigy beneath a fine feathered arch.

The chancel arch is Norman and extremely rich as well as in excellent preservation. It has 5 orders of moulding in which appear the roller, the chevron and the flat nail-head. The capitals of the shafts have rude foliage and an abacus of lozengy work. The chancel has on each side three windows mostly lancets. On the south are two single lancets (one of which is trefoiled) and one double lancet set within an obtuse arch almost of trefoil form, rising from shafts. On the north are two lancets foiled, and one very small Decorated window of 2 lights set within a trefoil arch.

The east window is Rectilinear of 4 lights with a little stained glass. In the south-east angle is a large, bold cinquefoiled niche with good mouldings, set obliquely and containing a double piscina. On the south of the chancel arch is the common transom opening from the transept towards the altar. The font is cylindrical upon steps, surrounded by two bands with the rope and lozenge ornament, clearly Norman.

Stowell

51/80–81 St. Mary 8 February, 1864

A small, mean church, mutilated and modernised, consisting of only a small nave and chancel, undivided, south porch and low west tower. The ceiling is flat and the windows all modernised. The tower is modernised at the top but the lower part is poor Perpendicular having a stair turret at the north-east, corner buttresses and doorway with continuous arch mouldings. The tower arch to the nave has also continuous mouldings. The church is in a lonely site amongst the meadows but near it is a fine old mansion house of excellent stone masonry of 15th century [date] and covered with ivy.

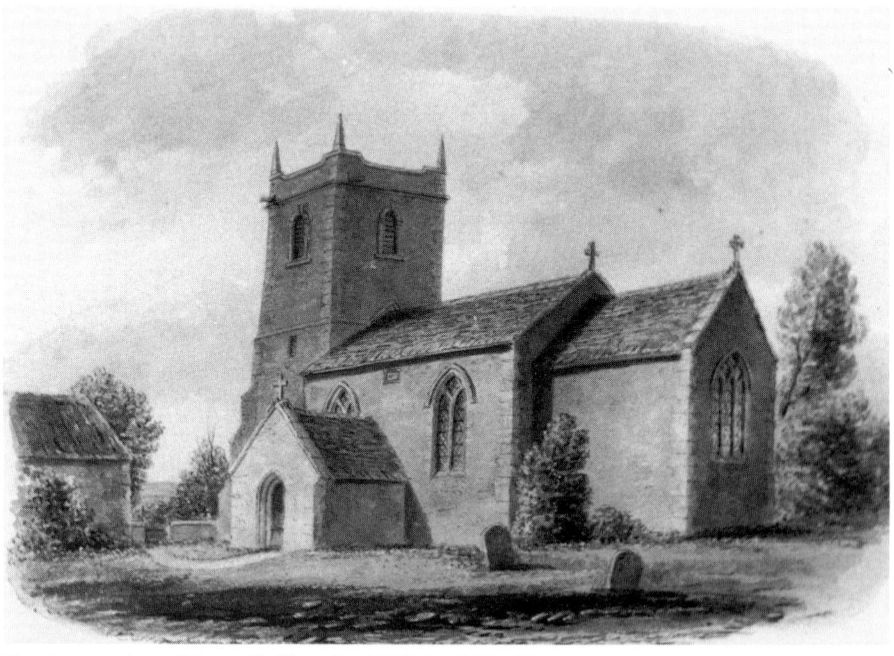

South east view of Stowell Church, 1843, by J. Buckler

Street

19/65–66 [Holy Trinity] Before 1830

The village of Street is situated at the junction of the roads from Glastonbury, Somerton and Bridgewater and is distant a mile and a half from Glastonbury.

The church is built of stone common in the neighbourhood, of a bluish-grey colour. It is not a large structure but stands within a burying ground of very great extent. It consists only of a nave and chancel without aisles and a tower at the west end. The tower is of Rectilinear work but of plain workmanship without any battlement and has belfry windows with square heads and of 2 lights. It contains six bells and is separated from the church by a pointed arch springing from octagonal shafts.

The south porch is large, but quite plain. On the north side of the nave is a curious doorway which, if genuine, appears to be of very early date being very high and extremely narrow, the arch just pointed and springing from rude imposts. The windows of the nave are Rectilinear with good tracery but having no dripstones.

The chancel opens to the nave by a pointed arch and has on each side 2 Curvilinear windows of 3 lights. In these are scraps of painted glass. On the south side of the altar are 2 good stone stalls with ogee canopies ornamented with crockets of a very small size and with feathering. There is also a piscina with a canopy of the same and flanked by elegant small buttresses and resting upon a bracket charged with the ballflower ornament peculiar to the

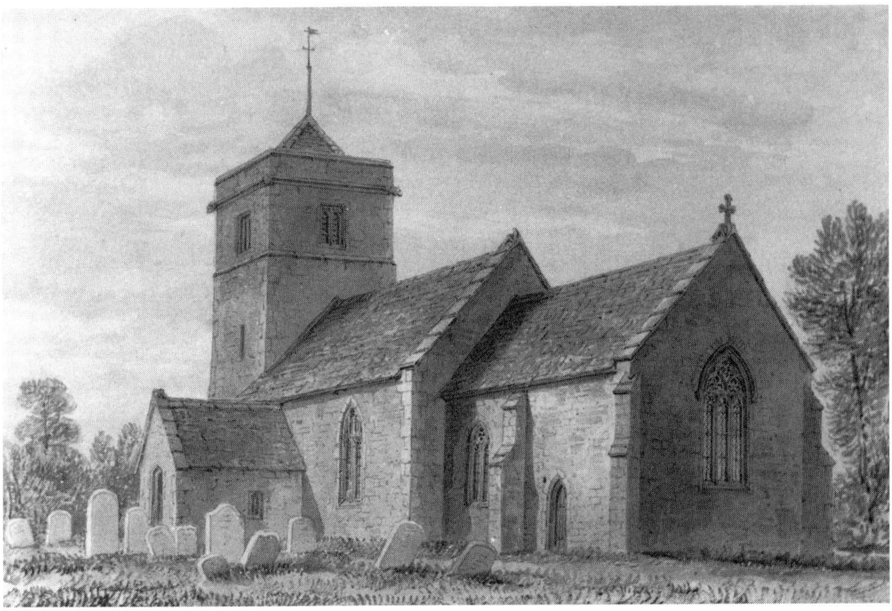

South east view of Street Church, 1834, by J. Buckler

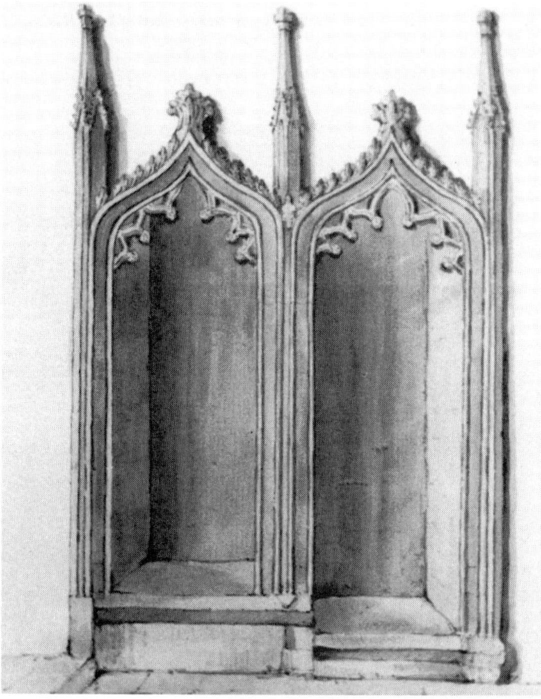

Street Church, in the chancel, 1845, by W.W. Wheatley

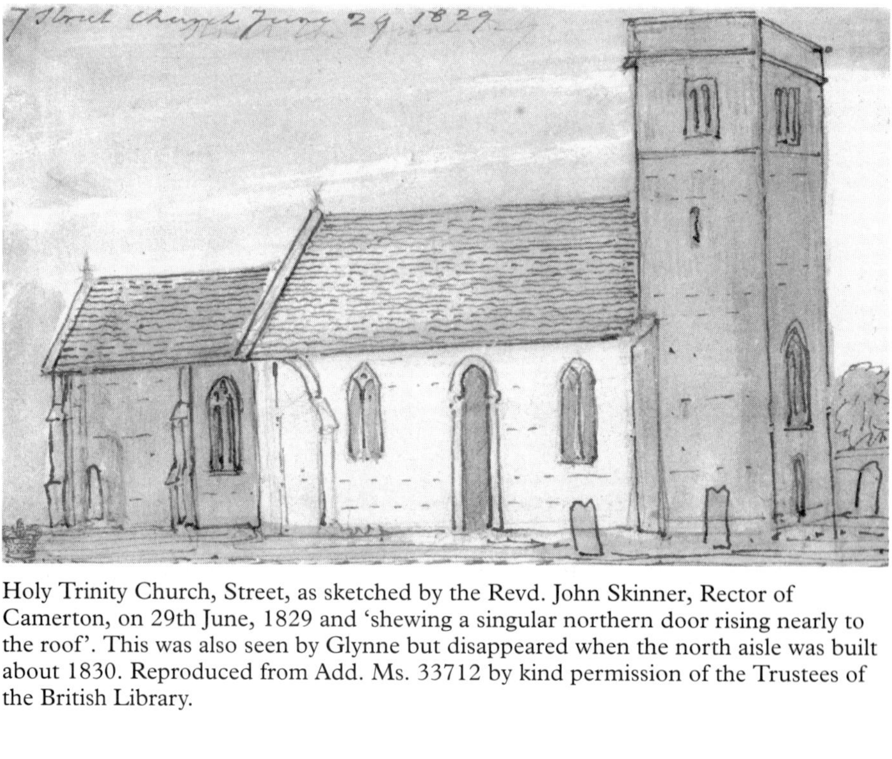

Holy Trinity Church, Street, as sketched by the Revd. John Skinner, Rector of Camerton, on 29th June, 1829 and 'shewing a singular northern door rising nearly to the roof'. This was also seen by Glynne but disappeared when the north aisle was built about 1830. Reproduced from Add. Ms. 33712 by kind permission of the Trustees of the British Library.

Curvilinear style. The church is kept neat. The pulpit is an ordinary one but rests on a stone bracket. The font is octagonal without ornament.

(A north aisle was added to the nave of Street church about 1830 with Perpendicular windows and a range of ungraceful flat arches. At a later period the church was also very considerably improved. The nave received a new open roof and the original fine timber roof of the chancel, hidden by a flat ceiling, was opened and restored. The whole church fitted up with open benches (pues being all abolished), the sedile in the church restored and the east window and 2 others in the church filled with fine stained glass, all the gifts of individuals.)

Sutton Bingham

51/36–37 [All Saints] 5 May, 1860

A small church of early work and little altered and presenting an uncommon specimen in this county where so little of early work is seen except in fragments and portions of churches.

There is only a small chancel and nave without aisles and with a north porch. On the south of the nave is one narrow Norman window and one trefoil lancet. On the north a similar Norman window and a single lancet. The west window is Decorated, of 2 lights, and over it, just below the gable are 2 lancet open arches (clearly original) in which hang 2 bells.

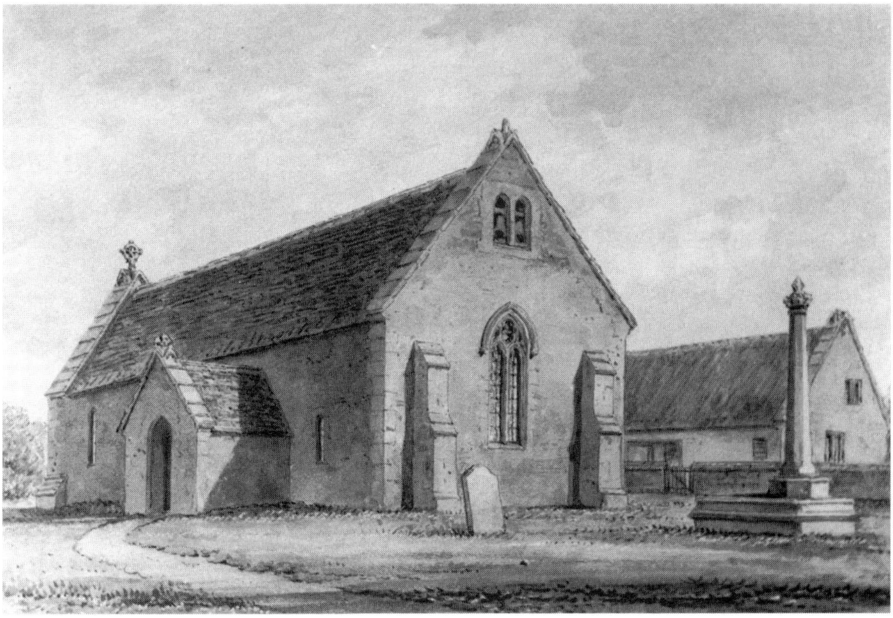

North west view of Sutton Bingham Church, 1838, by J. Buckler

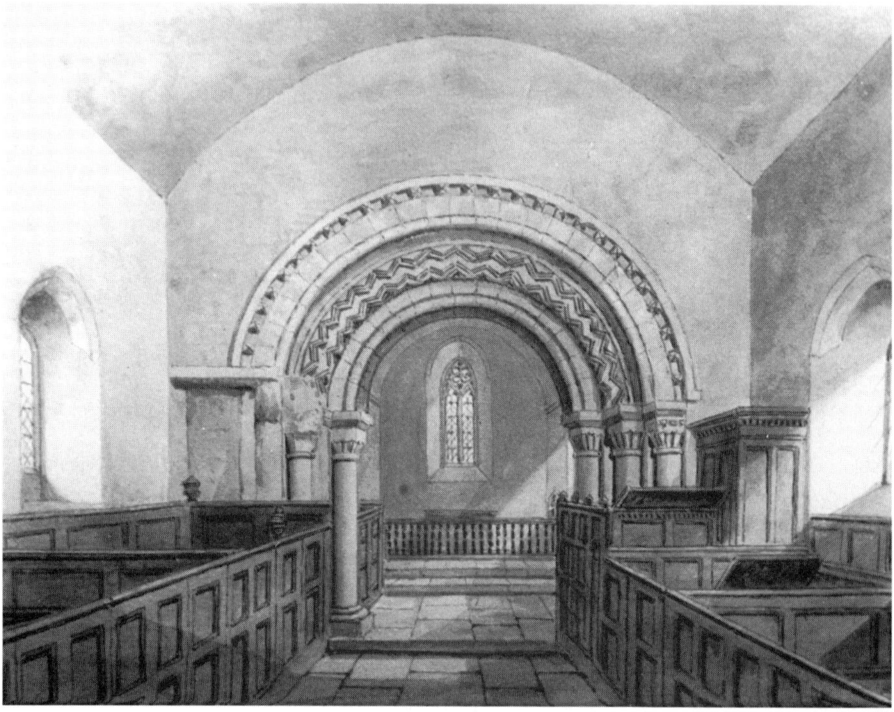

Interior view of Sutton Bingham Church, 1838, by J. Buckler

The chancel arch is Norman; semi-circular, small and low surrounded with much solid walling. On its west face are chevron mouldings, a nail-headed hood moulding and 3 orders of shafts. The eastern face is ruder and less ornamental. North of the chancel is one lancet window having the trefoil rear arch seen in Somersetshire. South of the chancel, 2 trefoil-headed lancets. The east window verging from Early English to Decorated, of 2 lights, with circle over them within an arch.

The font has a circular bowl on octagonal stem; cable moulding round the base of the bowl. Over the north door within the porch is a bracket for a statue. Over the east gable a floriated cross. In the churchyard the shaft of a cross set on what resembles an ancient tomb. The public path is on the north side.

Sutton, Long

49/31–32 Holy Trinity 1836

This is . . . a fine Rectilinear church of the kind so common in Somerset and seems to have no admixture of any other style. The tower is richer than at Curry and has four regular stages; has a good doorway, with label and bold foliage in the spandrels, set between 2 small niches over which is a 5 light

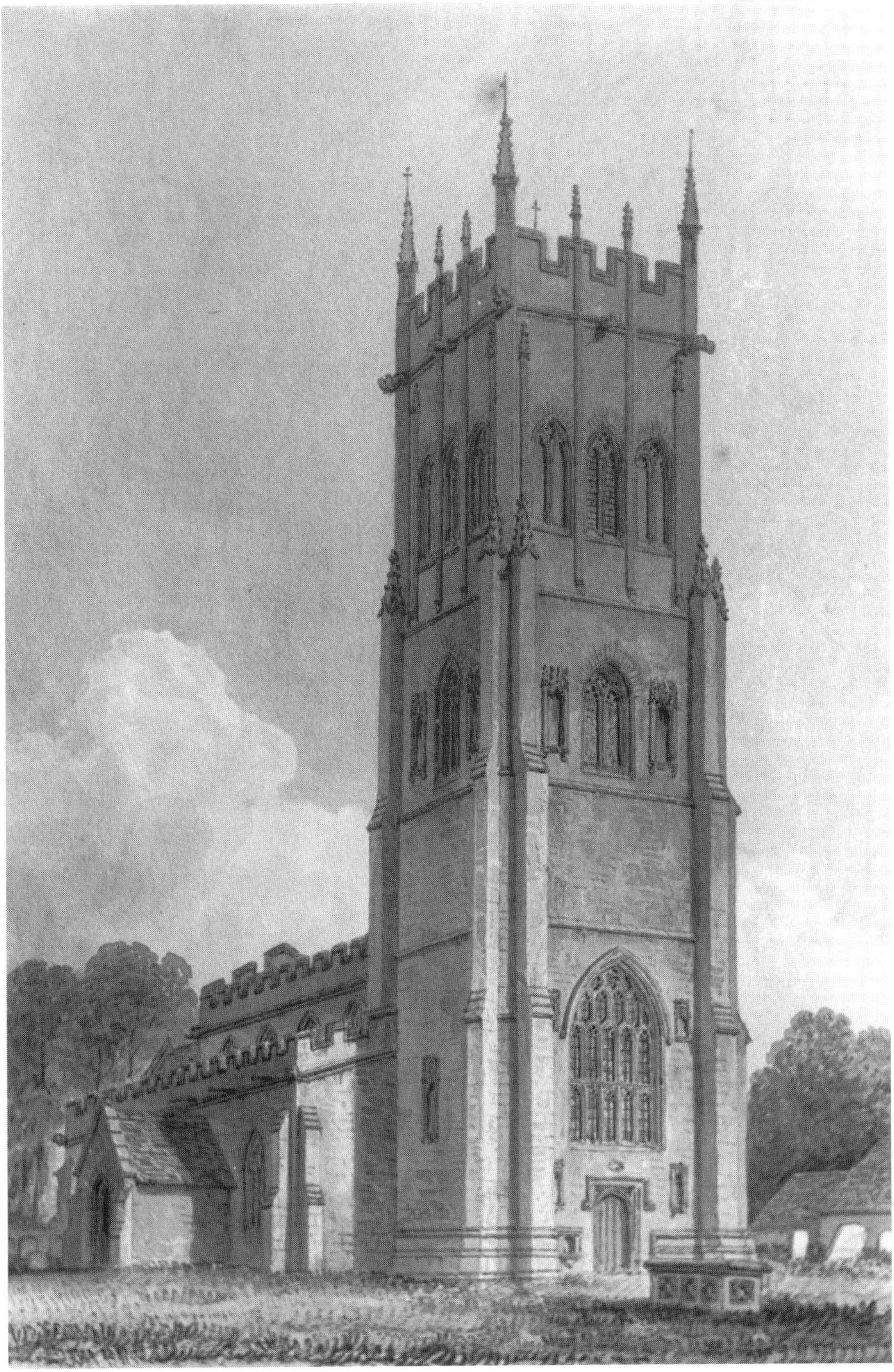

North west view of Long Sutton Church, 1832, by J.C. Buckler

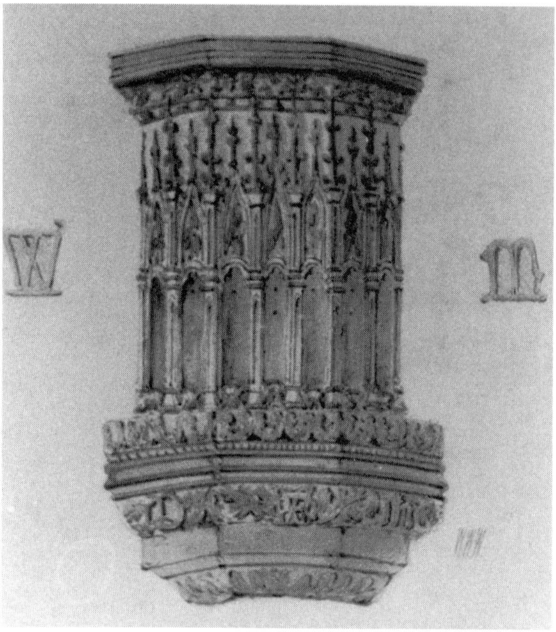

Pulpit of wood in Long Sutton Church, 1847, by W.W. Wheatley

window (also between niches). By this door is a stoup. The next stage is plain, the third has a 2 light window between niches, the highest 3 fine long belfry windows filled with ornamental lattice work in stone and having between them small pinnacles which run up above the battlements. The battlement is bold and good and at the 4 angles are larger crocketed pinnacles. There is a stair turret, as usual, on the south and the stages of the buttresses adorned with niches.

The battlements of the body and aisles are bold and good and there are fine gargoyles. There is an octagonal stair turret on the south for the roodloft and the south porch has fine niches within; the north porch also contains a niche. The nave and chancel have each side aisles and the nave a clerestory, the east gable of which has a niche with the figure of a saint. The interior is light and lofty; the nave has on each side 4 pointed arches with light piers as at Curry. The clerestory windows are of 2 lights, those of the aisles are of 3 and 4 lights (some having ancient stained glass). Those of the chancel have externally no dripstones; that at the east end is of 5 lights with a transom.

The tower opens to the nave by a lofty panelled arch. The nave has a fine open roof with open tracery above the tie beams which are enriched with square flower.

Between the body and chancel, across the whole breadth, is a magnificent woodscreen with the roodloft, painted and gilt and rich in bands of vine leaves etc. in fan groining and open tracery. The pulpit is of like character with rich niches and bands of foliage. The chancel opens to each aisle by panelled arches. The roof of the chancel is open, except a coved ceiling immediately over the altar. South of the altar are 3 plain sedilia (with flat arches) and a cinquefoiled niche with a piscina surmounted by a label. The font is octagonal, each face panelled with quatrefoils in lozenges, the shaft panelled and expanding, fan like, towards the basin.

Sutton Montis

52/6–7 Holy Trinity 10 June, 1871

A small church having nave and chancel with western tower. The chancel arch is Norman, has chevron ornament facing the west but plain soffit on shafts with sculptured capitals. There are no shafts to the east face. The nave has on the north doubtful windows of 2 lights without foliation; on the south Perpendicular windows of 3 lights and square-headed.

The chancel has on each side 2 Decorated windows of 2 lights with exterior hoods on head corbels. Beneath that on the north-west is a kind of lychnoscope, square-headed. The arch mouldings within are very good and are set upon shafts with moulded capitals and faces and the hoods on head corbels. The east window of 3 lights has been renovated. There is a square opening to the chancel on the south side of the chancel arch. The chancel has new fittings, stallwise.

The tower is low and apparently Perpendicular; has its east and west sides slightly gabled and a kind of saddle roof, but there is a battlement and small pinnacles. There are no buttresses, no string course, but a west window of 3 lights, belfry windows of 2 plain arched lights. On the south side a broad square turret for a staircase, not reaching to the top. The nave is unimproved, but the chancel in good state.

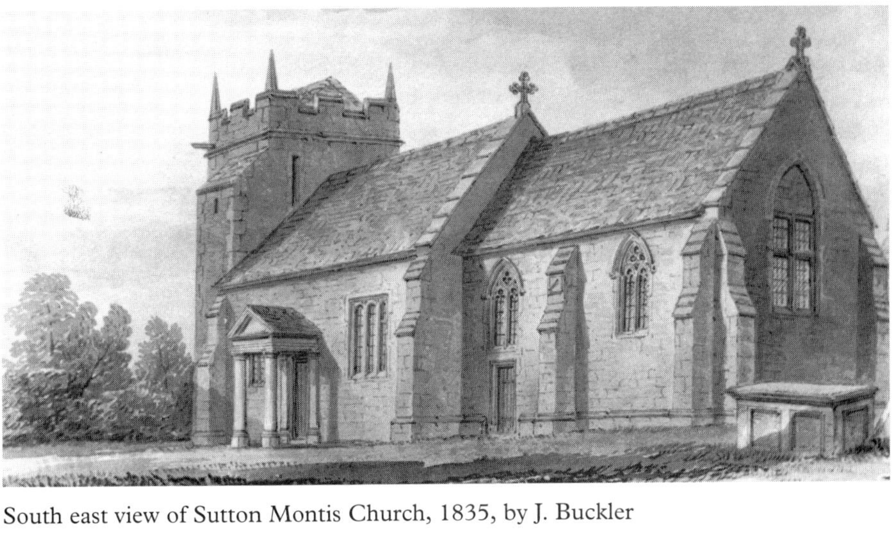

South east view of Sutton Montis Church, 1835, by J. Buckler

Swainswick

49/66 [St. Mary] Before 1840

The church of this retired village consists of a small west tower, a nave and chancel each with a north aisle and a south porch. The whole is very plain and

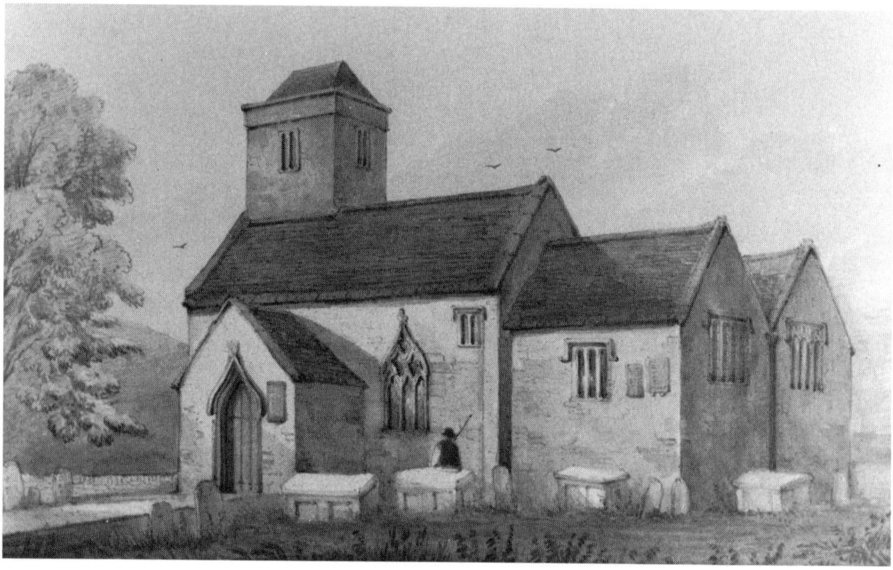

Swainswick, 1843, by W.W. Wheatley

neither tower nor body have any battlement. The tower is of unusually small dimensions with a square-headed late belfry window and opens to the nave by a very narrow arch. The south porch has a doorway with an ogee arch and finial. One of the south windows has an ogee head with good mouldings and tracery of rather odd character which appears to be Decorated.

All other features of the church are Perpendicular. The windows of the chancel are late and bad. In the north aisle of the church are some of better character and in the aisle of the nave a large one of 4 lights. The north doorway of the chancel is small with a label over it and shields in the spandrels. Near it is a stoup. The nave is divided from the aisle by 2 Tudor arches upon light clustered piers and a third low arched opening eastward of the arches. The chancel is divided from its aisle by a panelled arch. The font is a plain octagon.

Swell

50/34–35 St. Catherine April, 1845

A very small church having only a nave and chancel, south porch and a wooden bell turret. The south door within the porch is a very good Norman one having 2 courses of moulding and another one with net work, upon imposts. There are 2 orders of shafts, the outer ones the largest and the capitals vained, having the star on some of the abaci.

Everything else about the church is Perpendicular. The west window of 4 lights. The east window is of 3 lights. Other windows are of 2 and there are some pieces of ancient stained glass. The west door has an arch of Tudor form

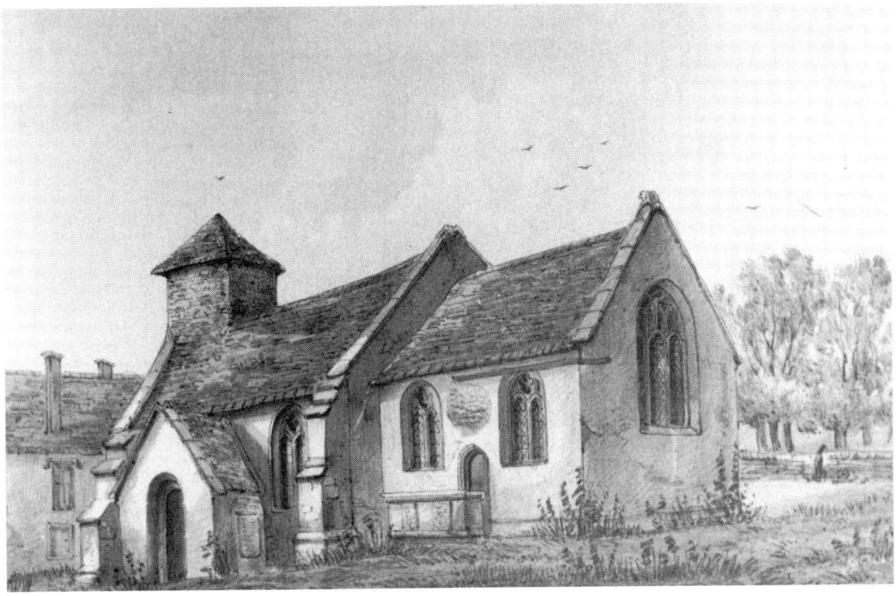

Swell, 1850, by W.W. Wheatley

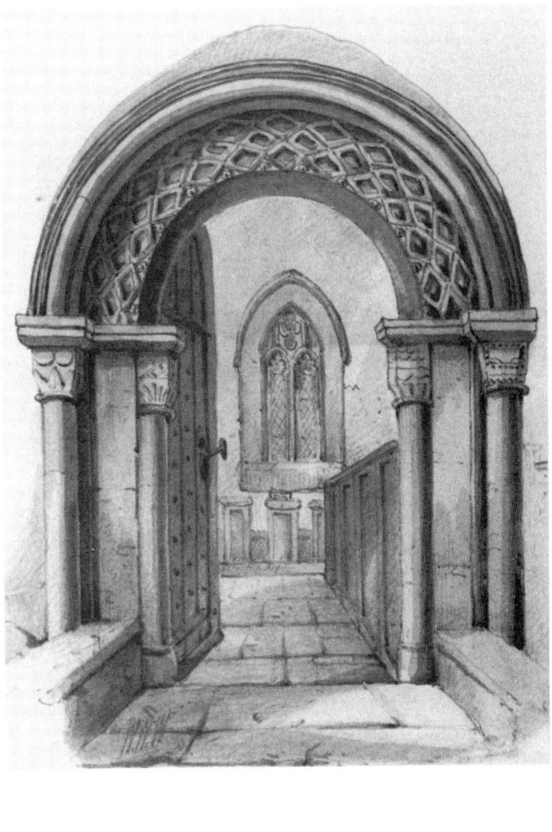

Swell Church, south porch, 1850, by W.W. Wheatley

with label and plain spandrels. The chancel is lower and smaller than the nave and opens to it by a good arch with panelled soffit. On the south of the altar is a plain trefoiled piscina. The font has an octagonal bowl on a cylindrical stem. There are some very plain open benches. The external walls are stuccoed.

Taunton

19/78–82 St. Mary Magdalene Before 1840

The town of Taunton is large and handsome containing several busy, fine and wide streets with well-built houses. There are several houses with ancient fronts and very good doorways with handsome enrichments of the 16th century or beginning of the 17th. The town contains 2 churches, both handsome structures, but that of St. Mary Magdalene is very much the largest and handsomest.

The church of St. Mary Magdalene is a very spacious and handsome structure and presents a good specimen of the rich Rectilinear style so prevalent in the Western counties, especially in its lofty and magnificent tower. The church consists of a nave with double aisles on either side which render the breadth very considerable, making in all 5 aisles, a chancel with side chapels and a lofty and beautiful tower at the west end of the nave.

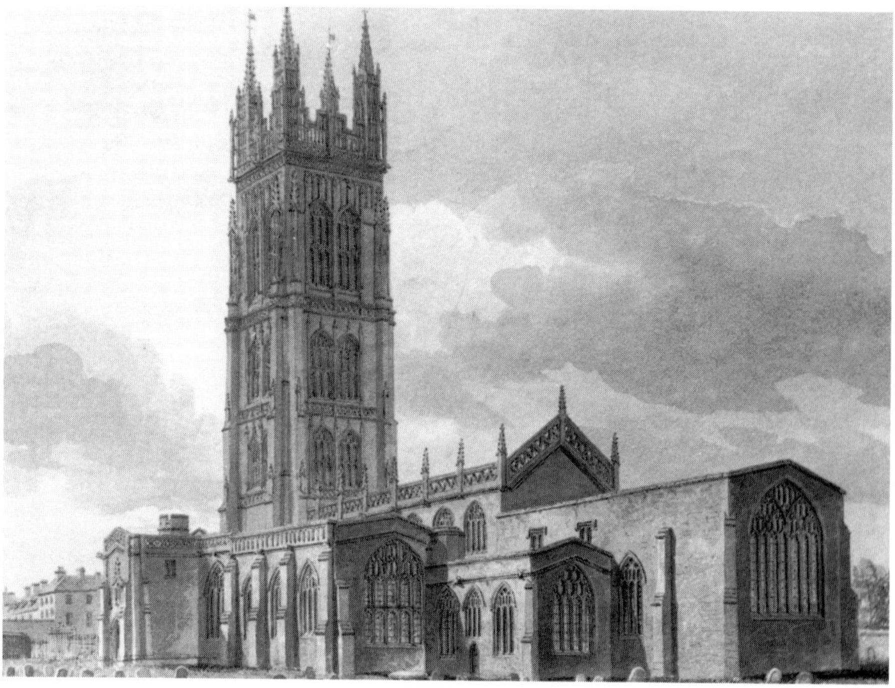

South east view of St. Mary Magdalen, Taunton, 1827, by J. Buckler

The tower is built of a dark coloured stone which is much worn in several places so that the tower loses some of its beauty on a near view, but the general effect is very fine and it appears to particular advantage terminating the view down Hammet Street. The tower is divided into 5 stages below the battlement. The lowest has on the west side a good doorway with contracted arch within a square compartment deeply recessed with mouldings and having the label returned over the side buttresses. The spandrels are filled with sculpture representing figures, etc. On each side of the upper part of the doorway is a fine niche with rich canopy.

Immediately over the doorway is a large, handsome window in the second stage and in the same stage on the south side are 2 handsome canopied niches. The 3 upper stages are each enriched with 5 double windows with Rectilinear tracery, ogee canopies with crockets and finials and wrought with elaborate stone lattice work pierced with ranges of quatrefoils. Between each stage is a rich band of division finely panelled with quatrefoils. The buttresses are fine and are in many places ornamented with fine crocketed pinnacles at their set offs. The battlement is exquisitely worked with pierced panelling and at each angle is a beautiful pierced turret crowned with a pinnacle forming a most elegant finishing to the tower. Between the large corner turrets are placed smaller crocketed pinnacles and the assemblage of pinnacles is very fine. The tower has within a stone goined ceiling and opens to the church by a lofty pointed arch with panelled soffit.

The south side of the church is considerably richer than the north in every respect. The western portion of the south aisle has a fine parapet of pierced panelling and a good porch with the same parapet and 3 fine niches over the doorways which themselves are comparatively plain. The eastern portion of the south aisle has a parapet of plain panelling. The exterior of the chancel is quite plain and devoid of ornament as is the whole of the exterior of the northern aisle being without either battlement or parapet. The clerestory is high and is enriched with a beautiful pierced parapet and pinnacles between the windows.

The interior, though of very fine space, has rather a gloomy appearance and is hardly sufficiently lighted with windows. The nave, or middle aisle, is very lofty and fine and enriched with a most beautiful wood roof having pierced tracery above the beams and various figures of angels, etc. The arches dividing the nave from its nearest side aisles are plain and pointed with plain lozenge piers having shafts at their angles and the intermediate spaces hollow and capitals with figures of half angels.

The two south aisles are divided by similar arches and piers and the two north aisles by lozenge piers with plain shafts and capitals without sculpture. The arches are not of elegant form and the piers generally too devoid of ornament for so large and rich a church. On one pier on the north side of the nave is a large and fine niche with very rich canopy ornamented with elegant crockets, finials, pinnacles, etc. and supported on a fine bracket sculptured with foliage and the bust of an angel.

The clerestory of the nave has a fine appearance. The windows are of 4 lights and between each window is a beautiful niche with rich crocketed canopy. The windows of the side aisles are too small and too low in number. They have some three, some four lights, with ordinary tracery. At the ends of the aisles are some larger ones of 4 or 5 lights. The western portion of the chancel has an aisle on each side divided from it by plain pointed arches with common lozenge pier of 4 shafts.

The east extremity is without aisles. The east window is large and of 7 lights. In the chancel are 2 panelled altar tombs, one of which has a contracted arch canopy. There is a small aperture in the wall with Rectilinear tracery between the most northerly aisle of the nave and the north aisle of the chancel. The chancel has a panelled ceiling partly painted blue with gilt stars. The font is an octagon panelled with quatrefoils. At the west end of the nave is a gallery (the only one in the church) containing a very large organ. Beneath it is a rather handsome screen of Italian work. There are some wooden carved seats in the church of Rectilinear character.

The dimensions of the church are as follows:-

Length of nave	98ft. by 86 in breadth including its 4 aisles.
Length of chancel	50ft by 56 in breadth including its 2 aisles.
Whole length	148ft

Height of the tower to the pinnacles 153ft.

Taunton

19/83–84 St. James Before 1840

St. James's church, although inferior in dimensions and magnificence to St. Mary Magdalene's is nevertheless a very elegant structure and has a handsome appearance. It consists of a nave with side aisles, chancel, and a tower at the west end.

The tower is of very good workmanship and much enriched and appears to be an imitation on a small scale of St. Mary Magdalene's tower, but the work is rather plainer and the whole much smaller. It has on its west side a door and window exactly resembling St. Mary's and 2 stages of fine double belfry windows with stone lattice work but without a canopy. In the upper stage are some rich niches on either side the belfry windows. The battlement is elegantly pierced and there are 4 handsome crocketed pinnacles. The buttresses have pinnacles on the set offs.

The church seems to be wholly of Rectilinear work. The body is covered with stucco. The south porch is of good plain work and there is a small doorway south of the chancel with Tudor arch and label. The windows are chiefly of 3 lights; the eastern one is of 5 lights and filled with modern painted glass. The arches are pointed and the piers of lozenge form with shafts having plain capitals at the angles and hollow spaces between them.

On the north side of the chancel is a very wide arch. The north aisle is recently added. On the south side of the nave is a low clerestory of square-headed windows. At the west end is an organ erected in the church in 1808. The font is a very fine one of octagonal form having round the top a band of square flowers and each compartment enriched with sculpture representing scripture subjects, the crucifixion, etc. The pedestal is enriched with large bold square flowers and is also octagonal and large.

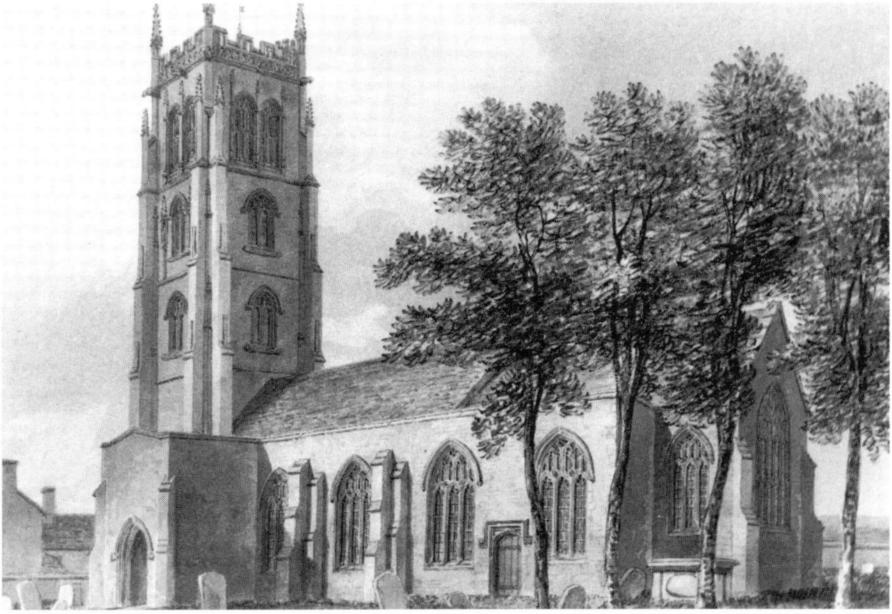

South east view of St. James, Taunton, 1832, by J. Buckler

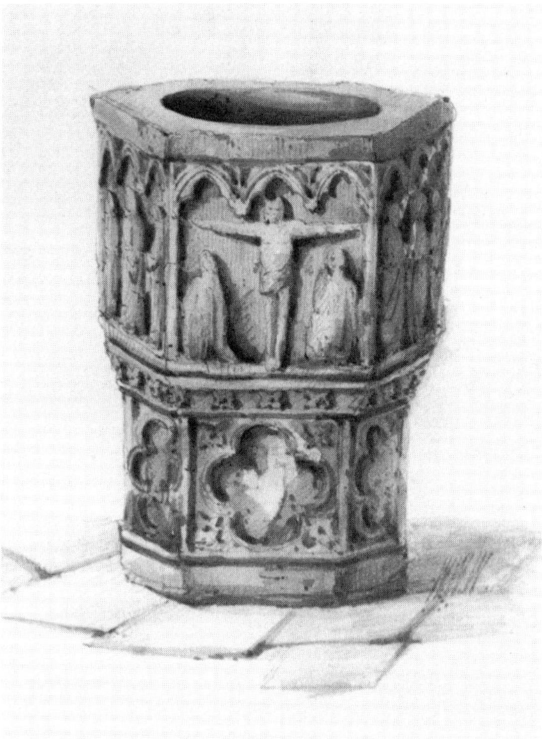

In St. James's Church,
Taunton, 1849,
by W.W. Wheatley

Templecombe

(or Abbas Combe)

50/46 St. Mary 1 August, 1849

An uninteresting church, mostly debased in style, comprising a nave and north aisle, chancel, south chapel and a tower on the south side of the nave which forms a porch. The latter is low and embattled with gargoyles, of plain Third Pointed work and [has] a 2 light window. The west door of the nave is labeled with foliage in the spandrels. The north windows of the nave are square-headed, the others very bad. The nave and aisles have separate and coved roofs. The chancel arch is pointed and continuous. The chapel arch of Tudor form with small shafts. The arcade between the nave and aisle consists of 4 pointed arches with channeled octagonal piers. There is a west gallery and organ.

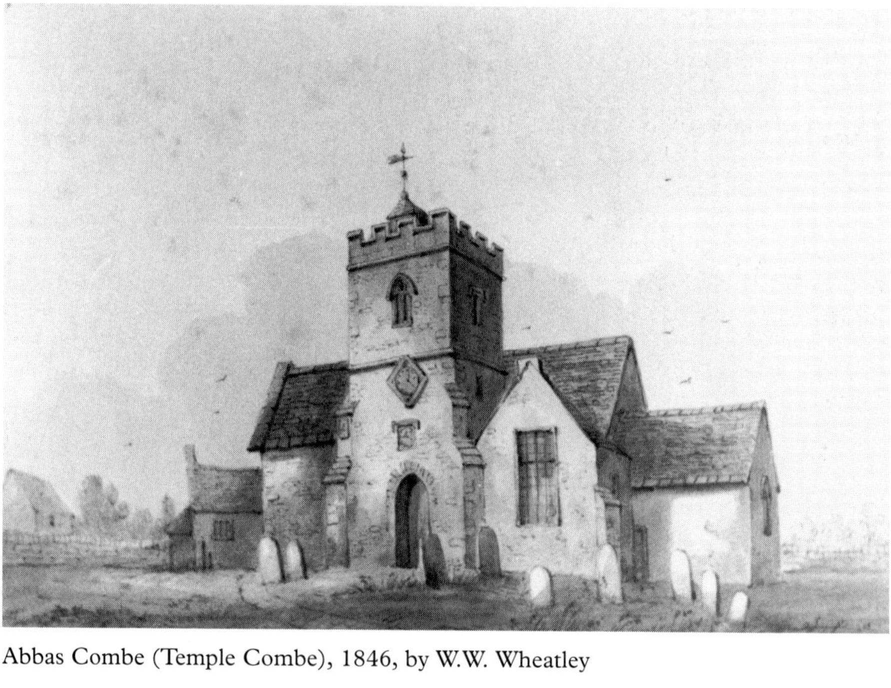

Abbas Combe (Temple Combe), 1846, by W.W. Wheatley

Thurloxton

51/38 St. Giles 30 January, 1861

A small church of little interest having chancel, nave and western tower; south porch, all of red stone and stripped of plaster. The roofs newly tiled. The tower arch is plain and pointed. There is no chancel arch, but part of a late

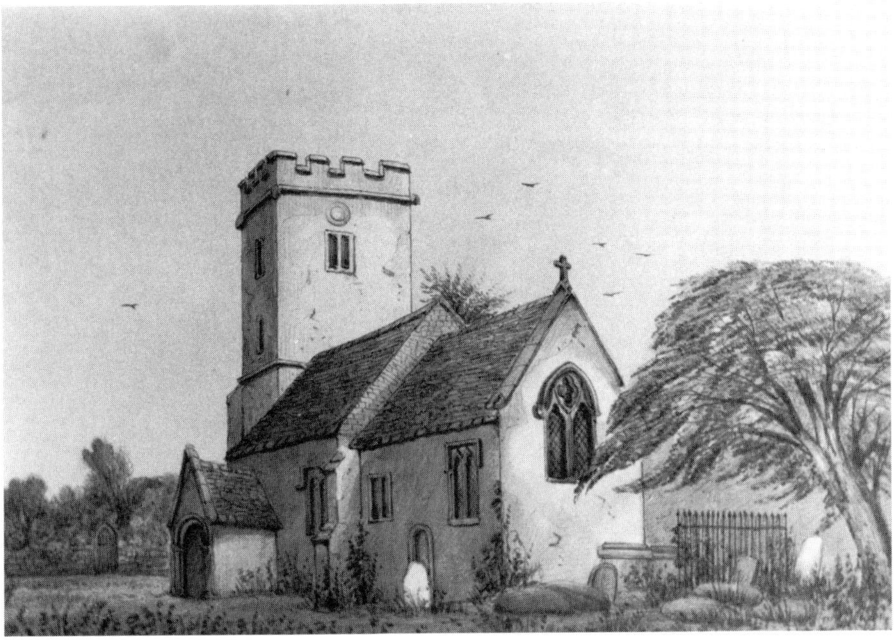

Thurloxton, 1850, by W.W. Wheatley

roodscreen remains. The windows small Perpendicular except a Decorated one of 2 lights at the east end, some being square-headed and labeled, but others with neither labels nor foil. The porch has an odd debased looking doorway. The tower low, embattled, with corner buttresses and one string, square-headed belfry window. The west window is of 2 lights, apparently late Decorated, having a wavy circle in the tracery.

Tickenham

51/61–63 St. Quericus and St. Julietta 15 August, 1862

An interesting church of very varied character comprising nave with north and south aisles, chancel with south aisle or chapel, western tower and south porch.

The nave has on each side an arcade of 3 arches. The northern has 3 pointed arches quite plain with square piers having no capitals. The southern has also 3 arches, all rather dissimilar in size, but all pointed and very plain. The eastern end rises from a large plain wall pier. The second arch is on Early English shafts set in the angles of the pier and having foliage capitals without. The western pier resembles those opposite. The north aisle is lofty, has a single trefoil-headed [window] at the west and one at the north. Two and three windows on this side are fine Decorated of 2 lights with square-heads and some fine pieces of ancient stained glass.

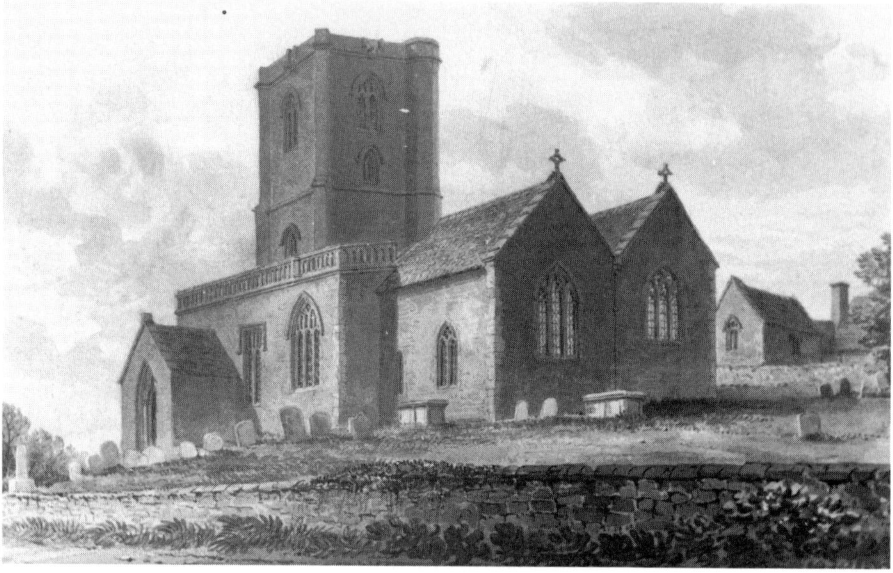

South east view of Tickenham Church, 1828, by J. Buckler

The eastern window is Perpendicular. In the east pier of the north arcade is a square recess closed and also a bracket. Beneath the northern windows is a stone bench. In this aisle are also 3 stone effigies, 2 are much injured; one of a lady with a whimple, one of a knight in chain helmet of the 15th century. The south aisle has some square-headed Perpendicular windows of 2 and 3 lights and a west window of 2 lights of Decorated character. The roofs have tie-beams and are open.

The chancel arch is a low plain Norman one on imposts set in piers of strong walling. The chancel has 2 rude pointed niches on plain pier without capital opening to the south chapel and eastward of the east end is a large amount of wall. The east window of the chancel is poor Decorated. On the north is one of Decorated character and square-headed. On the south is a piscina with pointed arch having a shelf of stone and projecting ledge. The jamb mouldings have bases but no capitals. There are some traces of the roodscreen.

The south chapel of the chancel is wider than the south aisle of the nave but does not open to it by an arch. The south chapel has its roof coved and ribbed as has the chancel. The south chapel is Decorated, has on the south 2 windows of 2 lights and at the east one of 3 lights, each simply trefoiled. There is a piscina with trefoil-headed arch; also 2 brackets; also some symptoms of a reredos.

The font is a curious Early English one; the bowl square, chamfered at the angles near the base, set upon 4 marble detached shafts having octagonal bases on square plinths and in the centre a rude cylindrical stem. From the capitals of the shafts rises on each face a trefoil niche. The tower arch is lofty and Perpendicular with continuous mouldings.

The south aisle has a fine Perpendicular parapet of the Somersetshire kind. The porch has an odd outer doorway with trefoiled arch of good mouldings within a pointed arch and shafts having octagonal capitals containing nail

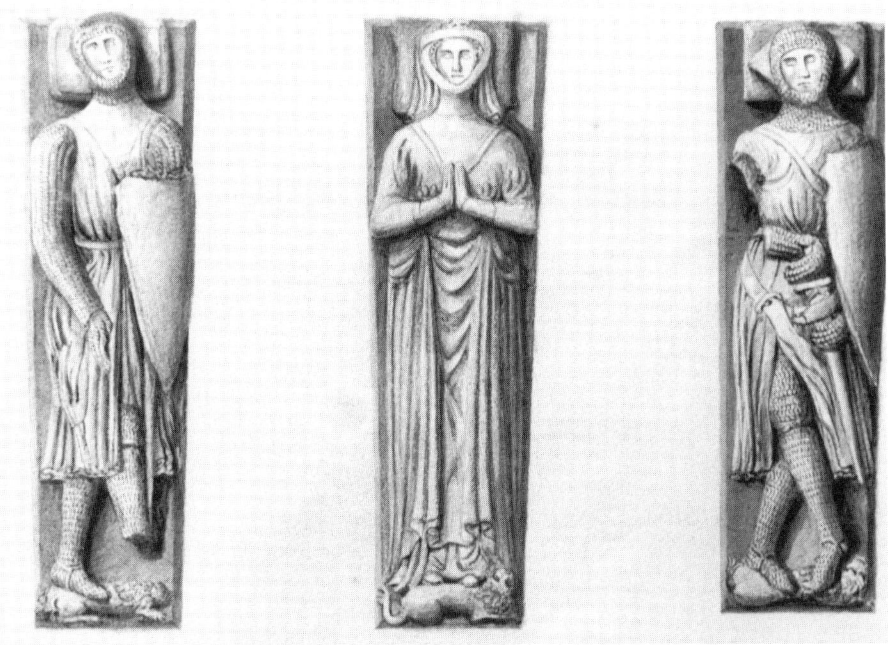

Effigies in Tickenham Church, 1828, by J. Buckler

heads. The inner doorway has circular mouldings; over it a niche and near it an octagonal stoup.

The tower is Perpendicular having corner buttresses and the top left unfinished without parapet; 3 string-courses; belfry windows of 2 lights and another below. On the west a 4 light window and good continuing arched doorway. At the north-east an octagonal stair turret. The north aisle is much modernised outside and has a new slate roof. There is the shaft of a cross in the churchyard.

(The nave has a coved roof. The chancel roof is flagged. The west pier on the north is wider than the others and has plinth and chamfer. There is trace of a niche on the west face of one of the south piers. Tickenham court near the church has some excellent ancient domestic architecture, especially a fine Edwardian hall, now in bad condition.)

Tintinhull

49/45–46 St. Margaret Before 1840

This church has also early features and in general character resembles [Stoke-Sub-Hamdon]. There is a nave and a chancel without aisles and a tower on the north side about the centre. There are tiled roofs and beneath them a corbel table of billet apparently of Early English character. There is an Early English string course under the windows on both sides of the nave and continued over

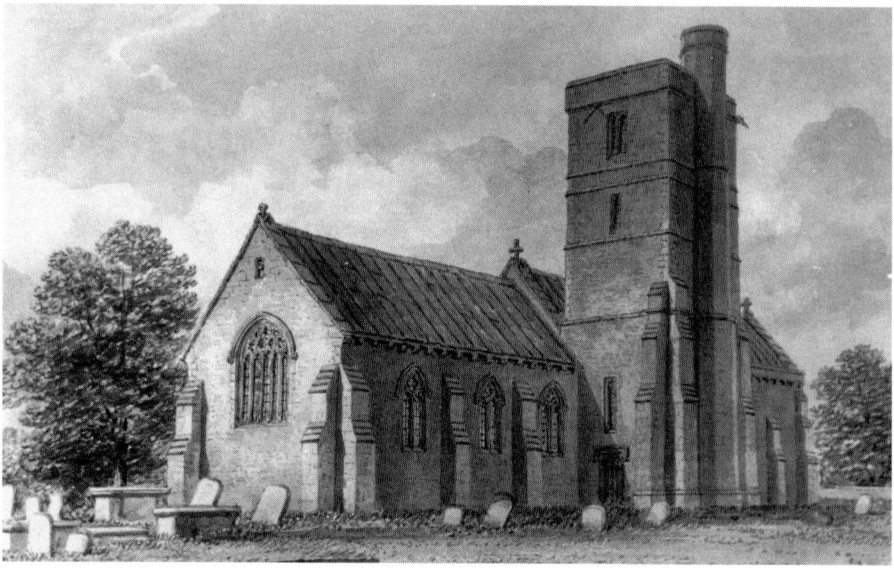

North east view of Tintinhull Church, 1835, by J. Buckler

the doorways. The windows themselves in the nave are Rectilinear of different sizes and shapes; that at the west end of 4 lights.

The tower has no battlement and an octagonal turret runs up the centre of the north side. The upper parts seem to be of later date, but the lower stage has on the east and west sides a single trefoiled lancet. There is also a plain Early English doorway and, communicating with the body in the second storey of the tower, is a trefoil lancet within an arch upon a longitudinal rib intersected by others and bosses at the crossings.

The chancel arch has given way and springs from small shafts upon heads having foliated capitals. The chancel has Early Decorated windows of 2 lights on the north and south opening within by arches upon shafts with bell capitals. The east window is bad and modern. A string course runs beneath the windows. There is a brass in the chancel to one John Stone, rector, 1416 and another with a half length figure of an ecclesiastic *Magist Johes Heth Rector*, etc. with the often recurring latin verse *Sis testis Xte*, etc.

The font is octagonal on a shaft of like form having a double range of panelling with quatrefoils. The south porch has a stone vaulted roof with strong arched ribs rising from shafts.

Tolland

50/88–89 St. John 7 May, 1855

A small church of no beauty but in a pretty secluded situation. It consists of 2 equal aisles, the east end of the southern being appropriated as chancel but no

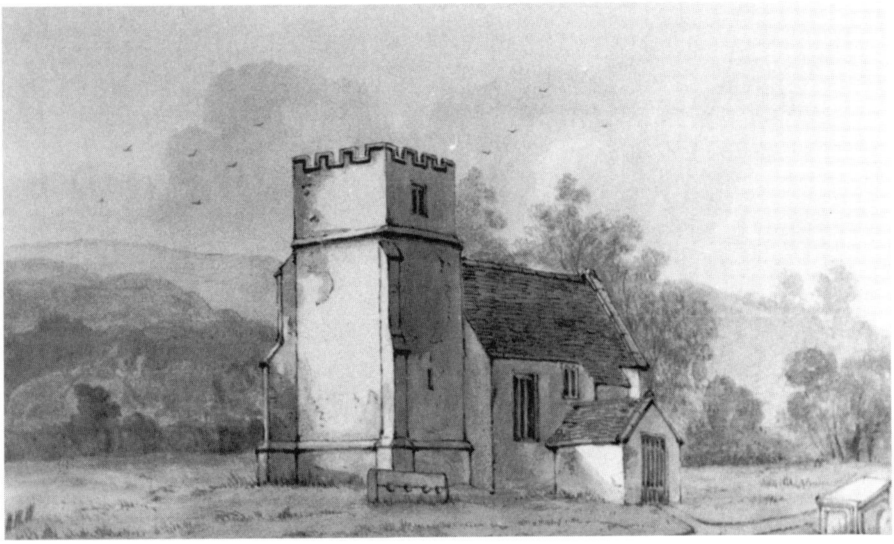

Tolland, 1845, by W.W. Wheatley

architectural distinction exists. At the west end a low, plain tower. The work is generally coarse. The arcade has 3 plainly moulded low pointed arches, the piers small and octagonal with capital overhanging.

The roofs are coved with ribs and bosses, except in the chancel which is ceiled, and there are small embattled cornices. On the south of the chancel are 2 small lancet windows rather questionable in character. The east window has 2 lights, obtuse in the heads and foliated within a square. The other windows are square-headed, late and poor. There is no respond to the arcade. There are several open standards with rich wood carving and square tops but some pues are frightfully high.

The west gallery exhibits some tracery which may have formed part of the roodloft. The pulpit has good Jacobean woodwork, arabesque, and round arches. The font has a circular bowl on cylindrical stem which has a square base which has cushion-like ornaments at the angles. The tower is low and small, of 2 stages, embattled with square 2 light belfry windows and corner buttresses, but no west window. On the south is a plain porch and square projection for the rood turret. The exterior walls roughcast. In the churchyard is the shaft of a cross.

Trull

50/75–76	All Saints	11 May, 1855

A neat church of genuine Somersetshire kind and wholly Perpendicular. The plan comprises nave and chancel with north and south aisles, west tower and south porch. There is the usual roughcast covering on the exterior and a

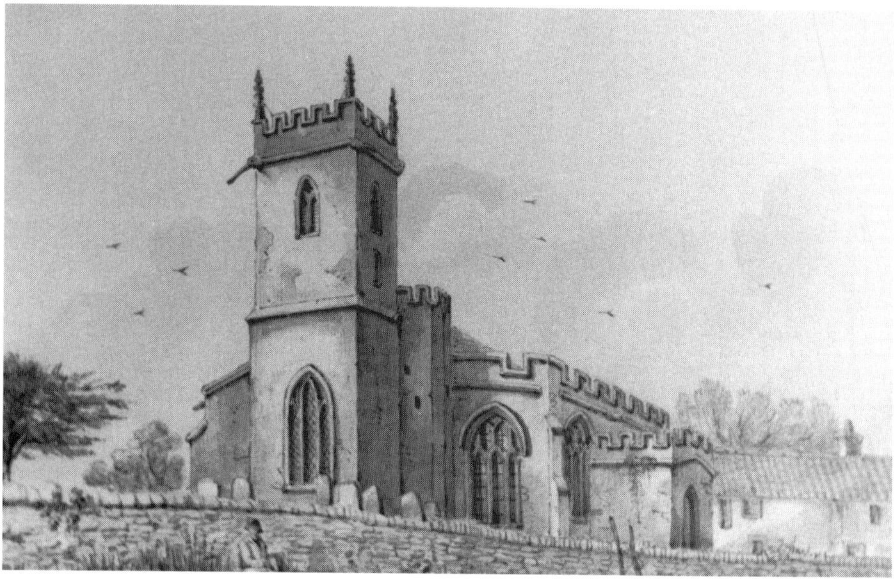

Trull, 1848, by W.W. Wheatley

battlement only on the south side. The windows throughout are very similar and of 3 lights. There is no architectural distinction of chancel but the division is marked by a fine roodloft screen which is continued across both aisles. The central or roodloft portion has 5 fine cornices of vine leaves and excellent fan groining enriched with foliage, the longitudinal mouldings being also foliaged and shafts under the groining which have for capitals angels bearing shields. The north and south screens are less rich.

The nave is of 3 bays, the chancel of one to the aisles, and extending one bay eastward with a window north and south of the sacrarium. The arcades are of the usual western Perpendicular sort, of good form with light piers having 4 shafts and intermediate hollow mouldings. The southern arcade is slightly different from the northern. The roofs are coved with ribs and bosses and no clerestory. Their arrangement more intricate and ornamental over the sacrarium. There is a trefoiled-headed piscina on the south of the altar on which is set a modern credence of wood.

There is a modern vestry north of the altar. The pulpit presents some good wood carving, figures of apostles and saints probably collected from elsewhere. On the north side of the nave are several very fine ancient benches, the ends flat-topped and exhibiting a great variety of beautiful carving, both of figures and tracery. There are several good fragments of stained glass in the east window; in the south-east window, St. Michael upon a Gothic pedestal. The font has a plain octagonal bowl on a stem of the same shape. There is a west gallery with a finger organ. The tower arch springs straight from the wall. The tower is plain with battlement but no buttresses, an octagonal stair turret on the south only part of the height. The belfry windows of 2 lights. On the west side a plain window of 3 lights without tracery within a pointed general arch.

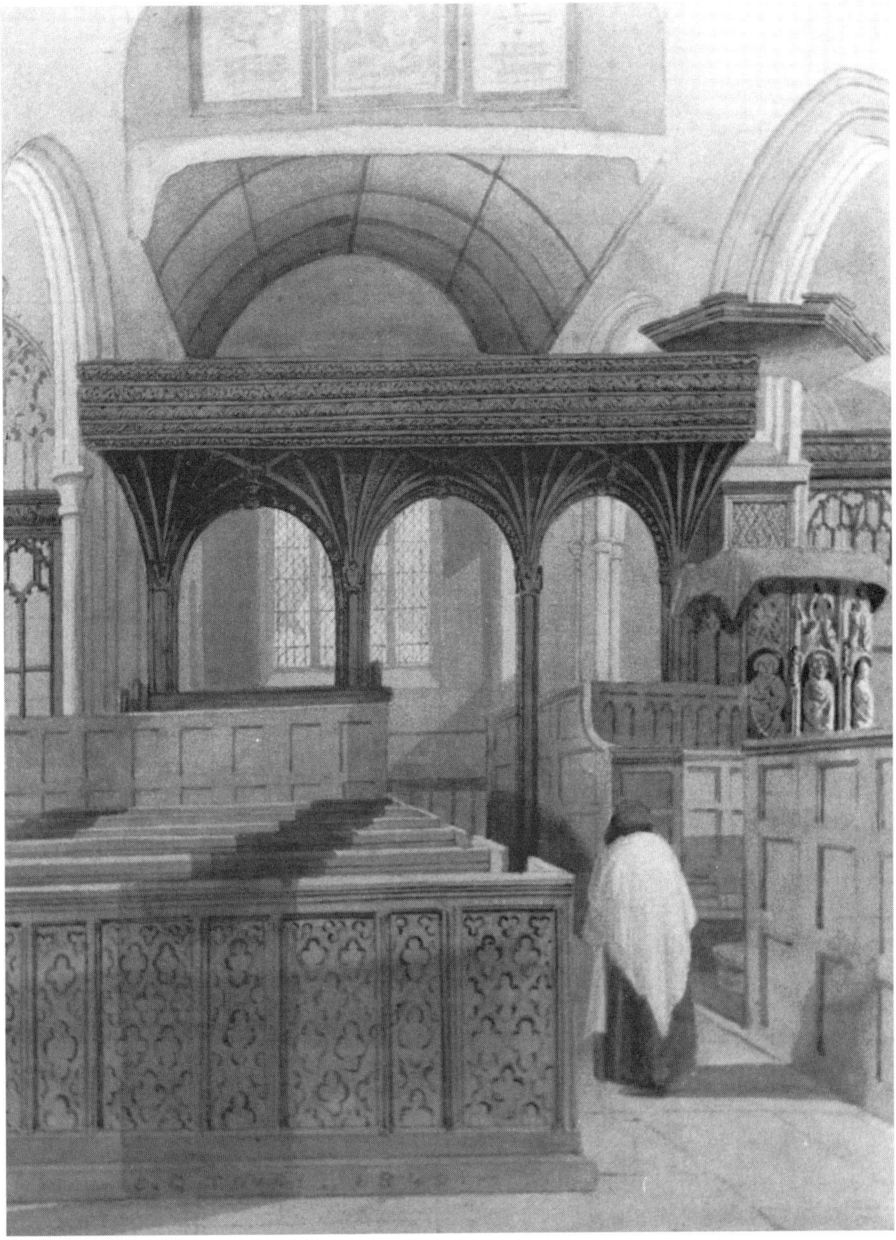

Trull Church, 1846, by S.G. Tovey

Twerton

50/58 St. Michael 21 April, 1850

This church has been entirely rebuilt except the tower which is rather low and of ordinary Third Pointed. It is embattled, has 4 small pinnacles, a 2 light belfry window and a labeled Tudor arch door. The body is modern Gothic, without aisles, pued and galleried with an organ.

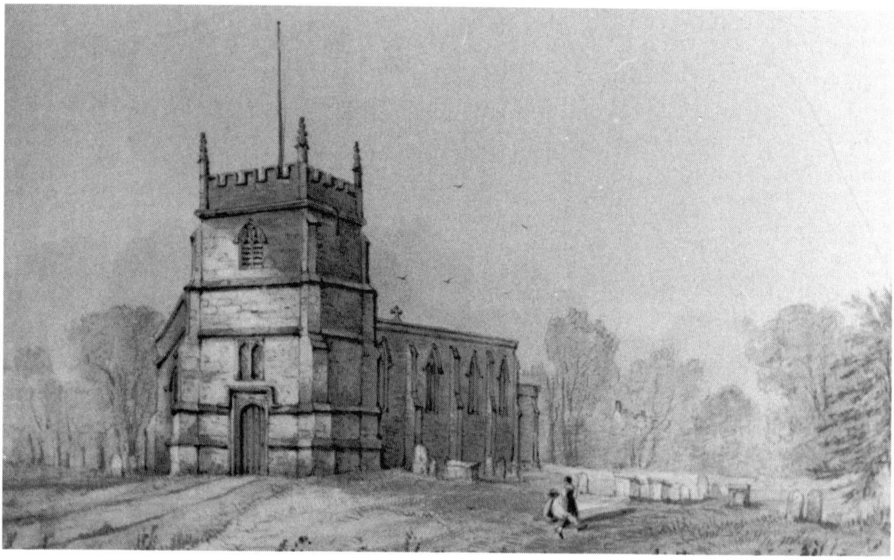

Twerton, 1843, by W.W. Wheatley

Ubley

50/25–26 St. Bartholomew April, 1845

This church consists of a nave with aisles, a chancel, also with aisles, a north porch and a low west tower crowned by a plain stone spire. The main features are Perpendicular. The north aisle has a good pierced parapet with quatrefoils in lozenges. The southern aisle has plain moulded parapet. The north porch has stone seats and within it is a door with continuous mouldings. The tower is low with a battlement and 4 pinnacles and a large square turret at the south-east corner. The west window is Perpendicular of 3 lights, the belfry windows of 2 lights. There is no west door or division by string courses. The spire is rather short and not particularly elegant.

The roofs are leaded and there is no clerestory; the aisles low. The windows of the north aisle are small with Tudor arches and Perpendicular tracery of 3 lights. In the south aisle are some square-headed windows of 2 and 3 lights and at its east end a pointed one of 3 lights. The nave is divided from each

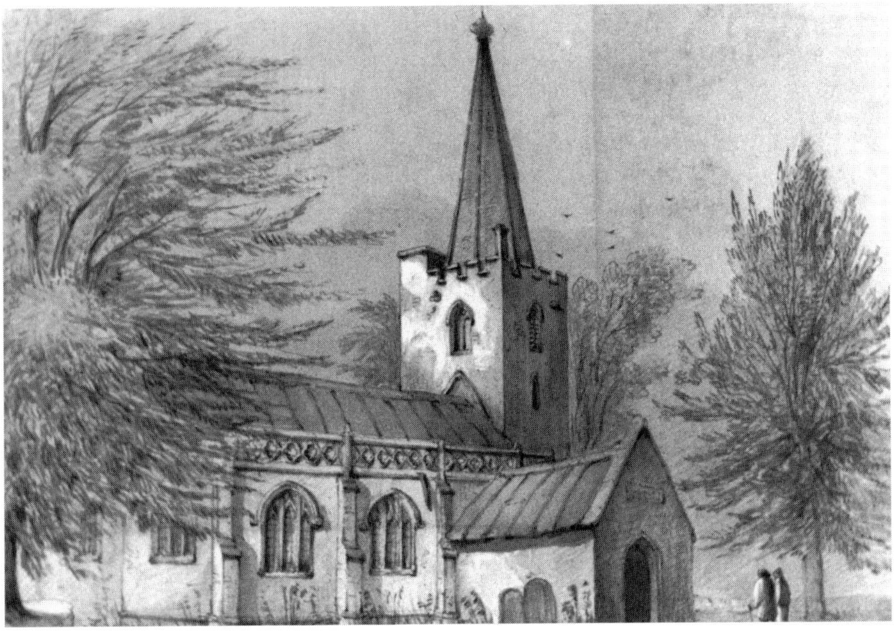

Ubley Church, 1844, by W.W. Wheatley

aisle by 4 small obtuse arches of late period springing from piers of lozenge form having 4 shafts with octagonal capitals and bases.

The chancel arch springs from one semi-octagonal pillar and on the south has the moulding continued. The tower arch is also pointed. The aisles are continued along part of the chancel and open to the chancel by arches resembling those of the nave. The chancel entirely beyond the aisles and has on each side a lancet window. The east window is Perpendicular of 3 lights. On the south side of the chancel is part of a plain trefoil niche with piscina but part cut off by the encroachment of a more modern wall.

On the north side there is also the trace of a niche. At the east end of the south aisle is a very small pointed arch with piscina. There are several plain old wood benches. The pulpit a tolerable specimen of the woodwork of James I. The font has a square bowl rounded below like a cushion capital and set on a short circular stem with a square base at the angles of which are the wedge-like ornaments not uncommon in specimens of this period.

Uphill

49/54–55 [St. Nicholas] 1843

This church, though small, is in a most conspicuous situation on the top of a high hill overhanging the sea, a very inconvenient position for the parishioners and much exposed to wind and weather.

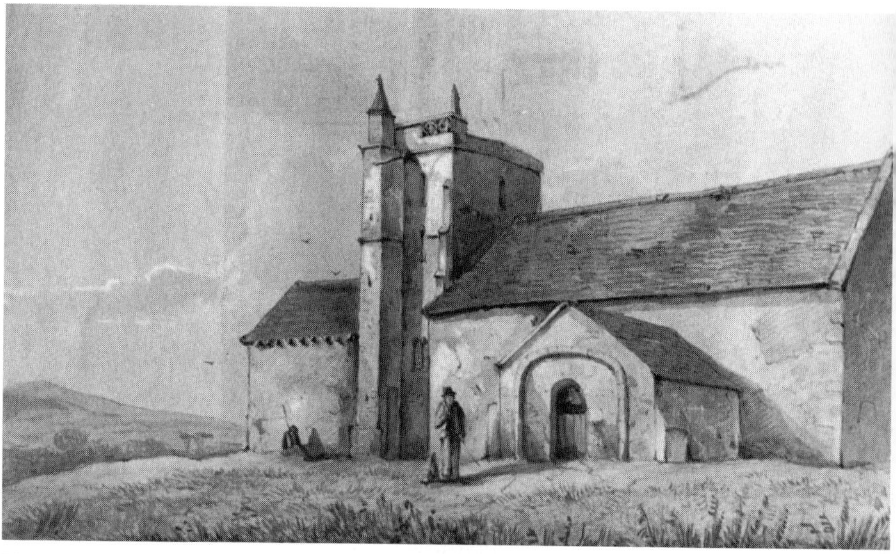

Uphill Old Church, 1842, by W.W. Wheatley

It consists of a nave and chancel with a low tower situated between them, a decidedly Norman arrangement and there are several features of that style: both north and south doorways partake of it, the former within a porch entirely of stone, is of singular shape. The arch is depressed and upon imposts and filled with stone work. The doorway is of the form often seen in castellated and domestic architecture. The stone ribs of the vault of the porch are continued down the sides. The outer doorway of this porch has an odd ellipical arch.

The south doorway, which is stopped up, has also a plain semi-circular arch upon imposts and the door head much resembling the northern. In the stonework of the arch head is a circle containing a cross. The tower is rude and low: in its lower part Norman having a rude window on the north, but the arches within under the tracery are pointed. The upper part of the tower is later. On the north are two small trefoil-headed openings with lattice work in stone and the parapet is only completed on the north side where it is pierced in panelling with quatrefoils. On the other three sides it has never been begun. On the north side of the tower is a projecting octagonal turret crowned with a stone pyramid and cornice of Tudor flower. The belfry windows are of Perpendicular character.

The west window of the nave is a single lancet, now closed. The windows are few. North of the nave, they are small and rude, but closed. On the south is one Perpendicular window. In the south wall is a projection with an ogee crocketed finialed arch in the thickness of the wall forming the entrance to the pulpit. The nave has a cradle roof in ribbed compartments. The chancel has 2 small Norman windows closed on the north side. On the south 2 Perpendicular ones square-headed, one of which, as well as the east window, is closed. On the north side of the chancel externally is an early corbel table. There being so many windows closed, the church is extremely dark and the whole, both within and without, is in bad repair.

(A new church has been built since 1843 in the village below the hill. The old church still remains, but no longer used for service.)

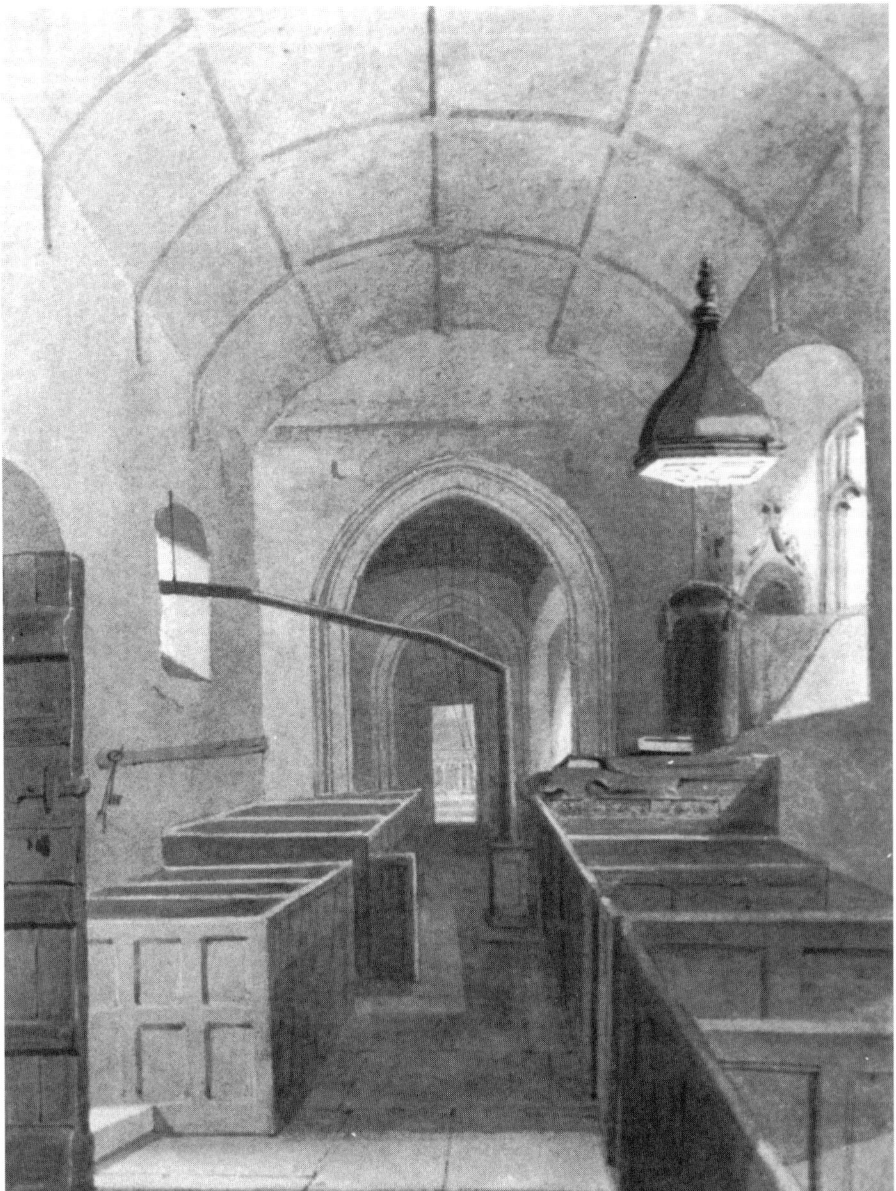

Uphill Old Church, 1844, by S.G. Tovey

Walton

19/66–67 [Holy Trinity] Before 1840

Walton is about a mile and a half from Street on the road to Bridgwater. The church is a chapel to Street and is an inelegant structure consisting of a nave and chancel with a heavy and clumsy tower placed between the nave and chancel. On the north side of the nave is a chapel or porch having its gable surmounted by an elegant small cross. The windows of the church are mostly of Curvilinear character with 2 lights but many of them have been despoiled by their tracery. The nave is well fitted up with pews painted oak colour.

The tower is of particularly clumsy formation. It has belfry windows of Curvilinear form and the lower windows of lancet form and on ye north side a plain, small doorway with a trefoiled head and very narrow. The tower is plain at top and without battlement. It contains 5 bells. The arches on which it rests and which open to the nave and chancel are of most inelegant form, clumsy, low, and of rather contracted form with plain mouldings and springing immediately from the ground without any shafts.

On the north side of the chancel beneath a plain trefoiled recess is a stone sepulchral effigy in good preservation, apparently of a priest, with his hands clasped. The font is octagonal of ugly design and probably of late workmanship. On the south side of the chancel is a small doorway having a dripstone supported at the ends by heads. This is a long church, but narrow, there being no aisles.

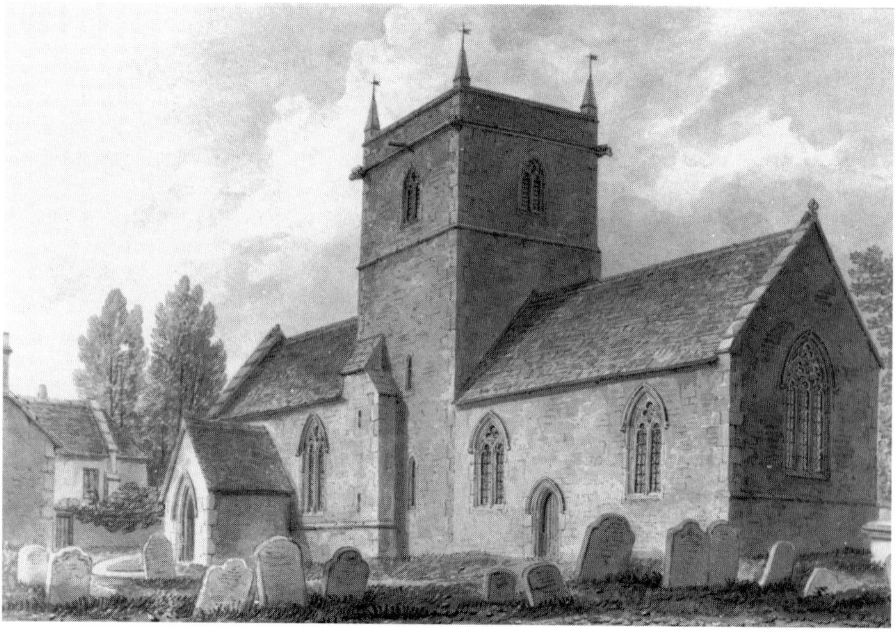

South east view of Walton Church, 1834, by J. Buckler

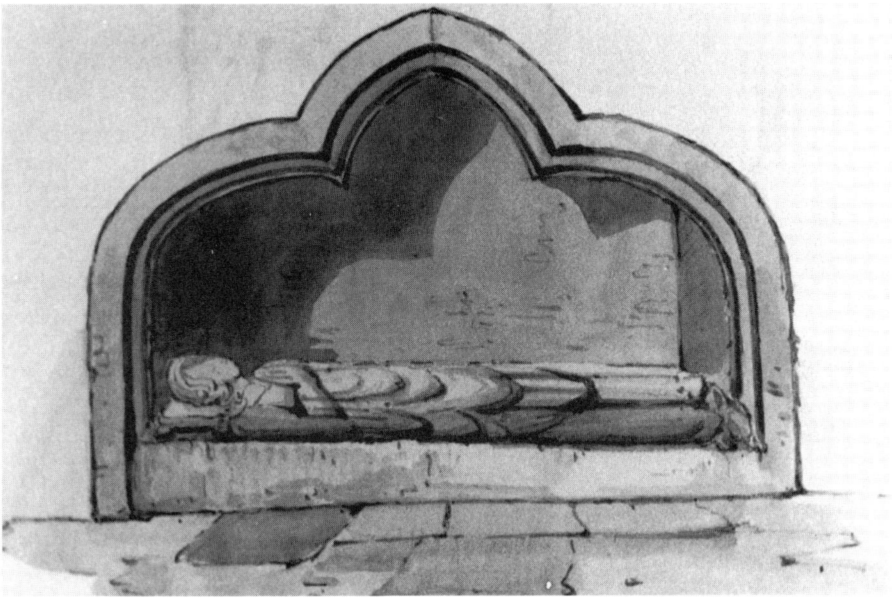

North side of the chancel of Walton Church, 1845, by W.W. Wheatley

Wellington

49/69–71 [St. John the Baptist] Before 1840

A handsome church consisting of a western tower, a nave, chancel, north and south aisles, and a south porch. The whole Perpendicular except the chancel which is early Decorated, just emerging from Early English. The tower is a fine Somersetshire one, though not of the most highly enriched sort. It is divided into 3 stages and has a battlement, grouped pinnacles at the angles and smaller ones at the intervals which rise from a kind of corbel between the heads of the belfry windows and all are crocketed.

The belfry windows are double on each side and have the stone lattice work. The buttresses are elegantly grouped. On the south side of the tower there is in the centre the common octagonal stair turret extending the whole height and rather disturbing the symmetry of the tower. (The turret rises above the parapet of the tower and is surmounted by a battlement. Its position in the centre of the most conspicuous side of the tower is rather unfortunate.) On the west side is a good window of 4 lights with tracery and under it a doorway which has good mouldings with a hollow band of foliage and spandrels, also with foliage. On either side of the door is a canopied niche.

The whole church is of a reddish stone. The north side, not being much seen, is plain, without battlement, and stuccoed. The south side is well finished with battlement and the clerestory has a high lead roof and cross on the east gable; also a flowered cornice. The south porch has plainly moulded arch of entrance with shafts. The chancel externally is plain and stuccoed. The

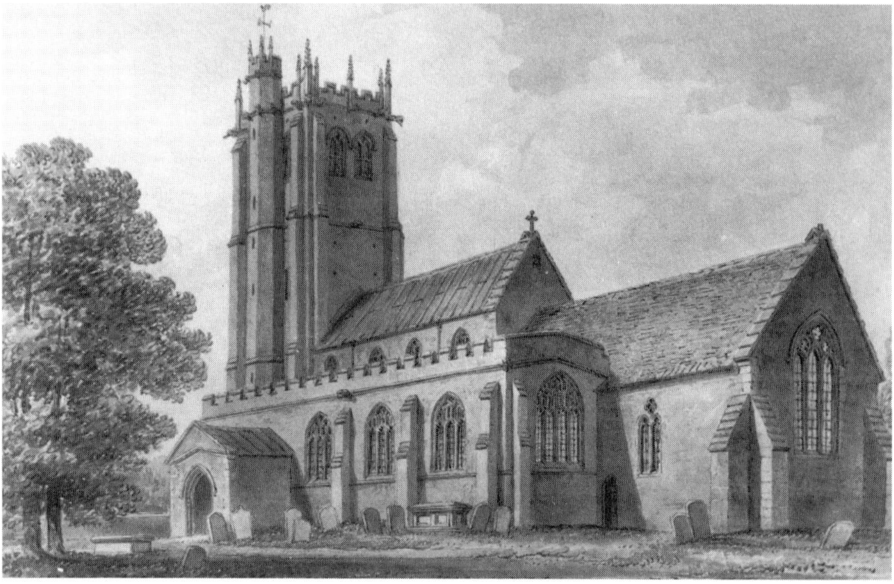

South east view of Wellington Church, 1837, by J. Buckler

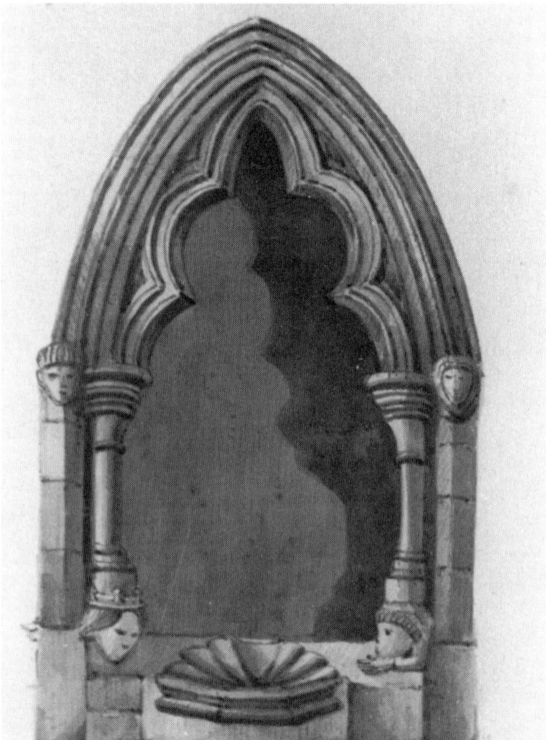

In the chancel of Wellington Church, 1849, by W.W. Wheatley

windows of the aisles are all of 3 lights, those at the east of 4 lights, those of the clerestory of 2 lights.

The interior is lofty and grand. On each side of the nave are 4 high pointed arches springing from light lozenge piers with alternate continuous mouldings and small shafts. The tower arch is very lofty and beautiful, with panelling and springing from single shafts. Through this is seen to advantage the fine west window of the tower, the organ being in the front of the west gallery and not encroaching upon the arch. The front of the gallery is adorned with wood sculpture, apparently ancient. The chancel arch has panelled soffit without shafts. There are small niches on two of the northern piers. The roof of the nave is coved and ribbed. The font is modern. In the north aisle is a projecting turret with stairs to the roodloft.

The chancel is coved and opens to each aisle by a wide pointed arch (in one is a niche in the soffit) springing from shafts and lower than those of the nave. The east window consists of 3 lancet lights with 3 quatrefoiled circles above, externally without a general arch but internally set within one elegantly moulded and the mullions within are enriched with shafts having moulded capitals. The north and south windows of the chancel are of similar character but with 2 lights and have no shafts.

On the south side of the altar is a fine niche with beautiful mouldings and cinquefoil feathering and shafts having bell capitals and set, the one upon a crowned head corbel, the other on the bust of a grotesque monkey figure with clasped hands. The piscina is a half octagon with quatrefoil orifice. On the north side of the altar in the wall is a piece of sculpture with 3 trefoiled niches, groining and a cornice of 4 half flowers.

There is a small piscina in the east wall of the north aisle. The altar piece is modern Italian. In the south aisle of the chancel is a sumptuous tomb of the time of James I to Lord Popham and his lady whose figures are recumbent on the slab, nicely painted gilt and surmounted by a lofty canopy on Corinthian columns. The sides of the tomb have sculpture of figures kneeling at desks, probably representing the whole family. The pews are mostly of deal. There is an ugly brick vestry north of the chancel.

Wellow

51/19–21 St. Julian 9 May, 1859

A fine church, altogether in very fair condition consisting of a lofty nave with aisles and clerestory, chancel with north chapel, west tower and south porch. The whole of the exterior of fine stone and excellent well-finished masonry and all Perpendicular except the chancel which is mainly Decorated. The aisles and clerestory are embattled and there are crocketed pinnacles surmounting the buttresses in the aisles. There is an octagonal turret at the south-east of the nave, embattled and crowned with pinnacles. The south porch has a battlement on the east and west. The central gable has an ogee finial and a lofty canopied niche.

The tower is lofty and fine, divided by 2 string courses, embattled, having buttresses not set at the angles, a square turret at the south-east rising into an

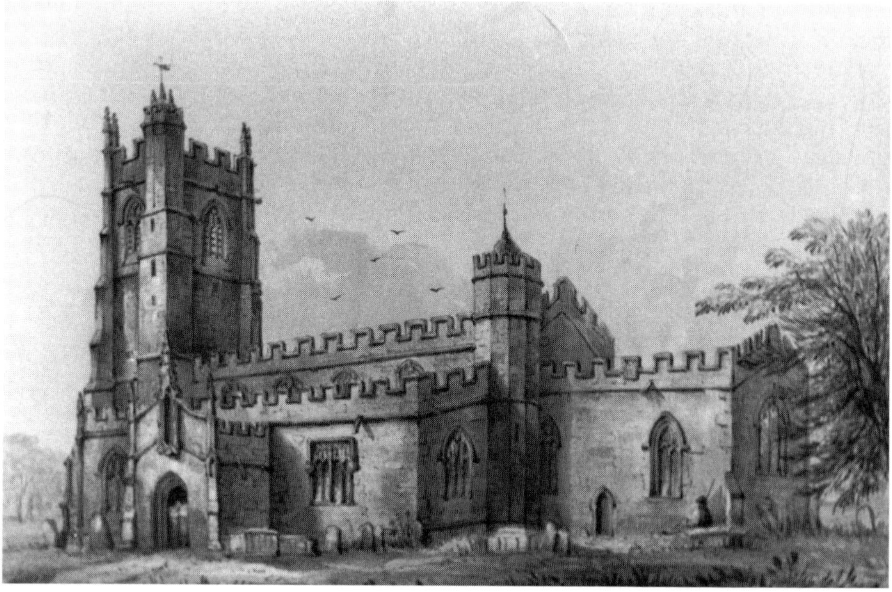

Wellow Church, 1842, by W.W. Wheatley

octagon and 2 pinnacles at each angle. On the west side a 3 light window with transoms and long belfry windows of 3 lights with corbeled hoods. The windows of the south aisle are Perpendicular, of 3 lights, one being square-headed.

The interior is lofty and striking. The nave has on each side a good arcade of 4 Perpendicular arches of good form with light clustered piers of the usual local type. The clerestory windows are of 3 lights with good Perpendicular tracery. The tower arch is on very strong piers with double shafts and is very deep. The lower part of the tower has a stone groined roof. The chancel arch is panelled upon shafts.

The roof of the nave is open and has well carved oak beams with foliated spandrels set on shafts on stone corbels representing figures bearing shields. The south aisle has a panelled roof; the northern roof is plain. The nave has several good open ancient seats with poppyheads on the standards. The roodscreen remains; has good wood panelling and a rich cornice of foliage, all painted and gilt.

On either side of the chancel arch is a squint with arch cinquefoiled. The chancel inclines very much to the north and has had the roof renewed and covered with lead. The east window has unfortunately been destroyed. The south windows are of 2 lights, Decorated, the south-east window having the cill extended for a sedile and having an angular piscina in the jamb with 3-foiled fenestella and pier of clustered shafts. The north-east window is plainer, of 2 lights, also early Decorated, and under it is a flat arch. On the north of the chancel is a sepulchral effigy of a priest bearing a chalice, beneath a flat arch.

The north chapel opens to the chancel by a panelled arch with small shafts near which is a hagioscope. Its roof is panelled with bosses and coloured and it contains a handsome Perpendicular tomb beneath an arch to the founder of the chantry. On its east wall is some colour representing large figures in niches. The chancel is stalled in deal. There are also pues, but the old open benches have ever remained uninjured. There is, however, a western gallery. The font is curious, the bowl surrounded with shafts resting on a cylinder.

(Pray for them that –
For the love of IHC and Mary sake
There is also a woodscreen in the north chapel).

Wells Cathedral

19/48–54 [St. Andrew] 25 October, 1825

October 25th went on a expedition to Wells which is small as a city and dull as a town, but situated in beautiful country diversified by bold hills and rich valleys. The first object in the place is the cathedral which is a most magnificent and interesting structure. Its plan comprehends a nave and choir with side aisles, a great transept, a small transept east of the choir, a Lady Chapel forming the eastern extremity of the building, a tower in the centre and two at the west end. On the north side of the transept is the chapter house with some of the prebendal houses, etc. On the south side of the nave are the cloisters forming 3 sides of a square.

The architecture of the church is principally Early English and without any

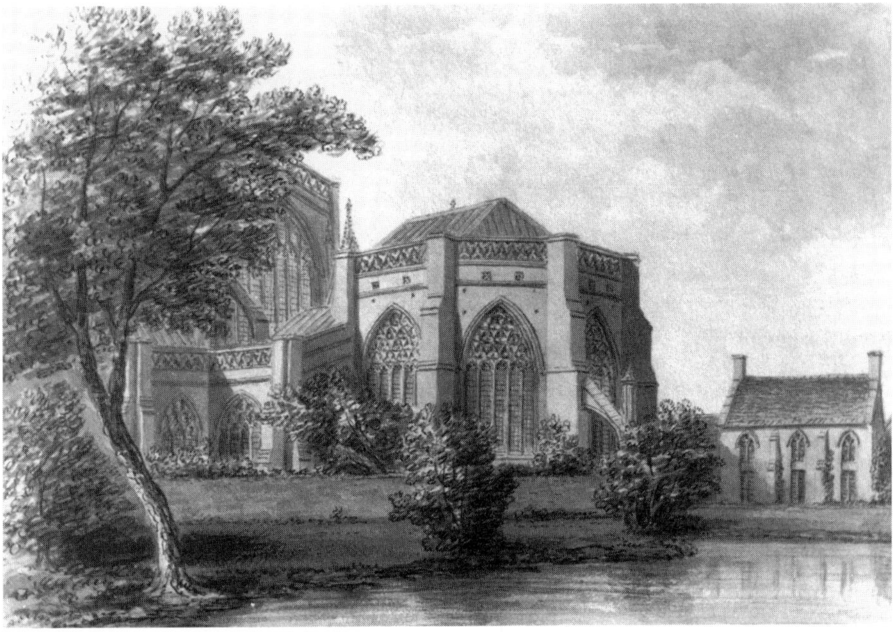

East view of Wells Cathedral, 1838, by J. Buckler

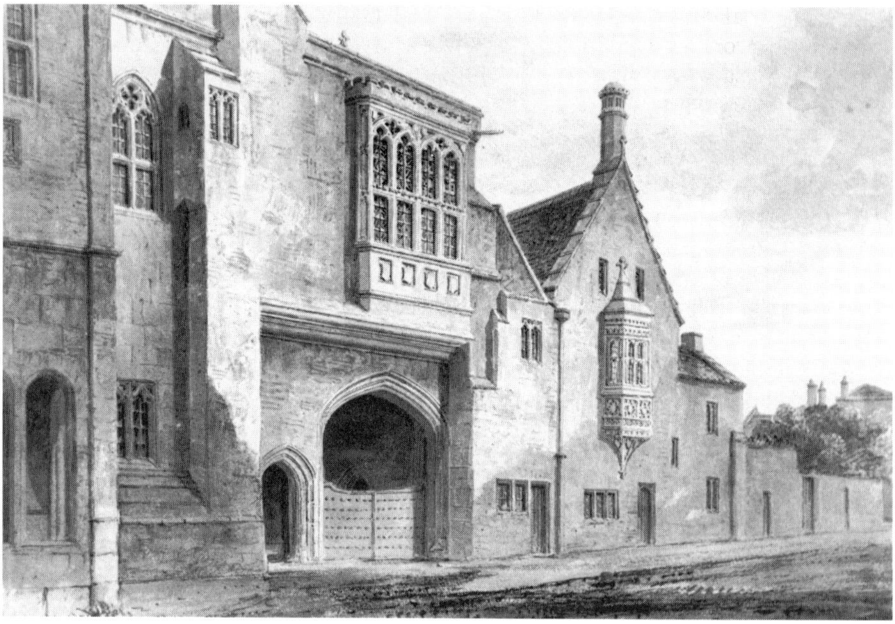

Entrance to Vicar's Close, Wells, 1804, by J. Buckler

traces of Norman work, but there are several later portions of Decorated and Perpendicular work. The most splendid part is undoubtedly the west front which, although equally Early English differs very considerably from the west fronts of Lincoln, Peterborough and Salisbury Cathedrals but is equally beautiful and even more gorgeous. It is nearly entirely covered with niches, mostly have plain triangular canopies and trefoiled heads and containing images which, from their great number, add materially to the richness of the general effect. The shafts are detached and stand free and the spaces between them and the wall are filled with Early English crockets which have a good effect.

The central division of the Front has buttresses entirely covered with rich niches containing images, etc. The buttresses are terminated by large Early English pyramidical pinnacles. In this central division is a fine window of 3 lancet lights and a fine doorway of double form with a quatrefoil between the heads of the arches. The mouldings are deep and bold and supported on fine shafts. The upper portion of the towers which flank the west front are of dissimilar work to the rest of the facade. They are of Perpendicular style and have fine long belfry windows and canopied buttresses, but are finished rather in an abrupt manner.

The north porch of the nave is a most splendid specimen of an Early English porch, the interior walls being enriched with ranges of fine niches with clustered filleted shafts having fine foliated capitals. The ceiling is groined with ribs springing from shafts. The outer door is amazingly fine and has deep receding bands of moulding, two of which are enriched with the double chevron work entwined with foliage. These are supported on fine shafts, filleted and standing free, having elegant capitals of foliage in some of which are worked grotesque heads and figures.

The external appearance of the nave and transepts is comparatively plain, but of good work and wholly built of fine durable stone. The windows in the aisles are of Early English origin, but have been filled up with Perpendicular tracery. The parapet is neat being worked with simple Early English niches. The transept ends are of good simple Early English work and have good windows and are flanked by large Early English turrets crowned by massive plain pinnacles. The central tower appears to be of Early Decorated work. It is large, and elegant in its ornament having a fine open work parapet and at each corner a turret crowned by a rich crocketed pinnacle. Between the large pinnacles are set at equal distances smaller ones making in all 12. The tower is enriched by 2 tiers of windows and small canopied buttresses.

The interior above the roof of the church is enriched with several ranges of niches of Early English character. The ceiling under it is very finely groined in stone. The western portion of the choir resembles the nave but the eastern part is much richer and is of Decorated work. It comprehends the 3 eastern windows of the choir which are rich and have very fine crocketed ogee canopies. This portion of the church has flying buttresses and a very beautiful pierced parapet.

The interior of the nave is handsome but inferior in lightness and loftiness to that of Salisbury. The west window of 3 lights has a good effect, being filled with fine painted glass and having shafts and toothed ornament in the soffit. The arches dividing the nave from the aisles are pointed and deeply moulded but somewhat low. The piers are massive and strong and have clusters of shafts set by 3's with foliated capitals.

The triforium is extremely plain being simply formed of lancet arches with plain mouldings and dripstone set by 3's over each main arch. The groining of the roof is also very plain having only plain ribs springing from foliated brackets between the triforium divisions. The clerestory windows have been filled with Perpendicular tracery. The transepts have side aisles as the nave and the triforium arches set in two's. The aisle roofs are groined simply with ribs and springing from foliated capitals of clustered shafts.

The eastern aisle of the south transept has some good plain Decorated windows and there is much Perpendicular open stone screenwork in the transepts. On the south side of the nave between two pillars is a beautiful Perpendicular chapel of rich and elegant work with fine groined ceiling and elegant tabernacle work which was erected to the memory of Bishop Beckington by his executors in the 15th century. On the north side of the nave, opposite the last mentioned chapel, is another chapel erected in memory of Bishop Bubwith, inferior in richness and elegance, but of tolerable Perpendicular work.

In the south transept is the font of circular form and moulded, with pointed arches and shafts of Early English character. In the north transept is a very curious and ancient clock of extraordinary mechanism which came from Glastonbury Abbey. In this transept is also the monument of Bishop Cornish, a good Perpendicular panelled one, of 1519. The piers supporting the central tower are strengthened with inverted arches opening to the nave and transepts. The organ screen at the entrance of the choir is plain and indifferent. The organ (although a noble and powerful instrument) has a very ugly, gaudy, painted case of the 17th century.

The choir has a beautiful appearance from the amazingly rich colours of the east window which is of 7 lights and early Perpendicular tracery and entirely filled with splendid painted glass. The arches opening behind the altar through which are seen elegant combinations of pillars and, in the distance, the rich painted windows of the Lady Chapel form a beautiful coup d'oeil. The arches and piers to the aisles resemble those of the nave, but the piers have one additional shaft which ascends to the ceiling. The ceiling is groined in a much richer style than the nave and is of complicated Perpendicular character. The 3 eastern windows of the clerestory have Decorated tracery and are filled with stained glass. In this portion there is a range of fine niches with rich crocketed canopies under the clerestory and forming a triforium of beautiful appearance.

The stalls are gaudy and covered with gilding and are neither elegant or in good taste. The Bishop's Throne was designed by Bishop Beckington and has some good Perpendicular tabernacle work mixed with much bad Italian work and tasteless gilding. The aisles of the choir have good Decorated windows and fine groined ceilings with foliated bosses. At the east end of the choir, beneath the great window, are 3 beautiful lancet arches with piers formed of clustered slender shafts with foliated capitals opening to the area leading to the Lady Chapel. Through these are seen the rich windows of the Lady Chapel. Above these arches and immediately below the great eastern window is a beautiful stone screen enriched with fine niches with crocketed canopies; the screen is crowned by an open parapet.

Behind the choir is an area forming a vestibule to the chapel of the Virgin and of the same elevation as the aisles of the choir. The middle aisle of the area is, as at Salisbury and Winchester, divided into three by rows of elegant pointed arches springing from very light clustered piers with foliated capitals. The effect produced by this is singularly beautiful from the lightness of the piers and elegant combinations of the numerous arches. There are on the north and south sides two chapels of the same elevation which form a small eastern transept. At the north and south ends of this transept are singular Decorated windows with contracted arches and a few others with rather uncommon tracery.

Near the south-west corner of the Lady Chapel is a light and elegant Perpendicular shrine to Bishop Bitton obviously erected long after his death which happened in 1264. In an elegant Perpendicular chapel on the south side of the choir is the tomb of Bishop Beckington of an altar form with the middle part open so that two slabs are seen in the upper of which is the figure of the Bishop in his episcopal robes and on the lower is a representation of him after death, a skeleton in a shroud.

The Lady Chapel is one of the most beautiful of the kind in England. It is of a hexagonal form and of beautiful Decorated work. It is of higher elevation than the chapel through which it is approached and has 5 large uniform windows of 5 lights entirely filled with the richest painted glass in fine preservation and presenting a wonderful effect. The groining of the roof is elegant and graceful, the ribs springing from clustered shafts at the angles of the building and all meeting at the centre and having at their intersection foliated bosses. The altar piece has been fine Perpendicular but is dreadfully mutilated. The Lady Chapel has a rich pierced parapet externally.

The Chapter House is a beautiful octagon of Decorated character and is approached by a passage from the north transept in which passage is a double stone staircase the top of which is level with the floor of the Chapter House, there being under it a crypt. One end of the staircase leads to the prebendal houses etc., the other to the north transept of the cathedral. This vestibule is of advanced Early English character and has fine windows resembling those of the cloisters of Salisbury Cathedral and a good groined ceiling.

The Chapter House itself has externally an enriched parapet, the upper portion of which is ornamented with quatrefoils, the lower with a range of niches. At each angle of the building is a buttress crowned with a rich crocketed pinnacle. The windows are of excellent Decorated character and externally are crowned with ogee crocketed canopies. Within the soffits are enriched with the Decorated ballflower. The windows are of 4 lights. The roof is groined with stone and is singularly beautiful, the ribs all springing from a central pier which supports the whole as in the chapter houses of Lichfield, Lincoln, Salisbury and Margam. This pier is formed of clustered slender shafts of Purbeck marble with fine foliated capitals. The ribs have foliated bosses at the intersections and are continued down the wall between the windows in clustered shafts with foliated capitals.

Beneath the windows are niches round the whole room. They are feathered and have rich triangular canopies with beautiful crockets and finials. The space between the head of the niche and the canopy is filled by a pierced trefoil. The niches are supported upon clustered shafts and between each is a false buttress terminating in a crocketed pinnacle. The doorway to the Chapter House is formed by two beautiful open stone screens with elegant Decorated tracery. The arch is deeply moulded and has beautiful shafts with foliated capitals. It consists of 2 feathered lights with a clustered pier between them. Between the apices of the lights is a triangle feathered and the space between that and the pier is occupied by a trefoil. Altogether it is a beautiful specimen.

The crypt beneath the Chapter House is a curious Early English apartment. The roof is arched with strong ribs which are supported upon substantial circular pillars, most of which have plain capitals, but a few have them enriched with the toothed ornament. In the centre is a very large massive pier surrounded with smaller Early English shafts. This pier is just beneath the pillar of the Chapter House. In the crypt against the wall is a stoup of octagonal form.

The cloisters are approached from the south transept by a fine Early English doorway with fine bands of foliage and filleted shafts with foliated capitals. The cloisters form three sides of a square and are of good Perpendicular work with good groined ceilings. Over the eastern cloister is the library, a fine old room built 1620, fitted up with wainscotting and having good windows of the period.

Adjoining the Chapter House are several collegiate buildings with some good specimens of ancient work and near the north side of the cathedral is a very fine Perpendicular gateway. In the town are several ancient buildings and conduit of octagonal form which is a most beautiful specimen of Perpendicular work.

Vol. 61

Wells. The West Front: superb. East window beautiful. Length of Lady Chapel, which is highly decorated, 47 feet. Tombs and Chapel of Bishop Beckington, Bubwith.

Wells

19/54–55 St. Cuthbert 25 October, 1825

Besides the cathedral, Wells has a parish church dedicated to St. Cuthbert which is an extremely spacious and handsome structure consisting of a nave, side aisles, north and south chapels, chancel and very beautiful Perpendicular tower at the west end which, though not particularly rich in its ornaments when compared with the gorgeous and elaborate towers of Glastonbury and Huish, is of most graceful proportion and extreme elegance and good taste in its decoration. This tower is lofty and has 4 turrets at the angles which terminate in lofty and graceful pinnacles. The belfry windows are double and of very great length and the buttresses are much enriched with pinnacles. There are some niches and panelling about the tower and good west door and window.

The nave is very lofty and magnificent and has a very fine timber roof with much excellent panelling and pierced work. The arches and piers dividing it from the aisles appears to be Early English, the piers being formed of shafts set in clusters, some having foliated capitals. On the north and south sides there are 2 additional aisles or chapels extending westward from the transepts, but they are only of 3 arches. These add considerably to the beauty and stateliness of the church from the beautiful combinations of arches and columns, there being in all 4 rows of arches. The south chapel is called Trinity Chapel and is divided from the church by pointed arches with [sic] . . .

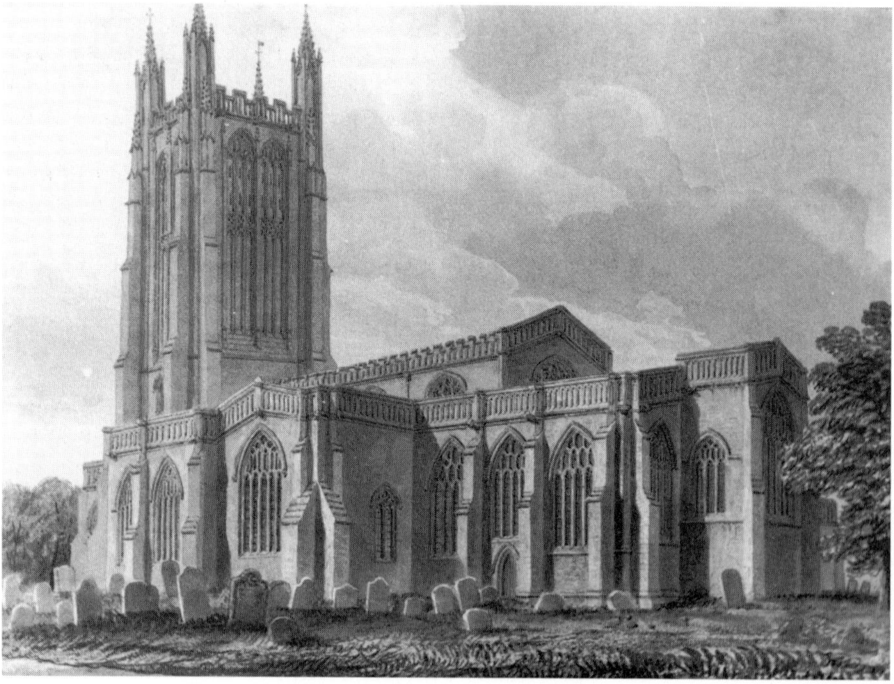

South east view of St. Cuthbert's, Wells, 1827, by J. Buckler

This chapel has a beautiful timber ceiling of rich Perpendicular work and large Perpendicular windows. The northern chapel has 3 Perpendicular arches with piers having shafts. The soffits of the arches have rich panelling. The arches to the transepts have piers of clustered Early English shafts. The nave has a clerestory of Perpendicular windows of which style nearly all the windows are fine and large specimens. There is, however, one at the east end of the south aisle which has the appearance of being very early Decorated.

The church has externally a panelled parapet and the chancel is divided from its side aisles by pointed arches with lozenge piers of shafts. In the nave there are stone shafts above the main piers of the nave extending to the roof. There are the beginnings of stone groins to the roof of the south aisle of the chancel. This chancel is very well and handsomely fitted up and has a beautifully carved pulpit. At the west end is a handsome organ.

February, 1849. Recently has been discovered at the east end of the north transept a curious reredos of stone with Third Pointed niche work representing the tree of Jesse having considerable remains of colour. There is a fresco of Our Lord with inscription **IHV MCY** and **Salvator Mundi.** The roof of the chapels blue and gilt. In the *domus inclusa* is now preserved a quantity of statues lately discovered, of fine execution with marks of painting and gilding, but all the heads are gone.

St. Cuthbert is a First Pointed church altered and greatly enlarged in the Third Pointed style. The nave is of 6 bays including that opening to the transepts, the last interval being of extraordinary width of wall and from its strength suggesting the idea of there once having been a central tower. These piers have impost mouldings. The other piers are quite First Pointed, the capitals varying. The clerestory has 5 light windows of large size. The roof beams rise on slender shafts with corbels. The roof is very fine, open and sloping, with panelled compartments, rich bosses and ornamental beams.

There is a short aisle or chapel on each side beyond the aisles extending to the transepts, the arcade of which has Third Pointed panelling down the piers. The transepts are of small proportion beyond the chapels. Over the chancel arch is a window corresponding with the clerestory. The chancel Third Pointed and the arcade to its aisles with light piers. It is unfortunately ceiled. On the south-east are shallow sedilia with double feathering and clustered shafts, a piscina with ogee canopy and stone shelf. The east window is blocked by a modern reredos.

At the east end of the south transept is an early Middle Pointed window of 2 lights. There are some open benches and a rich Jacobean pulpit. There is a fine panelled parapet to the exterior. On the north side is a simple chamber at first sight resembling a porch, but with no outer door and having a 2 light Middle Pointed window. It seems more like a *domus inclusa.*

Wembdon

49/12–13 [St. George] Before 1840

This church stands among fields at a distance from houses, but is a neat respectable edifice consisting of an embattled west tower, a nave with aisles and a chancel, the whole whitewashed externally. There is a good deal of Curvilinear work of which character is the west window of the tower, an elegant one of 3 lights; the belfry windows are square-headed. The nave and aisles are under one tiled roof without a clerestory.

Many of the windows of the nave are of 2 lights, very plain without feathering, apparently of early Curvilinear period and there is one square-headed Rectilinear one of 3 lights. The nave is divided from each aisle by 4 pointed arches of low proportions, the piers on the north being circular, those on the south octagonal. There are vestiges of painting upon the walls and texts inscribed over the piers. The arches to the tower and chancel are each pointed and within the latter is a wood screen.

The chancel has several Curvilinear windows of good character, those on the sides of 2 lights, the eastern ones of 4 lights and very elegant and has the outer arch springing from shafts with foliated capitals. On the south side is a Rectilinear window of 4 lights with a very wide arch but early in the style. There is an aperture on the north side of the chancel arch in a transverse direction. The altar table is small, but has very handsome carved legs temp. James I. On the north side of the chancel is a modern vestry. The font is octagonal, panelled with quatrefoils containing foliage.

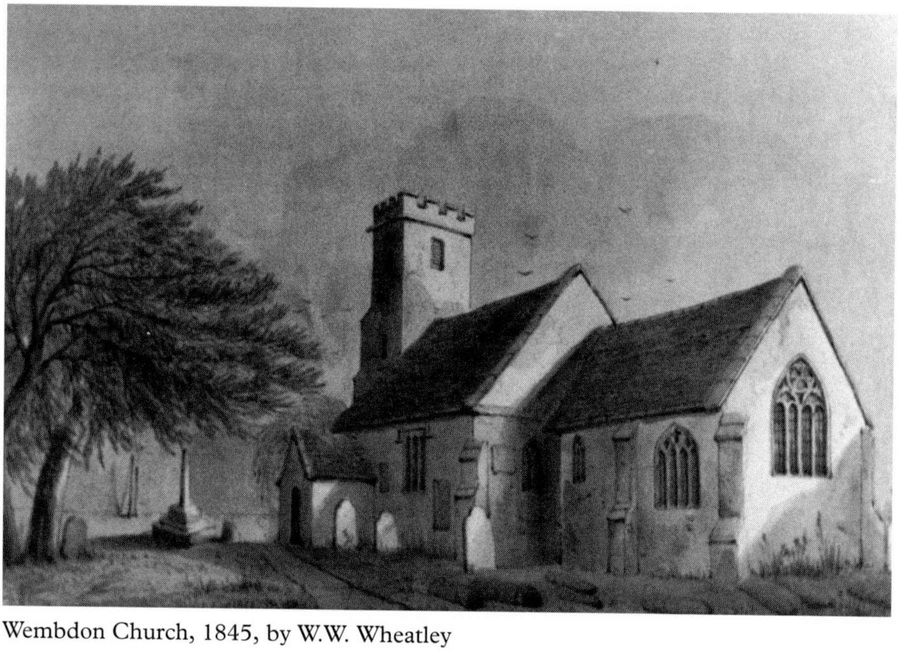

Wembdon Church, 1845, by W.W. Wheatley

Westbury Sub Mendip

51/54–55 St. Lawrence 27 January, 1862

Plan, nave with south aisle, chancel, west tower and south porch. On the north of the nave is an old early doorway with stilted segmental arch on shafts with capitals and abaci, now closed, and a buttress carried down the centre of it. The tower in its lower portion is Norman and has an early arch to the nave of 2 plain orders with shafts having sort of cushion capitals and abaci. The tower is very plain and has had Elizabethan insertions; the parapet embattled.

The walls are in great part covered with roughcast; the roofs of lead. On the north of the nave are Perpendicular windows of 2 and 3 lights, some square-headed. In the south aisle are 3 light Perpendicular windows. The nave has a flat ceiling with ribs upon corbel brackets and there are shafts to the timbers of the aisle roofs. The arcade is of the frequent Perpendicular character. The nave has 3 arches on light piers of shafts. The chancel arch is wide and ugly and misshapen with continuous mouldings.

The aisle is continued along one bay of the chancel with a similar arch. There is between the south aisle of the nave and that of the chancel a Decorated arch. The chancel has a flat ceiling. The east window Decorated of 2 lights having cinquefoil feathering to the rear arch as is sometimes seen in this county. On the south-east is a square-headed Perpendicular window of 2 lights and a piscina with trefoil feathering upon a corbel. In the south-east angle of the chancel and aisle is a door curiously placed and cutting off the angle. In the south aisle of the chancel, which is now a vestry, is a

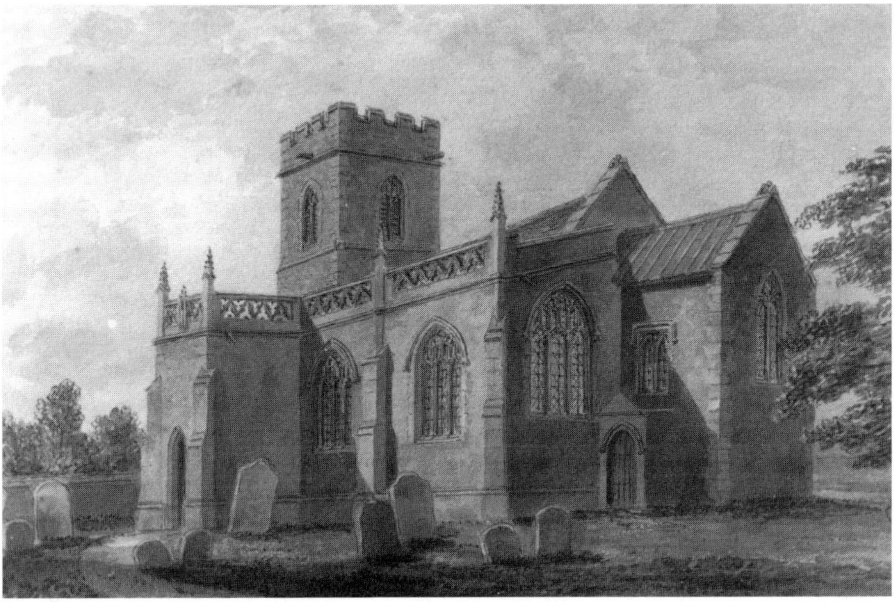

South east view of Westbury Church, 1844, by J. Buckler

Perpendicular piscina with cinquefoil feathering to the arch and pierced spandrels having an octagonal bowl.

The font has a plain octagonal bowl on a stem. The pulpit is of stone, Perpendicular, panelled. The pues are ugly. The porch and south aisle have the pierced parapet of the county. The porch has octagonal stair turret and pinnacles at the angles of the front. Over the outer door is a niche and another over the inner door which has continuous arch mouldings. Near it is a stoup with cinquefoiled arch and embattled cornice.

Weston in Gordano

51/63–65 St. Paul 15 August, 1862

A curious church in good order comprising a nave and chancel with south chapel to the latter only, a tower and porch each on the south of the nave. A recent restoration has been effected. The walls internally present the bare stone and the roof which is ribbed in cradle form is illuminated. The windows of the nave are Perpendicular of 3 lights, the internal fittings plain open benches. There is a piscina on the south of the nave with octagon basin, and, communicating with the tower, one pointed arch now closed and, adjoining it, a smaller one using Norman impost, partly built up.

The chancel arch is with continuous mouldings and there is a rood screen. On the north side of the nave is a very fine Perpendicular tomb of Richard de

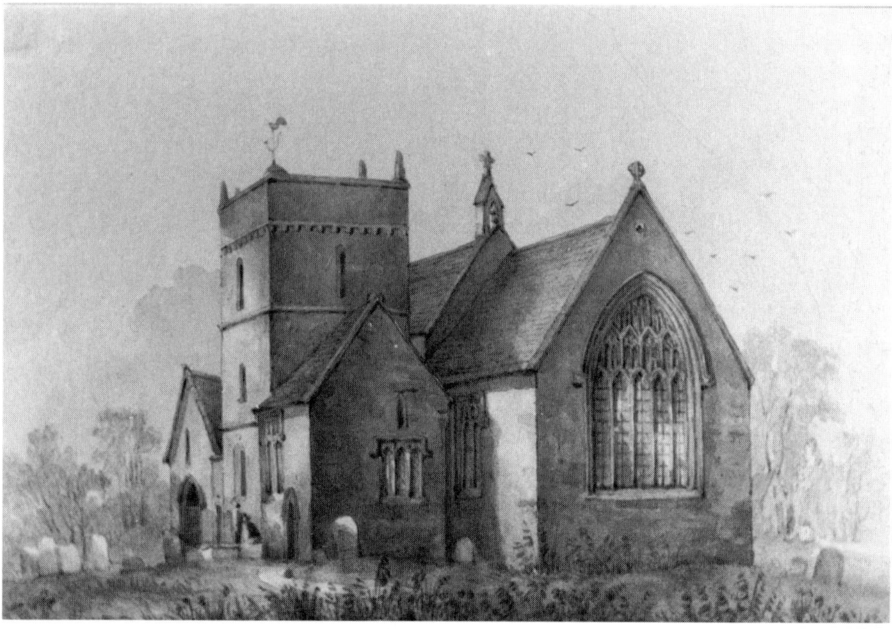

Weston in Gordano, 1842, by W.W. Wheatley

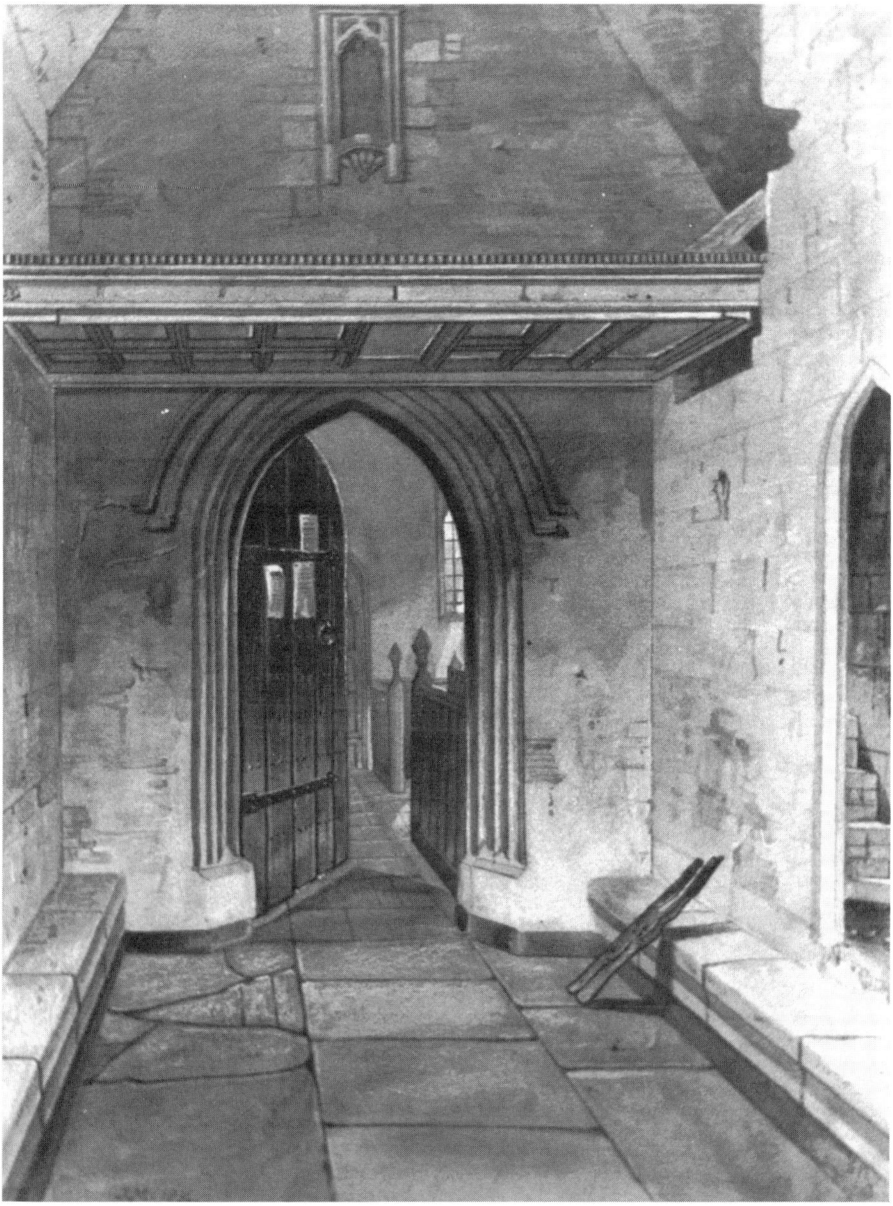

Weston in Gordano, 1834, by J. M(anning?)

Percyval quel morot l'an de Jesus MCCCCLXXVIII. The canopy has an ogee arch and the panelling enriched with angel figures bearing shields. This tomb has some illumination. The font is Norman, of cushion shape on a cylindrical stem.

The chancel has a coved roof and all its windows Perpendicular. Over the sacrarium the roof is boarded. The east window is of 5 lights, the others of 3 and square-headed, all having shafts. There is a piscina with shelf with pointed arch within a square compartment. There is a pointed arch on shafts of Perpendicular character opening to the south aisle. In this aisle, or chapel, is a bracket with foliage in the east wall and another, plainer, near the door, 2 oblong openings. The priest's door south of the chancel has corbel heads to the hood. The chancel is stalled and contains an organ.

The south chapel has on the west a low arch to the tower. The tower is Early English and rude, has 3 string courses forming divisions and a bald-looking, unfinished parapet to the upper storey which is probably a later addition. The upper string course has a corbel table of Early English character and the windows are obtuse headed kind of loops. There are 5 bells. The roofs have new slating externally. Over the east gable of the nave is a bellcote with trefoil arch for one bell and crowned by a new cross. The north doorway of the nave has an obtuse arch with continuous moulding. The south porch, which has a flagged roof, is remarkable; large and lofty; the outer doorway has Tudor Perpendicular arch; the inner has continuous arch mouldings and there is an illuminated niche over it. Over part of the porch is the curious woodloft, sometimes seen in Somersetshire, panelled and illuminated and approached by a staircase within the porch opening by an ogee doorway.

Westonzoyland

50/16–17 St. Mary 2 September, 1843

A large and handsome church comprising a fine and lofty west tower, nave with aisles, north and south porches, north and south transepts and chancel. The general character is the usual Perpendicular of the West of England with earlier indications in the chancel.

The tower is one of the finest in the neighbourhood and is 4 storeys high but the pinnacles unfinished. Under the battlement a band of quatrefoil panelling. The belfry storey has triple windows on each side of considerable length with pinnacles between them. The 2 next stages have each a 2 light window set between canopied niches which have had statues, some mutilated, some quite gone. There is a west door with plain mouldings and over it a large 4 light window. The buttresses are elegantly grouped and on the second stage have pinnacles. The battlement and buttresses are of fine stone, the rest of the coarse blue lias.

The south porch is large and extends somewhat further than the transepts. It has an open wood roof and a good battlement, the centrepiece at the apex of the gable being of ogee form. Over the entrance is a niche. The whole south side of the church has a fine battlement; that of the transept has at its apex an ogee head and is sculptured with a shield

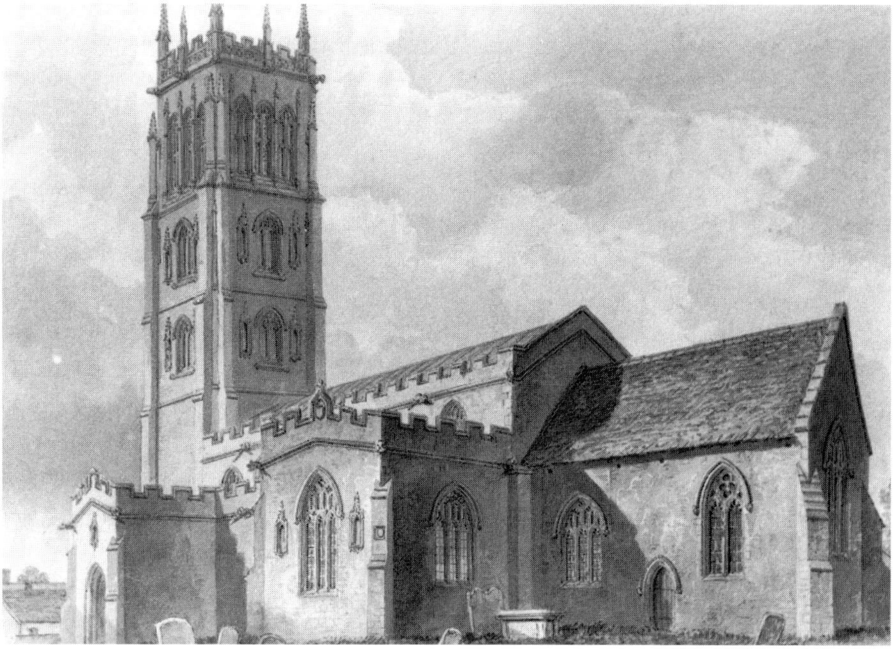

South east view of Westonzoyland Church, 1832, by J. Buckler

containing a cross Flory. On the buttress of the south transept are shields bearing the cypher BB and the figure of a pelican. The north side, as usual, is much plainer and without battlement. The windows of the aisles are very uniform, of 3 lights with good tracery. That of the south transept is externally flanked by elegant canopied niches.

The tower has internally a fine stone groined roof and opens to the nave by a lofty arch with panelled soffit. The nave has on each side 5 well-formed pointed arches with mouldings continued down light piers to which small shafts are attached and a sixth arch of greater width opens to each of the transepts. The clerestory windows are of 3 lights. The nave has a very fine wood roof, though the panelling is unfinished. The beams are moulded and decorated with flowers and pieces of foliage. The cornice has some quatrefoils and flowers and the beam brackets are on small shafts resting on stone angel figures. Above the beams is some pierced tracery which, though mutilated, has a very elegant effect. The nave is very wide and the church very light.

The transepts are small. The northern is higher than the southern so as to admit of a clerestory. Its end window is of 3 lights with transom and has some pieces of painted glass. Under it is a fine flattened arch with panelled spandrels and beautiful feathering with knobs at the points. Within this arch there must have been a tomb, now gone. In the east wall of the north transept is a small trefoil niche. Between the aisles and the transepts are fine Tudor arches with panelled soffit and small shafts. That on the south side is enriched with the figure of an angel bearing a shield.

The chancel opens to the nave by a large Perpendicular arch with panelled soffit and on the south side of this is a hagioscope, now closed. The chancel is originally early Decorated and has 3 windows of that character each of 2 lights. The inner arch rests on shafts. In 2 of these and also in that on the south (next the nave) in which is Perpendicular tracery inserted [*sic*]. The south-east window has no shafts, the others have one octagonal, one circular capital and one banded.

On the north side is a vestry. The east window has been mutilated. The altar is raised on 2 steps. In the nave are a great many fine, ancient wooden seats, the ends presenting some beautiful carving with shields, etc., late in the style, but very good. Against one of the northern piers is the octagonal base of a stone pulpit upon a shaft and enriched with flowers and shields. On this is erected a wooden pulpit now used. There are 6 bells and a barrel organ in the west gallery. The north porch is very small.

Whatley

50/50–51 St. George 31 July, 1849

This church has a nave and chancel without aisles, but a south transept and porch and a western tower surmounted by a stone spire. The whole of the body of the church has been much modernised and, excepting the steeple, the

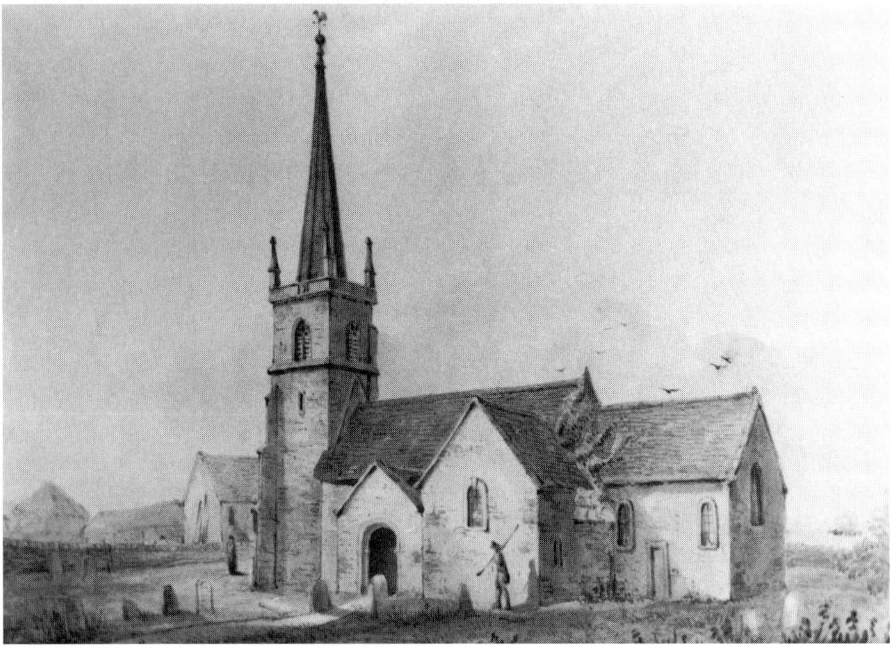

Whatley, 1842, by W.W. Wheatley

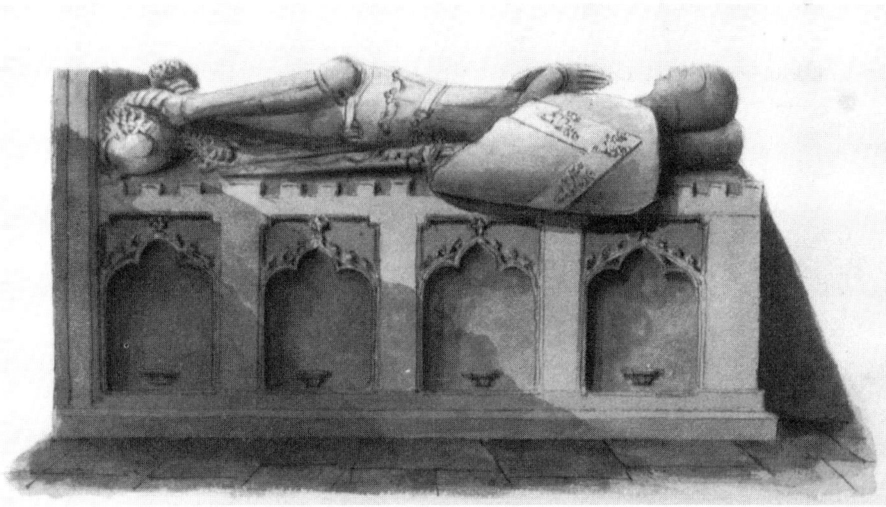

Monument in Whatley Church, 1844, by J. Buckler

exterior presents nothing worthy of notice. The steeple is situated very high and forms a pleasing object. It is Third Pointed but has no battlement, there being a flowered cornice under the parapet. At each angle is a pinnacle; the spire octagonal and ribbed, one of the most elegant in the county. The belfry window of 2 lights and there are stags head gargoyles at the angles. The tower arch to the nave is pointed, springing straight from the walls. The arch from the nave to the transept is First Pointed with octagonal corbels. On the east wall of the transept is a Third Pointed window; all other windows are mutilated. There is a hagioscope in the angle between the transept and chancel. The font is a circular bowl on a cylindrical stem with square base. In the transept is an altar tomb enriched with ogee canopies and embattled cornice and heraldic shields (arms, chevron between 3 stags heads) on which is the effigy of a cross-legged knight. The south porch has some base mouldings which have a Middle Pointed appearance. The outer door is rude, upon imposts; that within is rather less plain.

Wheathill

51/12–13 St. John 6 February, 1858

A very diminutive church now undergoing a restoration. It has only one space without distinction of chancel, a south porch and a pointed bellcote for 2 bells lately erected over the west end. There is neither west door nor window. The east window is a triplet; others are single and trefoiled, of Perpendicular character. There are remains of a Decorated window, cinquefoiled, now ejected. The roofs are ribbed within; the eastern part forming the chancel covered with tiles, the nave with slates.

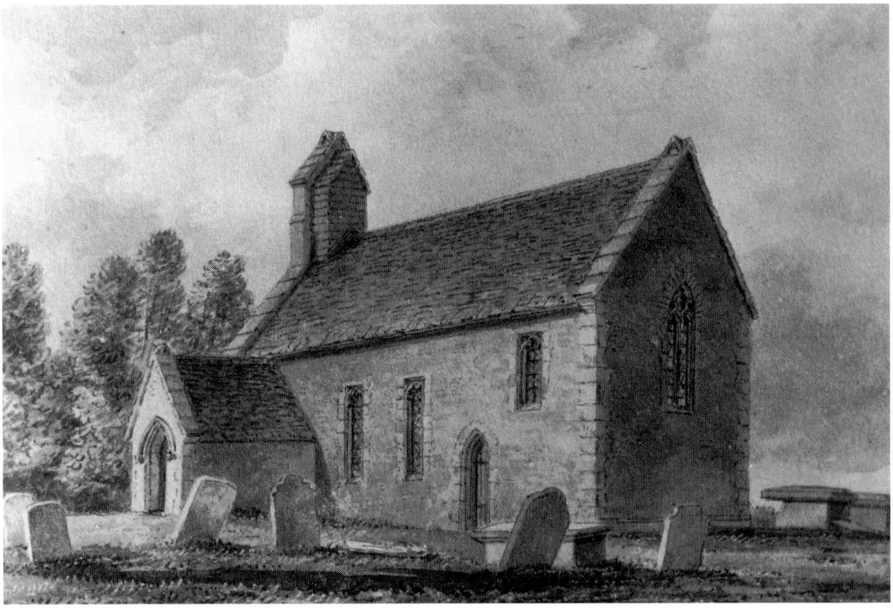

South east view of Wheathill Chapel, 1846, by J. Buckler

There is a small piscina on the south of the altar with a semi-octagonal bowl. In the porch is a stoup and on its south side a rude canopied niche, with coarsely executed pinnacles which probably once contained a statue. The font has an octagonal bowl, plain, on a square base and chamfered at the corners.

Whitchurch

51/66–68 St. Gregory 21 May, 1863

An interesting church lately put into very good condition and varying from the usual type of Somersetshire. No doubt it was original cruciform without aisles. The north transept remains undisturbed but the southern has been lost by the addition of a south aisle to the nave. There is also an aisle added on the south of the chancel. The tower is still in the centre and there are north and south porches. The walls have been externally new pointed. The north doorway within the porch has a plain semi-circular arch and may possibly be of Norman date.

In the north side of the nave 2 new Decorated windows have been [inserted]. The west window is Perpendicular of 3 lights and original, having internally shafts with foliated capitals and octagonal bases supporting the arch and smaller shafts on the mullions. At the west end of the aisle is also a Perpendicular window of 3 lights. In the aisle is a 2 light one of Decorated character and a square-headed Perpendicular one of 2 lights.

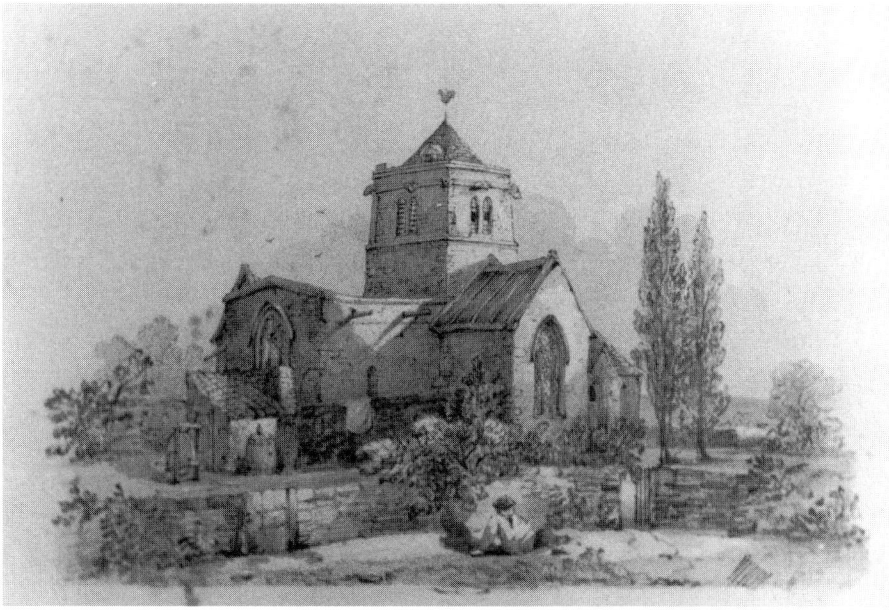

Whitchurch, by W.W. Wheatley

The roof of the nave and aisle are both open and of cradle form. The arcade to the aisle is Perpendicular of 3 Tudor-shaped arches on light piers of the common make, 4 shafts with cavettos. The south aisle is carried past the tower, supplanting the south transept. The inner walls are now of the bare stone and the seats are good plain open benches of ash. The font is ancient and much in the form of a Norman cushion capital on a cylindrical stem. The pulpit is a new one of stone.

The tower rises upon 4 Early English arches, pointed, of rather plain and rude make with edged soffits having impost mouldings and corbeled shafts, the capitals of which have no necks (as at Slimbridge and elsewhere in the west). The north transept has some Decorated windows of 3 lights with internal shafts both to the arch and to the mullions. There is a slab with incised cross rather mutilated.

The chancel is originally Early English but has received a new roof and is restored in richer style than the nave. On the north are 2 lancet windows one with stepped cill. The east window is early Decorated, of 3 lights with shafts to the arch and mullions internally. There is one single lancet remaining on the south-east now opening into the south aisle or chapel, and thus showing this to have been an outer wall. The other arch, broken in the wall, is Perpendicular upon shafts and contains a parclose screen.

The chancel is stalled and has a harmonium and laid with new polished tiles. The reredos of marble inlaid, the altar of oak, solid and good. The south chapel belongs to the Colston family and is altogether of Perpendicular character, inclosed with rich wood screens. The south porch is Perpendicular with tolerable doorways both without and within. There is also an octagonal

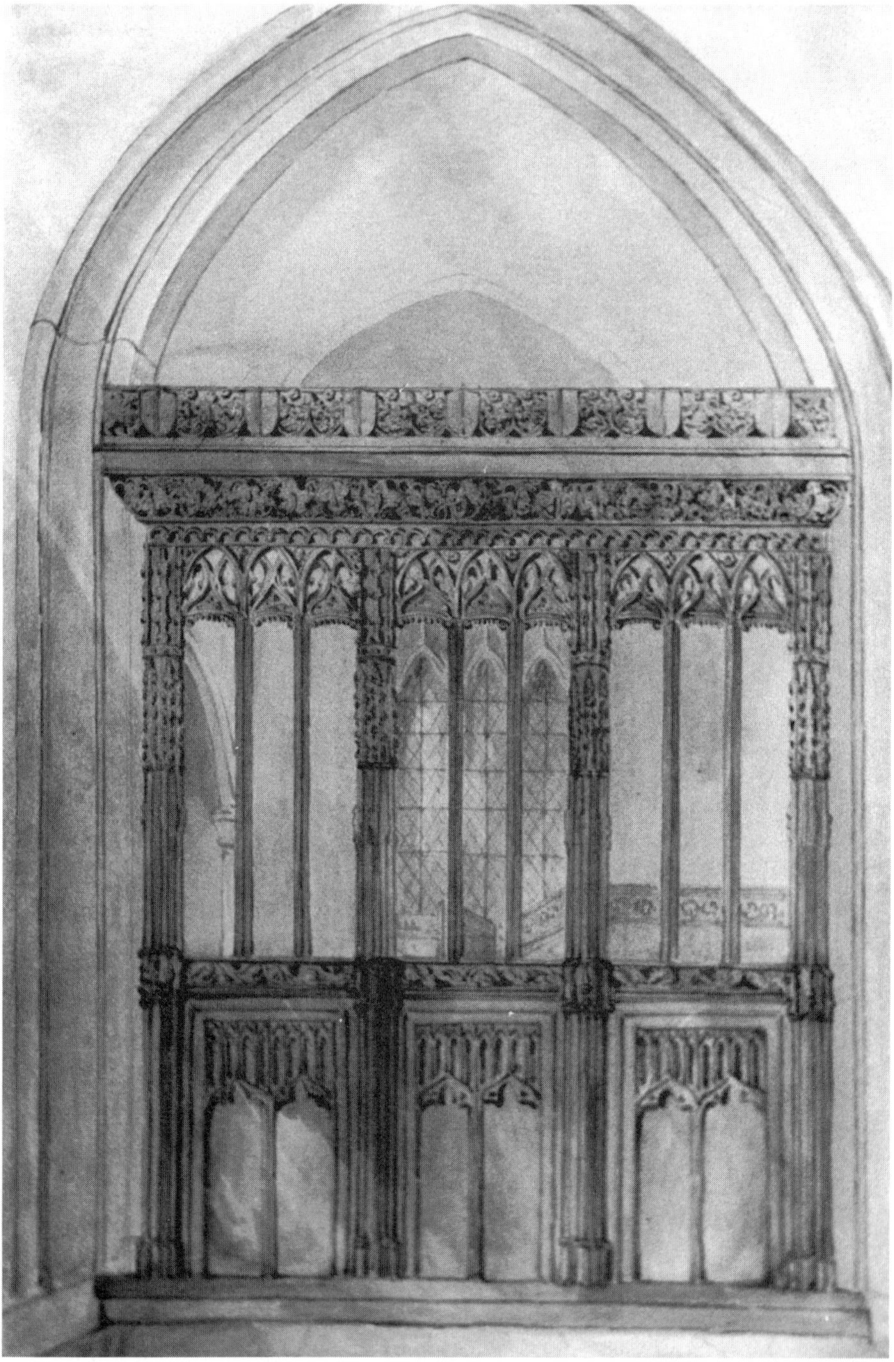

Entrance to chantry, south aisle, Whitchurch, 1843, by W.W. Wheatley

stoup. The roofs of the nave and transepts are steep and outwardly covered with lead.

There is some fair new obituary stained glass in a northern window. The tower is plain above the roof of the body with no battlement to the parapet and a pointed roof. The belfry windows of 2 very plain lights. The restoration is throughout of a very satisfactory character.

Widcombe

50/94 St. Thomas À Becket 16 January, 1857

A small Perpendicular church probably once sufficient for the population which has now greatly increased so as to form a regular portion of the City of Bath. The situation is pretty and retired on the hillside and the churchyard planted with evergreens etc. The plan comprises only a nave and chancel with western tower. The chancel seems to have been rebuilt. The nave has a good battlement and there is an octagonal rood turret to the north-east of the nave. The roof of the nave is of lead. The windows chiefly square-headed and labeled. The tower is embattled with corner buttresses and 4 pinnacles. The belfry windows of 2 lights and there is an octagonal turret at its north-east angle. The stone is good and well-preserved and some parts of the church covered with ivy.

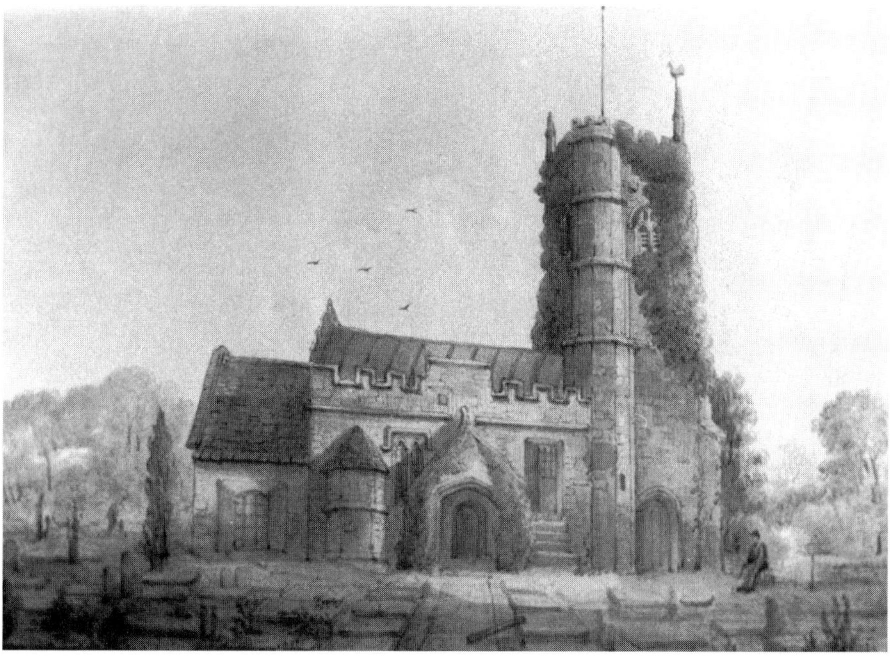

Widcombe, 1851, by W.W. Wheatley

Williton

50/18–19 16 July 1843

A chapelry of the parish of St. Decuman; a small Perpendicular building consisting of a nave with south aisle, chancel, and porch at the west end of the nave. The west gable is extended upwards and contains 2 arches with bells. The windows are mostly square-headed with labels except that at the west end which is pointed and of 3 lights. The porch is plain and the whole is in rather a coarse style.

The nave is divided from the aisle by 3 very rude pointed arches with clumsy circular piers which might be of any age and remind one rather of the coarse specimens of Cumberland and Westmoreland which, however, are generally late. The chancel arch is wider but similar in character. The roofs are cradle and in the chancel ribbed so as to form squares. There are some open seats. The font a small octagonal bowl quatrefoiled. There is a roodscreen with late tracery. There is along the outside of the north wall a kind of stone seat which seems original. And on the green north of the chapel the shaft of a cross.

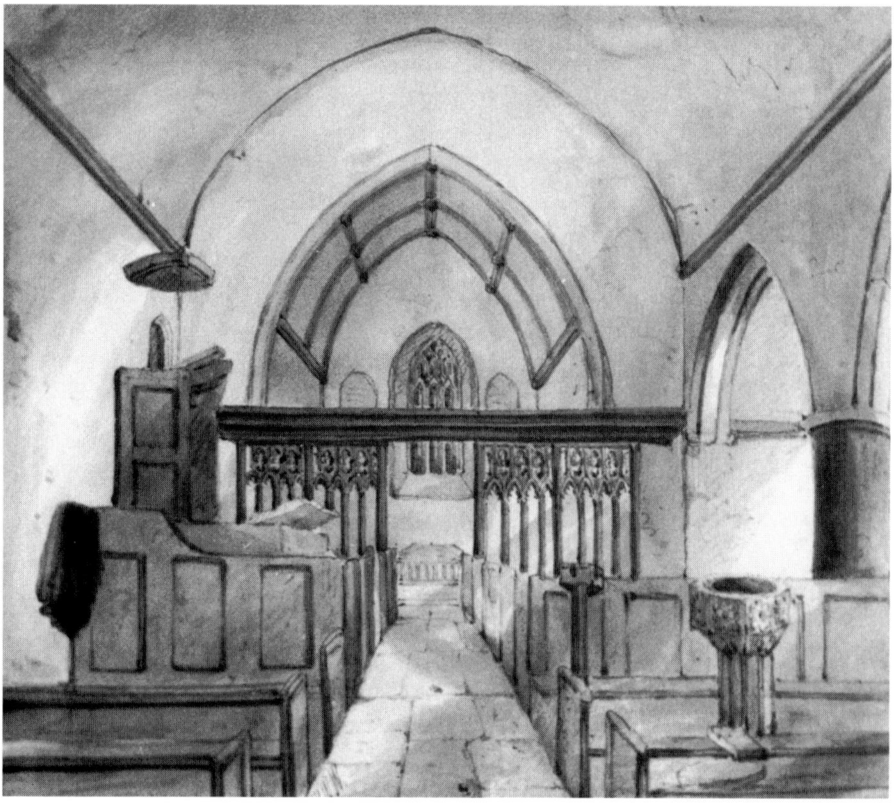

Williton Chapel, 1850, by W.W. Wheatley

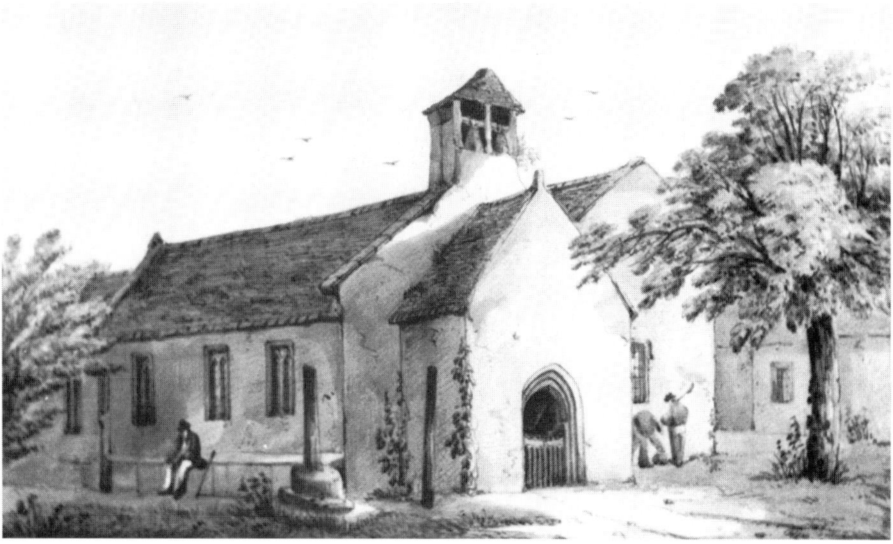

Williton Chapel, 1850, by W.W. Wheatley

Wilton

50/76 St. George 11 May, 1855

This church, now consisting of a nave and chancel with aisles and west tower, was almost wholly reconstructed and much enlarged in 1838. The tower and outer walls are all new and the only original portion is part of the south arcade

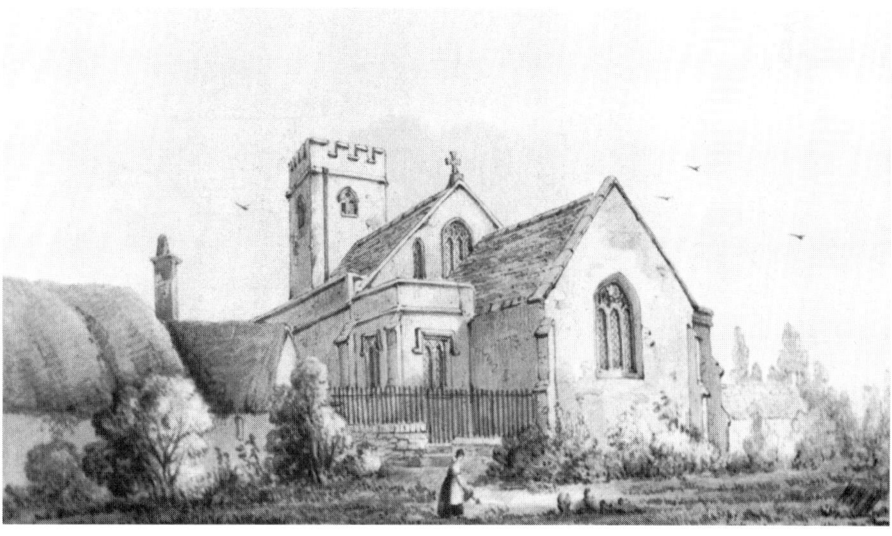

Wilton, 1848, by W.W. Wheatley

there having been originally only a south aisle. The present arcades are all uniform with Tudor shaped arches and the usual light piers of shafts. The nave of 5 bays, the chancel of one. The windows of 2 lights and Perpendicular. In fact the whole a very fair reproduction of the Perpendicular style considering the early period when it was done.

The east window contains stained glass with figures of SS. Paul, James and John and is in memory of Sir Benjamin Hammet, Knt., a native of the parish, Alderman of London, born 1737, died 1800, whose portrait is also introduced kneeling in the lower part of the window. The church is pued and has an organ. The font has a circular bowl, very plain, on a cylindrical stem, apparently mutilated. The tower is a successful imitation of the Somerset village steeple.

Wincanton

49/45–47 St. Peter and St. Paul Before 1840

This church has been so modernized as to be devoid of all interest. It consists of a nave with side aisles, a chancel and a western tower. There are 4 pointed arches on each side of the nave with piers of clustered shafts, but the capitals have been altered. The whole of the windows including the clerestory are of Venetian style and a similar character prevails in the decorations of the

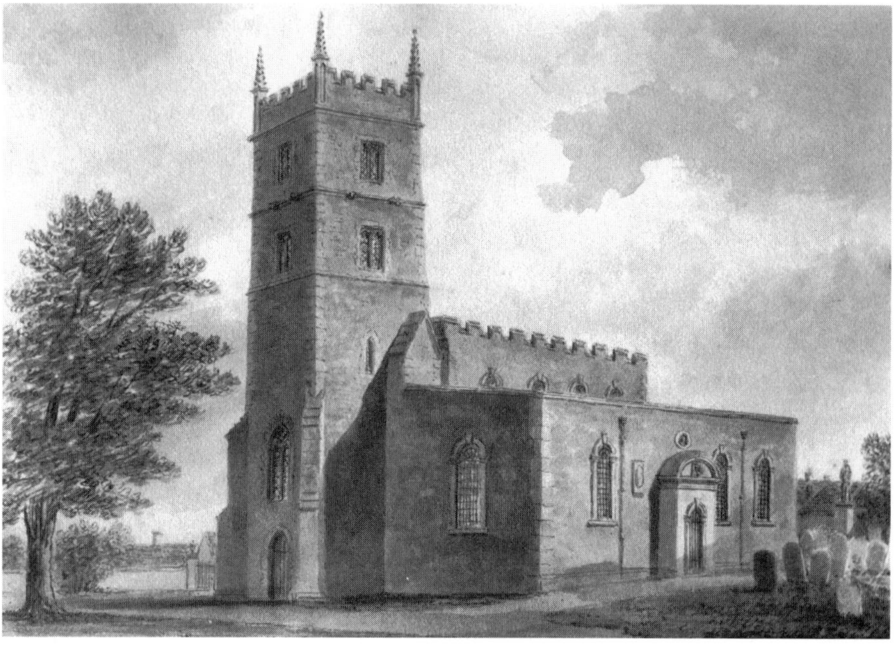

South east view of Wincanton Church, 1844, by J. Buckler

interior. There is a large organ with west gallery. The tower is plain Rectilinear, embattled, with modern pinnacles.

Winford

52/21–22 [St. Mary and St. Peter] 4 February, 1872

This church has been rebuilt except the tower and the work having been done in 1796 is far from satisfactory as an imitation of Perpendicular work. It is divided into nave with aisles and a small, poor chancel. The arcades of the nave are, however, of very fair Perpendicular character, each of 4 bays and either original or successful imitations. The arches and piers are tall, the latter have the usual type of Somersetshire in the 4 shafts and intermediate hollows and very stilted bases.

The font is a plain octagon. The tower is very good Perpendicular of the local character opening to the nave by a strong and deep arch on shafts. The tower is of excellent masonry and divided by 3 string courses into storeys, has pierced parapet with 4 crocketed pinnacles at the angles. The west door is lofty and has plain continuous arch mouldings. Over it is a poor window of 3 lights. The other stages have 2 light windows, those of the belfry pierced, the others blank. In the churchyard is the stump of a fine cross.

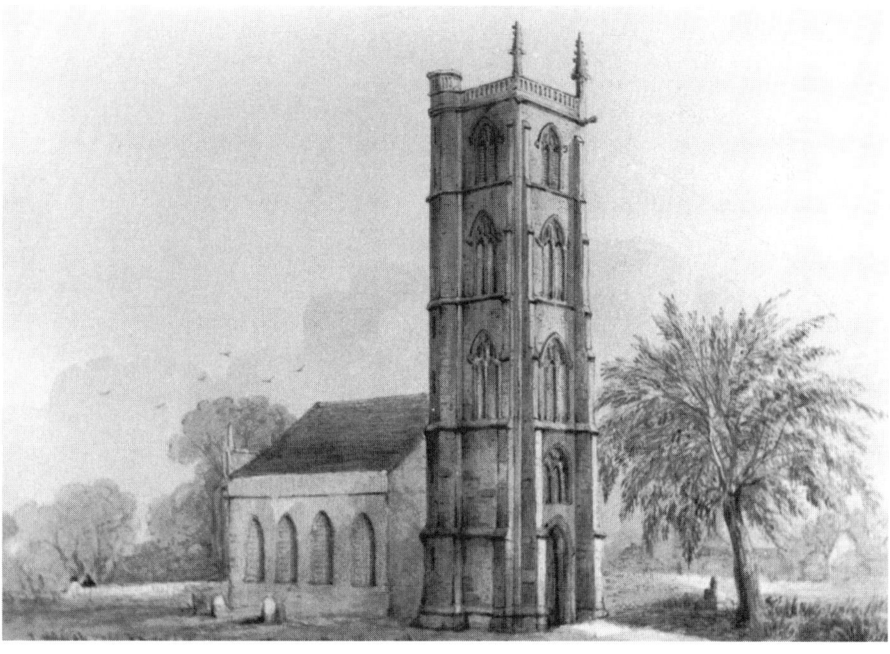

Winford, 1843, by W.W. Wheatley

Wookey

50/26–27 St. Matthew April, 1845

This church consists of a nave with aisles, chancel with south chapel, western tower and south porch. The principal external features Perpendicular but with earlier portions. The tower is a very good Perpendicular one divided into 3 stages by string courses with a good panelled battlement and pinnacles and an octagonal turret at the north-east angle which is crowned by a lofty pyramidical pinnacle. The belfry windows are of 2 lights with stone lattice work. On the west side a 4 light window and under it a door with good moulded arch and small shafts. The buttresses are at the angles.

The south porch is plain and leaded. The entrance to it is by a pointed arch which appears Decorated having shafts with moulded capitals. Within the porch is a plain door with continuous mouldings. There are no parapets to the body. The south chancel has a slated roof. The windows are nearly all Perpendicular of 2 lights except the east window of the chancel which appears Decorated and has 3 cinquefoiled lancet lights. In the south chancel are some Perpendicular ones square-headed. The nave is divided from each aisle by 3 very lofty pointed arches springing from light and elegant clustered piers, each of 4 shafts with moulded capitals. Those on the south side appear to be Decorated, but on the north the character is more Perpendicular.

The tower arch has continued moulding and is open. The chancel arch

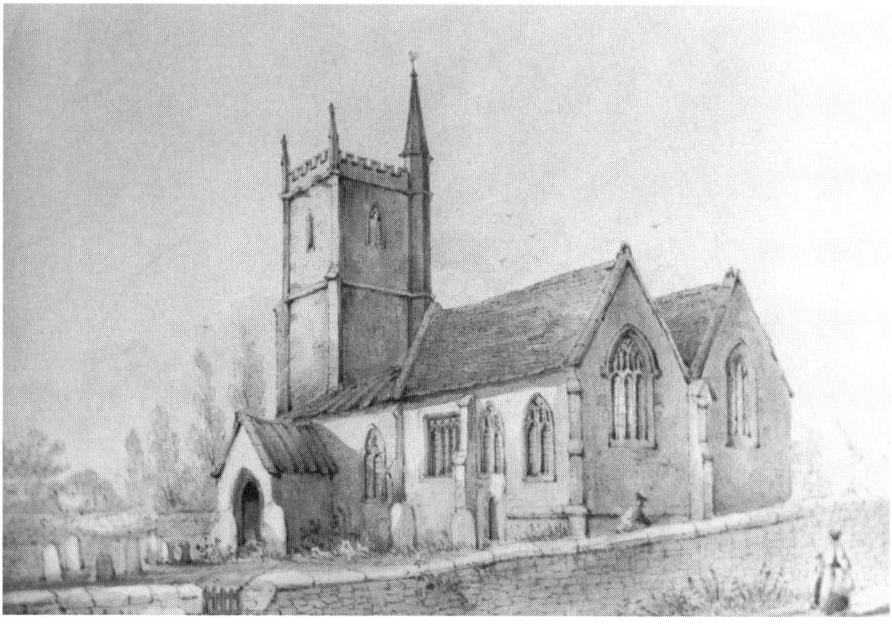

Wookey, 1843, by W.W. Wheatley

appears Perpendicular having good mouldings stopped by an impost or capital. The chancel is divided from the south chapel by 2 Perpendicular arches, much lower than those of the nave, springing from a pier with Perpendicular mouldings and shafts stilted with a plain general capital. In the south-east angle is a piscina with trefoil head set in a square and on the south of the altar is a large Perpendicular altar tomb with quatrefoil panelling containing shields and a cornice. In the south pier of the chancel arch is a square aperture. The font is of cylindrical form and plain upon a pedestal of like form. In the churchyard is the base of a cross.

Woolverton

50/41 St. Laurence 3 October, 1848

A very small church consisting only of a nave and chancel, south porch and a curious western steeple. The whole seems to be Third Pointed and the chancel is in course of rebuilding. The steeple is the principal feature consisting of a small square tower of 2 stages of which the belfry is smaller than the lower one crowned by a stone spire of no great height surrounded about the middle by a band of small battlements. The tower is also embattled with 4 little pinnacles but has no buttresses. The upper storey has square 2 light windows of a debased look, the lower has small trefoiled apertures.

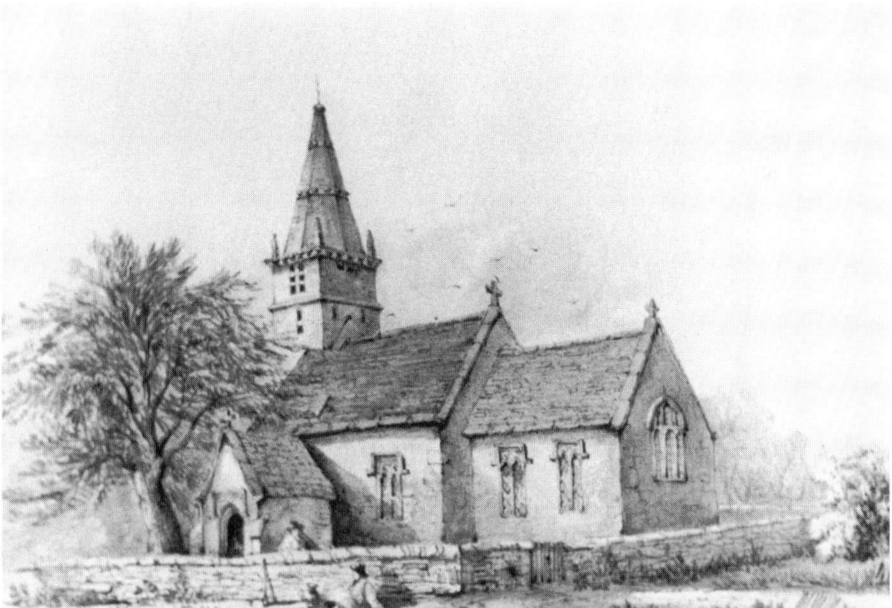

Woolverton Church, 1843, by W.W. Wheatley

The porch is small, but entirely of stone and groined, having strong ribs resting upon foliated corbels. The outer doorway has a label and foliated spandrels. The windows are all square-headed and of 2 lights in the nave. The chancel arch pointed on shafts with moulded capitals. The font has an octagonal bowl having quatrefoil panelling and a flowered band. The stem very short and painted brown.

Wootton Courtenay

51/9–10 All Saints 8 May, 1855

A nice church, as usual in this neighbourhood, beautifully situated in a fine sloping churchyard in which is a picturesque yew tree. The whole is Perpendicular. The plan consists of a chancel and nave, with north aisle to the latter, west tower and south porch.

The exterior is whitewashed and the interior unfortunately glaring with the same. The arcade of the nave has 3 very elegant arches with beautiful mouldings and tall light piers having the usual arrangement of 4 shafts having separate capitals and canopied niches at the front above the 2 piers. The roofs of the body and aisle are coved with moulded ribs and bosses; those in the aisle are boldest.

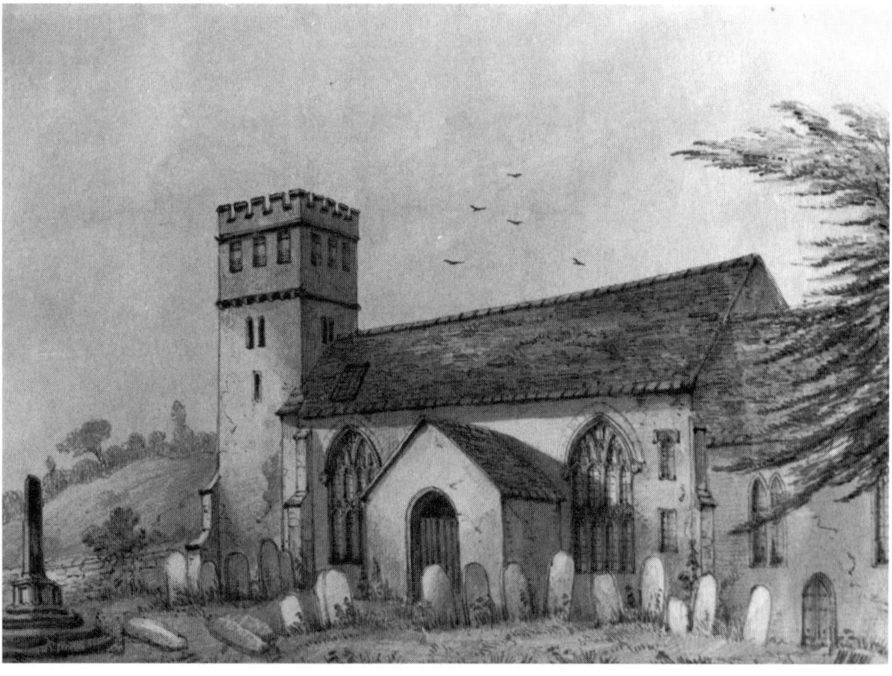

Wootton Courtenay, 1849, by W.W. Wheatley

There are 3 similar fine windows, 2 at the south side of the nave and at the east end of the aisle, like that at Minehead, square-headed with transom and subarcuated; of 4 lights. They have internally hood mouldings with angel figures bearing scrolls. Near the pulpit on the south is a single window set high up as if to light the pulpit. The other windows of the nave are poor and have no foliations. The roodscreen remains, though much mutilated, above which the space has been filled with wainscoting with the Decalogue and figures of Moses and Aaron.

The chancel has an east window which may be Early English, of 3 lancet lights within a pointed arch. On the south the windows are of 2 lights and square-headed. The font has an octagonal bowl, quatrefoils with shields, on a panelled octagonal stem. There is a west gallery and the whole is neat, but without the improvements that can be seen elsewhere. The tower is plain and rude with almost a Welsh character; a rude battlement with corbel table below it on the north and south and 3 plain oblong belfry windows. The other openings small and coarse, buttresses only to the lower part.

Worle

50/36–37 St. Martin 3 August, 1847

The church consists of a nave with north aisle and south porch, chancel and western tower with stone spire. The whole church is Third Pointed except the south doorway which is Norman and has a lofty arch upon imposts. The outer one which enclosed it has been destroyed but the strong Norman shafts

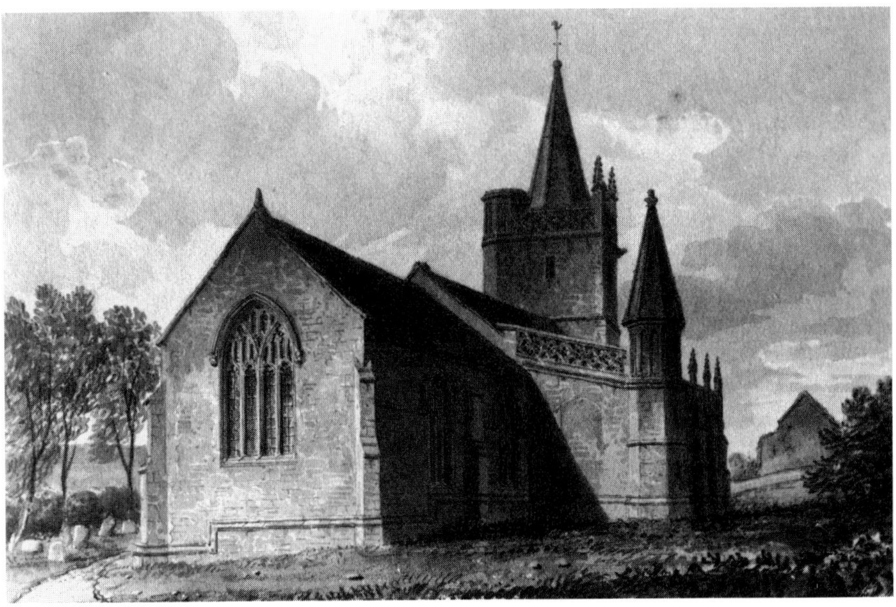

North east view of Worle Church, 1827, by J.C. Buckler

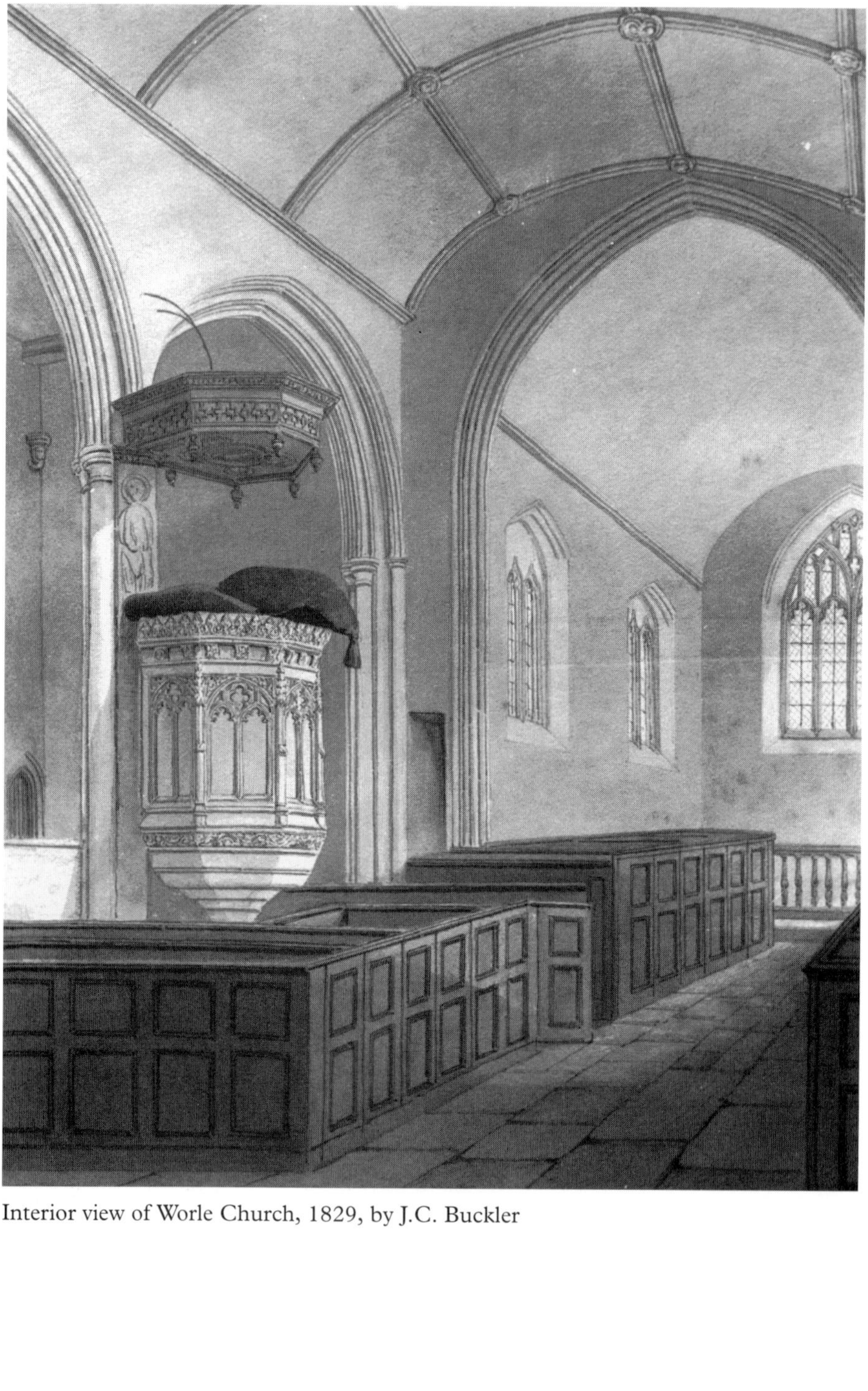

Interior view of Worle Church, 1829, by J.C. Buckler

remain. The north aisle has a fine parapet of pierced panelling, such as often occurs in Somersetshire, enriched with crocketed pinnacles on the buttresses. At the north-east angle of the aisle is a large octagonal stair turret with a panelled band and pyramidal finishing.

The tower has buttresses only in the lower part and is rather low, but has a pierced parapet like that of the north aisle, an octagonal turret at the south-east, panelled in its upper part and crocketed pinnacles at the angles of the tower. The spire is rather low but ribbed at the angles. The belfry window is of 2 lights, latticed in stone work except on the south side. On the west side is a 3 light window and below it a doorway with flowered hood.

The windows of the nave are mostly of 3 lights, but the tracery has been destroyed. The nave has a Third Pointed arcade on the north, of 4 arches with light piers of the sort frequent in this county. The tower arch is moulded dying into the wall. The chancel arch has continuous mouldings and on the north side of it is a square hagioscope. The pulpit is a fine one of stone with good panelling, Tudor flower and vine cornice. The chancel has an east window of 4 lights and some of 3 lights and a door on the south side. Those on the north are closed.

The arrangement on the south side is a little remarkable. There are 2 rather shallow sedilia ascending under the window (but without canopies) and a further ascent with the 4-foiled orifice of a piscina in the angle but no fenestella, eastward of which there is a square aumbrey deep in the wall. In the chancel remain most of the original stalls with misereres, having good carved woodwork. The font has an octagonal bowl with base of the same form.

Wraxall

51/23–26 All Saints 25 July, 1860

The church is well situated on the side of a picturesque hill and its fine tower forms a good object in the surrounding scenery. It has a nave with north aisle, south transept, chancel with north chapel, western tower and south porch.

The external character is almost wholly Perpendicular but there are small indications of earlier work, especially in the outer doorway of the south porch which is Early English with 2 orders of shafts which have capitals of foliage and a hood upon corbel heads, one a female, one a man mustacio'd. The porch joins the transept on the west and has a parvise or upper storey. The nave has a leaded roof. The north aisle has a moulded parapet and not being the show side is built of rougher stone masonry. There is on the side a projecting octagonal turret corresponding with the roodloft. The chancel has a priest's door on the south, of small size, with hood on corbels, one head, one foliage.

The interior is handsome and in neat condition. All its details are Perpendicular. The arcade of the nave is of that character and has 4 arches with clustered piers of 4 stilted shafts having moulded capitals. The roofs are coved and ribbed with bosses which are gilt and there is a flowered cornice just beneath the roof. The windows are mostly square-headed of 3 lights. The aisle has a flatter roof and the south transept is panelled. The transept opens to the

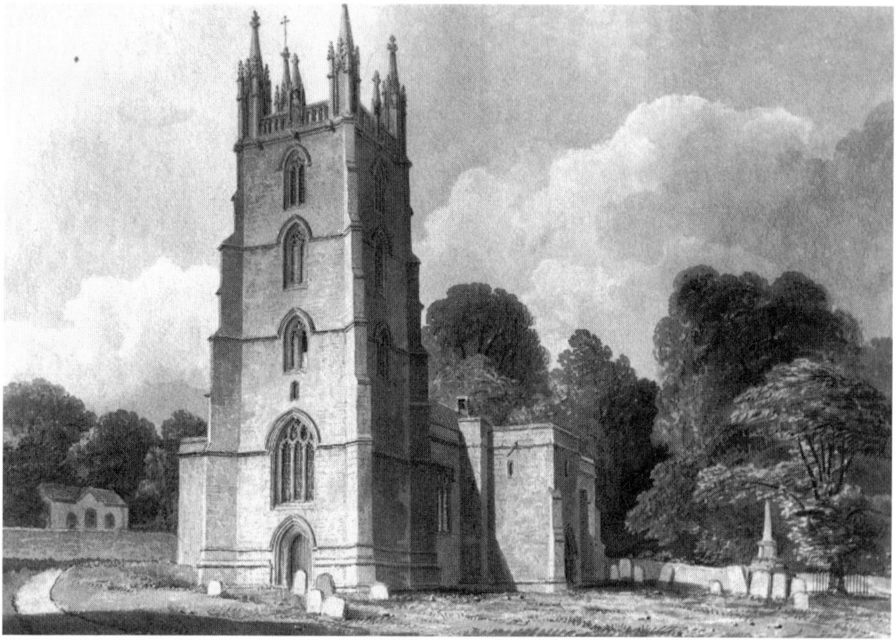

West view of Wraxall Church, 1827, by J.C. Buckler

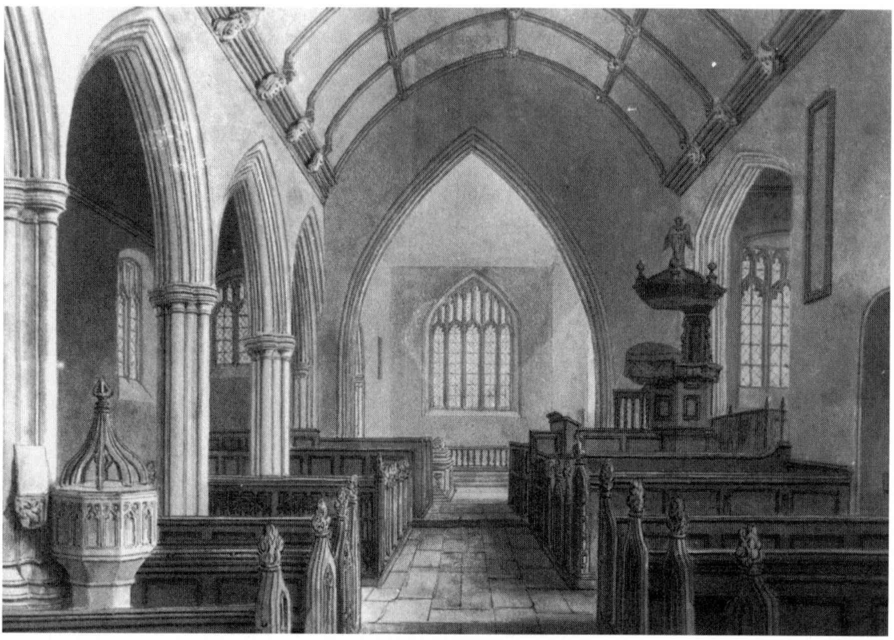

Interior view of Wraxall Church, 1829, by J.C. Buckler

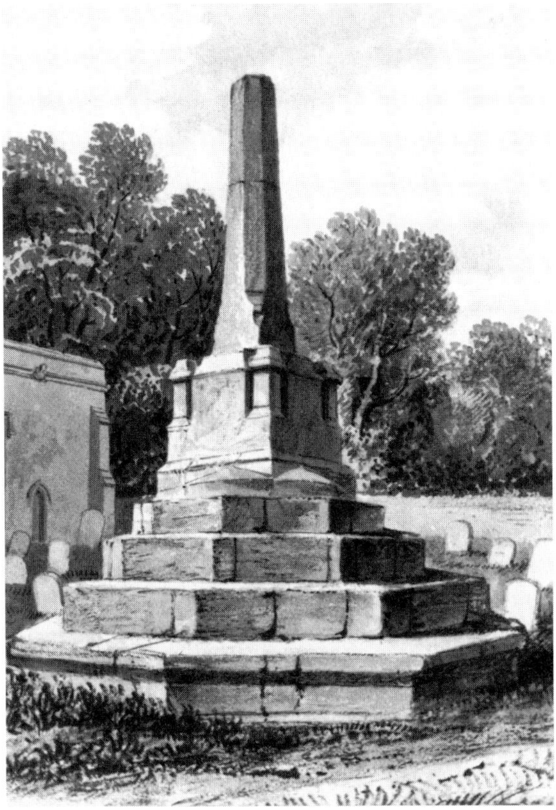

Cross in Wraxall churchyard, 1827, by J.C. Buckler

nave by a flat Tudor arch adjacent to which in the wall is a smaller arch not reaching to the ground which probably may have been a sepulchral niche. In the east wall of the transept is an arched hagioscope with a canopy.

The seats are partly open and partly with doors, some are ancient with panelling and poppyheads. The pulpit is a new one and panelled. The tower arch is lofty with continuous mouldings. The chancel arch is plain and ugly, its mouldings continuous. The chancel has one arch on the north opening to the aisle and a vestry eastward of it. The east window is of 5 lights; on the south are two square-headed windows, one set lower than the other.

The roof of the chancel is good, the beams upon angel figures bearing shields and having pierced panelling above. On the north of the altar is a tomb beneath an arch in the wall with recumbent effigies of a man and woman and lions at their feet, the sides charged with armorial bearings and blazoned. On the south of the altar is a piscina with trefoil head. The sacrarium is laid with tiles. There is a slab inscribed: Here lyeth Sir Tybbet Knyght and Baronet on Whose Soule God have mercy. Amen.

There is an arch over the south door opening from the parvise into the church. The font has an octagonal bowl, panelled with trefoiled arches, of Perpendicular character.

The tower is a very fine one lofty and well-finished and of the true Somersetshire type, has embattled parapet of pierced panelling and corner buttresses. There are 4 large corner pinnacles to which smaller ones are attached by flying buttresses and the centre battlement on each side has a canopied niche containing a statue. The tower is of 3 stages, each having windows of 3 lights with the pretty pierced stone lattice work which often is seen in Somersetshire. There is an octagonal turret at the north-east with a pierced parapet and large pinnacle. The west window is of 3 lights and the window below has good mouldings.

In the churchyard is the very lofty shaft of a cross upon 4 very high steps.

Wrington

50/71–73 All Saints 16 January, 1854

A fine church of the Somersetshire [type] and entirely Perpendicular except the east end of the chancel which is Decorated. The plan is as usual, nave with north and south aisles, chancel with north and south chapels, west tower and south porch.

The tower is a grand feature and is of very fine masonry with panelled battlements and 4 large pinnacles at ye angles, 4 smaller intermediate ones. Those at the angles have small ones attached. The belfry storey has 2 unusually long windows on each side, pierced stone work, the lower merely panelled. The lower parts of the tower are not highly ornamented, but the west window is an

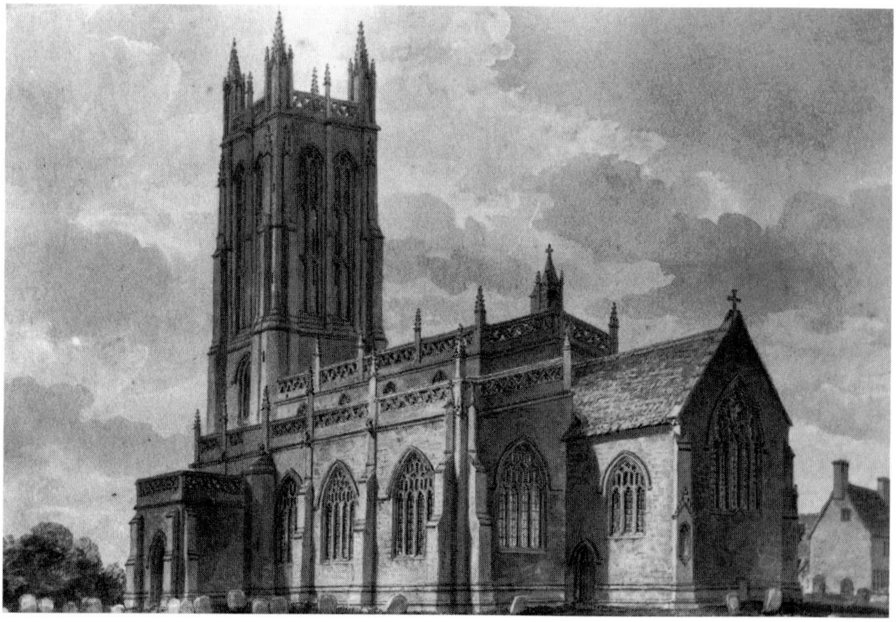

South east view of Wrington Church, 1828, by J. Buckler

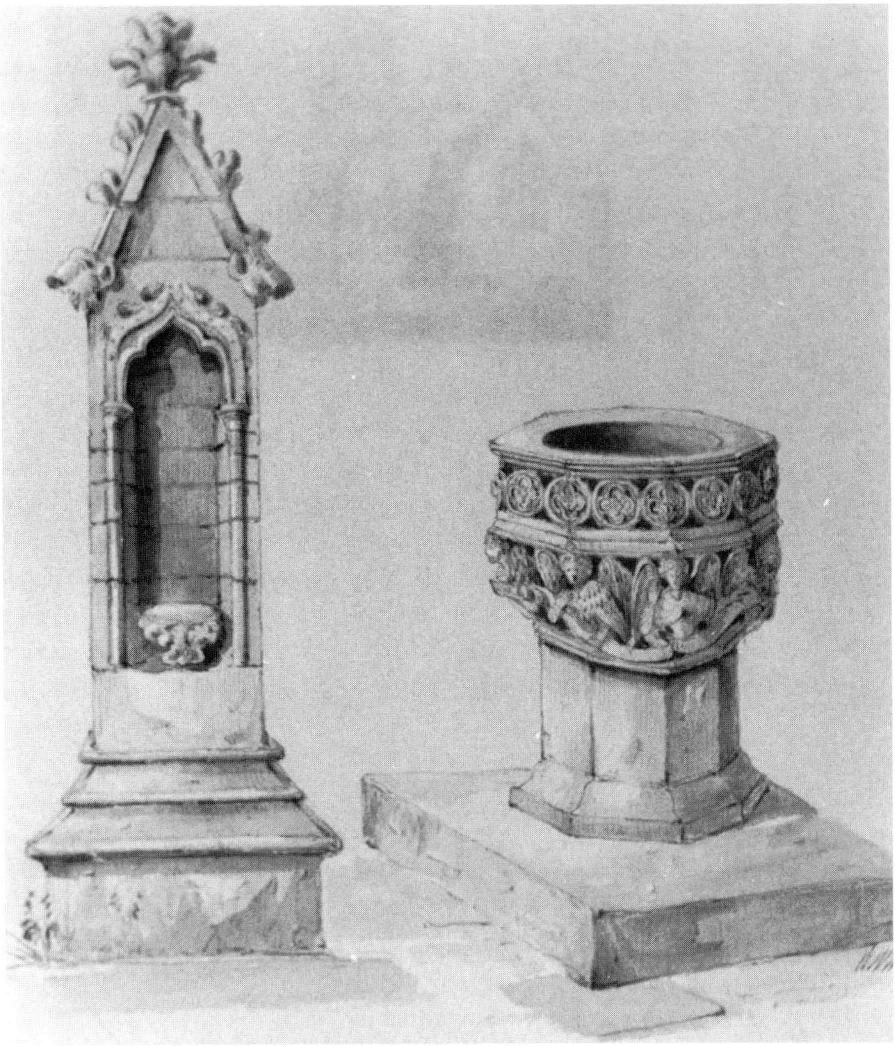

Wrington Church, 1843, by W.W. Wheatley

extremely fine one of 6 lights divided by 2 transoms. (This window has to its central part 3 transoms, one to each lateral division). Below it is a good door with panelled soffit and small shafts, the spandrels filled with armorial shields.

The buttresses are not set at the angles of the tower, but bold and having diagonal pinnacles at the set offs. The parapets of the aisles and of the clerestory and of the porch are fine open ones of pierced trefoils, a common pattern in Somersetshire. There is a small bellcote rising from the east gable of the clerestory with pointed top and little pinnacles and latticed sides. The outer door of the porch is continuous. There is a plain north door. There are bold gargoyles externally.

The east end of the chancel is good Decorated and flanked by bold buttresses which are enriched with canopied niches, the canopies being rather singular and rather like hoods, of pedimented form and crocketed but beginning in and ending in grotesque head corbels. The niches themselves are trefoiled. The mouldings ballflowers and small shafts. The lower part of the buttresses have triangular canopies. The east window is a very elegant one of 5 lights, rather early in the style and has its rear arch on shafts with moulded capitals. In the centre of the upper part is a multifoiled circle.

The other windows of the church are all Perpendicular; those of the aisles closely set and each of 4 lights. Those of the clerestory of 3 lights, having more of a Decorated character. The interior is very light and lofty. The nave is of 4 bays, the chancel of 1 bay. The roof of the nave is a good one of flat panelling with ribs and bosses and pierced spandrels. The clerestory windows have a curious kind of hood over them internally, in a trefoil form but spreading over the whole window and rising from foliated corbels on bosses.

The aisle roofs are flat, much like that of the nave. The tower arch is a lofty one with continued panelling and small shafts. The tower has a nice stone groined roof. The arcades of the nave are elegant and the piers very light, formed of 8 clustered shafts in lozenge form; the shafts stilted, the capitals of foliage and angel figures intermixed. The central shaft reaches to the spandrels of the roof. The chancel arch is wide, springing from shafts like the others and there are arches between the aisles of the nave and those of the chancel. On the north side is a rood turret with door. The screen of the roodloft remains across the entrance to the chancel and is a very fine one of wood consisting of elegant traceried compartments and door in the centre. There are crocketed pinnacles on the piers and fine cornice of vine foliage above.

The chancel is lower than the nave and has no clerestory. On each side a flattened arch opens to the side chapels upon shafts with foliated capitals, of later character than the arcades of the nave. Under the east window is a modern stone reredos lately erected, illuminated and of very fair character. The north-east and south-east windows are Perpendicular, of 3 lights with traces of stained glass. On the north is a small recess in the wall, perhaps an aumbrey. The chancel has been ceiled. The font is a fine one: Perpendicular, the bowl octagonal, the upper part of which has a range of circles containing quatrefoils with foliage. In the slope below it are half figures of angels with scrolls, the stem octagonal and panelled. There are 6 bells.

Yarlington

52/22–23 St. Mary 28 July, 1873

A small church having nave and chancel with a tower set transept fashion on the south side of the nave and north and south porches. There is not much of good work and the church is in an unimproved state. There are some poor windows on the south of the nave, small and Perpendicular of 2 lights. On the north one Perpendicular of 3 lights, 2 small of 2 lights of very ordinary character and one pointed of 2 lights unfoliated.

The west end has a square-headed labeled window of 2 lights. Both porches

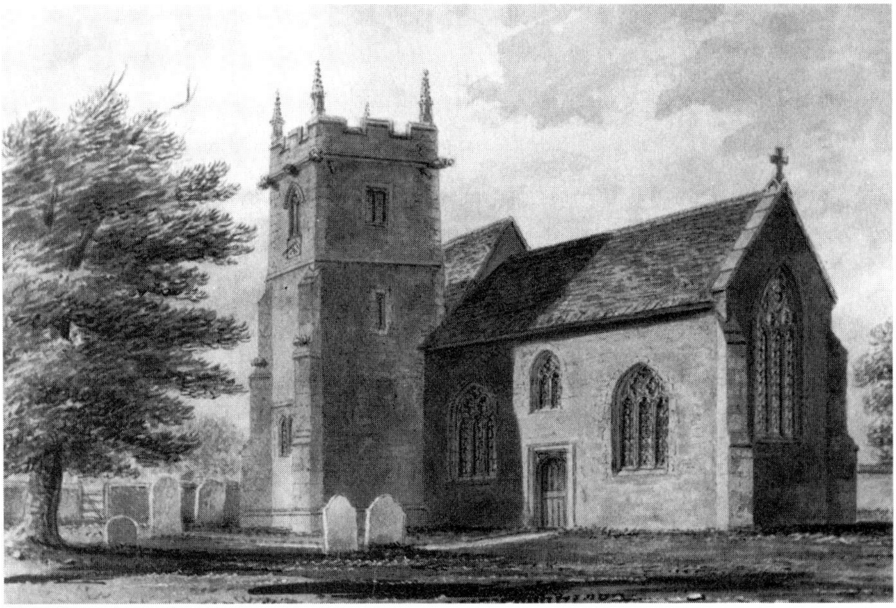

South east view of Yarlington Church, 1842, by J. Buckler

are small and poor. The nave has a coved roof with ribs. The tower arch is semi-circular and has a Norman character, with a hood, on imposts. The walls are very thick in the tower and eastern part of the nave. The tower is low, has 2 string courses, corner buttresses, embattled parapet and 4 corner pinnacles and gargoyles. The belfry windows of 2 lights. On the west side, a debased window of 3 round-headed lights.

There is no chancel arch. The chancel seems to have been rebuilt in stone of a false yellow colour and has pointed windows of 3 lights on the south and east of which the tracery has a Flamboyant and somewhat debased character; one small 2 light window being set high at the south-west. The altar rails are of iron and there is an ornate but debased door arch on the south. The font has a square bowl with the angles cut off, of Perpendicular character, panelled with shields.

The west gallery is painted with representations of an organ and of David playing the harp.

Yatton

49/57–61 St. Mary 1842

This very spacious and beautiful church is cruciform with a lofty tower at the centre of the cross surmounted by a turreted stone spire which appears never to have been finished. The nave is very lofty and has side aisles. The transepts are large, but, as well as the chancel, are lower than the nave and built of rougher stone. There is a large and rich south porch which, with a great

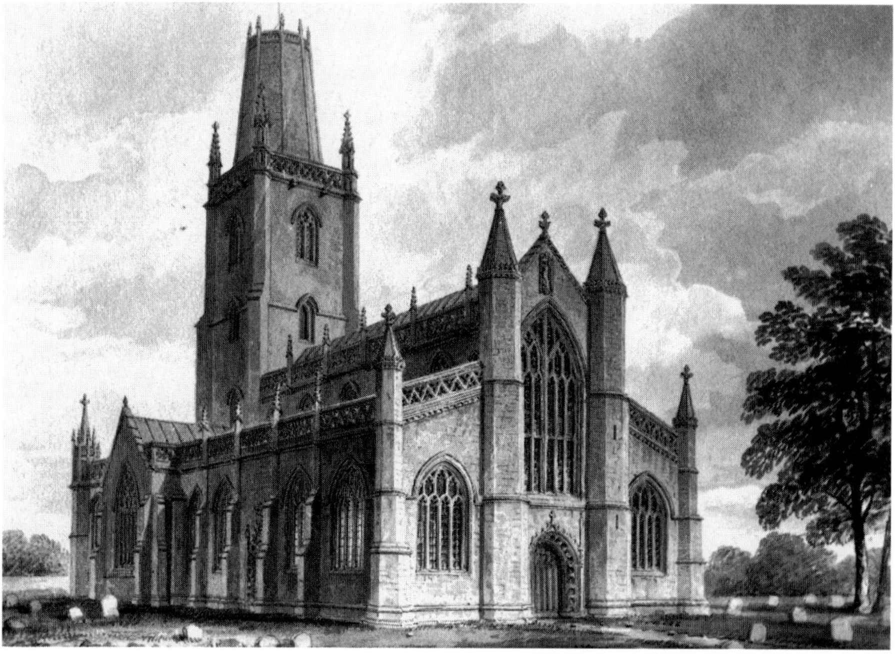

North west view of Yatton Church, 1827, by J.C. Buckler

portion of the exterior of the nave and the upper part of the tower, is Perpendicular. In the transepts and chancel are portions of early Decorated work. The clerestory has a high lead roof. The chancel has some curious ancient patterns in the lead of its roof.

The whole of the nave and aisles is of fine stone and beautiful masonry. The porch has a rich ogee arch doorway with a fine band of foliage and excellent mouldings, crockets and large finial. The front of the porch is covered with panelling, but it is not sunk deep and the execution is poor and imperfect. Over the doorway is a canopied niche terminated by a pinnacle. The porch is of 2 stages and has a fine groined ceiling.

The south aisle of the nave has a very rich pierced parapet and small pinnacles surmounting the buttresses. The north aisle and north clerestory have also fine pierced parapets, but not the south clerestory. The north doorway is without a porch and has a very fine crocketed and finialed ogee arch, beautifully moulded with a course of very bold flowers and flanked by pinnacles. The west front is handsome and striking, the centre gable surmounted by a cross and both the centre and the side aisles are flanked by octagonal turrets (4 in number) crowned by pyramidical pinnacles with finials on the top and round the cap of the turret below the pinnacles runs a course of Tudor flower.

The west window is a fine Perpendicular one of 6 lights and above it in the gable is a canopied niche containing a statue. Below the window is a string course round the turrets and continued as dripstone over the end windows of the aisles. These, as well as all the side aisle windows are Perpendicular of 4 lights. The west doorway is a very fine Perpendicular one with ogee arch

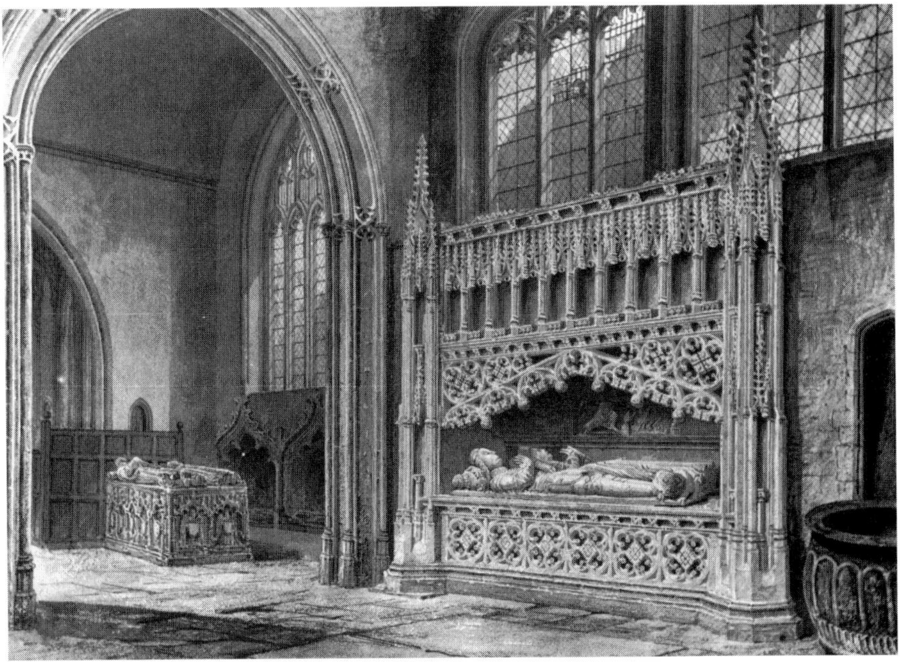

Interior of the chapel on the north side of Yatton Church, 1827, by J.C. Buckler

crocketed and finialed and elegant arch mouldings enriched with foliage and niches and flanked by pinnacles.

The transepts have lead high roofs. The tower is massive. The lower portion above the roof of the body appears to be Decorated and is simple in character. The belfry windows and the rest Perpendicular. The former have fine stone lattice work. The parapet is of open panelling and very fair. At the south-east angle is an octagonal turret rising a good deal above the parapet and crowned by a finial. At the other 3 angles rich crocketed pinnacles set diagonally.

The spire was evidently never finished, but was intended to be very lofty and has ribs at the angles. The interior of the nave is very grand and lofty. There are 5 fine moulded pointed arches on each side dividing the aisles which are clearly of Decorated character. The piers have small shafts attached at intervals of moulding with varied capitals sculptured with foliage and with heads. In the front of each pier is a large shaft which supports the ribs of the roof. The clerestory windows are each of 2 lights and Perpendicular tracery. In the western piers there are added bands to the shafts below the capitals.

The roof of the nave is coved and plastered with cornice of the time of James I. The south aisles have flat panelled ceilings of wood of great beauty with elegant tracery, foliated and very rich cornices. The windows of the side aisles have shafts to their arches internally. Above the western arch of the tower is seen an early Decorated window opening into the nave. There are two small ogee arch doorways in the soffit of the west window.

The tower rises upon 4 very large and fine moulded arches and under the tower is a strong groined ceiling with stone ribs springing from shafts which are set below the spring of the tower arches. The south transept has an early Decorated window of 5 lights without foils. The north transept has a Perpendicular window of 5 lights inserted in an earlier wall and below it are two fine Decorated ogee arches with feathering, crockets and finials, containing respectively the effigy of a man and woman with long hair, considered to be some of the De Wyck family, founders of the aisle.

The arch from this transept to the south aisle of the nave is plain and pointed, pierced in the original wall. The corresponding arch in the south transept is rich with mouldings and shafts. In the south transept an altar tomb of white marble, the sides of which are sculptured with niches and angel figures bearing shields upon which are the effigies of Sir Richard Caradoc Newton Chief Justice in the time of Henry VI, and his wife and heiress of the De Wyck family. The figures are coloured. The judge has 2 dogs at his feet, the lady 2 little dogs by her side.

The chancel is low in proportion to the nave and originally Decorated. It has on each side 3 windows of 2 lights with dripstone internally continued but on the south side the tracery has been altered to Perpendicular. (The outer moulding of these windows facing the interior terminate in octagonal bases.) On the south side is also a small doorway with a label over it. The east window is Perpendicular of 5 lights and filled with inferior stained glass.

The north chapel of the chancel is of rich and beautiful Perpendicular work having been added about 1470. The exterior is of very fine stone masonry and has at the north-east corner an elegant octagonal turret crowned with a kind of small spire and all the parapet is of rich open work. There are also small crocketed angular pinnacles. There are on the north side of the chancel two windows with good tracery of 3 lights with rather depressed arches. The east window is of 4 lights also Perpendicular and is said to have been originally in the east wall of the transept and moved on when this chapel, or aisle, was built.

Internally it is set between 2 extremely fine canopied niches with groining under the canopies. There is also against the wall rather a remarkable niche with a double canopy projecting in front and flanked by pinnacles. Within the niche is a shelf of stone and an octagonal piscina upon a shaft with a rose orifice. This is of remarkable arrangement, but seems to have been moved from its original place. Near it is the font, a large early circular basin with a moulded rim and swelling towards the centre, moulded with a range of plain, semi-circular arches and the base also circular moulded with a scaly ornament, clearly of Norman work.

This chapel is divided from the transept by a beautiful panelled arch with small delicate shafts and from the chancel by a similar one. By the latter arch there is also a small door set obliquely in the direction of the altar. Within the north chapel beneath the north window is one of the grandest tombs in the county and coeval with the chapel and probably commemorating the founder of it Sir John Newton Knt and his lady. The tomb has the sides enriched with quatrefoil panelling enclosing shields, the figures of the knight and his lady recumbent are in fine preservation; he rests his head on a wheatsheaf and both figures have chains round the neck.

The canopy has rather a depressed arch with the richest double feathering and the spandrels adorned with splendid pierced panelling. Above the canopy is a rich range of canopied niches and the whole is flanked by a large buttress having mouldings and elegant niches and crowned by large crocketed pinnacles. In the wall at the back of the monument is a bas relief representing the Annunciation of the Virgin Mary. This commemorates Sir John Newton and Isabella de Cheddar his wife, he being the son of the judge to whom the other tomb is erected.

(The south porch has beautiful groining with shields and foliage in the bosses, the ribs upon small shafts set in pairs with a kind of niche above them, rather a remarkable feature. Above the door within the porch is a canopied niche.

On the south side of the nave is a grotesque gargoyle representing an ape holding open the mouth of a toad.

There is an entry in the Church Book recording a legacy received by the wife of Sir Richard Newton for making a bell in 1451.)

Yeovil

19/63–65 [St. John] Before 1840

Yeovil is a large town surrounded by some very rich and beautiful scenery. The church is a very fine and spacious structure consisting of a nave with side aisles, a chancel, transept not extending far beyond the breadth of the body, and fine tower at the west end. The church is entirely of Perpendicular work, and very elegant in its ornament, although not extremely rich.

The exterior is elegant and the stone with which it is built good and durable. There is no clerestory but the roof is lofty and has a fine effect. The parapet is enriched with panelling. The south porch is a good Perpendicular composition. The tower very lofty and handsome though not rich. It has a panelled parapet at the top and a good western window. The buttresses of the church are finished with pinnacles and the south transept end flanked with turrets crowned with pinnacles.

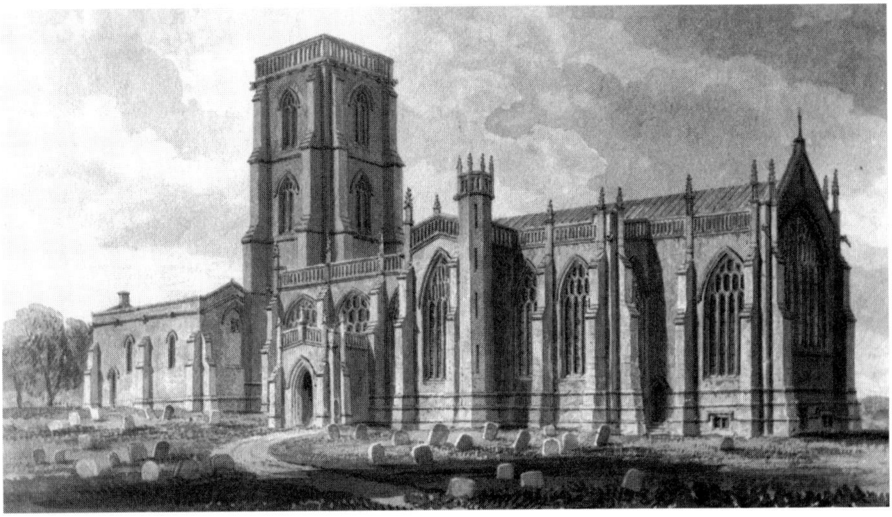

South east view of Yeovil Church, 1817, by J. Buckler

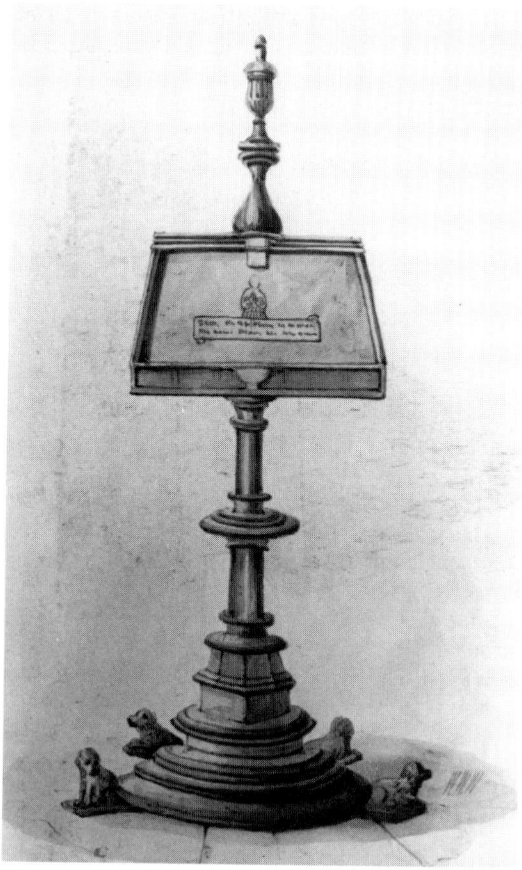

In Yeovil Church, 1847,
by W.W. Wheatley

The interior of the church is very fine and the furniture handsome. The nave is divided from the side aisles by lofty pointed arches springing from light piers of lozenge form having shafts at the angles. The windows are extremely numerous which gives the church a great lightness and elegance. They have mostly good tracery. The chancel is paved with marble. On the north side of the chancel is an elegant doorway leading to a vestry having a fine ogee canopy with rich crockets and feathering and at the extremeties 2 crocketed pinnacles.

The font is octagonal and of Perpendicular character, enriched with panelling, quatrefoils and the Tudor flower. At the west end of the church is an organ, erected by voluntary subscription in 1784. The tower has a peal of 8 bells. There is a handsome brass desk in the church bearing the following inscription in black letter but nearly unintelligible: Precibs mic 'poor cermus hinc cya rogate ferat Martins vita vigilet que beate'. The desk was formerly used for reading ye lessons and is supported upon a brass shaft with 4 claws supported by lions couchant.

There are 2 brasses in the church; the inscription of one is given Gent. Mag. vol. 84 pt. 2, page 18 with a view of ye church. There are some good niches and piscina south of ye chancel. The church has very good pews and galleries. In the churchyard on the west side of ye church is a large Perpendicular building now used as a school.

The dimensions of the church are thus:

Whole length exclusive of tower 113, nave being 88, chancel 25

Breadth of body and aisles 51

Length of transept from north to south 80.

Yeovilton

50/5–6 St. Bartholomew 5 September, 1843

This church has a west tower, nave, chancel, north and south porches. The tower is plain Perpendicular, 3 stages in height with corner buttresses, battlements and 4 small pinnacles, an octagonal turret on the south side, a canopied niche on the north, belfry windows of 2 lights and a west door with arch mouldings and spandrels and near it a stoup.

The whole church seems to be Perpendicular. The north porch is very large but plain, entered by a simple pointed arch. Within it is a stoup. Over the east end of the chancel is a cross. The interior is dark and solemn but the walls lean outwards very considerably. The nave is wide and the chancel large. The

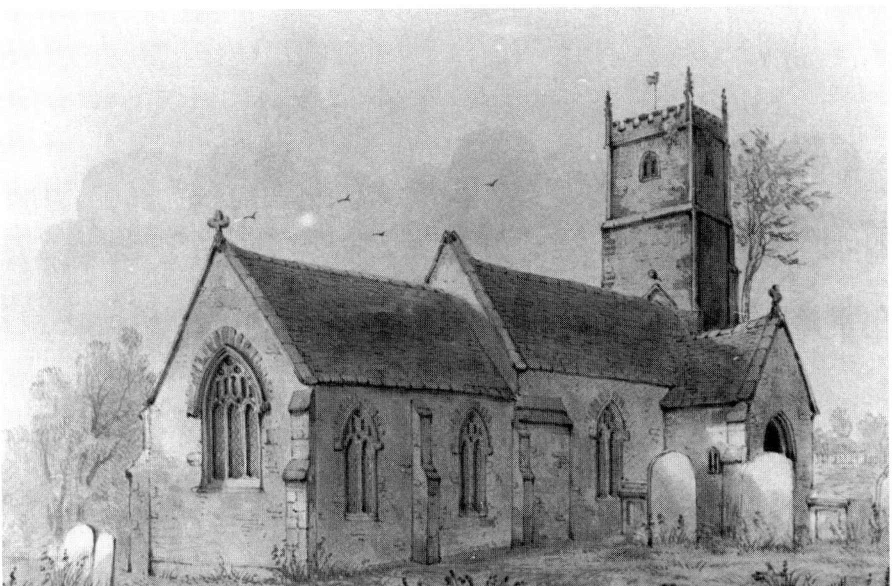

Yeovilton, 1847, by W.W. Wheatley

windows are all of 2 lights, except the eastern one which has 3. There is the common projection on the north side of the nave. The arches to the tower and chancel both have continuous mouldings. The roof has tie-beams. Against the south wall is a rich bracket for a statue with panelling and a flowered band terminating in a point or a head. Some of the windows have good pieces of stained glass.

On the south side of the chancel is a most elegant piscina of octangular form of a rose of 8 leaves resting on a grotesque corbel representing a half length figure. The canopy is in form of an ogee niche with trefoil feathering and excellent deep mouldings. There is a priest's door on the south of the chancel. In the thickness of the wall a pointed recess in the jamb as if for a bar. The screen is of Italian character. The font an octagonal bowl with quatrefoils, shields and lozenges diminishing and upon an octagonal shaft. There is a west gallery and a barrel organ.